Impact of Organizational Trauma on Workplace Behavior and Performance

Stanislav Háša
University of Economics, Czech Republic

Richard Brunet-Thornton
University of Economics, Czech Republic

A volume in the Advances in Human Resources Management and Organizational Development (AHRMOD) Book Series

IGI GLOBAL
DISSEMINATOR OF KNOWLEDGE
www.igi-global.com

Published in the United States of America by
IGI Global
Business Science Reference (an imprint of IGI Global)
701 E. Chocolate Avenue
Hershey PA, USA 17033
Tel: 717-533-8845
Fax: 717-533-8661
E-mail: cust@igi-global.com
Web site: http://www.igi-global.com

Library of Congress Cataloging-in-Publication Data

Names: Hasa, Stanislav, 1974- editor. | Brunet-Thornton, Richard, 1953- editor.
Title: Impact of organizational trauma on workplace behavior and performance / Stanislav Hasa and Richard Brunet-Thornton, editors.
Description: Hershey : Business Science Reference, [2017]
Identifiers: LCCN 2016052328| ISBN 9781522520214 (hardcover) | ISBN 9781522520221 (ebook)
Subjects: LCSH: Quality of work life. | Industrial psychology. | Psychic trauma. | Organizational sociology.
Classification: LCC HD6955 .I47 2017 | DDC 331.25/6--dc23
LC record available at https://lccn.loc.gov/2016052328

This book is published in the IGI Global book series Advances in Human Resources Management and Organizational Development (AHRMOD) (ISSN: 2327-3372; eISSN: 2327-3380)

British Cataloguing in Publication Data
A Cataloguing in Publication record for this book is available from the British Library.

Advances in Human Resources Management and Organizational Development (AHRMOD) Book Series

Patricia Ordóñez de Pablos
Universidad de Oviedo, Spain

ISSN:2327-3372
EISSN:2327-3380

Mission

A solid foundation is essential to the development and success of any organization and can be accomplished through the effective and careful management of an organization's human capital. Research in human resources management and organizational development is necessary in providing business leaders with the tools and methodologies which will assist in the development and maintenance of their organizational structure.

The **Advances in Human Resources Management and Organizational Development (AHRMOD) Book Series** aims to publish the latest research on all aspects of human resources as well as the latest methodologies, tools, and theories regarding organizational development and sustainability. The **AHRMOD Book Series** intends to provide business professionals, managers, researchers, and students with the necessary resources to effectively develop and implement organizational strategies.

Coverage

- Process Improvement
- Organizational Development
- Diversity in the Workplace
- Workplace Culture
- Talent Identification and Management
- Job Enrichment
- Organizational Behavior
- Employment and Labor Laws
- Compliance
- Personnel Retention

IGI Global is currently accepting manuscripts for publication within this series. To submit a proposal for a volume in this series, please contact our Acquisition Editors at Acquisitions@igi-global.com or visit: http://www.igi-global.com/publish/.

The Advances in Human Resources Management and Organizational Development (AHRMOD) Book Series (ISSN 2327-3372) is published by IGI Global, 701 E. Chocolate Avenue, Hershey, PA 17033-1240, USA, www.igi-global.com. This series is composed of titles available for purchase individually; each title is edited to be contextually exclusive from any other title within the series. For pricing and ordering information please visit http://www.igi-global.com/book-series/advances-human-resources-management-organizational/73670. Postmaster: Send all address changes to above address.

Titles in this Series

For a list of additional titles in this series, please visit: www.igi-global.com

Handbook of Research on Human Resources Strategies for the New Millennial Workforce
Patricia Ordoñez de Pablos (University of Oviedo, Spain) and Robert D. Tennyson (University of Minnesota, USA)
Business Science Reference • copyright 2017 • 523pp • H/C (ISBN: 9781522509486) • US $310.00 (our price)

Management Education for Global Leadership
Neeta Baporikar (HP-GSB, Namibia University of Science and Technology, Namibia)
Business Science Reference • copyright 2017 • 321pp • H/C (ISBN: 9781522510130) • US $185.00 (our price)

Innovation and Shifting Perspectives in Management Education
Neeta Baporikar (HP-GSB, Namibia University of Science and Technology, Namibia)
Business Science Reference • copyright 2017 • 352pp • H/C (ISBN: 9781522510192) • US $190.00 (our price)

Strategic Labor Relations Management in Modern Organizations
Ana María Lucia Casademunt (Universidad Loyola Andalucía, Spain)
Business Science Reference • copyright 2016 • 313pp • H/C (ISBN: 9781522503569) • US $205.00 (our price)

Bridging the Scholar-Practitioner Gap in Human Resources Development
Claretha Hughes (University of Arkansas, USA) and Matthew W. Gosney (Hillcrest HealthCare Systems, USA)
Business Science Reference • copyright 2016 • 267pp • H/C (ISBN: 9781466699984) • US $185.00 (our price)

Quantitative Multidisciplinary Approaches in Human Capital and Asset Management
Meir Russ (University of Wisconsin-Green Bay, USA)
Business Science Reference • copyright 2016 • 317pp • H/C (ISBN: 9781466696525) • US $205.00 (our price)

Strategic Information Technology Governance and Organizational Politics in Modern Business
Tiko Iyamu (Cape Peninsula University of Technology, South Africa)
Business Science Reference • copyright 2015 • 326pp • H/C (ISBN: 9781466685246) • US $210.00 (our price)

Cross-Cultural Collaboration and Leadership in Modern Organizations
Nancy D. Erbe (California State University Dominguez Hills, California) and Anthony H. Normore (California State University Dominguez Hills, California)
Business Science Reference • copyright 2015 • 388pp • H/C (ISBN: 9781466683761) • US $225.00 (our price)

Handbook of Research on Internationalization of Entrepreneurial Innovation in the Global Economy
Luisa Cagica Carvalho (Universidade Aberta, Portugal & CEFAGE, Universidade de Évora, Portugal)
Business Science Reference • copyright 2015 • 547pp • H/C (ISBN: 9781466682160) • US $335.00 (our price)

IGI GLOBAL
DISSEMINATOR OF KNOWLEDGE
www.igi-global.com

701 E. Chocolate Ave., Hershey, PA 17033
Order online at www.igi-global.com or call 717-533-8845 x100
To place a standing order for titles released in this series, contact: cust@igi-global.com
Mon-Fri 8:00 am - 5:00 pm (est) or fax 24 hours a day 717-533-8661

Editorial Advisory Board

Table of Contents

Detailed Table of Contents

The chapter summarizes research studies as well as case studies from companies worldwide that show how organizational changes followed by downsizing create a traumatic experience for all organization members. The author's focus is on the psychological perspective on traumatic experience by all employees (victims and survivors) and managers whose task is to organize and implement changes in the organization. Based on the literature review, the chapter describes symptoms and psychological effects of organizational change trauma on individuals and the ways to minimize the traumatic effects. The author believes that outplacement and therapeutic approach are effective tools for overcoming the layoff trauma and also send positive signals to employees and to general public.

This chapter will evaluate the correlation between change management and the employee and/or management behaviors detrimental to the wellbeing of those individuals and the overall productivity and efficiency of an organization. The potential relationship between change and organizational behaviors, the effects of change on the wellbeing of individuals, the well-documented resistance to change would analyzed as well as potential techniques that managers, consultants and HR departments could implement to minimize the detrimental influence of organizational change on the wellbeing of individuals. The traumatic effects of change on the employee, both physical and psychological effects would be included in this chapter. These effects on the wellbeing of employees have been correlated to diminishing job satisfaction, increased absenteeism and turnover, reduced productivity and effectiveness and overall lower engagement with the organization. The chapter will include the introduction and brief analysis of organizational change and effectiveness models in particular the Burke-Litwin Model.

Increasing human interaction creates extra stress on individuals and organisations as well. The nature of such stress results in economic shocks and large societal and organisational traumas. Although recent social science is capable of addressing the complexity of international interplay such as culture, acts of multinational corporations or cross-cultural team management, little attention was paid on the cultural aspects of removing organisational trauma. Since the 1980s, social science has experienced lively development in cross-cultural studies via the work of Hofstede, the Globe Group, the World Value Survey initiative, Trompenaars, Schwartz and others. Although major models are sufficient for defining national culture, there is lack of work explaining the managerial implications for crisis management or mitigating trauma in organisations.The authors of this chapter intend to critically review the latest literature on national culture, while discussing the relevant models and introducing the theoretic framework applicable for crisis/ trauma management.

Section 3
Trauma and the Workplace

The global progression of human rights advocating for marginalized communities, especially LGBTQ, has seen tremendous change over the past several decades, including the conditions for disclosure of sexual identity in the workplace. The decision-making process of disclosure and the necessity for others to know is key to understanding how best to support and address the potential organizational trauma that may result. Not all disclosure of minority identity is negative and the availability of positive policy development within organizations can assist in smooth transitions toward more equal inclusion and dispel previous heteronormative and heterosexist ideologies. Through increased knowledge about the LGBTQ community and case analysis, a cross cultural lens will be utilized from Brazil, Turkey and the U.S.; prominent sexual identity disclosure perspectives for numerous occupations, as well as recommendations for systemic awareness and change will be offered.

Research suggests that a significant number of people are exposed to persistent abusive treatment within the workplace, with the majority of studies within Europe indicating that between 10% and 15% of the workforce are exposed to workplace bullying, with North American research reporting similar prevalence rates. This is a significant, ongoing dilemma for researchers and practitioners, for which an agreed resolution would be useful because of legal and policy implications. Hence, the purpose of this chapter is on the impact of organizational trauma on workplace behavior and performance based on workplace bullying. The chapter is based on a case study regarding a program that is funded by the Department of Education within a community college in the State of California. The community college is one of four community colleges under the same community college district.

Section 4
Case Studies

Organizational trauma is traditionally associated with negative effects on organizational behavior and performance. In this chapter the authors seek to answer the question how organizational trauma, and in particular near-death experiences, can positively influence organizational culture in the long term. In doing

Foreword

I am especially delighted to have been requested by the Editors to fulfil this role as a contributor by providing a foreword to this reference text. The contributions contained herein are of significance to the study of the influence of critical situations on employee well-being and engagement. Even more so, they address the ultimate research question as to whether organizational trauma exists.

Upon review of the chapters, one feels a subtle sense of urgency to reveal and share individual experiences and scientific findings. This is probably derived from the premise that currently this topic lacks sufficient attention. Extensive literature reviews on organizational trauma have identified few manuscripts that are explicitly dedicated to organizational trauma (de Klerk, 2007; Kahn, 2003; Gabriel, 2012). In addition, prevailing studies focus on specific aspects such as the effects of massive layoffs and their emotional impact on employees. Consequently, the resultant traumatization is described and treated in terms of its manifestations of employee dysfunctional behavior (Stuart, 1996; Sahdev, 2004; Brenner, 2004). Furthermore, there is no comprehensive conclusion as to whether organizational trauma influences employee performance. Some studies suggest that layoffs exhibit a negative impact on survivors and individual performance (Allen, et al., 2001); organizational performance is adversely affected only by ineffective change management (Sahdev, 2004) and that employee injuries occur more frequently in transitional workplaces (Brenner, et al., 2004). However, there are considerations about the impact on employee engagement (Sahdev, 2004). Other studies propose a strong relationship between engagement, well-being and performance. (Harter, et al., 2002; Vanhala & Tuomi, 2006; Van De Voorde, et al., 2012).

Overall, each chapter aims to define organizational trauma as a separate phenomenon, describes the mechanisms of its origins, manifestations and effects on member performance. As output, propose possible methods to minimize and/or mitigate the impact. In addition, they singularly and as a set, contribute to an area that is not elaborated in the extant literature; upgrade current topic treatment from a purely psychological perspective to one that comprises management and organizational development, and finally, examine organizational impact from trauma to employee performance.

In closing, I highly recommend this text for both academicians and practitioners who share an interest in this subject matter. Each segment as well as the book in its entirety, enhances the current body of knowledge and serves to highlight possibilities for future research and scientific endeavors.

Ivan Nový
University of Economics, Czech Republic

Ivan Nový, *an established academic and business consultant, has authored numerous manuscripts, articles, and reference books on the topics of managerial psychology, sociology, and cross-cultural management. He currently sits on numerous scientific and editorial boards. Due to his acknowledged reputation in these professional areas, Professor Nový works closely with other educational institutions and businesses in both Central and Eastern Europe. His professional interests include Managerial Psychology and Sociology, intercultural communication and management, intercultural training, sociological research and consultancy in the field of personnel development, international business, and managerial training on social and managerial skills. Professor Nový is the current dean of the Faculty of Business Administration and the Department of Managerial Psychology and Sociology of the University of Economics, Prague.*

REFERENCES

Allen, D., Freeman, D. M., Russell, E. A., Reizenstein, R. C., & Rentz, J. O. (2001, June). Survivor reactions to organizational downsizing: Does time ease the pain? *Journal of Occupational and Organizational Psychology*, *74*(2), 145–164. doi:10.1348/096317901167299

Brenner, M. D., Fairris, D., & Ruser, J. (2004). Flexible work practices and occupational safety and Health: Exploring the Relationship between cumulative trauma disorders and workplace transformation. *Industrial Relations*, *43*(1), 242–266. doi:10.1111/j.0019-8676.2004.00325.x

De Klerk, M. (2007, Summer). Healing Emotional Trauma in Organizations: An O.D. Framework and Case Study. *Organization Development Journal*, *25*(2), 49–55.

Gabriel, Y. (2012). Organizations in a State of Darkness: Towards a Theory of Organizational Miasma. *Organization Studies*, *33*(9), 1137–1152. doi:10.1177/0170840612448154

Harter, J. K., Schmidt, F. L., & Hayes, T. L. (2002). Business-Unit-Level Relationship Between Employee Satisfaction, Employee Engagement, and Business Outcomes: A Meta-Analysis. *The Journal of Applied Psychology*, *87*(2), 268–279. doi:10.1037/0021-9010.87.2.268 PMID:12002955

Kahn, W. A. (2003). The revelation of Organizational Trauma. *The Journal of Applied Behavioral Science*, *39*(4), 364–380. doi:10.1177/0021886303261954

Sahdev, K. (2004). Revisiting the survivor syndrome: The Role of Leadership in Implementing downsizing. *European Journal of Work and Organizational Psychology*, *13*(2), 165–196. doi:10.1080/13594320444000056

Stuart, R. (1996). The trauma of organizational change. *Journal of European Industrial Training*, *20*(2), 11–16. doi:10.1108/03090599610110420

Van De Voorde, K., Paauwe, J., & Van Veldhoven, M. (2012, December). Employee Well-being and the HRM-Organizational Performance Relationship: A Review of Quantitative Studies. *International Journal of Management Reviews*, *14*(4), 391–407. doi:10.1111/j.1468-2370.2011.00322.x

Vanhala, S., & Tuomi, K. (2006). HRM, Company Performance and Employee Well-being. Management Revue, 17(3), 241-255.

Preface

When confronted with a stressful event that surpasses the ability to cope, this experience may lead to trauma. This condition, an emotional response that jeopardises psychological integrity, produces a series of symptoms that includes flashbacks, strained relationships, and physical manifestations. If such an event affects a significant portion of a group as in the case of an ethnic cluster or a nation, it disrupts the social structure and the sense of community. Incidental reports in the literature suggest that formally established institutions, organisations, and businesses are not immune from suffering symptoms of collective trauma. When affected by events with a strong adverse impact, an organisation, all or part, may exhibit signs of collective traumatization that in turn, deteriorates social bonds, damages external relations, and possibly instigate secondary and transgenerational traumatisation. In addition, due to the varied components of the organisation: hierarchy, roles, and functions, a collective trauma displays certain specifics such as typical causative mechanisms and characteristic symptomatology. The former includes massive redundancies, abuse of power and rank, catastrophic events, hostile take-overs and other considerable transformations. The symptomatology is characterised by the emergence of specific in-groups identified as victims, witnesses, perpetrators, the creation of new coalitions as a reaction to trauma, organisational rumours, emotional disengagement from the organisation, performance decline, scapegoating, and others. Despite these conditions and circumstances, the word "trauma" is seldom used as a description. As largely demonstrated in research on collective trauma, the absence of recognition of the traumatizing nature of distressing events, inhibits the healing process in the affected community. Therefore, when trauma-like events occur, it is essential for leaders to acknowledge the distressing nature and to obtain awareness and insight into the reality of the situation to mitigate emotional as well as functional consequences.

ORGANISATIONAL TRAUMA

Despite the turmoil, stress and constant change often experienced in today's organisations, the employee's life has bettered when compared with the situation observed decades ago. National labour codes especially those in the European Union, Canada and other western states establish limits to the number of hours worked and protect workers' rights. A work-life balance is no longer a taboo concept and many employees focus on leisure activities to replenish their energy. There exists an ongoing discussion on employee engagement, which implies that a "job" can also be a source of fulfilment and self-realisation. Under favourable circumstances, organisational life can be quite comfortable. However, in an environment of volatility, uncertainty, complexity and ambiguity (VUCA) many organisations confront sudden unexpected changes that impact the worker negatively. These are often amplified through mergers and acquisitions, transformations, downsizing, and outsourcing to name a few. When such turbulence overwhelms the employees' coping capacity, this leads to psychological wounds that require time to heal. When such "wounding" affects a group or a large portion of the organisation, circumstances prone to group trauma arise. Organisational trauma has an impact not only on employee well-being, but also on individual performance that ultimately affects organisational performance of the entire organisation. De Klerk (2007) identifies that unresolved emotional trauma is a significant barrier to employee performance.

Trauma: A Psychological Perspective

Current research in the field of trauma and post-traumatic stress disorder (PSTD) provides a detailled description of individual trauma that includes causative mechanisms, symptoms and impact of the level of dysfunctional behaviour of the individual. Trauma is understood as a reaction to the disconcerting events that the individual has no control or lacks a perception of control. This perception, real or imagined, then floods the psyche in a way that the person can no longer integrate and comprehend what is happening. The event and related traumatisation thus dramatically undermines the sense of personal integrity and welfare. Shock and an altered state of consciousness accompany the trauma complemented by confusion and a *freezing reaction*. In turn, feelings of anger, helplessness and depression follow. The intensity of traumatic experience depends on the subjective perception. The more intensely the individual experiences the traumatic event, the deeper and longer-lasting is the impression regardless of the event's "objective strength" (Stuart, 1996). When a trauma is not recognised as such within the given social context, victims attempt to detach from the traumatic event without processing it. The trauma then tends to be replayed in the forms of flashbacks, nightmares, and physical symptoms (Audergon, 2004). Subsequently, the trauma exercises an extremely negative impact on the psyche and significantly undermines the ability to fully utilise and fulfil potential and skills.

An unprocessed trauma is subsequently transformed into a post-traumatic stress disorder, which can be characterised by the following symptomatology (Courtois, 2008):

- Alterations in the regulation of affective impulses, difficulty with modulation of anger, self-destructiveness
- Alterations in attention and consciousness, amnesia, dissociative episodes, depersonalisation
- Alterations in self perceptions, chronic sense of guilt and responsibility, intense shame
- Alterations in perceptions of the perpetrator, incorporation of their beliefs
- Alterations in relationships to others, not able to trust, not able to feel intimate
- Somatisation and/or medical problems
- Alterations in systems of meaning, hopeless to find anyone who understands.

At present, numerous studies also explore the topic of collective trauma that is a traumatic experience that affects a larger group who thereafter exhibit similar maladaptive behaviour and emotional patterns. In the long term, these symptoms shape social norms of the affected group and create a long-term mood and anxiety within the community. The most researched collective traumas comprise war, genocides, and the severe marginalisation of ethnic and other minority groups (Luszczynska, Benight, & Cieslak, 2009; Audergon, 2004).

According to Erikson (1995), individual trauma interferes "only" with the intrapersonal structure of the individual, while collective trauma disrupts and alters the structure of social bonds of a community or a group of people. An important conclusion relative to collective trauma is that the traumatic events does not only affect the direct participants, but is trans-generational. More specifically, the next generation that has not personally experienced the incident may replicate the maladaptive behaviour patterns of the direct victims. The same phenomenon is observed in individual traumas wherein grandchildren may demonstrate similar behavioural patterns of their traumatised grandparents. Thus, while group trauma is always experienced subjectively, it possesses at the same time, a collective dimension that transcends the individual experience.

Organisational Trauma: A Definition

Trauma research that focuses on organisational context deals with individual trauma who have been directly or indirectly affected by challenging situations within their working environment. Most studies emphasise professions that are more likely to be exposed to events of a traumatic nature as integral components of their occupation as with the case of medical personnel, fire-fighters, armed and police forces. However, only few studies explore the collective dimension of organisational trauma and a minority of experts directly mention the existence of *organisational trauma* as a distinctive phenomenon. Employees exposed to a negative and intensive event that overrides their cope-capacity, trauma exists. Similarly, other traumas affect groups when a significant portion of their population is either directly or indirectly influenced by the circumstances, the trauma acquires a new collective dimension. Employees share their experience, approximate their behaviour patterns and gradually create a "shared story" that records the events thus enabling to interpret the reality. A shared identity in the affected group emerges and begins to define itself as "we" and views itself apart from the rest ("them"). The trauma, as well as the role of the "perpetrator" and the traumatised, the victim, acquires a collective dimension even though the trauma itself remains anchored in the distinctive experience of everyone concerned (Kahn, 2003; Gabriel, 2012).

Gabriel (2012) discusses organisational "darkness" where unspoken injuries are hidden, while on the exterior, individuals behave as if everything was "alright". There permeates a sense that in the background there is an invisible power, which determines the individuals' fate; who searches for scapegoats, victims and oppressors (Gabriel, 2012). Thus, the organisational trauma is characterised by deadlock within the entire affected group that remains trapped in patterns of dysfunctional behaviours and collective relationships with the outside world damaged. At the same time, a trans-generational traumatisation (Kahn 2003) is equally possible. Per Hormann and Vivian (2005), an organisation can suffer a trauma in a similar fashion as an individual when its self-defence mechanisms are overwhelmed and feelings of helplessness emerge in the collective. Comparably, Burke (2012) defines organisational trauma as a set of responses to one or more events that reach beyond the organisation's ability to handle the situation adaptively, which culminates to dysfunctional patterns of behaviour.

The authors suggest that the emergence of a common identity of "we", collective patterns of behaviour and shared experiences of the event in the affected group distinguishes organisational from an individual trauma without a collective dimension. Through these elements, a traumatic event in an organisation acquires a collective dimension. Moreover, in the same way as the individual trauma diminishes individual performance, the organisational trauma results in a reduction of organisational performance or the performance of its affected parts.

Based on the above, organisational trauma exists and possess both an individual and a collective dimension that manifests though a shared story and the collective identity of 'we' versus 'them'.

Proposition 1: Organisational trauma exists and comprises both an individual and collective dimension that manifests through a shared story and a subsequent identity of *us* versus *them*.

Three distinctive roles are described: the survivors affected directly, the witnesses affected indirectly, and the perpetrators. Gabriel (2012) describes five stages of survivors' reaction to trauma:

1. Denial
2. Idealisation of the lost ones
3. Anger at their disappearance
4. Guilt, self-accusation and blame for not having done enough
5. Scapegoating others

Quite interestingly, the "perpetrators" group in organisations tend to respond similarly. Stuart (1996) asserts that these individuals also exhibit stress, worry, angst and grief, feelings often associated with victims of disasters, catastrophes or abuse. Organisational trauma thus affects those who are directly involved in the event, both victims and perpetrators as well as those affected indirectly as with the survivors and witnesses (De Klerk, 2007). Moreover, in the same fashion that individual trauma diminishes individual performance, organisational trauma reduces organisational performance or at least within the affected parts.

Symptomatology of Organisational Trauma

The emergence of a shared collective identity is characteristic of groups affected by organisational trauma; the sense of "we" is created through which the survivors' group defines itself and separates from the rest of the organisation, the management and/or the owners. The "shared story" is replayed through social interactions that revolve around the traumatic event. Rumours emerge, that include anxiety about the future. Hormann and Vivian (2005) enumerate several symptoms of organisational trauma:

- Isolation of the group from the outside: the traumatised group sets itself aside from the rest of the organisation. The "rest" or its parts is perceived as a source of danger, is vilified and while the perception of the in-group, "we" is often progressively idealised. The group closes inwards and becomes more defensive and resistant to change.
- Loss of perspective: the ability to objectively assess external events is disrupted.
- Centrality of Insider Relationships: the internal life of the organisation is intensified, personal relationships become more and more important.
- Traumatic infection: Stress and anxiety can be transmitted to individuals who were affected by the events only indirectly or not at all, secondary traumatisation.
- Symptoms in affected individuals: People affected by the organisational trauma show signs of PSTD.
- Emergence of new perceived roles: the perpetrator or oppressor, perceived as omnipotent and the victims or oppressed, perceived as powerless
- Loss of the sense of meaningfulness of the work or the organisation detachment from the organisation's mission, transactional approach to work: "I do only what I am paid for.".

Gabriel (2012) also suggests that the present of the traumatised organisation is perceived as a divide or break from its past.

There lacks attention to the collective process and phenomena that are created by the trauma. One assumes that there is a disproportionate distribution in power in which one group suffers while the other speaks of the necessity of change and the move forward. This dominant group refuses to incorporate the traumatic story into their own. At the same time, there is no protective mechanism to confront the trauma itself and comfort the traumatised group.

These notions lead to the following:

Proposition 2: Organisational trauma exhibits strong collective behavioural patterns rooted in group identity. The latter being the marginalised and powerless group. The dominant group discards their perception and story of the events and strives to move on. The central process is one of victimisation and marginalisation.

Proposition 3: Long-term organisational trauma is displayed at the individual level as an aggressor introject that subsequently leads to feelings of helplessness as a victim and as such, promotes future aversion to change.

CAUSES AND MECHANISMS OF ORGANISATIONAL TRAUMA

Burke (2012) advocates that possible causes of organisational trauma include organisational restructuring associated with headcount reduction, mergers and acquisitions, sudden deaths and suicides at the workplace, terrorism, natural disasters and severe accidents at work. Organisational trauma can affect the whole organisation most frequently because of extraordinary external events, as with the terrorist attacks of 9/11, hostile takeovers by a competitor or only its parts. Emotional wounding in organisations may also be caused by an abuse of power and rank, manipulation, demeaning negative feedback, cynicism, gossip, humiliation and insensitive cost-cutting and redundancies (De Klerk, 2007).

Events leading to organisational trauma are categorised following several criteria:

- **Origin of the Trauma:** Internal or external events. According to Byron and Peterson (2002), most existing studies focus on internal events and study the impact of trauma on mental health and less on the organisational performance.
- **Time:** Acute or chronic stressors. According to Beehr et al (2000), the acute stressors tend to have a more devastating impact and last longer than the chronic stressors.
- **Visibility:** Visible causes as with restructuring, deaths, etc. or "invisible" causes, typically, bullying, manipulation, abuse of power.

Gabriel (2005) describes the process of projective identification through which the traumatised group creates a shared identity and sets itself apart from the rest of the organisation. When a trauma is not dealt with properly, it tends to spread to groups who did not experience the trauma themselves. In doing so, this results in a secondary or vicarious traumatisation (White & Rollins, 1981; Figley, 1982; Pearlman & Saakvitne, 1995) and compassion fatigue (Figley, 1995). According to Hormann and Vivian (2005), when the trauma imprints onto the organisation's culture, becomes part of the organisation's identity through a mechanism of emotional contagion and socialisation, the trauma spreads to the next generation of workers who have not experienced the actual trauma.

The way in which an organisational change is announced, presented and handled may induce trauma in a similar fashion as the change itself (Stuart, 1996). When a transformation is performed, and communicated impersonally, cynically, or without respect, the employees affected by the event may internalise this methodology. This ultimately leads to numbness and emotional withdrawal (Gabriel, 2012). Employees perceive themselves as a resource that translates to a transactional approach to work and consequently, a reduction in performance.

The existing literature is silent as to the origins and processes relevant to organisational trauma. However, there is recognition of the emotional wounds and the lack of acknowledgement as well as the victims attempt to cope.

Proposition 4: Organisational trauma is treated as a taboo. It is not accredited but overlooked. In doing so, the victims are re-traumatised through their failure to acquire recognition.

ORGANISATIONAL TRAUMA AND PERFORMANCE

The phenomenon of organisational trauma lacks depth in empiric research. Prevailing studies focus on the impact of trauma on individual performance. Nonetheless, it is to be expected that negative effects on performance should also appear at the organisational level. Allen et al (2001) report the negative effect of redundancies on survivors' performance. More specifically, they observe a decrease of organisational commitment and job involvement, lower satisfaction with job security and increased intent to turnover. While satisfaction with top management continues to increase with time, job involvement decreases. High-involvement employees appear to be the most sensitive group to such changes.

Although no definite data is available on the impact of organisational trauma on the performance of the organisation as a whole, available studies tend towards that direction. Sahnev (2004) suggests that organisational performance can be negatively influenced by the fact that management announces organisational changes. After downsizing, attitudes such as job satisfaction, organisational commitment, job involvement and intention to turnover become less favourable (Kozlowski, et al., 1993). Noer (1993) mentions the phenomenon of 'lay off survivor sickness', a term that describes common symptoms of guilt, lack of organisational commitment and fear typical of survivors towards downsizing. Sahnev (2004) reports a negative influence on employee engagement, while other studies demonstrate a strong relationship between employee engagement and well-being with employee performance (James, et al., 2002; Vanhala, et al., 2006; Van De Voorde, et al., 2012). Byron and Peterson (2002) indicate that people who experience an acutely stressful event exhibit a higher rate of absenteeism in the following period and decreased job satisfaction. Brenner et al. (2004) reports that occupational injuries occur more frequently in workplaces undergoing transformation.

Proposition 5: Organisational trauma impacts individual well-being and employee engagement and thus, organisational performance is negatively influenced.

INFLUENCING AND HEALING ORGANISATIONAL TRAUMA

An active approach to traumatic organisational changes should become an integral part of change management and transformation programmes (De Klerk, 2007; Gabriel, 2012). Firstly, the negative consequences of traumatic events can be mitigated through public recognition. Leaders can have a major positive impact to heal organisational wounds by acknowledging the existence of the trauma, providing a safe place, bringing the trauma to awareness, and allowing the expression and dealing with the emotion (Burke, 2012). Seeking an insight into what is happening and accepting the feelings associated with the trauma is essential (Moules, 2004), as well as recognising the role of managers as facilitators of group processes associated with experiences around the trauma (Kahn, 2003; De Klerk, 2007; Dutton, 2002). More compassion can promote the healing of organisational wounds (Dutton, 2002; Audergon, 2004). The managers' ability to enable sympathetic responses to trauma as opposed to suppressing them directly affects organisational ability to maintain high performance during difficult times (Dutton, 2002). Active listening and an attempt to understand the experience from the victims' and survivors' viewpoint are essential (Stuart, 1996).

Most change management models focus on "selling" changes to organisational members. However, many employees must grieve and mourn before they are open to the new exciting future full of possibilities (De Klerk, 2007). De Klerk (2007) proposes four steps to treat the trauma:

1. "Acknowledge the existence of trauma - organisations must and be willing to deal with it openly. By doing so, victims, survivors, witnesses and even perpetrators reach contentment. Acknowledging the existence of trauma and supporting process of trauma healing is the role of the leader;
2. Provide a safe space to work through the trauma – as symptoms of trauma are often associated with weakness many victims are ashamed. They need to be provided with a safe space where they can express their feelings without embarrassment
3. Symbolising the trauma and putting it into perspective – trauma experiences need to be brought into awareness. Effective way is to develop a narrative. This helps to find meaning in traumas.
4. Allowing emotions and dealing with the emotions – time need to be granted to allow to complete the grieving process."

Some authors also suggest that strengthening of organisational resilience can reduce the vulnerability to suffer organisational trauma. For instance, Sheffi (2005) emphasises the concept of "resilient organisational culture" where teamwork, collaborative spirit, engagement and personal relationships act as protective factors for the organisation in the time of crisis.

Proposition 6: There is a significant difference between trauma groups wherein the trauma is acknowledged and those for which the trauma is ignored. Methods dealing with the trauma influence the perception ad experience.

Proposition 7: Organisational trauma serves the collective learning process for both the organisation and member and possibly increase organisational resilience.

RESEARCH PROSPECTS

The research project seeks empirical answers to the following questions:

- Is it possible to demonstrate the existence of organisational trauma as a phenomenon with distinctive characteristics?
- What are the causative mechanisms of organisational trauma?
- How does the group process operate?
- What is the impact of organisational trauma on employees' engagement and well-being?
- What metrics may be applied to measure organisational trauma?
- What are the most effective methods to mitigate organisational trauma?
- How to develop a process model for learning?

The research focuses on a specific type of potentially traumatic event, the organisational change affecting the organisation or its parts. The research design combines a qualitative approach necessary to study the causative mechanisms of organisational trauma and its phenomenology with quantitative methods aimed to measure the impact of organisational trauma on member engagement and well-being. A series of commercial and non-profit organisations, an expected sample of 10 were identified, wherein a major restructuration has been implemented recently or is in process. These include downsizing, change management, post-merger and merger related projects. Within these organisations, the focus centres on departments and/or teams that are directly or impacted indirectly.

The following methods are employed to gather data:

- *Semi-structured individual in-depth interviews* with employees who have been directly/indirectly affected by the event. These interviews aim to explore the process of possible traumatisation, to study its causative mechanisms and symptoms at individual and group level.
- *Focus groups* to study the impact of the organisational change on the well-being of employees. The discussion will not identify the event as "traumatic" as not to influence the participants; information about the potentially traumatic nature of the event is expected to emerge spontaneously throughout facilitated group discussion.
- *A measure of well-being* administered to focus groups participants. The specific tool/questionnaire yet to be selected.
- *A measure of engagement* by using an ad hoc engagement questionnaire and/or by using data available from the organisation such as, employee satisfaction surveys.

In addition to verifying the traumatizing nature of organisational changes and their expected impact on well-being and engagement of the affected groups, the Grounded Theory approach is used (Strauss & Corbin, 1998) to derive a model of organisational trauma based on data gathered in the individual interviews and focus groups. Based on the results, possible ways of intervention to "heal" the organisational trauma and, should the cooperation with selected organisations be successfully prolonged, to examine the effectiveness of such interventions through further research.

ORGANIZATION OF THE BOOK

Chapter 1: The phenomenon of organizational trauma (OT) is mentioned by an increasing number of researchers. However, there is a large heterogeneity of definitions and practices related to this notion. This chapter reviews the existing literature about the subject focusing on three key elements: its definition, typology and the processes involved.

Chapter 2: This chapter proposes that a typology of "potentially traumatic events" (PTEs) and the taxonomy of these events' attributes can be developed by conducting a comprehensive literature review. As the final step, the proposed taxonomy was applied to real traumatic business cases happened in 2015 and early 2016 so that the taxonomic model was tested.

Chapter 3: This chapter examines the usefulness of the conceptualization of trauma in contemporary French theory for a better understanding of the core of organizational trauma. The aim of this chapter is also to bridge conceptual gaps, understanding critical differences in clinical practice and offering a more integrative view of psychological trauma.

Chapter 4: The purpose of this chapter is to provide an overview of the interrelationship between personal characteristics, such as resilience, emotional intelligence, and optimism, and the ability to cope with occupational stress and organizational trauma. The proposal of the authors is that the nurturing of specific personality traits, attitudes, and behaviors can prove beneficial both on an individual and organizational level.

Chapter 5: The chapter summarizes research studies as well as case studies from companies worldwide that show how organizational changes followed by downsizing create a traumatic experience for all organization members. The author's focus is on the psychological perspective on traumatic experience by all employees (victims and survivors) and managers whose task is to organize and implement changes in the organization.

Chapter 6: This chapter evaluates the correlation between change management and the employee and/or management behaviors detrimental to the wellbeing of those individuals and the overall productivity and efficiency of an organization. It also includes the introduction and brief analysis of organizational change and effectiveness models the Burke-Litwin Model.

Chapter 7: Increasing human interaction creates extra stress on individuals and organisations as well. Although major models are sufficient for defining national culture, there is lack of work explaining the managerial implications for crisis management or mitigating trauma in organisations. The authors of this chapter intend to critically review the latest literature on national culture, while discussing the relevant models and introducing the theoretic framework applicable for crisis/ trauma management.

Chapter 8: The decision-making process of disclosure and the necessity for others to know is key to understanding how best to support and address the potential organizational trauma that may result. Through increased knowledge about the LGBTQ community and case analysis, a cross cultural lens will be utilized from Brazil, Turkey and the U.S.; prominent sexual identity disclosure perspectives for numerous occupations, as well as recommendations for systemic awareness and change will be offered.

Chapter 9: The purpose of this chapter is on the impact of organizational trauma on workplace behavior and performance based on workplace bullying. The chapter is based on a case study regarding a program that is funded by the Department of Education within a community college in the State of California.

Chapter 10: In this chapter the authors seek to answer the question how organizational trauma, and near-death experiences, can positively influence organizational culture in the long term. In doing so, the authors briefly review the recent literature on organizational trauma and near death experiences, and discuss how these negative traumatic experiences can turn into prosocial organizational behaviour.

Chapter 11: The aim of this chapter is to describe a trauma experienced among blue collar employees at the XYZ car factory in Turkey. This study focuses on the pre-intervention, pilot intervention and main intervention programs. The theoretical perspective is put forward; the implemented program is described and the descriptive findings are presented then the findings and implications are discussed.

Chapter 12: This chapter begins by exploring subjective well-being and its origins dating back to ancient thinkers such as Aristotle. In addition, this chapter also presents the latest research from neuroscience and discusses how neuroscience potentially challenges personality and set-point theories. A few practical steps for subjective well-being are also discussed.

Chapter 13: This chapter attempts to show the complexity of the problem through getting over the traditional framework of managerial psychology as defined by modern Western thought. It tackles the potential of spirituality (human faith and hope) that gives a new meaning to life and work. Spirituality relates to some religious systems.

Chapter 14: This chapter endeavors to contribute to knowledge about organizational trauma and leader behaviors- specifically what leaders can do when there are signs of trauma in the organization due to organizational change. The authors also link professional identity to the trauma of organizational change.

Richard Brunet-Thornton
University of Economics, Czech Republic

Stanislav Háša
University of Economics, Czech Republic

REFERENCES

Allen, D., Freeman, D. M., & Russell Joyce, E. A. (2001, June). Survivor reactions to organisational downsizing: Does time ease the pain? *Journal of Occupational and Organizational Psychology*, *74*(2), 145–164. doi:10.1348/096317901167299

Audergon, A. (2004). Collective trauma: The nightmare of History. *Psychotherapy and Politics International*, *2004*(1), 16–31. doi:10.1002/ppi.67

Baruch, Y., & Hind, P. (2000). Survivor syndrome - a management myth? *Journal of Managerial Psychology*, *15*(1), 29–45. doi:10.1108/02683940010305289

Beehr, T. A., Jex, S. M., Stacy, B. A., & Murray, M. A. (2000). Work stressors and coworker support as predictors of individual strain and job performance. *Journal of Organizational Behavior*, *21*(4), 391–405. doi:10.1002/(SICI)1099-1379(200006)21:4<391::AID-JOB15>3.0.CO;2-9

Brenner, M. D., Fairris, D., & Ruser, J. (2004). Flexible work practices and occupational safety and health: Exploring the relationship between cumulative trauma disorders and workplace transformation. *Industrial Relations*, *43*(1), 242–266. doi:10.1111/j.0019-8676.2004.00325.x

Burke, R. J. (2012). International Handbook of Workplace Trauma Support. In R. Hughes, A. Kinder, & C. L. Cooper (Eds.), Workplace Trauma Support. Wiley-Blackwell.

Byron, K., & Peterson, S. (2002). The impact of a large-scale traumatic event on individual and organisational outcomes. *Journal of Organizational Behavior*, 895–910. doi:10.1002/job.176

Courtois, C. A. (2008). Complex trauma, complex reactions: Assessment and treatment. *Psychological Trauma: Theory, Research, Practice, and Policy, S*(1), 86-100.

De Klerk, M. (2007, Summer). Healing Emotional Trauma in Organisations: An O.D. Framework and Case Study. *Organization Development Journal, 25*(2), 49–55.

Dutton, J.E., Frost, P. J., Worline, M.C., Lilius, J.M., & Kanov, J. M. (2002, January). Leading in Time of Trauma. *Harvard Business Review*, 55-61.

Erikson, K. (1995). Notes on trauma and community. In C. Caruth (Ed.), Trauma: explorations in memory (pp. 183–199). Academic Press.

Evers, Prochaska, Castle, Johnson, Prochaska, Harrison, … Pope. (2012). Development of an individual well-being scores assessment. *Psychology of Well-Being: Theory, Research and Practice.*

Figley, C. R. (1982). *Traumatization and comfort: Close relationships may be hazardous to your health.* Conference on Families and Close Relationships: Individuals in social interaction, Lubbock, TX.

Figley, C. R. (Ed.). (1995). *Compassion Fatigue: Coping with secondary traumatic stress disorder in those who treat the traumatized.* Florence, KY: Brunner/Mazel.

Gabriel, Y. (2012). Organisations in a State of Darkness: Towards a Theory of Organisational Miasma. *Organization Studies, 33*(9), 1137–1152. doi:10.1177/0170840612448154

Harter, J. K., Schmidt, F. L., & Hayes, T. L. (2002). Business-unit-level relationship between employee satisfaction, employee engagement, and business outcomes: A meta-analysis. *The Journal of Applied Psychology, 87*(2), 268–279. doi:10.1037/0021-9010.87.2.268 PMID:12002955

Hormann, S., & Vivian, P. (2005). Toward An Understanding of Traumatized Organisations and How to Intervene in Them. *Traumatology, 11*(3), 159–169. doi:10.1177/153476560501100302

Kahn, W. A. (2003). The revelation of Organisational Trauma. *The Journal of Applied Behavioral Science, 39*(4), 364–380. doi:10.1177/0021886303261954

Kozlowski, S. W. J., Chao, G. T., Smith, E. M., & Hedlund, J. (1993). Organisational downsizing: Strategies, interventions, and research implications. *International Review of Industrial and Organizational Psychology, 8*, 263–332.

Luszczynska, A., Benight, C. C., & Cieslak, R. (2009). Self-efficacy and health-related outcomes of collective trauma: A systematic review. *European Psychologist, 14*(1), 51–62. doi:10.1027/1016-9040.14.1.51

Harter, Schmidt, & Hayes. (2002). Business-Unit-Level Relationship Between Employee Satisfaction, Employee Engagement, and Business Outcomes: Meta-Analysis, . *The Journal of Applied Psychology, 87*(2), 268–279.

Moules, N. J., Simonson, K., Prins, M., Angus, P., & Bell, J. M. (2004). Making room for grief: Walking backwards and living forward. *Nursing Inquiry*, *11*(2), 99–107. doi:10.1111/j.1440-1800.2004.00204.x PMID:15154889

Noer, D. M. (1993). *Healing the wounds*. San Francisco, CA: Jossey-Bass Inc.

Pearlman, L. A., & Saakvitne, K. W. (1995). *Trauma and the therapist: Countertransference and vicarious traumatization in psychotherapy with incest survivors*. New York, NY: W.W. Norton and Company.

Sahdev, K. (2004). Revisiting the survivor syndrome: The role of Leadership in implementing downsizing. *European Journal of Work and Organizational Psychology*, *13*(2), 165–196. doi:10.1080/13594320444000056

Sheffi, Y. (2005). *The resilient enterprise*. Cambridge, MA: Ballinger.

Strauss, A. L., & Corbin, J. (1998). *Basics of qualitative research: Grounded theory procedures and techniques* (2nd ed.). Thousand Oaks, CA: Sage.

Stuart, R. (1996). The trauma of organisational change. *Journal of European Industrial Training*, *20*(2), 11–16. doi:10.1108/03090599610110420

Van De Voorde. (2012, December). Employee Well-being and the HRM-Organisational Performance Relationship: A Review of Quantitative Studies. *International Journal of Management Reviews*, *14*(4), 391–407. doi:10.1111/j.1468-2370.2011.00322.x

Vanhala, S., & Tuomi, K. (2006). HRM, Company Performance and Employee Well-being. *Management Review*.

White, P. N., & Rollins, J. C. (1981). Rape: A family crisis. *Family Relations*, *30*(1), 103–109. doi:10.2307/584243

Acknowledgment

The editors wish to acknowledge the assistance of all those involved in this project and, more specifically, to the authors and reviewers that took part in the assessment process. Without their support, this book would not have become a reality.

First, the editors wish to thank each author for their contributions. Our sincere gratitude to those who contributed their time and expertise to this endeavour.

Second, the editors recognise the valuable contributions of the reviewers to the improvement of quality, coherence, and content presentation of chapters. Many authors also served as referees; we highly appreciate this double task.

Lastly, special thanks to our Editorial Advisory Board members.

Section 1
Defining and Understanding Organizational Trauma

Chapter 1
Definitions, Typologies, and Processes Involved in Organizational Trauma:
A Literature Review

Pablo Alonso Pena
Royal Military Academy, Belgium

Michel Sylin
Université Libre de Bruxelles, Belgium

Stephan Van den Broucke
Université Catholique de Louvain, Belgium

Jan Leysen
Royal Military Academy, Belgium

Erik de Soir
Royal Higher Institute of Defence, Belgium

ABSTRACT

The phenomenon of organizational trauma (OT) is mentioned by an increasing number of researchers. However, there is a large heterogeneity of definitions and practices related to this notion. In view of developing a more consensual understanding of OT, this paper reviews the existing literature with regard to the subject focusing on three key elements: its definition, typology and the processes involved. For each element, the existing models are reviewed and an integrated conceptualization is introduced, providing a basis for further empirical research and enabling comparisons between existing studies. As such, the paper contributes to the consensus that is necessary to advance the research with regard to this subject.

INTRODUCTION

The economic crisis of 2008 and the austerity measures that followed, making many people redundant, the terrorist attacks of New-York, London, Madrid, Paris, or Brussels, and natural or man-made disasters such as Hurricane Katrina or the nuclear disaster in Fukushima have changed our way of life. These events made many victims, and traumatized many more. However, the victims of these events were not only individuals. Organizations also were directly or indirectly impacted. How did organizations react to

DOI: 10.4018/978-1-5225-2021-4.ch001

these events? How will they respond to future events? In this paper we will try to answer these question by developing a conceptualization of organizational trauma and its processes.

Etymologically, the word trauma comes from the Greek word τραυμα. As stated by De Soir, Daubechies, and Van den Steene (2012, p. 111), a "trauma" in fact means an "injury" that is inflicted by a confrontation with an event that is terrifying and/or life-threatening, difficult to manage on an emotional level for a "normal" human being, and which threatens to overwhelm and completely control that person. As such, a traumatic experience can change individual peoples' perceptions of their environment, themselves, or the people surrounding them. Continued exposure to trauma will have repercussions on individuals' biological, cognitive and emotional existences, and also on their social interactions and identities (De Clercq, 1999).

A potentially traumatising experience is generally considered to be an event that affects people who are confronted with a sudden situation that is potentially threatening, either physically or emotionally. That might be a serious accident or a natural catastrophe (Guiho-Bailly & Guillet, 2005). This individual-centred approach to trauma is the classic approach adopted in the literature. However, organisations, just like individuals, can also be confronted with trauma. Indeed, at the time of potentially traumatising events, organisations also undergo changes that affect their founding principles in such a way that they no longer operate as before.

Despite the various indications that highlight the existence of such an "organisational pathology" and the burgeoning interest in this concept, there are currently only a few publications dealing with organisational trauma (OT). In addition, the emerging literature on this topic, stemming from only a handful of researchers (Brown, 1997; Byron & Peterson, 2002; Vivian & Hormann, 2002; Kahn, 2003; Farragher & Yanosy, 2005; Hormann & Vivian, 2005; Hormann, 2007; Pross & Schweitzer, 2010; Klein & Alexander, 2011; Burke, 2012; Gantt & Hopper, 2012; Hopper, 2012; Vivian & Hormann, 2013), reveals such disparities that a consensual model of OT does not exist yet. Such a model would nevertheless be very useful, not only to study the phenomenon, but also to diagnose OT through organisational assessment or to develop and implement preventive interventions.

This chapter aims to provide the elements for such an analytic model of OT by reviewing the existing literature with regard to organisational trauma. While taking the divergent and convergent definitions of OT into account, it will propose a consensual model. Using this model, the characteristics of OT will be discussed and a typology of OTH will be established. Finally, the traumatising process will also be analysed and conceptualised.

METHOD

Information Sources and Search Terms

In order to perform the literature review, a search of virtual databases was performed, using the matrix method proposed by Goldman and Schmalz (2004). As the concept of OT is relatively new and described in very few publications, the first task was to find every article dealing with this concept as its main or subsidiary focus.

To trace potentially relevant publications, the search was performed using the electronic interfaces Ebscohost and Proquest, as well as the Cairn and PubMed databases and Google Scholar. Within Ebscohost, the following databases were consulted: Academic Search Elite, Business Source Premier, EconLit,

ERIC, and Library Information Science & Technology abstract. In Proquest, Psychinfo was consulted. As the general Boolean expression (oragni* AND trauma*) produced too results that were too heterogeneous, five Boolean combinations of search terms were used, covering different languages (i.e., English, French, Spanish, and Italian). These combinations were: (organizational AND trauma); (trauma AND impact AND organization); (Traumatisme organisationnel); (Trauma* AND organizacion*); (Trauma AND organizzazion*); and ("Trauma* AND organisation*"). In Pubmed, a specific Boolean expression was used to exclude the high number of publications involving physiological trauma: (institution AND "XXX" NOT Wounds NOT injuries), where XXX represents the Booleans sentences given above. In Google Scholar, the same Boolean sentences were used but restricted by the addition of quotations marks. Finally, all relevant reference lists from the identified articles were hand searched for additional relevant articles. As a result of this procedure, a total of 4148 papers were found. Of these, 1292 were found through Cairn, 1109 via Proquest, 869 via Ebscohost, 621 via PubMed, and 257 via Google Scholar.

Given the larger number of references found, a first selection was made based on the abstracts, enabling us to focus on those publications that were most relevant. In order to be considered for inclusion, an article had to have OT or pathologies close to OT (such as organisational stress) as its subject. Articles dealing with organisational crisis that could lead to organisational trauma but which did not focus on the concept specifically were excluded. This was the case for articles dealing with physical trauma and/or trauma centres, and/or organisational causes of individual trauma, and/or only mentioning OT without further developing the issue.

In total, 15 publications in English were retained.

RESULTS

Definitions

Of the fifteen articles retained, five suggest a definition for OT, while also listing the causes, symptoms and consequences. None of the definitions was adopted by another author and their content is heterogeneous. The definitions are set out in Table 1.

All of the five definitions are characterised by a twofold structure: the triggers that induced the OT, and the consequences of the appearance of that trauma. This structure is illustrated in the two right-hand columns of Table 1.

1. Triggers

The triggers of an OT have few common characteristics. Two definitions even present contradictions: According to Hormann (2005), the traumatic event arises due to an unusual event, whereas according to Brown (1997) the event is an institutionalized feature of the organisational system, its inevitable character implying that it belongs to the "normal" trajectory of an organisation. If an organisation often faces crises, the "traumatic" crisis is typical. Amongst other things, this is what distinguishes it from a crisis that is not traumatic. For example, the organisation *Medecins sans Frontières* ("Doctors without Borders") often has face crisis situations, to the effect that it becomes part of the normal functioning of this organisation. However, the same events and crises can be traumatic for other organisations that are not supposed to face them.

Table 1. OT definition

	Definitions	Triggers	Consequences
Hormann and Vivian (2005)	An injury to the body of an organization resulting from a single event or an accumulation of injuries	A single event or an accumulation of injuries	An injury to the body of an organization
	Severe distress from experiencing a disastrous event outside the range of usual experience, as the bombing of a building or embezzlement	Experiencing a disastrous event outside the range of usual experience, as the bombing of a building or embezzlement	Severe distress
Stein (1991)	The protective emotional membrane was penetrated, violated, perhaps destroyed	The protective emotional membrane was penetrated, violated, perhaps destroyed	
	At any level, trauma is an experience for which a person-family-group is emotionally (not only cognitively) unprepared, that overwhelms ones' defensive (self-protective) structure and leaves one feelings totally vulnerable and at least temporarily helpless	Experience for which a person-family-group is emotionally (not only cognitively) unprepared, that overwhelms ones' defensive (self-protective) structure	Leaves one feelings totally vulnerable and at least temporarily helpless
Hopper (2012)	A set of potential organizational responses to internal or external acts or events	Internal or external acts or events	A set of potential organizational responses
Burke (2012)	[Trauma] « Caused » by one or more individuals or by natural forces that result in psychological distress, property damage, injury, or death to one or more employees of an organization.	[« Caused » by one or more individuals or by natural forces	Result in psychological distress, property damage, injury, or death to one or more employees of an organization
	Can affect one or more organizations simultaneously.		Can affect one or more organizations simultaneously
Brown (1997)	Institutionalized pattern of pathology [...], reflects the trauma which can cripple an organization [...], is inevitable in a system. It is not good or bad	Is inevitable in a system	Institutionalized pattern of pathology

2. Consequences

The five definitions of OT all offer different descriptions of the consequences of a traumatic event. The review shows that this event can cause physical or non-physical injuries. Physical injuries are marked by physical damage such as the deterioration of buildings or injury or death inflicted upon one or more employees (Burke, 2012). The non-physical injuries refer to a sense of vulnerability (Stein, 2005), to various organisational responses (Hopper, 2005) and to institutionalised disease patterns (Brown, 1997). Hormann (2007) looks at two possibilities, characterising the consequences as injuries to the body of an organisation and acute stress.

Characteristics of OT

1. Triggers

The literature review shows that a parallel can be drawn between things that trigger an OT and "potentially traumatising events" that are mentioned in theories of individual trauma. The concept of a potentially traumatising event is defined by Crocq (2007; cited by Salmona, 2013) as: "*a phenomenon involving the rupture of the psyche and the overcoming of its defences by violent stimulations relating to the occurrence of an assault or threat against the life or integrity (physical or psychological) of an individual exposed to it as a victim, witness or party*" (p. 72). When translated to an organisation, the "rupture of the psyche" and the "overcoming of its defences" becomes the "penetration, violation and perhaps destruction of the protective emotional membrane" (Stein, 2005; cited by Hormann & Vivian, 2005). On the other hand, the "occurrence of an assault or threat against the life or the physical or psychological integrity of an individual exposed to it as a victim, witness or party" in an organisational context would refer to "a disastrous event outside the range of usual experience, caused by one or more individuals or by natural forces that result in psychological distress, property damage, injury, or death to one or more employees of an organization [that] can affect one or more organizations simultaneously" (Burke 2012).

2. Consequences

As outlined in the definitions of OT, the consequences can be many, and as such give rise to a lack of precision. This imprecision is due to the difficulty to differentiate normal progress of an organisation's experience from a pathological consequence. According to Hopper (2012), it is even impossible to define a normal state for an organisation, as an organisation does not have "natural" lines of development, and, therefore, their lines of regression and progression cannot be assumed in advance. Nevertheless, other authors mention various organisational consequences of a traumatic event which they consider as pathological, without referring to the normal or natural state. It is however important to understand why these consequences are considered as "pathological" by comparing them to a state that can be considered as "normal".

In this regard, our review of the consequences of OT found in the literature allows us to distinguish between 5 categories of consequences: (a) Groupthink type behaviours, (b) trauma propagation, (c) loss of points of reference and emotional security, (d) expression of stress, and (e) structural dysfunction.

a. Groupthink type behaviours.

The first category of consequences are the symptoms of organisations that suffer from the "groupthink" phenomenon (Hart, 1991), also known as the "Janis effect". This phenomenon was first used to describe the group dynamics affecting the decision-making of group leaders. The term "Groupthink" was chosen in reference to the term "Doublethink" in George Orwell's "1984". The concept has since then been extended to include the way in which group realities are affected in their entirety.

With regard to OT, this first category covers three symptoms of Groupthink. The first is an over-estimation of the group, characterised by illusions of invulnerability and an unquestioned belief in the morality of the group. The second, closed-mindedness, refers to collective rationalisation and stereotyping of other groups. The third, pressure towards uniformity, refers to self-censorship, illusions of unanimity and direct pressure on those who do not agree with the group consensus. This creates a context in which rational decisions cannot be taken in a coherent manner.

A consequence of OT that is often highlighted in the literature is closing the borders of the organisation (Brown, 1997; Hormann, 2007; Stein, 1991; Vivian & Hormann, 2013). It is directly linked to the first and second type of Groupthink symptoms. Similarly, the centrality of domestic relations (Hormann & Vivian, 2005; Klein & Alexander, 2011) is also linked to this effect.

The best predictor of whether or not Groupthink will appear is the context. This context is defined by Hart (1991) as "a situation with stressful characteristics, whether they be internal or external to the group" (pp. 258-259). As such, the context of an organisational trauma lends itself perfectly to the progression of Groupthink. This is illustrated by Farragher and Yanosy (2005) who noted that in the healthcare centres where the work is very stressful, behaviours linked to Groupthink are notably present.

Hopper (2012) points out the propensity of organisations to behave like large groups when confronted with an OT, and for large groups to behave like restricted groups. According to this author, traumatised organisations "tend to lose their formal structure and become large groups or like large groups." (Hopper, 2012, p. xxi) It is not unreasonable therefore to propose Groupthink as a symptom of OT.

b. Trauma propagation.

The second category of consequences of OT refers to vicarious trauma theories. These suppose that trauma propagates not only from one person to another, but also from one generation to another (Gantt & Hopper, 2012). In other words, whereas the OT may only affect a part of the organisation at first instance, it will eventually spread to the entire organisation. An explanation for this phenomenon is given by Vivian and Hormann (2013), who advance the idea that trauma changes the organisational culture. The latter incorporates the trauma which is then transmitted to other generations.

Examples of this form of propagation can be seen in corporate restructuring. When a decision is taken to restructure (a part of) an organisation, the news of this restructuring often spreads more quickly than the official information. In a same way, the trauma that a restructuration may cause is also propagated.

c. Loss of reference points and emotional security.

The third category are the consequences found in classic definitions of trauma. As for post-traumatic stress, the loss of reference points caused by the organisational identity crisis resulting from the trauma is a fundamental consequence of organisational trauma. The crisis will disrupt the organisation, its identity and any other constituent elements. An organisation that normally has meaning and creates an identity for the individuals that belong to it loses its characteristics (Koninckx & Teneau, 2010), which has for a direct consequence that the organisational reference points are lost. This also has consequences for the organisations' group behaviour (Hopper, 2012).

When an event causes the organisational identity to change, the values of the organisation change as well. For example, when the Youth Division of the Norwegian Labour Party was attacked by Anders Breivik on the island of Utøya near Oslo in 2011, it was also the values shared by the workers that were attacked. Questions like "How can we deal with this event? Should we stop working for what we believe in? Is our work safe?" indicates the loss of reference points.

d. Expression of stress.

Of all the different consequences of an OT, stress is the most visible one. The stress that is caused by the trauma can be expressed in a whole range of behaviours of the individuals within the organisation. These behaviours are the ones that are most often reported in the literature on OT. For instance, Byron and Peterson (2002) noted an increase in absenteeism and dissatisfaction at work. Kibel (2012) mentioned the appearance of rumours within an organisation due to OT, which characteristically induce paranoid behaviours in individuals. Another example of this type of consequence is the increase of suicides within the company France Telecom in 2008-2009 mentioned by Burke (2012).

e. Structural dysfunction.

Pross and Schweitzer (2010) mention that as a consequence of an OT a chaotic, unstructured and unpredictable environment, accompanied by an increase of the role of informal structures. The latter is due to the fact that informal structures govern organisational dynamics more than formal structures. As for the previously mentioned consequences, the structural dysfunction is a direct consequence of the identity crisis. Since the structure of an organisation is an essential element in the definition of its identity, an identity crisis will have a destructive effect on the organisation.

This consequence can be illustrated by the crisis that occurred in the Volkswagen company following the environmental software scandal. As the trust in the organisation is damaged due to the scandal, employees are trying to develop a new structure through informal networks which they trust.

The different categories of consequences outlined above do not all impact on the OT in the same way. Groupthink behaviours and the emergence of informal structures are important for the preservation of the organisational identity: Groupthink results in the preservation of a positive and stable image of a group (Turner & Pratkanis, 1998), while the emergence of informal structures compensates the tensions within the formal structures arising from the identity crisis (Gombault, 2002). The other consequences do not play such a protective role.

3. Differentiation from related concepts

The outline of the triggers and consequence of OT in the preceding paragraphs allow to understand what has thus far been considered an OT. However, they are not sufficient to give a full account of what an OT is, as many of these characteristics are also found to describe other pathologies. It is therefore necessary to specify the issues that allow to distinguish OT from other phenomena.

a. OT and individual trauma

A first distinction that must be made is that between OT and individual trauma. Our literature review identified a large number of articles that dealt with individual trauma caused by organisations. Admittedly, there are strong similarities between the conceptualizations of OT and those relating to individual trauma, which refers to a post-traumatic state defined as "anxiety-producing distress that appears following the occurrence of a disturbing event in the patient's life" and can be acute, chronic or delayed (Bathia, 2009). The DSM V (2013) defines six diagnostic characteristics of trauma: threat to life and severity of the peri-traumatic response, flashbacks, avoidance and dullness symptoms, state of arousal, significant duration of disturbance and suffering or changes in functioning. These characteristics are very similar to those of organisational trauma, in the way that the threat to life is comparable to the potentially traumatic event; the peri-traumatic event can be compared to the identity crisis; the avoidance and dullness symptoms are similar to the Groupthink behaviours; the significant suffering are linked to the expression of stress; and the changes in functioning are comparable to structural dysfunction. Moreover, flashbacks can also be considered in OT, as it is conceivable that the organisational culture integrates aspects of the events that triggered the OT and a comparable situation can trigger the same responses.

Despite these parallels, however, organisational and individual traumas are two distinct phenomena, as the "subjects" affected by the "pathology" are fundamentally different. It must be realized that an organisation is not just the sum of the individuals that are part of it, and is not an entirely distinct entity either (Klein & Kozlowski, 2013). The view of an organisation as an assembly of individuals neglects the structure, aims, common beliefs and values, and collective responses of an organisation. On the other hand, the anthropomorphic view of an organisation neglects the singularity of individuals within the organisation and attributes thoughts to the organisation itself. Consequently, defining OT as the sum of the individual traumas is reductive, as is ignoring its repercussions for the members of the organisation. That is why the effect of an OT on individuals is important to measure and understand (Byron & Peterson, 2002; Pross & Schweitzer, 2010), but it is not the point to consider.

b. OT and organisational "pathologies"

The literature on OT describes the five characteristics described in point 2.2. as being relevant to traumatised organisations. However, as noted above, these characteristics are not always pathological: They can be part of the "normal" operation of an organisation or, at least, a stage of its development.

For instance, Groupthink is a reflection of the operation of an organisation that includes the massification of individuals as one of its fundamental values (Hopper, 2012). These must remain solid no matter what, without questioning the legitimacy of the group and the instructions given to them. Organisations that are impacted by this effect mainly comprise emergency response units, such as the army and the emergency services etc. Likewise, the propagation of trauma is a daily recurring event for organisations that work with victims. It does not necessarily entail an organisational pathology, as long as the phenomenon is controlled and remains within acceptable parameters. The loss of reference points and structural dysfunction are also aspects that can be normal or even beneficial for an organisation. According to Brown (1997), the changes at the heart of an organisation subsequent to a trauma allow for a better understanding of the organisation and a revitalization of its structures.

As a consequence, only the expression of stress is pathological in and of itself. However, the presence of stress alone is not sufficient to consider the existence of an OT, as other causes might potentially be triggers. It is therefore necessary to analyse these characteristics, taking into account the individuality of the organisation affected.

The consequences of an organisational trauma are not considered pathological in the individual psychology sense, which means pathological in comparison to the norm. They are pathological in the sense that they are dependent upon a state that the organisation considers negative.

Another element adds nuance to the specific characteristics of OT: their strong resemblance to those caused by other "pathological" organisational reactions. Two of these have strong similarities to OT: Organisational stress and the non-traumatic organisational identity crisis.

1. OT and organisational stress

Organisational stress is strongly related to OT. Indeed, the symptoms of organisational stress as defined by Bloom (2006) correspond well to the categories defined for OT (cf. Table 2). At first glance, only one element distinguishes both phenomena: the potentially traumatising event. In certain cases, the distinction can be very subtle. If you take the example of a vicarious trauma, there is no single event that pierces the organisation's protective emotional membrane, but a trauma that pierces the membrane bit by bit and has its impact over time.

As such, the difference between organisational stress and OT is similar to that between stress and post-traumatic stress (PTSD). This difference is structured around three elements. The first one is time. One of the criteria of PTSD is that the symptoms must persist for over a month (APA, 2013). As such, we must also take into consideration that an OT may continue even after the end of the threatening event or assault. The second element is that the potentially traumatising events are inherently violent and thus allow the rupture of the protective membrane (Stein et al, 2005). The third element is the fact that the theories of organisational stress make no reference to a possible identity crisis.

2. OT and the organisational identity crisis

Table 2. Comparison of consequences between organizational trauma and organizational stress

TO	Organisational Stress
Groupthink Behaviors	Loss of Emotional Management
	Impaired Cognition and Silencing of Dissent
	Increased Authoritarianism
	Systematic Error
	Dissociation, Amnesia, and Fragmentation of Function
Trauma propagation	Chronic Stressors and Collective Trauma
Loss of boundaries and emotional security	Loss of Meaning and Demoralization
	Unresolved Grief
	Lack of Basic Safety
	Disempowerment and Helplessness
Expression of stress	Increased Aggression
Structural dysfunctions	Impoverished Relationships

Although an OT includes an organisational identity crisis by virtue of its impact on the organisation's identity and reference points, not all organisational identity crises actually entail an OT. Gombault (2002) introduced the process leading to an identity crisis as "a break in continuity", which is due to the fact that differences are subjectively perceived as being too significant for the assumption of a degree of continuity. "When the differences are perceived as ruptures, then crises of identity appear" (Mucchielli, 1986; cited by Gombault, 2002, p. 13).

An organisational identity crisis (OIC) implies various consequences. Apart from the loss of reference points, which is also a consequence of OT, these consequences are defined by their own nomenclature. However, a comparison of the consequences of an OIC with those of an OT shows that both look at the same aspects, and that only the terms used to describe the phenomena are different:

- A first consequence of OIC described in the literature is the "autopoietic system" mode of operation. This is characterised by a "*self-referential closing-off vis-à-vis its environment*" (Gombault, 2002, pp. 17). The characteristics of this mode of operation are very similar to those of Groupthink.
- The second consequence of OIC highlighted in the literature is "solipsism", defined by Gombault (2002) as "*a situation where there is no other reality for the parties other than their perceptions of the organisation's identity*" (pp 17). This entails communication difficulties and internal conflicts. These elements resemble the expression of stress that is observed in an OT. Paranoid and psychodramatic thoughts have also been mentioned for OIC, and have also been reported by Kibel (2012) in traumatised organisations.
- A third and final consequence mentioned for OIC is the division that is observed between the employees and the management, along with the formation of informal groups. These can be likened to the characteristics of structural dysfunction mentioned for OT.

Despite these similarities, OIC differs from OT in the sense that there is no trauma propagation, nor stress or loss of emotional security. Indeed, OIC do not assume that a trauma is involved. They may be due, for example, to simple organisational change. The issue of violence, and even suffering, is not a prerequisite for the crisis and may not be present.

These similarities between organisational stress, organisational identity crises and OT refer back to the premises of the stress theories as developed by Selye (1936; cited by Rimé, 2005). His work has enabled the demonstration of a sole defensive response in the face of an extreme situation. By analogy, the similarities that are found between the consequences mentioned by authors who study different organisational pathologies are due to the fact that they echo the same, single response to an extreme situation.

PROCESS

Throughout this paper, we have stated that an OT is structured around two significant dimensions: the potentially traumatising event that triggers the trauma, and the consequences of this trauma on the employees and on the organisation. As already mentioned, these two dimensions are not particular to OT: other organisational pathologies, such as organisational stress or organisational identity crisis, are described on the basis of the same dimensions. This poses a problem because it does not allow to differentiate an OT from the other phenomena. It is therefore appropriate to understand organisational trauma as a process and not as the state of an organisation following from a potentially traumatising event.

1. Individual Process

The importance of considering the process aspect is also evident in the literature relating to individual trauma. An individual trauma does not appear as a result of the simple appearance of a traumatising event, but of its intrusion into the person's psyche. This intrusion can be conceived of as the penetration of the traumatising object into the psyche. The traumatic image will subsequently be internalised and as such affect the psychological functioning of the victim from within. According to Lebigot (2004), this internal stimulation of the psyche is the actual trauma.

2. From the individual process to the collective process

The concepts of psyche and intrusion that are central to individual trauma can also be applied to the organisational context, whereby the "psyche" corresponds to the mental representation of the organisation and includes the organisation's identity. According to Albert and Whetten (1985, cited by Gombault, 2002), the latter refers to "*the perceptions of all the organisation's members of the central, distinctive and stable characteristics of the organisation. It is a subjective and intersubjective construction of the members of an organisation regarding the organisation's identity, of what it is, that is to say its constituent, central, distinctive and continuous features*"

Intrusion, applied to the organisational context, is described by Stein et al (2005; cited by Hormann and Vivian, 2005) as the rupture of the organisation's protective emotional membrane by a threatening event or assault. This membrane refers to the Freudian concept of a protective shield, like a cell membrane that keeps out all excess energy attempting to penetrate it (Lebigot, 2004). This concept of a protective shield is also found in Anzieu's notion of the "skin-ego" (1995). It was introduced to the organisational context by Abbassi (Anzieu et al., 1986) with the introduction of the concept of "psychological institution" which "*ensures at an institutional group level a certain number of psychological functions, certain of which would be derived from propping up the skin-ego, a sort of collective skin-ego, an institution-ego that would perform functions similar to those of the skin-ego at an institutional group level [...] protective shield, composure, recording memories, individuation in the sense of identity, and perhaps also self-destruction*" (pp. 41). Conceptualised in this way, the rupture of the protective membrane will provoke organisational symptoms that are particular to an OT (Stein et al, 2005), and consequently produce emotional responses to the violence that is inherent to the destruction of the membrane.

3. Collective processes

Some authors have also studies the process of collective trauma in contexts other than that of organisations. For example, a traumatising process was described by Tyhurst (1951; cited by Klein & Alexander, 2011) in the form of potentially traumatising events impacting upon communities faced with war, disasters, etc. The author subdivided this process into three phases. The "impact phase" appears just after the potentially traumatising event. During that phase, only 15% of people behave in a reasonable manner. Nearly 75% are stunned or lost and the remaining 10% are paralysed by fear, anxiety and confusion. The second phase is the "recoil phase". When the first, chaotic moments have passed, the group begins to discuss what has just happened. Through this discussion process, people become closer and close ranks. In the third, "post-trauma" phase, people achieve a clearer insight, gradually become fully aware of what has happened and can begin to move forward. However, this awareness also raises the disappointment with the fact that actions were not or poorly undertaken by everyone during the ordeal.

4. Establishing a model for an OT process

In order to avoid the anthropomorphic view that is inherent to the use of the concept of psychological rupture and penetration, as well as the additional view of organisations as advanced by Tyhurst (1951; cited by Klein & Alexander, 2011), we propose a five-phase model of an OT based on the triggers, consequences and processes discussed above (see. Figure 1).

a. **Phase I:** The first phase of an OT is the first response to a potentially traumatising event. This response is not yet processed by the organisation. The potentially traumatising event gives rise to two kinds of "organisational disruptions", namely the expression of stress and the propagation of trauma. During this phase, the symptoms of an OT develop and stress is created. This phase can be compared to the immediate stress reaction affecting individuals after a traumatic event.
b. **Phase II:** During the second phase, the repercussions of the potentially traumatising event are being processed. This will have repercussions for the organisation's identity. It will create a rupture (Gombault, 2002) between two perceptions of the organisation's identity: one reflecting an idealized identity and another that corresponds with the reality of individuals "on the ground" (Albert & Whetten; 1985). This difference will be a source of cognitive dissonance and create an organisational crisis.
c. **Phase III:** As the previous phase created an organisational crisis, negative emotions will appear in the third phase. A crisis can trigger various negative emotions such as anxiety, fear, sadness or dread (Fox, Amichai-Hamburger and Evans, 2001; Jin, Liu, Anagondahalli, and Austin, 2014). The consequences of these emotions will be the production of emotional disturbances that decrease workers' motivation and satisfaction (Klarner, By and Diefenbach, 2011). These negative emotions may also arise from the direct confrontation with the potentially traumatising event. The organisational crisis will also lead to a loss of points of reference and emotional security.
d. **Phase IV:** In the fourth phase, the negative emotions provoke identity-defending behaviours that can be referred to as "emotional defence mechanisms". As seen previously, the two main defence mechanisms to cope with negative emotions are Groupthink-type behaviours and structural dysfunction.
e. **Phase V:** The fifth phase is the adaptation phase. For the organisation to successfully adapt to the new situation created by the potentially traumatising event, it is necessary that the emotional protection mechanisms succeeded to diminish the negative emotions and impact. When strong negative emotions persist, it is difficult to adapt as these emotions reinforce the links between resistance to change and irrational ideas (Bovey & Hede, 2001). So if the adaptation phase is not completed successfully because of persisting negative emotions, the organisation will retain its defence mechanisms. Additionally, the failure to adapt will entail a continued presence of cognitive dissonance and a continued impact on the organisation of the consequences linked to the potentially traumatic event.

The persistence of these adaptation mechanisms and the consequences of the potentially traumatic event are specific to OT. Indeed, organisational stress and the organisational identity crisis ultimately lead the organisation towards an adaptation that is appropriate for each pathology. This adaptation to the new situation may inhibit the defence mechanisms and the consequences linked to the potentially traumatic event. As such, this model enables to differentiate an OT from organisational stress and organisational identity crises from a process point of view.

As a result, we can propose the following definition of an OT.

An OT happens when: (1) there is a rupture of the protective emotional membrane of the organisation, and (2) the adaptation mechanisms following the rupture of the protective membrane continue even when the conditions no longer require so.

The rupture of the organisation's protective membrane (a) is the result of a potentially traumatic event, and (b) involves the appearance of emotional and organisational disturbances.

It must be noted that this definition differentiates an OT from other organisational pathologies by the fact that it emphasises the trauma process. It is not limited to the description of triggers and consequences but introduces the trauma process that is necessary for an OT to occur.

CONCLUSION

It is a well-known fact that the analysis of the changes in organisations requires an understanding of the structural issues which underlie them. In this paper, we have analysed the structural issues underlying organisational trauma as a particular process of organisational change. As opposed to the concept of individual trauma, which has been extensively studied and described in a comprehensive body of literature, the concept of OT is much less understood and therefore merits closer scrutiny.

In this paper, we have defined an OT as "an organisation's "over"-adaptation to the rupture of its protective emotional membrane caused by a potentially traumatising event and involving the appearance of emotional and organisational disturbances". Based on the typologies of organisational change (Malarewicz, 2012), two forms of adaptation should be considered to differentiate an OT from related phenomena: al diagnosis. The organisational stress leading to minor changes (type I) can be defined as: "an organisational adaptation to the rupture of the organisational protective emotional membrane caused by a potentially traumatising event and involving minor changes". The organisational identity crisis, leading to major changes (type II), can be defined as: "an organisational adaptation to the rupture of the organisational protective emotional membrane caused by a potentially traumatising event and involving major changes".

The above conceptual definition is based on an integrative review of the existing literature about OT. As such, it remains theoretical. More empirical research is needed to consolidate the process of organisational traumatization and thereby also the definition of OT. The intention of this paper was to propose a model for OT that can serve as a base for studying the organisational realities of OT, to provide a common basis for support and allow a meaningful advancement in the understanding of this field. Future research will need to consider the construction and validation of a diagnostic tool on the basis of the model that is proposed here. This tool will allow a systematic analysis of the symptoms of OT, and allow the development and application of relevant and efficient intervention and prevention strategies.

Figure 1. Establishing a model for an OT process
Legend: - R: Identity consistent with the Albert and Whetten 1985 definition corresponding to the reality of individuals close to the "ground"- I: Identity defended by the parties involved that reflects the organisation's ideal

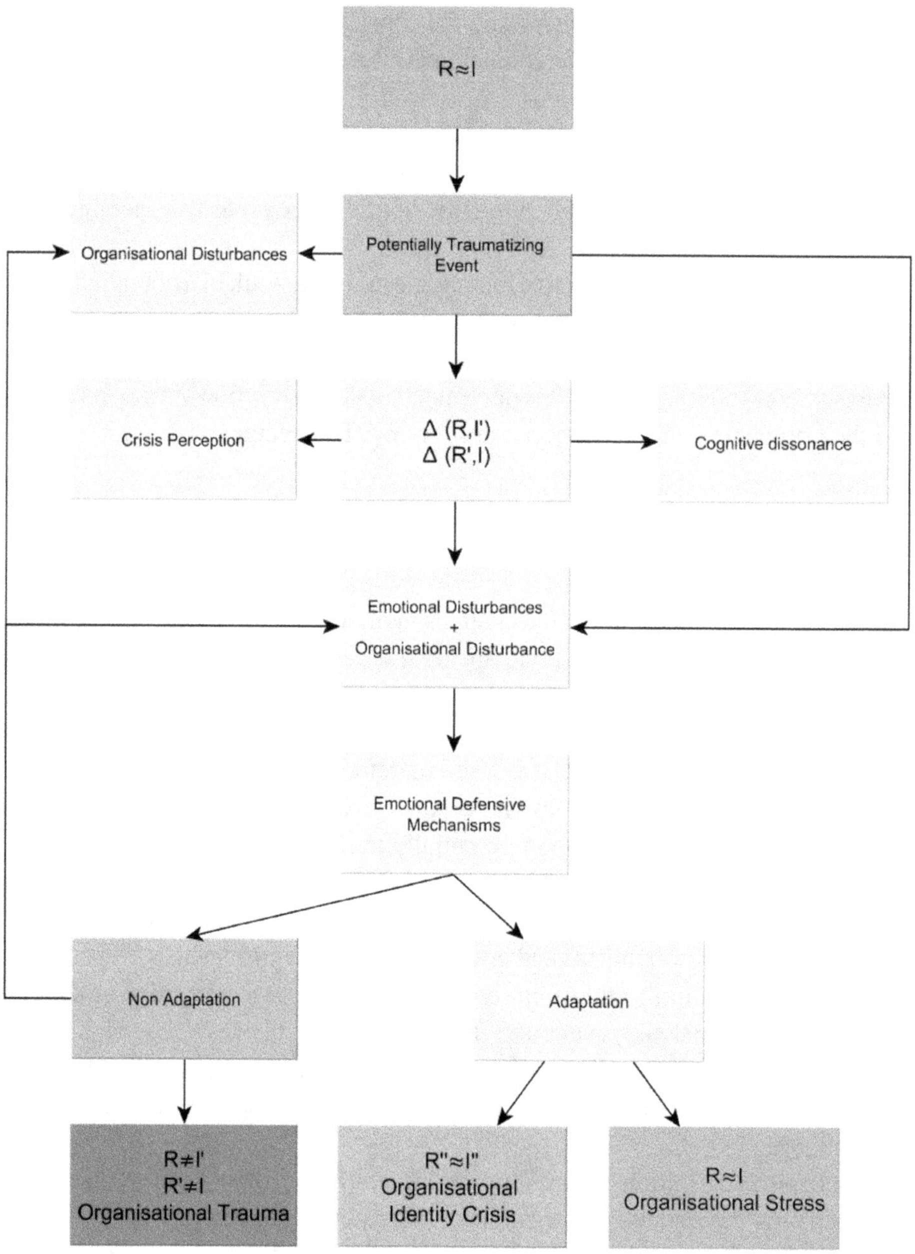

Legend:
- **R** : Identity consistent with the Albert and Whetten 1985 definition corresponding to the reality of individuals close to the "ground"
- **I** : Identity defended by the parties involved that reflects the organisation's ideal
- **R' & I'** : Identities that have undergone minor changes during the traumatising process
- **R'' & I''** : Identities that have undergone major changes during the traumatising process

REFERENCES

American Psychological Association. (2013). DSM 5. American Psychiatric Association.

Anzieu, D., & Séchaud, E. (1995). *Le moi-peau*. Dunod.

Anzieu, D. B., Chabert, J., Chouvier, B., Ciccone, A., Clancier, A., … Vidal, J. P. (1986). *L'Oeuvre Ouverte*. Paper presented at the Journées d'Etudes de Psychologie Sociale Clinique Organisées par le C.O.R sur le thème L'œuvre Ouverte: Autour Du Concept De Moi-Peau Et Des Travaux De Didier Anzieu.

Bathia, M. S. (Ed.). (2009). *Dictionary Of Psychology And Allied Sciences*. New Age International Pvt Ltd Publisher.

Bloom, S. (2006). *Organizational stress as a barrier to trauma-sensitive change and system transformation*. Alexandria, VA: National Technical Assistance Center for State Mental Health Planning Pulications and Reports.

Bloom, S. L., & Farragher, B. (2011). *Destroying sanctuary: The crisis in human service delivery systems*. New York, NY: Oxford University Press.

Bovey, W. H., & Hede, A. (2001). Resistance to organizational change: The role of cognitive and affective processes. *Leadership and Organization Development Journal, 22*(8), 372–382. doi:10.1108/01437730110410099

Brown, E. H. (1997). Improving organizational health by addressing organizational trauma. *Journal of Organizational Change Management, 10*(2), 175–178. doi:10.1108/09534819710160835

Burke, R. J. (2012). Organizations: Causes, Consequences, and Remedies. International Handbook of Workplace Trauma Support, 71.

Byron, K., & Peterson, S. (2002). The impact of a large-scale traumatic event on individual and organizational outcomes: Exploring employee and company reactions to September 11, 2001. *Journal of Organizational Behavior, 23*(8), 895–910. doi:10.1002/job.176

Crocq, L. (2007). Traumatismes psychiques: prise en charge psychologique des victimes. Paris: Masson.

De Clercq, M. (1999). Les répercussions psychiatriques et psycho-sociales des catastrophes et trauma graves. *Médecine de Catastrophe - urgences collectives, 2*(3–4), 73-78. doi:10.1016/S1279-8479(00)80006-3

De Soir, E. (2009). Le modèle CRASH. *Revue internationale de psychosociologie et de gestion des comportements organisationnels, 36*, 157-198. doi: 10.3917/rips.036.0157

De Soir, E., Daubechies, F., & Van den Steene, P. (2012). *Stress et trauma dans les services de police et de secours*. Antwerpen, Apeldoorn: Maklu Uitgevers.

Farragher, B., & Yanosy, S. (2005). Creating a trauma-sensitive culture in residential treatment. *Therapeutic Communities, 26*(1), 93–109.

Fox, S., Amichai-Hamburger, Y., & Evans, E. A. (2001). The Power of Emotional Appeals in Promoting Organizational Change Programs [and Executive Commentary]. *The Academy of Management Executive (1993-2005), 15*(4), 84-95. doi: 10.2307/4165788

Gantt, S. P., & Hopper, E. (2012). *Two perspectives on a trauma in a training group: The systems-centred approach and the theory of incohesion. In Trauma and organizations* (pp. 233–254). London: Karnac Books.

Goldman, K. D., & Schmalz, K. J. (2004). The Matrix Method of literature reviews. *Health Promotion Practice, 5*(1), 5–7. doi:10.1177/1524839903258885 PMID:14965430

Gombault, A. (2002). Clinique d'une crise d'identité organisationnelle. L'adolescence du Grand Louvre. Paper presented at the Actes de la 11 è Conférence de l'Association Internationale de Management Stratégique (AIMS).

Guiho-Bailly, M. P., & Guillet, D. (2005). Psychopathologie et psychodynamique du travail. *EMC - Toxicologie-Pathologie, 2*(3), 98-110. doi:10.1016/j.emctp.2005.04.001

Hart, P. (1991). Irving L. Janis Victims of Groupthink. *Political Psychology, 12*(2), 247–278. doi:10.2307/3791464

Hopper, E. (2012). *A theory of Incohesion: Aggregation/massification as the fourth basic assumption in the unconscious life of groups and group-like social systems. In Trauma and organizations* (pp. xxxi–li). London: Karnac Books.

Hormann, S., & Vivian, P. (2005). Toward An Understanding of Traumatized Organizations and How to Intervene in Them. *Traumatology, 11*(3), 159–169. doi:10.1177/153476560501100302

Hormann, S. D. L. (2007). *Organizational trauma: A phenomenological study of leaders in traumatized organizations* (AAI3276967). PsycINFO database.

Jin, Y., Liu, B. F., Anagondahalli, D., & Austin, L. (2014). Scale development for measuring publics emotions in organizational crises. *Public Relations Review, 40*(3), 509–518. doi:10.1016/j.pubrev.2014.04.007

Kahn, W. A. (2003). The revelation of organizational trauma. *The Journal of Applied Behavioral Science, 39*(4), 364–380. doi:10.1177/0021886303261954

Kibel, H. D. (2012). *A study in institutional change: The experience of trauma and the role of rumour in a case of paranoiagenesis. In Trauma and organizations* (pp. 3–22). London: Karnac Books.

Klarner, P., By, R. T., & Diefenbach, T. (2011). Employee emotions during organizational change—Towards a new research agenda. *Scandinavian Journal of Management, 27*(3), 332–340. doi:10.1016/j.scaman.2011.06.002

Klein, K. J., & Kozlowski, S. W. J. (2013). *Multilevel Theory, Research, and Methods in Organizations: Foundations, Extensions, and New Directions*. Wiley.

Klein, S., & Alexander, D. (2011). The impact of trauma within organisations. In Managing trauma in the workplace: Supporting workers and organisations (pp. 117-138). Routledge/Taylor et Francis Group.

Koninckx, G., & Teneau, G. (2010). *Résilience organisationnelle: Rebondir face aux turbulences*. Brussels/Paris: De Boeck Supérieur

Lebigot, F. (2004). Le traumatisme psychique. *Revue Francophone du Stress et du Trauma, 4*(1), 5–11.

Malarewicz, J. A. (2012). *Systémique et entreprise: Mettre en oeuvre une stratégie de changement*. Pearson Education France.

Pross, C., & Schweitzer, S. (2010). The culture of organizations dealing with trauma: Sources of work-related stress and conflict. *Traumatology, 16*(4), 97–108. doi:10.1177/1534765610388301

Rimé, B. (2005). *Le partage social des émotions*. Paris: Presses universitaires de France.

Salmona, M. (2013). *Le livre noir des violences sexuelles*. Dunod.

Stein, H. F. (1991). Metaphors of organizational trauma and organizational development: A case example. *Organization Development Journal, 9*(4), 22–30.

Terr, L. C. (1994). Childhood traumas. *Psychotraumatology: Key papers and core concepts in post-traumatic stress*, 301.

Turner, M. E., & Pratkanis, A. R. (1998). A social identity maintenance model of groupthink. *Organizational Behavior and Human Decision Processes, 73*(2), 210–235. doi:10.1006/obhd.1998.2757 PMID:9705803

Vivian, P., & Hormann, S. (2002). Trauma and Healing in Organizations. *O.D. The Practitioner, 34*(4), 52–57.

Vivian, P., & Hormann, S. (2013). *Organizational Trauma and Healing*. CreateSpace Independent Publishing Platform.

KEY TERMS AND DEFINITIONS

Autopoietic System: Self-maintaining system.

Janis Effect: Group pathology in which rational decisions cannot be taken in a coherent manner.

Organisation: A complex and structured system wherein the modification of a single element changes the whole system.

Organisational Identity Crisis: Organisational adaptation to the rupture of the organisational protective emotional membrane caused by a potentially traumatising event and involving major changes.

Organisational Stress: Organisational adaptation to the rupture of the organisational protective emotional membrane caused by a potentially traumatising event and involving minor changes.

Organisational Trauma: Organisation's "over"-adaptation to the rupture of its protective emotional membrane caused by a potentially traumatising event and involving the appearance of emotional and organisational disturbances.

Chapter 2
Organizations and Exposure to Trauma at a Collective Level:
The Taxonomy of Potentially Traumatic Events

Idil Isik
Istanbul Bilgi University, Turkey

ABSTRACT

Organizational trauma is a contemporary construct that highlights long-lasting negative psychological consequences of various internal and external events that overwhelm the capacity of people in organizational settings. This chapter proposes that a typology of "potentially traumatic events" (PTEs) and the taxonomy of these events' attributes can be developed by conducting a comprehensive literature review. The search of databases for the period of 1995-2016 revealed 81 articles on which inductive qualitative content analysis was conducted. Analysis brought three PTEs: "events resulting from organizational processes"; "adverse experiences in trauma-prone occupations/sectors", and "catastrophic events caused by economic/social/environmental conditions". These events' attributes appeared distinctive under three themes: "features of traumatic events";"human behaviours";"internal and external organizational environment". As the final step, the proposed taxonomy was applied to real traumatic business cases happened in 2015 and early 2016 so that the taxonomic model was tested.

INTRODUCTION

This chapter aims to bring forward a taxonomy of potentially traumatic events that organizations and their members may be exposed to. Organizations are idiosyncratic social systems that are composed of sub-systems with particular technology, structure, culture, and human capital at managerial and non-managerial levels. This peculiarity emerges as a consequence of the interaction of these sub-systems, which can be defined as the internal environment of organizations. Of course organizations are open systems that both affect and are affected by their proximal and distal external conditions. Employees perform in the settings where these internal and external conditions are continuously interacting and

DOI: 10.4018/978-1-5225-2021-4.ch002

are presumably productive and constructive. Nevertheless, internal dynamics and external conditions of organizational systems can be destructive at individual and collective levels. Dysfunctional processes, improper methods, imprudent decisions, unacceptable behaviours, or catastrophic interpersonal relationships, to list a few as weaknesses may be present in the layers of organizational hierarchy and may ignite failures at individual and organizational levels and cause damage. Besides, environmental, economic, social, political, and technological external conditions may threaten survival and bodily integrity of people. The amalgam of organizations' unique internal and external attributes intending to be beneficial for all may suddenly transform into a circumstance that potentially harms people and sometimes with long-lasting impact which is named as trauma.

Although researchers have diverse perspectives related to trauma as a construct, they unanimously agree on the fact that trauma is the consequence of overwhelming events (e.g., Herman, 1992; Saakvitne, Tennen, & Ameck, 1998; Steinkamp, 2014) that exceed people's capacity to deal with them. Akin to this definition, staggering events that unfold in organizational settings can cause strain at collective levels and people may experience negative emotions like anxiety, depression, rage, and helplessness. Problem solving skills, concentration on tasks, performance, and interpersonal relations may be negatively affected (Kahn, 2003). This emotional state at the collective level can be named as organizational trauma. Steinkamp (2014) underpins that if not handled properly, the traumatic experience leads to dysfunctional behaviours as a collective phenomenon. However, responses to traumatic conditions show enormous interpersonal differences. The same traumatic event may create enduring effect on physical and/or psychological health and well-being of some people; but for others, it is simply a distraction and recovery happens in the blink of an eye. How intolerable the adverse event is experienced certainly varies from person to person, but it would be doubtful to claim that people show persistent tolerance levels across time and space; indeed, there is intrapersonal variance. The same is true at the organizational level. Organizations at the collective level show diverse reactions when a traumatic condition is faced. A traumatic event may paralyze functionality of some organizations and may cause decline and even death if we borrow the terms from organizational life cycle research (Adizes, 1979; Miller & Freisen, 1980; Lester, Parnell, & Carraher, 2003); as the others rebound easily and convert this adverse experience to organizational learning to polish their resilience.

Organizations' capacity and strength in dealing with the unfavourable conditions and recovering from them, their speed in taking action, collective reactions, and solidarity among the members are the distinct features to understand elasticity of organizations facing traumatic conditions. The characteristics of adverse conditions are critical determinants of traumatic consequences; how extraordinary the event is, severity of its consequences, if it is man-made or natural, or if its impact is only on a single organization or exceeds to other stakeholders out of the company are among a few characteristics or attributes of traumatic events that researchers are addressing. Some conventional concepts like organizational failures/errors (Aini and Fakhru'l-Razi, 2013; Reason, 2002), crisis (Antonacopoulou & Sheaffer, 2014; Constantinides, 2013; Powley & Piderit, 2008), disasters (Bozeman, 2011a, 2011b; Waring, 2015), and catastrophe (Kumar, Gupta, Agarwal, & Singh, 2016); or more contemporary terms like organizational wounds (Kahn, 2011), implosion (Bozeman, 2011b), miasma (Gabriel, 2012; Stein, 2007), darkness (Gabriel, 2012; Griffin, & Lopez, 2005; Griffin, & O'Leary-Kelly, 2004; Linstead, Maréchal, & Griffin, 2014; Stein, 2007), and zemblanity (Giustiniano, Cunha, & Clegg, 2015) are cited in the literature in order to differentiate the adverse events that organizations may encounter.

Bozeman (2011a) attempted to distinctively summarize the definition of various conventional concepts currently available in the literature. Errors are defined as the unintended deviations from organizational rules or procedures that cause losses and are most often the conduct of more than one individual. Organizational failure is posted as the deviation from the objectives due to avoidable and unavoidable errors, and risk taking. Crises are defined as unexpected events, which result in uncertainty and consequently anxiety among the members of organizations that have to be responded to in limited time. Alternatively, catastrophe is defined as trauma in the workplace, due to injuries, accidents or violence. Errors, crisis, and catastrophe are not so severe that they may cause damage to the degree of termination of organizational operations, and their effects are presumably short-term. Disasters are considered to be more intense, large-scale, and costly; physical, cultural, and emotional events that cause dramatic loss not only for the organization but also for the public. As the definitions show, distinctions among these constructs are based on how intense their consequences are and if they affect only the organizational stakeholders or society in general. These events are presumed to be rare but when revealed, prompt actions are needed.

Even if researchers attempted to differentiate between the various concepts, we recognize that one concept is denoted by another term. For example, Aini and Fakhru'l-Razi (2013) articulated organizational failures and disasters back and forth and underpin the role of failures and human errors in the emergence of disasters. Their premise is that "humans are fallible and errors are to be expected, even in the best organization. It posits that an individual is rarely the sole cause of disaster but rather due to factors within the system, which abet the occurrences of the event." (p.285). Similarly, Constantinides (2013) stated that crises range from natural or environmental disasters to economic crises and frequently erroneous human behaviours contribute to their emergence. These explanations also indicate that differentiating the concepts is not an easy task.

However, we recognize more contemporary conceptualizations arising in order to scrutinize the distinctions among various conditions that disturb the routine flow of organizational processes. Kahn (2011) defines organizational wounds as the pain, betrayal, anger, sadness, despair, and shame caused by events that damage organizational identity due to organizational scandals, accidents, non-adaptive strategies to changing external conditions, and operational errors. Kahn defines this state as "emotional fallout of organizational crises" (p. 76). Bozeman (2011b) posts the concept of organizational implosion to refer to damage directly caused by the organizations' own members. Members' agency by acting in their official role and their externally constrained responses, i.e., the reactions activated by external conditions are two distinct features of implosions. Besides, Giustiniano et al. (2015) adds the concept of organizational zemblanity, which was first presented by Boyd (1998). This term emphasizes how the members of organizations cause avoidable disasters unintentionally in the structures that have been designed to be resistant to errors and damages. Key organizational actors worsen the conditions both for themselves and for their organizations when disaster erupts.

Besides organizational miasma (Gabriel, 2012) is defined as a toxic state, which is highly contagious, and distinct characteristic that especially occurs in the process of sudden and traumatic organizational changes. Gabriel (2012) states that "miasma brings about a state of moral and spiritual decay, a corruption of all values and human relations of trust, love and community – people suspect their neighbours of being the cause, scapegoating and witch hunts are rife" (p.1146).

Linstead, Maréchal, and Griffin (2014) highlight organizational darkness which underscores the dark side of organizational behaviour like workplace violence, aggression, and incivility. Two major categories of darkness are mentioned. The harm caused by verbal and psychological abuse, physical violence, sexual harassment, and discrimination is the first category. The second one consists of counterproductive behaviours like absenteeism, turnover, revenge, theft, destruction of organization's properties, violations of regulations, and injustice which are injurious to overall organization.

As the literature review in the current chapter shows, organizational trauma is a recent construct that especially highlights long-lasting negative psychological consequences of these events. Among early academic attempts we see Brown (1997), Kahn (2003), Hormann and Vivian (2005), and Hormann (2007) who directly articulated the concept of "organizational trauma" in their publications. There are prominent incidents that led the researchers to systematically investigate various internal and external events with adverse consequences for organizations at individual and collective level. The Chernobyl nuclear reactor failure in 1986 and Bhopal toxic release in 1984 (Waring 2015); the World Trade Centre attack in September 11, 2001 (Burke, 2012; Kleinberg, 2012); the explosion of the space shuttle Columbia in 2003 (Kauffman, 2005), and the hurricane Katrina in 2005 (Abulnour, 2014) are to mention a few. More recent events like the economic crises in 2008 (Constantinides, 2013; Cornand, & Gimet, 2012), the Great East Japan Earthquake and damage to the Fukishima nuclear plant in 2011 (Davis, Keilis-Borok, Kossobokov, & Soloviev, 2012) also affected researchers to concentrate on traumatic influences of various catastrophic events. David M. Noer's book (2010a) entitled "Healing the wounds: Overcoming the trauma of layoffs and revitalizing downsized organizations, Revised & Updated"; Noreen Tehrani's (2011) "Managing trauma in the workplace: Supporting workers and organisations"; Earl Hopper's (2012) "Trauma and organizations"; and Rick Hughes, Andrew Kinder, Cary L. Cooper's (2012) "International handbook of workplace trauma support" are the contemporary books that focus on the phenomena of organizational trauma.

As Burke (2012) mentions, collective trauma is the emotional response to traumatic events which are caused "by one or more individuals or by natural forces that result in psychological distress, property damage, injury, or death to one or more employees of an organization. These acts or events can affect one or more organizations simultaneously." (p. 72). Accordingly, we may propose that events affecting organizations' routine and creating distress among its members, stakeholders and society in general might be covered by the concept of "potentially traumatic events" and the resulting collective psychological state is "organizational trauma". Organizations affected by these traumatic events can be named as "traumatized organizations" following Hughes, Kinder, and Cooper (2012) where catastrophic processes take place and the organizational members experience helplessness and trouble in coping with accompanying negative emotions.

Since the literature is like a patchwork of various concepts and cases that needs to be more theoretically structured, an initiative is needed to develop a taxonomy of adverse events that can delineate the distinctive characteristics of traumatic experiences, i.e., a model to systematically categorize them. Carper and Snizek (1980) emphasized, "the most important and basic step in conducting any form of scientific inquiry involves the ordering, classification, or other grouping of the objects or phenomena under investigation." (p.65) and taxonomies serve that function. Accordingly, the primary aim that the current chapter pursues is to develop a taxonomic framework that shows the pattern of events under the general term of organizational trauma. The need for the development of taxonomies is well embraced by organizational studies and organizational theory literature that frequently cites Haas, Hall, and Johnson (1966), Pugh, Hickson, and Hinings (1969), McKelvey (1975), Pinder and Moore (1979), Carper and Snizek (1980), and Fleishman and Quaintance (1984). These researchers assert taxonomies as analytical devices with the following functions: (i) It is a multidimensional classification and large amounts of information are systematically structured into more convenient categories to ease processing, storing, and comprehending. (ii) It is comprehensive where each item is conceptually independent, and each item has its own research history. (iii) It is considered a preliminary step for theory development which pertains to hypothesis generation and refinement. (iv) It provides a holistic framework for operationalization of the constructs so that attributes will be specified in a measurable way and will be empirically analysed. (v) It sets forth broadly applicable principles to explain phenomena.

Accordingly, the current chapter attempts to develop a taxonomy of potentially traumatic events by systematically categorizing the previous researchers' highlighted conceptualizations, specific cases that they focused on, and an analytic scope that they applied to define and explain the traumatic condition. The objective of such taxonomy is to provide a tool to enhance the systematic portrayal of events with negative outcomes without being restricted by one word descriptions like disasters, crisis, implosion, or darkness. Such a systematic description will provide an opportunity to compare the events so that countermeasures at the levels of individual, group, organization, and society can also be effectively specified.

In order to develop the taxonomy, a content analysis of selected literature was conducted for the current chapter. The following sections first present the methodology, and then the results of the content analysis. The results section is comprised of:

1. Potentially traumatic events' typology;
2. A taxonomic model of the attributes of these diverse events with potential negative outcomes, and;
3. The application of the taxonomic model to selected real life cases.

The last section demonstrates how functional the taxonomy is in depicting the events with potential traumatic consequences and in systematically analysing them so that the implications for the proposed taxonomy in research and practice are discussed.

METHODOLOGY

In order to develop the taxonomy for organizational trauma, a literature review with two phases was conducted. In the first phase, the keyword "organizational trauma" (in quotation marks) was searched in the databases of Academic Search Complete, Sage Journals Online, SpringerLink, Emerald Management Xtra 175, PsycArticle, Science Direct, Wiley Online Library, and Taylor & Francis Online. The search was limited to the period of 1995-2016 and only to the scientific articles published in peer-reviewed journals. In the second phase of literature review, the references of articles obtained from the first phase were further investigated to reach additional studies related to traumatic experiences that affect organizations and their members. At this phase, the distinctiveness of traumatic events were taken as a criterion to pick an article for inclusion in the set of relevant papers since the aim of the current research is to identify a variety of experiences that disturb the routine flow of activities in organizational settings. Books and dissertations were excluded.

Consequently, the inductive qualitative content analysis was conducted on the designated list of organizational trauma related papers. MAXQDA 12, Qualitative Data Analysis Software was utilized for systematic coding and data analysis.

The aim of the content analysis was twofold. First was to attain the typology of traumatic experiences. Various concepts and highlighted adverse events like crisis, disasters, failures, violence, toxic conditions, and violations were coded inductively following an open coding procedure. Then, the open codes of the events were grouped in terms of their similarity to each other so that the major traumatic event categories were depicted. The second aim of content analysis was to code the attributes that a particular paper articulates in order to describe the nature and dynamics of the traumatic event. As with any scientific inquiry, with the objectives of describing and explaining a phenomenon, the organizational trauma literature also attempts to describe the features and characteristics of traumatic events, and highlights the causes of these events. These analytical scopes were coded, as well, to model the taxonomy.

Coding processes for the typology of traumatic experiences as well as the taxonomy of attributes for potentially traumatic events were conducted by using "The Coding Manual for Qualitative Researchers" (Saldaña, 2013) as the major guideline. The coding to attain the typology was "descriptive coding" which aims to summarize segments from the qualitative data in a word or short phrase which highlights the basic topic of the statement. The articles were reviewed to see which adverse events were highlighted, their themes were openly coded, and then re-grouping of the open codes were done to name them as the major types of potentially traumatic events.

The approach for coding the attributes of events was based on the design that Saldaña (2013) calls "versus coding" which aims to "identify in dichotomous or binary terms the individuals, groups, social systems, organizations, phenomena, processes, concepts, etc., in direct conflict with each other." (p.115). We see that researchers frequently describe various characteristics of the traumatic events in binary terms like man-made vs natural, acute vs chronic, or internal vs external. Therefore, our coding process attempted to capture the dichotomous description of the events.

In the qualitative content analysis, the context and the cases that each research paper addressed were used to develop the themes without targeting the quantification. Both open coding and re-grouping of open codes were inductively realized; there were no pre-defined codes, themes or categories.

As mentioned earlier, this chapter also aims to apply the proposed taxonomy to real traumatic cases that impact organizations and business life in order to test how functional the taxonomic model is. The cases relevant to organizational trauma were obtained through the search of selected business news websites (www.bbc.com, www.bloomberg.com, www.fortune.com, www.theguardian.com) and websites that provide news on the world's current political, economic, social, and environmental incidents. Cases were selected from the events that happened in 2015 and in the first few months of 2016. The reification of the cases and the analysis according to the taxonomy are presented in the final part of the results section.

Results

As Table 1 shows, the first phase of literature review identified 98 articles matching the keyword of "organizational trauma" from the selected databases. Six of the publications that appeared more than one database were counted under a single database. A review of abstracts showed that 17.35% of these publications were also relevant to traumatic organizational experiences; the full-texts were accessible so that the pool of the articles obtained from the first phase of the literature review consisted of 17 articles.

These 17 articles were downloaded and read thoroughly. Then an additional literature review was conducted by tracking the reference lists of these papers as well as by searching the more recent research that cite these papers and their references. As a consequence of stepwise access to other papers, 64 additional academic papers were added to the pool. Therefore, 81 articles in total were accumulated.

The final set of 81 articles were coded according to the procedure summarized in the methodology section. The emerging themes within the typology of potentially traumatic events and within the taxonomy of these events in terms of their distinctive attributes are delineated in the following sections.

Table 1. Organizational trauma related studies obtained from the first phase of literature review

	Hits	Relevant articles	Multiple occurrence in different databases	Final number of relevant articles
Taylor & Francis Online	20	5		5
Sage Journals Online	16	3		3
Wiley Online Library	16	4		4
Academic Search Complete	12	6	4	2
Emerald Management Xtra 175	12	2		2
SpringerLink	10	0		0
Science Direct	10	1		1
PsycArticles	2	2	2	0
TOTAL	98	23	6	17

Typology of Potentially Traumatic Events

The "descriptive coding" used in the process of inductive qualitative content analysis showed that three main types of potentially traumatic events can be identified to cover the cases, experiences, and events investigated by the designated papers. The types of events were named as "traumatic events resulting from organizational processes"; "adverse experiences in trauma-prone occupations/organizations", and "catastrophic events caused by economic, social, and environmental conditions". The concept map in Figure 1 presents sub-themes of the typology.

Figure 1. Concept map of the potentially traumatic events typology

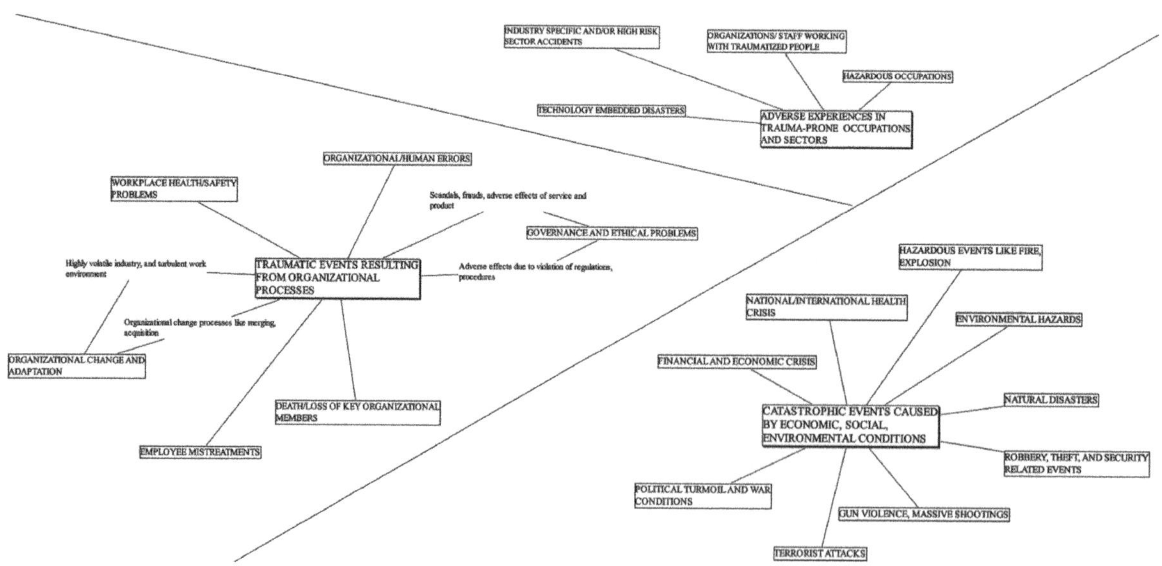

1. **Traumatic events resulting from organizational processes:** The first major type of traumatic events includes those caused by organizational processes. Table 2 shows that 26 articles in the pool of selected papers were coded under this category.

Table 2. List of 26 articles and their categorisation according to the typology of potentially traumatic events (Traumatic events resulting from organizational processes)

Traumatic events resulting from organizational processes	Articles
Governance and ethical problems	
Adverse effects due to violation of regulations, procedures, governance problems	Martin, G., Farndale, E., Paauwe, J., & Stiles, P.G. (2016)
	Reason, J. (2000)
	Zaloznay, M. (2015).
Scandals, frauds, adverse effects of service and product on public health that creates inquiry on business ethics	Kahn, W. A. (2011)
	Kleinberg, J. (2014)
	Kleinberg, J. (2016)
Employee mistreatments	
Employee mistreatments including workplace bullying and mobbing, toxic work setting, prejudice and discrimination especially for disadvantaged groups like employees with disability, LGBTs	Bragg, K. (1997)
	Griffin, R. W., & Lopez, Y. P. (2005)
	Lutgen-Sandvik, P. (2008)
	Miller, D. (1996)
	Seymour, K. (2009)
Organizational change and adaptation	
Organizational change processes like merging, acquisition, lay-offs, re-engineering	Brown, E.H. (1997)
	Gabriel, Y. (2012)
	Kantur, D. and İşeri Say (2012)
	Lennerfors, T.T. (2013)
	Noer, D. M (2010b)
	Sellers, R.D., Fogerty, T.J., & Parker, L.M. (2014)
	Werther, W. B. (2003)
Highly volatile industry, turbulent work environment, uncertainty and subsequent stressful conditions	deKlerk, M. (2007)
	Eskildson, L. (1997).
Organizational/human errors	
Organizational errors, human errors	Goodman, P.S., Ramanujam, R., Carroll, J.S., Edmondson, A.C., Hofmann, D.A., & Sutcliffe, K.M. (2011)
	Kumar, P., Gupta, S., Agarwal, M., & Singh, U. (2016)
Death/loss of key organizational members	
Bereavement, attrition, and loss of key organizational members	Dutton, J. E. Frost, P. J., Worline, M.C., Lilius, J. M., & Kanov, J. M. (2002)
Workplace health and safety problems	
Workplace health and safety problems, risks, and accidents	Busby, J.S. & Iszatt-White, M. (2016)
	Coze, J. C. L. (2013)
	Sklet, S. (20016)

As the left hand corner of the concept map in Figure 1 shows, we see that "governance and ethical problems", "employee mistreatments", "organizational change and adaptation", "organizational/human errors", "death/loss of key organizational members", and "workplace health and safety problems" appear as the distinct individual types of potentially traumatic events. Among these "governance and ethical problems" and "organizational change and adaptation" appeared to have sub-dimensions. Governance and ethical problems dimension incorporates; (i) violation of regulations, procedures, and related governance problems; and (ii) scandals, frauds, adverse effects of services/products on public health that create inquiry on business ethics. On the other hand, the "organizational change and adaptation" dimension includes; (i) organizational change processes like merging, acquisitions, lay-offs, and re-engineering; and (ii) highly volatile industries, turbulent work environment, uncertainty and subsequent stressful conditions.

2. **Adverse experiences in trauma-prone occupations and sectors:** The literature shows that there are more frequently addressed sectors and occupations which can be considered more prone to potentially traumatic events. For instance, manufacturing companies have a higher potential for the emergence of traumatic incidents especially if they operate in hazardous conditions like storage and handling of dangerous chemicals; if they utilize complex/high-risk technologies; and if they are open to hazards that arise from uncertain and uncontrollable external conditions. Additionally, particular occupations' main duty is to intervene in emergency conditions like natural disasters, fires, and criminal offenses to mention a few. These occupations are by nature dangerous and employees are trained to be qualified and accredited in order to secure people's life and their possessions. However, being trained and competent does not diminish the risk for trauma. We see that the literature is also focusing on the events that these professionals are handling and their traumatic impact. We also recognize that particular service sector companies are more frequently mentioned as a focal point in the literature. These are; hospitals; care giving organizations for vulnerable groups like elderly people, people with mental and physical disabilities, and children with special needs; organizations that deliver support for traumatized people like veterans, victims of terror, domestic violence, and survivors of any form of physical violence, and; organizations of psychological counselling. Staff in these organizations who can be named as trauma workers (Hormann & Vivian, 2005) are consistently exposed to secondary/vicarious trauma (Pearlman, 1999) and the research literature extensively concentrates on this issue as well. In summary, these sectors and occupations were entitled as "trauma-prone" (Table 3) and 25 of the articles were relevant to this category.

Content analysis showed the emergence of four dimensions under the category of "adverse experiences in trauma-prone occupations and sectors". As the concept map depicts at the upper section of Figure 1, the first dimension is named as the industry specific and/or high risk sector accidents like in mining, gas, energy, aviation, maritime accidents, aerospace, transportation, and nuclear sectors. Second dimension includes hazardous occupations like police, armed forces, paramedics, firefighters, and similar occupations. The third dimension is related to technology embedded disasters that occur within specific industries, especially the ones with highly complex technologies. The last dimension is the secondary exposure to trauma by staff working with traumatized people in health care organizations.

Table 3. List of 25 articles and their categorisation according to the typology of potentially traumatic events (Adverse experiences in trauma-prone occupations and sectors)

Adverse experiences in trauma-prone occupations and sectors	Articles
Industry specific and/or high risk sector accidents like mining, gas, energy, aviation, maritime accidents, aerospace, transportation, and nuclear	Antonacopoulou, Elena and Sheaffer, Z. (2014)
	Bozeman, B. (2011a)
	Bozeman, B. (2011b)
	Chauvin, C., Lardjane, S., Morel, G., Clostermann, J. P., & Langard, B. (2013)
	Constantinides, P. (2013)
	Giustiniano, L., Cunha, M. P., & Clegg, S. (2016)
	Hyungju, K., Stein, H., & Bouwer, U. I. (2016)
	Kauffman, J. (2005)
	Park, H. (2011)
	Plant, K. L., & Stanton, N. A. (2012)
	Siomkos, G. J. (2000)
	Stenson, J. (2006)
	Tansel, B. (1995)
Technology embedded disasters	McBride, N. (2015)
	Schaluf, I. M., Ahmadun, F., & Scariff, A. R. (2003)
Health care people, staff working with traumatized people	Bassuk, E. L., Unick, G. J., Paquette, K., & Richard, M. K. (2016)
	Dagan K., Itzhaky H., & Ben-Porat, A. (2015)
	Hormann & Vivian (2005)
	Kahn, W.A. (2003)
	Nuttman-Shwartz, O. (2015)
	Paton, D. (2005).
	Shepard, B.C. (2013)
Policeman, paramedics, firefighters, and similar hazardous occupations	Hong,O., Chin, D.L, Phelps, S., Feld, J., & Vogel, S. (2012)
	Regehr, C., Hill, J., Goldberg, G., & Hughes, J. (2003)
	Papazoglou, K. (2013)

3. **Catastrophic events caused by economic, social, and environmental conditions:** This category pertains to the events that organizations have less control over the sources and impact of adverse factors. This category additionally includes the ecosystem of organizations since the acts of other institutions may be the source of threat and multiple institutions can be affected by this single traumatic event. Table 4 shows the list of 30 articles that were coded under the catastrophic events category of the typology.

Table 4. List of 30 articles and their categorisation according to the typology of potentially traumatic events (Catastrophic events caused by economic, social, environmental conditions)

Catastrophic events caused by economic, social, environmental conditions	Articles
Natural disasters like floods, earthquakes, tsunami, hurricane, volcano	Abulnour, A. H. (2014)
	Davis, C., Keilis-Borok, V., Kossobokov, V., & Soloviev, A. (2012)
	Mutch, C. (2015)
	Raju, E., & Becker, P. (2013)
Environmental hazards like toxic release, oil spill	Waring, A. (2015)
	Plater Z. (2010)
Hazardous events like fire, explosion, collapse of buildings, crash of platforms	van der Velden, P. G., Bosmans, M. W. G., Bogaerts, S., & Veldhoven, M. J. P. M. (2014)
	Aini M. S., & Fakhru'l-Raz, A. (2013)
National/international health crisis	Leidner, D. E., Pan, G., & Pan, S. L. (2009)
Financial and economic crisis	Brewis, J. & Őzbilgin, M. (2013).
	Cornand, C., & Gimet, c. (2012)
	De Cock, C., Vachhani, S. & Murray, S. (2013)
Political turmoil and war conditions	Cruz, J. (2014)
	Dahles, H., & Susilowati, T. P. (2015)
	Sousa, C.A., Haj-Yahia, M.M., Feldman, G. & Lee, J. (2013)
	Veronese, G., & Pepe, A. (2015)
Terrorist attacks	Ackoff, R. L., & Strümpfer, J. P. (2003)
	Kendra, J.M. and T. Wachtendorf (2003)
	Mendonça, D., & Wallace, W. A. (2015)
	Myer, R.A., & Moore, H.B. (2006)
	Paul, R. & Thompson, C. (2006).
	Rose, A., & Krausmann, E. (2013)
Gun violence, massive shootings, organized crime and civilian violence	Defraia, G.S. (2013).
	Fein, A.H., & Isaacson, N.S (2009)
	Fox, J.A. & Savage, J. (2009)
	Powley, E.H., & Piderit, S.K. (2008)
	Leppaniemi, A.K. (2009)
Robbery, theft, security related traumas	Jones, C.A. (2002)
	Vickers, M. H. & Kouzmin, A. (2001)
	Bowman, B., Bhamjee, B., Eagle, G., & Crafford, A. (2009)

The right corner in Figure 1 depicts the concept map for this category that incorporates following themes;

1. Natural disasters like floods, earthquakes, tsunami, hurricane, and volcano;
2. Environmental hazards like toxic release, and oil spill;
3. Hazardous events like fire, explosion, collapse of buildings, and crash of platforms;
4. National/international health crisis;
5. Financial and economic crisis;
6. Political turmoil and war conditions;
7. Terrorist attacks;
8. Gun violence, massive shootings, organized crime and civilian violence;
9. Robbery, theft, and security related events.

In summary, extensive literature exists on events that have adverse effects on organizations at individual and collective levels. The typology of potentially traumatic events asserts that categorization is possible by investigating if these events are triggered by organizations' internal processes, if the nature of occupations and sectors is making the organizations more susceptible for traumatic events, or if detrimental events are caused by external factors. Further elaboration of the designated articles leads to the abstraction of a model on how various attributes or characteristics of potentially traumatic events can be structured as a taxonomy.

Taxonomy of Potentially Traumatic Events' Attributes

As previously mentioned, in the second phase of inductive qualitative content analysis, the "versus coding" approach was implemented. Content analysis led us to categorize traumatic events' distinctive attributes into three major components. The first component scrutinizes the nature and dynamics of the traumatic events. The next one addresses the behaviours of organizations' members that contribute to the emergence of the event. The last component specified the internal and external organizational environment as the context in which the traumatic events occur.

Figure 2 demonstrates this taxonomic model in which various traumatic events can be evaluated according to its features, the role of human behaviours and the internal and external organizational conditions as context. This figure also shows how the taxonomy of traumatic events' attributes is incorporated with the typology of potentially traumatic events. The figure manifests the idea that the attributes and characteristics of potentially traumatic events -including those that are caused by organizational processes, catastrophic events, or proneness to traumatic events- can be investigated by following components:

1. Features of the traumatic event,
2. Involvement of human behaviour, and
3. Organizations' internal and external conditions.

Three components of the taxonomy were modelled on its dimensions, which were again depicted in terms of the dichotomies of specific characteristics of the traumatic events. Each main taxonomic structure is summarized with a figure in the following section where the black circle at the centre is the main component of the taxonomy; the rectangular boxes with bold lines are the dimensions of the component

Figure 2. Taxonomy of traumatic events' attributes

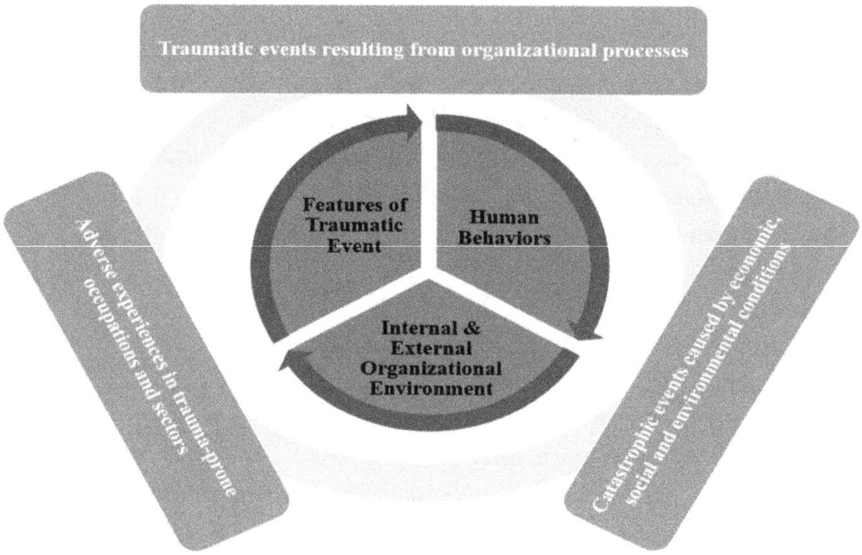

in the taxonomic structure; and the dashed boxes represents the binary themes that identify the mutually distinctive attributes of the events. In the following section, the emerging structure of taxonomy with its components, dimensions and dichotomous attributes is elaborated upon by linking them with the literature that the current chapter is incorporating.

Features of Traumatic Events

Various features that are covered in the literature as distinctive dimensions of traumatic events, include their inducers, origin, control over event, emergence, exposure, availability of time to react, and impact.

Figure 3. Features of traumatic events

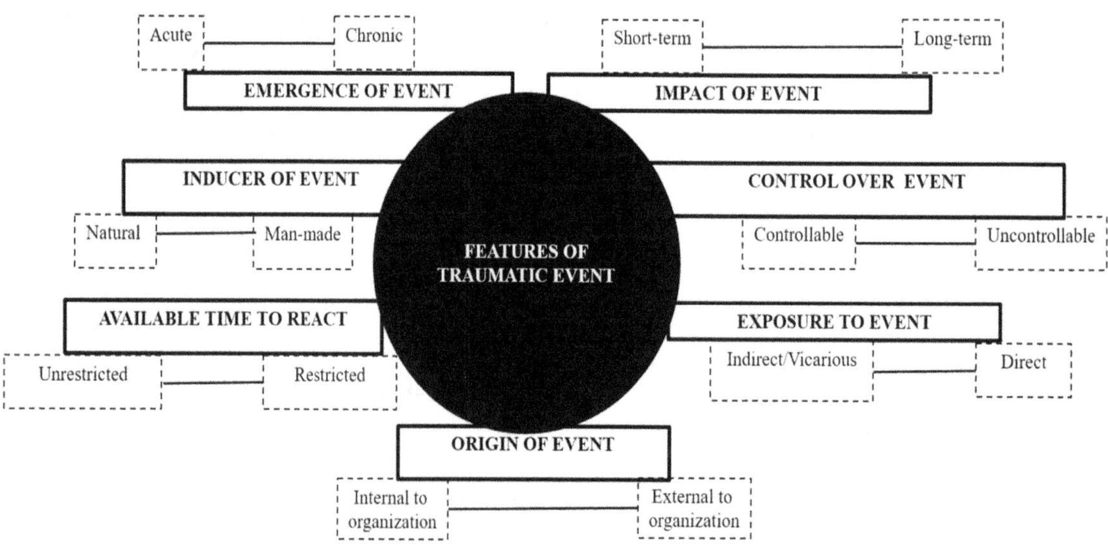

These form the first component of the taxonomy. Figure 3 displays the dimensions and their dichotomy of attributes.

1. **Inducers:** Park (2011) investigated the man-made disasters and mentioned that catastrophic accidents may happen due to "human factors such as poor judgment, poor working condition, poor maintenance of equipment and/or the negligence of the operators" (p.466) or due to exogenous factors like bad weather. Studies categorize the events as "man-made" if the event is induced by direct or indirect involvement of people who can be the organizational members or someone from outside. The event is conceptualized as "natural" if the event is the result of natural anomalies or disasters. Accordingly, for our taxonomy, inducers of the traumatic event were conceptualized with the binary themes of "natural" vs "man-made".
2. **Origins:** Factors igniting the adverse events are discussed as "internal" and "external" to organizations. Internal organizational processes, the organizations' own members and their work related behaviours may trigger the event. Or, the event may be the consequence of external conditions. Hormann (2007) differentiated between external and internal injurious events, which can be catastrophic for the organizations. The bombing of an organization is given as an example as an external event; whereas sexual abuse, corporate members' misbehaviours, leader's termination, workplace mistreatments, and layoffs exemplify internal injurious events.
3. **Control Over:** The traumatic event can be rooted to factors that are within or beyond the control of organizations' members. This feature, conceptually, has the binary attributes of "controllable" vs "uncontrollable". Park (2011) stated that hurricanes, tsunamis or other types of natural forces are beyond human control. Giustiniano et al. (2016) talked about "avoidable" disasters that affect organizations designed to be "high-reliability" structures, i.e., organizational mechanisms and managerial control are assumed to inhibit emergency conditions. This is indeed an example of conceptualization based on controllability.
4. **Emergence:** Traumatic events are posited as "acute" when emergence is sudden and early symptoms are not recognized. The other extreme is related to "chronic" characteristics of the event that organizational members are periodically exposed. Chronic problems might be those that the organizations show efforts to solve but fail or organizational members may overlook the problem so that no initiative over time is taken to resolve it. For example, Kahn (2011) used this differentiation and mentioned that chronic organizational wounds happen by suppression of events like organizational scandals; where acute wounds emerge suddenly, like 2010 oil spill in the Gulf of Mexico.
5. **Exposure:** Hormann and Vivian (2005) define trauma as indirect when the nature of work that organizations particularly engage in creates continuous exposure to trauma as in the trauma-prone occupations and organizations. Literature also poses that even if people don't experience traumatic event directly, they may still show reactions of trauma by observing the others who are affected by the event (Kahn, 2003; Pearlman and Mac Ian, 1995). Secondary traumatic stress (Stamm, 1999) and vicarious traumatization (Pearlman, 1999; Shepard, 2013) are highlighted by Hormann and Vivian (2005) by borrowing the concept from clinical psychology literature that investigates trauma workers' psychological well-being. Therefore, exposure of organizational members to traumatic event may be "indirect/vicarious" or "direct".
6. **Available Time to React**: Organizational members may have "unrestricted" time to evaluate an event, its causes and effects, to plan the steps to cure the adverse effects, to solve the aftermath of these events, and to initiate measures with the aim of preventing reoccurrence. But especially when

the event emerges suddenly and when the organizations are not prepared for it, time is "restricted" to handle detrimental effects (Antonacopoulou & Sheaffer, 2014). Bozeman (2011a) defined crisis as the events that present a restricted amount of time in which a response can be made. Mendonça and Wallace (2015) worked out the case of the electric power restoration in New York City after September 11 and discussed organizational resilience to show immediate reaction under restricted time. Mutch (2015) discussed how the 2010/2011 earthquakes in Canterbury, New Zealand directed the school principals to take immediate actions, which let us categorize earthquakes as conditions with restricted response time. However, Mutch (2015) also described short and mid-term recovery efforts following the disasters to improve management of emergencies and leadership under crisis conditions. Moreover, Schmitt and Klarner (2015) talked about the organizational adaptation to external changes and emphasized the necessity for long-term perspectives in order to choose appropriate strategic responses. These studies lead us to think that traumatic conditions can also be analysed in terms of the available time to react to them with the dichotomy of "restricted" vs "unrestricted" time.

7. **Impact:** In order to differentiate negative events from organizational disasters, Bozeman (2011b) proposed an assessment whether the event has enduring effects or not, and mentioned that "although it is difficult to be precise as to duration, a good rule of thumb is that any negative events whose effects essentially vanish within 1 year cannot be classified as a disaster" (p.122). He elaborated on the case of information technology collapse which had enormous financial costs, but the negative publicity of event was mentioned as more critical because of potential long-term implications (Norris et.al, 2002; Bonanno, Brewin, Kaniasty, & La Greca, 2010). For example, Fox and Savage (2009) mention that massive shootings on college campuses generate long-lasting, devastating consequences, for students, faculty, and staff of the university. Disasters' serious long term effects on victim's health and well-being is a well-established issue of literature (Mutch, 2015). Therefore, impact of traumatic events can be grouped as "short-term" and "long-term".

Human Behaviours in Emergence of Traumatic Events

Human behaviour is the next component of taxonomy with attributes that can be categorized under three dimensions: involvement of human behaviour in the occurrence of traumatic events, exceptionality of the behaviour and types of error (Figure 4).

Figure 4. Dimensions of human behaviours involved in the emergence of traumatic events

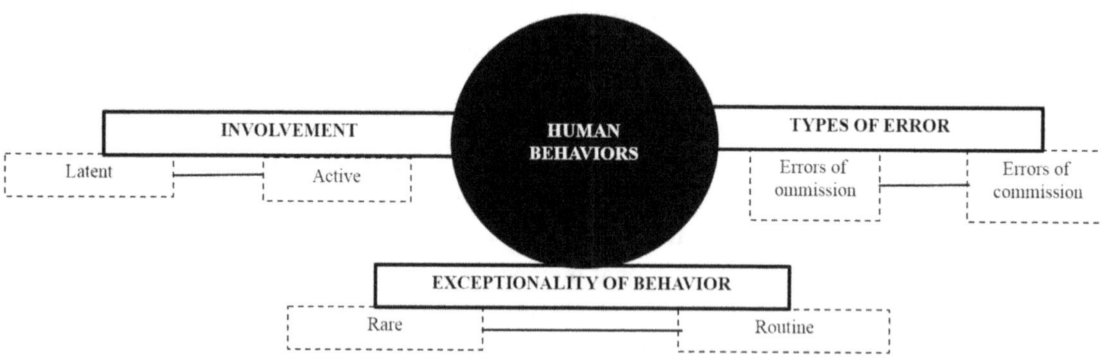

1. **Involvement**: When a traumatic event is man-made, internal or external people as passive or active actors may involve in the rise of events. Reason's (2002) categorization of human errors as "active" and "latent" is consistent with this idea. The former is related to unsafe behaviours that create direct and immediate adverse effects and contains slips, lapses, mistakes, and violations. For instance, Reason evaluated and determined the Chernobyl case as being caused by procedural violations. Giustiniano et al. (2016) by articulating the concept of zemblanity referred to how employees actively but unintentionally construct adverse consequences for themselves and their organizations. Latent errors emerge because of defects in the system of the organization such as poor design, ineffective management, procedural inadequacies that mainly arise from decisions made not only by organizational members but also by other stakeholders like the government, and manufacturers. These references let us talk about the dichotomy of human involvement as "active" vs "latent".
2. **Exceptionality of the Behaviours:** Goodman et al. (2011) discussed organizational errors by presenting a case study about the treatment procedures in a neonatal intensive care unit. They discuss that staff may start overlooking some of the vital procedures of medicine verification because of the assumptions that organizational routines are functioning effectively therefore the behaviours that deviate from safe procedures are not perceived risky. This pattern leads other members to repeat erroneous procedures so that it becomes a collective phenomenon. This is considered as an indication that some behaviours that ease the emergence of adverse events become part of the organizational daily "routine". Kauffman (2005) scrutinized NASA's crisis communication in the Columbia space shuttle accident in 2003 and mentioned that reports on accident analysis stress "normalized deviance" (p.272) which means that deviance from the safety and quality procedures becomes routine and normal. Chauvin, Lardjane, Morel, Clostermann, and Langard (2013) adapted a human factor analysis and classification system in a maritime context and reported that routine and rare violations, as the twofold categories of employees' unsafe acts, are critical in the emergence of shipping industry accidents. Moreover, research on organizational darkness depicts rare but highly detrimental organizational behaviours like sexual abuse, harassment, and theft (Linstead et al., 2014). These studies guide us to affirm that potentially traumatic events can be investigated in terms of the exceptionality of human behaviours involved in it with the binary themes of "rare" vs "routine".
3. **Types of Error:** Ackoff (2006) claimed that there are two types of organizational mistakes: "errors of commission" and "errors of omission". The first is related to the mistakes "when an organization or individual does something that should not have been done" (p.706). The second happens when "an individual or organization fails to do something it should have done" (p.706). Similarly, Kumar et al. (2016) depicted similar categories of errors by enhancing Reason's (2000) conceptualization for human errors and added "errors of commission" and "errors of omission" to their model as "mode of response" (p.90). Slips and lapses were considered as part of errors of commission; rule based and knowledge-based mistakes, and violations as belonging to errors of omission as they applied their model to underground coal mining accidents in India. Busby and Iszatt-White (2016) cited the intentionality to further explore the rule violations. Accordingly, our taxonomy proposes to incorporate the type of errors as "error of commission" vs "error of omission".

Figure 5. Internal Environment as the context for traumatic events

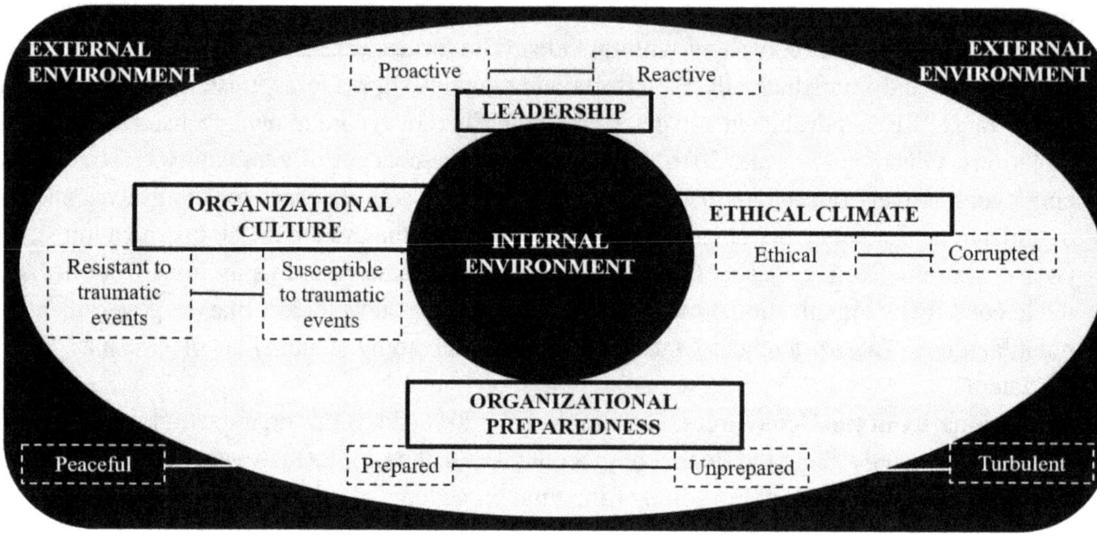

Internal and External Environment

The context in which the traumatic event occurs as it is depicted by the taxonomy is the third major component of the attributes of traumatic events (Figure 5). This context helps to see which internal and external environmental conditions are creating a baseline for the emergence of traumatic events.

1. **Internal Environment:** The content analysis depicts that the components of the organization as a system which is composed of technology, organizational culture, leader behaviours, and organizational ethics unveil the internal environment as a potential contextual catalyst of traumatic events.
   a. **Organizational Culture**: The first theme within the dimension of internal environment is organizational culture. Organizational culture is defined as a frame of reference that guides the members of organizations about what behaviours are good or bad, right or wrong, and acceptable or unacceptable (Waring, 2015). If organizations as social entities lead their members to develop common assumptions, values, ideologies, attitudes, and beliefs that help to develop social identity and unique corporate DNA at a collective level, then existence of strong culture may either incubate positive organizational behaviours and outcomes or counterproductive organizational behaviours, such as toxicity, malfunction, pathology and trauma. Researchers apply the construct of organizational culture to various domains of work life relevant to traumatic experiences. For instance, Waring (2015) states weak safety culture as one of the determinants of human-created disasters which was mentioned as valid for the BP Texas City refinery disaster (the US Chemical Safety & Hazard Investigation Board, 2007). Similarly, Kauffman (2005) cites The Columbia Accident Investigation Board's report (2003) where flaws in NASA's organizational culture were indicated as the key cause of accident. These guide us to the conclusion that some organizations are culturally "susceptible to traumatic events". On the other hand, Bozeman (2011b) answers the question of which organizational attributes affect organizations' capacity to mitigate the risks for disasters and notices that organizations

with strong two-way communications ties, without tense resource constraints, and those which are innovative, and autonomous in using their resources are less prone to disasters. Therefore, we may entitle organizations with these attributes as "resistant to traumatic conditions".

b. **Leadership**: Schmitt and Klarner (2015) stated that organizational adaptation efforts to changing environmental conditions, specifically climate change, can be conceptualized along a continuum from proactive to reactive. By assessing organization's strengths and weaknesses under the conditions of external threats and opportunities, organizations can ameliorate their "absorptive capacity" (p.6) to initiate effective adaptation. Such a proactive approach needs to be fostered by the leaders since leading organizational change is vital for organizational survival especially under the conditions that physical and social environment provokes potentially traumatic experiences. Hyungju, Stein, and Bouwer (2016) presented proactivity and reactivity as one of the classification for "safety barriers" in their research that amplifies the ferry accident happened in South Korea in 2014 where 304 people died. Sklet (2006) defines the means to prevent, control, or mitigate undesired events or accidents as the indication of proactivity. Additionally, Annarelli and Nanino (2015) elaborated the defensive/reactive and proactive approaches to organizational resilience. Initiating efforts for organizational adaptation, developing organizational resilience or endorsing safety systems certainly requires effective leadership; in conclusion, related research sets a ground to propose a leadership dimension in our taxonomy to have the binary themes of "proactive" vs "reactive".

c. **Ethical Climate of Organization**: Victor and Cullen (1988) asserted that organizations have unique ethical climates, which are "the perceived prescriptions, proscriptions, and permissions regarding moral obligations in organizations." (p.101). Members form aggregated perceptions about their organizations' normative systems. In their research they derived five distinct types of perception: (i) Members perceive their organization as "caring" when a company's major consideration focuses on what is best for all members. (ii) Organization's emphasis on compliance with "law and professional codes" may dominate the members' perception. (iii) Members may think that following the company's "rules" and procedures is critical. (iv) Protection of members' own benefits and interests may cause "instrumentalism" as the dominant perception. (v) Perception of "independence" might be predominant so that people are allowed to follow their own personal and moral values. Kleinberg (2014) described some of the leaders and founders' exploitation of organizational resources for their personal gains against collective benefits, and how tolerance to unethical, illegal, and unprofessional approaches becomes prevalent. From Victor and Cullen's (1988) perspective, in these organizations instrumentalism is dominant. Kleinberg (2014) propounds these structures as "corruptogenic organizations" that portray vulnerability to corruption. Consequently, "corrupted" is proposed to be one edge of dichotomy for the dimension of organizations' ethical climate. On the other hand, organizations with caring climate where law, professional codes, and rules are perceived as dominant can be considered as the organizations with strong ethical values. With that being said, entitling the other edge of the ethical climate dichotomy as "ethical" is plausible.

d. **Organizational Preparedness**: Organizational preparedness for traumatic events incorporates loss control measures. Assessment of the risks, implementation of preventive measures and development of contingency plans are needed to increase organizational preparedness so that the destructive impact of traumatic events is reduced. In order to discuss how ready, the organizations are to deal with potentially traumatic events, we may talk about "trauma control" as the derivative of "hazard control" which is indeed industrial safety management literature's prime construct. Hazard control is the removal of root causes so that the emergence of accidents would be hindered. Fox and Savage (2009) report the collection of various task forces' recommendations on the massacres committed in the university campuses. Among these recommendations, we see emergency planning, training of staff on emergency plans, establishing teams of employees to assess reported threats to students and university staff, implementation of emergency plans, and following up conditions until the problematic situation ceases. Such a structure aims to enhance the level of preparedness in the organizations to deal with potentially traumatic events. Furthermore, Aini and Fakhru'l-Razi (2013) underscored the latent conditions that trigger organizational failures and the role of risk management in order to identify conditions in the organization that may stimulate adversity. Accordingly, organizational efforts to identify risks, to take countermeasures, develop contingency plans, develop models to deal with the aftermath of traumatic events and implement techniques to increase employee readiness at individual and collective levels may represent the dichotomy of "prepared" vs "unprepared".

2. **External Environment:** The taxonomy proposes that external environment can be investigated on the dichotomy of "peaceful" vs "turbulent". Researchers discuss the external environment as setting a ground for potential traumatic conditions. Social, economic and political conditions at sectoral, national, and international layers may result in traumatic consequences for the members of organizations. The external environment may show variance in terms of how volatile, competitive and violent the conditions are, how much uncertainty is imposed by external factors, how turbulent the political conditions may be and how strong the regulations and legislations are to control these just to list a few. For example, Bowman, Bhamjee, Eagle, and Crafford (2009) investigated external workplace violence in the telecommunication sector of South Africa where interviewees described their everyday working conditions to be like a war "resulting in wounds, death, and devastation" (p.305). Technicians who especially work in violent communities portrayed their daily activities like being in a "battlefield" (p.305). They talk about hijacking, armed robbery, encounters with violent protestors, and being in the crossfire of police and perpetrators as the incidents that let them to be potential victims. Park (2011) stated that national culture determines the effect of human errors on man-made disasters, and specifically, identified level of corruption as one of the societal variables of national culture. For example, public servants' readiness to accept bribes instead of applying strict rules in a particular organization is identified as a jeopardizing factor. Respectively, description and evaluation of external environment as peaceful or turbulent depicts various attributes that researchers focus as they explain the dynamics of traumatic events.

Application of Potentially Traumatic Events Taxonomy to Real Life Cases

This section will demonstrate how the proposed taxonomy can be applied to a variety of events with potential for traumatic consequences. Six cases were described (Table 5) which can be categorized according to the typology of potentially traumatic events: the events caused by organizational processes; events faced in trauma-prone occupations and sectors; catastrophic events caused primarily by external conditions.

These cases serve to implement the proposed taxonomy in real life events. Table 6 summarizes the evaluation of cases according to the outlined taxonomy. In Table 6, the attributes of the traumatic events

Table 5. The cases to be analysed by the taxonomy of potentially traumatic events' attributes

Case	Potentially Traumatic Events Category	Themes under the Potentially Traumatic Events
Case 1: Toshiba accounting scandal	Traumatic events resulting from organizational processes	Scandals, frauds, adverse effects of service and product on public health that creates inquiry on business ethics
Case 2: Nestlé lawsuit on forced labour		Employee mistreatments
Case 3: Peru oil pipeline leaks	Adverse experiences in trauma-prone occupations and sectors	Industry specific and/or high risk sector accidents like mining, gas, energy, aviation, maritime accidents, aerospace, transportation, and nuclear
Case 4: Australian emergency services workers		Events that hazardous occupations like policemen, armed forces, paramedics, firefighters, and similar occupations face traumatic events frequently.
Case 5: Terrorist attack in Paris	Catastrophic events caused by economic, social, environmental conditions	Terrorist attacks
Case 6: Flood of a century, India		Natural disasters like floods, earthquakes, tsunami, hurricane, volcano

are provided in the left column and the dichotomy of attributes on the right; one edge of the dichotomy is represented with light grey, and the other with dark grey. Each case is placed in a separate column so that their evaluation was depicted with related colours of the cell. However, for some cases the attributes were non-applicable to the analysis and indicated in Table 6 with "NA". In other cases, the attributes' direction couldn't be determined and are shown with question marks in the white coloured cells.

Table 6. Evaluation of cases by the taxonomy of potentially traumatic events' attributes

Components of Taxonomy	Attributes of traumatic event (Dimensions)	Binary Characteristics (Themes of Versus Coding)		Traumatic events resulting from organizational processes		Adverse experiences in trauma-prone occupations and sectors		Catastrophic events caused by economic, social, and environmental conditions	
		From	To	Case 1: Toshiba accounting scandal	Case 2: Nestlé lawsuit on forced labour	Case 3: Peru oil pipeline leak	Case 4: Australian emergency services workers	Case 5: Terrorist attack in Paris	Case 3: Flood of a century, India
Features of Traumatic Event	Inducers	Natural	Man-made						
	Origin	External to organization	Internal to organization						
	Control over	Controllable	Uncontrollable						
	Emergence	Acute	Chronic						
	Exposure	Vicarious/Indirect	Direct						
	Reaction time	Unrestricted	Restricted						
	Impact	Short-term	Long-term						
Human Behaviours	Involvement	Latent	Active				NA	NA	NA
	Exceptionality	Rare	Routine				NA	NA	NA
	Type of error	Errors of omissions	Errors of commissions				NA	NA	NA
Context of traumatic event – Internal Environment	Organizational preparedness	Prepared	Unprepared						?
	Organizational culture	Resistant to traumatic events	Susceptible to traumatic events					?	?
	Leadership	Proactive	Reactive					?	?
	Ethical Climate	Ethical	Corrupted		?	?		?	?
Context of traumatic event	External Environment	Peaceful	Turbulent			?			

In the following section, cases are briefly described and their analysis according to the taxonomy of potential traumatic events is conveyed.

Traumatic Events Resulting from Organizational Processes

Case 1: Toshiba Accounting Scandal, September 2015.

The news reported that Toshiba overstated their earnings by nearly $2 billion over a seven-year period which is more than four times its initial estimate in April of 2015 (Exhibit 1). It was further reported that employees were forced to postpone loss reports or move certain costs into later years by applying inappropriate accounting procedures (Paddison, 2015; Smith, 2015).

In such a man-made, direct, and internally ignited problem, involvement of human behaviour is identified as active, because, scandal is the collective outcome of repeated unethical behaviour at both managerial and non-managerial levels. It is routine and there is a direct violation of regulations so that errors of commission exist. Its chronic characteristics indeed provided unrestricted time to recognize and intervene with the violations which meant there was an opportunity to extinguish and prevent this scandal's emergence. But, leaders didn't act proactively. Organizational culture and corrupted ethical climate appear to put pressure on employees to conform to "commands" of their supervisors to engage in unethical behaviours. Therefore, the organizational culture become susceptible for the occurrence of such a traumatic event. The organization seems to be missing appropriate countermeasures to prevent governance problems and is not prepared for the event because of minimal effort to assess the risks. Leaders have to scrutinize how the current organizational culture elevates other man-made problems and how the external environment shapes it. The external environment may be predicted to be turbulent due to the hypercompetitive and volatile characteristics of the sector, which is a reality today for any industry. The effort of Toshiba to overstate their revenue implies an external environment where the survival of the company is based in misleading financial reporting. However, Toshiba's well-established history and presence in the business world may hinder the effect of this scandal's long-term negative impact if leaders decide to act proactively for future prospects.

Case 2: Nestlé lawsuit, use of fish sourced from Thai company using slave labour, September 2015.

Nestlé had been a target of scandal (Pettersson & Burnson, 2015, August 28) due to seafood used in the production of cat food that claimed to be coming from slave ships wherein kidnapped workers were forced to work (Business & Human Rights Resource Centre, 2015, August 27). Nestlé's official response (Business & Human Rights Resource Centre, 2015, September 1) is given in Exhibit 2.

Exhibit 1. Toshiba scandal (Paddison, 2015, December 30; Smith, 2015, July 21)

The news are attributing Toshiba's scandal to "a broken corporate culture". A report filed to the Tokyo Stock Exchange by the company spoke of a broken corporate culture: "Within Toshiba, there was a corporate culture in which one could not go against the wishes of superiors. According to regulators, the company set unrealistic targets and employees were discouraged from questioning the actions of their bosses. Independent investigators found that both the president and chief executive of the 140-year old company were aware of the overstatement. There is clearly much more work to be done to achieve corporate transparency."

Exhibit 2. Nestlé's official response (Business & Human Rights Resource Centre, 2015, September 1)

Forced labour has no place in our supply chain. Our mandatory Nestlé Supplier Code and Responsible Sourcing Guideline (RSG) on Fish and Seafood require all of our suppliers to respect human rights and to comply with all applicable labor laws. Over the past 12 months, we have been working with the independent supply chain consultancy Achilles to better understand the multi layered supply chain in the Thai seafood industry which supplies some ingredients for our products. Nestlé is participating in a multi-stakeholder International Labour Organisation (ILO) Working Group, consisting of representatives from the Government of Thailand, local seafood suppliers, and international buyers. This group has developed training guidelines for factories, primary processors and fish farms to help end unfair practices, and tools to support the inspection of fishing vessels to identify where forced and child labour is taking place.

This case represents a traumatic organizational process in which potential employee mistreatment exists. This event is man-made, its origin is external and it is not within the direct control of the organization. Its emergence is acute, exposure is direct, and time is restricted to take action. There is the latent involvement of human behaviour here since the people responsible from the supply-chain management overlooked the multi-layered system in the Thai seafood industry and leaders couldn't act proactively on the issue. Therefore, we may hypothesize that this event is the consequence of errors of omission that people do not frequently engage in. Organizational preparedness appears to be low, making the organizational culture susceptible to traumatic events. The external environment in the seafood supply chain can be assessed as turbulent since learning that this industry is still operating with modalities against civilized labour law and human rights. The estimation of the Nestlé's ethical climate, as ethical or corrupted, is not possible based on the available information from the news; it is a task that Nestlé should deeply concentrate its efforts on and inform all stakeholders. The impact of such adverse events might be short-term due to the organization's strong reputation and positive image within business society and may serve to veil the negative image created by this event. The perception of this event by Nestlé employees is crucial and how their psychological well-being and work related behaviours are affected by the idea of being a member of a company that is accused with inhumane activities should also be assessed.

Adverse Experiences in Trauma-Prone Occupations and Sectors

Case 3: Peru pipeline leak in the Amazon, February 2016.

Peru's main oil pipeline, owned by Petroperu, had an oil spill in the Amazonian region (Exhibit 3) and two rivers that native villages relied on for water were polluted (Taj & Aquino, 2016, February 23). This case is an example of industry specific accidents and took place in a high risk sector; this is representative for similar cases in the sectors of gas, energy, aviation, marine, aerospace, transportation, and nuclear.

This case was man-induced, it is controllable -under the condition that preventive measures could have been taken-, its origin is internal to the organization, its emergence is chronic, and the exposure is

Exhibit 3. Peru pipeline leaks in Amazon (Taj & Aquino, 2016, February 23)

Two breaks in the pipeline have halted transportation of 5,000 to 6,000 barrels of oil per day. Peru's health ministry declared a water quality emergency in five districts near the spill. State-owned Petroperu faces some 60 million soles ($17 million) in fines if tests confirm that the spills, in late January and early February, hurt the health of locals, said OEFA. Velasquez said the company was conducting an evaluation of the pipeline, built in the 70s, to prevent any future spills, a process that could take up to two months.

direct for that specific company. Other companies from the same industry may start taking action such as evaluating their as-is conditions, starting with periodic maintenance, and training their employees for emergency conditions even if they are not exposed to direct threat, but vicariously. After the oil spill began, time was restricted to stop it, however, if organizational preparedness were high, leaders and its members' could have taken action to prevent it. The internal environment of the organization creates susceptibility to traumatic events and leaders behave in a reactive manner. This case appears to be caused by latent involvement of staff and by errors of omission that are rooted in a work setting where the technology is old and prone to defects especially under the conditions that periodic maintenance is not executed. Consequently, employee behaviours that contribute to the events with negative consequences may not be considered exceptional; they are routine elements of that system. The ethical climate and external environment cannot be concluded from the available information but it should be an area of focus for the leaders.

Case 4: Australian emergency services workers suicide, June 2015.

The news about Australian emergency service workers' psychological well-being is our second case that represents adverse experiences in trauma-prone occupations and sectors. This news highlighted that police officers, paramedics, and firefighters experience post-traumatic stress disorder (PTSD) and commit suicide (Koubaridis, 2015).

The stories of Al Briggs who worked with ambulance services and Ross Beckley who is a former firefighter proclaimed that they were suffering from PTSD. Al Briggs had complained that emergency services workers witness people on their worst days, and Ross Beckley had mentioned that he could not stand to drive down a road where he'd been to a fatal crash and then avoided certain roads.

Using our taxonomic model to evaluate this case, we see that emergency service workers by the essence of their occupations have to intervene in a variety of nature-driven or man-driven dangerous conditions. These workers are exposed to trauma of other people. The source of traumatic events is uncontrollable. The origin of the event is external to their organization, and events' emergence is acute. Exposure to traumatic event is both direct and vicarious. As the dangerous conditions that emergency workers show performance create a setting for direct exposure; witnessing how others are victimized is vicarious or indirect trauma. They have restricted time to intervene in the traumatic event. Within the scope of the current case, the impact of the traumatic event is long-term because of the reports that the workers suffered from PTSD through repeated exposure to traumatic conditions. However, the human behaviour component of the taxonomy is considered non-applicable to the current case. Emergency service workers' behaviours may or may not be regarded as a stimulus for the traumatic condition. Specific cases must be examined to check the involvement and exceptionality of behaviours, as well as to understand which type of errors may intensify the traumatic effects of emergency conditions for these

Exhibit 4. Australian emergency services workers in committing suicide (Koubaridis, 2015)

New figures reveal one police officer, paramedic or firefighter is taking their own life every six weeks. But the true extent of the problem is unknown and the actual number may be much higher. The Intentional Self-Harm Fact Sheet is based on coronial cases around Australia and shows 110 police officers, paramedics and firefighters died by suicide between July 2000 and December 2012. It is the first time the number of suicides among emergency service personnel has been officially quantified in Australia. A breakdown of the 110 deaths shows 62 cases involved police officers, 22 involved firefighters and 26 were paramedics.

professionals. Emergency organizations should have a high level of preparedness since their services require expertise and accreditation at the individual level. They need effectively executed measures at the organizational level to mitigate the risk for the life of job incumbents. The organizational culture is susceptible to traumatic events, the leadership is reactive, and the organizational climate is ethical. The external environment is turbulent because emergency services are delivered following the events with enormous uncertainty.

Catastrophic Events Caused by Economic, Social, and Environmental Conditions

Case 5: Paris terrorist attack organized by the Islamic State (IS) militant group, November, 2015.

The Paris terrorist attack simultaneously targeted several sites on November, 13, 2015. One of the sites was a popular live music venue, the Bataclan, where three gunmen claimed the lives of 90 victims (BBC News, 2015, December 9). As Exhibit 5 shows, this attack caused the Bataclan to stop its business (Aubourg, 2015, November 25). However, they later notified that they would start to host concerts again prior to the end of 2016 (J. Goodman, 2016). The dilemma between being an entertainment centre and now converting to a crime site requires unique organizational efforts to recover from this devastating experience.

As this case displayed, organization are not isolated as traumatic events impinge on them, but within the ecology of a particular organization, all stakeholders are affected. In the Bataclan Concert Hall case, business owners, employees, musicians, service providers and customers, in this case concertgoers, were all jeopardized.

This traumatic event is man-made, it is uncontrollable, the origin is external to the organization, its emergence is acute, the exposure is direct, and there is restricted time to react. The human behaviour component of the taxonomy is non-applicable for this specific case since staff's direct involvement in this attack is not assumed. The socio-economic-political environment at both national and international levels are critical determinants. Terrorism itself is the product of a turbulent/war like external environmental conditions and the Bataclan seems to be unprepared for such an attack. In this particular case and in similar incidents of terrorism, external environmental conditions surpass the internal conditions as the determinants of traumatic event. Therefore, the role of leadership, organizational culture and ethical climate of organizations in the occurrence of a terrorist attack are difficult to foreseen. Because of the world wide political turbulence all nations experience in recent days, we may predict that terrorism to be one of the components in risk assessment and contingency planning for organizations. The terrorist

Exhibit 5. Bataclan Concert Hall announcement from their official website

The Bataclan's website had the following remark after almost four months (Mansell, 2015, November 18): "Dear friends, No words can express the magnitude of our grief. Our thoughts are with the victims, the injured and their families. You are likely to want to come together and pay your respects at the Bataclan, but unfortunately the authorities still need to work on site. We will inform you when it will be possible to gather in front of the venue." In February, 23, 2016 the website announced (J. Goodman, 2016, February 11): "Today we wish to share with you an important new: we decided to renovate the Bataclan. We will do our best to accommodate new shows before the end of 2016.Of course, we will keep you informed as soon as our project will become clearer. We also wish to thank all those who have expressed us their support. Your sympathy touch us deeply. The Bataclan team".

attack's impact on the business of the Bataclan seems relatively short term since advertisement for concert performances by November, 2016 started as evidenced by their website. However, the psychological effects of this attack may still stay deeply rooted.

Case 6: Flood of the century, Chennai, India, November 2015.

The flooding in Chennai, India was reported to be the worst flood that took place in the last 100 years (Pereira, 2015, December 4). At least 379 people were reported to have died. Agricultural areas were demolished. Since Chennai is accepted as the industrial centre of automobile manufacturing and information technologies, business was disrupted by the disaster on a large scale (Exhibit 6).

This uncontrollable disaster of flooding was induced by nature and identified as acute, direct and forced reaction in a restricted time. Its origin is external, and impact is long-term. The dimension covering the involvement of human behaviour seems non-applicable for this case. However, preparedness of organizations is critical since this can really mitigate the potential traumatic impact. Since the case doesn't elaborate the individual cases of organizations, it is hard to speculate about the sub-dimensions of the internal environment. But it is absolutely the leaders' task to ponder how their internal environment -namely the organizational preparedness, culture, leadership, and ethical climate- created a context to evade the devastating consequences of this natural disaster as a totally destructive experience. Proactive leadership is necessary to motivate responsible parties to analyse potential natural disasters before they are directly experienced. Since the external environment is presumably turbulent knowing that the organizations are geographically sited in regions with a higher risk of natural disasters (i.e. floods and earthquakes) stronger organizational preparation is necessary in the form of organizational contingency plans and preventive measures in order to minimize potential loss.

DISCUSSION

The comprehensive literature review in this chapter demonstrates that organizations and their members have significant vulnerability against a variety of threats that emerge from external and internal conditions of their companies. Researchers assort a variety of events with negative consequences like natural disasters, terrorism, frauds, financial crises, workplace bullying, or industrial accidents by labelling them as organizational crises, disasters, failures, implosions, or zemblanity. The current chapter asserts that what differentiates these threats and events from each other is not how they are denominated, but the distinction becomes visible when their attributes are specified. One of the crucial attributes of these events is their long term impact on individuals, groups, and organizations, which is defined in the recent researches as "organizational trauma".

Exhibit 6. Flood of a century, Chennai, India (Pereira, 2015, December 4)

Chennai hosts over 165 BSE-listed companies (registered in the city) with an aggregate market capitalisation of over Rs 285,000 crore. A big automobile manufacturing and IT hub, the floods have badly derailed the business activity in the city as companies stopped their production activity and shut down offices with instruction for employees to stay home or work from home. According to Assocham, "the financial loss due to record-breaking rainfall in Chennai and several parts of Tamil Nadu may even exceed Rs 15,000 crore mark as Chennai has come to a virtual standstill and is in the grip of fear and panic."

The content analysis of the literature showed that a typology can be developed to sketch the variety of potentially traumatic events into a coherent structure. There are primarily three types of events with potential traumatic consequences. The first type of event is caused by internal organizational processes as the cases of Toshiba and Nestlé exemplify. Governance problems, including the violation of regulations and procedures; and conducts contrary to business ethics such as scandals, frauds, harm and mistreatment of workers are illustrated by these specific corporate cases. The literature also underscores that workplace health and safety problems/accidents, organizational/human errors, death/loss of key organizational members, technology embedded disasters, and social accidents experienced during organizational change processes (Factor, Mahalel, and Yair, 2007) are in fact potentially traumatic events.

The second type of potentially traumatic events contain adverse experiences in trauma-prone occupations and sectors. The oil pipeline leak in Peru illustrates an industry specific and/or high risk sector accident which is an example for trauma-prone sectors. The literature highlights major accidents in the mining, gas, energy, aviation, maritime, aerospace, transportation, and nuclear industries as threats to human and material resources for both organizations and societies. Moreover, the Australian emergency service workers' case represents the adverse experiences for trauma-prone occupations. Security staff, police officers, armed forces, paramedics, firefighters, and other similar occupations are potentially traumatizing for the employees by direct exposure to adverse events or by witnessing the victims of such events. Additionally, secondary exposure to trauma is also a risk for professionals who work in health care organizations where contact to traumatized individuals is prevalent.

The third type of "potentially traumatic event" revealed in the content analysis, is the catastrophic events caused by economic, social, and environmental conditions. The flood in the India case belongs to the category of natural disasters, as the Bataclan case in Paris resides in the terrorist attack theme. However, this type of potentially traumatic events also includes environmental hazards like toxic waste releases, fires, explosions, and collapse of buildings; national/international health crisis; financial and economic crisis; political turmoil and war conditions; gun violence, massive shootings, organized crime and civilian violence; and robbery, theft, and security related events.

In summary, the typology for potentially traumatic events outlines the wide array of events into a solid and compact threefold structure. Potentially traumatic events that are highlighted in the literature are sometimes nurtured by the internal organizational processes. Sometimes they are the output of sectoral and occupational proneness to trauma. Or some are the consequence of external socioeconomic and political conditions. However, such a typology is not sufficient to encompass the highly sophisticated evaluations that take place in the literature. A taxonomic model is needed to summarize the available analytic choices of researchers to make sense of such events. The current chapter's goal was to transform the discussion of traumatic events from a "conceptual level" to one of a "sense making level" by specification of various attributes that make the adverse events unique. The content analysis highlighted that the components, dimensions, and binary attributes of such a taxonomy can effectively scrutinize potentially traumatic events.

The taxonomy of attributes for potentially traumatic events illustrates that events' distinctiveness is refined when the features of traumatic events are analysed by searching if; (i) the event is induced by nature or human being, (ii) its origin is external or internal to the organization, (iii) the members of the organizations have the chance to control it or if the event is uncontrollable, (iv) its emergence is acute or chronic, (v) the members are exposed to the event directly or witness how others become traumatized, (vi) the time to respond is restricted so that immediate actions are necessary or unrestricted so that actions can be taken over time, and (vii) the consequences are short-term or long-lasting. These features constitute the first component of the taxonomic structure and demonstrate how Toshiba accounting scandal and Peru oil pipeline leak cases are similar to each other. Both are man-made, internal, controllable, direct, chronic and require responses in a restricted time. What differs is the impact of these events. Financial scandals' may have a temporary effect if the organizations are strong and resilient enough to rebuild their reputation and regain the trust of their stakeholders. However, harm caused by organizations toward their own employees, overall society or the environment has the potential to be remembered over generations and recovery is likely to be long term. The Toshiba and Peru pipeline cases show a divergence in terms of their impact in this sense.

The potentially traumatic events occur in unique environmental settings where the conduct of people can either facilitate or inhibit the emergence and endurance of events. Some behaviours are so critical in the emergence of an adverse event that if this behaviour can be precluded then the event may never occur. Errors, omissions, lapses or violations of individuals may contribute directly to the emergence of accidents, failures, or crises. People's active or latent involvement, if they engage in these critical behaviours frequently or exceptionally, or if these behaviours are the output of errors of omissions or commissions are distinctive attributes of human behaviours. In the Toshiba case, human involvement is active, (i.e., staff was intentionally manipulating the financial records), and the event was the consequence of a culmination of behaviours that violated legal or organizational procedures. With these characteristics, Toshiba's case is unlike Nestlé and the Peru pipeline cases which were caused by latent behaviours of people, such as limited competence of staff, operational shortcomings or deficiencies in decision-making. On the other hand, involvement of human behaviour, its exceptionality and types of errors couldn't be estimated for the cases of Australian emergency service workers, terrorist attack in Paris, and flood that happened in India because these events' origin was external to the organization. If these events' analysis is conducted for particular organizations, or for specific groups/operations within a particular organization, different scenarios can be detected. For example, in the case of the flooding, latent behaviours of staff may either have mitigated or aggravated the risks, and the adversity changes depending if the measures to maximize organization's preparedness were effectively deployed or not. Eventually, the taxonomy guides leaders and members of organizations to undertake an in-depth analysis of the events to explore case specific characteristics so that future corrective measures can be implemented.

The taxonomy also has a contextual component, which is comprised of the internal and external environment. It presents the internal environmental attributes that help to identify; (i) how susceptible or resistant the organization is against traumatic events; (ii) if the leaders perform in a proactive or reactive style; (iii) if the organizational climate is ethical or corrupted, and; (iv) if the organization has a sufficient level of preparedness for addressing traumatic conditions. For the cases of Toshiba, Nestlé and PetroPeru, insufficient level of organizational preparedness, susceptibility to traumatic events, and reactive leadership style appears as common characteristics. Even if the ethical climate for Toshiba can be predicted as corrupted, for the other two, it is hard to determine. For the later cases, leaders should explore if the ethical climate of their organizations also has an effect on the occurrence of traumatic events and if so, reasons have to be investigated. For trauma-prone occupations, organizations have to maximize their readiness against adverse events because by the essence of their organizations inclination toward traumatic events is higher.

The external environment of organizations for majority of cases is estimated as turbulent. Hypercompetitive characteristics of the business market in the case of Toshiba, uncertainties of global markets in the case of Nestlé, war-like conditions of contemporary international politics as occurred in the case of the Paris terror attacks, extreme climate events that emerged from climate change as the one India encountered, and the highly stressful working conditions of emergency service workers represent a turbulent external environment even if each has its unique nature.

In the majority of the illustrated cases, leadership has been estimated as reactive. In this vein, leaders and professionals' competencies to better depict the background of traumatic events in terms of technology, structure, psycho-social, and management subsystems of the organization must be developed. Leaders shouldn't be alerted only when other companies or geographic regions of the world are traumatized, or wait until their organizations directly face the threat. Instead leaders have to proactively assess the conditions for potential risks within their organizations and appropriate countermeasures have to be activated. As the system activates effective tools to prepare against risks, people are trained and socialized; organizational preparedness will improve subsequently.

Moreover, management teams at all levels within the organization should be guided to become aware of organizational trauma as a phenomenon. This is indeed a process of recognizing major risks proactively, taking preventive measures, testing the capabilities of the organization to act under emergency conditions, handling the event if it really emerges, and "healing the wounds" that follow devastating experiences. Besides engaging in daily business activities, attention to potentially chaotic conditions needs to be addressed as a key component of any managerial role. Both leader development as well as organizational development efforts should embrace this perspective to decrease the potential effects of organizational trauma.

FUTURE RESEARCH DIRECTIONS

During the literature review for the current chapter, it was remarkable to observe that vast majority of available research utilize theoretical level of analysis for organizational trauma related constructs and phenomena. These studies focus on description of traumatic events, and attempt to explain them according to researchers' preferred theoretical approach to propose particular measures to control future occurrences. In these studies, object of the analysis is mostly "the organizations". This underpins the need for empirical research on organizational trauma from the perspectives of employees, employers, managers, customers and the other third parties. Not only the individual and psychological level of analysis, and but also collective and social level of analysis on organizational trauma seems missing. Therefore, future studies should investigate organizational members' and other stakeholders' perspectives about the traumatic events. Rigorous approaches, and quantitative and qualitative research methodologies should be used to understand the cognitive, emotional and behavioral processes involve before, during, and after the traumatic events. The effects of various adverse conditions at collective level have to be investigated by in-depth evaluation of social psychological processes.

The capacity to learn from traumatic experiences need to be investigated too. How the individuals, groups and organizations improve their adaptability following their survival from the conditions of threat, stress, and uncertainty is critical to investigate which routes the research toward individual and organizational resilience. The way that the survival experience can be used as an organizational development opportunity and who will take the lead role in this process seem to be among future's appealing research issues.

Moreover, the phenomena of organizational trauma may set a base to initiate multi-disciplinary and even trans-disciplinary research. Organizational trauma can be conceptualized as intersection where industrial/organizational psychologists and clinical psychologists may collaboratively work. This interactionist approach can be enhanced with the inclusion of expert views from diverse scientific disciplines like engineering, law, business, and sociology just to mention a few.

CONCLUSION

In conclusion, the typology of potentially traumatic events, and the taxonomy of attributes assist a systematic and complex investigation of various organizational and sector specific cases. The analysis can be utilized to initiate the; (i) design of preventive and corrective measures by informing, motivating, and coordinating members and various groups within the organization; (ii) healing of traumatic impacts, and; (iii) feeding the "lessons learned" from these experiences to organizational processes. First, the culture has to be well understood in order to determine if the organization, as a social entity, is creating its own hurdles. Then, organizational adaptiveness has to be reinforced since it is the key to dealing with the changing conditions that may create a baseline for trauma; it is also the core competency used to recover from the adverse effects of these events. Last but not least, trauma resistant climate and culture with a focus both on employee and environment have to be addressed within the vision and mission of the organizations. One crucial role of leaders will be to systematically analyse the traumatic events at both causal and contextual layers in order to provide unique answers to all questions within the taxonomy. The peculiarity of the problem will be refined once the features of the trauma, types of human behaviour involved in it, level of organizational preparedness, and the internal and external environments are known. Moreover, understanding the impact of traumatic events in the short and long term, with small or large industrial and organizational level of effect will aid to anticipate the consequences that will circularly be used to design interventions that maximize organizational preparedness.

REFERENCES

Abulnour, A. H. (2014). The post-disaster temporary dwelling: Fundamentals of provision, design and construction. *Housing and Building National Research Center Journal*, *10*, 10–24.

Ackoff, R. L. (2006). Why few organizations adopt systems thinking. *Systems Research and Behavioral Science*, *23*(5), 705–708. doi:10.1002/sres.791

Ackoff, R. L., & Strümpfer, J. P. (2003). Terrorism: A systemic review. *Systems Research and Behavioral Science*, *20*(3), 287–294. doi:10.1002/sres.544

Adizes, I. (1979). Organizational passagesdiagnosing and treating lifecycle problems of organizations. *Organizational Dynamics*, *8*(1), 3–25. doi:10.1016/0090-2616(79)90001-9

Aini, M. S., & Fakhrul-Raz, A. (2013). Latent errors of socio-technical disasters: A Malaysian case study. *Safety Science*, *51*(1), 284–292. doi:10.1016/j.ssci.2012.07.004

Annarelli, A., & Nanino, F. (2015). *Strategic and operational management of organizational resilience: Current state of research and future directions*. Retrieved from: http://www.sciencedirect.com/science/article/pii/S0305048315001590

Antonacopoulou, E., & Sheaffer, Z. (2014). Learning in crisis: rethinking the relationship between organizational learning and crisis management. *Journal of Management Inquiry, 23*(1), 5-21.

Aubourg, L. (2015, November 25). This is what happened at the Bataclan Concert Hall during the Paris attacks. *Vice News*. Retrieved August 16, 2016, from https://news.vice.com/article/this-is-what-happened-at-the-bataclan-concert-hall-during-the-paris-attacks

Bassuk, E. L., Unick, G. J., Paquette, K., & Richard, M. K. (2016). Developing an Instrument to measure organizational trauma-informed care in human services: The TICOMETER. *Psychology of Violence*. 10.1037/vio0000030

BBC News. (2015, December 9). Paris attacks: What happened on the night? *BBC News*. Retrieved August 16, 2016, from http://www.bbc.com/news/world-europe-34818994

Bonanno, G., Brewin, C., Kaniasty, K., & La Greca, A. (2010). Weighing the costs of disaster: Consequences, risks, and resilience in individuals, families and communities. *Psychological Science in the Public Interest, 11*(1), 1–49. doi:10.1177/1529100610387086 PMID:26168411

Bowman, B., Bhamjee, F., Eagle, G., & Crafford, A. (2009). A qualitative study of the multiple impacts of external workplace violence in two Western Cape communities. *South African Journal of Psychology. Suid-Afrikaanse Tydskrif vir Sielkunde, 39*(3), 300–313. doi:10.1177/008124630903900305

Boyd, W. (1998). *Armadillo*. London: Hamish Hamilton.

Bozeman, B. (2011a). The 2010 BP Gulf of Mexico oil spill: Implications for theory of organizational disaster. *Technology in Society, 33*(3-4), 244–252. doi:10.1016/j.techsoc.2011.09.006

Bozeman, B. (2011b). Toward a theory of organizational implosion. *American Review of Public Administration, 41*(2), 119–140. doi:10.1177/0275074010381781

Bragg, K. (1997). Being a gay or lesbian professional in a psychiatric hospital for adolescents. *Journal of Gay & Lesbian Social Services, 6*(4), 25–38. doi:10.1300/J041v06n04_03

Brewis, J., & Őzbilgin, M. (2013). Introducing recovery and organization. *Culture and Organization, 19*(5), 371–376. doi:10.1080/14759551.2013.848631

Brown, E. H. (1997). Improving organizational health by addressing organizational trauma. *Journal of Organizational Change Management, 10*(2), 175–178. doi:10.1108/09534819710160835

Burke, R. J. (2012). The trauma impact on organizations: causes, consequences, and remedies. In R. Hughes, A. Kinder, & C.L. Cooper (Ed.), International handbook of workplace trauma support (pp. 71-86). Noida, India: John Wiley & Sons. doi:10.1002/9781119943242.ch5

Busby, J. S., & Iszatt-White, M. (2016). Rationalizing violation: Ordered accounts of intentionality in the breaking of safety rules. *Organization Studies, 37*(1), 35–53. doi:10.1177/0170840615593590

Business & Human Rights Resource Centre. (2015, August 27). *Hagens Berman: Class action filed against Nestlé for slave labor, human trafficking used to produce top-selling pet food*. Business & Human Rights Resource Centre. Retrieved August 16, 2016, from http://www.businesswire.com/news/home/20150827006036/en/Hagens-Berman-Class-Action-Filed-Nestl%C3%A9-Slave#.VeCqmZerog4

Business & Human Rights Resource Centre. (2015, September 1). *Nestlé's response*. Business & Human Rights Resource Centre. Retrieved August 16, 2016, from http://business-humanrights.org/sites/default/files/documents/BHRRC%20Response_Thailand%20Slave%20Labour_English%2002%2009%2015.docx

Carper, W. B., & Snizek, W. E. (1980). The nature and types of organizational taxonomies: An overview. *Academy of Management Review*, *5*, 55–75.

Chauvin, C., Lardjane, S., Morel, G., Clostermann, J. P., & Langard, B. (2013). Human and organizational factors in maritime accidents: Analysis of collisions at sea using the HFACS. *Accident; Analysis and Prevention*, *59*, 26–37. doi:10.1016/j.aap.2013.05.006 PMID:23764875

Columbia Accident Investigation Board. (2003). *Columbia Accident Report* (vol. 1). Burlington, Ontario: Apoge. Retrieved May, 6, 2016 from http://www.nasa.gov/columbia/home/CAIB_Vol1.html

Constantinides, P. (2013). The failure of foresight in crisis management: A secondary analysis of the Mari disaster. *Technological Forecasting and Social Change*, *80*(9), 1657–1683. doi:10.1016/j.techfore.2012.10.017

Cornand, C., & Gimet, C. (2012). The 2007–2008 financial crisis: Is there evidence of disaster myopia? *Emerging Markets Review*, *13*(3), 301–315. doi:10.1016/j.ememar.2012.02.001

Coze, J. C. L. (2013). What have we learned about learning from accidents? Post-disasters reflections. *Safety Science*, *51*(1), 441–453. doi:10.1016/j.ssci.2012.07.007

Cruz, J. (2014). Memories of trauma and organizing: Market womens susu groups in post-conflict Liberia. *Organization*, *21*(4), 447–462. doi:10.1177/1350508414527254

Dagan, K., Itzhaky, H., & Ben-Porat, A. (2015). Therapists working with trauma victims: The contribution of personal, environmental, and professional-organizational resources to secondary traumatization. *Journal ofTrauma & Dissociation*, *16*(5), 592–606. doi:10.1080/15299732.2015.1037038 PMID:26158393

Dahles, H., & Susilowati, T. P. (2015). Business resilience in times of growth and crisis. *Annals of Tourism Research*, *51*, 34–50. doi:10.1016/j.annals.2015.01.002

Davis, C., Keilis-Borok, V., Kossobokov, V., & Soloviev, A. (2012). Advance prediction of the March 11, 2011 Great East Japan Earthquake: A missed opportunity for disaster preparedness. *International Journal of Disaster Risk Reduction*, *1*, 17–32. doi:10.1016/j.ijdrr.2012.03.001

De Cock, C., Vachhani, S., & Murray, S. (2013). Putting into question the imaginary of recovery: A dialectical reading of the global financial crisis and its aftermath. *Culture and Organization*, *19*(5), 396–412. doi:10.1080/14759551.2013.815618

de Klerk, S. (2007). Healing emotional trauma in organizations: An O.D. framework and case study. *Organization Development Journal*, *25*, 49–55.

Defraia, G. S. (2013). Organizational outcomes following traumatic workplace incidents: A practice-based exploration of impact of incident severity level. *Social Work in Mental Health*, *11*(5), 404–433. doi:10.1080/15332985.2013.784224

Dutton, J. E., Frost, P. J., Worline, M. C., Lilius, J. M., & Kanov, J. M. (2002). Leading in times of trauma. *Harvard Business Review*, *80*(1), 54–61. PMID:12964467

Eskildson, L. (1997). Surviving and thriving in a hypercompetitive economy. *National Productivity Review*, *16*(2), 9–24. doi:10.1002/npr.4040160203

Factor, R., Mahalel, D., & Yair, G. (2007). The social accident: A theoretical model and a research agenda for studying the influence of social and cultural characteristics on motor vehicle accidents. *Accident; Analysis and Prevention*, *39*(5), 914–921. doi:10.1016/j.aap.2006.12.015 PMID:17291438

Fein, A. H., & Isaacson, N. S. (2009). Echoes of Columbine the emotion work of leaders in school shooting sites. *The American Behavioral Scientist*, *52*(9), 1327–1346. doi:10.1177/0002764209332549

Fleishman, E. A., & Quaintance, M. K. (1984). *Taxonomies of human performance*. New York, NY: Academic Press.

Fox, J. A., & Savage, J. (2009). Mass murder goes to college: An examination of changes on college campuses following Virginia Tech. *The American Behavioral Scientist*, *52*(10), 1227–1245. doi:10.1177/0002764209332558

Gabriel, Y. (2012). Organizations in a state of darkness: Towards a theory of organizational Miasma. *Organization Studies*, *33*(9), 1137–1152. doi:10.1177/0170840612448154

Giustiniano, L., Cunha, M. P., & Clegg, S. (2016). Organizational zemblanity. *European Management Journal*, *34*(1), 7–21. doi:10.1016/j.emj.2015.12.001

Goodman, J. (2016, February 11). Paris attacks: Le Bataclan to reopen before end of 2016. *Entertainment Weekly*. Retrieved August 16, 2016, from http://www.ew.com/article/2016/02/11/le-bataclan-reopen-2016-paris-attacks

Goodman, P. S., Ramanujam, R., Carroll, J. S., Edmondson, A. C., Hofmann, D. A., & Sutcliffe, K. M. (2011). Organizational errors: Directions for future research. *Research in Organizational Behavior*, *31*, 151–176. doi:10.1016/j.riob.2011.09.003

Griffin, R. W., & Lopez, Y. P. (2005). Bad behavior in organizations: A review and typology for future research. *Journal of Management*, *31*(6), 988–1005. doi:10.1177/0149206305279942

Griffin, R. W., & O'Leary-Kelly, A. M. (2004). *The dark side of organizational behaviour*. San Francisco: Jossey-Bass.

Haas, J. E., Hall, R. H., & Johnson, N. J. (1966). Toward an empirically derived taxonomy of organizations. In R. V. Bowers (Ed.), Studies on Behavior in Organizations (pp. 157-180). Athens, GA: University of Georgia.

Herman, J. (1992). *Trauma and Recovery: The Aftermath of Violence – from Domestic Abuse to Political Terror*. New York, NY: Basic Books.

Hong, O., Chin, D. L., Phelps, S., Feld, J., & Vogel, S. (2012). Occupational injuries, duty status, and factors associated with injuries among firefighters. *Workplace Health and Safety*, *60*(10), 517–523. doi:10.3928/21650799-20121116-08 PMID:23163314

Hopper, E. (2012). *Trauma and organizations*. London, UK: Karnac Books Ltd.

Hormann, S. (2007). *Organizational trauma: A phenomenological study of leaders in traumatized organizations* (Doctoral dissertation). Antioch University, Ohio.

Hormann, S., & Vivian, P. (2005). Toward an understanding of traumatized organizations and how to intervene in them. *Traumatology*, *11*(3), 159–169. doi:10.1177/153476560501100302

Hughes, R., Kinder, A., & Cooper, C. L. (2012). *International handbook of workplace trauma support*. Noida, India: John Wiley & Sons. doi:10.1002/9781119943242

Hyungju, K., Stein, H., & Bouwer, U. I. (2016). Assessment of accident theories for major accidents focusing on the MV SEWOL disaster: Similarities, differences, and discussion for a combined approach. *Safety Science*, *82*, 410–420. doi:10.1016/j.ssci.2015.10.009

Jones, C. A. (2002). Victim perspective of bank robbery trauma and recovery. *Traumatology*, *8*(4), 191–204. doi:10.1177/153476560200800402

Kahn, W. A. (2003). The revelation of organizational trauma. *The Journal of Applied Behavioral Science*, *39*(4), 364–380. doi:10.1177/0021886303261954

Kahn, W. A. (2011). Treating organizational wounds. *Organizational Dynamics*, *40*(2), 75–84. doi:10.1016/j.orgdyn.2011.01.001

Kantur, D., & İşeri-Say, A. (2012). Organizational resilience: Conceptual integrative framework. *Journal of Management & Organization*, *18*(06), 762–773. doi:10.1017/S1833367200000420

Kauffman, J. (2005). Lost in space: A critique of NASAs crisis communications in the Columbia disaster. *Public Relations Review*, *31*(2), 263–275. doi:10.1016/j.pubrev.2005.02.013

Kendra, J. M., & Wachtendorf, T. (2003). Elements of resilience after the world trade center disaster: Reconstituting New York Citys emergency operations center. *Disasters*, *27*(1), 37–53. doi:10.1111/1467-7717.00218 PMID:12703151

Kleinberg, J. (2012). Building individual resilience and organizational hardiness: addressing post-trauma worker's block. In E. Hopper (Ed.), Trauma and organizations (pp. 255-276). London, UK: Karnac Books Ltd.

Kleinberg, J. (2014). Corruptogenic organizations. *International Journal of Group Psychotherapy*, *64*(4), 420–443. doi:10.1521/ijgp.2014.64.4.420 PMID:25188561

Kleinberg, J. (2016). How organizational hunger may have contributed to the American Psychological Association's scandal over the ethics of torture. *International Journal of Group Psychotherapy*. doi:10.1080/00207284.2016.1176482

Koubaridis, A. (2015, June 5). *Every six weeks an emergency services worker in Australia commits suicide*. Retrieved August 16, 2016, from http://www.news.com.au/finance/work/every-six-weeks-an-emergency-services-worker-in-australia-commits-suicide/news-story/728bedaac0840e4a6214c0e525324d44

Kumar, P., Gupta, S., Agarwal, M., & Singh, U. (2016). Categorization and standardization of accidental risk-criticality levels of human error to develop risk and safety management policy. *Safety Science*, *85*, 88–98. doi:10.1016/j.ssci.2016.01.007

Leidner, D. E., Pan, G., & Pan, S. L. (2009). The role of IT in crisis response: Lessons from the SARS and Asian tsunami disasters. *The Journal of Strategic Information Systems*, *18*(2), 80–99. doi:10.1016/j.jsis.2009.05.001

Lengnick-Hall, C. A., Beck, T. E., & Lengnick-Hall, M. L. (2011). Developing a capacity for organizational resilience through strategic human resource management. *Human Resource Management Review*, *21*(3), 243–255. doi:10.1016/j.hrmr.2010.07.001

Lennerfors, T. T. (2013). Organizational diaspora: The aftermath of the Saléninvest bankruptcy. *Culture and Organization*, *19*(5), 430–450. doi:10.1080/14759551.2013.824447

Leppaniemi, A. K. (2009). Update on global trends in trauma. *Trauma*, *11*(1), 37–47. doi:10.1177/1460408608100461

Lester, D. L., Parnell, J. A., & Carraher, S. (2003). Organizational life cycle: A five-stage empirical scale. *The International Journal of Organizational Analysis*, *11*(4), 339–354. doi:10.1108/eb028979

Linstead, S., Maréchal, G., & Griffin, R. W. (2014). Theorizing and researching the dark side of organization. *Organization Studies*, *35*(2), 165–188. doi:10.1177/0170840613515402

Lutgen-Sandvik, P. (2008). Intensive remedial identity work: Responses to workplace bullying trauma and stigmatization. *Organization*, *15*(1), 97–119. doi:10.1177/1350508407084487

Mansell, W. (2015, November 18). *Eagles of death metal share first message since Paris attack*. Retrieved August 16, 2016, from http://www.idigitaltimes.com/eagles-death-metal-share-first-message-paris-attack-491231

Martin, G., Farndale, E., Paauwe, J., & Stiles, P. G. (2016). Corporate governance and strategic human resource management: Four archetypes and proposals for a new approach to corporate sustainability. *European Management Journal*, *34*(1), 22–35. doi:10.1016/j.emj.2016.01.002

McBride, N. (2015). *The application of an extended hierarchy theory in understanding complex organizational situations: The case of FIReControl*. Retrieved from http://onlinelibrary.wiley.com/doi/10.1002/sres.2350/epdf

McKelvey, B. (1975). Guidelines for the empirical classification of organizations. *Administrative Science Quarterly*, *20*(4), 509–525. doi:10.2307/2392019

Mendonça, D., & Wallace, W. A. (2015). Factors underlying organizational resilience: The case of electric power restoration in New York City after 11 September 2001. *Reliability Engineering & System Safety*, *141*, 83–91. doi:10.1016/j.ress.2015.03.017

Miller, D. (1996). Equality management-towards a materialist approach. *Gender, Work and Organization*, *3*(4), 202–214. doi:10.1111/j.1468-0432.1996.tb00060.x

Miller, D., & Freisen, P. H. (1980). Momentum and revolution in organizational adaptation. *Academy of Management Journal*, *23*(4), 591–614. doi:10.2307/255551

Mutch, C. (2015). Leadership in times of crisis: Dispositional, relational and contextual factors influencing school principals actions. *International Journal of Disaster Risk Reduction*, *14*, 186–194. doi:10.1016/j.ijdrr.2015.06.005

Myer, R. A., & Moore, H. B. (2006). Crisis in context theory: An ecological model. *Journal of Counseling and Development*, *84*(2), 139–147. doi:10.1002/j.1556-6678.2006.tb00389.x

Noer, D. M. (2010a). *Healing the wounds: overcoming the trauma of layoffs and revitalizing downsized organizations, revised & updated*. San Francisco: Jossey-Bass.

Noer, D. M. (2010b). Six crucial leadership competencies for an era of downsizing. *Leader to Leader*, *2010*(56), 8–11. doi:10.1002/ltl.407

Norris, F. H., Friedman, M. J., Watson, P., Byrne, C. M., Diaz, E., & Kaniasty, K. (2002). 60,000 disaster victims speak: Part I. An empirical review of the empirical literature, 1981–2001. *Psychiatry: Interpers. Biol. Process.*, *65*(3), 207–239. doi:10.1521/psyc.65.3.207.20173 PMID:12405079

Nuttman-Shwartz, O. (2015). Shared resilience in a traumatic reality: A new concept for trauma workers exposed personally and professionally to collective disaster. *Trauma, Violence & Abuse*, *16*(4), 466–475. doi:10.1177/1524838014557287 PMID:25427830

Paddison, L. (2015, December 30). From VW to Brazil's mining disaster: 5 corporate scandals that defined 2015. *The Guardian*. Retrieved August 16, 2016, from http://www.theguardian.com/sustainable-business/2015/dec/30/vw-exxon-lobbying-brazil-mining-tragedy-toshiba-corporate-scandals-greenwashing-climate-change

Papazoglou, K. (2013). Conceptualizing police complex spiral trauma and its applications in the police field. *Traumatology*, *19*(3), 196–209. doi:10.1177/1534765612466151

Park, H. (2011). Man-made disasters: A cross-national analysis. *International Business Review*, *20*(4), 466–476. doi:10.1016/j.ibusrev.2010.08.004

Paton, D. (2005). Posttraumatic growth in protective services professionals: Individual, cognitive and organizational influences. *Traumatology*, *11*(4), 335–346. doi:10.1177/153476560501100411

Paul, R., & Thompson, C. (2006). Employee assistance program responses to large scale traumatic events. *Journal of Workplace Behavioral Health*, *21*(3-4), 1–19. doi:10.1300/J490v21n03_01

Pearlman, L. A. (1999). Self-care for trauma therapists: Ameliorating vicarious traumatization. In B. H. Stamm (Eds.), Secondary traumatic stress: Self-care issues for clinicians, researchers, and Educators (pp. 51-64). Baltimore, MD: Sidran Press.

Pearlman, L. A., & Mac Ian, P. S. (1995). Vicarious traumatization: An empirical study of the effects of trauma work on trauma therapists. *Professional Psychology, Research and Practice*, *26*(6), 558–565. doi:10.1037/0735-7028.26.6.558

Pereira, A. (2015, December 4). Chennai floods: Decoding the city's worst rains in 100 years. *The Indian Express*. Retrieved August 16, 2016, from http://indianexpress.com/article/india/india-news-india/chennai-floods-rains-jayalalithaa-imd-reasons-rescue-news-updates/

Pettersson, E., & Burnson, R. (2015, August 28). Nestle accused of putting fish from slave labor in cat food. *Bloomberg*. Retrieved August 16, 2016, from http://www.bloomberg.com/news/articles/2015-08-27/nestle-accused-of-putting-fish-from-slave-labor-in-cat-food

Pinder, C. C., & Moore, L. F. (1979). The resurrection of taxonomy to aid the development of middle range theories of organizational behavior. *Administrative Science Quarterly*, *24*(1), 99–118. doi:10.2307/2989878

Plant, K. L., & Stanton, N. A. (2012). Why did the pilots shut down the wrong engine? Explaining errors in context using Schema Theory and the Perceptual Cycle Model. *Safety Science*, *50*(2), 300–315. doi:10.1016/j.ssci.2011.09.005

Plater, Z. (2010). Learning from disasters: Twenty-one years after the Exxon Valdez oil spill, will reactions to the Deepwater Horizon blowout finally address the systematic flaws revealed in Alaska? *Environmental Law Reporter*, *40*, 391–408.

Powley, E. H., & Piderit, S. K. (2008). Tending wounds elements of the organizational healing process. *The Journal of Applied Behavioral Science*, *44*(1), 134–149. doi:10.1177/0021886308314842

Pugh, D. S., Hickson, D. J., & Hinings, C. R. (1969). An empirical taxonomy of work organizations. *Administrative Science Ouarterly*, *14*(1), 115–126. doi:10.2307/2391367

Raju, E., & Becker, P. (2013). Multi-organisational coordination for disaster recovery: The story of post-tsunami Tamil Nadu, India. *International Journal of Disaster Risk Reduction*, *4*, 82–91. doi:10.1016/j.ijdrr.2013.02.004

Reason, J. (2000). Human error: Models and management. *British Medical Journal*, *320*(7237), 768–771. doi:10.1136/bmj.320.7237.768 PMID:10720363

Reason, J. (2002). *Managing the risks of organizational accidents*. Burlington: Ashgate.

Regehr, C., Hill, J., Goldberg, G., & Hughes, J. (2003). Postmortem inquiries and trauma responses in paramedics and firefighters. *Journal of Interpersonal Violence*, *18*(6), 607–622. doi:10.1177/0886260503251131

Rose, A., & Krausmann, E. (2013). An economic framework for the development of a resilience index for business recovery. *International Journal of Disaster Risk Reduction*, *5*, 73–83. doi:10.1016/j.ijdrr.2013.08.003

Saakvitne, K. W., Tennen, H., & Ameck, G. (1998). Exploring thriving in the context of clinical trauma theory: Constructivist self-development theory. *The Journal of Social Issues*, *54*(2), 279–299. doi:10.1111/j.1540-4560.1998.tb01219.x

Saldaña, J. (2013). *The Coding Manual for Qualitative Researchers*. London: Sage Publications Ltd.

Schaluf, I. M., Ahmadun, F., & Scariff, A. R. (2003). Technological disaster factors. *Journal of Loss Prevention in the Process Industries*, *16*(6), 513–521. doi:10.1016/j.jlp.2003.08.002

Schmitt, A., & Klarner, P. (2015). From snapshot to continuity: A dynamic model of organizational adaptation to environmental changes. *Scandinavian Journal of Management*, *31*(1), 3–13. doi:10.1016/j.scaman.2014.06.003

Sellers, R. D., Fogerty, T. J., & Parker, L. M. (2014). Mobility and structural change through traumatic organizational events. *Journal of Accounting & Organizational Change*, *10*(3), 382–408. doi:10.1108/JAOC-02-2011-0007

Seymour, K. (2009). Women, gendered work and gendered violence: So much more than a job. *Gender, Work and Organization*, *16*(2), 238–265. doi:10.1111/j.1468-0432.2009.00437.x

Shepard, B. C. (2013). Between harm reduction, loss and wellness: On the occupational hazards of work. *Harm Reduction Journal*, *10*(5). doi:10.1186/1477-7517-10-5 PMID:23548032

Siomkos, G. J. (2000). Managing airline disasters: The role of consumer safety perceptions and sense-making. *Journal of Air Transport Management*, *6*(2), 101–108. doi:10.1016/S0969-6997(99)00030-7

Sklet, S. (2006). Safety barriers: Definition, classification, and performance. *Journal of Loss Prevention in the Process Industries*, *19*(5), 494–506. doi:10.1016/j.jlp.2005.12.004

Smith, G. (2015, July 21). Toshiba just lost its CEO to a huge accounting scandal. *Fortune*. Retrieved August 16, 2016, from http://fortune.com/2015/07/21/toshiba-just-lost-its-ceo-to-a-huge-accounting-scandal/

Sousa, C. A., Haj-Yahia, M. M., Feldman, G., & Lee, J. (2013). Individual and collective dimensions of resilience within political violence. *Trauma, Violence & Abuse*, *14*(3), 235–254. doi:10.1177/1524838013493520 PMID:23793902

Stamm, B. H. (Ed.). (1999). *Secondary traumatic stress: Self-care issues for clinicians, researchers, and educators*. Baltimore, MD: Sidran Press.

Stein, M. (2007). Toxicity and the unconscious experience of the body at the employee–customer interface. *Organization Studies*, *28*(8), 1223–1242. doi:10.1177/0170840607079527

Steinkamp, M. (2014). *Behind the masks of silence: How leaders can overcome organizational trauma* (Unpublished master's thesis). INSEAD, Fontainebleau.

Stenson, J. (2006). Disaster management as a tool for sustainable development: A case study of cyanide leaching in the gold mining industry. *Journal of Cleaner Production*, *14*(3-4), 230–233. doi:10.1016/j.jclepro.2005.03.003

Taj, M., & Aquino, M. (2016, February 23). *Peru pipeline leaks in Amazon; two rivers polluted, agency says* (A. Hay, Ed.). Retrieved August 16, 2016, from http://uk.reuters.com/article/us-peru-oil-spill-idUKKCN0VW064

Tansel, B. (1995). Natural and manmade disasters: Accepting and managing risks. *Safety Science*, *20*(1), 91–99. doi:10.1016/0925-7535(94)00070-J

Tehrani, N. (2011). *Managing trauma in the workplace: Supporting workers and organisations*. New York, NY: Routledge/Taylor & Francis Group.

US Chemical Safety & Hazard Investigation Board. (2007). *Refinery Explosion and Fire, BP Texas City 23 March 2005*. Washington, DC: Author.

van der Velden, P. G., Bosmans, M. W. G., Bogaerts, S., & Veldhoven, M. J. P. M. (2014). Social organizational stressors and post-disaster mental health disturbances: A longitudinal study. *Psychiatry Research*, *219*(1), 177–182. doi:10.1016/j.psychres.2014.05.032 PMID:24915898

Veronese, G., Pepe, A. (2015). Sense of coherence as a determinant of psychological well-being across professional groups of aid workers exposed to war trauma. *Journal of Interpersonal Violence*.

Vickers, M. H., & Kouzmin, A. (2001). Resilience in organizational actors and rearticulating voice: Towards a humanistic critique of New Public Management. *Public Management Review*, *3*(1), 95–119. doi:10.1080/14616670010009478

Victor, B., & Cullen, J. (1988). The organizational bases of ethical work climates. *Administrative Science Quarterly*, *33*(1), 101–125. doi:10.2307/2392857

Waring, A. (2015). Managerial and non-technical factors in the development of human-created disasters: A review and research agenda. *Safety Science*, *79*, 254–267. doi:10.1016/j.ssci.2015.06.015

Werther, W. B. Jr. (2003). Strategic change and leader-follower alignment. *Organizational Dynamics*, *32*(1), 32–45. doi:10.1016/S0090-2616(02)00136-5

Zaloznay, M. (2015). Does authoritarianism breed corruption? Reconsidering the relationship between authoritarian governance and corrupt exchanges in bureaucracies. *Law & Social Inquiry*, *40*(2), 345–376. doi:10.1111/lsi.12076

KEY TERMS AND DEFINITIONS

Catastrophe: Trauma in the workplace experienced due to injuries, accidents or violence.

Crises: Unexpected events, which result in uncertainty and consequently anxiety among the members of organizations that have to be responded to in limited time.

Disasters: Intense, large-scale, and costly physical, cultural, and emotional events that cause dramatic loss not only for the organization but also for the public.

Errors: The unintended deviations from organizational rules or procedures that cause losses and are most often the conduct of more than one individual.

Organizational Darkness: Organizational behaviours like workplace violence, aggression, and incivility.

Organizational Failure: The deviation from the objectives due to avoidable and unavoidable errors, and risk taking.

Organizational Miasma: A toxic state, which is highly contagious, and distinct characteristic that especially occurs in the process of sudden and traumatic organizational changes.

Organizational Trauma: Long-lasting collective and negative psychological state that emerge as a consequence of various traumatic events.

Organizational Wounds: The pain, betrayal, anger, sadness, despair, and shame caused by events that damage organizational identity due to organizational scandals, accidents, non-adaptive strategies to changing external conditions, and operational errors.

Organizational Zemblanity: Avoidable disasters caused unintentionally by key organizational actors.

Potentially Traumatic Events: Adverse events that may affect organizational members' psychological states negatively and log-lastingly, however, these negative consequences may or may not emerge.

Traumatized Organizations: Organizations where the catastrophic processes take place and the organizational members experience helplessness and trouble in coping with accompanying negative emotions.

Chapter 3
Understanding the Core of Psychological Trauma:
Trauma in Contemporary French Theory

Erik de Soir
Royal Higher Institute of Defence, Belgium

Rolf Kleber
Utrecht University, The Netherlands

ABSTRACT

This chapter examines the usefulness of the conceptualization of trauma in contemporary French theory for a better understanding of the core of organizational trauma. Starting with a short historical background, it investigates the contribution from contemporary French authors to current knowledge on psychotraumatology. The current position of the most influential contemporary French authors is that stress and trauma do not necessarily fit into the same concept. The French clinical description of psychological trauma is based on the concept of frozen fright in the face of death (effroi de la mort) and the repetition syndrome (syndrome de répétition). This may have implications for the analysis of what constitutes an organizational trauma since these clinically relevant but largely unknown theories shed another light on the currently used concepts in mainstream literature. The aim of this chapter is also to bridge conceptual gaps, understanding critical differences in clinical practice and offering a more integrative view of psychological trauma.

INTRODUCTION

Scientific research in recent decades has provided a clear, evidence-based description of the serious consequences of trauma-related experiences (Breslau & Davis, 1992; Carlson, Furby, Armstrong, & Shlaes, 1997; Foa & Rothbaum, 1998; Horowitz, 1986). Various concepts have been developed to explicate the consequences of these experiences (Gersons & Carlier, 1992; Kinzie & Goetz, 1996; Wilson, 1989, 1994). *Post-Traumatic Stress Disorder* (PTSD) and other mental disorders (including anxiety, depression, substance abuse, dissociative disorders and psychosomatic disorders) can result from psychological

DOI: 10.4018/978-1-5225-2021-4.ch003

trauma (Brewin, 2000). *Acute Stress Disorder* (ASD) and *Post-Traumatic Stress Disorder* (PTSD) are described in DSM-IV-TR (APA, 2000) as mental disorders which may occur after traumatic experiences such as severe accidents, rape, torture, violence and war. The risk for PTSD increases with the degree of exposure to trauma and both the frequency and the severity of the traumatic events (e.g. Bramsen, 1995).

Over the years, a scientific consensus has appeared in the Anglo-American scientific literature about the symptoms of both acute and posttraumatic stress – i.e. intrusive recollections of the traumatic event, a profound sense of numbness, avoidance, increased arousal and hyperactivity and/or exaggerated startle response and dissociative reactions (Foa, Riggs & Gershuny, 1995). If these reactions – intrusive re-experience, avoidance and hyperarousal – persist (at least for one month) causing significant distress or loss of function, PTSD can be diagnosed according to the DSM-IV-TR (APA, 2000).

In DSM-5 (APA, 2013), PTSD was included in a new section on trauma- and stress-or-related disorders. This move from DSM-IV-TR, which addressed PTSD as an anxiety disorder, is among several changes approved for this condition that is increasingly at the center of public as well as professional attention (APA, 2013). In PTSD, the trigger is exposure to an actual or threatened death, serious injury or sexual violation. The exposure must result from one or more of the following scenarios, in which the individual: directly experiences the traumatic event, witnesses the traumatic event in person, learns that the traumatic event occurred to a close family member or close friend (with the actual or threatened death being either violent or accidental); or experiences first-hand repeated or extreme exposure to aversive details of the traumatic event (not through media, pictures or movies unless work-related). The disturbance, regardless of its trigger, is supposed to cause clinically significant distress or impairment in the individual's social interactions, capacity to work or other important areas of functioning and was not the result of another medical condition, medication, drugs or alcohol.

In DSM-IV (APA, 2000), the controversy as to the definition of PTSD's traumatic stressor criterion, since PTSD first appeared in the DSM-III (APA, 1980), may have implications for pointing at trauma in organizational context. This criterion (A1, in DSM-IV) represented an attempt to provide an objective definition of the traumatic event – such as a terror attack on an airport - that was necessary for the validity of the PTSD diagnosis. Despite a long controversy, there was little empirical research exploring whether events meeting DSM-IV-TR's Criterion A1 were better associated with the diagnosis or severity of PTSD than non-Criterion A1 stressful events. In fact, the trauma literature of recent years is not well linked to the research that has been conducted on the psychological and physiological impact of "mere" stressful life events over the past century (e.g. Holmes & Rahe, 1967; Vinokur & Selzer, 1975).

In each subsequent version of the DSM, the potential range of events that would satisfy Criterion A1 has grown such that currently, in DSM-5, the traumatic stress criterion can be satisfied based on an indirectly experienced trauma (e.g., by witnessing or learning about a trauma occurring to someone else). This broadening of the stressor definition may result in concerns that is has become too lenient (Elhai, Kashdan, & Frueh, 2005; Frueh, Elhai, & Kaloupek, 2004; McNally, 2003; Mikkelsen & Einarsen, 2002). However, other researchers argued that Criterion A1 had to be expanded to include less severe, but still serious life events such as chronic illness, childbirth complications, sexual harassment, or bullying (Matthiesen & Einarsen, 2004; Olde, van der Hart, Kleber, & Van Son, 2006; Palmieri & Fitzgerald, 2005; Smith, Redda, Peyserb, & Vool, 1999).

For organizations such as armed forces, police, fire and rescue or NGOs, regularly confronted with trauma, a clear definition of psychological trauma, is essential with respect to the consequences coupled to the appearance of potentially traumatizing events in the context of daily routine. Compared to DSM-IV, the diagnostic criteria for DSM-5 draw a clearer line when detailing what constitutes a traumatic event.

The PTSD A2-criterion stipulating an individual's response to the event – intense fear, helplessness or horror – has been deleted and the manual pays more attention to the behavioural symptoms that accompany PTSD. It also proposes four distinct diagnostic clusters instead of three. They are described as re-experiencing, avoidance, negative cognitions and mood, and arousal. DSM-5 requires that a disturbance continues for more than a month and eliminated the distinction between acute and chronic phases of PTSD. It includes two subtypes: PTSD Preschool Subtype and PTSD Dissociative Subtype (APA, 2013).

Significantly different perspectives, largely dependent on historical and cultural differences, exist in the international trauma literature and they have broad implications for the identification of trauma victims, allocation of resources, and clarification of trauma-related research. Among these perspectives, the contemporary French conceptualization remains largely unknown to the Anglo-Saxon field of traumatic stress studies. While this mainstream literature often serves as the reference point, the viewpoints of contemporary French-language authors continue to provide the basis of clinical practice for trauma clinicians and researchers in France, Belgium and Switzerland. Moreover, these French concepts also remain influential in Latin countries across Europe and South-America and may inspire managers of trauma prone organizations with respect to the identification of what may cause both individual and collective traumas. They are metaphorical and continue to be driven by classical hermeneutical interpretations, psychodynamic theories and clinical experience. The depth and breadth of the theoretical and conceptual gap which exists between trauma concepts in different language groups is striking. While the existing professional societies for traumatic stress studies struggle to create greater openness to cultural diversity, to our knowledge no attempts have been undertaken to define or integrate these very different descriptive and conceptual views or investigate their relative usefulness for clinical and practical use.

It is important to present current French trauma theories along with the conceptual trauma terminology used by influential contemporary French authors along with a brief review of historical background from which these ideas arose. Therefore, the objective of this chapter is to explore how contemporary French trauma theory might contribute to a more integrative view of the variety of terminologies and concepts used by trauma practitioners in different language groups. The hermeneutical description of what constitutes trauma may inspire managers of risk organizations to develop a taxonomy of potentially traumatizing events which may occur as a result of their specific mission.

BACKGROUND

From Ancient History to the Traumatic Neurosis

The history of French trauma theory goes back to the concept of traumatic neurosis as originally defined by the German psychiatrist Oppenheim (1884). Oppenheim was one of the first to identify this posttraumatic disorder as an independent entity in a study on the psychological sequelae caused by fear experienced during train accidents. The theory which Oppenheim formulated posited that post-traumatic nervous symptoms constituted a distinct diagnostic entity and resulted from the direct – anatomical or psychic – effects of traumatic experiences. His suggestion was opposed by Charcot (1887) who saw 'traumatic neurosis' as nothing more than a particular etiologic form of hysteria, or – at the most – of 'hysteroneurasthenia' and prompted his students to write a number of theses defending his views. Charcot (1825-1893) studied trauma during the second half of his career, from the later 1870s through to his death in the early 1890s. By this time, he had already completed his major clinical and scientific work in neurology and was a figure of international fame throughout the world of Western medicine. Included among Charcot's voluminous clinical publications are approximately twenty detailed case studies that carry the primary diagnoses "névrose traumatique" (traumatic neurosis), "hystérie traumatique" (traumatic hysteria), "hystero-traumatisme" (hysteric trauma), or "hystero-neurasthénie traumatique" (hysteric-neurasthenic trauma) (Micale & Lerner, 2011). Clinically, what Charcot observed in his practice during the 1880s were curious syndromes following a diversity of (sometimes minor) bodily injuries, marked by disabling physical and psychological features but in the complete absence of any indication of structural damage. The most common symptoms seemed to be motoric and sensory disturbances – anesthesias, hyperesthesias, paralyses, and contractures of all kind. Fatigue, headache, back pain, heart palpitations, chest pain, irregular pulse rate, constipation, dizziness and fainting spells, and the trembling of the hands and legs also occurred frequently. In current times, these symptoms would be seen as bodily trauma symptoms resulting from the limbic activation in threatening situations. Emotional troubles could be part of the symptom profile as well: depressive states, sleep disorders (including insomnia and nightmares), phobias, mental confusion, and lowered intellectual efficiency. At times, these symptoms disappeared suddenly and spontaneously, in a matter of hours. At other times, they persisted for months or even years (Micale & Lerner, 2011).

From Graeco-Roman times onward, conversion hysteria has been well documented. A well-known example is the case of the Athenian warrior who fought the Marathon battle – mentioned by Herodotus – and became 'blind' for the rest of his life because he had been frightened by the sudden sight of a colossal enemy whom he had taken for a spectre (Crocq, 1999). Another famous case, mentioned by Pinel (1798), is that of the philosopher Pascal, who – after being nearly thrown with his coach into the Seine river by his runaway horses – suffered from repetition nightmares and could fall asleep only after placing a chair near his bed to reassure himself that he was not on the brink of void.

The cases of 'nostalgia' in campaigning armies during the 18th century and the syndromes of 'cannonball wind' exhibited by Napoleon's armies probably included a large number of (post)traumatic stress reactions, named 'traumatic neurosis' in classical literature. Pierre Janet (1889), and then Freud (1893), looked into the pathogenic role of psychological trauma and memories 'forgotten by consciousness' of traumatic events and 'moral emotions', and each contributed to the discovery of the unconscious and of the 'cathartic' method for curing these disorders. For Freud, Charcot's cases opened the way toward the possibility of a purely psychological explanation of physical symptoms, that is, a theory of conversion, and, beyond this, to a general psychological theory of the neuroses based on Charcot's clinical writings on hysteron-traumatic paralyses (Freud & Breuer, 1893).

Etiologically, Charcot believed that his cases resulted from the combined action of a hereditary *diasthèse,* or constitutional predilection to nervous degeneration, and an environmental provoking agent *(agent provocateur).* Throughout the second half of the nineteenth century, a doctrine of hereditary determination dominated French mental medicine (Dowbiggin, 1985). According to this view, which Charcot endorsed unreservedly, nervous and neurological diseases manifested a latent flaw or defect of the nervous system – a *tare nerveuse* – that at all times was waiting to be activated by appropriate circumstances. In Charcot's medical thinking, traumatic stimuli acted on this prior constitutional susceptibility, and the fact that some individuals developed elaborate neurotic symptoms following a trauma while others did not was explained by the presence or absence of this background (Bertrand, 1990).

According to Freud's initial psychoanalytic theory, hysteria has traumatic origins (Freud, 1956). Hysteria is seen as a neurotic state in which an experience cannot be admitted into consciousness and is instead expressed in a body part. This is what Freud (1956) referred to as the *deferred effect* or *Nachträglichkeit*; that is an event is not experienced as traumatic at the time at which it occurs but becomes so later once it is given a meaning within the frame of mental representations. This experience cannot be admitted into consciousness and is only expressed in a symptom. In his two most important early works, *L'Automatisme psychologique* (1889) and *l'Etat mental des hystériques* (1893), Pierre Janet (one of Charcot's most influencial students) focuses on the mental, rather than the neurological, stigmata of the neuroses, including phobias, abulias, obsessions, and states of "dual" or "double consciousness". Many of these symptoms result from emotional traumata the memory of which became unconsciously fixed in the patient's mind causing a weakening of the ability for mental and emotional synthesis. The vocabulary (*obnubilation of consciousness, dissociation of the ego*) used by Charcot in the case of "Le Log" – a 29-year-old Breton who had been crossing the *Pont des Invalides* in Paris and sideswiped with a wheelbarrow by a passing horse-drawn carriage – is close to the language of early Janetian psychology.

War Neurosis

Actually, the two World Wars were the most instrumental events in establishing the existence of traumatic neurosis, in its etiologic form of 'war neurosis' (*névrose de guerre*), in which the role of a 'shock-emotion' and emphasizing the specific 'post-emotional' character of combat which started to be seen instead of the previous hypothesis related to 'post-commotional' etiology or the 'war psychoneurosis' (*psychonévrose de guerre*) as described by Roussy & Lhermitte (1919). French medical writing about *la neurologie de guerre* (*war neurology*) during World War I was largely inspired by Charcot's ideas on the neurology of human trauma. Suddenly confronted with outbreaks of psychogenic paralysis, blindness, and amnesia among soldiers at the front lines, French physicians returned to the ideas of Charcot. Publications in military psychiatry in France between 1914 and 1918 repeated the fin-de-siècle debate about the origins of the traumatic neuroses. Neurophysicians during World War I increasingly came to acknowledge that so-called shell-shocked soldiers suffered not from the direct concussive effects of exploding shells and poisonous gas but from extreme levels of fear, anxiety and fatigue. The war seemed to illustrate on a huge scale Charcot's emphasis on the terribly pathogenic potency of fear (Cygielstrejch, 1916). Many wartime doctors openly characterized shellshock as *hystérie de guerre* (war hysteria) (Lefebvre & Barbes, 1984). The 'infantile' or 'regressive' attitude of the war neurosis patients was also mentioned (Charpentier, 1917; Ferenczi, Abraham, Simmel & Jones, 1921), and Freud (1918) as well as the American authors of World War II (Kardiner & Spiegel, 1947) revealed the 'conflictual' interweavings (war superego against peacetime superego, fight or flight) entwined with the 'fright' and 'surprise' dimensions of the trauma.

Renewed interest in traumatic neurosis and related disorders was generated by the development of victim psychopathology – in victims of the Holocaust, rape, accidents or abduction and disaster psychiatry (immediate and delayed sequelae of accidents and disasters) (Wilson et al., 1988).

This historical background makes clear that the original French idea of trauma differs from the psychiatric concept as described in the Diagnostic and Statistical Manual of Mental Disorders (DSM) (APA, 1980; 1984; 1994, 2000, 2013). According to the DSM, an overwhelming event can only be traumatizing when it is observable by others and directly and causally linked to the disorder. In contrast to the latter, the psychoanalytic idea proclaims that events not directly observable by others may also be traumatic. This is of utmost importance for managers: according to this theory, some events which may not be seen as spectacular or overwhelming will have the potential to produce effects of trauma.

PSYCHOLOGICAL TRAUMA IN CONTEMPORARY FRENCH LITERATURE: THE WORK OF LOUIS CROCQ

Louis Crocq and his Perspective on Traumatic Neurosis

Louis Crocq, who was the recipient of the 2006 Lifetime Achievement Award of the International Society for Traumatic Stress Studies, should be considered as the most influential contemporary French trauma theoretician, closely followed by his contemporary colleagues François Lebigot and Claude Barrois. Crocq (1999) tried to fulfil a bridging role between the classical French trauma interpretation and the current view on psychological trauma in mainstream literature. He pointed out that posttraumatic stress disorder (PTSD, APA, 1994, 2000), except in some etiological differences, corresponds closely to the former 'traumatic neurosis' in the classification of neuroses. Freud, who devoted memorable pages to this condition as early as 1893-'95 (*Studies on Hysteria*), then shortly after World War I, in 1921 (*Beyond the Pleasure Principle*), never disclaimed its existence since he recognized – towards the end of his life – in 1938, that traumatic neuroses had always eluded the infantile conflict hypothesis. In his writings, he elevated the medical idea of trauma from secondary to primary etiological status and linked trauma to the notions of psychosexual motivation and unconscious repression (Micale, 2001).

Traumatic neurosis is recognized by Crocq (1999) as an independent neurosis, i.e. as a structured and lasting neurotic disorder, including both specific symptoms (symptoms of repetition) and general neurotic symptoms such as anxiety and asthenia, and involving a typical organization (which in this case is a reorganization) of the personality which produces and perpetuates symptoms.

Crocq (1999) presents the traumatic neurosis as a persistent residual state that should not be mistaken for an immediate stress reaction. It develops after a latent period that varies across situations and individuals (from several days to several months). This latent period, previously called 'incubation', 'meditation', 'rumination' or 'contemplation' by trauma clinicians, corresponds to a dynamic readjustment of personality, which must elaborate new defences in order to cope with the intrusion of an event that the subject was unable to control at the time of its occurrence. During this latency period, which is apparently silent, the knowledgeable observer can nevertheless detect various signs or symptoms including self-isolation, solitary mental rumination, depressive withdrawal, or, on the contrary, paradoxical and voluble euphoria predicting subsequent problems.

The Repetition Syndrome in Traumatic Neurosis

Every neurosis is characterized by its constellation of symptoms: anxiety attacks in anxiety neurosis, specific fears in phobic neurosis, conversion and/or dissociation in hysteria, rites and obsession in obsessive-compulsive neurosis. In traumatic neurosis, the characteristic finding is a set of symptoms related to what is called the 'repetition syndrome'.

Crocq (1999) describes the repetition nightmare as the most important feature in the disturbances after a traumatizing experience. The repetition nightmare is experienced rather than contemplated; the traumatized subject relives – under the original form or as a transposition developed to the dream-formation rules of displacement, condensation, and symbolization – the inaugural traumatic scene that overwhelmed his defences. The repetition nightmare is experienced intensely; the subject screams, struggles, occasionally falls out of bed and wakes up, terrified and covered with sweat.

The repetition syndrome also includes other forms of repetition, including resurgence of irresistible thoughts recalling the traumatic scene, mental ruminations, fleeting, near-hallucinatory visions, an irresistible tendency to look for and contemplate scenes of violence in real life or in visual reproductions, impulsive motor behaviours improvising motions of defence or aggression, and, last but not least, startle reactions – either in response to minimal stimuli or spontaneously – that may be considered as the most archaic form of repetition.

PSYCHOLOGICAL TRAUMA IN CONTEMPORARY FRENCH LITERATURE: QUESTIONING TERMINOLOGIE

Terminology and Key Concepts

Contemporary French authors (Barrois, 1998; Crocq, 1992, 1999, 2001; Lebigot, 2001, 2002, 2005) have questioned the terminology of '(post)traumatic stress' used by Anglophone authors, claiming that stress and trauma are two distinct concepts and that the most immediate human reaction to a traumatizing stimulus is a typical state of petrified shock or dread. In French literature (ibid) this state is referred to as *effroi*, close to Kraepelin's old concept of *Shreck* (1899), which will be named *frozen fright of death* in this chapter. According to this view, intense fear and stress reactions only follow after this first and basic reaction of shivering tremor. In his clinical cases, Charcot conjectured that such a state induced a kind of "somnambulism" or "hypnotic trance" in which there is an increased psychological suggestibility which leads to a reproduction or imprinting of the traumatic sensation as a mental representation. A "traumatic idea" or *idée fixe* is then lodged in the mind of the individual. It is interesting to note that, according to the Oxford English Dictionary, the word "trance" derives from a Middle French word for "being frightened to death".

In line with this view, these French authors have proposed a clinical uncoupling of psychotraumatic syndromes – i.e. syndromes directly linked to the potentially traumatizing impact of a sudden, massive and/or brutal confrontation with death – and the psycho-emotional consequences of disturbing events and life crises (Crocq, 1992, 2001). The accent is put on the unique personal truth of the traumatic experience, which can never be reduced to merely experiencing an overwhelming event and a consecutive biophysical reality of extreme stress (Crocq, 2001; De Clercq & Lebigot, 2001; Lebigot, 2001). In this view, the immediate, post-immediate and delayed stages of the reaction to a potentially traumatizing event are clearly distinguished and therefore a disorder (previously described as 'traumatic neurosis'), for which the repetition syndrome (*syndrome de répétition*) is the pathognomonic expression, can be clearly identified. This interpretation is strongly inspired by psychoanalytic theories based on concepts such as the traumatic unconscious (*inconscient traumatique*), psychological automatism (*automatisme psychologique*) and the reality of death (*réel de la mort*), respectively inspired by the theories of Freud (1895), Janet (1889, 1904) and Lacan (1973).

François Lebigot and l'effroi de la mort (The Frozen Fright of Death)

In this classically oriented French theoretical approach of stress and trauma, the core of a potentially traumatizing event is the confrontation with the 'reality of death' (*le reel de la mort*). Due to the sudden and unexpected confrontation with death, the subject enters into a temporary state of petrified shock – i.e. seems to turn into a stone as numerous soldiers in the old Greek Medusa tale (Crocq, 1999). In this state of *effroi de la mort* (*frozen state of shock in the face of death*), the subject encounters the complete and absolute *emptiness* and *nothingness of death*, and experiences it as being totally abandoned by the world of the living.

This interpretation is well-documented by numerous clinical vignettes in the work of Lebigot (2005). The notion of *effroi de la mort* is essential in this approach: it describes the impact of an event which involves extreme anxiety, horror, total abandonment and powerlessness, which also appeared in DSM-IV under the A2 criterion (APA, 2000) but which has since been dropped in DSM-5 on the basis of statistical studies of its predictive power in assessing PTSD. This classical trauma interpretation is inspired by the early Freudian viewpoints on trauma in which the psyche is represented by a restricted volume in which there is a network of representations, between which small amounts of energy (affect) can freely circulate. This restricted volume is surrounded by a membrane which is seen as a stimulus barrier, protecting the psyche from being overwhelmed by over-stimulation and being charged with positive energy. This metaphorical view on the psyche is used to explain the difference between stress and trauma. The stimulus barrier protects the psyche from excessive stimulation which could, from the outside, influence the psychological equilibrium on the inside and deform the shape of the stimulus barrier. The tension on the outside of the stimulus barrier can be seen as a kind of strain ('to stress' literally means 'to increase the strain') which will have a negative impact on the free circulation of energy between the representations within the psychological system. The anxiety which results from this specific state will lead to an increase of energy on the outside of the stimulus barrier (i.e. the subject will draw on its own resources and react). The psyche defends itself against the aggression coming from the outside. When the tension from the outside decreases or disappears, the stimulus barrier takes its previous shape again. In this interpretation, the subject defends itself against a threat from the outside and manages to recover from stress: an apt metaphor for psychological resilience.

In the case of a traumatic impact, the story becomes different. Trauma is seen as the vital threat, life-threatening and striking unexpectedly and very suddenly. It is an overwhelming amount of energy coming from the outside which abruptly penetrates the stimulus barrier. It infiltrates into the network of representations and discharges an enormous amount of energy within it which instantaneously disrupts the psychological equilibrium. The breaking-in of a life-threatening event – called *l'effraction traumatique* in French - leaves a strange nucleus – a *corps étranger* – in place i.e. an element which has no representation, no symbolic shape and which can therefore not be integrated in the existing network of mental representations. According to this psychodynamic view, this strange corpus is related to the close encounter with the 'reality of death' and cannot be 'metabolized' because there is no representation, no symbolisation, for death in the broader network of representations. The traumatizing experience literally stops time in the psyche and leaves the subject in a state of total abandonment.

A: Shows how the stimulus barrier is reinforced and protects the psyche from to much stimulation; it filters and fragments sensorial inputs, allowing them to be assimilated in the network of representations.

B: Shows how a stimulus with maximum excitation breaks into the stimulus barrier and penetrates deeply into (non-verbal part of) the network of representations where it finds no signifying link.

In this metaphoric interpretation, the psyche is considered as a restricted volume surrounding a network of representations, separated from the outside world by a membrane. This view illustrates the difference

Figure 1.

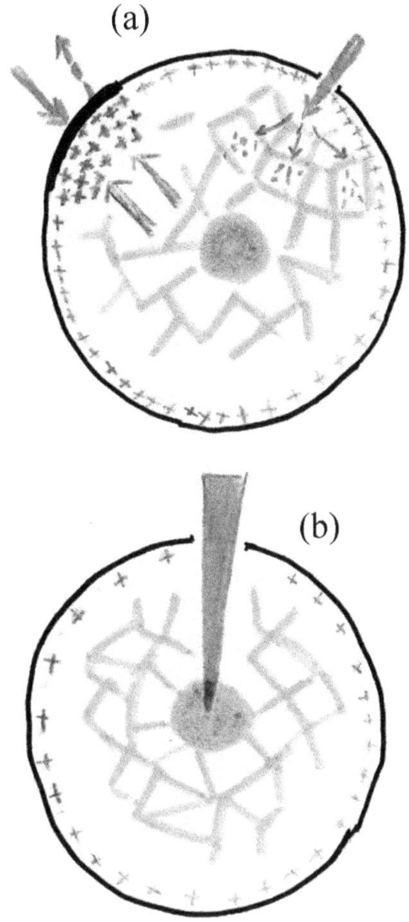

between vital – i.e. threats for the integrity - and non-vital aggressions on the psyche. The way in which the psyche remains affected by a (potentially) vital aggression from the outside and/or tries to recover from it, as a function of time, is determined by the possibilities of symbolizing or representing the experience. The inability to symbolize the traumatic experience through verbal expression and language excludes the traumatized subject from the world of those who are able to speak and renders integration within the network of mental representations impossible. Social relations and all of the internal and external networks based on that world of internal representations are profoundly disrupted resulting in loss of the ability to relate to self or others.

According to this view, organizational trauma would result from a sudden and invasive threat that instantly threatens the further existence and the continuity of the organization itself, beyond the imaginable. The current state of permanent threat and terror attacks, seems to create that kind of impact in Western communities which have not been confronted with war scenes and massive casualties since the ending of World War II. The cruelty of terror attacks such as in Paris (13th November 2015), Brussels (22th March 2016) and Nice (14th July 2016) left the victims and their caregivers in a state of petrified shock and provoked disruption in their capacity to verbalize the impact.

Trauma penetrates deep into the psyche. Stress involves a psychological suffering which persists for as long as the external pressure (strain) lasts; when the 'stress' disappears, the membrane or stimulus barrier slowly takes back its previous shape and the system recovers. The internal functioning of the psyche can continue, even in the light of small internal changes which might have occurred due to the losses provoked by the external aggression. On the other hand, trauma leaves – potentially forever – an internal source of disruption, an indigestible strange corpus (corps étranger) within the psyche; this disruption will persist, even when the threat is over. But stress and trauma often go hand in hand: in these cases, there is first the crushing and transforming impact due to the strain from the outside of the membrane, and then the penetration by the strange, disrupting element. In the case of trauma, the protective function of the stimulus barrier fails and is penetrated: the psychic apparatus becomes the subject of an effraction, which literally means break-in or brutal impact. Once penetrated, the psychic apparatus will do everything it can to assimilate or reject the new source of excessive stimuli but these attempts fail. It appears impossible to metabolize the pathogenic nucleus of trauma. On the clinical level, first symptoms of severe stress will appear before the appearance of the repetition syndrome (syndrome de répétition) which may begin much later. In this syndrome, there will always be the re-appearance of the strange nucleus (corps étranger) under its various forms, like a testimony of the effraction of the psychic apparatus.

The above example of terror attacks on Western countries may illustrate this effect: the images of amputated dead bodies, the smells of blood and nitrate, the senseless apathy of victims in search for help and the complete chaos created a unique experience which seems impossible to express in words. The typical loss of integration and sense of time, creates a trauma nucleus which will constantly reappear during daily activities and after confrontation with places and people reminding the terror attacks.

The hermeneutic aspect of this metaphorical trauma view, which is proposed by contemporary French authors (Barrois, 1998; Crocq, 1999, 2001; Lebigot, 2001, 2005), indicates that a potentially traumatizing event, simply called *le trauma* in French, is experienced subjectively. But what is traumatizing for one survivor, will not necessarily be traumatic for the other. The essence of trauma has to be seen as an encounter between an event and a subject. From this angle of incidence, each event could be seen as potentially traumatizing, but a subject with sufficient defensive resources (i.e. a strong enough stimulus barrier) will be able to formulate an adapted response to it.

The Specificity of Traumatization in the French: From the Close Encounter with Death to the Repetition Syndrome (Syndrome De Répétition).

Barrois (1998) presented psychological trauma as a disruption in the connection with the external world. The subject is confronted with *the unthinkable*, namely his own death. This confrontation, for which one can never be fully prepared, triggers a reaction of *effroi* (frozen fright or dread) in the individual, in which *death of the self* is announced as the ultimate truth. Trauma is experienced as a disruption in the continuity of one's existence. And even if we all know that death is the inescapable end for every human being, we do not have a (mental) representation of death in our psyche. We live our lives as if we all know that we will die, but without believing that this will actually happen. We all know what a dead body is, but we do not know what death in itself is really about. The real cognition of death (*I will die*) suddenly appears as a consequence of an intimate encounter with death; our own death or the death of another human being who matters to us.

According to this theoretical approach, the psychological trauma response will be an answer, a syndrome of adaptation, to the disruption of the continuity of life: there will also be a disruption between the life prior to the trauma, on the one hand, and the post-trauma life, on the other hand. But in the light of a potentially traumatizing event, not everyone will be traumatized. If the subject can resist/prove resilient and find a way to cope with the confrontation with death and complete the necessary series of survival reactions in the face of the confrontation with the reality of death, the neurobiological symptoms will dissolve and disappear. In the psyche, there will still be a conscious memory of the potentially traumatizing event, but this memory will become less intense and vaguer over time. The opposite is also true: when there is no fulfilment or completion of coping with the potentially traumatic event, there will be no final narrative to insert the traumatic memory into the personal life story and psychotraumatic symptoms will tend to coalesce and persist.

In this view, trauma is viewed as a repetition syndrome through which the traumatic experience, containing the 'irrepresentable nucleus' in the original event (e.g., cruel images of terror victims), reappears over and over again, plays an essential role in the work of contemporary French authors (Andreoli & Damsa, 2005: Barrois, 1998; Crocq, 1999, 2001; Lebigot, 2001, 2005). Symptoms of intrusion are described as repeated involuntary reminiscences with distinct manifestations, expression registers and circumstantial appearances (Crocq, 1999). Beyond the automatic replication of the experience of frozen fright (*effroi*) and petrification (*sidération*), this approach also highlights the memory and personality disturbances which often develop after some time (cf. the delayed onset of symptoms as described in DSM) and involves psychological functions which are both complex and independent from the direct effects of overwhelming stress (Crocq, 1999; Crocq, 2002; Lebigot, 2002).

Through the repetition syndrome, these authors describe how the traumatizing event instantly stops or freezes the time in the psyche and installs itself, instantly or after a given amount of time, as a strange object which creates a permanent reiteration of the traumatic experience, accompanied by exactly the same somatosensory and psychological phenomena as those present at the time of the original event. The nature of the alterations in memory and consciousness occurring during the repetition syndrome have been described by Crocq (1999, 2001), and Crocq and De Verbizier (1989) with the use of the concepts of 'traumatic unconscious (*inconscient traumatique*)', dissociation from consciousness and catharsis.

The 'black hole' of the traumatic memory is considered as the characteristic trait of posttraumatic pathology. The French authors describe the concept of 'traumatic unconscious' as a result from the close encounter with the reality of death ('*réel de la mort*'). The experience of perplexity, absurdity and annihilation, which typically appears in clinical descriptions of trauma survivors, constitutes a 'short circuit' of symbolic function i.e. the cognitive action responsible for the symbolization of experience is suspended, rendering the subject without words or mental representation of the experience. In this view, psychological traumatisation is brought back to disruption in 'signifiers' – i.e. the Lacanian concept for meaningful representation carriers, words, which are needed to structure knowledge – due to the sudden confrontation with the unthinkable and the inconceivable. In line with this view, trauma means a disruption between the 'signified' (i.e. death) and the 'signifier' (i.e. the representation or symbolisation of death in the network of representations in the psyche). What really happens is that the previously symbolic references to death prove insufficient in the face of the *réel de la mort* which then leaves a break between the signified and the signifier. Thus, the psychological disturbances occurring in the repetition syndrome are not the direct consequences of the stress created by the apperception of an event, but of the psychic impact of this same apperception and its total inconceivable (irrepresentable) or unthinkable aspect. It should be noted that the '*réel de la mort*' does not exactly equate with the 'reality of death' even if that is the closest literal translation available in English. *Réel de la mort* more specifically refers to a fundamental confrontation with the 'wordless shadow of life', the 'nothingness', the 'hole' left by trauma in the current psychological functioning of the stricken subject and the annihilating effect which will continue over time, upon each automatic reiteration of this experience through the repetition compulsion.

These metaphoric French trauma interpretations, influenced by the terminology and the clinical concepts of Freudian and Lacanian psychoanalytic theories, lead to a more phenomenological approach which is relevant for the interpretation of trauma-related accounts of survivors. They illustrate the specific meanings and position of stress and trauma concepts in the French-oriented trauma literature as they are widely known in Latin countries (i.e. France, Spain, Italy and the South-American countries). Clinically, these interpretations may allow us to make a better sense of the accounts of trauma survivors who always repeat the fact that their experience is impossible to express in words while clinicians are always in search for the right therapy protocol or technique which make the expression of trauma-related experiences possible.

Managers of organizations which are at risk for trauma should be attentive to the accounts of their personnel in the aftermath of unexpected or overwhelming crises in order to assess whether or not a disruptive event may lead to an organizational trauma. In these weeks and months following the terror attacks on Brussels airport and the Maalbeek metro station (on 22nd March 2016), police, fire and rescue personnel, emergency medical technicians and doctors continued their daily activities but many among them were left without a complete story. In the absence of a coherent narrative of that dramatic day, the traumatic experiences will stay unintegrated and continue to haunt too many minds.

DISCUSSION AND CONCLUSION

The classical French authors can be credited with an important descriptive clinical contribution to the field of psychological trauma. This chapter explored how contemporary French authors, inspired by classical psychodynamic theories, have contributed to a more integrative view on a broad range of terms and concepts used by trauma practitioners in different language groups. A problem with the French terminology is that *le trauma* (*the trauma*) is used both as a trauma-eliciting event and as a chronic state of psychological trauma thus conflating cause and origin.

Furthermore, these theoretical viewpoints are clinically interesting but difficult to confirm or to falsify through empirical research. This may be the primary reason why the current mainstream Anglo-Saxon literature, which is essentially driven by empirical research rather than by clinical experience, has not taken these insights into account till now. In the context of organizational trauma, it seems important to analyse the subjective experiences of personnel and invest more in case studies, instead of only using the sometimes superficial and descriptive diagnostic methods based on lists of symptoms and standardized measure instruments.

French theory separates the pattern of psychological trauma on two distinct levels: the level of post-traumatic symptoms and the level of the underlying personality which creates and sustains the explicit symptoms. The lack of filtration of stimuli, the loss of interest in former activities and emotional withdrawal are in fact only expressions of this alteration of the personality in the wake of a traumatizing event. Instead of focusing on the biological, behavioural and cognitive aspects of psychological trauma, French theories focus on the phenomenological variety and the underlying meaning of trauma symptoms.

Organizations may also be described in terms of character traits and specificities. Therefore, it seems acceptable that some organizations will be more trauma-prone, due to their mission and their 'organizational personality', than others. This aspect merits more research in organizational psychology.

One of the weak points in the mainstream Anglo-Saxon literature is its considerable variation in terminology, while there is a huge amount of research on the determinants and predictors of (both neurobiological and psychological) pre-, peri- and posttraumatic symptoms. The translation of the empirical results into relevant clinical or managerial concepts or therapeutic approaches seems sometimes difficult. In DSM-IV, DSM-IV-TR and DSM-5 (APA, 1994, 2000, 2013), PTSD is essentially approached from a quantitative point of view as defined by a set of symptoms, belonging to three different clusters, and by time-related criteria of dysfunction. A possible bridge toward the French clinical trauma interpretations was the split of the *stressor criterion* of PTSD into two parts (in DSM-IV-TR); Criterion A1 and Criterion A2. Criterion A1 referred to the objective elements of the trauma (e.g. physical threat of the event to self and others), and Criterion A2 related to subjective components (e.g. the individual's response): intense fear, helplessness, and/or horror (APA, 1994; 2000), yet this potential crosswalk between theoretical approaches has been lost following the redefinition of the Stressor Criterion in DSM-5. The subjective aspect of the trauma diagnosis, focusing on the meaning that a potentially event had for its survivor, could receive even more attention since recovering from trauma should not only be reduced to showing less symptoms or a reduction in the intensity (severity) of the trauma symptoms listed in the typical symptom clusters. The phenomenology of trauma, as it appears in French contemporary trauma theories, insists on the adaptive ability to reach a level of integration of the traumatic experience into one's psychic existence by transforming the 'traumatizing experience' into a narrative, accompanied by a catharsis of affects and the cessation of the compulsive repetition syndrome ('*syndrome de répétition*'). This is in line with the opinion of Van der Hart, Nijenhuis & Steele (2006) who consider failed integration on the perceptual, cognitive and somatic levels as essential features of psychological trauma and of Krystal (1988) who described psychological trauma in terms of alexithymia.

According to this view on trauma, essentially a failure in integration, organizations confronted with severe trauma will have to recover from the impact by re-framing the experience, re-adapting and re-adjusting to the post-impact reality, re-authoring the organizational history and re-constructing the bonds between subsystems of the organization. The development of a healing theory and a recovery narrative, inspired by the metaphorical view of the theories exposed in this chapter, could be very useful.

French trauma theories lead to a more psychodynamic and hermeneutic trauma interpretation which is relevant from both a clinical and a managerial point of view – i.e. closely matches the accounts of trauma survivors – and offers insights which go beyond the descriptive approach of psychological trauma in the diagnostic nomenclature.

It would be meaningful to integrate both approaches within a more holistic trauma view and bridge the gap between the quantitative (empirical) trauma approach, on the one hand, and more qualitative (clinical) interpretations, on the other hand. There should also be a search for a more restrictive terminology in the field of psychotraumatology, aiming at what psychological trauma really is: a close encounter with the inconceivable, the irrepresentable, which leads to a loss of integration of the various levels of the personality.

DSM-5 (APA, 2013) lists symptoms which are essentially applicable in the stress and HPA-activation paradigm, while the persisting symptoms of trauma survivors appear to be of psychodynamic origin. In the light of French theory, the following question might be raised: Should the new stressor criterion of DSM V, i.e. the exposure to actual or threatened death, serious injury or sexual violation, remain in the definition of PTSD? The current nosography of posttraumatic stress disorder suffers from a lack of conceptual richness or of words which fit with the actual experience of trauma survivors. While the French interpretation of psychological trauma might be the unspeakable experience of the confrontation with the 'reality of death', a more nuanced view might be the confrontation with an aspect of life which one cannot fully integrate, associated with manifest neurobiological correlates and a typical constellation of stress and anxiety symptoms. Therefore, from a classical hermeneutical and clinical point of view, it would make more sense to broaden the A2 criterion for PTSD instead of eliminating it from the set of diagnostic criteria.

The scientific evidence in neurosciences and behavioural sciences which have appeared over the past two decades, should make it possible to bridge the phenomenological description of trauma in French theory with DSM-5 criteria: intrusion symptoms, persistent avoidance, negative alternations in cognitions and mood, alteration in arousal and reactivity, duration of these symptoms and the distress or impairment in social, occupational, or other important areas of functioning. The increase of cross cultural and 'cross conceptual' research, in a context of global integration of trauma societies, will hopefully lead to the development and further improvement of evidence-based clinical treatment for trauma survivors which should show more respect for cultural and global diversity.

REFERENCES

American Psychiatric Association. (1980). *Diagnostic and statistical manual of mental disorders* (3rd ed.). Washington, DC: Author.

American Psychiatric Association. (1987). *Diagnostic and statistical manual of mental disorders* (3rd ed. Rev.). Washington, DC: Author.

American Psychiatric Association. (1994). *Diagnostic and statistical manual of mental disorders* (4th ed.). Washington, DC: Author.

American Psychiatric Association. (2000). Diagnostic and statistical manual of mental disorders (4th ed.). Rev. Washington DC: Author.

American Psychiatric Association. (2013). *Diagnostic and statistical manual of mental disorders* (5th ed.). Washington, DC: Author.

Andreoli, A., & Damsa, C. (2005). Stress, dissociation ou trauma psychique? Incidence des travaux francophones dans le débat international. *Revue Francophone du Stress et du Trauma*, *5*(2), 61–65.

Barrois, C. (1998). *Les névroses traumatiques*. Paris: Editions Dunod.

Belenky, G. (1987). *Contemporary studies in combat psychiatry*. Westport, CT: Greenwood Press.

Bramsen, I. (1995). *The longterm psychological adjustment of World War II survivors in the Netherlands*. Delft: Eburon Press.

Breslau, N., & Davis, G. C. (1992). Posttraumatic stress disorder in an urban population of young adults: Risk factors for chronicity. *Journal of Psychiatry*, *149*, 671–675. PMID:1575259

Breuer, J., & Freud, S. (1973). *Studies on Hysteria: Physical Mechanisms of Hysteria*. New York: Penguin.

Brewin, C. R., Andrews, B., & Valentine, J. D. (2000). Meta-Analysis of Risk Factors for Posttraumatic Stress Disorder in Trauma-Exposed Adults. *Journal of Consulting and Clinical Psychology, 68*(5), 748–766. doi:10.1037/0022-006X.68.5.748 PMID:11068961

Carlson, E. B., Furby, L., Armstrong, L., & Shlaes, J. (1997). A conceptual framework for the long-term psychological effects of traumatic childhood abuse. *Child Maltreatment, 2*(3), 272–295.

Charcot, J.-M. (1887). *Leçons sur les maladies du système nerveux faites à la Salpêtrière*. Paris: Progrèm Médical Delahaye & Lecrosnie.

Charpentier, R. (1917). Allocution de M. René Charpentier. *Annales Médico-Psychologiques, 74*(8), 273–329.

Crocq, L. (1992). Le syndrome de répétition dans la névrose traumatique. Ses variations cliniques, sa signification. *Perspectives Psy, 32*(2), 59–65.

Crocq, L. (1999). *Les traumatismes psychiques de guerre*. Paris: Odile Jacob.

Crocq, L. (2001). Le traumatisme psychique dans la pensée psychiatrique francophone: Introduction. In M. De Clercq & F. Lebigot (Eds.), *Les traumatismes psychiques*. Paris: Masson.

Crocq, L. (2002). Persée, la Méduse et l'effroi. *Revue Francophone du Stress et du Trauma, 2*(3), 133–138.

Crocq, L., & De Verbizier, J. (1989). Le traumatisme psychologique dans l'oeuvre de Pierre Janet. *Annales Médico-Psychologiques, 147*, 983–987.

De Clercq, M., & Lebigot, F. (2001). *Les traumatismes psychiques*. Paris: Masson.

Cygielstrejch, A. (1916). La psychologie de la panique pendant la guerre. *Annales Médico-Psychologiques, 7*, 172–192.

Dowbiggin, I. (1985). Degeneration and Hereditarianism in French Mental Medicine, 1840-1890: Psychiatric Theory as Ideological Adaptation. In W. F. Bynum, R. Porter, & M. Shepherd (Eds.), *The Anatomy of Madness: Essays in the History of Psychiatry* (Vol. 1, pp. 188–232). London: Tavistock.

Elhai, J. D., Grubaugh, A. L., Kashdan, T. B., & Frueh, B. C. (2008). Empirical examination of a proposed refinement to posttraumatic stress disorders symptom criteria using the National Comorbidity Survey Replication data. *The Journal of Clinical Psychiatry, 69*(4), 597–602. doi:10.4088/JCP.v69n0411 PMID:18294026

Fenichel, O. (1945). *The psychoanalytic theory of neurosis*. New York: Norton & Company Inc.

Ferenczi, S., Abraham, K., Simmel, E., & Jones, E. (1921). Psychoanalysis and the war neuroses. *The International Psycho-Analytical Library, 2*, 1–59.

Foa, E. B., Riggs, D. S., & Gershuny, B. S. (1995). Arousal, numbing, and intrusion: Symptom structure of PTSD following assault. *The American Journal of Psychiatry, 152*(1), 116–120. doi:10.1176/ajp.152.1.116 PMID:7802101

Foa, E. B., & Rothbaum, B. O. (1998). *Treating the trauma of rape*. New York: Guilford Press.

Freud, S. (1918). *Reflections on war and death*. New York: Moffat, Yard & Co.

Freud, S. (2001). Some points for a comparative study of organic and hysterical paralyses. In J. Strachey & A. Strachey (Eds.), *Standard edition of the complete Psychological Works of Sigmund Freud, 1*. London: Hogarth. (Original work published 1893)

Freud, S., & Breuer, J. (1893). Preliminary Communication. Studies on Hysteria, 2(17).

Freud, S., & Breuer, J. (1956). Etudes sur l'hystérie (7th ed.). Paris: PUF.

Frueh, B. C., Elhai, J. D., & Kaloupek, D. G. (2004). Unresolved issues in the assessment of trauma exposure and posttraumatic reactions. In G. M. Rosen (Ed.), *Posttraumatic stress disorder: issues and controversies* (pp. 63–84). New York, NY: Wiley. doi:10.1002/9780470713570.ch4

Gersons, B. P. R., & Carlier, I. V. E. (1992). Post-Traumatic Stress Disorder: The History of a Recent Concept. *The British Journal of Psychiatry, 161*(6), 742–748. doi:10.1192/bjp.161.6.742 PMID:1483159

Holmes, T. H., & Rahe, R. H. (1967). The Social Readjustment Rating Scale. *Journal of Psychosomatic Research, 11*(2), 213–218. doi:10.1016/0022-3999(67)90010-4 PMID:6059863

Horowitz, M. (1986). Stress-response syndromes: A review of posttraumatic and adjustment disorder. *Hospital & Community Psychiatry, 37*, 241–249. PMID:3957267

Janet, P. (1889). *L'automatisme psychologique*. Paris: Alcan.

Janet, P. (1904). L'amnésie et la dissociation des souvenirs par l'émotion. *Journal für Psychologie, 1*, 417–453.

Janoff-Bulman, R. (1985). The aftermath of victimization: Rebuilding shattered assumptions. In C. R. Figley (Ed.), *Trauma and its wake: The study and Treatment of Post-Traumatic Stress Disorder*. Brunner-Mazel.

Jones, D. W. (1982). The Vietnams of Michael Herr and Tim OBrien: Tales of Disintegration and Integration. *Canadian Review of American Studies, 13*(3), 309–200. doi:10.3138/CRAS-013-03-03

Kardiner, A., & Spiegel, H. (1947). *War stress and neurotic illness*. New York: Paul B. Hoeber Inc.

Kinzie, J. D., & Goetz, R. R. (1996). A Century of Controversy Surrounding Posttraumatic Stress-Spectrum Syndromes: The Impact on DSM-III and DSM-IV. *Journal of Traumatic Stress, 9*(2), 159–179. doi:10.1002/jts.2490090202 PMID:8731540

Kleber, R. J., & Brom, D. (1992). *Coping with trauma*. Amsterdam: Swets & Zeitlinger.

Kraepelin, E. (1899). *Ein Lehrbuch für Studierende und Aertze (vols. 1-2)*. Leipzig: Johann Ambrosius Barth.

Krystal, H. (1988). *Integration and Self Healing: Affect – Trauma – Alexithymia*. New York: Routledge.

Lacan, J. (1973). *Les quatre concepts fondamentaux de la psychanalyse*. Paris: Seuil.

Lebigot, F. (2001). Prises en charge psychothérapeutiques psychodynamiques. In Les traumatismes psychiques. Paris: Masson.

Lebigot, F. (2002). L'effroi du traumatisme psychique. Le regarder en face ou s'en protéger. *Revue Francophone du Stress et du Trauma*, *2*(3), 139–146.

Lebigot, F. (2005). *Traiter les traumatismes psychiques. Cliniques et prise en charge*. Paris: Editions Dunod.

Lefebvre, P., & Barbes, S. (184). L'Hystérie de guerre: Étude comparative de ses manifestations au cours de deux derniers conflits mondiaux. *Annales Médico-Psychologiques*, *142*(February), 262–266.

Lindy, J., Green, B., & Grace, M. (1987). The stressor criterion and posttraumatic stress disorder. *The Journal of Nervous and Mental Disease*, *175*, 269–272. doi:10.1097/00005053-198705000-00004 PMID:3572377

Matthiessen, S. B., & Einarsen, S. (2004). Psychiatric distress and symptoms of PTSD among victims of bullying at work. *British Journal of Guidance & Counselling*, *32*(3), 335–356. doi:10.1080/030698 80410001723558

McNally, R. J. (2003). Progress and controversy in the study of posttraumatic stress disorder. *Annual Review of Psychology*, *54*(1), 229–252. doi:10.1146/annurev.psych.54.101601.145112 PMID:12172002

Micale, M. S. (1985). The Salpêtrière in the Age of Charcot: An Institutional Perspective on Medical History in the Late Nineteenth Century. *Journal of Contemporary History*, *20*(October), 703–731. doi:10.1177/002200948502000411 PMID:11617298

Micale, M. S. (1996). Paradigm and Ideology in Psychiatric History Writing: The Case of Psychoanalysis. *The Journal of Nervous and Mental Disease*, *184*(3), 146–152. doi:10.1097/00005053-199603000-00002 PMID:8600217

Micale, M. S., & Lerner, P. (Eds.). (2001). Traumatic Pasts. History, Psychiatry, and Trauma in the Modern Age, 1870-1930. New York: Cambridge University Press.

Mikkelsen, E. G., & Einarsen, S. (2002). Basic assumptions and symptoms of post-traumatic stress among of bullying at work. *European Journal of Work and Organizational Psychology*, *11*(1), 87–111. doi:10.1080/13594320143000861

Olde, E., van der Hart, O., Kleber, R., & van Son, M. (2006). Posttraumatic stress following childbirth: A review. *Clinical Psychology Review*, *26*(1), 1–16. doi:10.1016/j.cpr.2005.07.002 PMID:16176853

Palmieri, P. A., & Fitzgerals, L. F. (2005). Confirmatory factor analysis of posttraumatic stress symptoms in sexually harassed women. *Journal of Traumatic Stress*, *18*(6), 657–666. doi:10.1002/jts.20074 PMID:16382424

Pinel, P. (1798). *Nosographie philosophique, ou la method de l'analyse appliquée à la Médecine*. Paris: Richard, Caille, & Ravier.

Roussy, G., & Lhermitte, J. (1919). *Les psychonévroses de guerre*. Paris: Masson.

Smith, M. Y., Redda, W. H., Peyserb, C., & Vool, D. (1999). Posttraumatic stress disorder in cancer.: A review. *Psycho-Oncology*, *8*(6), 521–537. doi:10.1002/(SICI)1099-1611(199911/12)8:6<521::AID-PON423>3.0.CO;2-X PMID:10607985

Van der Hart, O., Brown, P., & Van der Kolk, B. A. (1989). Pierre Janets Treatment of Post-Traumatic Stress. *Journal of Traumatic Stress*, *2*(4), 379–395. doi:10.1002/jts.2490020404

Van der Hart, O., & Friedman, B. (1989). A Reader's Guide to Pierre Janet on Dissociation: A Neglected Intellectual Heritage. *Dissociation*, *2*, 3–16.

Van der Hart, O., Nijenhuis, E., & Steele, K. (2006). *The haunted Self: Structural dissociation and the treatment of chronic traumatization*. New York: Norton.

Vinokur, A., & Selzer, M. L. (1975). Desirable versus undesirable life events: Their relationship to stress and mental distress. *Journal of Personality and Social Psychology*, *32*(2), 329–337. doi:10.1037/0022-3514.32.2.329 PMID:1239500

Wilson, J. P. (1989). A person-environment approach to traumatic stress reactions. In J. Wilson (Ed.), Trauma, transformation and healing: An integrative approach to theory, research, and post-traumatic therapy, (pp. 75-110). New York: Brunner/Mazel.

Wilson, J. P. (1994). The Historical Evolution of PTSD Diagnostic Criteria: From Freud to DSM-IV. *Journal of Traumatic Stress*, *7*(4), 1994. doi:10.1002/jts.2490070413 PMID:7820357

Wilson, J. P., Harel, Z., & Kahana, B. (Eds.). (1988). Human Adaptation to Extreme Stress From the Holocaust to Vietnam. New York: Springer Science.

KEY TERMS AND DEFINITIONS

DSM: Diagnostic and Statistical Manual of Mental Disorders, currently in the 5th edition (DSM-5), the 2013 update to the American Psychiatric Association's (APA) classification and diagnostic tool. In the United States the DSM serves as a universal authority for psychiatric diagnosis and treatment recommendations, as well as payment by health care providers.

Effroi de la Mort (Frozen State of Shock): Subjective state of frozen fright and petrified state of shock, described in French trauma theory and due to a sudden and unexpected confrontation with death.

PTSD Criterion A2: DSM-IV (2000) criterion of Post-Traumatic Stress Disorder (see below) related to subjective components (e.g. the individual's response) such as intense fear, helplessness and/or horror.

Post-Traumatic Stress Disorder (PTSD): Mental disorder which is described as a stress-related disorder in the DSM-5 and which may occur after traumatic experiences such as severe accidents, rape, torture, violence and war.

Psychological Traumatization (in French Lacanian Theory): Disruption between the 'signifier' (words and symbols available for representation) and the 'signified' (the real face of death).

Repetition Syndrome: Syndrome following psychological trauma, characterized by various forms of mental repetition, such as resurgence of irresistible thoughts recalling the traumatic scene, mental ruminations, fleeting, near-hallucinatory visions, an irresistible tendency to look for and contemplate scenes of violence in real life of visual reproductions, impulsive motor behaviors and startle reactions.

Traumatic Neurosis: Diagnostic entity which may result from direct – anatomical or psychic – effects of traumatic experiences including specific symptoms (symptoms of repetition) and general neurotic symptoms such as anxiety and asthenia, and involving a typical organization of the personality.

War Neurosis: Traumatic neurosis in which the role of a 'shock emotion' and the emphasis of the specific 'post-emotional' character of combat play an essential role.

Section 2
Incidents of Organizational Trauma

Chapter 4
The Stress Profile:
The Influence of Personal Characteristics on Response to Occupational Trauma

Ilona Jerabek
PsychTests AIM Inc., Canada

Deborah Muoio
PsychTests AIM Inc., Canada

ABSTRACT

The purpose of this chapter is to provide an overview of the interrelationship between personal characteristics, such as resilience, emotional intelligence, and optimism, and the ability to cope with occupational stress and organizational trauma. Although the availability of stress management resources can offer some pre-emptive measures to reduce the mental, physical, and organizational impact of trauma, this is but part of the prevention equation. The role of the individual, and the person's character in particular, is of paramount importance, as it can also offset and even deter the impact of trauma, and the effects of stress in general. Even in situations where individuals are exposed to the same type of stressor and same degree of pressure, the ability to cope can vary a great deal from person to person. The proposal of the authors is that the nurturing of specific personality traits, attitudes, and behaviors can prove beneficial both on an individual and organizational level.

INTRODUCTION

Companies have made great strides toward understanding the value of "human capital"; after all, the web overflows with articles on how to lead, Top 10 lists of Dos and Don'ts for managers, and tips on how to structure salary and benefit packages. However, many companies still fail to grasp the importance of employee well-being, paying only lip service to the concept of work-life balance. Some even feel that catering to employee well-being would detract from productivity. The truth, of course, is that efforts to promote well-being at work makes a lot of business sense, and failure to do so can be expensive in terms of increased risk for accidents, absenteeism, productivity cost, and stress-related health issues.

DOI: 10.4018/978-1-5225-2021-4.ch004

The Statistic Brain Research Institute (2015) quotes the annual cost of stress-related healthcare and absenteeism at $300 billion, with nearly a third of the American sample indicating that they are "always" or "often" stressed at work.

Well-being is a broad concept that can represent and include many things. It can encompass physical, mental, emotional, and social well-being. It takes into account everything from healthy personal relationships to sleep hygiene, leisure, and a fulfilling career. Moreover, well-being extends far beyond financial prosperity. In a nutshell, well-being is a state of being content, healthy, and prosperous. At the bare minimum, it is a satisfactory condition of existence. However, in order to truly grasp the concept of well-being, it is important to understand what it isn't: Well-being is not the absence of stress, because stress can be healthy, at least to some degree. In the right circumstances and with the right mindset, it offers people a motivational push or the momentum to take action and to keep trying. It is only when stress reaches an unhealthy level that it starts to affect well-being (Müeller, Heiden, Herbig, Poppe, & Angerer, 2016).

What is an unhealthy level of stress? The answer to this loaded question is: "It depends." While all humans go through the same pattern of stress response, there are major individual differences in how we react to stressors. People's perception of the same stressor will vary widely, and their reaction can go from a mild annoyance to a full-blown panic. Some people take on a challenge with ease and enthusiasm, while others are paralyzed when faced with the same obstacle. In the same vein, people react to trauma in a variety of ways, depending on their psychological make-up, physical and mental fortitude, attitudes, beliefs, past experiences, support network and available resources. In fact, psychological trauma can be conceptualized as a case of extreme, acute stress, resulting from exposure to a severely distressing event, oftentimes outside the realm of normal human experience.

There are many factors that influence our reaction to stress and trauma. Our genetic make-up may predetermine our level of reactivity, but it is modulated by life experiences, training, and environment. This chapter focuses on clusters of personal characteristics; it explains how they influence the stress reaction and how they impact a person's response to trauma. Certain personality traits, attitudes, emotional processes, behaviors and competencies, if developed and nurtured, can help employees deal with traumatic experiences, while other characteristics can predispose them to an exaggerated stress response. Research on paramedics revealed that those who practiced adaptive coping strategies in response to trauma experienced better post-traumatic adjustment (positive psychological changes as a result of the trauma), while extroversion, one of the Big Five personality traits, can offer the same benefits for police officers (Paton, 2005). In times of distress, these characteristics come into play on 1) an individual level, with personal constellations of adaptive or maladaptive characteristics determining how a person copes, and 2) on an organizational level, in which employees may feed off each other's fears *or* strengths, based on the combination of the team's individual personal characteristics and team dynamics. The authors' propose the theory that the best way to make an organization resilient, particularly when dealing with trauma, is to help individuals develop and nurture specific protective traits, attitudes, and skills. Stress and trauma may be inevitable, but they do not have to completely impede the operational functions and progress of an organization. The goal of this chapter is to offer insight into how to reduce employee stress as a result of trauma and mitigate its impact on the company. In order to do so, it is essential to understand the different personal factors that can contribute to a person's response to stress and trauma, and how both the individual employee and management can play a role in reducing their impact.

BACKGROUND

The term "stress" is often used as an umbrella term to account for a psychological and/or physical shift from homeostasis and its ensuing physiological impact, in response to both unpleasant and pleasant stimuli. There are, however, several facets of stress - different types of stress and different degrees of it. Simply, not all stressors are universally stressful, nor are all forms of stress damaging. Relative to individuals, the ability to cope with stress and/or trauma can vary significantly, and is contingent on each person's constellation of personality traits and competencies.

Experiencing trauma in the workplace as a result of the nature of one's work is not a new concept – nor does a person need to experience trauma directly in order to experience its negative effects. Figley (1995) conducted extensive research on the experience of "secondary trauma" in the helping professions (therapy, emergency response, child protection) resulting from contact with patients who were a victim of a traumatic experience. The need to listen to and empathize with a patient's experience and offer emotional support can lead to "compassion fatigue," making it difficult for care providers to remain objective and to regulate their own emotional response to stress and trauma (Adams, Boscarino, & Figley, 2006; Hensel, Ruiz, Finney, & Dewa, 2015). On a wider scale, the experience of organizational trauma can come from a number of sources, both internal and external. The organization might be the target of a terrorist attack (e.g. Charlie Hebdo case); subjected to layoffs, mergers, downsizing and other factors that affect job security, or rocked by controversy (e.g. embezzlement or fraud accusations) (Hormann & Vivian, 2005). An organization can be traumatized by suicides blamed on the company climate (e.g. France Telecom) (Willsher, 2014), or fatal/near-fatal work accidents. Hormann and Vivian (2005) also argued that an organization may be vulnerable to trauma from its very inception because the products or services it offers are steeped in controversy (e.g. abortion clinics, Planned Parenthood, tobacco companies, etc.). According to Hormann and Vivian, organizational trauma can be the result of a single, unexpected traumatic event or a build up of a series of adverse situations. Trauma and extreme stress can affect not only the direct victims of the events, but also those who witnessed them first or even second-hand, as well as the organization as a whole.

Although workers in high-risk or high-stress occupations (e.g. protective services, emergency medical personnel, therapists) are more likely to be directly or indirectly exposed to traumatic events or traumatized people, employees from a variety of occupations have the potential to face traumatic circumstances. For example, frequent exposure to interpersonal conflict with colleagues and, more notably, with customers, was associated with higher levels of burnout and decreased ability to perform job tasks effectively (Sliter, Pui, Sliter, & Jex 2011) as well as gastrointestinal issues and interrupted sleep patterns (Nixon, Mazzola, Bauer, Krueger, & Spector, 2011). Employees working under the threat of downsizing and job insecurity are more likely to struggle with physical and mental health problems (Moore, Grunberg, & Greenberg, 2004). Meta-analytical studies have also uncovered disconcerting links between occupational stress and significant physical health issues, including an increased need for disability leave for employees diagnosed with diabetes (Ervasti, et al., 2016), persistent coronary heart disease in patients who already have heart issues (Li, Zhang, Loerbroks, Angerer, & Siegrist, 2014) as well as increased risk of stroke (Booth et al., 2015).

Several initiatives have been taken in the United States and in Europe to reduce troublesome occupational hazards. According to the Institute of Work, Health and Organizations (I-WHO) (2008), the threat of downsizing and outsourcing and other sources of job insecurity, as well as psychosocial risk factors (e.g. lack of social or managerial support, oppressive company culture), and work design issues (e.g. excessive workload, lack of job control, role confusion) can also lead to stress-related problems. I-WHO's "risk management paradigm" is a proposed initiative to reduce two worrisome trends in the work world: musculoskeletal disorders and an increase in work-related stress (I-WHO, 2004; I-WHO, 2008; National Institute for Occupational Safety and Health, 1999). In the United States, the 1999 *Stress At Work* report by the National Institute for Occupational Safety and Health (NIOSH) proposed that job stress reduction initiatives must encompass two approaches: Stress management training for employees through Employee Assistance Programs (EAP) and organizational changes to decrease job stress risks, such as transparency and improved communication between management and employees, encouraging social interaction between employees to foster social support, and creating reasonable and flexible work schedules that allow for work/life balance.

OCCUPATIONAL STRESS AND TRAUMA: THE ROLE OF PERSONAL CHARACTERISTICS

Undeniably, people tend to disagree on what is and what is not traumatic. However, the magnitude of perceived stress in response to the same traumatic event varies considerably from one individual to another. Also, there are major individual differences in terms of tolerance to stressful conditions. The thresholds or tipping points for the stages of the stress response depend on many factors, including the individual's emotional reactivity (Rzeszutek, Partyka, & Gołąb, 2015), the circumstances and gravity of the situation (seriousness and longevity of consequences) (Zandberg et al., 2016), the individual's coping skills (Brandt et al., 2015; Denollet, Martens, Nyklíček, Conraads, de Gelder, 2008) and support system (Rzeszutek et al., 2015), among other factors.

A number of personal characteristics have been linked to a higher vulnerability to stress-related symptoms. The authors' define these personal characteristics as traits, attitudes, values, beliefs, skills, and competencies that can enhance or diminish an individual's ability to cope with stressful events and trauma. They theorize that having a greater number of adaptive personal characteristics can result in better posttraumatic outcomes, whereas having certain maladaptive personal characteristic, such as hostility (Lemogne, et al., 2015), and an external locus of control (Zhou, Yan, Che, & Meier, 2015), can make vulnerable individuals more prone to the effects of traumatic conditions.

Several studies using the well-established Five-Factor model of personality (consisting of Openness, Conscientiousness, Extroversion, Agreeableness, and Neuroticism or Emotional Stability) have revealed a notable influence on an individual's capacity to cope with stress. Traits like neuroticism (De Hoogh & Den Hartog, 2009; Hyun, Kang, & Swanger, 2009), low openness, low conscientiousness (Törnroos et al., 2013), and emotional reactivity (Rzeszutek et al., 2015) have been linked to a higher susceptibility to stress. In Bowling and Eschleman's research (2010), vulnerable employees who tended to engage in "counterproductive work behaviors" in response to stress (i.e. intentionally harmful behaviors against the organization, colleagues, or clients) were not only more likely to lack the personal resources to cope with work stressors, they also scored low in conscientious as well as agreeableness. A study on the link between burnout and personality of frontline staff at a psychiatric residential treatment center for children revealed that employees who were low in emotional stability and who also rated their patients as severely ill were at an increased risk of experiencing depersonalization, a burnout symptom in which the individual feels detached from his or her reality (Leon, Visscher, Sugimura, & Lakin, 2008). In Alarcon, Eschlemn, & Bowling's (2009) as well as Swider & Zimmerman's (2010) meta-analyses, all five traits demonstrated a significant relationship with burnout as measured by the Maslach Burnout Inventory (Maslach, Jackson, & Leiter, 1996). When looking at the Big Five traits in groupings rather than as independent constructs, Grant and Langan-Fox (2006) discovered that managers high in neuroticism (or low in emotional stability) and low in conscientiousness were more likely to suffer the ill-effects of stress, deficient coping ability, physical ailments, and low job satisfaction.

It is clear that occupational stress can have detrimental effects on work performance as well as physical and mental health, but this may not be the case in all circumstances and for all people. Several studies have shown that the use of effective coping strategies can buffer the effects of stress and reduce task interference, even in fields where workers are exposed to trauma and even under circumstances in which symptoms of burnout are already in play (Demerouti, Bakker, & Leiter, 2014). Nursing, for example, presents major risk factors for burnout, including long work hours, heavy work load, shift work, lack of work-life balance, lack of effective coping strategies, and lack of social support (Lasebikan & Oyetunde, 2012; Ribeiro, et al., 2014). Yet nurses who display a greater sense of self-efficacy in their ability to solve problems and who describe themselves as being tolerant of stress at work are less likely to experience burnout (Elliott, Shewchuck, Hagglund, Rybarczyk, & Harkins, 1996). However, when the demands of a job begin to outweigh any professional gains that work effort renders (e.g. increased salary, self-efficacy, job security), the resulting job strain increases propensity for emotional exhaustion and stress-related health issues (Feuerhahn, Kühnel, & Kudielka 2012). Employees' inability to function at full mental, emotional, and physical capacity will be reflected in their diminished job performance, often in the form of tardiness, absenteeism, lack of attention, poor work quality, inadequate client care, poor customer service, attitude problems, and work accidents (Bakker & Heuven, 2006; Greiner, Krause, Ragland, & Fisher, 1998; Sherman & Thelen, 1998; Stoneman & Jinnah, 2015).

Personal Characteristics That Exacerbate the Impact of Stress and Trauma

There are certain personal characteristics that can heighten stress levels and prevent certain vulnerable people from coping effectively with change, trauma, and hardship in general. In fact, people with a specific cluster of traits and attitudes can perceive even innocuous situations as threatening or highly stressful. The authors' theorize that individuals who display the characteristics below – perfectionism, Type A and D personality traits, workaholism, and a toxic personality in general - are more likely to be prone to the negative effects of stressful conditions. They also suggest that for individuals whose stress threshold is already low as a result of these problematic personal characteristics, a major trauma can further deplete their already limited personal resources. Table 1 provides a breakdown of the key problem traits that outline the types of employees discussed below.

Perfectionism

Researchers Hamachek (1978), Frost, Marten, Lahart, and Rosenblate (1990) as well as Blankstein and Dunkley (2002) propose that perfectionism should be viewed from a multidimensional perspective. Essentially, perfectionism is not necessarily a problematic trait in all circumstances. Those who take pride in doing their work well and who set high yet reasonable expectations for themselves (an achievement-striving aspect of perfectionism) display an adaptive style of perfectionism; those who take accountability to an extreme and have difficulty overcoming the fear of other people's opinion of them, of making

Table 1. Key problematic traits of perfectionists, Type A and D personalities, workaholics, and toxic personalities

Personal Characteristic	Key Problematic Issues
Perfectionism	Avoidance coping strategies
	Extreme sense of accountability
	Fear of failure
	Fear of criticism
	Fear of judgment
Type A Personality	Hostility
	Neuroticism
	Impatience
Type D Personality	Negative Affect
	Social Inhibition
Workaholism	Compulsive tendency to work
	Perfectionism
	Extreme Achievement Orientation
Toxic Personalities	Poor emotional regulation (EQ competency)
	Lack of empathy (EQ competency)
	Poor social skills (EQ competency)
	Abusiveness (verbal, psychological, sexual, physical)
	Maladaptive or ineffective coping strategies
	Narcissism (Dark Triad)
	Machiavellianism (Dark Triad)
	Psychopathy (Dark Triad)

mistakes and of failure, display a maladaptive form of perfectionism (Frost, Heimberg, Holt, Mattia, & Neubauer, 1993; Hamachek, 1978). Research by Moate, Gnilka, West, and Bruns (2016) also found that maladaptive perfectionists perceive their work environment as more stressful, and were more likely to be at risk for work-related burnout. Jerabek and Muoio's (2013c) research on maladaptive perfectionists revealed that they were more likely to have consulted a medical or mental health professional for stress-related problems, which was also supported by Mandel, Dunkley and Moroz's (2015) study of highly self-critical perfectionists. Maladaptive perfectionists are also more likely to use ineffective or avoidant stress management strategies, like drinking alcohol (R. C. O'Connor & D. B. O'Connor, 2003; Rice & Van Arsdale, 2010) and misusing prescription drugs (Hartung et al., 2013).

Type A Personality

Although not an official diagnosis in the DSM-5, the Type A Behavioral Profile (often called Type A Personality or TABP) has been shown in several studies as far back as the 1950's to pose a serious physical health risk (Friedman, 1977). Type A Personality is generally characterized by hostility, neuroticism, extreme drive and ambition, and impatience (Bokenberger, Pedersen, Gatz, & Dahl, 2014). Friedman and Rosenman (1959), along with contemporary researchers, have discovered a notable link between problematic Type A Personality traits and vulnerability to stress, mental health issues, and cardiovascular risk (Bokenberger et al., 2014). A study by Jamal and Baba (2003) of Canadian employees with Type A Personality indicated that the sense of time pressure and competitiveness/drive aspect of the TABP was associated with a greater degree of job stress, health issues, and turnover intention. While the achievement striving aspect of the TABP (drive, ambition) can translate into higher productivity, goal achievement and job satisfaction, and is generally conducive to success (Bluen, Barling, & Burns,

1990; Day & Jreige, 2002; Jerabek & Muoio, 2011), the hostility, neuroticism, and impatience aspect makes Type A people feel more stressed, particularly in situations where Type A employees have little job control and a great deal of role ambiguity (Day & Jreige, 2002), two major sources of work-related stress (I-WHO, 2004).

A meta-analytical study by Orth and Wieland (2006) revealed that hostility on its own is linked with Posttraumatic Stress Disorder (PTSD) in adults who have suffered a trauma. Although depression and anxiety in particular are commonly associated with PTSD, some individuals exposed to trauma can also react with anger and hostility (Orth & Wieland, 2006). In terms of neuroticism, aside from frequently coexisting with PTSD (Cox, MacPherson, Enns, & McWilliams, 2004), individuals who experienced trauma and who were regularly exposed to stress throughout their lifespan were at an increased risk for depression, particularly if they scored high in neuroticism (Vinkers et al., 2014). A neurotic temperament is also one of the risk factors for PTSD in journalists who cover traumatic events (Marais & Stuart, 2005).

Despite the potential benefits of social support in times of stress and trauma in particular (Jones, 2002), research from Jerabek and Muoio (2015a) revealed that people with Type A personality are less accustomed to seeking assistance from others. In fact, their abrasive behavior and habitual complaining can strain their social interactions, thus eroding their support network and prevent them from forming meaningful relationships. Even if the help comes from respected medical professionals, in these authors' consulting experience, Type A are cynical by nature, and more likely to doubt medical opinions or refuse to consult a doctor or psychologist for health problems. In addition, their difficulty and reluctance to relax, unwind and simply enjoy the moment contributes to their higher baseline levels of stress (Jerabek and Muoio, 2015a).

Type D Personality

Although a relatively new construct, Type D Personality has been associated with several stress-related, health-related, and job-related issues. Johan Denollet, the author who proposed the construct, characterized Type D individuals as having a propensity for "Negative Affectivity" or negative emotions, such as unease and a dissatisfaction with self and life, and "Social Inhibition," defined as a tendency to avoid expressing one's emotions and social interaction in general (Denollet, 2000). Meta-analyses reveal that patients diagnosed with cardiovascular disease and categorized as Type D were at an increased risk for developing elevated levels of stress, mental health problems, and were more likely to suffer a heart attack or cardiac-related death (Denollet, 2012). While additional research is required to solidify the link between Type D and cardiovascular issues, it is clear that negative affect and social inhibition, which have been positively correlated with neuroticism and negatively correlated with extroversion respectively (Denollet, 2005), can prove to be detrimental to an individual's mental and physical health. Moreover, research by van der Tooren and Rutte (2016) indicates that employees characterized as Type D are less likely to be engaged in their work, and more likely to be at risk for emotional exhaustion, one of the typical symptoms of burnout (Maslach et al., 1996). Van der Tooren and Rutte (2016) wisely suggested that while the characteristics of a job (job design, task design) can have a significant impact on employee well-being, the role of employee personality on mental health cannot be ignored.

Workaholism

Although there is much divergence on the proper definition of workaholism and characterization of workaholics, it is in these authors' opinion that the concept was best captured by the work of Scott, Moore, and & Miceli (1997), who described three main workaholic constructs: a compulsive tendency to work, a tendency toward perfectionism, and a strong achievement orientation. Despite having certain advantages in relation to productivity, workaholism comes at a significant psychological cost (Bovornusvakool, Vodanovich, Ariyabuddhiphongs, & Ngamake, 2012; Jerabek & Muoio, 2015a; Mazzetti, Schaufeli, & Guglielmi, 2014). On the one hand, workaholics are driven, dedicated and determined to get work done. The stress and constant pressure to be productive, however, results in a build-up of resentment, frustration, and fatigue. Despite admitting that they find their life stressful, workaholics regularly overwork and overbook themselves and feel like they are constantly rushing to get somewhere (Jerabek & Muoio, 2015a). This leads to a higher risk for absenteeism due to physical ailments, burnout, and a reduced sense of happiness and satisfaction (Bonebright, Clay, & Ankenmann, 2000; Bovornusvakool et al., 2012; Schaufeli, Bakker, van der Heijden, & Prins, 2009; van Beek, Taris, & Schaufeli, 2011).

The negative repercussions of workaholism are not limited to the psychological distress of the workaholic himself/herself; it also leads to significant work-family conflict. Workaholics are more likely to bring work home or worry about their work during their leisure time (Bovornusvakool et al., 2012; Jerabek & Muoio, 2015a). They are also less likely to enjoy their time off and more likely to neglect loved ones, resulting in lower relationship satisfaction (Andreassen, 2014; Bakker, Demerouti, & Burke, 2009; Brady, Vodanovich, & Rotunda, 2008) and cutting them off from protective factors against stress like relaxation (Brady et al., 2008), leisure, and a healthy social life (Bovornusvakool et al., 2012). In these authors' opinion, even the protective factor of exercise, which has been shown to lead to lower levels of task stress (Sliter & Yuan, 2015) and reduce the incidence of depression, anxiety, and burnout (Lindwall, Gerber, Jonsdottir, Börjesson, & Ahlborg, 2014), would likely be viewed by workaholics as just another chore, or time that would be better spent working on something they consider productive.

Toxic Personalities

Abusive or narcissistic leaders, or leaders who lack personal resources to cope with stress, can be toxic to an organization by not only creating stress for their staff, but also reducing job satisfaction and breeding resentment between management and subordinates, "infecting" the organizational climate in general (Byrne et al., 2014; Farh & Chen, 2014; Gallus, Walsh, van Driel, Gouge, & Antolic, 2013; Keller-Hansbrough & Jones, 2014; Mawritz, Dust, & Resick. 2014; Skogstad, et al., 2014). Research by Hoobler and Brass (2006) and Restubog, Scott, and Zagenczyk (2011) revealed that verbally abusive behavior from leaders - like insults, put-downs, bringing up past mistakes, breaking promises made to employees - can carry over into an employee's family life. Employees who were being undermined and abused at work were more likely to displace their anger by taking their frustration out on loved ones, often by belittling them in turn. When under stress themselves, team leaders in Byrne et al's study (2014) and Li, Wang, Yang, and Liu's study (2016) who were unable to remain psychologically strong became verbally abusive toward others, which in turn resulted in psychological distress in employees. Toxic leaders can also have a negative impact on morale and the job satisfaction of their employees, and are often the reason for high turnover and talent exodus (Jerabek & Muoio, 2015b), making a bad situation worse when the company is faced with restructuring, layoffs, or other organizational traumas. In a study on probability of turnover, Jerabek and Muoio (2015b) asked 256 employees who were actively looking for a new job opportunity about the role that management played in their decision to leave. Their study revealed that:

- 53% indicated that issues or concerns they brought up to management tended to fall on deaf ears and went unresolved.
- 55% asserted that management made promises to employees that they did not keep.
- 56% explained that their manager did not provide them (or employees in general) with sufficient learning opportunities or opportunities to develop their skills.

Although they can be charismatic, leaders with narcissistic traits, such as an exaggerated sense of self-importance, a sense of superiority and entitlement, a lack of empathy, and the belief that others are envious of them (American Psychological Association, 2013), are more likely to endorse the belief that employees are insubordinate and dishonest. They use this belief to justify their tendency to use abusive leadership techniques (e.g. verbal abuse, harsh feedback, and public ridicule) to keep employees in line (Hansbrough & Jones, 2014). Along with other competencies related to emotional intelligence, poor social skills, the inability to manage one's emotions or emotional situations, and a lack of sensitivity and empathy on the part of leaders not only foster a hostile work environment, it can also erode employee motivation and organizational commitment (Goleman, 1998). Essentially, when employees are treated disrespectfully and their leader models negative and abrasive behaviors, they in turn are more likely to direct their resentment outward, by being less committed to their work and the organization, by mistreating their colleagues, or by carrying work stress into their family life (Farh & Chen, 2014; Gallus et al., 2013; Mawritz et al., 2014; Mitchell & Ambrose, 2007; Zellars, Tepper, & Duffy, 2002).

Leaders are not the only members of an organization that can breed a toxic work environment. The social, emotional, and organizational consequences of workplace incivility on the part of employees can be severe. Prominent researchers in this area, Pearson, Andersson, and Porath (2005), defined workplace incivility as disrespectful behaviors that go against workplace norms and that are designed to harm the intended target. Pearson et al argue that potentially traumatic organizational changes, such as downsizing, outsourcing, and mergers can foster anger and fear in employees, who may in turn express these emotions by lashing out at their colleagues. On an individual level, employees who are the target of incivility may react in a number of ways. Some may find their morale faltering, affecting their sense of well-being and job satisfaction (Pearson et al., 2005; Tahnee & Griffin, 2015). Others may choose to quit or retaliate by becoming equally disrespectful toward fellow employees, or toward the organization as a whole by slacking off (Pearson et al., 2005). If organizations do not deal with workplace incivility promptly, Pearson et al (2005) caution that mildly deviant or aggressive behavior can escalate and initiate more aggressive and violent acts in the workplace, leading to a highly toxic and uncivil work environment. Research has also found that leaders or employees characterized by the "Dark Triad" traits – narcissism, Machiavellianism (propensity for manipulativeness, cynicism, justification of deception and immorality), and psychopathy (propensity for remorselessness, impulsive behavior, selfishness, lack of empathy) – are more forceful and antagonistic when interacting with others, particularly if they are men (Jonason, Slomski, & Partyka, 2012). The Dark Triad has also been associated with bullying behavior in the workplace (Linton & Power, 2013), as well as counterproductive work behaviors and lower productivity (O'Boyle, Forsyth, Banks, & McDaniel, 2012).

Personal Characteristics That Act as Protective Factors Against Stress and Trauma

Certain personal characteristics can alter how trauma and hardship affect an individual's psychological and physical health (Blackie, E. Jayawickreme, Forgeard, & N. Jayawickreme, 2015; Felix et al., 2015; Kurian, Currier, Rojas-Flores, Herrera, & Foster, 2016; López-Fuentes & Calvete, 2015; Yablon, 2015). These protective factors play a significant role in a person's reaction to major stressors at several levels. They influence cognitive appraisal of a situation (Dueweke, Hurtado, & Hovey, 2015; Felix et al., 2015; Ford, Mauss, Troy, Smolen, & Hankin, 2014; Larsen, Clauss-Ehlers, & Cosden, 2015; López-Fuentes & Calvete, 2015; Novak & Davidson, 2013), impact emotional reaction (Larsen et al., 2015; Craigie et al., 2016), and invoke specific coping mechanisms (Larsen et al., 2015; López-Fuentes & Calvete, 2015; Moody, Fuks, Peláez, Smith, 2015). Research has shown that certain personal characteristics can buffer the effects of stress, potentially reduce the effects of trauma, and improve post-trauma outcomes. The authors propose the following protective characteristics: Optimism/Positive mindset, Resilience/Hardiness, Emotional Intelligence, Resourcefulness, Internal locus of control, and Assertiveness.

Optimism and Positive Mindset

While a great deal of research in the 20th century focused on mental illness, theorists like Maslow and Seligman attempted to shift attention toward human strengths rather than weaknesses, and on optimism, hope, and self-actualization rather than psychopathy, negative affect, and conflict. The advent of Positive Psychology shifted focus toward *prevention* of mental health issues, not just the study of them (Peterson & Seligman, 2004). Optimism is one of the many traits that research has shown to have protective characteristics in response to adversity (Seligman & Csikszentmihalyi, 2000).

Optimism and a positive outlook have a major impact on how people cope with stress, failure, and hardship (Jerabek & Muoio, 2013b), particularly in high-pressure occupations or occupations where professionals are required to deal with trauma (Harrison & Westwood, 2009). When Gallavan and Newman (2013) looked at antecedents of burnout in mental health professionals in correctional facilities, those who displayed a more positive disposition and attitude toward their subjects (prisoners) reported more positive work experiences. Clinicians characterized by optimism and a proactive approach to problems are less likely to experience "vicarious traumatisation" when dealing with patients who have experienced a trauma (Harrison & Westwood, 2009). On the other hand, low optimism, coupled with an external locus of control and poor self-efficacy, is linked to increased likelihood of depression, particularly in cases where the demands on an employee exceed the person's abilities (Park, Beehr, Han, & Grebner, 2012). Not only does optimism act as a protective factor against stress, it is also a valuable personal asset in occupations where organizational resources for stress management are limited, as it lowers the probability of burnout (Riolli & Savicki, 2003).

Core Self-Evaluation

The manner in which an individual interprets events in his or her general environment and responds to these events is influenced by his/her core self-evaluation (CSE), which encompasses self-esteem, sense of self-efficacy, locus of control, and emotional stability (van Doorn & Hülsheger, 2015). When confronted with stress, the health of an individual's core self-evaluation determines how they perceive the stressor and the type of coping strategies they use (Kammeyer-Mueller, Judge, & Scott, 2009; Tavousi, 2014). A strong CSE can also help employees cope with conflict at work (Liu, Li, Fan, and Nauta, 2015) and temper the effects of job demands and job strains on level of distress (Tavousi, 2014; van Doorn and Hülsheger, 2015)

Research on a specific facet of core self-evaluation, self-esteem, indicates that individuals with high self-esteem experience less job stress (Brunborg, 2008), and are less likely to experience burnout-related symptoms such as emotional exhaustion, depersonalization, and reduced productivity (De Cuyper, Raeder, Van der Heijden, & Wittekind, 2012). In cases of low self-esteem, even in work environments where employees have a great deal of control over their circumstances at work, a lack of belief in one's capacity to cope with high job demands is more likely to result in frustration, disappointment, self-condemnation, and stress-related issues (Hystad, Eid, & Brevik, 2011). Employees with low self-esteem, engage in more self-critical thinking and self-sabotaging behaviors and experience high levels of anxiety and depression (Jerabek & Muoio, 2013d). Similarly, self-efficacy itself also plays a role in buffering the effects of occupational stress and trauma. A strong sense of self-efficacy, in conjunction with an optimistic and resilient attitude, has been shown to help new entrepreneurs weather on often volatile business climate (Baron, Franklin, & Hmieleski, 2016). Teachers who have trust in themselves and in their skills are less likely to experience emotional exhaustion (Tuxford & Bradley, 2015), while firefighters who believe that they are capable of coping with stress and trauma tend to experience less psychological stress (Lambert, Benight, Harrison, & Cieslak, 2012). Overall, research seems to strongly suggest that employees who have confidence in their ability to handle work tasks and demands and cope with stressors not only experience less distress, they are also less likely to engage in counterproductive work behavior when under pressure or in emotionally charged work situations (Fida, Paciello, Tramontano, Barbaranelli, & Farnese, 2015).

Locus of Control

When an individual takes active steps to adapt to a problem or traumatic situation, even if it's only a matter of making the situation tolerable, this offers the person a sense of control. It is these authors' belief that adopting an internal locus of control - or the belief that one has the power to change one's circumstances - is an important factor in coping with occupational trauma. This may be particularly true in circumstances where employees don't have a great deal of job control, and where having an internal locus of control can act as a protective factor against stress and reduce the likelihood of engaging in counterproductive coping behaviors (Sprung & Jex, 2012; Zhou et al. 2015). For example, when faced with stressful situations at work, those in Sprung & Jex's (2012) study who had an internal locus of control were less likely to engage in unproductive or vengeful behavior directed toward colleagues or the company. Clinicians working with survivors of trauma in Killian's study (2008) were more likely to experience a sense of satisfaction from helping others, in spite of the traumatic nature of their job, if they possessed an internal locus of control and a strong social support at work.

In the same vein, individuals with an external locus of control are more likely to struggle in situations of stress and trauma. In Regehr, Hill, and Glancy's study (2000) and Brown, Mulhern, and Joseph's study (2005) with firefighters who were exposed to trauma on the job, an external locus of control played a major role in a firefighter's likelihood of experiencing posttraumatic stress symptoms and depression. Similarly, two of the factors that acted as a precursor to "peritraumatic dissociation" a predictive factor of PTSD in rescue personnel after the 1989 earthquake in San Francisco Bay, was an external locus of control as well as avoidance coping strategies (Marmar, Weiss, Metzler, & Delucchi, 1996). These studies thus strongly imply that individuals with an external locus of control are at a disadvantage in traumatic situations. Individuals with an external locus of control attribute difficult circumstances to factors that are not within their ability to change, and therefore, feel helpless, creating a sense of victimhood (Jerabek & Muoio, 2014a). Continual exposure to stressful situations that a person feels powerless to change can lead to a state of "learned helplessness," which can further manifest as anxiety or depression (Havranek et al., 2016).

Resilience/Hardiness

In his book, *Hardiness: Turning stressful situations into resilient growth* (2013), author Salvatore R. Maddi, one of the leading hardiness theorists and researchers, saw hardiness as a group of attitudes and strategies that help individuals use stressful situations as opportunities to learn and grow. This in turn contributes to a person's resilience, which Maddi considers to be the capacity to not just survive but thrive even when in the midst of stressful events. Although resilience and hardiness can be seen as two unique constructs, for practical consideration, the authors use these terms interchangeably.

Resilience is very much a matter of perspective. Resilient individuals tend to view their job as less demanding (Boudrias et al., 2011; Ferris, Sinclair, & Kline, 2005; Hystad, et al., 2011), and this fortitude plays a particularly crucial role in jobs that present an element of danger, as is the case with service members. Lo Bue, Taverniers, Mylle, and Euwema's study (2013) of members of the International Security and Assistance Force revealed that hardy soldiers found more meaning in their missions than less hardy members. They felt more committed to their work and were less likely to suffer from emotional and physical exhaustion, despite being exposed to highly stressful experiences. Essentially, they recognized that the work they engaged in offered benefits not only to the people whom they were helping, it also contributed to their own growth and resilience (Britt, Adler, & Bartone, 2001). This awareness, it would appear, is the key to thriving even in the face of traumatic circumstances. In his book, Maddi discusses a 12-year longitudinal study (starting in 1975) that followed the progress of employees at the Illinois Bell Telephone company. After being forced to endure the ever-looming cloud of deregulation of the telecommunication industry, when it finally came to pass six years later, almost half the employees were relieved of their job as a result of downsizing; the remaining staff were left to struggle with ever-changing job roles in an effort to cope with a now highly competitive market. The impact on former and current employees' mental and physical health was staggering: Maddi discovered that two-thirds of them had suffered from physical ailments such as heart attacks, strokes, and cancer. Others had fallen into addictions, depression, and anxiety, or committed suicide. The remaining one-third, however, displayed strong signs of resilience, using their job experience to pursue other positions, or venturing out to start their own company. Maddi's study emphasized that how a person reacts to hardship and trauma can mean the difference between failing and thriving.

In her research comparing two groups of executives in high-stress jobs, a study by Kobasa (1979) revealed that those characterized by hardiness were less likely to fall ill than their less hardy yet equally stressed counterparts. This result is supported by research by Hystad et al (2011) and Jerabek and Muoio (2013a), in which hardy employees took fewer sick days than less hardy employees. In contrast, Ferris et al's research (2005) indicated that a lack of resilience along with a negative perception of one's job increased biopsychosocial strain and cardiovascular disease risk. Like Maddi, Kobasa also theorized that *how* a person interprets a stressful event impacts his or her ability to cope with the hypothetical threat. When faced with stressful life events, hardy individuals proactively search for solutions; they believe in their ability to change their life and destiny (Hystad, et al., 2011; Jerabek & Muoio, 2013a) and actively look for ways to improve their circumstances, even if it is just to make them bearable. These authors theorize that this persevering attitude helps hardy individuals view negative events as less stressful, enables them to put the stressful situation in perspective, and helps them maintain a high level of motivation.

Emotional Intelligence

Emotions can impact decisions individuals make, the way they approach problems, and the manner in which they handle challenges and conflict (Mayer, Caruso, & Salovey, 2000), all of which can factor into the potential for success. Emotional intelligence (EQ) has also been shown to play a role in a person's ability to cope with and move on from trauma. Goleman (1995) suggested that when an individual experiences a traumatic event, their "emotional brain" creates emotional memories that are relived as a result of Posttraumatic Stress Disorder. By retraining the emotional brain to express a more appropriate emotional response to the trauma, they can gain mastery over the feelings, and overcome the trauma. Veterans with strong emotional intelligence, for example, are less likely to display PTSD symptoms and problems related to alcohol (Gaher et al., 2014).

EQ studies by Jerabek and Muoio (2014c) comparing subjects with high and low levels of life satisfaction revealed that satisfied individuals not only displayed higher emotional intelligence, they also outscored their discontent counterparts on 14 EQ competencies, including resilience, problem-solving, positive mindset, self-motivation, and coping ability. Individuals high in emotional intelligence also showed more determination and persistence when faced with major challenges, displayed greater self-motivation, more proactive behavior at work, and higher self-confidence (Jerabek & Muoio, 2012a). Other important facets of EQ, including emotional regulation and the ability to appraise emotions in self and others, have been linked to lower levels of physiological inflammation (Appleton, Buka, Loucks, Gilman, & Kubzansky, 2013) and burnout (Nizielski, Hallum, Schütz, & Lopes, 2013; Robinson, Moeller, Buchholz, Boyd, and Troop-Gordon, 2012). Programs to improve communication skills and social skills, also facets of emotional intelligence (Goleman, 1998), have shown promising results as an intervention strategy to reduce stress and burnout symptoms in medical practioners (Bar-Sela, Lulav-Grinwald, & Mitnik, 2012; Doulatabad, Mohamadhosaini, Shirazi, Hamid, & Mohebbi, 2015; Emold, Schneider, Meller, & Yagil, 2011; Goldsmith, Ferrell, Wittenberg-Lyles, & Ragan, 2013; Pereira-Lima & Loureiro, 2015; van Mol, Kompanje, Benoit, Bakker, & Nijkamp, 2015; Vitinius, et al., 2013).

This raises the question, and not for the first time, about the benefits of emotional intelligence training in the workplace, if not at the academic level. In a dissertation thesis by Colonel Ramona Fiorey (2010), she proposed a change to existing military protocols to incorporate emotional intelligence training in the development of combat unit leaders. The goal: To reduce the negative repercussions of PTSD. "Leaders set the environmental climate in their units," she writes. "This greatly influences the monitoring of Soldier wellness, acceptance of psychological stress as an expected consequence of combat, and encouragement to seek early treatment ..." (p. 10). Even outside a military framework, emotional intelligence training in the general population has the potential to reduce stress and improve not just the quality of personal and professional relationships, but also quality of life (Kotsou, Nelis, Grégoire, & Mikolajczak, 2011).

Resourcefulness

In 1928, in an effort to create a clear-cut, more apropos definition of what constituted intelligence, theorist Austin S. Edwards proposed that the ability to apply knowledge learned, and to be resourceful in challenging situations was a differentiating factor between the intelligent and the non-intelligent, or lesser and more advanced organisms. This ability to find ways to adapt and resolve problems, by using one's own faculties as well as outside sources of information, can also be applied to stress management and response to trauma.

After a traumatic job loss, the majority of older adults in Gabriel, Gray, and Goregaokar's study (2013), who had once enjoyed high-status positions, were compelled to set their job expectations much lower. While for many the loss of their job triggered a loss of identity, those who were resourceful, flexible, and opportunistic had a greater capacity to acclimate to their new circumstances. Research has also demonstrated that resourcefulness can be a protective factor in stressful situations in which the risk for burnout, mental health issues, and substance abuse is high, as in health professions (Sauter, Murphy, & Hurrell, 1990). For instance, rehabilitation providers who are highly resourceful are less likely than their counterparts to suffer from burnout (Clanton, Rude, & Taylor, 1992), while caregivers who display resourcefulness are less prone to work stress and, as an extension, depression (M.C. Chen, K. M. Chen, & Chu, 2015; Wang et al., 2015).

Job Control/Autonomy

The relationship between job control and occupational stress is not a straightforward one. Having control over one's job can reduce or increase stress, depending on the circumstances and the person. On the one hand, the need to be accountable for decisions and the result of assignments, be they a success or a failure, can result in a great deal of work strain, but research by Schmitt, Den Hartog, and Belschak (2015) reveals that this is less so for employees who are proactive and autonomous at work. Autonomy, along with a host of other protective factors, like social support and effective leadership, can reduce the strain that comes with taking initiative or taking on additional responsibilities (Bakker, Demerouti, & Euwema, 2005). In Theorell et al's meta-analytical study (2015), occupations in which employees experience a high degree of job strain (a combination of psychologically demanding work and little decision-making power), are associated with symptoms of depression.

In general, job control offers a sense of personal control. When employees are given the power to determine how their work is done, or are given a say in decisions that affect them directly, they are more satisfied with their job, feel less stressed, and are likely to be more committed to their work and to the company (Igic, Ryser, & Elfering, 2013; Rodwell & Fernando, 2015). Research from Igic et al (2013) also indicates that a lack of job control in office workers could increase the risk of "spinal shrinkage," a potential consequence of psychological stress in which back muscles become tense for a prolonged period of time, putting pressure on the disks. Similarly, a meta-analysis conducted by Eijckelhof et al (2013) found an association between work-related stressors (e.g. noise, time pressure, increased work pace) and neck, shoulder, and forearm pain. Yet while job control can act as a protective factor against stress under some circumstances, it could also prove to be risk factor. Meier, Semmer, Elfering, & Jacobshagen (2008) found a unique "loophole" in control theory: Employees with an internal locus of control were more likely to benefit from having autonomy at work because it aligns with their belief system: They perceive events in their environment (and their subsequent outcomes) as controllable. In contrast, despite having a degree of control over their work environment, employees with an *external* locus were more likely to experience emotional and physical symptoms of stress. The more demanding their job, the less *in control* they felt. The burden of responsibility that comes with autonomy and job control (making decisions independently, being accountable) appears to be too overwhelming for employees who already see themselves as being helpless to control their fate to begin with.

Assertiveness

In response to challenge and stress, research indicates that assertive individuals are more likely to thrive and have a more productive approach to coping (Tavakoli, Lumley, Hijazi, Slavin-Spenny, & Parris, 2009; Tomaka, et al., 1999). The ability to take action in response to stressful situations is important when seeking social support, a particularly useful coping mechanism when dealing with stress. Rather than trying to carry the burden of a problem alone, assertive people are more likely to seek help from others, which has the potential to improve both stress levels and depressive symptoms (Elliott & Gramling, 1990). Research by Tomaka et al (1999) has shown that the degree to which a person is assertive - women in particular - determines how they will react to stress. Submitted to an impromptu speech task, assertive women in Tomaka et al's study saw the challenge as less demanding and easier to adapt to than unassertive women. Not only were their speeches considered better than those of the unassertive group, they also experienced less stress about having to prepare a last-minute speech, less negative affect, and a greater sense of accomplishment once the task was completed.

Based on these authors' opinion, the ability to express one's needs and, perhaps more importantly, speaking up when those needs are being ignored or encroached upon, is crucial in stressful situations - whether it is a matter of approaching a supervisor when an environmental stressor (noise, lighting, workload) is affecting performance, or asserting oneself when the source of the stress is an actual person (e.g. a manager with a toxic leadership style).

ADDITIONAL INDIVIDUAL AND SOCIAL FACTORS THAT PROTECT AGAINST STRESS AND TRAUMA

Personality and attitude have been shown to impact a person's appraisal of and consequent response to occupational stress and trauma. However, research also proposes several other protective factors, on a personal and organizational level, that can reduce the impact of stress and trauma.

Spirituality and Mindfulness Practices

Although the services and dedication of emergency personnel and individuals in the helping professions are sorely needed and valued, their job regularly exposes them to direct or secondary trauma through the people they help (Dombo & Gray, 2013; Setti & Argentero, 2014). Several researchers have looked at the role of spiritual and mindfulness practices in helping this particularly vulnerable group deal with trauma-related physical and psychological symptoms. The practice of mindfulness, which involves consciously focusing one's attention on the present by tuning into feelings and bodily sensations (Brown & Ryan, 2003), can be particularly helpful to firefighters in order to cope with psychosomatic symptoms as a result of stress and trauma (Setti & Argentero, 2014). Optimists and people with strong religious or spiritual beliefs are also more likely to experience a positive outcome of their traumatic experience (Helgeson, Reynolds, & Tomich, 2006), whether it be a lesson learned, growth, stronger faith, or better personal resources to cope with hardship in the future. Research by Pack (2014) indicated that counselors who work with victims found it easier to overcome the effects of vicarious trauma through social support, spirituality, and humor as a coping mechanism. In Hardiman and Simmonds study (2013), the strength of a counselor's "existential well-being" (i.e. sense of purpose, ability to find meaning in what one does, acceptance of suffering and one's mortality as part of the human condition) reduced the potential for emotional exhaustion, as a result of dealing with severely traumatized patients. Brady, Guy, Poelstra, and Brokaw (1999) argued that while constant exposure to trauma on the part of therapists may often compel them to question their spirituality, their purpose, their work, and the goodness of humanity, it also has the potential to enhance it. Their research revealed that psychotherapists working with victims of abuse actually displayed a stronger sense of existential well-being and spirituality than those who rarely worked with them. For individuals in high-trauma fields, it appears that engaging in spiritual practices may enhance their ability to cope with, learn from, and overcome trauma (Dombo & Gray, 2013; Killian, 2008), especially if they are already spiritually or religiously inclined.

Coping Skills

Lazarus and his colleagues updated coping theory in the 1960's and proposed two well-established strategies in current coping research: 1) Problem-focused coping, which involves confronting and finding solutions to the problem that triggered the stress reaction, and 2) Emotion-focused coping, which revolves around finding ways to deal with the emotions that arise as a result of the stressor (Folkman & Lazarus, 1985). Although problem-focused methods of managing hardship are generally seen as adaptive, the appropriateness of this coping method varies by situation. Lazarus (1993) emphasized that in situations where a stressor cannot be changed (e.g. an incurable illness, death of a loved one), the use of problem-focused methods would be counterproductive, perhaps even resulting in further distress. In such cases, opting for emotion-focused coping strategies, like seeking emotional support from others, is the better option. Overall, however, people who consistently use problem or emotion-focused strategies when under stress or, as Lazarus (1993) put it, "adaptive" coping strategies, tend to be better equipped to handle emotionally taxing situations. In fact, research by Riolli and Savicki (2010) indicated that the moderate use of even just a few adaptive coping strategies was better for a person's well-being than frequent use of a multitude of maladaptive strategies.

People who have endured or continue to endure trauma as a part of their job greatly benefit from adaptive coping strategies. Powell, Cassematis, Benson, Smallbone, and Wortley's study (2014) of police officers who investigate cases of child exploitation revealed that they use a variety of adaptive strategies to cope with the often disturbing nature of their work, including physical exercise, temporary mental distraction, or by simply recognizing the importance of their role in keeping children safe. Aid workers deployed on humanitarian missions who not only found meaning in their work but who also adopted proactive coping techniques like social support and healthy lifestyle habits, experienced lower levels of stress surrounding their mission (Dolan, Adler, Thomas, & Castro, 2005; Eriksson et al., 2013). As it relates to job stress, both unemployed and employed participants in Mantler, Matejicek, Matheson, and Anisman's study (2005) benefited from the use of proactive, problem-focused coping techniques, despite the fact that they were dealing with different stressors.

The use of *maladaptive* strategies, particularly in high-stress and high-trauma fields, can be extremely counterproductive. In a study where employees were forced to work with an abusive supervisor, those who had a tendency to withdraw from conflict experienced more distress and a more difficult relationship with their direct supervisor (May, Wesche, Heinitz, & Kerschreiter, 2014; Nandkeolyar, Shaffer, Li, Ekkirala, & Bagger, 2014). Employees exposed to community violence who coped by using substances, disengaging emotionally from their work, or lashing out at others exacerbated their stress symptoms (Cox, Johnson, & Coyle, 2015). Ambulance workers who adopted avoidance coping strategies, such as disengagement, denial or engaging in self-blame were more likely to have negative posttraumatic outcomes when dealing with traumatic experiences (Kirby, Shakespeare-Finch, & Palk, 2011). A study by J. Shapiro, Astin, S. L. Shapiro, Robitshek, and D. H. Shapiro (2011) found that physicians who dealt with seemingly uncontrollable medical situations (e.g. patients who refuse to follow medical advice; the uncertainty of illness prognosis, progression, and treatment) by simply giving up, avoiding them, or in contrast, by becoming angry and forceful with others, were less capable of offering effective patient care, and more likely to experience higher levels of job stress. Evidently, in contrast to healthy coping strategies, the use of maladaptive coping strategies is detrimental to psychological health (Capielo, Delgado-Romero, & Stewart, 2015) and significantly exacerbates job stress.

Psychological Well-Being and Health

The detrimental effects of stress on psychological health are well-established. Burnout and depression are often inextricably tied together (Bianchi, Schonfeld, & Laurent, 2014), and the more stressful an employee perceives his or her job to be, the greater his/her likelihood of being diagnosed with a mental health issue (Szeto & Dobson, 2013). Although Sauter et al (1990) found that mental health problems were more common among people who had a low-status job and less income, education, and skills, they also discovered that individuals in medical professions, like nurses, doctors, and dentists were more likely to struggle with alcohol and drug abuse and mental disorders, and higher suicide rates. Nurses who were characterized by negative affect were more likely to experience secondary traumatic stress and burnout (Craigie, et al., 2016), while 911 operators with higher levels of distress and a lower sense of self-worth had a higher likelihood of experiencing symptoms of depression (Lilly & Pierce, 2013). This suggests, in the authors' opinion, that with the right mindset, the effects of stress can be reduced, and the outcome post-trauma can be improved. However, if people who are vulnerable to mental disorders are more likely to experience stress (and vice versa) it stands to reason that good mental health might act as a protective factor against stress and trauma.

Social Support at Work

Research has shown that support from colleagues and supervisors can reduce the negative effects of work demands (Bakker et al., 2005) and has also been associated with a reduced risk of physical health problems, such as diabetes (Toker, Shirom, Melamed, & Armon, 2012) and musculoskeletal disorders (Pekkarinen et al., 2013). In response to organizational trauma, social support from colleagues can prove valuable to recovery. Jones' study (2002) with bank employees exposed to a robbery revealed that they were particularly vulnerable to recurring posttraumatic stress symptoms as a result of having to carry on working in the place where the trauma occurred. Talking through their experience and feelings with other employees helped reduce their distress and enhanced their recovery. When Zacher, Jimmieson, and

Bordia (2014) uncovered a curvilinear relationship between well-being at work and age, they discovered that employees in their late 20s and early 40s (as opposed to younger and older employees) not only struggled with elements of time pressure, they also perceived themselves as having less social support at work. The sense of belonging that comes with social interactions and friendships in the workplace provides a source of motivation and sympathy during difficult days, which in turn can increase engagement, job satisfaction, and commitment, and reduce turnover intention (Riordan & Griffeth, 1995; Venkataramani, Labianca, & Grossier, 2013).

Employee Development

U. S. companies spend approximately 165 billion dollars on training and employee development (Association for Talent Development, 2013). Hiring an executive coach to mentor and develop top-level employees can run anywhere from $200 to $500 per hour (The Conference Board, 2008). Research may, however, offer sufficient justification for such an expense. Employees who are more amenable to coaching are resilient in the face of failure, willing to accept criticism and learn from their mistakes, and are driven and perseverant when confronted with challenges or obstacles in the achievement of their goals (Jerabek & Muoio, 2014b). Moreover, research from McGonagle, Beatty, and Joffe (2014) reveals that coaching can be particularly beneficial to employees who have been diagnosed with a chronic illness (but who are still capable of working). Those who participated in a coaching program to help them cope with their illness saw noticeable improvement in their work performance, their mental faculties, their level of resilience, and their self-esteem. Coaching also helped reduce exhaustion from burnout.

SOLUTIONS AND RECOMMENDATIONS For coping with Stress and Trauma

Stress is a common issue in almost all jobs, and can be the result of a combination of factors, making it difficult to control. Although it is possible in some cases to reduce or completely remove a particular stressor (e.g. a problematic team member, a demanding project), unexpected stressors like organizational trauma require a different approach. In these cases, the authors recommend that organizations take a pre-emptive approach to improve posttraumatic outcomes should trauma occur.

Using Pre-Employment and Personality Assessments

Personality and attitude assessments delve into the core of who a person is. Unlike tests that assess knowledge, there is no "right" or "wrong" as it relates to personality. As such, in order for an employee to thrive, his or her personality needs to be a good match to the position and the work environment. Moreover, while certain traits would be considered a disadvantage in some jobs (e.g. fierce competitiveness or ambition when working for a non-profit organization or in the mental health field), they could be an asset in others (e.g. sales). Personality assessment has been shown to be a good predictor of job performance (Barrick & Mount, 1991; Hebl, Madera, & Martinez, 2014; R. Hogan, J. Hogan, & Roberts, 1996).

A reliable and valid psychological assessment can cut costs and save time by increasing the size and quality of a candidate pool, and by allowing test administrators to assess a large number of people at the same time. Assessments can be designed to evaluate traits and skills that are relevant to the job and identify a person's strengths and areas that need development and training. They can also ascertain a good

Table 2. Pre-employment and personality assessments

Construct assessed	Assessment	Authors
Emotional Intelligence	Mayer-Salovey-Caruso Emotional Intelligence Test	John D. Mayer, Peter Salovey, and David R. Caruso
	The Emotional Quotient Inventory	Reuven Bar-On
	Emotional and Social Competence Inventory	Daniel Goleman, Richard Boyzatis, and Hay Group
	MEIQ – HR (Multidimensional Emotional Intelligence Quotient – Human Resources Version)	PsychTests AIM Inc.
Personality	NEO Personality Inventory-3 (Five Factor Model)	Paul T. Costa, Jr. and Robert R. McCrae
	HEXACO Personality Inventory-Revised (HEXACO-PI-R)	Mike Ashton and Kibeom Lee
	Clifton StrengthsFinder	Donald O. Clifton
	Sixteen Personality Factor Questionnaire (16PF)	Raymond B. Cattell, Maurice Tatsuoka, and Herbert Eber
	AMPM – Ab – R2 (Advanced Multidimensional Personality Matrix Abridged – 2nd Revision)	PsychTests AIM Inc.
	Values in Action Survey of Character Strengths	Christopher Peterson and Martin E. P. Seligman

fit with the organization's culture and values. Most importantly, they provide an objective, standardized evaluation of an individual that is free of interviewer bias. As it relates to organizational trauma, the use of pre-employment and personality assessments can help HR managers find people who can deal with change and pressure productively; people who possess traits like resilience and emotional intelligence and who are equipped with healthy coping strategies. This allows HR managers to immediately identify and filter out candidates who are not a right fit, in terms of skills, personality, and attitude. Table 2 provides a list of reliable and valid assessments that can help with this process.

Assessing Company-Wide Attitudes and Trends

In 2014-2015 in Great Britain, 35% of employees surveyed reported that they had suffered from stress-related health issues and 43% missed work as a result of excessive stress (Health and Safety Executive, 2015). Statistics Canada reported that in 2010, 1 in 4 workers stated in a survey that they are "highly stressed" (Crompton, 2014). In the United States, a Stress in America™ survey conducted between August 4 and 29, 2014, revealed that while stress levels are not as high as they used to be, they are still at an unhealthy level (American Psychological Association, 2015). Companies may only realize the degree to which stress is rampant in the organization after the fact - after a traumatic event or change, and after chronic stress has taken its toll and resulted in absenteeism, low morale and productivity, and health-related issues. In their aptly titled article "Work-related stress – it's time to act," Levi, Sauter, & Shimomitsu (1999) emphasized the importance of taking initiatives to counteract stress-related issues *before* they reach problematic levels:

Such stress should be prevented or remedied at the collective level. Such actions are the obligation of the employer, who should analyze the working situation, detect possible stressors, evaluate such risks, and take appropriate measures for prevention or remedy, in an attempt to adapt work to the worker (p. 394)

Assessing company-wide trends with monthly or quarterly surveys via a "stress checklist" (see Table 3) or other mental health assessments (see Table 4) such as the well-established and well-researched Maslach Burnout Inventory (Maslach et al., 1996) can be a simple and cost-effective way to evaluate employee stress levels, job satisfaction and level of engagement. This pre-emptive approach can alert management to disturbing trends and allow them to implement strategies to deal with stress, trauma-related problems or other unhealthy tendencies promptly. Many government health organizations are well aware of increases in job demands and other forms of occupational stress, but in addition to conducting investigations and offering recommendations on how to deal with the problem, more initiative must be taken to truly resolve the issue (Levi et al., 1999).

Recent research has shown that stress management intervention programs can have a positive impact on employee well-being, as demonstrated by Brough, Dollard, and Tuckey's editorial (2014) reviewing various stress management initiatives across the globe. For example, in Australia, employees who were actively involved in a program to reduce work stressors saw improvement in job design, training, and

Table 3. Stress-check quiz (PsychTests AIM Inc., 2016)

Make a checkmark under the answer option that best describes how you feel.	Not at all	Somewhat	Totally
1) I feel overwhelmed			
2) I feel overly emotional, like I want to cry or bite someone's head off.			
3) I am having difficulty focusing on my work or making decisions.			
4) I feel like people are demanding more of me than I can handle.			
5) I feel rushed, like I don't or won't have enough time to get everything done.			
6) I feel helpless, discouraged, or depressed.			
7) I just want to shut down and go home.			
8) I don't find any joy in my work.			
9) The quality of my work is declining.			
10) I can't stop worrying or thinking about my problems.			
11) I feel like at any moment, I am going to crack under the pressure.			
12) At the end of the day, I find it hard to relax and unwind.			
Scoring • Each response of "Totally" is worth 10 points. • Each response of "Somewhat" is worth 5 points. • Each response of "Not at all" is worth 0 points.			
Results • Score of 0 to 39: Current stress level is low. • Score of 40 to 80: Current stress level is moderate. • Score of 81 to 120: Current stress level is high.			

morale, among other job factors. Another Australian program aiming to develop leaders in police service in order to improve the psychological health of their team lead to better social support and improved work engagement and job satisfaction in employees. In Hong Kong, a stress intervention program for teachers and healthcare employees designed within the framework of positive psychology resulted in better recovery rates after burnout. Employees on sick leave in Lagerveld, Blonk, Brenninkmeijer, Wijngaards-de Meij, & Schaufeli's study (2012) who were administered Cognitive-Behavioral Therapy that focused specially on work behaviors, not only returned to work earlier than the control group, they were also less likely to have stress-related psychological issues over time.

Table 4. Recommended mental health assessments

Construct assessed	Assessment	Authors
Burnout	Maslach Burnout Inventory	Christina Maslach, Susan E. Jackson, Michael P. Leiter, Wilmar B. Schaufeli, and Richard L. Schwab
	Burnout Symptom Screener – For Non-Service Fields) BSS-NSF Burnout Symptom Screener – For Service Fields) BSS-SF	PsychTests AIM Inc.
Perfectionism	Perfectionism Scale	Greta Mazzetti, Wilmar B. Schaufeli, and Dina Guglielmi
	Multidimensional Perfectionism Cognitions Inventory (MPCI)	Joachim Stoeber, Osamu Kobori, and Yoshihiko Tanno
	Perfectionism Inventory (PI)	Robert W. Hill, Timothy J. Huelsman, Michael R. Furr, and Jason Kibler
	Perfectionism Test	PsychTests AIM Inc.
Type A/D Behavior	Type A Behavior Pattern Scales	Kathleen Bokenberger, Nancy L. Pedersen, Margaret Gatz, and Anna K. Dahl
	Type D Scale-14	Johan Denollet
	Type A Personality Profile (TAPP)	PsychTests AIM Inc.
Workaholism	Overwork Climate Scale	Greta Mazzetti, Wilmar B. Schaufeli, and Dina Guglielmi
	Work Addiction Risk Test (WART)	Bryan E. Robinson
Toxic Personality	Perceptions of Toxic Leadership Scale (PTLS)	Kathie L. Pelletier
	Counterproductive Work Attitude Scale	Peter Belmi, Rodolfo Cortes Barragan, Margaret A. Neale, and Geoffrey L. Cohen
	Bullying Behavior Scale	C. M. Brotheridge, Raymond T. Lee
	Short Dark Triad (SD3)	Daniel N. Jones and Delroy L. Paulhus
Optimism / Positive Mindset	Life Orientation Test – Revised (LOT-R)	Michael F. Scheier, Charles S. Carver, and Michael W. Bridges
	Beck Hopelessness Scale	Aaron T. Beck
Core Self-Evaluation	Core Self-Evaluations Questionnaire	Timothy A. Judge, Remus Illies, and Zhen Zhang
	General Core Self-Evaluations Scale – Revised	Nathan A. Bowling, Qiang Wang, Han Ying Tang, and Kellie D. Kennedy
	Self-Esteem Assessment (SEA)	PsychTests AIM Inc.
Resilience / Hardiness	Workplace Resilience Inventory (WRI)	Matthew J. W. McLarnon and Mitchell G. Rothstein
	The HardiSurveyIII-R	Salvatore R. Maddi and Deborah Khoshaba
	Psychological Hardiness Profile (PsyHP)	PsychTests AIM Inc.
Resourcefulness	Self-Control Schedule (SCS)	Michael Rosenbaum
Locus of Control, Job Control and Autonomy	Job Crafting Scale (JCS)	Maria Tims, Arnold B. Bakker, and Daantje, Derks
	Attributional Style Questionnaire	Martin E. P. Seligman
	Perceived Control Over Stressful Events Scale	Patricia Frazier, Nora Keenan, Samantha Anders, Sulani Perera, Sandra Shallcross, and Samuel Hintz
	Rotter's Locus of Control Scale	Julian B. Rotter
	Job External Control Measure	Jessica Vitak, Julia Crouse, and Robert LaRose

Implementing an Employee Well-being Program

It is estimated that psychological and physical health issues related to stress cost $300 billion in the US and €20 billion in the EU annually (European Agency for Safety and Health at Work, 2014). Employee Assistance Programs (EAPs) are offered by many companies with the goal of helping team members manage a number of personal issues (e.g. substance abuse, relationship problems, work-family conflict), and work performance problems (e.g. job stress, harassment). However, there is likely to be some reluctance on the part of organizations to implement an EAP, particularly as it relates to the financial cost and the potential for stigma for those who choose to seek help. Still, in light of the psychological and financial toll of organizational trauma, work stress and the ensuing stress-related problems (illness, absenteeism, loss in productivity), the benefits of EAPs outweigh the risks. Even implementing something as simple as a yoga or mindfulness training program has been shown to yield significant benefits, including better sleep hygiene and lower perceived stress levels. In addition, the cost per employee is fairly low and is justified by the savings brought about by reduction of stress-related problems. Although the fees for an EAP program can vary based on the degree of usage, the Employee Assistance Trade Association (2009) estimates the annual cost to be $12 to $40 per employee. Clavelle (2009) also outlined several initiatives (adopted by the U.S. Intelligence Community) that can allay fears of the potential professional repercussions of utilizing EAP services, including encouragement from management to make use of assistance programs and ensuring that EAP staff are well-informed about their legal and ethical responsibilities to those whom they counsel.

It is important to outline to employees that seeking the services of a counselor through an EAP program is strictly confidential, even in circumstances in which the recommendation comes from management as a result of sub-par job performance or behavioral issues. A third-party EAP program that provides a 24-hour crisis phone number can provide anonymity and easily accessible help should an employee require it. Ensuring confidentiality can also be achieved by taking the following precautions (Employee Assistance Trade Association, 2013):

- Providing confidentiality agreements that clearly outline what constitutes confidential information, and with whom information can be shared. Information cannot be shared without an employee's signed consent.
- Any records that are kept during the course of an employee's treatment should contain only the most pertinent information, like the issue being treated, the type of treatment provided, and dates of treatment. Sharing information in an employee file can only be done with the express written consent of the employee, and his or her identity must be protected.

Stress in the Workplace: Action Tips

Not all employees are comfortable speaking up to management after experiencing a trauma, let alone admitting that they are suffering ill-effects as a result. This is why it is important to not only create an atmosphere in which employees will be at ease sharing concerns, but also to train managers to recognize distress in their staff. Table 5 provides a detailed breakdown of stress and distress symptoms. Table 6 clarifies the differentiation between stress and burnout. Table 7 offers advice to managers on how to approach an employee in distress. Table 8 includes a tip-sheet designed to help employees improve their coping skills.

Table 5. Recognizing stress in others

The physiological, emotional, and cognitive symptoms of stress can translate into the following behaviors in employees:

Their demeanor changes:

- They become angry or agitated more easily
- They are restless and can't sit still or relax
- They show little interest in their appearance
- They develop nervous habits, like twitching, fidgeting, or biting their nails
- They look tired or are low on energy

Their performance changes:

- They are coming in late or calling in sick more often
- They are procrastinating or avoiding tasks
- They are "scatterbrained" and forget important deadlines, appointments, or tasks
- They are less productive than usual
- They are less motivated and driven than usual, and seem to be just going through the motions
- They become less engaged, and stop caring about their work
- They make up excuses as to why their work is not up to par
- They are making more mistakes or, in the case of manual labor, are prone to work accidents

They are acting out of character and treating people differently:

- They are more judgmental, critical, and tactless than before
- They have little patience with others and get into arguments more often
- They overreact to minor annoyances that normally wouldn't bother them
- They withdraw from other people
- They complain more

CONCLUSION

The occurrence of organizational trauma is not easy to anticipate, let alone the aftermath on employees and the organization as a whole. This can leave unprepared organizations scrambling to adapt. Any endeavor to assess employee well-being and most importantly, to implement an intervention initiative and, ideally, a prevention program, is one that requires the acknowledgement of the role that both the individual employee and the organization must play. This chapter has outlined the correlation between certain protective and problematic personal characteristics and stress and trauma but more to the point, the importance of developing personal resources to combat and circumvent the effects of stress and improve post-trauma recovery.

Table 6. Differentiating between stress and burnout

After a while, intense, chronic stress can lead to burnout. There is only so much the body can take; like a car that's constantly running at full speed, a body that is overwhelmed with constant stress hormones will eventually tire and give out. Even if the person has no intention of taking a rest or giving up, their body will.

Stress becomes burnout when:

- The employee feels physically drained and emotionally numb at the end of the day.
- The employee feels like he or she doesn't have the energy to get up in the morning, let alone go through a full day's work.
- The employee feels there is too much weight on his or her shoulders and he/she can't handle it anymore.
- The employee doesn't care about clients or the quality of his or her work anymore, and is no longer motivated to put an effort into tasks.
- The employee's tasks no longer offer a sense of fulfillment and he or she feel like his/her efforts don't make a difference.

Table 7. Dealing with distressed employees

If you notice signs that an employee is stressed, broach the subject diplomatically and with compassion. Try the following:

- State why you are concerned. The employee might be having performance issues, is snapping at people, or looks stressed, sad, or anxious.
- Remain calm and open-minded. Validate the employee's feelings. You don't have to agree with the person in order to empathize with his or her feelings.
- Identify the source of the stress. Ask the employee if there is a work-related or personal issue behind the problem.
- Assess *your* ability to deal with the issue and the appropriateness of your participation in the intervention.
- Make it clear that you are trying to help, and offer some options. The employee can choose to speak to you, talk to a local HR contact, or take advantage of the Employee Assistance Program (if you have one implemented).

An organization may not be able to limit the potential for trauma or all sources of stress, but they can provide the means to help employees cope, a step that has already been taken in some high-trauma fields (protective services, nursing). By nurturing certain traits, competencies, and attitudes, fostering a positive, supportive work environment, keeping an eye on unhealthy trends and providing the necessary psychological and occupational resources, companies can reduce the impact of trauma both on an individual and organizational level. With the implementation of stress management interventions through EAPs and other initiatives, organizations can help employees cultivate "immunizing" traits and

Table 8. Stress tip-sheet for employees

Reducing the physical impact of stress:

- **Exercise:** Not only does regular exercise promote good health, research also shows that it helps battle stress. Exercise releases tension as well as endorphins, the feel-good hormones. Try working out for a half hour or more at least 3 times a week. Choosing activities where you're outside in nature is also a naturally soothing experience.
- **Meditation or Yoga:** This relaxing activity allows you to detach yourself from all the clutter that is filling your mind. It helps you to gain perspective and accept the present situation. You can also try "walking meditation," which combines the benefits of meditation with a change of scenery, fresh air, and a little bit of exercise. It involves walking slowly but very deliberately while breathing deeply, so that every breath in, you take 3 or so steps, and for every breath out you take 3 or so steps. A number of free online resources also offer guided meditation, which is especially suitable for beginners.
- **Mindfulness Techniques:** Try playing this simple yet surprisingly effective game to calm your nerves and stay focused on the present moment. For each letter of the alphabet, try to come up with a word or short phrase that is synonymous with calmness. Example: "All is well," "Blissful," "Composed," "Docile," "Easygoing," "Fluid," "Gentle," etc. Soon enough, you'll be so focused on trying to come up with words that you won't be thinking about the situation that is stressing you out.
- **Visualization Techniques:** When athletes use visualization as part of their training, they imagine themselves engaging in their sport. Runners visualize themselves running a race from start to finish; hockey players visualize themselves scoring or in the case of goaltenders, stopping the puck; gymnasts visualize themselves going through each part of their routine. Essentially, they visualize themselves completing a goal successfully. If you have to deal with a situation or problem that is stressing you out, visualize yourself accomplishing it successfully. When you prime yourself for success, you are more likely to achieve it.
- **Deep breathing and progressive relaxation:** When you're anxious or under stress, you are more likely to take shallow rather than deep breaths. Deep breathing from your diaphragm is a simple yet very effective technique to bring your body back to homeostasis, physiologically and emotionally. And it can easily be done at work while sitting at your desk:
  - Sit comfortably and close your eyes.
  - Stay focused on the present. Clear your mind of any thoughts. If you find yourself being pulled away by a distracting thought, repeat "Be here now" to yourself and bring your attention back. Don't get frustrated if your thoughts keep intruding; just keep bringing your focus back.
  - Allow each part of your body to relax, starting from your head and working your way down to your toes.
  - Take deep breaths. Breathe in through your nose for a count of 5, then slowly exhale from your mouth for a count of 5.
  - Focus on the rise and fall of your diaphragm as you breathe in and out. Continue to do this for as long as you can remain focused.
  - When you want to stop, just allow your thoughts to re-enter and bring yourself back to reality.

skills, and provide a safe haven for them to seek help should they require it. Organizations must fully comprehend the duality of occupational trauma and stress, as their impact on the individual level (i.e. human cost) and at the macro level are significant and costly.

REFERENCES

Adams, R. E., Boscarino, J. A., & Figley, C. R. (2006). Compassion fatigue and psychological distress among social workers: A validation study. *The American Journal of Orthopsychiatry*, *76*(1), 103–108. doi:10.1037/0002-9432.76.1.103 PMID:16569133

Alarcon, G., Eschleman, K. J., & Bowling, N. A. (2009). Relationships between personality variables and burnout: A meta-analysis. *Work & Stress: An International Journal of Work, Health, & Organisations*, *23*(3), 244–263.

American Psychiatric Association. (2013). *Diagnostic and statistical manual of mental disorders* (5th ed.). Arlington, VA: American Psychiatric Publishing.

American Psychological Association. (2015). *Stress in America. Paying With Our Health.* Retrieved December 3, 2015, from https://www.apa.org/news/press/releases/stress/2014/stress-report.pdf

Andreassen, C. S. (2014). Workaholism: An overview and current status of the research. *Journal of Behavioral Addictions*, *3*(1), 1–11. doi:10.1556/JBA.2.2013.017 PMID:25215209

Appleton, A. A., Buka, S. L., Loucks, E. B., Gilman, S. E., & Kubzansky, L. D. (2013). Divergent associations of adaptive and maladaptive emotion regulation strategies with inflammation. *Health Psychology*, *32*(7), 748–756. doi:10.1037/a0030068 PMID:23815767

Association for Talent Development. (2013). *$164.2 Billion Spent on Training and Development by U.S. Companies.* Retrieved February 10, 2016, from https://www.td.org/Publications/Blogs/ATD-Blog/2013/12/ASTD-Releases-2013-State-of-the-Industry-Report

Bakker, A. B., Demerouti, E., & Burke, R. (2009). Workaholism and relationship quality: A spillover-crossover perspective. *Journal of Occupational Health Psychology*, *14*(1), 23–33. doi:10.1037/a0013290 PMID:19210044

Bakker, A. B., Demerouti, E., & Euwema, M. C. (2005). Job Resources Buffer the Impact of Job Demands on Burnout. *Journal of Occupational Health Psychology*, *10*(2), 170–180. doi:10.1037/1076-8998.10.2.170 PMID:15826226

Bakker, A. B., & Heuven, E. (2006). Emotional dissonance, burnout, and in-role performance among nurses and police officers. *International Journal of Stress Management*, *13*(4), 423–440. doi:10.1037/1072-5245.13.4.423

Bar-Sela, G., Lulav-Grinwald, D., & Mitnik, I. (2012). Balint group meetings for oncology residents as a tool to improve therapeutic communication skills and reduce burnout level. *Journal of Cancer Education*, *27*(4), 786–789. doi:10.1007/s13187-012-0407-3 PMID:22923383

Baron, R. A., Franklin, R. J., & Hmieleski, K. M. (2016). Why entrepreneurs often experience low, not high, levels of stress: The joint effects of selection and psychological capital. *Journal of Management*, *42*(3), 742–768. doi:10.1177/0149206313495411

Barrick, M. R., & Mount, M. K. (1991). The Big Five Personality Dimensions and Job Performance: A meta-analysis. *Personnel Psychology*, *44*(1), 1–26. doi:10.1111/j.1744-6570.1991.tb00688.x

Bianchi, R., Schonfeld, I. S., & Laurent, E. (2014). Is burnout a depressive disorder? A reexamination with special focus on atypical depression. *International Journal of Stress Management*, *21*(4), 307–324. doi:10.1037/a0037906

Blackie, L. E. R., Jayawickreme, E., Forgeard, M. J. C., & Jayawickreme, N. (2015). The protective function of personal growth initiative among a genocide-affected population in Rwanda. *Psychological Trauma: Theory, Research, Practice, and Policy*, *7*(4), 333–339. doi:10.1037/tra0000010 PMID:26147518

Blankstein, K. R., & Dunkley, D. M. (2002). Evaluative Concerns, Self-critical, and Personal Standards Perfectionism: A Structural Equation Modeling Strategy. In G. L. Flett & P. L. Hewitt (Eds.), *Perfectionism: Theory, Research, and Treatment* (pp. 285–315). Washington, DC: American Psychological Association. doi:10.1037/10458-012

Bluen, S. D., Barling, J., & Burns, W. (1990). Predicting sales performance, job satisfaction, and depression using the Achievement Strivings and Impatience/Irritability dimensions of Type A behavior. *The Journal of Applied Psychology*, *75*(2), 212–216. doi:10.1037/0021-9010.75.2.212

Bokenberger, K., Pedersen, N. L., Gatz, M., & Dahl, A. K. (2014). The Type A behavior pattern and cardiovascular disease as predictors of dementia. *Health Psychology*, *33*(12), 1593–1601. doi:10.1037/hea0000028 PMID:24364377

Bonebright, C. A., Clay, D. L., & Ankenmann, R. D. (2000). The relationship of workaholism with work–life conflict, life satisfaction, and purpose in life. *Journal of Counseling Psychology*, *47*(4), 469–477. doi:10.1037/0022-0167.47.4.469

Booth, J., Connelly, L., Lawrence, M., Chalmers, C., Joice, S., Becker, C., & Dougall, N. (2015). Evidence of perceived psychosocial stress as a risk factor for stroke in adults: A meta-analysis. *BMC Neurology*, *15*(233). doi:10.1186/s12883-015-0456-4 PMID:26563170

Boudrias, J. S., Desrumaux, P., Gaudreau, P., Nelson, K., Brunet, L., & Savoie, A. (2011). Modeling the experience of psychological health at work: The role of personal resources, social-organizational resources, and job demands. *International Journal of Stress Management*, *18*(4), 372–395. doi:10.1037/a0025353

Bovornusvakool, W., Vodanovich, S. J., Ariyabuddhiphongs, K., & Ngamake, S. T. (2012). Examining the antecedents and consequences of workaholism. *The Psychologist Manager Journal*, *15*(1), 56–70. doi:10.1080/10887156.2012.649994

Bowling, N. A., & Eschleman, K. J. (2010). Employee personality as a moderator of relationships between work stressors and counterproductive work behavior. *Journal of Occupational Health Psychology*, *15*(1), 91–103. doi:10.1037/a0017326 PMID:20063961

Brady, B. R., Vodanovich, S. J., & Rotunda, R. (2008). The impact of workaholism on work-family conflict, job satisfaction, and perception of leisure activities. *The Psychologist Manager Journal*, *11*(2), 241–263. doi:10.1080/10887150802371781

Brady, J. L., Guy, J. D., Poelstra, P. L., & Brokaw, B. F. (1999). Vicarious traumatization, spirituality, and the treatment of sexual abuse survivors: A national survey of women psychotherapists. *Professional Psychology, Research and Practice*, *30*(4), 386–393. doi:10.1037/0735-7028.30.4.386

Brandt, C. P., Zvolensky, M. J., Vujanovic, A. A., Gover, K. W., Hogan, J., Bakhshaie, J., & Gonzalez, A. (2015). The mediating role of anxiety sensitivity in the relation between avoidant coping and posttraumatic stress among trauma-exposed HIV+ individuals. *Psychological Trauma: Theory, Research, Practice, and Policy*, *7*(2), 146–153. doi:10.1037/a0037236 PMID:25793690

Britt, T. W., Adler, A. B., & Bartone, P. T. (2001). Deriving benefits from stressful events: The role of engagement in meaningful work and hardiness. *Journal of Occupational Health Psychology*, *6*(1), 53–63. doi:10.1037/1076-8998.6.1.53 PMID:11199257

Brough, P., Dollard, M. F., & Tuckey, M. R. (2014). Theory and methods to prevent and manage occupational stress: Innovations from around the globe. *International Journal of Stress Management*, *21*(1), 1–6. doi:10.1037/a0035903

Brown, J., Mulhern, G., & Joseph, S. (2005). Incident-related stressors, locus of control, and psychological distress among firefighters in Northern Ireland. *Journal of Traumatic Stress*, *15*(2), 191–168. PMID:12013068

Brown, K. W., & Ryan, R. M. (2003). The benefits of being present: Mindfulness and its role in psychological well-being. *Journal of Personality and Social Psychology*, *84*(4), 822–848. doi:10.1037/0022-3514.84.4.822 PMID:12703651

Brunborg, G. S. (2008). Core self-evaluations: A predictor variable for job stress. *European Psychologist*, *13*(2), 96–102. doi:10.1027/1016-9040.13.2.96

Byrne, A., Dionisi, A. M., Barling, J., Akers, A., Robertson, J., Lys, R., & Dupré, K. et al. (2014). The depleted leader: The influence of leaders diminished psychological resources on leadership behaviors. *The Leadership Quarterly*, *25*(2), 344–357. doi:10.1016/j.leaqua.2013.09.003

Capielo, C., Delgado-Romero, E. A., & Stewart, A. E. (2015). A focus on an emerging Latina/o population: The role of psychological acculturation, acculturative stress, and coping on depression symptoms among central Florida Puerto Ricans. *Journal of Latina/o Psychology (Savannah, Ga.)*, *3*(4), 209–223.

Chen, M. C., Chen, K. M., & Chu, T. P. (2015). Caregiver burden, health status, and learned resourcefulness of older caregivers. *Western Journal of Nursing Research*, *37*(6), 767–780. doi:10.1177/0193945914525280 PMID:24608748

Clanton, L. D., Rude, S. S., & Taylor, C. (1992). Learned resourcefulness as a moderator of burnout in a sample of rehabilitation providers. *Rehabilitation Psychology*, *37*(2), 131–140. doi:10.1037/h0079105

Clavelle, P. R. (2009). Consulting to the intelligence community: An employee assistance program model. *Consulting Psychology Journal: Practice and Research*, *61*(1), 14–24. doi:10.1037/a0015101

Cox, B. J., MacPherson, P. S. R., Enns, M. W., & McWilliams, L. A. (2004). Neuroticism and self-criticism associated with posttraumatic stress disorder in a nationally representative sample. *Behavior Therapy*, *42*(1), 105–114. doi:10.1016/S0005-7967(03)00105-0 PMID:14744527

Cox, C. B., Johnson, J., & Coyle, T. (2015). Coping styles moderate the relationship between exposure to community violence and work-related outcomes. *Journal of Occupational Health Psychology*, *20*(3), 348–358. doi:10.1037/a0038556 PMID:25528686

Craigie, M., Osseiran-Moisson, R., Hemsworth, D., Aoun, S., Francis, K., Brown, J., & Rees, C. et al. (2016). The influence of trait-negative affect and compassion satisfaction on compassion fatigue in Australian nurses. *Psychological Trauma: Theory, Research, Practice, and Policy*, *8*(1), 88–97. doi:10.1037/tra0000050 PMID:25961866

Crompton, S. (2014). *What's stressing the stressed? Main sources of stress among workers.* Retrieved December 2, 2015, from http://www.statcan.gc.ca/pub/11-008-x/2011002/article/11562-eng.htm

Day, A. L., & Jreige, S. (2002). Examining Type A behavior pattern to explain the relationship between job stressors and psychosocial outcomes. *Journal of Occupational Health Psychology*, *7*(1), 109–120. doi:10.1037/1076-8998.7.2.109 PMID:12003364

De Cuyper, N., Raeder, S., Van der Heijden, B. I. J. M., & Wittekind, A. (2012). Psychodynamics of normal and neurotic perfectionism. *Journal of Occupational Health Psychology*, *17*(2), 162–174. doi:10.1037/a0027348 PMID:22352292

De Hoogh, A. H. B., & Den Hartog, D. H. (2009). Neuroticism and locus of control as moderators of the relationships of charismatic and autocratic leadership with burnout. *The Journal of Applied Psychology*, *94*(4), 1058–1067. doi:10.1037/a0016253 PMID:19594244

Demerouti, E., Bakker, A. B., & Leiter, M. (2014). Burnout and job performance: The moderating role of selection, optimization, and compensation strategies. *Journal of Occupational Health Psychology*, *19*(1), 96–107. doi:10.1037/a0035062 PMID:24447224

Denollet, J. (2000). Type D personality a potential risk factor refined. *Journal of Psychosomatic Research*, *49*(4), 255–266. doi:10.1016/S0022-3999(00)00177-X PMID:11119782

Denollet, J. (2005). DS14: Standard assessment of negative affectivity, social inhibition, and Type D personality. *Psychosomatic Medicine*, *67*(1), 89–97. doi:10.1097/01.psy.0000149256.81953.49 PMID:15673629

Denollet, J. (2012). Type D or not Type D: That's the question. *The European Health Psychologist Bulletin of the European Health Psychology Society*, *14*(3), 58–63.

Denollet, J., Martens, E. J., Nyklíček, I., Conraads, V. M., & de Gelder, B. (2008). Clinical events in coronary patients who report low distress: Adverse effect of repressive coping. *Health Psychology*, *27*(3), 302–307. doi:10.1037/0278-6133.27.3.302 PMID:18624593

Dolan, C. A., Adler, A. B., Thomas, J. L., & Castro, C. A. (2005). Operations Tempo and Soldier Health: The Moderating Effect of Wellness Behavior. *Military Psychology*, *17*(3), 157–174. doi:10.1207/s15327876mp1703_3

Dombo, E. A., & Gray, C. (2013). Engaging spirituality in addressing vicarious trauma in clinical social workers: A self-care model. *Social Work & Christianity*, *40*(1), 89–104.

Doulatabad, S. N., Mohamadhosaini, S., Shirazi, H. R. G., & Mohebbi, Z. (2015). Nursing students in Iran identify the clinical environment stressors. *International Journal of Nursing Practice*, *21*(3), 297–302. doi:10.1111/ijn.12276 PMID:24840020

Dueweke, A. R., Hurtado, G., & Hovey, J. D. (2015). Protective psychosocial resources in the lives of Latina migrant farmworkers. *Journal of Rural Mental Health, 39*(3-4), 162–177. doi:10.1037/rmh0000038

Edwards, A. S. (1928). Intelligence as the capacity for variability or versatility of response. *Psychological Review, 35*(3), 198–210. doi:10.1037/h0073234

Eijckelhof, B. H., Huysmans, M. A., Bruno, G. J. L., Blatter, B. M., van Dieën, J. H., Dennerlein, J. T., & van der Beek, A. J. (2013). The effects of workplace stressors on muscle activity in the neck-shoulder and forearm muscles during computer work: A systematic review and meta-analysis. *European Journal of Applied Physiology, 113*(12), 2897–2912. doi:10.1007/s00421-013-2602-2 PMID:23584278

Elliott, T. R., & Gramling, S. E. (1990). Personal assertiveness and the effects of social support among college students. *Journal of Counseling Psychology, 37*(4), 427–436. doi:10.1037/0022-0167.37.4.427

Elliott, T. R., Shewchuk, R., Hagglund, K., Rybarczyk, B., & Harkins, S. (1996). Occupational Burnout, Tolerance for Stress, and Coping Among Nurses in Rehabilitation Units. *Rehabilitation Psychology, 41*(4), 267–284. doi:10.1037/0090-5550.41.4.267

Emold, C., Schneider, N., Meller, I., & Yagil, Y. (2011). Communication Skills, working environment and burnout among oncology nurses. *European Journal of Oncology Nursing, 15*(4), 358–363. doi:10.1016/j.ejon.2010.08.001 PMID:20863757

Employee Assistance Trade Association. (2009). *Selecting and Strengthening Employee Assistance Programs: A Purchaser's Guide.* Retrieved December 3, 2015 from https://www.easna.org/wp-content/uploads/2010/08/EASNA-PURCHSERS-GUIDE-TO-EAPs-FINAL-102209.pdf

Employee Assistance Trade Association. (2013). *Code of Ethics.* Retrieved February 11, 2016 from http://www.easna.org/research-and-best-practices/what-is-eap/code-of-ethics/

Eriksson, C. B., Lopes, C. B., Foy, D. W., Sabin, M., Ager, A., Snider, L., & Simon, W. et al. (2013). Predeployment mental health and trauma exposure of expatriate humanitarian aid workers: Risk and resilience factors. *Traumatology, 19*(1), 41–48. doi:10.1177/1534765612441978

Ervasti, J., Kivimäki, M., Dray-Spira, R., Head, J., Goldberg, M., Pentti, J., & Virtanen, M. et al. (2016). Psychosocial factors associated with work disability in men and women with diabetes: A pooled analysis of three occupational cohort studies. *Diabetic Medicine, 33*(2), 208–207. doi:10.1111/dme.12821 PMID:26036141

European Agency for Safety and Health at Work. (2014). *Calculating the costs of work-related stress and psychosocial risks – A literature review.* Retrieved December 3, 2015 from https://osha.europa.eu/en/tools-and-publications/publications/literature_reviews/calculating-the-cost-of-work-related-stress-and-psychosocial-risks

Farh, C. I. C., & Chen, Z. (2014). Beyond the individual victim: Multilevel consequences of abusive supervision in teams. *The Journal of Applied Psychology, 99*(6), 1074–1095. doi:10.1037/a0037636 PMID:25111251

Felix, E., Afifi, T., Kia-Keating, M., Brown, L., Afifi, W., & Reyes, G. (2015). Family functioning and posttraumatic growth among parents and youth following wildfire disasters. *The American Journal of Orthopsychiatry*, *85*(2), 191–200. doi:10.1037/ort0000054 PMID:25822609

Ferris, P. A., Sinclair, C., & Kline, T. J. (2005). It Takes Two to Tango: Personal and Organizational Resilience as Predictors of Strain and Cardiovascular Disease Risk in a Work Sample. *Journal of Occupational Health Psychology*, *10*(3), 225–238. doi:10.1037/1076-8998.10.3.225 PMID:16060726

Feuerhahn, N., Kühnel, J., & Kudielka, B. M. (2012). Interaction effects of effort-reward imbalance and overcommitment on emotional exhaustion and job performance. *International Journal of Stress Management*, *19*(2), 105–131. doi:10.1037/a0028338

Fida, R., Paciello, M., Tramontano, C., Barbaranelli, C., & Farnese, M. L. (2015). Yes I can: The protective role of personal self-efficacy in hindering counterproductive work behavior under stressful conditions. *Anxiety, Stress, and Coping*, *28*(5), 479–499. doi:10.1080/10615806.2014.969718 PMID:25265506

Figley, C. R. (1995). Systemic traumatization: Secondary traumatic stress disorder in family therapists. In R. H. Mikesell, D.-D. Lusterman, & S. H. McDaniel (Eds.), *Integrating family therapy: Handbook of family psychology and systems theory* (pp. 571–581). Washington, DC: American Psychological Association. doi:10.1037/10172-033

Fiorey, R. M. (2010). *Mitigating PTSD: Emotionally intelligent leaders* (Doctoral dissertation). Retrieved from PsycEXTRA. (Accession Order No. ADA526234)

Folkman, S., & Lazarus, R. S. (1985). If it changes it must be a process: Study of emotion and coping during three stages of a college examination. *Journal of Personality and Social Psychology*, *48*(1), 150–170. doi:10.1037/0022-3514.48.1.150 PMID:2980281

Ford, B. Q., Mauss, I. B., Troy, A. S., Smolen, A., & Hankin, B. (2014). Emotion regulation moderates the risk associated with the 5-HTT gene and stress in children. *Emotion (Washington, D.C.)*, *14*(5), 930–939. doi:10.1037/a0036835 PMID:24866526

Friedman, M. (1977). Type A behavior pattern: Some of its pathophysiological components. *Bulletin of the New York Academy of Medicine*, *53*(7), 593–604. PMID:196708

Friedman, M., & Rosenman, R. H. (1959). Association of Specific Overt Behavior Pattern with Blood and Cardiovascular Findings: Blood cholesterol level, blood clotting time, incidence of arcus senilis, and clinical coronary artery disease. *Journal of the American Medical Association*, *169*(12), 1286–1296. doi:10.1001/jama.1959.03000290012005 PMID:13630753

Frost, R. O., Heimberg, R. G., Holt, C. S., Mattia, J. I., & Neubauer, A. L. (1993). A comparison of two measures of perfectionism. *Personality and Individual Differences*, *14*(1), 119–126. doi:10.1016/0191-8869(93)90181-2

Frost, R. O., Marten, P., Lahart, C., & Rosenblate, R. (1990). The Dimensions of Perfectionism. *Cognitive Therapy and Research*, *14*(5), 449–468. doi:10.1007/BF01172967

Gabriel, Y., Gray, D. E., & Goregaokar, H. (2013). Job loss and its aftermath among managers and professionals: Wounded, fragmented and flexible. *Work, Employment and Society*, *27*(1), 56–72. doi:10.1177/0950017012460326

Gaher, R. M., Simons, J. S., Hahn, A. M., Hofman, N. L., Hansen, J., & Buchkoski, J. (2014). An experience sampling study of PTSD and alcohol-related problems. *Psychology of Addictive Behaviors*, *28*(4), 1013–1025. doi:10.1037/a0037257 PMID:25134021

Gallavan, D. B., & Newman, J. L. (2013). Predictors of burnout among correctional mental health professionals. *Psychological Services*, *10*(1), 115–122. doi:10.1037/a0031341 PMID:23421364

Gallus, J. A., Walsh, B. M., van Driel, M., Gouge, M. C., & Antolic, E. (2013). Intolerable cruelty: A multilevel examination of the impact of toxic leadership on U.S. military units and service members. *Military Psychology*, *25*(6), 588–601. doi:10.1037/mil0000022

Goldsmith, J., Ferrell, B., Wittenberg-Lyles, E., & Ragan, S. L. (2013). Palliative care communication in oncology nurses. *Clinical Journal of Oncology Nursing*, *17*(2), 163–167. doi:10.1188/13.CJON.163-167 PMID:23538251

Goleman, D. (1995). *Emotional intelligence: Why it can matter more than IQ*. New York: Bantam.

Goleman, D. (1998). *Working with Emotional Intelligence*. New York: Bantam.

Grant, S., & Langan-Fox, J. (2006). Occupational stress, coping and strain: The combined/interactive effect of the Big Five traits. *Personality and Individual Differences*, *41*(4), 719–732. doi:10.1016/j.paid.2006.03.008

Greiner, B. A., Krause, N., Ragland, D. R., & Fisher, J. M. (1998). Objective stress factors, accidents, and absenteeism in transit operators: A theoretical framework and empirical evidence. *Journal of Occupational Health Psychology*, *3*(2), 130–146. doi:10.1037/1076-8998.3.2.130 PMID:9585913

Hamachek, D. E. (1978). Psychodynamics of normal and neurotic perfectionism. *Psychology: A Journal of Human Behavior, 15*(1), 27-33.

Hansbrough, T. K., & Jones, G. E. (2014). Inside the minds of narcissists: How narcissistic leaders cognitive processes contribute to abusive supervision. *Zeitschrift fur Psychologie mit Zeitschrift fur Angewandte Psychologie*, *222*(4), 214–220. doi:10.1027/2151-2604/a000188

Hardiman, P., & Simmonds, J. G. (2013). Spiritual well-being, burnout and trauma in counselors and psychotherapists. *Mental Health, Religion & Culture*, *16*(10), 1044–1055. doi:10.1080/13674676.2012.732560

Harrison, R. L., & Westwood, M. J. (2009). Preventing vicarious traumatization of mental health therapists: Identifying protective practices. *Psychotherapy (Chicago, Ill.)*, *46*(2), 203–219. doi:10.1037/a0016081 PMID:22122619

Hartung, C. M., Canu, W. H., Cleveland, C. S., Lefler, E. K., Mignogna, M. J., Fedele, D. A., & Clapp, J. D. et al. (2013). Stimulant Medication Use in College Students: Comparison of Appropriate Users, Misusers, and Nonusers. *Psychology of Addictive Behaviors*, *27*(3), 832–840. doi:10.1037/a0033822 PMID:24059834

Havranek, M. M., Bolliger, B., Ross, S., Pryce, C. R., Quednow, B. B., & Seifritz, E. (2016). Uncontrollable and unpredictable stress interacts with subclinical depression and anxiety scores in determining anxiety response. *Stress: The International Journal of the Biology of Stress*, *19*(1), 53–62. doi:10.3109/10253890.2015.1117449 PMID:26669536

Health and Safety Executive. (2015). *Work related Stress, Anxiety and Depression Statistics in Great Britain 2015*. Retrieved December 2, 2015, from http://www.hse.gov.uk/statistics/causdis/stress/

Hebl, M. R., Madera, J. M., & Martinez, L. R. (2014). Personnel selection. In F. T. L. Leong, L. Comas-Díaz, G. C. Nagayama Hall, V. C. McLoyd, & J. E. Trimble (Eds.), APA handbook of multicultural psychology, Vol. 2: Applications and training. APA handbooks in psychology (pp. 253-264). Washington, DC: American Psychological Association. doi:10.1037/14187-015

Helgeson, V. S., Reynolds, K. A., & Tomich, P. L. (2006). A meta-analytic review of benefit finding and growth. *Journal of Consluting and Clinical Psychology, 74*(5), 797-816.

Hensel, J. M., Ruiz, C., Finney, C., & Dewa, C. S. (2015). Meta-analysis of risk factors for secondary traumatic stress in therapeutic work with trauma victims. *Journal of Traumatic Stress*, *28*(2), 83–91. doi:10.1002/jts.21998 PMID:25864503

Hogan, R., Hogan, J., & Roberts, B. W. (1996). Personality measurement and employment decisions: Questions and answers. *The American Psychologist*, *51*(5), 469–477. doi:10.1037/0003-066X.51.5.469

Hoobler, J. M., & Brass, D. J. (2006). Abusive supervision and family undermining as displaced aggression. *The Journal of Applied Psychology*, *91*(5), 1125–1133. doi:10.1037/0021-9010.91.5.1125 PMID:16953773

Hormann, S., & Vivian, P. (2005). Toward an understanding of traumatized organizations and how to intervene in them. *Traumatology*, *11*(3), 159–169. doi:10.1177/153476560501100302

Hystad, S. W., Eid, J., & Brevik, J. I. (2011). Effects of psychological hardiness, job demands, and job control on sickness absence: A prospective study. *Journal of Occupational Health Psychology*, *16*(3), 265–278. doi:10.1037/a0022904 PMID:21728435

Hyun, J. K., Kang, H. S., & Swanger, N. (2009). Burnout and engagement: A comparative analysis using the Big Five personality dimensions. *International Journal of Hospitality Management*, *28*(1), 96–104. doi:10.1016/j.ijhm.2008.06.001

Igic, I., Ryser, S., & Elfering, A. (2013). Does work stress make you shorter? An ambulatory field study of daily work stressors, job control, and spinal shrinkage. *Journal of Occupational Health Psychology*, *18*(4), 469–480. doi:10.1037/a0034256 PMID:24099165

Institute of Work, Health and Organizations. (2004). *Protecting Workers' Health (Series 3)*. Retrieved from http://www.who.int/occupational_health/publications/stress/en/

Institute of Work, Health and Organizations. (2008). *Towards the Development of a European Framework for Psychosocial Risk Management at the Workplace*. Retrieved from http://www.prima-ef.org/preliminary-report.html

Jamal, M., & Baba, V. V. (2003). Type A behavior, components, and outcomes: A study of Canadian employees. *International Journal of Stress Management, 10*(1), 39–50. doi:10.1037/1072-5245.10.1.39

Jerabek, I., & Muoio, D. (2011). *Type A Personality and Striving for Success*. Unpublished raw data.

Jerabek, I., & Muoio, D. (2012a). *Why emotional intelligence matters more than traditional intelligence*. Unpublished raw data.

Jerabek, I., & Muoio, D. (2013a). *The Hardy Personality*. Unpublished raw data.

Jerabek, I., & Muoio, D. (2013b). *The Power of a Positive Mindset*. Unpublished raw data.

Jerabek, I., & Muoio, D. (2013c). *The Pitfalls of Perfectionism*. Unpublished raw data.

Jerabek, I., & Muoio, D. (2013d). *Protective Factor of High Self-esteem*. Unpublished raw data.

Jerabek, I., & Muoio, D. (2014a). *Self-made martyr: Locus of control and victim mentality*. Unpublished raw data.

Jerabek, I., & Muoio, D. (2014b). *Goal Achievement and Coaching*. Unpublished raw data.

Jerabek, I., & Muoio, D. (2014c). *Emotional Intelligence and Life Satisfaction*. Unpublished raw data.

Jerabek, I., & Muoio, D. (2015a). *The Splendors and Miseries of Workaholics*. Unpublished raw data.

Jerabek, I., & Muoio, D. (2015b). *The Role of Management in Turnover*. Unpublished raw data.

Jonason, P. K., Slomski, S., & Partyka, J. (2012). The Dark Triad at work: How toxic employees get their way. *Personality and Individual Differences, 52*(3), 449–453. doi:10.1016/j.paid.2011.11.008

Jones, C. A. (2002). Victim Perspective of Bank Robbery Trauma and Recovery. *Traumatology, 8*(4), 191–204. doi:10.1177/153476560200800402

Kammeyer-Mueller, J. D., Judge, T. A., & Scott, B. A. (2009). The role of core self-evaluations in the coping process. *The Journal of Applied Psychology, 94*(1), 177–195. doi:10.1037/a0013214 PMID:19186903

Keller-Hansbrough, T., & Jones, G. E. (2014). Inside the minds of narcissists: How narcissistic leaders cognitive processes contribute to abusive supervision. *Zeitschrift fur Psychologie mit Zeitschrift fur Angewandte Psychologie, 222*(4), 214–220. doi:10.1027/2151-2604/a000188

Killian, K. D. (2008). Helping till it hurts? A multimethod study of compassion fatigue, burnout, and self-care in clinicians working with trauma survivors. *Traumatology, 14*(2), 32–44. doi:10.1177/1534765608319083

Kirby, R., Shakespeare-Finch, J., & Palk, G. (2011). Adaptive and maladaptive coping strategies predict post-trauma outcomes in ambulance personnel. *Traumatology, 17*(4), 25–34. doi:10.1177/1534765610395623

Kobasa, S. C. (1979). Stressful life events, personality, and health: An inquiry into hardiness. *Journal of Personality and Social Psychology, 37*(1), 1–11. doi:10.1037/0022-3514.37.1.1 PMID:458548

Kotsou, I., Nelis, D., Grégoire, J., & Mikolajczak, M. (2011). Emotional plasticity: Conditions and effects of improving emotional competence in adulthood. *The Journal of Applied Psychology, 96*(4), 827–839. doi:10.1037/a0023047 PMID:21443316

Kurian, A. G., Currier, J. M., Rojas-Flores, L., Herrera, S., & Foster, J. D. (2016). Meaning, Perceived Growth, and Posttraumatic Stress Among Teachers in El Salvador: Assessing the Impact of Daily Spiritual Experiences. *Psychology of Religion and Spirituality*, *8*(4), 289–297; Advance online publication. doi:10.1037/rel0000070

Lagerveld, S. E., Blonk, R. W. B., Brenninkmeijer, V., Wijngaards-de Meij, L., & Schaufeli, W. B. (2012). Work-focused treatment of common mental disorders and return to work: A comparative outcome study. *Journal of Occupational Health Psychology*, *17*(2), 220–234. doi:10.1037/a0027049 PMID:22308965

Lambert, J. E., Benight, C. C., Harrison, E., & Cieslak, R. (2012). The Firefighter Coping Self-Efficacy Scale: Measure development and validation. *Anxiety, Stress, and Coping*, *25*(1), 79–91. doi:10.1080/10615806.2011.567328 PMID:21476153

Larsen, J. L., Clauss-Ehlers, C. S., & Cosden, M. A. (2015). An exploration of army wives responses to spousal deployment: Stressors and protective factors. *Couple and Family Psychology: Research and Practice*, *4*(4), 212–228. doi:10.1037/cfp0000049

Lasebikan, V. O., & Oyetunde, M. O. (2012). Burnout among Nurses in a Nigerian General Hospital: Prevalance and Associated Factors. *ISRN Nursing, 2012*(1), 1-6.

Lazarus, R. S. (1993). Coping Theory and Research: Past, Present, and Future. *Psychosomatic Medicine*, *55*(3), 234–247. doi:10.1097/00006842-199305000-00002 PMID:8346332

Lemogne, C., Schuster, J. P., Levenstein, S., Melchior, M., Nabi, H., Ducimetière, P., & Consoli, S. M. et al. (2015). Hostility and the risk of peptic ulcer in the GAZEL cohort. *Health Psychology*, *34*(2), 181–185. doi:10.1037/hea0000129 PMID:25110845

Leon, S. C., Visscher, L., Sugimura, N., & Lakin, B. L. (2008). Person-job match among frontline staff working in residential treatment centers: The impact of personality and child psychopathology on burnout experiences. *The American Journal of Orthopsychiatry*, *78*(2), 240–248. doi:10.1037/a0013946 PMID:18954187

Levi, L., Sauter, S. L., & Shimomitsu, T. (1999). Work-related stress - its time to act. *Journal of Occupational Health Psychology*, *4*(4), 394–396. doi:10.1037/1076-8998.4.4.394 PMID:10526843

Li, J., Zhang, M., Loerbroks, A., Angerer, P., & Siegrist, J. (2014). Work stress and the risk of recurrent coronary heart disease events: A systematic review and meta-analysis. *International Journal of Occupational Medicine and Environmental Health*, *28*(1), 8–19. PMID:26159942

Li, Y., Wang, Z., Yang, L. Q., & Liu, S. (2016). The crossover of psychological distress from leaders to subordinates in teams: The role of abusive supervision, psychological capital, and team performance. *Journal of Occupational Health Psychology*, *21*(2), 142–153. doi:10.1037/a0039960 PMID:26652269

Lilly, M. M., & Pierce, H. (2013). PTSD and depressive symptoms in 911 telecommunicators: The role of peritraumatic distress and world assumptions in predicting risk. *Psychological Trauma: Theory, Research, Practice, and Policy*, *5*(2), 135–141. doi:10.1037/a0026850

Lindwall, M., Gerber, M., Jonsdottir, I. H., Börjesson, M., & Ahlborg, G. Jr. (2014). The relationships of change in physical activity with change in depression, anxiety, and burnout: A longitudinal study of Swedish healthcare workers. *Health Psychology*, *33*(11), 1309–1318. doi:10.1037/a0034402 PMID:24245832

Linton, D. K., & Power, J. L. (2013). The personality traits of workplace bullies are often shared by their victims: Is there a dark side to victims? *Personality and Individual Differences*, *54*(6), 738–743. doi:10.1016/j.paid.2012.11.026

Liu, C., Li, C., Fan, J., & Nauta, M. M. (2015). Workplace conflict and absence/lateness: The moderating effects of core self-evaluation in China and the United States. *International Journal of Stress Management*, *22*(3), 243–269. doi:10.1037/a0039163

Lo Bue, S., Taverniers, J., Mylle, J., & Euwema, M. (2013). Hardiness promotes work engagement, prevents burnout, and moderates their relationship. *Military Psychology*, *25*(2), 105–115. doi:10.1037/h0094952

López-Fuentes, I., & Calvete, E. (2015). Building resilience: A quantitative study of Spanish women who have suffered intimate partner violence. *The American Journal of Orthopsychiatry*, *85*(4), 339–351. doi:10.1037/ort0000070 PMID:26011382

Maddi, S. R. (2013). Personal hardiness as the basis for resilience. In S. R. Maddi (Ed.), *Hardiness: Turning stressful circumstances into resilient growth* (pp. 7–17). New York: Springer. doi:10.1007/978-94-007-5222-1_2

Mandel, T., Dunkley, D. M., & Moroz, M. (2015). Self-critical perfectionism and depressive and anxious symptoms over 4 years: The mediating role of daily stress reactivity. *Journal of Counseling Psychology*, *62*(4), 703–717. doi:10.1037/cou0000101 PMID:26191980

Mantler, J., Matejicek, A., Matheson, K., & Anisman, H. (2005). Coping With Employment Uncertainty: A Comparison of Employed and Unemployed Workers. *Journal of Occupational Health Psychology*, *10*(3), 200–209. doi:10.1037/1076-8998.10.3.200 PMID:16060724

Marais, A., & Stuart, A. D. (2005). The role of temperament in the development of post-traumatic stress disorder amongst journalists. *South African Journal of Psychology. Suid-Afrikaanse Tydskrif vir Sielkunde*, *35*(1), 89–105. doi:10.1177/008124630503500106

Marmar, C. R., Weiss, D. S., & Metzler, T. J. (1996). Characteristics of emergency services personnel related to peritraumatic dissociation during critical incident exposure. *The American Journal of Psychiatry*, *153*(7), 94–102. doi:10.1176/ajp.153.7.94 PMID:8659646

Maslach, C., Jackson, S. E., & Leiter, M. P. (1996). *The Maslach Burnout Inventory* (3rd ed.). Palo Alto, CA: Consulting Psychologists Press.

Mawritz, M. B., Dust, S. B., & Resick, C. J. (2014). Hostile climate, abusive supervision, and employee coping: Does conscientiousness matter? *The Journal of Applied Psychology*, *99*(4), 737–747. doi:10.1037/a0035863 PMID:24512026

May, D., Wesche, J. S., Heinitz, K., & Kerschreiter, R. (2014). Coping with destructive leadership: Putting forward an integrated theoretical framework for the interaction process between leaders and followers. *Zeitschrift fur Psychologie mit Zeitschrift fur Angewandte Psychologie, 222*(4), 203–213. doi:10.1027/2151-2604/a000187

Mayer, J. D., Caruso, D. R., & Salovey, P. (2000). Emotional intelligence meets traditional standards for an intelligence. *Intelligence, 27*(4), 267–298. doi:10.1016/S0160-2896(99)00016-1

Mazzetti, G., Schaufeli, W. B., & Guglielmi, D. (2014). Are workaholics born or made? Relations of workaholism with person characteristics and overwork climate. *Journal of Counseling Psychology, 62*(4), 703–717.

McGonagle, A. K., Beatty, J. E., & Joffe, R. (2014). Coaching for workers with chronic illness: Evaluating an intervention. *Journal of Occupational Health Psychology, 19*(3), 385–398. doi:10.1037/a0036601 PMID:24796227

Meier, L. L., Semmer, N. K., Elfering, A., & Jacobshagen, N. (2008). The double meaning of control: Three-way interactions between internal resources, job control, and stressors at work. *Journal of Occupational Health Psychology, 13*(3), 244–258. doi:10.1037/1076-8998.13.3.244 PMID:18572995

Mitchell, M. S., & Ambrose, M. L. (2007). Abusive supervision and workplace deviance and the moderating effects of negative reciprocity beliefs. *The Journal of Applied Psychology, 92*(4), 1159–1168. doi:10.1037/0021-9010.92.4.1159 PMID:17638473

Moate, R. M., Gnilka, P. B., West, E. M., & Bruns, K. L. (2016). Stress and burnout among counselor educators: Differences between adaptive perfectionists, maladaptive perfectionists, and nonperfectionists. *Journal of Counseling and Development, 94*(2), 161–171. doi:10.1002/jcad.12073

Moody, C., Fuks, N., Peláez, S., & Smith, N. G. (2015). Without this, I would for sure be already dead: A qualitative inquiry regarding suicide protective factors among trans adults. *Psychology of Sexual Orientation and Gender Diversity, 2*(3), 266–280. doi:10.1037/sgd0000130

Moore, S., Grunberg, L., & Greenberg, E. (2004). Repeated Downsizing Contact: The Effects of Similar and Dissimilar Layoff Experiences on Work and Well-Being Outcomes. *Journal of Occupational Health Psychology, 9*(3), 247–257. doi:10.1037/1076-8998.9.3.247 PMID:15279519

Müeller, A., Heiden, B., Herbig, B., Poppe, F., & Angerer, P. (2016). Improving Well-being at Work: A Randomized Controlled Intervention Based on Selection, Optimization, and Compensation. *Journal of Occupational Health Psychology, 21*(2), 169–181. doi:10.1037/a0039676 PMID:26322438

Nandkeolyar, A. K., Shaffer, J. A., Li, A., Ekkirala, S., & Bagger, J. (2014). Surviving an abusive supervisor: The joint roles of conscientiousness and coping strategies. *The Journal of Applied Psychology, 99*(1), 138–150. doi:10.1037/a0034262 PMID:23978107

National Institute for Occupational Safety and Health (NIOSH) – Center for Disease Control and Prevention. (1999). *Stress At Work* (Publication No. 99-101). Retrieved from http://www.cdc.gov/niosh/topics/stress/

Nixon, A. E., Mazzola, J. J., Bauer, J., Krueger, J. R., & Spector, P. E. (2011). Can work make you sick? A meta-analysis of the relationships between job stressors and physical symptoms. *Work & Stress: An International Journal of Work. Health & Organisations*, *25*(1), 1–22.

Nizielski, S., Hallum, S., Schütz, A., & Lopes, P. N. (2013). A note on emotion appraisal and burnout: The mediating role of antecedent-focused coping strategies. *Journal of Occupational Health Psychology*, *18*(3), 363–369. doi:10.1037/a0033043 PMID:23834450

Novak, R. J., & Davidson, S. (2013). Journalists reporting on hazardous events: Constructing protective factors within the professional role. *Traumatology*, *19*(4), 313–322. doi:10.1177/1534765613481854

OBoyle, E. H. Jr, Forsyth, D. R., Banks, G. C., & McDaniel, M. A. (2012). A meta-analysis of the Dark Triad and work behavior: A social exchange perspective. *The Journal of Applied Psychology*, *97*(3), 557–579. doi:10.1037/a0025679 PMID:22023075

OConnor, R. C., & OConnor, D. B. (2003). Predicting Hopeless and Psychological Distress: The Role of Perfectionism and Coping. *Journal of Counseling Psychology*, *50*(3), 362–372. doi:10.1037/0022-0167.50.3.362

Orth, U., & Wieland, E. (2006). Anger, hostility, and posttraumatic stress disorder in trauma-exposed adults: A meta-analysis. *Journal of Consulting and Clinical Psychology*, *74*(4), 698–706. doi:10.1037/0022-006X.74.4.698 PMID:16881777

Pack, M. (2014). Vicarious resilience: A multilayered model of stress and trauma. *Affilia: Journal of Women & Social Work*, *29*(1), 18–29. doi:10.1177/0886109913510088

Park, H. I., Beehr, T. A., Han, K., & Grebner, S. I. (2012). Demands-abilities fit and psychological strain: Moderating effects of personality. *International Journal of Stress Management*, *19*(1), 1–33. doi:10.1037/a0026852

Paton, D. (2005). Posttraumatic growth in protective services professionals: Individual, cognitive and organizational differences. *Traumatology*, *11*(4), 335–346. doi:10.1177/153476560501100411

Pearson, C. M., Andersson, L. A., & Porath, C. L. (2005). Workplace Incivility. In S. Fox & P. E. Spector (Eds.), *Counterproductive workplace behavior: Investigations of actors and targets* (pp. 256–309). Washington, DC: American Psychological Association. doi:10.1037/10893-008

Pekkarinen, L., Elovainio, M., Sinervo, T., Heponiemi, T., Aalto, A. M., Noro, A., & Finne-Soveri, H. (2013). Job demands and musculoskeletal symptoms among female geriatric nurses: The moderating role of psychosocial resources. *Journal of Occupational Health Psychology*, *18*(2), 211–219. doi:10.1037/a0031801 PMID:23458058

Pereira-Lima, K., & Loureiro, S. R. (2015). Burnout, anxiety, depression, and social skills in medical residents. *Psychology Health and Medicine*, *20*(3), 353–362. doi:10.1080/13548506.2014.936889 PMID:25030412

Peterson, C., & Seligman, M. E. P. (2004). *Character strengths and virtues: A handbook and classification.* American Psychological Association.

Powell, M., Cassematis, P., Benson, M., Smallbone, S., & Wortley, R. (2014). Police officers strategies for coping with the stress of investigating Internet child exploitation. *Traumatology: An International Journal*, *20*(1), 32–42. doi:10.1037/h0099378

Regehr, C., Hill, J., & Glancy, G. D. (2000). Individual predictors of traumatic reactions in firefighters. *The Journal of Nervous and Mental Disease*, *188*(6), 333–339. doi:10.1097/00005053-200006000-00003 PMID:10890341

Restubog, S. L. D., Scott, K. L., & Zagenczyk, T. J. (2011). When distress hits home: The role of contextual factors and psychological distress in predicting employees responses to abusive supervision. *The Journal of Applied Psychology*, *96*(4), 713–729. doi:10.1037/a0021593 PMID:21280933

Ribeiro, V. F., Filho, C. F., Valenti, V. E., Ferreira, M., de Abreu, L. C., de Carvalho, T. D., & Ferreira, C. et al. (2014). Prevalence of burnout syndrome in clinical nurses at a hospital of excellence. *International Archives of Medicine*, *7*(22), 1–14. PMID:24860618

Rice, K. G., & Van Arsdale, A. C. (2010). Perfectionism, perceived stress, drinking to cope, and alcohol-related problems among college students. *Journal of Counseling Psychology*, *57*(4), 439–450. doi:10.1037/a0020221

Riolli, L., & Savicki, V. (2003). Optimism and Coping as Moderators of the Relation Between Work Resources and Burnout in Information Service Workers. *International Journal of Stress Management*, *10*(3), 235–252. doi:10.1037/1072-5245.10.3.235

Riolli, L., & Savicki, V. (2010). Coping effectiveness and coping diversity under traumatic stress. *International Journal of Stress Management*, *17*(2), 97–113. doi:10.1037/a0018041

Riordan, C. M., & Griffeth, R. W. (1995). The opportunity for friendship in the workplace: An underexplored construct. *Journal of Business and Psychology*, *10*(2), 141–154. doi:10.1007/BF02249575

Robinson, M. D., Moeller, S. K., Buchholz, M. M., Boyd, R. L., & Troop-Gordon, W. (2012). The regulatory benefits of high levels of affect perception accuracy: A process analysis of reactions to stressors in daily life. *Emotion (Washington, D.C.)*, *12*(4), 785–795. doi:10.1037/a0029044 PMID:22775136

Rodwell, J. J., & Fernando, J. W. (2015). Improving employee outcomes among an often-neglected occupational group in healthcare: Stimulating work and job control keep hospital administrators happy. *International Journal of Stress Management*, *22*(4), 395–419. doi:10.1037/a0039358

Rzeszutek, M., Partyka, M., & Gołąb, A. (2015). Temperament traits, social support, and secondary traumatic stress disorder symptoms in a sample of trauma therapists. *Professional Psychology, Research and Practice*, *46*(4), 213–220. doi:10.1037/pro0000024

Sauter, S. L., Murphy, L. R., & Hurrell, J. J. (1990). Prevention of work-related psychological disorders: A national strategy proposed by the National Institute for Occupational Safety and Health (NIOSH). *The American Psychologist*, *45*(10), 1146–1158. doi:10.1037/0003-066X.45.10.1146 PMID:2252233

Schaufeli, W. B., Bakker, A. B., van der Heijden, F. M. M. A., & Prins, J. T. (2009). Workaholism among medical residents: It is the combination of working excessively and compulsively that counts. *International Journal of Stress Management*, *16*(4), 249–272. doi:10.1037/a0017537

Schmitt, A., Den Hartog, D. N., & Belschak, F. D. (2015). Is outcome responsibility at work emotionally exhausting? Investigating employee proactivity as a moderator. *Journal of Occupational Health Psychology*, *20*(4), 491–500. doi:10.1037/a0039011 PMID:25798719

Scott, K. S., Moore, K. S., & Miceli, P. (1997). An exploration of the meaning and consequences of workaholism. *Human Relations*, *50*(3), 287–314. doi:10.1177/001872679705000304

Seligman, M. E. P., & Csikszentmihalyi, M. (2000). Positive psychology: An introduction. *The American Psychologist*, *55*(1), 5–14. doi:10.1037/0003-066X.55.1.5 PMID:11392865

Setti, I., & Argentero, P. (2014). The role of mindfulness in protecting firefighters from psychosomatic malaise. *Traumatology: An International Journal*, *20*(2), 134–141. doi:10.1037/h0099398

Shapiro, J., Astin, J., Shapiro, S. L., Robitshek, D., & Shapiro, D. H. (2011). Coping with loss of control in the practice of medicine. *Families, Systems & Health*, *29*(1), 15–28. doi:10.1037/a0022921 PMID:21417521

Sherman, M. D., & Thelen, M. H. (1998). Distress and professional impairment among psychologists in clinical practice. *Professional Psychology, Research and Practice*, *29*(1), 79–85. doi:10.1037/0735-7028.29.1.79

Siu, O. L., Cooper, C. L., & Phillips, D. R. (2014). Intervention studies on enhancing work well-being, reducing burnout, and improving recovery experiences among Hong Kong health care workers and teachers. *International Journal of Stress Management*, *21*(1), 69–84. doi:10.1037/a0033291

Skogstad, A., Aasland, M. S., Nielsen, M. B., Hetland, J., Matthiesen, S. B., & Einarsen, S. (2014). The relative effects of constructive, laissez-faire, and tyrannical leadership on subordinate job satisfaction: Results from two prospective and representative studies. *Zeitschrift fur Psychologie mit Zeitschrift fur Angewandte Psychologie*, *222*(4), 221–232. doi:10.1027/2151-2604/a000189

Sliter, M., & Yuan, Z. (2015). Workout at work: Laboratory test of psychological and performance outcomes of active workstations. *Journal of Occupational Health Psychology*, *20*(2), 259–271. doi:10.1037/a0038175 PMID:25347682

Sliter, M. T., Pui, S. Y., Sliter, K. A., & Jex, S. M. (2011). The differential effects of interpersonal conflict from customer and coworkers: Trait anger as a moderator. *Journal of Occupational Health Psychology*, *16*(4), 424–440. doi:10.1037/a0023874 PMID:21688916

Spetch, A., Howland, A., & Lowman, R. L. (2011). EAP utilization patterns and employee absenteeism: Results of an empirical, 3-year longitudinal study in a national Canadian retail corporation. *Consulting Psychology Journal: Practice and Research*, *63*(2), 110–128. doi:10.1037/a0024690

Sprung, J. M., & Jex, S. M. (2012). Work locus of control as a moderator of the relationship between work stressors and counterproductive work behavior. *International Journal of Stress Management*, *19*(4), 272–291. doi:10.1037/a0030320

Statistic Brain Research Institute. (2015). *Stress Statistics*. Retrieved November 30, 2015, from http://www.statisticbrain.com/stress-statistics/

Stoneman, Z., & Jinnah, H. A. (2015). Stress on the farm: Father stress and its association with unsafe farm behaviors of youth. *Journal of Rural Mental Health, 39*(2), 73–80. doi:10.1037/rmh0000026

Swider, B. W., & Zimmerman, R. D. (2010). Born to burnout: A meta-analytic path model of personality, job burnout, and work outcomes. *Journal of Vocational Behavior, 76*(3), 487–506. doi:10.1016/j.jvb.2010.01.003

Szeto, A. C. H., & Dobson, K. S. (2013). Mental disorders and their association with perceived work stress: An investigation of the 2010 Canadian Community Health Survey. *Journal of Occupational Health Psychology, 18*(2), 191–197. doi:10.1037/a0031806 PMID:23458060

Tahnee, N., & Griffin, B. (2015). Here today but not gone tomorrow: Incivility affects after-work and next-day recovery. *Journal of Occupational Health Psychology, 20*(2), 218–225. doi:10.1037/a0038376 PMID:25402225

Tavakoli, S., Lumley, M. A., Hijazi, A. M., Slavin-Spenny, O. M., & Parris, G. P. (2009). Effects of assertiveness training and expressive writing on acculturative stress in international students. *Journal of Counseling Psychology, 56*(4), 590–596. doi:10.1037/a0016634 PMID:20357910

Tavousi, M. N. (2014). Job stress and affective well being: The mediating effects of core self-evaluations. *Journal of Iranian Psychologists, 10*(38), 103–122.

The Conference Board. (2008). *Executive Coaching Fee Survey.* Retrieved February 10, 2016, from https://www.conference-board.org/pdf_free/councils/TCBCP006.pdf

Theorell, T., Hammarström, A., Aronsson, G., Träskman Bendz, L., Grape, T., Hogstedt, C., & Hall, C. et al. (2015). A systematic review including meta-analysis of work environment and depressive symptoms. *BMC Public Health, 15*(1), 1–14. doi:10.1186/s12889-015-1954-4 PMID:26232123

Toker, S., Shirom, A., Melamed, S., & Armon, G. (2012). Work characteristics as predictors of diabetes incidence among apparently healthy employees. *Journal of Occupational Health Psychology, 17*(3), 259–267. doi:10.1037/a0028401 PMID:22746366

Tomaka, J., Palacios, R., Schneider, K. T., Colotla, M., Concha, J. B., & Herrald, M. M. (1999). Assertiveness predicts threat and challenge reactions to potential stress among women. *Journal of Personality and Social Psychology, 76*(6), 1008–1021. doi:10.1037/0022-3514.76.6.1008 PMID:10402683

Törnroos, M., Hintsanen, M., Hintsa, T., Jokela, M., Pulkki-Råback, L., Hutri-Kähönen, N., & Keltikangas-Järvinen, L. (2013). Associations between Five-Factor Model traits and perceived job strain: A population-based study. *Journal of Occupational Health Psychology, 18*(4), 492–500. doi:10.1037/a0033987 PMID:24099167

Tuxford, L. M., & Bradley, G. L. (2015). Emotional job demands and emotional exhaustion in teachers. *Educational Psychology, 35*(8), 1006–1024. doi:10.1080/01443410.2014.912260

Van Beek, I., Taris, T. W., & Schaufeli, W. B. (2011). Workaholic and work engaged employees: Dead ringers or worlds apart? *Journal of Occupational Health Psychology, 16*(4), 468–482. doi:10.1037/a0024392 PMID:21787085

Van der Tooren, M., & Rutte, C. (2016). Explaining Emotional Exhaustion and Work Engagement: The role of job demands-resources and Type D Personality. *International Journal of Stress Management*; Advanced online publication. doi:10.1037/a0039754

Van Doorn, R. A., & Hülsheger, U. R. (2015). What makes employees resilient to job demands? The role of core self-evaluations in the relationship between job demands and strain reactions. *European Journal of Work and Organizational Psychology*, *24*(1), 76–87. doi:10.1080/1359432X.2013.858700

Van Mol, M. M. C., Kompanje, E. J. O., Benoit, D. D., Bakker, J., & Nijkmap, M. D. (2015). The prevalence of compassion fatigue and burnout among healthcare professionals in intensive care units: A systematic review. *PLoS ONE*, *10*(8), e0136955. doi:10.1371/journal.pone.0136955 PMID:26322644

Venkataramani, V., Labianca, G., & Grossier, T. (2013). Positive and negative workplace relationships, social satisfaction, and organizational attachment. *The Journal of Applied Psychology*, *98*(6), 1028–1039. doi:10.1037/a0034090 PMID:23915428

Vinkers, C. H., Joëls, M., Milaneschi, Y., Kahn, R. S., Penninx, B. W. J. H., & Boks, M. P. M. (2014). Stress exposure across the life span cumulatively increases depression risk and is moderated by neuroticism. *Depression and Anxiety*, *31*(9), 737–745. doi:10.1002/da.22262 PMID:24753162

Vitinius, F., Sonntag, B., Barthel, Y., Brennfleck, B., Kuhnt, S., Werner, A., & Keller, M. et al. (2013). KoMPASS – Design, implementation, and experiences concerning a structured communication skills training for physicians dealing with oncology. *PPmP: Psychotherapie Psychosomatik Medizinische Psychologie*, *63*(12), 482–488. PMID:23677627

Wang, S. M., Lai, C. Y., Chang, Y. Y., Huang, C. Y., Zauszniewski, J. A., & Yu, C. Y. (2015). The relationships among work stress, resourcefulness, and depression level in psychiatric nurses. *Archives of Psychiatric Nursing*, *29*(1), 64–70. doi:10.1016/j.apnu.2014.10.002 PMID:25634877

Willsher, K. (2014, March 19). Orange France investigates second wave of suicides among staff. *The Guardian*. Retrieved from https://www.theguardian.com

Yablon, Y. B. (2015). Positive school climate as a resilience factor in armed conflict zones. *Psychology of Violence*, *5*(4), 393–401. doi:10.1037/a0039600

Zacher, H., Jimmieson, N. L., & Bordia, P. (2014). Time pressure and coworker support mediate the curvilinear relationship between age and occupational well-being. *Journal of Occupational Health Psychology*, *19*(4), 462–475. doi:10.1037/a0036995 PMID:24885685

Zandberg, L. J., Rosenfield, D., McLean, C. P., Powers, M. B., Asnaani, A., & Foa, E. B. (2016). Concurrent treatment of posttraumatic stress disorder and alcohol dependence: Predictors and moderators of outcome. *Journal of Consulting and Clinical Psychology*, *84*(1), 43–56. doi:10.1037/ccp0000052 PMID:26460570

Zellars, K. L., Tepper, B. J., & Duffy, M. K. (2002). Abusive supervision and subordinates organizational citizenship behavior. *The Journal of Applied Psychology*, *87*(6), 1068–1076. doi:10.1037/0021-9010.87.6.1068 PMID:12558214

Zhou, Z. E., Yan, Y., Che, X. X., & Meier, L. L. (2015). Effect of workplace incivility on end-of-work negative affect: Examining individual and organizational moderators in a daily diary study. *Journal of Occupational Health Psychology*, *20*(1), 117–130. doi:10.1037/a0038167 PMID:25347686

KEY TERMS AND DEFINITIONS

Burnout: A state of being in which an individual's stress level has become extreme, resulting in physical and emotional exhaustion, and an inability to do his or her job to the best of his/her ability.

Emotional Intelligence: Ability to identify with other people's emotions, regulate and make practical use one's own emotions, and orient oneself in emotional situations.

Mindfulness: The state of being consciously present in the moment, not thinking about the past or the future.

Personality: A cluster of traits that define one's character.

Stress: A state of being in which an individual's sense of physiological, psychological, emotional, and behavioral homeostasis has shifted.

Toxic Personality: A single trait or group of traits that an individual possesses that makes interaction with him or her unpleasant, uncomfortable, and psychologically or physically destructive.

Trauma: An event that happens to a person or that a person witnesses or hears about, that results in significant distress that negatively affect a person's emotional, psychological and/or physical well-being.

Well-Being: A sense of contentment and satisfaction with one's physical, emotional, and psychological health.

Chapter 5
Psychological Impacts of Downsizing Trauma

Jozef Simuth
City University of Seattle, USA

ABSTRACT

The chapter summarizes research studies as well as case studies from companies worldwide that show how organizational changes followed by downsizing create a traumatic experience for all organization members. The author's focus is on the psychological perspective on traumatic experience by all employees (victims and survivors) and managers whose task is to organize and implement changes in the organization. Based on the literature review, the chapter describes symptoms and psychological effects of organizational change trauma on individuals and the ways to minimize the traumatic effects. The author believes that outplacement and therapeutic approach are effective tools for overcoming the layoff trauma and also send positive signals to employees and to general public.

INTRODUCTION

This chapter is based on a thorough summary and critical analysis of relevant available research and non-research literature with the aim of summarizing the valid findings about the traumatic impacts of downsizing on members of organizations. The author used the traditional literature review of Google Scholar, Business Source Complete and Psych Web databases. The main research task was to find relevant research studies describing the traumatic impacts of downsizing on all organization members. Only studies with relevant research and reliable sources were selected for the chapter. The main goal of the selection process was to bring the reader up-to-date with available and reliable literature on the traumatic effects of organizational restructuring resulting in downsizing. This serves as the basis for practical proposals of procedures to minimize the traumatic effects of downsizing. The proposals are intended to be useful for practitioners such as managers, consultants, psychologists.

Trauma in organization is a consequence of a situation which causes traumatic experiences to individuals within the organization. Before the symptoms of organizational trauma and ways to cure or prevent them are discussed, the reasons that lead to such situations need to be revealed. Traumatic events

DOI: 10.4018/978-1-5225-2021-4.ch005

are quite often results of rational business decisions to optimize business efficiency. One of the frequent strategies is a restructuring the company that is accompanied by downsizing. As the definition states: downsizing is a deliberate organizational design which reduces the manpower and is planned to improve organizational performance. It is an approach that influences the workforce size, operational costs and work processes (Appelbaum, Patton, & Shapiro, 2003). Fisher & White (2000) say that like "rightsizing" and "reengineering", downsizing is a class of management tools for attaining desired change. The decision to downsize a company is among the toughest managerial decisions. It is a legitimate managerial approach to solving critical problems in an organization. Among the main reasons for downsizing are, for example, declining profits, increased pressure from competitors, a merger, the introduction of new technology, the desire to decrease levels of management, and getting rid of unproductive employees.

There are various approaches to this process. Companies follow a structured and planned procedure or they run this process in a haphazard manner, in which layoffs are happening without planning or prior warning. In this case, employees even do not realize what is happening or why. It is obvious that the first-case scenario has much less impact on the members of the organization. However, even in such a process there are negative impacts on the victims – people who are laid off as well as on survivors – people who remain in the company, including employees and managers. Unfortunately, there is no indication that downsizing in organizations, despite its negative effects, is declining.

On the contrary, there are several assumptions that tend to persist in managerial decision making. First, downsizing and decline are natural and even desirable phases of an organization´s development. There is a need to reduce waste and inefficiency that builds up in organizations. Downsizing then leads to efficiency, higher productivity and flexibility as "agility and leanness go together" (Cameron, 1994). Therefore, a common assumption is that organizational downsizing will spur business performance. The usual belief is that organizational restructuring accompanied by downsizing will provide a better alignment with the external competitive environment, improve financial indicators, and ultimately improve stock price performance (Lee & Teo, 2005). Trends like technological advances, environmental emergencies, and global economy are shaping the world. They affect corporate culture and the employees who support the culture. Environmental forces such as technology as well as political/regulatory, economic, and socio-cultural challenges, coupled with bad decision-making, a lack of resources and knowledge, and global competition, are all factors driving change. A good example could be the growth of mergers and acquisitions which result in restructuring frequently accompanied by downsizing. The internationalization of companies is on a growth pattern. This brings the necessity to restructure the companies where one of the necessities of such a process is the change in employee structure and/or downsizing. The number of multinational companies was around 17,000 in 1980; this figure had increased to more than 63,000 in 2000 and had increased further to 70,000 by 2004. At the same time, the number of subsidiaries of multinational companies in 2004 stood at approximately 690,000. Consequently the size and power of Multinational Corporations (MNCs) has grown steadily during recent decades through mergers and acquisitions: between 1990 and 1999 the number of global mergers increased from 9,000 to nearly 25,000. The number of transnational mergers during the same period increased from 2,500 to more than 7,000 in 1999 and over 8,000 in 2000 (Voss et al, 2007). Just in Europe in period from 2002 to 2010, more than 11 000 cases of restructuring were recorded by the European Restructuring Monitor, with the ratio of announced job losses/job creations standing at 1.8:1. In the period 2008-2010, that ratio increased to 2.5:1(Voss et al, 2007). A similar trend in US as well as globaly can be assumed.

MAIN FOCUS OF THE CHAPTER

Even though organizations keep coming up with new expressions for their organization restructuring methods, it is still the same old strategy for hitting financial targets. These methods have been called names like "restructuring," "termination," "permanent layoffs," "resource alignment," "downsizing," and "rightsizing" (Schiro & Baker, 2009). So it is obvious that organizational downsizing has become an important part of business life. Burke (2005) indicated that organizational restructuring and downsizing are a complex and difficult task quite often resulting in completely missing the original strategic goal. Interestingly, there is growing amount of literature suggesting that restructuring fails to reach the stated objectives (usually financial) about half the time" (p. 21). Downsizing is especially hazardous to learning organizations, which is another trend. Because a single individual has multiple relationships in such an organization, unselective, nonselective downsizing has the potential to cause significant damage to the learning and memory capacity of organizations. That damage is far greater than might be implied by a simple count of the number of employees laid off. One needs to consider the multiple relationships generated by one individual. It is obvious that restructuring that involves significant reductions in employees can inflict damage and create the loss of significant "chunks" of organizational memory. Such a loss damages ongoing processes and operations, loses current contacts, and may lead to missing business opportunities. Moreover, this process may increase stress and influence the well-being of employees (Amabile & Conti, 1999; Reynolds-Fisher & White, 2000). There are further disadvantages to downsizing regardless of the type of the organization. For example according to Schiro & Baker (2009), the drawbacks of downsizing could include:

1. Morale issues can surface,
2. Growth is stymied,
3. Productivity can go down, and
4. Employee health and behavioral problems can appear.

It is well-known that organizational change (including layoffs, downsizing, acquisitions, and mergers, but also job relocations, technological innovations at work, management restructuring, introduction of team-based work, and the like) may have adverse effects on employee well-being.

In this chapter, the author is going to look inside the organization during and after the downsizing process. The focus will be primarily at the individuals within an organization. The author strongly believes that organizational trauma is a concept referring to experience of trauma by the members of the organization.

After one looks inside the organization, s/he can see that the whole organism of the company is traumatized. Separate parts of the system undergo various symptoms of the trauma. The psychological impacts are most severe for victims of downsizing. However, the survivors - the remaining employees - also suffer from this traumatic situation. The survivor literature provides convincing evidence that organizational downsizing has negative consequences for remaining employees (e.g. Brockner, 1988, Makawatsakul & Kleiner 2003; Devine, et al., 2003). Similarly, evidence shows that organization restructuring can be a traumatic event for middle as well as for top managers.

Although organizational trauma originates at the individual level, the individual projects his or her trauma into the larger organizational system. The human body cannot differentiate between an emotional emergency and physical danger, trauma that results from experiences which represent psychological emergencies can trigger significant emotional trauma. Unresolved emotional trauma blocks people's capacity to be effective and ability to perform (DeKlerk, 2007).

The trauma is understood, according to American Psychiatric Association, as a

situation when the person has experienced and event that is perceived as a serious threat to his or her life or physical integrity; serious threat or harm to his or her children spouse, or other close relatives or friends; sudden destruction of his home or community; or seeing a friend or a close person experiencing such an traumatic event (American Psychiatric Association, 2013)

Quite often organizations approach downsizing with sheer ignorance of the emotional dimension of the organizational setting. They focus on articulating a vision, selling the positive rational aspects of the change. This is an important aspect; however, it doesn't help to overcome the emotional wounds that lead to experiencing of trauma. It is like telling a person who just lost a partner about new opportunities for new partners. This ignores the pain and harm that comes with a change.

The next part is a description of the symptoms and causes of downsizing trauma on organizational members. It is important to realize that these symptoms are natural and are part of the healing process; therefore, they need to be acknowledged. Feeling sadness caused by the downsizing should not be considered as a weakness but as a natural part of the organizational healing process. As DeKlerk (2007) states it is not the trauma itself that produces disorders such as post-traumatic stress disorder, but rather the failure to process trauma adequately that can lead to pathological behavior.

The Victim

Losing a job is very difficult life situation. Holmes & Rahe (1967) consider this as the 8th the most stressful situation in life. It does not only mean losing a job. With the job loss, a person loses social networks that one developed at the work place. The person also loses the daily routine and activities. Losing a job may quite often mean losing a hook to one identity related to the job performed. All this leads to numerous emotional and physical side effects of losing a job. The emotions that accompany a job loss actually resemble the Kubler-Ross grief cycle experienced when losing a loved one. Most people report feeling a rush of emotions, but the most typical are denial, shock, sadness, anxiety and anger.

The typical reactions to the layoff trauma based on the Kubler-Ross grief cycle consists of 5 stages:

- **Stage 1**: Denial — "I feel fine."; "This is not happening, not to me."

Denial is usually only a short-term defense mechanism. Denial can be conscious or unconscious denial to accept the reality and factual information. It is a defense mechanism and some people can become locked in this stage.

- **Stage 2**: Anger — "Why me? It's not fair!"; "How can this happen to me?"; '"Who is to blame?"

During this stage, the individual grasps that denial cannot continue. Person feels anger that is directed toward the organizations as such, to manager personally, other colleagues or even toward him/herself. The person is very difficult to deal with for misplaced feelings of rage and envy to the survivors of the downsizing.

- **Stage 3**: Depression — "I'm so sad, why bother with anything?"; "I invested so much time, energy and effort in the company and this is the result? So what's the point?"; "I miss my job, my daily routine so why to go on?"

During the fourth stage, the person begins to understand the certainty of job loss. Because of this, the individual may become silent; refuse social contact not only in the company but also with relatives and friends. Colleagues usually try to show sympathy or attempt to cheer the person up. However, this only allows the victim of downsizing to avoid looking into future opportunities. So it is not recommended to attempt to cheer up an individual who is in this stage. It is an important time for grieving that must be processed. For example, Greenglass, Burke, & Moore (2003) conducted a study with 488 unemployed hospital nurses whose units had closed as the result of restructuring. Their findings suggested that anger, cynicism, and emotional exhaustion operationalized distress, indicating the importance of studying patterns of negative reactions and their consequences for depression.

- **Stage 4**: Bargaining — "I'll do anything for a few more days, months at the company." This stage involves the hope that the individual can somehow postpone or delay the job termination decision. Psychologically, the individual is saying, "I understand I will lose the job, but if I could just do something to get another chance at least for some time..."
- **Stage 5**: Acceptance — "It's going to be okay."; "I can't fight it, I may as well accept it and move on."

In this last stage, individuals begin to come to terms with the fact of job loss. (Adapted from Kübler-Ross, E. (2005).

However, the person who just lost a job may suffer of further symptoms in various stages of the cycle. These symptoms can lead to trauma formation:

- **Anxiety**: Irrational anticipation that danger is about to happen, which causes unhealthy nervousness.
- **Apprehension**: A dreaded and fearful anticipation that something bad will happen to oneself in the organization
- **Cynicism**: Having distrust of action and intentions of other, accompanied by skepticism, suspicion and sarcasm.
- **Decreased Commitment**: Reduced willingness to take up time or energy to fulfil obligations.
- **Distrust** - Losing faith or confidence about organizations trustworthiness and honesty.
- **Emotional Numbness**: Apathy demonstrated by absence of emotional sensations and reactions such as feeling good, happy or sad.
- **Higher Absenteeism and Turnover**: Being more inclined to take sick leave or resign.
- **Lack of Focus**: Inability to concentrate on one's work.
- **Lack of Involvement**: Reluctance to immerse oneself in the work or organization.
- **Perception of Betrayal**: Feeling that organization was disloyal unfaithful and deceitful.
- **Rejection**:The experience of not being accepted, but rather pushed aside by the organization.
- **Sadness**: Intense feelings of unhappiness, grief and sorrow.
- **Uncertainty**:Being undecided and not knowing what to do or where to go with one's actions.
- **Withdrawal**: Removing oneself emotionally from organizational obligations and relations (DeKlerk, 2007).

Naturally, one cannot expect that every individual will undergo the same cycle. Especially in reaching acceptance, many victims will fight before reaching the acceptance stage. A lot depends on the strength of psychological contract between the individual and organization. A psychological contract is according to Armstrong (2014), a group of unwritten expectations that exists between the employee and the organization. It is a sum of beliefs that includes the expectations of organization from the employee as well as the employee´s expectations that the organization will meet. These expectations usually include fair and consistent treatment, job security, opportunity for using of the talent, and believing in the promise fulfilment from the management. To many of the victims and survivors downsizing may imply a one-sided renegotiation of the terms of the psychological contract between the organization and its employees, such that the latter receive less from this relationship and invest more in this relationship.

There are also other variables that influence the intensity of the traumatic effect of downsizing on the laid-off employees. Cascio (2002) published an Australian study with71 individuals who had accepted voluntary buyout packages (after 7 to 44 years of service, with an average of 25 years) and were contacted 2 to 7 years after leaving their firms. Almost 90 percent were married, and about half had dependent children. Surprisingly, 61 percent considered their health to be about the same, and 29 percent considered it to be "better" or "much better."

Cascio (2002) also cites research showing that one's financial situation is a major factor in how people perceive and respond to job loss, both physiologically and psychologically. Financial incentives, which often accompany voluntary severance agreements, may well moderate the ill effects of job loss. As one set of authors noted, "evidence is mounting that events viewed as uncontrollable and undesirable are more likely to be associated with psychological and physical distress." The findings of this study suggest that rather than considering themselves to be "victims," individuals who are offered voluntary buyouts may see themselves as having the opportunity to make choices about their future prospects that are not available to the "survivors." As a result, they experience less distress later on (Cascio, 2002). However, our empirical evidence from working in outplacement projects for companies after takeovers shows that job loss generates substantial distress above and beyond the loss of income.

Terminating employees, even when it seems an absolute and obvious necessity, is extremely unpleasant for all involved. At worst, the victim can quickly get into a severe state of anxiety, stress, self-doubt, and depression. Devine et al. (2003) reported that individuals are called downsizing victims because the literature documents job loss and the psychological and physical consequences. Devine et al. explained that "based on a small number of empirical investigations it is accepted that those who lose a job through no consequence of their own become anxious, depressed, unhappy, and dissatisfied with life in general" (2003, p. 110).

To summarize, the downsizing has obviously traumatic effects on employees who are victims of this process. Despite the fact that people react to this situation differently, losing a job is more than losing an income, it often means losing the social connections and quite often also losing the self fulfilment. The main symptoms that indicate the trauma formation in the downsizing victim are anxiety, distrust, and lack of focus and perception of betrayal. However, similar symptoms can also be noticed in people who remain in the organization.

The Survivor

It is a mistake to believe that downsizing would not affect the remaining employees. The employees who remain with the organization after downsizing are identified as "survivors".

These employees are responsible for new business performance and ultimately the success of implementation of restructuring (Baker, 2006). However, it is quite common that these people are taken somehow for granted are often neglected in the organization restructuring process. As Chipunza & Berry, (2010) show, survivors are the greater losers than those laid-off, because they have to bear cynicism, irritation and in general feel insecure. Research (e.g., Noronha & D'Cruz, 2005) indicated that in the new situation emerged after downsizing; an organizational success depends on the well-being of the survivors in terms of their attitudes, loyalty and eagerness to work. Travagione & Cross (2006), claim that survivors feel a reduction in affective commitment, performance and job satisfaction and increase in health problems. The research findings show that downsizing is negatively correlated with survivors" organizational commitment, work motivation and psychological well-being (Faheem et al, 2013). The survivors usually have feelings of guilt, stress, anxiety, distrust, fear, insecurity, and depression.

Thus, it is rather naïve to believe that downsizing employees may automatically boost profit. Cascio (2002) shows the data that clearly prove this point. Data from the S&P 500, 1982-2000, showed that profitability, as measured by the return on assets, does not necessarily follow downsizing, even as long as two years later. The 2001 Layoffs and Job Security Survey, conducted by the Society for Human Resources Management, reported that only 32 percent of respondents indicated that layoffs improved profits. Even massive staff cutbacks at firms such as Eastman Kodak, Apple Computer, and AT&T have not produced increased earnings years later. Furthermore, Cascio (2002) shows data indicating that downsizing employees does not improve productivity. The American Management Association surveyed 700 companies that had downsized in the 1990s. In 34 percent of the cases, productivity rose, but it fell in 30 percent of them. These results are consistent study of 250,000 manufacturing plants by the National Bureau of Economic Research which concluded that the productivity-enhancing role of employment downsizing has been exaggerated. While some plants did downsize and post healthy gains in productivity, even more (including many of the largest facilities) managed to raise output per worker while expanding employment. They contributed about as much to overall productivity increases in manufacturing as did the successful downsizes.

A review of the adverse effects of downsizing on the remaining employees: For example, Cascio (2002) found that 70 percent of senior managers who remained in downsized firms reported that morale and trust declined. Survivors felt overworked (54 percent), overwhelmed by workload (55 percent), having a lack time for reflection (59 percent), not having time to complete tasks (56 percent), and having the need to multitask too much (45percent). Similar situation is with the managers. Cascio (2002) cites a study that asked a simple question. How had the restructuring changed the nature of the managers' jobs? More than 30 percent of the managers said they now had more staff reporting to them,64 percent had increased responsibility, 69 percent had a wider range of duties,77 percent worked longer hours, 83 percent experienced increased stress, and 85percent had increased workload overall. Against all that, however, only 37 percent said they'd received a salary increase. Is it any surprise that 49 percent felt a decreased sense of commitment to one bank or that 64 percent experienced decreased job satisfaction? Asked about their level of commitment and their views on working for the bank, the managers offered 8 positive and 390 negative comments. There is other substantial evidence that organizational downsizing has negative consequences for remaining employees (Beylerian & Kleiner, 2003; Brockner, 1988; Devine, Reay, Stainton, & Collins-Nakai, 2003; Makawatsakul & Kleiner, 2003).

Vahtera et al. (1997) noted that some common changes in mental health surface during and after a downsizing or an organizational change:

Stress is “a dynamic condition in which an individual is confronted with an opportunity, demand, or resource related to what the individual desires and for which the outcome is perceived to be both uncertain and important” (Schuler, 1980. p. 189).

Self-esteem is the individuals’ perception of liking or disliking themselves and the degree to which they think they are worthy (Brockner, 1988).

Anxiety is common when stressed. It helps individuals to cope with various tense situations (National Institute of Mental Health [NIMH], n.d.a).

Depression is another issue that may surface in the wake of downsizing, according to the (NIMH, n.d.b)

Besides these negative symptoms, there are other accompanying symptoms that the victims may experience. According to Rice & Dreilinger (1991), survivors can experience:

- **Low Morale**: Survivors have the tendency to become depressed when their friends and associates leave the organization. They are not sure what to do to save their own jobs, so they maintain a low profile.
- **Decrease in Productivity**: Survivors usually face worker overload because there are fewer employees to get the work done. They can get confused about their specific roles or responsibilities, as well as what management thinks about them.
- **Distrust Management**: Survivors have seen that competence and performance no longer equate with continued employment. Their psychological contract with management has been unilateral, and they question management’s trustworthiness.
- **Excessive Caution**: Survivors usually discontinue risk taking and decision-making, and innovation. Shifting the responsibility or playing it safe is the new rules of conduct.

Similarly, Noer (1993) shows that the survivors typically experience a number of emotional reactions, including fear; sadness, depression, and quilt. Betrayal, distrust, and anger; unfairness; anxiety and stress are also among the emotional reactions as the social network gets damaged during downsizing. Comparable results were noted by Schiro et al (2009); the employees who had remained with the organization in transition exhibited a lack of confidence, distrust, high levels of stress, and doubts about their roles.

Review the most prevalent trauma symptoms of survivors such as stress, anxiety, depression and survivor syndrome in detail:

Faced with the possibility of a layoff, increased workload, the unknown, or an early retirement, many employees experience an increase in their stress level. Situations that results in stressful reactions affect virtually everyone in the organization. Stress can be good or bad, and by itself, it might not alter behavior. However, the cumulative effects of stress can reach an individual’s coping threshold (Gilmore, 1994). Beehr & Newman (1978) had defined stress as a situation which will force a person to deviate from normal functioning due to the change (i.e. disrupt or enhance) in his/her psychological and/or physiological condition, such that the person is forced to deviate from normal functioning.

Behavior can be changed at certain levels of stress given that a person’s ability to function is at risk. The continued threat of possible victimization as the causative agent in deteriorating psychological health induces such stress-related illnesses as heart disease and ulcers (Leana & Feldman, 1988). Stress also can reform a person’s character. It may change feelings, perceptions, social relations, well-being, behavior, and almost all social or individual reactions. It is very damaging, and if it is not controlled, it can lead to serious health consequences.

Torkelson & Muhonen (2003) conducted a study to determine how men and women cope with stress during a period of change and how there is a relationship between coping strategies to health. Ninety-eight health care administrators participated in the study. Denial explained a significant proportion of variance in the health problems. A study to systematically separate and combine the effects of organizational downsizing and work-related stress on a measure of health in survivors of layoffs included 240 men and 319 women ages 16 to 59 (Dragano, Verde, & Siegrist, 2005). The researchers found that although health associated with organizational downsizing was partly related to an increase in work-related stress, the findings showed an additional synergy produced by the combined exposure to both conditions.

Cheng et al (2005) administered a survey to 8,705 male and 5,986 female Taiwanese individuals' ages 25 to 65 years old from the general population. The findings reported that job insecurity was an important source of stress and that adverse psychosocial work conditions and poor health followed. Rose (2003) studied the results that the stress in work environment reduces the intention of employees to perform better in jobs with the increasing level of stress the employees thinking demoralize and his tendency to work well also decreases.

Similar to victims, survivors may show symptoms of anxiety. The feeling of anxiety can be infinite, and many emotions can be apparent during the period of uncertainty at a wok place. The emotional, psychological, physical, and job-related problems of the survivors influence them and their families. The emotional and psychological toll is similar to the grieving associated with death and the devastation of fighting in military conflicts. It means that survivors may go through a similar grieving cycle as the victim. Of course, not all necessarily undergo such emotional distress. But Greenglass & Burke (2000) surveying 1,363 nurses found that the heavier was the nurse's workload, the greater were their levels of emotional exhaustion, cynicism, depression, and anxiety. This means that not only the survivor's social network and relationships get damaged. The increased workload pressure combined with job insecurity causes further traumatic experience.

The enormous exposure to traumatic and stressful situations in which a person feels symptoms of anxiety can lead to developing a depression. There is a strong connection between depression and high-risk behaviors. Excessive drinking and drug abuse are all self-injurious behaviors that individuals may use to provide temporary relief from intense emotional pain. These behaviors are observable with victims as well as with the survivors. In any case such a behavior can have devastating effect on the future recovery from the trauma.

The emotional symptoms of depression potentially include the following:

- Withdrawal from socializing;
- Loss of interest in previously enjoyed activities;
- Constant irritability or sadness;
- Constant pessimism;
- Feelings of inadequacy and self-loathing (Sue, et al, 1990)

All these symptoms obviously influence the performance, attitude and behavior of the employees. This makes it very difficult to make these people to behave so they are in line with the company's strategic goals.

Moreover, the employees who remain on the job face some of the same symptoms as the survivors of catastrophic accidents. Survivor syndrome is a set of attitudes, feelings, and perceptions that occur in employees who remain in organizations following staff reductions (Devine, Reay, Stainton, & Collins-

Nakai, 2003). Doherty & Horsted (1995) described survivor syndrome as the expression of many different emotions by the surviving employees after a downsizing. The survivors may suffer of survivor syndrome as they feel the guilt of surviving (Conway, 1993). According to Gandolfi (2008) survivors feel positive inequity, anger, relief, and job insecurity. Research to date has suggested that the various reasons for survivor syndrome include a violation of the psychological contract, an act of unfairness by the management, or an organization's lack of vision (Schiro et al 2009).

The syndrome first affects morale and then influences the company's productivity at the bottom line. Moreover, downsizing has been linked to elevated levels of burnout, cortisol and testosterone, cardiovascular complaints, psychosomatic complaints, absenteeism, and sickness and absenteeism of the remaining employees (Kalimo et al, 2003).

Paterson & Cary (2002) surveyed 71 employees in an organization that had just downsized. Their analysis showed that procedural justice and change anxiety explained the effects of change management procedures on acceptance of downsizing. Although distributive justice did not have the predicted direct effect on employee morale, it did help to explain the effects of procedures on the employees' acceptance of change and morale by helping reduce anxiety about the change. By showing that procedural justice and change anxiety explained the effects of change management procedures on acceptance of downsizing. Although distributive justice did not have the predicted direct effect on employee morale, it did help to explain the effects of procedures on the employees' acceptance of change and morale by helping reduce anxiety about the change. The results disclosed that all employees needed specific leadership behaviors pertaining to inspiration, encouragement, and challenging the process to ensure that they achieved the best performance results. All in all their research clearly pointed out that the most severe and frequent job stress events occurred because of a lack of organizational support and stress due to inadequate pay and insufficient staff.

Manager

Managers are not immune to the traumatic effects of downsizing, either. A growing amount of literature draws attention to the fact that managers may also suffer from the traumatic effects of downsizing. This especially true for mid-level managers. As the previous discussion suggests, managers in firms undergoing significant restructuring are much more likely to feel that their psychological contracts have been violated and to respond with reduced loyalty and increased attempts to leave the organization.

Armstrong-Strassen, (2005) in her analyses of the empirical evidence, shows that management-level survivors are not immune from the adverse effects of downsizing. The author examined number of studies related to management reactions to downsizing in general without differentiating among the management levels.

Downs (1995) contended that middle managers have the hardest job of all during downsizing because they are usually the ones who are responsible for laying off employees and, at the same time, they worry about the permanence of their own jobs. The findings of the present study indicate that middle managers perceived a significantly greater sense of powerlessness over decisions affecting the future of their job than executive-level managers prior to the downsizing and that this sense of powerlessness increased significantly during the involuntary departure period.

Laying people off can be a traumatic situation for managers as this is an unusual and emotionally tense situation to which they are not trained and psychologically equipped. Quite often the managers make mistakes in communication that only contribute to damage of the company culture and social interactions. While top executives may make general, almost abstract, decisions about the total number of employees to be laid off, first- and second-line supervisors are often the ones who have to select and then personally inform the particular individuals to be let go. These front-line managers are caught in the middle, between their responsibilities to the organization and to their subordinates (DeWitt, Trevino, & Mollica, 2003). To dismiss employees who may be long-term colleagues or even friends is a traumatic situation that leaves a permanent label on managers who carry these decisions out. The layoffs cause so huge amount of much discomfort for managers that psychologists note a common tendency among them to try to minimize the discomfort by avoidance and distancing behaviors.

REDUCING THE TRAUMATIC EFFECTS

The most effective way to reduce the traumatic effects of downsizing is to avoid it. There are alternatives to layoffs such as:

- Internal transfers
- Restricting overtime
- Reducing the hours in a standard workweek
- Not renewing contracts for temporary and part-time workers
- Offering temporary leaves
- Job sharing
- Retraining
- Giving early retirement with preferential conditions
- Reducing executive salaries and incentive pay (Jackson et al, 2009).

However, downsizing can become an inevitable approach in situations when all the other alternatives are not realistic. To make this process the least painful for everyone, we need to look at methods which can minimize the traumatic effect of such processes. Some available methods that can assist the victims, survivors and managers follow.

The Victim

Companies usually offer the downsizing victims a severance package. Nevertheless, offering only monetary compensation is insufficient. One of the services that may help to reduce the traumatic effect of a lay off is outplacement. This service can be used as a part of the complex severance package.

Outplacement can be defined as a service that assists the management during the lay off period maintaining the positive image of the company. The service starts with the psychological assistance during the announcement of the decision of downsizing to group of employees or to individuals. The outplacement counselors are available to the victim of the lay off right from the moment of learning about the decision. This is important factor as the emotional support is needed from the first seconds to minimize later traumatic reactions which can be directed inward or outward toward the company, manager and other survivors. Our experience in coordinating large outplacement project clearly proves that this is the basis for the success of later intervention which is on more rational level. So, this psychological assistance should not be underestimated. It can contribute to shortening of the grieving cycle. In some cases, managers undergo training and coaching sessions aimed at managing emotionally distressing situations during the announcing of terminations. The timing of an outplacement offer is important because as time passes people tend to lose interest in such services after lay off.

After the psychological support during which the employees are accompanied through the emotional distress, the outplacement consultants start to work with the victims on analyzing their reemployment potential, auditing their experience, knowledge and skills and also proposing further training areas necessary for the labor market. The next stage of the outplacement process is the job search counselling and training starting with preparing resumes, and training in job search techniques. This is supposed to keep the victims activated and focused on future rather than dwelling in the past. Experience proves that people tend to look back and focus too much on what they did for the company and how unethical and unfair it was to lay them off. Therefore, these people need to be focusing on job search, training activities that concentrate their attention toward future. The important factor is to maintain the momentum in job search. Quite often employees who are left without this assistance tend to lose the work habits and routines. The critical period seemed to be around 6 months. After this time people struggle to be motivated in their job search.

The main goal of outplacement is reemployment of the laid off employee. We can call this service also a last benefit for the employee. It can actually help to maintain the image of the company, trust and reputation in the eyes employees as well as the public. The research of Messenger (2003) confirms that the outplacement improves the image of the company inward and outward as well. It reduces the level of managerial stress and improves the morale of remaining employees. The company is showing that it cares for employees and will not ignore them in the future if similar situation happens.

One of the conditions of successful outplacement is selection of outplacement experts. The external experts should be preferred. Victims accept the assistance from a different person or entity preferably to the one who actually caused the situation and laid them off. The main criteria for outplacement expert should be:

- Reputation and references
- The communication strategies and professionalism
- The professional background of outplacement consultants
- Flexibility in delivering the assistance methods

De Vitte et al. (2005) state the emotional support; education and individual coaching are the most important methods. Psychological assistance is necessary to minimize the reactions such as anger, denial and apathy. In some cases, it is necessary to include family member in the process of trauma healing after lay off.

Next, very important procedures lead to identification of skills, abilities and needs for further education and training. The career counselling should consist of resume writing, active job search, successful interview, establishing professional contacts, entrepreneurial training, etc.

After the identification of educational needs, the outplacement professionals should recommend the educational institutions the victim should attend (any fees related to this should be part of the severance compensation).

Above all complex entrepreneurial training seems to be the most effective way in overcoming the unemployment especially in regions with high unemployment.

The recent trends indicate that the use of outplacement as a part of severance package is widely used. As revealed in the 2015 study by Lee Hecht Harrison (LHH) (Phuong, 2015) surveying nearly 400 employers worldwide, the majority of respondents stated that their organization offers outplacement, either full or partial, to all levels of employee. The study confirms our recommendations stating that 90% of respondents prefer human interaction in outplacement programs. They indicated that in-person meetings, seminars and coaching are deemed to be the most important elements of a successful outplacement program.

Despite of this, there is obvious trend to use information and communication technology (ICT) as main and/or supporting tool in outplacement programs. Using platforms that can support a variety of self-development options such as e-learning courses, virtual interview center, personality assessments along with consolidated job-search database seem to be very effective and efficient tools. The LHH study showed that more than 50 per cent of respondents praised such platforms. However, only 2 per cent of respondents prefer a technology-based outplacement program. These findings may seem a little confusing. The main reason for this discrepancy is the difference between using a blended approach with personal face to face contact and purely online outplacement program. A research study (Simuth, Sarmany-Schuller, 2010) clearly indicates that the lack of direct social interactions is one of the main barriers of using ICT as the only tool for communication in adult educational settings. Moreover, offering online help to traumatized employee is completely missing the point of what outplacement program is supposed to achieve. Based on this, the main recommendation is to use blended learning program with in-person interventions with a support of the ICT tools.

It is clear that the victims of downsizing go through a traumatic experience and depending on individual need to get through emotional healing process. The outplacement service can help to minimize the impact of the downsizing process.

The Survivors

As with the victims of downsizing, there are several ways to minimize the traumatic impacts of downsizing on surviving employees and managers. The main actors in the trauma reduction process for employees are managers themselves.

Therefore let´s, look at what would help managers. According to Ramsey (2004), following simple recommendations could minimize the negative impact of downsizing on managers:

- Make a big deal out of full disclosure.
- Radiate confidence and a "we'll get through this" attitude.
- Show true care about former co-workers who have been let go and about those still on the job.
- Remind employees that the mission of the organization is still the mission.
- Rally the staff or crew by emphasizing the best insurance against further layoffs is to make them more productive, more profitable and more indispensable to the overall organization.
- Provide additional training and growth opportunities for employees.
- Do whatever possible to lighten the load of your downsized workforce that is overstretched and over-stressed.
- Make a case to the front office for retaining all remaining employees.
- Take care of yourself so you have the resilience and energy to offer others all the support they need during tough times (Schiro, 2005).

A manager needs to create an environment where the emotional wounds could be open in creative non-threatening way to make a team of survivors up and running in the direction of new strategic goals. This can, however; be done by trained manager or by a trained specialist or by psychologist.

De klerk & Sasol (2007) propose a therapeutic model for healing emotional trauma caused by downsizing. This model consists of four interconnected steps.

1. Acknowledging the existence of trauma;
2. Providing a safe place to work through the trauma;
3. Symbolizing the trauma;
4. Allowing emotions and dealing with emotions.

First the organization needs to accept the existence of organizational trauma. Managers need to take action against the as Iancovini (1993 in De Klerk, 2007) described "the unconscious conspiracy of silence about the feelings of sadness, anger, denial and fear that employees experience" (p.66). As with physical wound, De Klerk (2007) claim, the wounds of emotional trauma should be open, the problem correctly addressed and emotions must be symbolized and dealt with before employees can progress to acceptance of the situation and it consequences. This is the role of managers and leaders. They not only have to allow the organizational members to deal openly with the traumatic emotions, they need to deal with their own trauma openly. Among the most powerful strategies for handling this are sensitivity to the traumatic, effects of change, compassion, emphatic listening skills, introspection to understand own emotions and ability to show and talk about their own traumatic symptoms.

The second step lies in providing a safe place where even the most irrational thoughts and emotions can be expressed openly. Many of the trauma victims do not understand the symptoms and get confused by their feeling and thoughts. They quite often blame themselves and feel that there is something wrong with them. The symptoms of trauma are very often associated with weakness; people tend to be ashamed of their thoughts and feeling and try to hide them. This can lead to traumatic residue that may last for years in some individuals. Therefore, De Klerk (2007), stress that such an environment needs to allow the traumatized people to express their fears, anger, and helplessness without being judged, moralized.

The third step is based on a therapeutic approach using the combination of expressive art therapy (e.g. drawing, painting, writing etc.) with narrative therapy (especially story telling). This approach is particularly important as adults tend to suppress their traumatic feelings and thoughts into their unconsciousness. Then, it is very difficult to express the true thought and emotions in front of a group of colleagues. As De Klerk (2007) clearly demonstrate, developing one's story can bring order to the emotional chaos of recollections and emotions. Putting the negative experience in words and /or images allows the victims of trauma to stop the inhibition process of their negative thoughts and feelings. They also describe how important it could be to use metaphors in this process. It eases discussing difficult emotions. This kind of approaches offer an environment providing emotional safety that makes the trauma visible explicitly and clearly.

The last step refers to the grieving process during processing the trauma. Grieving is an emotionally heathy process that takes some time. Therefore, to fully overcome the trauma, a lot of patience is necessary. Hasty resolution of grieving usually leads to anger and resentment. The trauma victim needs to go through the whole grieving cycle as described previously.

A very important factor in this healing process is the use of humor. De Klerk (2007), stress that humor is a great way to deal with trauma. Humor and laughter can be reflecting and distancing from the grief at the same time, allowing the victim to recover and enjoy current life more fully. It is generally believed that laughter can be therapeutic. As the writer Leo Rosten says "Humor is the affectionate communication of insight."

Of course, we are aware that this approach is psychological and not every manager or leader would be able to pursue these steps. However, it is important to realize that the survivors of the downsizing process are the victims as well. They undergo emotional upheaval that quite often leads to traumatic experience with all the symptoms and consequences. Trauma in organization is a psychological phenomenon and needs to be treated by psychological methods.

Another way to look at the traumatic experience is from the perspective of psychological contract between the organization and the employee. During the restructuring and downsizing process the psychological contract can be broken and therefore it needs to be renegotiated. From this perspective managers must communicate clearly with employees about the scope of the changed psychological contract and the time frame within which violations will be remedied. One of the conditions for this is carefully and honestly explain any external forces which cause organizations to "change the deal" to all survivors. After the change, managers should avoid micro-managing employees during, otherwise employees would get the feeling of decreased autonomy and responsibility which would contribute to their feelings of hopelessness.

CONCLUSION

This chapter has shown the trend of using organizational restructuring accompanied by downsizing as a common strategic tool. Whatever the expectations of this process are, it always entails some degree of organizational trauma. The author indicated that organizational trauma is actually a trauma for specific individuals who happen to be members of the organization. A body of research was provided clearly demonstrating that this process can be very traumatic and have serious consequences for individuals. The people who are affected the most are those who lose their jobs. As a consequence, they suffer displaying clear trauma symptoms such as anxiety, decreased commitment, and emotional numbness, lack of focus, sadness, uncertainty and withdrawal. One way to minimize the impact is to offer to these victims of downsizing the benefit of outplacement services. We have shown that outplacement can be an effective method if it follows certain principles. The core principle is to maintain a personal contact of the outplacement consultant with the victim right from the moment of learning about the job loss until reemployment. This principle needs to be stressed nowadays when there is a trend of using ICT in supporting victims. The author recommended a blended approach including regular personal contact with a support of ICT in some aspects of learning and job search.

The author has also provided enough evidence to show that downsizing can have negative impact also on people who remain in the company. These survivors show the trauma symptoms such as higher level of stress, anxiety, depression accompanied by loss of interest in socializing with colleagues, irritability, pessimism and feeling of inadequacy. As a result these employees show lower morale, decrease in productivity and tendencies to distrust management. This, then, can have negative impact on the productivity, customer satisfaction resulting in loses rather than higher profits. As noted, downsizing has traumatic effects on the employees who remain in the company as well as on managers. In some instances, the effect can be very similar to the experiences of the terminated employees if not even more severe. Managers need to carry on with the trauma survivors, provide them with support and keep the business running toward the new strategic goals at the same time. Therefore, the author proposed a procedure based on a therapeutic model that can help the managers to go through the traumatic experience in a healthy way. This would enable the manager to create an environment where the emotional suffering can be discussed in a creative and non-threatening way. The author firmly believes that this is the only way to make the remaining employees loyal again, and to keep them productive and innovative even after such turbulent period.

REFERENCES

Amabile, T. M., & Conti, R. (1999). Changes in the work environment for creativity during downsizing. *Academy of Management Journal*, *42*(6), 630–640. doi:10.2307/256984

American Psychiatric Association. (2013). *Diagnostic and statistical manual of mental health* (5th ed.). Washington, DC: Author.

Appelbaum, S. H., Patton, E., & Shapiro, B. (2003). The early retirement incentive program: A downsizing strategy. *Journal of European Industrial Training*, *27*(1), 22–35. doi:10.1108/03090590310456500

Armstrong-Stassen, M. (2005). Coping With Downsizing: A Comparison of Executive-Level and Middle Managers. *International Journal of Stress Management*, *12*(2), 117–141. doi:10.1037/1072-5245.12.2.117

Baker, D. (2006). *Fairness in downsizing: Judgement and complexity*. Adelaide: University of South Australia.

Beehr, T. A., & Newman, J. E. (1978). Job stress, employee health, and organizational effectiveness: A facet analysis, model, and literature review. *Personnel Psychology*, *31*(4), 665–699. doi:10.1111/j.1744-6570.1978.tb02118.x

Beylerian, M., & Kleiner, B. H. (2003). The downsized workplace. *Management Research News*, *26*(2/3/4), 97–108.

Blyth, A. (2003). The art of survival. *People Management*, *9*(9), 38–40.

Boronson, W., & Burgess, L. (1992). Survivors' syndrome. *Across the Board*, *29*(11), 41–45.

Brand, J. E. (2015). The Far-Reaching Impact of Job Loss and Unemployment. *Annual Review of Sociology*, *41*(1), 359–375. doi:10.1146/annurev-soc-071913-043237 PMID:26336327

Brockner, J. (1988). The effects of work layoffs on survivors: Research, theory, and practice. In B. M. Staw & L. L. Cummings (Eds.), Research in organizational behavior (pp. 213–255). Greenwich, CT: JAI Press.

Burke, R. J. (2005). Hospital restructuring stressors, support, and nursing staff perceptions of unit functioning. *The Health Care Manager*, *24*(1), 21–28. doi:10.1097/00126450-200501000-00004 PMID:15825816

Cameron, K. S. (1994). Strategies for Successful Organizational Downsizing. *Human Resource Management*, *33*(2), 189–211. doi:10.1002/hrm.3930330204

Cascio, W. F. (2002). *Managing Human resources* (9th ed.). San Francisco: Berrett-Koehler Publishers.

Cheng, Y., Chen, C. W., Chen, C. J., & Chiang, T. L. (2005). Job insecurity and its association with health among employees in the Taiwanese general population. *Social Science & Medicine, 61*(1), 41–52. doi:10.1016/j.socscimed.2004.11.039 PMID:15847960

Chipunza, C., & Berry, D. M. (2010). The relationship among survivor qualities – attitude, commitment and motivation – after downsizing. *African Journal of Business Management, 4*(5), 604–613.

Conway, S. (1993). Advice from a corporate casualty. *Industry Week, 242*, 22–24.

De Vitte, H., Vandoorne, J., Verlinder, R., & De Cuyper, N. (2005). Outplacement and Re-Employment Measures during Organizational Restructuring in Belgium: Overview of the Literature and Results of Qualitative Research. *Journal of European Industrial Training, 29*(2), 148–164. doi:10.1108/03090590510585109

DeKlerk, M. (2007). Healing emotional trauma in organizations: An O.D. Framework and Case study. *Organization Development Journal, 25*(2), 49–56.

Devine, K., Reay, T., Stainton, L., & Collins-Nakai, R. (2003). Downsizing outcomes: Better a victim than a survivor? *Human Resource Management, 42*(2), 109–124. doi:10.1002/hrm.10071

Dewitt, R. L., Trevino, L. K., & Mollica, K. A. (2003). Stuck in the middle: A control based model of managers' reactions to subordinates' layoffs. *Journal of Managerial Issues, 15*, 32–49.

Doherty, N., & Horsted, J. (1995). Helping survivors stay on board. *People Management, 1*(1), 26–31.

Downs, A. (1995). *Corporate executions: The ugly truth about layoffs: How corporate greed is shattering lives, companies, and communities*. New York: American Management Association.

Dragano, N., Verde, P. E., & Siegrist, J. (2005). Organisational downsizing and work stress: Testing synergistic health effects in employed men and women. *Journal of Epidemiology and Community Health, 59*(8), 694–699. doi:10.1136/jech.2005.035089 PMID:16020648

Dwyer, D. J., & Arbelo, M. (2012). The role of social cognition in downsizing decisions. *Journal of Managerial Psychology, 27*(4), 383–405. doi:10.1108/02683941211220199

Eriebach, A. C., Amundson, N. E., Borgen, W., & Jordan, S. A. (2004). Survivors of downsizing: Helpful and hindering experiences. *Career Development Quarterly*. Retrieved on January 5, 2016 from http://www.allbusiness.com/human-resources/workforce-management-hiring/770709-1.html

Faheem, Q. J., & Khan, A. M. (2013). Association of downsizing with survivor's organizational commitment, work motivation and psychological wellbeing in secondary and tertiary sectors of economy of Pakistan. *Journal of Behavioural Science, 23*(1), 68–79.

Fisher, S. R., & White, M. A. (2000). Downsizing in a learning organization: Are there hidden costs? *Academy of Management Review, 25*(1), 244–251. doi:10.5465/AMR.2000.2791613

Gandolfi, F. (2008). Reflecting on downsizing: What have mangers learned? *S.A.M. Advanced Management Journal, 73*(2), 46–55.

Gilmore, G. (1994). Coping with the realities of rightsizing. *Risk Management, 41*, 42–46.

Gowan, M. A. (2012). Employability, well-being and job satisfaction following a job loss. *Journal of Managerial Psychology*, *27*(8), 780–798. doi:10.1108/02683941211280157

Greenglass, E. R., Burke, R. J., & Moore, K. A. (2003). Reactions to increased workload: Effects on professional efficacy on nurses. *Applied Psychology*, *52*(4), 580–597. doi:10.1111/1464-0597.00152

Holmes, T. H., & Rahe, R. H. (1967). The Social Readjustment Rating Scale. *Journal of Psychosomatic Research*, *11*(2), 213–218. doi:10.1016/0022-3999(67)90010-4 PMID:6059863

Jackson, S. E., Schuler, S. W., & Werner, S. (2009). *Managing Human Resources*. Mason, OH: Cengage Learning.

Jamal, F. Q., & Khan, A. M. (2013). Association of downsizing with survivor's organizational commitment, work motivation and psychological well-being in secondary and tertiary sectors of economy of Pakistan. *Journal of Behavioural Science*, *23*(1), 1–25.

Kalimo, R., Taris, T. W., & Schaufeli, W. B. (2003). The effects of Past and Anticipated Future Downsizing on Survivor Well-Being: An Equity Perspective. *Journal of Occupational Health Psychology*, *8*(2), 91–109. doi:10.1037/1076-8998.8.2.91 PMID:12703876

Kates, N., Greiff, B. S., & Hagen, D. Q. (1990). *The Psychosocial Impact of Job Loss*. Washington, DC: American Psychiatric Association.

Kübler-Ross, E. (2005). *On Grief and Grieving: Finding the Meaning of Grief Through the Five Stages of Loss*. New York: Simon & Schuster Ltd.

Leana, C. R., & Feldman, D. C. (1988). Individual responses to job loss: Perceptions, reactions, and coping behaviors. *Journal of Management*, *14*(3), 375–389. doi:10.1177/014920638801400302

Lee, G., & Teo, A. (2005). Organizational restructuring: Impact on trust and work satisfaction. *Asia Pacific Journal of Management*, *22*(1), 23–39. doi:10.1007/s10490-005-6416-6

Makawatsakul, N., & Kleiner, B.H. (2003). The effect of downsizing on morale and attrition. *Management Research News, 26*(2/3/4), 52-62.

Maki, N. E. (2005). The Responses of Male and Female Managers to Workplace Stress and Downsizing. *North American Journal of Psychology*, *7*(2), 295–312.

Malik, M. I., & Ahmad, D. M. (2011). Lucky or unlucky people: Layoff Survivors. *Far East Journal of Psychology and Business*, *2*(3), 23–35.

Mandemakers, J. J., & Monden, C. S. (2013). Does the effect of job loss on psychological distress differ by educational level? *Work, Employment and Society*, *27*(1), 73–93. doi:10.1177/0950017012460312

Messenger, A. (2003). *Breakthrough research by DBM finds Investment in outplacement services positively impacts the bottom line*. Thomson DBM. Retrieved January 5, 2016, from http://www.amgr.com/pdf/02-06-03OPCReturnOnInvestment.pdf

Neves, P. (2014). Taking it out on survivors: Submissive employees, downsizing, and abusive supervision. *Journal of Occupational and Organizational Psychology*, *87*(3), 507–534. doi:10.1111/joop.12061

Noer, D. (1993). Four new realities. *Executive Excellence, 10*(11), 16–17.

Noronha, E., & DCruz, P. (2005). Achieving downsizing. Managerial perspectives. *Global Business Review, 6*(1), 77–94. doi:10.1177/097215090500600106

Paterson, J. M., & Cary, J. (2002). Organizational justice, change anxiety, and acceptance of downsizing: Preliminary tests of an AET-based model. *Motivation and Emotion, 26*(1), 83–103. doi:10.1023/A:1015146225215

Ramsey, R. D. (2004). Humanizing a downsized workplace. *Super Vision, 65*(7), 3–5.

Reynolds-Fisher, S., & White, M. (2000). Downsizing in a learning organization: Are there hidden costs? *Academy of Management Review, 25*(1), 244–251. doi:10.5465/AMR.2000.2791613

Rice, D., & Dreilinger, C. (1991). After the downsizing. *Training & Development, 45*(5), 41–44.

Rose, M. (2003). Good Deal, Bad Deal? Job Satisfaction in Occupations. *Work, Employment and Society, 17*(3), 503–530. doi:10.1177/09500170030173006

Schiro, J.B., & Baker, R.L. (2009). Downsizing and organizational change survivors and victims: mental health issues. *The International Journal of Applied Management and Technology,7*(1), 91-121.

Schuler, R. S. (1980). Definition and conceptualization of stress in organizations. *Organizational Behavior and Human Performance, 25*(2), 189–202. doi:10.1016/0030-5073(80)90063-X

Scire, P. (2007). *Applying Grief Stages to Organizational Change. An attributional analysis of Kubler-Ross Model of dying*. Cambridge, MA: Harvard University.

Simuth, J., & Sarmany-Schuller, I. (2010). Online learning barriers. In *Technological Developments in Education and Automation* (pp. 113–118). New York: Springer. doi:10.1007/978-90-481-3656-8_21

Sue, D. et al.. (1990). *Understanding abnormal behavior* (3rd ed.). Boston: Houghton Mifflin company.

Torkelson, E., & Muhonen, T. (2003). Coping strategies and health symptoms among women and men in a downsizing organization. *Psychological Reports, 92*(3), 899–907. doi:10.2466/pr0.2003.92.3.899 PMID:12841464

Travagione, A., & Cross, B. (2006). Diminishing the social network in organizations: Does there need to be such a phenomenon as „survivor syndrome" after downsizing? *Strategic Change, 15*(1), 1–13. doi:10.1002/jsc.743

Vahtera, J., Kivimaki, M., & Pentti, J. (1997). Effect of organizational downsizing on health of employees. *Lancet, 350*(9085), 1124–1128. doi:10.1016/S0140-6736(97)03216-9 PMID:9343499

Voss, E., & Maack, P. (2007). *Overview of restructuring in Europe*. Hamburg, Germany: European Trade Union Confederation. ETUC.

Voss, T. (2007). *Overview of restructuring in Europe. European Trade Union Confederation*. European Commission.

Young, C. (2012). Losing a Job: The Nonpecuniary Cost of Unemployment in the United States. *Social Forces, 91*(2), 609–634. doi:10.1093/sf/sos071

KEY TERMS AND DEFINITIONS

Downsizing Survivor: An employee or a manager who remain at the company after the organizational restructuring accompanied by downsizing.

Downsizing Victim: A person whose contract is terminated due to the organizational restructuring accompanied by downsizing.

Organizational Downsizing: Process in which a company attempts to optimize its human resources by reducing the number of employees.

Organizational Trauma: A situation in which the members of the organization go through an unpleasant situation that causes traumatic symptoms.

Outplacement: Service provided to assists the management during the lay off period maintaining the positive image of the company.

Trauma Healing: A directed process in which a manager or specialist use therapeutic methods to help the employees to deal with their negative emotions during and after the traumatic period.

Trauma Symptoms: Typical reaction to organizational change that is dramatic. Such symptoms include, stress, anxiety, depression and fear.

Chapter 6
Organizational Trauma and Change Management

Juan-Maria Gallego
Regis University, USA

ABSTRACT

This chapter will evaluate the correlation between change management and the employee and/or management behaviors detrimental to the wellbeing of those individuals and the overall productivity and efficiency of an organization. The potential relationship between change and organizational behaviors, the effects of change on the wellbeing of individuals, the well-documented resistance to change would analyzed as well as potential techniques that managers, consultants and HR departments could implement to minimize the detrimental influence of organizational change on the wellbeing of individuals. The traumatic effects of change on the employee, both physical and psychological effects would be included in this chapter. These effects on the wellbeing of employees have been correlated to diminishing job satisfaction, increased absenteeism and turnover, reduced productivity and effectiveness and overall lower engagement with the organization. The chapter will include the introduction and brief analysis of organizational change and effectiveness models in particular the Burke-Litwin Model.

INTRODUCTION

Change is a permanent characteristic in most industries. As an important factor in the strategic success and survival of many organizations (Cameron & Quinn, 2011; Kotter, & Schlesinger, 2008), it is also a key competence for an organization to properly predict, adapt to and maximize the opportunity of market changes, technology disruptions, technological evaluation, economic and social transformations, and competitive changes, determining the long-term survival and success of an organization. For example, the telecommunications (Telecom) industry has been one of fastest changing industries over the last two decades (Atluri, Jubas, Patel, & Schneider, 2012; Hwang & Lee, 2000). With the introduction of new technologies, the constant and fast evolution of existing technologies, the merger of the Information Technology (IT), entertainment and Telecom industries, the convergence of mobile telephony, fixed telephony, internet and cable technologies, the global growth and maturation of mobile

DOI: 10.4018/978-1-5225-2021-4.ch006

telecommunications, the Internet of Things and the decrease in demand of fixed telephone services, the Telecom industry has undergone global changes that have affected its workforce in immeasurable ways (Atluri, Jubas, Patel, & Scheneider, 2012; Bughin, Chui, & Manyika, 2013; Bughin, Ferruz-Aguilar, Gil-Gómez, & Spittaels, 2013; Hwang & Lee, 2000; Van der Hoeven & Sziraczki, 1998). A recent study supported that this perceived frequency of change within the telecom industry impacted the wellbeing of its employees (Gallego-Toledo, 2015).

Nora, a customer service representative at a call center for Telmex, a large Mexican telecommunications operator, documented some traumatic behaviors witnessed and lived through a period of organizational change (Ramírez-Velazquez, 2006). In her interview with the researcher, she noted an instance when a co-worker poured a full bottle of perfume on another employee´s head, commenting how the victim "stunk". Another employee keyed the car of a colleague because the victim "pushed her" during office hours and did not apologize. Nora also reported on the reaction (or inaction) of management and the union representatives when some of these actions were reported, attributing the behaviors to "women issues" or "gossiping". This contributed to an organizational climate of employee frustration, magnifying the workplace stress, chastising the victims and normalizing the behaviors of the perpetrators. But it is not just the employees that suffered from these traumatic behaviors. In other instances, customers became the victims of rude responses, misleading answers, phone hang-ups and/or quick dismissals. The working climate was conducive to aggressive and bullying behaviors towards other co-workers, negatively affecting the wellbeing of employees, negatively influencing the level of customer service, negatively impacting the organizational performance and the change implementation within the TelMex organization.

Changes are stressful events, met in many instances with resistance and often resulting in sabotaging actions (Kotter & Schlesinger, 2008). Disengagement, either passive or active, is another resulting factor negatively impacting the organization´s effectiveness and productivity. Passive aggressive behaviors between employees, or toward suppliers and customers, including acts of incivility, cynicism and other socially deviant behaviors could transform the organizational climate during periods of change. Ultimately, those become traumatic events that negatively impact the physical and psychological wellbeing of employees (Andersson, & Pearson, 1999; Cortina, Magley, Williams, & Langhout, 2001; Gallego-Toledo, 2015; Leiter, Laschinger, Day, & Oore, 2011; Maslach, 2003).

Dark Side behaviors are magnified during periods of change, leading to increased absenteeism, higher turnover, negative effects on psychological and physical wellbeing of employees (Cortina, Magley, Williams, & Langhout, 2001; Rafferty, & Griffin, 2006), higher levels of job disengagement (Ace & Parker, 2010), lower rates of job satisfaction and motivation (Burnes, 2009; Burnes & Jackson, 2011), higher rates on manifestation of aggressive behaviors towards others (Andersson, & Pearson, 1999; Griffin, & O´Leary-Kelly, 2004), resulting in lower productivity and efficiency in the organization (Beer & Nohria, 2000; Burke & Litwin, 1992; Kusy & Holloway, 2009; Kotter 1996), and an overall failure to adopt the new changes. Dark side behaviors are those behaviors that are injurious to human welfare, having an indirect and direct cost on the employees and the organization as a whole (Griffin & Oleary-Kelly, 2004). In other words, change may lead to Dark Side behaviors, inhibiting the change process and thus, creating more change.

This chapter evaluates the relationship between change management, organizational health and the employee and/or management behaviors detrimental to the wellbeing of those individuals and the overall effectiveness of an organization. With this purpose in mind, the chapter will analyze the potential relationship between change and organizational behaviors, the effects of change on the wellbeing of individuals, the well-documented resistance to change, (Bringselius, 2014; Burnes, 2015) as well as potential techniques that managers, Organizational Development (OD) practitioners, consultants and Human Resource (HR) departments could implement to minimize the detrimental effects of organizational. The traumatic effects of change on employees foment Dark Side behaviors including violence and aggression, incivility, sexual harassment, organizational cynicism, and toxic leadership.

Researchers and practitioners have argued that the results of change could be correlated to diminishing job satisfaction, increased absenteeism and turnover, reduced productivity and effectiveness and overall lower engagement with the organization. Studies suggested that Dark Side behaviors resulting from organizational change negatively affected the level of employee engagement with the organization. The level of employee engagement has been correlated to the profitability of an organization (Gallup, 2011). Finally, certain organizational change and diagnosis models such as Pascale and Athos´s 7S model, Weisbord´s Leadership model, the Nadler-Tushman model or the Burke-Litwin Model identify elements such as staff relationships, individual motivation, work unit climate and values. Climate and values are important elements for the effective implementation of change in an organization. In a circular manner, factors such as the deterioration of organizational climate, employee motivation, or the staff relationships resulted in an increase in deviant and Dark Side behaviors, negatively impacting those same elements, resulting in a magnification of those dark-side behaviors and further negatively impacting the organizational effectiveness.

ORGANIZATIONAL HEALTH

An organization is an entity that has been constructed based on the founder(s)´s beliefs, values, vision and mission to develop a product or service that fills a certain perceived need in society (Stone, 2015). Some researchers have compared organizations to living organisms (Morgan, 2011). As such, organizations could be prescribed an organizational level of health, based on a series of elements such as employee wellbeing, organizational climate, processes and employees´ efficiency and productivity. According to Patnaik (2011), organizational health refers to the ability of an organization to meet its performance goals while functioning within competitive and working environments that encourages employee wellbeing and the search for the optimization of stakeholders´ value. For the purpose of this chapter, wellbeing would be defined as a "complex framework composed of factors such as mental health, psychological health, and aspects of an employee´s behaviors and tendencies" (Gallego-Toledo, 2015, p. 71). Organizational change introduces uncertainty and ambiguity in those goals, therefore, potentially impacting the organizational health. Improperly introduced or implemented changes, or frequent change could negatively affect the organizational health and the wellbeing of its employees (Arnetz, 2005). The relationship between change management and organizational performance has been suggested and supported in different research studies, as well as change management models such as the ones included in this chapter.

During a 2002 interview, professor and author Yiannis Gabriel commented the following in relation to a "sick" organization:

I am convinced that 'sick' organizations, i.e. organizations with very high levels of anxiety, acrimony, and even delusion, can be effective over substantial periods of time, not in spite but because of these unpleasant circumstances . . . I have strongly believed that organizations can prosper on the back of individual neurosis, delusion and suffering. This, of course, does not mean that only organizations that inflict a lot of suffering on their members are successful or indeed the opposite. (Driver, 2003, p. 46-47)

In other words, Gabriel believed that an organization could be productive (to a certain degree) despite potentially being inflicted with its burnt-out employees, an uncivil culture, a deviant climate and/or a toxic leadership. Just as it holds true for humans, stress may be a productive and desirable factor for organizations in the short-term. In humans, stress produces biological and brain changes that enhance awareness, energy levels and productivity. Enhancement in these areas may also be apparent in organizations experiencing stress. But just as long term exposure to stress proves to have detrimental effects on human health (Lubit, 2008), organizations that learn to work with certain "sickness" such as deviant behaviors could eventually transform their organizational culture to incorporate new norms such as a decline in employees´ physical and psychological wellbeing, eroding morale, an increase in leadership and employee toxicity, a diminishing job satisfaction rate, compromised organizational citizen behavior and engagement, and the subsequent and potentially long-term deterioration and metamorphosis of a once-productive and effective organizational culture. Studies have shown that those before-mentioned factors would eventually impact productivity, organizational climate, and employee morale in a disruptive manner (Burnes & Jackson, 2011; Cortina et al., 2001; Coyle-Shapiro, 2002; Gallego-Toledo, 2014; Holloway & Kusy, 2010; Kusy & Holloway, 2010). Furthermore, organizational change or perceived high frequency of change catalyzes those hostile factors within the organization's health, magnifying the potential symptoms of the organizational "sickness" such as employee burnout, incivility and organizational cynicism (Andersson & Pearson, 1999; John, Arnon, & James, 2000; Maslach, 2003; Maslack & Leiter, 2008; Rafferty & Griffin, 2006;Wanous, Reichers, & Austin, 2000).

ASSESSING ORGANIZATIONAL HEALTH DURING CHANGE

Just as individuals undergo regular physical exams with their physicians to prevent and detect potential health issues, organizations use assessments to identify, monitor and control different important factors during organizational change. Relying on the perceptions of individuals within the organization, these assessments permit HR managers, consultants and other OD professionals to diagnose the organizational health issues that may disrupt the productivity of an organization. Those assessments also facilitate the development of recommendations to improve the productivity and effectiveness of an organization (Stone, 2015).

Assessing Change

Goldratt (2010), the physicist and father of *Theory of Constraints*, argued that employees were not opposed to change if they understood (1) the risks of staying with the same business model or not changing; (2) the incentives and benefits of changing were underscored; (3) leadership curtailed the existing benefits and incentives to maintain the current status quo; and (4) leadership minimized the obstacles to change by providing the knowledge, skills and training necessaries to employees to make the migration. Kotter (1995) noted that 70% of change implementations failed within the first year. A similar failure ratio also supported by other studies (Burnes & Jackson, 2011; Cameron & Quinn, 2011). Kotter presented several factors that explained the high failure rate such as the negligence to properly communicate the changes, ignoring the organizational culture or situational constraints, lack of or weak continuous support from leadership, and a failure to develop the right skills in the change agents and employees. Kotter (1995, 2011) identified an 8-step process used to reduce those resistance risk factors.

Leadership and Change

Following a rationale similar to Goldratt´s, Kotter (1995) urged leadership to first clearly communicate the risks of not changing by "establishing a sense of urgency", then to implement an effective leadership style to communicate and support a clear mission and strategy, empowering other change sponsors at all levels, and anchoring the new changes into the organizational culture. Effective employee training, the right leadership, the proper culture, clear communication, addressing situational constraints and developing supporting policies for the introduced changes were some of the factors recommended to properly motivate change within an organization. Change failure strikes at an individual´s sense of safety, belonging and esteem. Several organizational assessments look at those factors to provide guidance-during organizational change, providing a snapshot on the organization health throughout the change process.

A CAUSAL MODEL OF ORGANIZATIONAL PERFORMANCE AND CHANGE

Change is the new normal for most organizations and industries. Change occurs under many names such as organizational change, downsizing, re-organization, strategic realignment, right sizing, reengineering, restructuring and cultural realignment. In their book *Diagnosing and changing organizational culture: Based on the competing values framework*, Cameron and Quinn (2011) noted that the velocity of change would exponentially accelerate during the second decade of the XXI century, establishing a business environment intolerant to organizational status quo. While change itself is not one of the goals for this chapter, it is important to understand the types of change assessments and change categories that an organization faces. Organizational change can be classified into two categories – transactional and transformational changes (Gallego-Toledo, 2015; Waclawski, 2002). Transactional change, also known as a first-order change, requires recurrent, gradual and continuous adjustments to existing processes and other factors to gradually adapt to the changing environment or strategy. Transformational changes such as re-engineering or revolutionary changes, are more drastic in nature and involve a fundamental and radical change within the organizational culture, strategy and mission, and/or leadership that requires a major adjustment or transformation in employees and group behaviors. Transformational changes have a tendency to metamorphose the character of an organization, significantly altering the organizational performance and employee behaviors (Waclawski, 2002).

During the 1970s and 1980s, different models were developed, supported by various organizational change assessment tools. To understand the logic and the theory upon which some of the present models were built, it is important to understand the essence of those models. These assessment theories and tools help OD and HR practitioners and consultants diagnose the organizational health and effectiveness of change. Table 1 summarizing the different models can be found below.

Weisbord´s Leadership Model

In 1976, Marvin Weisbord introduced one of the first organizational assessment tools (Weisbord, 1976; 1971). This model was important for several reasons. First, the model was constructed on the idea that an organization was an open-system, with inputs coming from the external environment and outputs shaping, to a lesser degree, the environment in which it existed. The model was composed of six elements that Weisbord proposed needed to be considered during organizational change, without ever

Table 1. Summary of organizational design and change management models

Model	Weisbord's Leadership Model (1976)	Nadler-Tushman Congruence Model (1980)	7-S Framework (1981)	Burke-Litwin Model (1992)
Elements	• Purpose • Structure • Rewards • Helpful Mechanisms • Relationships	• Inputs (Environment, Resources, History) • Strategy • Culture • Work • Structure • People • Output (Organizational, Group and Individual performance)	• Strategy • Structure • Systems • Skills • Style • Staff	• External Environment • Mission & Strategy • Leadership • Organizational Culture • Structure • Management Practices • Systems (Policies, Procedures) • Work Unit Climate • Task Requirements and Individual Skills and Abilities • Motivation • Individual Needs and Values • Individual and organizational Performance
Specifics	Semi-open system involving environment input	Open System with defined inputs and outputs	Close System with no feedback loop	Open System with Feedback Loop, inputs and outputs
Assessment	Model includes some diagnostic questions in each box or quadrant to assist with analysis	Model includes an eight-step process to analyze each element.		Burke-Litwin Organizational Assessment Survey

losing sight of the whole picture - the organization. Five of the elements (purpose, structure, rewards, helpful mechanisms, and relationships), were interconnected with the sixth element leadership, at the center of the circle created by the previous five elements. The "purposes" of the organization defined what the company did, its mission, and it was mutually influenced by "structure", or how the work was divided, and "relationships", or how management and employees dealt with the interpersonal conflict or technological conflict. "Helpful mechanisms", such as ways of dealing with internal coordination or proper use of technology within the organization, were connected to "relationships" on one side and closing the circle, to "rewards", the incentives applied to certain or all tasks required to accomplish the goals of the organization. In the center, "leadership" kept the other five elements in balance, ensuring harmony and effectiveness.

The Nadler-Tushman Congruence Model for Diagnosing Organizational Behavior

Originally developed at the end of the 1970s, Nadler and Tushman argued that planned organizational change affected organizational values. In short, the relationship between the organization, the leadership and the employees, and ultimately, the organizational performance, were all affected by the external inputs of environment, resources, and history and the organizational strategy (Nadler & Tushman, 1989,1980).

The researchers argued that external forces such as environment, resources and history provoked an evolution or transformation of an organization´s strategy. Those strategic alterations resulted in adaptations within the organization at:

- The work-level
- The people-level
- The processes-level
- The organizational structure-level.

The effectiveness and success of change implementation would be determined by the congruence of the changes at the different levels or how well the changes could be implemented at all levels of the organization logically, effectively and taking into account the existing relationships. Nadler and Tushman (1989) developed a series of principles or recommendation on how to properly evaluate change, starting with the initiation of change, that led to the definition of the content of the change and the style of leadership required for change implementation. The last phase involved the achievement of the change, through qualitative and quantitative goal measurements, as well as feedback and lessons learned. To successfully implement change, a diagnosis of the organization was essential. For this diagnosis phase, the organization had to properly address the "what to" change to, the "what" to change, and the "how" to change in order to react, anticipate and conquer the new environmental challenges.

The 7-S Framework

In 1981, Pascale and Athos, with the support of other McKinsey consultants such as Tom Peters and Robert Waterman, developed a framework that allowed OD practitioners and consultants to depict seven key elements for the effective strategy implementation (Burke & Litwin, 1992; Kaplan, 2005). Unlike the other framework mentioned, the 7-S Framework did not consider the environment as an input or output, and focused on the interrelationship and definition of seven key elements: style, staff, shared values, skills, structure, strategy and systems. The model argued that a company reached excellence when harmony or balance could be reached among the three hard "S" elements, defined as strategy, structure, and systems and the four soft "S" elements, defined as style, staff, skills, and shared values (Kaplan, 2005). Two transformational elements, organizational culture, what Pascale and Athos referred to as "shared values" and leadership, referred to as "style" were classified as part of the "soft" category with two other transactional elements "staff" and "skills". Two transactional elements, informal and formal processes, or "systems" and hierarchical structure and power distribution, or "structure" were placed in the same category as "strategy", a transformational element.

On the other hand, no performance variables were defined in the 7-S model, even though organizational patterns could be clearly defined (Burke & Litwin, 1992; Kaplan, 2005). Kaplan (2005) suggested supplementing the 7-S Framework with their concept of the Balanced Score Card. This combination would provide a complete 360-view of the current organizational situation and provide clear quantitative and qualitative measures to guide, monitor and control change implementation. While some of these seven elements could possibly help address the wellbeing of employees in an organization, for the purpose of diagnosing the organizational health, this model would provide OD practitioners or consultants with a very limited perspective (Burke & Litwin, 1992).

A Causal Model of Organizational Performance and Change

Organizational change is a form of chaos (Burke & Litwin, 1992). This change-induced chaos could negatively affect the employees´ wellbeing and organizational performance (Abrahamson, 2004; Waisfisz, 2015). Burke and Litwin (Burke, 2011; Burke & Litwin, 1992) built a causal-based model for their theoretical diagnosis model. Behaviorist, author and consultant Aubrey Daniels (2000) explained how scientific studies have supported the concept that an antecedent resulted in a personal or group behavior, which was either reinforced or discouraged by the resulting consequence(s). External factors, or antecedents such as changes in the legal, technological, market, social or competitive environments cause employees and management either proactively or reactively to emit new behaviors, or consequences, that affect the employees´ wellbeing and organizational performance. The nature of that consequence would determine if the behavior in question would be repeated or not.

The two first models initially mentioned, Weisbord´s and Nadler and Tushman´s models, depicted a listing of inputs, outputs and other components that could affect the performance of an organization and the change management. Organizations operate in dynamic environments where change is frequent and recurring (Burnes, 2009; Burnes & Jackson, 2011; Cameron & Quinn, 2011; Waisfisz, 2015) implying the need to develop open-system-based assessment. An organization depends on its environment and other external factors to survive (Goodstein & Burke, 1991). Burke and Litwin´s causal model aimed to address the "what" and "how" of effective performance and change implementation (1992). The Burke-Litwin model was built upon some of the models and concepts previously mentioned, and shared concepts with other organizational change theories. For example, Abrahamson (2004) argued that successful change needed modification at five different levels -- people, processes, culture, networks, and structure. Studies have tied leadership to the organizational commitment of employees and their motivation (Hong et al., 2016). Finally, it should be mentioned that the Burke-Litwin model was built around the research work conducted by George Litwin in the 1960´s, based on the works of McClelland, a needs theorist that believed that human needs could increase or decrease depending on the corresponding environment (Burke, 2011; Burke & Litwin, 1992). Litwin concluded in his research work that organizational climate affected motivation, as well as employee health and retention (Burke, 2011). Waisfisz (2015) specified that the "stay motivation", similar to Herzberg´s Hygiene factors (Herzberg, 2003), corresponded to the concept of work climate, mentioned in various models, including the Burke-Litwin model, detailed below.

Climate was defined "in terms of perceptions that individuals have on how their local work unit is managed and how effectively they and their day-to-day colleagues work together on the job" (Burke & Litwin, 1992, p. 526). Organizational culture, not to be confused with organizational climate, was defined as the enduring set of explicit and implicit behaviors, norms, shared values, expectations and assumptions that governed the relationship among employees within an organization (Cameron & Quinn, 2011). The researchers identified culture as a fundamental factor to properly seal new organizational changes beyond superficial changes in the processes. They noted that "without an alteration of the fundamental goals, values, and expectations of organizations or individuals, change remains superficial and of short duration" (Cameron and Quinn, 2011, p. 13).

A Practioner's Model

Burke and Litwin (1992) developed a practitioner´s model meant to help HR professionals, OD practitioners, managers, and consultants diagnose, plan, monitor and manage change initiatives aimed at improving the effectiveness of an organization. The resulting model has been tested in companies such as British Airways (Goodstein & Burke, 1991), SmithKline Beecham (Burke & Jackson, 1991), Citibank (Burke, 2011), and also validated by other research studies (Burke, 2011; DiPofi, 2002; Martins & Coetzee, 2009; Stone, 2015, 2010).

The Burke-Litwin model contains twelve elements, classified as transformational elements and transactional elements (Burke, 2011; Burke & Litwin, 1992). Based on studies published by Burke (2011) and Litwin (Burke & Litwin, 1992), those elements could be defined as follows. The transformational elements include; (1) The input or *external environment* defined as the outside conditions or situations that could affect the organizational performance (2) Mission and strategy, or the purpose and goals of the organization as well as the way to reach those goals; (3) Leadership, focused on the most senior level managers and executives of the organization; (4) Individual and organizational performance, an output that reflects the results and other indicators related to the individual and organizational achievement; and (5) Culture, or the set of values, beliefs, and norms shared by the employees of an organization which govern individuals´ and groups´ actions and behaviors. The transactional elements involve (1) Structure, or the design of the organization and power flow; (2) Systems, defined as the policies, processes, rewards and IT systems that support people´s actions; (3) Management practices, or the actions and behaviors exhibited by managers and supervisors during the day-to-day work; (4) Climate, previously defined; (5) Motivation, or the individual´s or group´s desire to pursue the established performance goals and individual satisfaction; (6) Individual needs and values, or the individual perception of what is a good behavior versus a bad one; and (7) Tasks requirements and individual skills or abilities, or the knowledge, skills, abilities and others factors that employees need to develop in order to meet the performance expectations.

THE BURKE-LITWIN ORGANIZATIONAL ASSESSMENT SURVEY

In addition, the Burke-Litwin model Organizational Assessment Survey (BLOAS) was developed to help OD practitioners identify what elements to change and how to change to maintain organizational effectiveness (Burke, 2011: Stone, 2015). The BLOAS consists of 90 questions, 79 questions in 5-point Likert scales and 11 open-ended questions allowing the participants to expand on their responses (DePofi, 2002; Stone, 2015, 2010). Scholastic research has found that the BLOAS has strong content validity and internal consistency reliability measures with the exception of the *external environment* element, which has a low internal consistency (Stone, 2015, 2010). By asking questions on each of the twelve organizational variables, the BLOAS provides a picture-in-time on the organizational health, including a diagnosis on those elements that employees and management believe to be working correctly and those that could be improved to achieve the desired change.

Finally, it is important to understand that change assessment surveys such as the BLOAS, based on Burke-Litwin model allow OD practitioners, HR professionals and consultants to visualize individual elements that have been shown to affect individual employee wellbeing. For example, by defining the current organizational climate, one could predict potential issues with the morale and performance of individuals. Job satisfaction and the individual need to achieve could be explained by the motivation factor. Studying the organizational culture, climate and leadership could illuminate potential deviant behaviors such as toxic leadership, uncivil behaviors among employees or the level of burnout or organizational cynicism. Understanding the organizational environment and the effect of change on the organizational health provides the first hints of possible employee trauma that one could find in an organization during times of change.

EMPLOYEE TRAUMA AND WELLBEING

Culture could be defined as what a group believes to be true and right (Hay Group, 2004). Hence, the resistance of many individuals to adapt to or to implement change. Change questions "the way things have been done", forcing employees and managers to doubt their previous actions – could they have done something different to achieve better results? – and their future decisions – how will things be different now? For almost two decades, this author worked globally for a large telecommunications company. The motto of the Scandinavian company was that "if it ain´t broken, break it". Change was perceived as the essence of success and competitiveness. Throughout the years, the author saw how change affected individual's wellbeing. During those years of frequent organizational changes, many employees developed organizational cynicism due to change fatigue. Those employees would silently doubt all decisions, projecting a passive-aggressive attitude to the leadership. Other employees showed different change fatigue symptoms such as distrust of management, emotional detachment from their jobs and palpable frustration when confronted by challenging situations. Others would reduce their productivity and organizational engagement to a minimum, surviving below the radar until the next change occurred. Employees questioned the leadership´s behavioral integrity, defined as the "perceived pattern of alignment between the leader´s words and deeds" (Leroy, Palanski, & Simons, 2012, p. 256). Furthermore, a few colleagues showed burnout symptoms such as depression, unhappiness and a lack of motivation and organizational engagement. Some of the remaining, especially those in managerial positions, turned against their peers and colleagues, using sarcasm and uncivil behaviors to manage their fear of, resistance to or disagreement with the new processes, policies, strategies or mission. Employees reacted differently to change depending on their exposure to previous changes and their own personality types, predisposition to change being a characteristic that varies greatly among individuals (Barger & Kirby, 1995). Change could also precipitate presenteeism, a wellbeing phenomenon found in the developed West, and classified by some as costlier than actual abseenteism (Cooper & Lu, 2016). Presenteeism refers to the physical presence of employees that are functionally absent, deterring from any individual contribution to the productivity of the organization, and possibly demoralizing and demotivating other surrounding employees.

The chaos introduced by change, when poorly managed, results in traumatic effects on motivation, and motivation plays a central role on employee wellbeing and organizational health, as shown in many change management assessment models previously described. Furthermore, studies have linked employees´ lower wellbeing levels to employees´ job dissatisfaction, and to higher job-related costs and lower productivity for an organization (Dana & Griffin, 1999). Transformational change specifically, impacts all elements presented in the Burke-Litwin model. Adaptation within each element is required to successfully implement and seal those desired changes. Motivation is one of the main pulpits of successful transformational change.

MOTIVATION

Musculu and Muntean (2013) defined motivation as the "sum of psychological motives that initiates and directs an employee´s behavior towards a goal/objective" (p. 306). Motivation has the ability to energize, direct and/or sustain a behavior as well as affect the intensity of the behavior and its recurrence. It is important to understand that motivation derives from the frustration of unsatisfied needs or unachieved goals. After the introduction of Maslow´s Hierarchy of Needs (1943), McGregor´s Theory X & Y (1960), and McClelland´s Human Motivation Theory (1961), Herzberg introduced his motivation-hygiene theory (Locke & Latham, 2009). Differentiating between factors that created job satisfaction versus those that prevented job dissatisfaction, Herzberg argued for the importance of motivating factors such as recognition, responsibility, professional growth and achievement and career advancement-because of their ability to positively affect employee motivation. The other factors, known as hygiene factors, which included elements such as supervision, working conditions, relationships with subordinates and supervisors, and salary, contributed to dissatisfaction if improperly managed but only marginally to job satisfaction, and hence had a limited motivating factor (Herzberg, 2003).

A review of research studies on emotions and organizational change conducted by Kiefer (2005) found that daily changes or continuous change could trigger negative emotions in employees. Those negative emotions included a decline in motivation and an increase in employee anxiety, anger and frustration. This is not surprising since, as previously mentioned, motivation provides individuals with the ability and desire to execute or sustain a specific behavior, and that behavior aims at fulfilling an unmet need or desire. Additionally, Kiefer (2005) listed five consequences related to those negative emotions such as (1) the deterioration of the work climate; (2) the rise in improper management practices; (3) the reduction on the level of employee motivation; (4) conflicting, confusing and unclear employee roles and responsibility descriptions; and (5) ineffective reward systems. One should recognize those elements as factors included in the Burke-Litwin model, and therefore measurable by the Burke-Litwin Organizational Assessment Survey.

TRAUMA

Change causes stress in a work environment. The reaction to stress by individuals or by groups of individuals within an organization could potentially lead to organizational and employee trauma. Those reactions could be the result of the change itself, the reaction to behaviors developed to resist the change or a combination of both. Behaviors and reactions have a symbiotic relationship. For example, reactionary leaders use toxic behaviors such as humiliation, bullying and other uncivil behaviors as a source of power. Those behaviors eventually create a toxic system within the work unit or the whole organization that corrodes the organizational climate and in the long term, the organizational culture, transforming those toxic behaviors into the working norm for other managers, supervisors and employees. This path of destructive behaviors may spawn greater psychological distress to its victims and witnesses of the toxic behaviors, lower productivity levels and job satisfaction, and higher levels of turnover, resulting in legal and absenteeism costs for the organization. The toxic system would survive until the organization collapses under the pressure of an unhealthy culture, lower efficiency and lost productivity or until the leadership is changed.

Deviant Behaviors

After conducting a longitudinal study, researchers Meier and Spector (2013) posited the existence of a positive correlation between work stressors and counterproductive work behaviors (CWB). The authors defined CWB as behaviors that damaged the organization or its contributors (Gallego-Toledo, 2015). CWB include deviant behaviors such as uncivil behaviors, organizational cynicism, toxic behaviors and more aggressive behaviors such as sabotage and sexual harassment. Kusy and Holloway (2009) argued that those individuals who showed a pattern of CWB, "debilitate individuals, teams, and even organizations over the long term" (p. 4), and should be considered as displaying toxic personalities. Some have argued that a toxic personality could be hiding more serious psychological disorders such as narcissism, antisocial personality and psychopathic behaviors (Cavaiola, & Lavender, 2000).

The negative effects of deviant behaviors on an organization and its employees have been widely documented (Lubit, 2008; Holloway & Kusy, 2010; Kusy & Holloway, 2009). Those effects included higher levels of absenteeism, lower employee engagement and commitment to the organization, higher levels of turnover and desire to leave the organization, resistance to change directive, lower employee morale, and increased organizational costs related to higher levels of stress leading to higher rates of workplace-related accident and litigation. The correlation between CWB and presenteeism has yet to be researched but as previously mentioned, presenteeism could result in a higher financial impact to organizations in the developed West than absenteeism (Cooper & Lu, 2016). Studies have shown that toxic leadership did lead to abusive verbal attacks and other types of employee abuse and mistreatment that resulted lower morale, higher job dissatisfaction and an increase of hostility in the work unit climate (Kusy & Holloway, 2010). Toxic behaviors include bullying, humiliation, sarcasm, passive hostility, shaming, and/or sabotage (Kusy, & Holloway, 2009).

Organizational changes such as mergers and acquisitions, reengineering, restructuring or realignments present ideal situations for toxic behaviors to grow, as adjustments to organizational culture are necessary. Employees are adjusting to leadership changes and strategy realignments, and confusion and ambiguity in communication may occur. The fear caused by transformational changes could feed the overall resistance to change from employees, unless the communication from leadership is clear and concrete.

The toxicity in an organization can be measured and evaluated. Kusy and Holloway (2010) provided an extensive explanation on how to identify, provide solutions for and address toxic behaviors in an organization. Using the National Survey of Toxic Personalities, the researchers measure four different components – Toxic behaviors (12 questions); Leader reaction to toxic behaviors (7 questions); Personalities: Leader strategies (13 questions); and Organizational culture (8 questions). Each question is rated using a 6-point Likert scale from "1-Not at all likely" to "6-Completely likely". The results of the survey determine the best way to address the toxicity of an organization.

Toxic behaviors such as bullying and incivility are part of counterproductive work behaviors, resulting in employee mistreatment. Civility is defined by the organizational culture. Employees could perceive behaviors that stray from the norms, ethics or values defined by the organizational culture as a form of mistreatment. In a 1999 publication, Anderson and Pearson listed different forms of mistreatment within an organization.

Those forms of mistreatment included:

1. Antisocial behaviors
2. Deviant behaviors

3. Violence
4. Aggression
5. Incivility

Anderson and Pearson (1999) argued that mistreatment within an organization encompassed the concept of antisocial behaviors. Antisocial behaviors are those behaviors that deviate from the expected norms, ethics, moral standards, values and beliefs and defined as the organizational culture. Deviant behaviors, a sub-group of antisocial behaviors that violates behavioral norms based on the organizational and national culture, included violence, aggression and incivility.

All violent behaviors were considered high-intensity aggressive behaviors but not all aggressive behaviors are violent, despite the intention to harm. Uncivil behaviors are included in the deviant behaviors as well as the aggressive behaviors as the intent to harm is very ambiguous (Anderson & Pearson, 1999; Cortina et al., 2001). All antisocial behaviors listed above would cause trauma within an organization and to its employees (Andersson & Pearson, 1999; Cortina et al., 2001; Grawitch et al., 2006; Holloway & Kusy, 2010; Martínez et al., 2009; Pearson, Andersson, & Porah, 2000).

Burnout

Studies support the idea that the stress created by organizational change could affect the psychological and physical health of employees. Chronic levels of stress or an elevated, negative perceived frequency of change resulted in higher levels of burnout in organizations (Gallego-Toledo, 2015; Lubit, 2008; Maslach, 2003; Maslach & Leiter, 2008). Maslach defined burnout as "a syndrome of emotional exhaustion, depersonalization, and reduced personal accomplishment that can occur among individuals who do 'people-work' of some kind" (2003, p. 2). Burnout is a psychological syndrome borne from the long-term exposure to chronic interpersonal stressors within the workplace (Maslach & Leiter, 2008; Leiter, Laschinger, Day, & Oore, 2011). Factors in the workplace such as workload, control over one´s work, the reward system, the work-unit climate, the perception of fairness and the values of the organization, all contributed to the burnout syndrome (Maslach & Leiter, 2008).

Maslach (2003) developed several types of surveys, such as the Maslach Burnout Indicator- General Survey (MBI-GS) and the Maslach Burnout Indicator- Human Services Survey (MBI-HSS) that measured the burnout level of employees based on three factors – depersonalization, exhaustion and Professional Efficiency, also known as reduced personal accomplishment. The first element, professional efficiency or reduced personal accomplishment is defined as the loss of individual personal performance. Depersonalization, commonly referred to as cynicism, indicates an uncaring attitude towards clients, other employees, organizational goals, and even the organizational vision and mission. This phenomenon is defined by a distancing from other colleagues, peers and work-related issues. Finally, emotional exhaustion presents itself as a lack of energy or the belief that one´s emotional resources are depleted. By measuring those three factors, the Maslach burnout surveys determine the level of burnout at an individual- and/or organizational- level. Studies have supported the idea that burnout level is affected by change or perceived frequency of change (De Cuyper, Raeder, Van Der Heijden & Wittekind, 2012; Gallego-Toledo, 2015; Leiter, Gascón, & Martínez-Jarreta, 2010).

There are two versions of the MBI, each with a distinct use. The original MBI-HSS was mostly used in people-focused industries such as teaching, mental health, the legal system, law enforcement, and social work. As previously mentioned, the survey covers three specific subscales: exhaustion, depersonalization and professional efficiency. These elements factor into the total burnout score. The participants would receive four scores: three subscales plus the overall burnout score ranked as "high", "moderate" and "low" depending on their responses, with the thresholds being subscale-specific (Maslach, 2003; Leiter & Maslach, 2005). However, the MBI-GS is the most commonly used burnout survey, as it covers all other industries. The MBI-GS includes 22-questions measured with a 7-point Likert scale and as a tool has been validated in many studies, different languages and across different cultures (Gallego-Toledo, 2015; Leiter et al., 2011; Maslach, 2003).

Incivility

Incivility is defined as a "low-intensity deviant behavior with ambiguous intent to harm the target, in violation of workplace norms for mutual respect. Uncivil behaviors are characteristically rude and discourteous, displaying a lack of regard for others" (Anderson & Pearson, 1999, p. 457). Due to the ambiguity and uncertainty of the behavior, the victim is left confused and unsure about the aim and nature of the comment, action or decision. Did the instigator aim the uncivil behavior explicitly towards the victim or is the victim reading "too much" into the behavior? In some instances, the victim will retaliate. Pearson, Andersson and Porah (2000) posited that the victim may choose to reciprocate against the instigator, against individuals connected to the instigator, against other co-workers or subordinates, or against "safer" targets such as friends or family members. A reciprocated uncivil behavior could result in an incivility spiral, where the instigator and target engage in a series of behaviors that could eventually lead to more aggressive deviant behaviors (Anderson & Pearson, 1999).

There is a cost to incivility. Kusy and Holloway (2010) noted that "almost 50% of those who experienced incivility at work reported that they lost time worrying about this and its future consequences" while "more than 25% of individuals who were targets of incivility acknowledged that they cut back on their work" and 12% actually left their jobs (p. 14). In another study, 75% of 1043 students surveyed had experienced incivility by other members of their higher learning institution resulting in psychological distress that led to disengagement from and dissatisfaction with their institution itself and a decline in school performance (Caza & Cortina, 2007). Several studies (Cortina et al., 2001; Martínez, et al., 2009) identified other consequences of uncivil behaviors such as a disruption of the relationships with other employees and managers and a loss of productivity. The targets of the incivility, as well as witnesses of the acts, could suffer from physical and psychological ailments related to stress such as anxiety, depression, stomach- and heart-related diseases and confusion. Job satisfaction and organizational commitment would most likely decline in these situations.

Cortina and colleagues (2001) developed a simple survey to measure incivility in an organization. The Workplace Incivility Scale originally included 7-questions using a 5-point Likert scale and covered over a five-year period of employment. Subsequent studies suggested that validity remained the same or improved if a 7-point Likert scale was used and covered fewer recent years of employment (Blau & Andersson, 2005; Caza & Cortina, 2007; Gallego-Toledo, 2015).

Organizational Cynicism

Another measurement of individual trauma within an organization is organizational cynicism. This indicator is directly related to organizational change. Reichers, Wanous and Austin defined organizational cynicism as "the attitude borne from repeated exposure to failed or partially successful and mismanaged change efforts by management and leadership in an organization" (Gallego-Toledo, 2015, p. 95). The researchers argued that a potential loss of trust in the leadership could occur when an organization has undergone repeated and frequent change initiatives with moderate to no success. Employees would seek to put some distance between themselves and the organizational management, mostly through lack of support of or lack of active engagement with the change process.

The Measure of Cynicism about Organizational Change (MoCaOC) was developed by Reichers, Wanous and Austin to evaluate the level of organizational cynicism present in an organization during and in between change initiatives. The survey is composed of eight questions that could be answered by the respondent with a "agree" or "disagree". "Agree" answers are counted as one point while "Disagree" answers are counted as zero. The higher the total score, the higher the level of organizational cynicism and therefore, the lower the trust in the management of the organization.

MEASURING AND PREVENTING TRAUMA DURING ORGANIZATIONAL CHANGE

Previously, it was established that organizational change, when improperly managed, could result in organizational trauma at the organizational and employee level. The change-induced chaos creates a stressing environment for employees. The magnitude of change ranging from organic growth to disruptive innovation determines the risk level to the organization, with transactional or organic growth resulting in the lesser risk, while transformative change such as disruptive innovation or a merger and acquisition resulting in higher risk levels. Employees react to stress and the perceived frequency of change in different ways, before change fatigue settles on the individual. Change fatigue manifests as mental fatigue, disengagement, anxiety and even depression. Other employees could convert those psychological effects into physical effects such as headaches, digestive disorders and heart diseases. Employees with both physical and psychological symptoms could be classified in the burnout category.

Still, a portion of traumatized employees could react by changing their behaviors to defend and adapt to the new situation. Those changes could lead to organizational cynicism, toxic behaviors and incivility. Those deviant behaviors would potentially create a spiral that would magnify the "sickness" felt by other employees when faced with organizational change, increasing the number of traumatized employees and negatively impacting the organizational health and the successful implementation of the change initiatives. Failures in change implementation usually lead to losses in performance and profitability.

Measuring and Preventing Trauma

To measure and prevent trauma during organizational change, the author has presented an array of tools that HR professionals, consultants and OD practitioners could use to monitor the rate of success of the organizational change initiatives and the health of the employees and the organization during the transitional period. Different organizational change assessment models were presented. One of the most used models is the Burke-Litwin model and the Burke-Litwin Organizational Assessment Survey. Based on twelve key organizational elements, the BLOAS provides a roadmap to the efficient change implementation in regards to the "what to" change and "how to" change it. The survey provides a picture of the current situation in the organization and a diagnostic instrument to monitor and control the migration to the desired state.

During the change process, it is important to monitor the organizational health to identify and react to potential detrimental reactions. For this purpose, the chapter listed four potential measurements of employee and organizational wellbeing. First, it is important to monitor the toxicity level of an organization. On its own, the National Survey of Toxic Personalities only provides the consultant with potential areas of concerns. The Toxic Organization Change System helps the consultant address the workplace toxicity using three potential change strategies related to the organization strategies, the team strategies and the individual strategies (Kusy & Holloway, 2010). There is an array of OD and psychological surveys such as the Myers-Briggs Type Indicator (MBTI), 360-degree feedback surveys, the Campbell-Hallam-Team Development Survey, the Belbin Team Roles, Cameron and Quinn´s Organizational Culture Assessment Inventory (OCAI) or the Hofstede´s Organizational Culture Scan Light (Waisfisz, 2015), to mention only a few, that would provide additional guidance during this process.

In addition to monitoring the toxicity level of the organization during change, the consultant should also rely on the Maslach Burnout Inventory – General Survey (MBI-GS), the Workplace Incivility Scale (WIS) and the Measure of Cynicism about Organizational Change (MoCaOC). A consultant uses the MBI-GS to measure the burnout level of individual employees and in the overall organization. By analyzing the three subscales (depersonalization, exhaustion, and efficacy), one could determine what modifications to the change strategy need to be made at the individual and organizational level. For example, resentment and apathy could be the result of a perceived lack of personal efficacy that could be resolved by further focusing on the process and not the end-point (Lubit, 2008). The MoCaOC should complement the results obtained in the depersonalization subscale of the MBI-GS. High levels of organizational cynicism denote a need to change the communication and leadership strategies. For example, greater levels of delegation or a reduction in micro-management may be called for at this stage. Greater involvement of the employees would help clarify the processes and goals. Finally, the WIS would provide another snapshot of the organizational climate and to a certain degree, of the organizational culture.

CONCLUSION

Using the tools mentioned above provides consultants with a diagnosis of the organizational health during change while permitting the monitoring and management of the employee wellbeing. A traumatized employee is an unproductive employee. It is in the best interest of an organization to ensure that trauma is monitored and controlled over the change process. While it may be hard to prevent, acting on potential reasons or sources of stress and trauma could improve the chances of success of an organization implementing change.

Change is inevitable. But the effects of change on the wellbeing of employees could be diagnosable with the help of different tools such as the ones presented in this chapter. Models such as the Burke-Litwin model, provide a list of factors that should be considered during times of change, as well as diagnostic tools to evaluate those factors. By identifying the potential negative effects that change could cause on the wellbeing level of employees, the management of an organization, consultants or HR practitioners could anticipate and neutralize the Dark Side of change, supporting the productivity and effectiveness of the overall organization. Those same diagnostic tools could provide organizational leaders with a better evaluation of the success (or failure) of the change plan, providing opportunities to adapt or modify specific actions. Change is inevitable but the dark side of change does not need to be.

REFERENCES

Abrahamson, E. (2004). *Change without pain: How managers can overcome initiative overload, organizational chaos, and employee burnout*. Boston, MA: Harvard Business School Press.

Ace, W., & Parker, S. (2010). Overcoming change fatigue through focused employee engagement. *OD Practitioner*, *42*(1), 21–25.

Andersson, L. M., & Pearson, C. M. (1999). Tit for tat? The spiraling effect of incivility in the workplace. *Academy of Management Review*, *24*(3), 452–471. doi:10.5465/AMR.1999.2202131

Arnetz, B. B. (2005). Subjective indicators as a gauge for improving organizational well being. An attempt to apply the cognitive activation theory to organizations. *Psychoneuroendocrinology*, *30*(10), 1022–1026. doi:10.1016/j.psyneuen.2005.03.016 PMID:15955637

Atluri, V., Jubas, J., Patel, D., & Schneider, J. (2012). *Mobile industry at a crossroads*. Retrieved from https://tmt.mckinsey.com/

Barger, N., & Kirby, L. (1995). *The challenge of change in organizations: Helping employees thrive in the New Frontier*. Mountain View, CA: Davies-Black Publishing.

Beer, M., & Nohria, N. (2000). Cracking the code of change. *Harvard Business Review*, *78*(3), 133–141. PMID:11183975

Blau, G., & Andersson, L. (2005). Testing a measure of instigated workplace incivility. *Journal of Occupational and Organizational Psychology*, *78*(4), 595–614. doi:10.1348/096317905X26822

Bringselius, L. (2014). Employee objections to organizational change: A framework for addressing management responses. *Organization Development Journal*, *32*(1), 41–54.

Bughin, J., Chui, M., & Manyika, J. (2013). *Ten IT-enabled business trends for the decade ahead*. Retrieved from http://www.mckinsey.com/insights/high_tech_telecoms_internet/ten_it-enabled_business_trends_for_the_decade_ahead

Bughin, J., Ferruz-Aguilar, P., Gil-Gómez, J., & Spittaels, S. (2013). *Evolve or perish: Digital Darwinism for telecom companies*. Retrieved from http://www.mckinsey.com/~/media/mckinsey/dotcom/client_service/Telecoms/PDFs/Evolve_or_Perish.ashx

Burke, W. W. (2011). *Organization change: Theory and Practice* (3rd ed.). Thousand Oaks, CA: Sage Publications.

Burke, W. W., & Jackson, P. (1991). Making the SmithKline Beecham merger work. *Human Resource Management*, *30*(1), 69–87. doi:10.1002/hrm.3930300105

Burke, W. W., & Litwin, G. H. (1992). A causal model of organizational performance and change. *Journal of Management*, *18*(3), 523–545. doi:10.1177/014920639201800306

Burnes, B. (2009). *Managing Change* (5th ed.). London, UK: FT/Prentice Hall.

Burnes, B., & Jackson, P. (2011). Success and failure in organizational change: An exploration of the role of values. *Journal of Change Management*, *11*(2), 133–162. doi:10.1080/14697017.2010.524655

Cameron, K., & Quinn, R. (2011). *Diagnosing and changing organizational culture: Based on the competing values framework*. San Francisco, CA: Jossey-Bass.

Cameron, K., Quinn, R., DeGraff, J., & Thakor, A. (2006). Competing values leadership: Creating value in organizations. MPG Books Group. doi:10.4337/9781847201560

Cavaiola, A., & Lavender, N. (2000). *Toxic coworkers: How to deal with dysfunctional people on the job. Working with narcissists, borderlines, sociopaths, schizoids, and others*. Oakland, CA: New Harbinger Publications Inc.

Caza, B., & Cortina, L. M. (2007). From insult to injury: Explaining the impact of incivility. *Basic and Applied Social Psychology*, *29*(4), 335–350. doi:10.1080/01973530701665108

Cooper, C. L., & Lu, L. (2016). Presenteeism as a global phenomenon. *Cross Cultural & Strategic Management*, *23*(2), 216–231. doi:10.1108/CCSM-09-2015-0106

Cortina, L. M., Magley, V. J., Williams, J., & Langhout, R. (2001). Incivility in the workplace: Incidence and impact. *Journal of Occupational Health Psychology*, *6*(1), 64–80. doi:10.1037/1076-8998.6.1.64 PMID:11199258

Coyle-Shapiro, J. A. (2002). A psychological contract perspective on organizational citizenship behavior. *Journal of Organizational Behavior*, *23*(8), 927–946. doi:10.1002/job.173

Daniels, A. C. (2000). *Bringing out the best in people: How to apply the astonishing power of position reinforcement*. New York, NY: McGraw-Hill.

Danna, K., & Griffin, R. W. (1999). Health and wellbeing in the workplace: A review and synthesis of the literature. *Journal of Management*, *25*(3), 357–384. doi:10.1177/014920639902500305

De Cuyper, N., Raeder, S., Van der Heijden, B. M., & Wittekind, A. (2012). The association between workers employability and burnout in a reorganization context: Longitudinal evidence building upon the conservation of resources theory. *Journal of Occupational Health Psychology*, *17*(2), 162–174. doi:10.1037/a0027348 PMID:22352292

DiPofi, J. A. (2002). Organizational diagnostics: Integrating qualitative and quantitative methodology. *Journal of Change Management*, *15*(2), 156–168. doi:10.1108/09534810210423053

Driver, M. (2003). Nothing clinical, just business? Reflections on psychoanalytically grounded organizational diagnosis and intervention. *Human Relations*, *56*(1), 39–59. doi:10.1177/0018726703056001449

Frost, P. J. (2004). Handling toxic emotions: New challenges for leaders and their organization. *Organizational Dynamics*, *33*(2), 111–127. doi:10.1016/j.orgdyn.2004.01.001

Gallego-Toledo, J. M. (2015). *The Relationship between perceived frequency of change and the wellbeing of telecom professionals*. Ann Arbor, MI: UMI Dissertation Services.

Gallos, J. V. (2008). Learning from the toxic trenches. *Journal of Management Inquiry*, *17*(4), 354–367. doi:10.1177/1056492608320580

Gallup Consulting. (2011). *State of the global workplace 2011*. Retrieved from http://www.gallup.com/strategicconsulting/145535/State-Global-Workplace-2011.aspx

Goldratt, E. (2010, July 17). *Overcoming resistance to change: Isn't it obvious?* [YouTube]. The World with Theory of Constraints. Retrieved from https://youtu.be/hcz1aZ60k7w

Goodstein, L. D., & Burke, W. W. (1991). Creating successful organization change. *Organizational Dynamics*, *19*(4), 4–17. doi:10.1016/0090-2616(91)90050-J

Grawitch, M. J., Gottschalk, M., & Munz, D. C. (2006). The path to a healthy workplace: A critical review linking healthy workplace practices, employee wellbeing, and organizational improvements. *Consulting Psychology Journal: Practice and Research*, *58*(3), 129–147. doi:10.1037/1065-9293.58.3.129

Gregory, B. T., Harris, S. G., Armenakis, A. A., & Shook, C. L. (2009). Organizational culture and effectiveness: A study of values, attitudes, & organizational outcome. *Journal of Business Research*, *62*(7), 673–679. doi:10.1016/j.jbusres.2008.05.021

Griffin, R. W., & O'Leary-Kelly, A. M. (2004). *The dark side of organizational behavior*. San Francisco, CA: Jossey-Bass – A Wiley Imprint.

Hay Group. (2004, March 4). *A culture for learning: An investigation into the values and beliefs associated with effective schools*. Retrieved from http://www.haygroup.com/Downloads/uk/misc/Culture_for_Learning.pdf

Herzberg, F. (2003). One more time: How do you motivate employees? *Harvard Business Review*, *81*(1), 87–96. PMID:12545925

Hofstede, G. H., Hofstede, G. J., & Minkov, M. (2010). *Cultures and organizations: Software of the mind: Intercultural cooperation and its importance for survival* (3rd ed.). McGrawHill.

Holloway, E., & Kusy, M. (2010). Detox your workplace. *Marketing Health Services*, *30*(3), 24–27. PMID:20804081

Hong, G., Cho, Y., Jintae-Froese, F., & Shin, M. (2016). The effect of leadership styles, rank, and seniority on affective organizational commitment. *Cross Cultural & Strategic Management*, *23*(2), 340–362. doi:10.1108/CCSM-03-2014-0034

Hwang, G., & Lee, J. (2000). The process innovation in a competitive telecommunications market: A case study. *Total Quality Management,11*(4/5/6), S728-S733.10.1080/09544120050008138

Igo, T., & Skitmore, M. (2006). Diagnosing the organizational culture of an Australian engineering consultancy using the competing values framework. *Construction Innovation*, *6*(2), 121–139. doi:10.1108/14714170610710659

John, P., Arnon, E., & James, T. (2000). Cynicism about organizational change. *Group & Organization Management*, *25*(2), 132–153. doi:10.1177/1059601100252003

Kaplan, R. S. (2005). How the balanced scorecard complements the McKinsey 7-S model. *Strategy and Leadership*, *33*(3), 41–46. doi:10.1108/10878570510594442

Kiefer, T. (2005). The real reason people won't change. *Harvard Business Review*, *79*(10), 85–92.

Kotter, J. (1995). Leading change: Why transformation efforts fail. *Harvard Business Review*, *73*(2), 59–67. doi:10.1002/npr.10055

Kotter, J. (2011, March 23). *John Kotter- Dealing with resistance to change* [YouTube]. Retrieved from https://youtu.be/Wdroj6F3VlQ

Kotter, J. P., & Schlesinger, L. A. (2008). Choosing strategies for change. *Harvard Business Review, 86*(7/8), 130–139. PMID:10240501

Kusy, M., & Holloway, E. (2009). *Toxic workplace! Managing toxic personalities and their systems of power*. San Francisco, CA: John Wiley & Sons, Inc.

Kusy, M., & Holloway, E. (2010). Cultivating a culture of respectful engagement. *Leader to Leader, 2010*(58), 50–56. doi:10.1002/ltl.442

Leiter, M. P., Gascón, S., & Martínez-Jarreta, B. (2010). Making sense of work life: A structural model of burnout. *Journal of Applied Social Psychology, 40*(1), 57–75. doi:10.1111/j.1559-1816.2009.00563.x

Leiter, M. P., Laschinger, H., Day, A., & Oore, D. (2011). The impact of civility interventions on employees social behavior, distress, and attitudes. *The Journal of Applied Psychology, 96*(6), 1258–1274. doi:10.1037/a0024442 PMID:21744942

Leroy, H., Palanski, M., & Simons, T. (2012). Authentic leadership and behavioral integrity as drivers of follower commitment and performance. *Journal of Business Ethics, 107*(3), 255–264. doi:10.1007/s10551-011-1036-1

Locke, E. A., & Latham, G. P. (2009). What should we do about motivation theory? *Academy of Management Review, 29*, 388–403.

Lubit, R. H. (2008). *Coping with toxic managers, subordinates.... and other difficult people: Using emotional intelligence to survive and prosper*. Upper Saddle River, NJ: FT Press.

Martinez, M. E., Morales, O., Rodríguez, O., Rosa, W., & Sánchez, S. (2009). Civilidad, incivilidad y el bienestar asociado al trabajo en un grupo de personas empleadas en Puerto Rico[Civility, incivility and the wellbeing associated with the workplace on a group of Puerto Rican employees]. *Revista Interamericana de Psicología Ocupacional, 28*(1), 45–55.

Maslach, C. (2003). *Burnout: The cost of caring*. Cambridge, MA: Marlor Books.

Maslach, C., & Leiter, M. P. (2008). Early predictors of job burnout and engagement. *The Journal of Applied Psychology, 93*(3), 498–512. doi:10.1037/0021-9010.93.3.498 PMID:18457483

Meier, L., & Spector, P. (2013). Reciprocal effects of work stressors and counterproductive work behavior: A five-wave longitudinal study. *The Journal of Applied Psychology, 98*(3), 529–539. doi:10.1037/a0031732 PMID:23379915

Moreno-Jiménez, B., Bustos, R., Matallana, A., & Miralles, T. (1997). La Evaluación del burnout: Problemas y Alternativas. El CBB como evaluación de los elementos del proceso[A burnout evaluation: Problems and alternatives. The CBB as an evaluation tool of process elements]. *Revista de Psicología del Trabajo y de las Organizaciones, 13*(2), 185–207.

Morgan, G. (2011). Reflections on Images of Organization and its implications for organization and environment. *Organization & Environment, 24*(4), 459–478. doi:10.1177/1086026611434274

Muscalu, E., & Muntean, S. (2013). Motivation - A stimulating factor for increasing human resource management performance. *Review of International Comparative Management, 14*(2), 303-309.

Nadler, D. A., & Tushman, M. L. (1980). A model for diagnosing organizational behavior. *Organizational Dynamics, 9*(2), 35–51. doi:10.1016/0090-2616(80)90039-X

Nadler, D. A., & Tushman, M. L. (1989). Organizational frame bending: Principles for managing reorientation. *Academy of Management Executive, 3*(3), 194-204. doi:10.5465/AME.1989.4274738

O'Leary-Kelly, A. M., Griffin, R. W., & Glew, D. J. (1996). Organization-motivated aggression: A research framework. *Academy of Management Review, 21*(1), 225–253. doi:10.5465/AMR.1996.9602161571

Patnaik, J. B. (2011). Role of work culture in improving organizational health. *Amity Journal of Applied Psychology, 2*(1), 40–48.

Pearson, C. M., Andersson, L. M., & Porath, C. L. (2000). Assessing and attacking workplace incivility. *Organizational Dynamics, 29*(2), 123–137. doi:10.1016/S0090-2616(00)00019-X

Pearson, C. M., Andersson, L. M., & Wegner, J. W. (2001). When workers flout convention: A study of workplace incivility. *Human Relations, 54*(11), 1387–1419. doi:10.1177/00187267015411001

Rafferty, A. E., & Griffin, M. A. (2006). Perceptions of organizational change: A stress and coping perspective. *The Journal of Applied Psychology, 91*(5), 1154–1162. doi:10.1037/0021-9010.91.5.1154 PMID:16953776

Rafferty, A. E., & Griffin, M. A. (2006). Perceptions of organizational change: A stress and coping perspective. *The Journal of Applied Psychology, 91*(5), 1154–1162. doi:10.1037/0021-9010.91.5.1154 PMID:16953776

Ramírez-Velázquez, J. (2006). *El Estudio de las Emociones en el Ámbito Laboral* [A study of emotions in the workplace]. Presentation at V Congreso National AMET: Trabajo y Reestructuraci6n: Los Retos del Nuevo Siglo.

Reichers, A. E., Wanous, J. P., & Austin, J. T. (1997). Understanding and managing cynicism about organizational change. *The Academy of Management Executive, 11*(1), 48–59. doi:10.5465/AME.1997.9707100659

Shull, A. C., Church, A. H., & Burke, W. W. (2014). Something old, something new. *OD Practitioner, 46*(4), 23–30.

Stanley, D. J., Meyer, J. P., & Topolnytsky, L. (2005). Employee cynicism and resistance to organizational change. *Journal of Business and Psychology, 19*(4), 429–459. doi:10.1007/s10869-005-4518-2

Stone, K. B. (2010). *Relationships between organizational performance and change factors and manufacturing firms´leanness*. Retrieved from http://dspace.library.colostate.edu/webclient/DeliveryManager/digitool_items/csu01_storage/2011/04/22/file_1/96022

Stone, K. B. (2015). Burke-Litwin Organizational Assessment Survey: Reliability and Validity. *Organization Development Journal, 33*(2), 33–50.

Van der Hoeven, R., & Sziraczki, G. (1998). *Lessons from privatization: Labour issues in developing and transitional countries*. Geneva, Switzerland: ILO Publications.

Waclawski, J. (2002). Large-scale organizational change and performance: An empirical examination. *Human Resource Development Quarterly*, *13*(3), 289–305. doi:10.1002/hrdq.1032

Waisfisz, R. (2015). *Constructing the best culture to perform*. Helsinki, Finland: Itim Publications.

Wanous, J. P., Reichers, A. E., & Austin, J. T. (2000). Cynicism about organizational change: Measurements, antecedents, and correlates. *Group & Organization Management*, *25*(2), 132–153. doi:10.1177/1059601100252003

Weisbord, M. R. (1971). Eight most important issues managers should look into. *Industrial Management (Des Plaines)*, *13*(6), 11.

Weisbord, M. R. (1976). Organizational Diagnosis: Six places to look for trouble with or without a theory. *Group & Organization Studies*, *1*(4), 430–447. doi:10.1177/105960117600100405

KEY TERMS AND DEFINITIONS

Climate: A perception developed by individuals within an organization related to how well and effective their local work unit is managed and how their day-to-day colleagues work together to accomplish the organization´s common goals.

Dark Side Behaviors: Those behaviors that could be perceived as injurious to human welfare, and result in an indirect and direct economic and wellbeing cost on the employees and the organization as a whole.

Motivation: The ability to energize, direct and/or sustain a behavior as well as affect the intensity of the behavior and its recurrence.

Organizational Culture: Organizational climate refers to the enduring set of explicit and implicit behaviors, norms, shared values, expectations and assumptions that governed the relationship among employees within an organization.

Organizational Health: The ability of an organization to meet its performance goals while functioning within competitive and working environments that encourages employee wellbeing and the search for the optimization of stakeholders´ value.

Transformational Changes: Organizational changes that are more drastic in nature and require a fundamental and radical change to several key factors such as the organizational culture, strategy and mission, and/or leadership. This type of changes calls for a major adjustment on the part of employees´ actions, objectives and behaviors.

Transactional Change: This type of changes, also known as a first-order change, require recurrent, gradual and continuous adjustments to existing processes and organizational elements such as management, motivation, and procedural systems.

Wellbeing: This term refers to the complex framework constructed upon factors such as mental health, psychological health, and aspects of an employee´s behaviors and tendencies.

Chapter 7
National Culture Influence on Organisational Trauma:
A Conceptual Framework Review

Pavel Cejka
University of Economics, Czech Republic

Hana Mohelska
University of Hradec Kralove, Czech Republic

ABSTRACT

Increasing human interaction creates extra stress on individuals and organisations as well. The nature of such stress results in economic shocks and large societal and organisational traumas. Although recent social science is capable of addressing the complexity of international interplay such as culture, acts of multinational corporations or cross-cultural team management, little attention was paid on the cultural aspects of removing organisational trauma. Since the 1980s, social science has experienced lively development in cross-cultural studies via the work of Hofstede, the Globe Group, the World Value Survey initiative, Trompenaars, Schwartz and others. Although major models are sufficient for defining national culture, there is lack of work explaining the managerial implications for crisis management or mitigating trauma in organisations.The authors of this chapter intend to critically review the latest literature on national culture, while discussing the relevant models and introducing the theoretic framework applicable for crisis/ trauma management.

INTRODUCTION

Natural disasters, acts of terrorism, or losing a family member have a strong psychological impact not only on individuals, but societies and organizations as well (Dutton, et al., 2002). Trauma's role in having a negative influence on the national culture was described in the example of Saadat Hasan Manto's genocide (Saint, 2012). The author Saint (2012) argues that under extreme external pressure, cultural norms can be re-forged. In his review, Norburn (1987) suggests that managerial attitudes, beliefs or values are a function of their country of origin. He (Norburn & Hall, 1987) also claims that it is not an

DOI: 10.4018/978-1-5225-2021-4.ch007

individual decision, but rather the national culture of the decision maker which impacts that organization. Culture plays a crucial role in recovering from organizational trauma (Brewis & Ozbilgin, 2013).

"A program of the mind" (Hofstede, 1990) is a definition introduced by Hofstsede for the concept of culture. Although there is a vivid debate on the definition, application, and robustness of culture as a concept, one is generally used in the literature: the importance and impact of the culture on the behaviour of individuals, communities, countries or organizations. The concept of culture shapes social sciences and is gaining significant momentum in the field of management too.

This chapter aims to explore conceptual models of national culture and their relationship to organizations and their traumas and trauma recovery. This is important, as one's occupation has a direct influence on their mental health (Champagne, 2009). An extensive literature review will be carried out to fulfil the goal of the research. The desired outcome is a conceptual map comparing major national culture-related studies (such as Hofstede, Schwartz, Trompenaars and Globe) and their influence on organizational traumas and mitigating them. We also intend to introduce a critical discussion of the concepts of national culture vs. the corporate stream of thoughts culture.

BACKGROUND

National Culture vs. Corporate Culture

The cultural concept debate started in 1955 when Herskovitz (1995) suggested culture to be "the human-made part of the environment", and Shwered and LeVine (1984) introduced the importance of the shared meaning of cultural systems, or the "Collective programming of a mind" as Hofstede defines culture. An important aspect of this view of culture is the collective understanding of it. Perhaps the most complex understanding of culture was demonstrated in the original study by Rohner (1984) "the largest unit of a territorially bounded, multigenerational population recruited largely through sexual reproduction, and organized around a common culture and a common social system", describing the social system also known as society. He also describes culture as "the totality of equivalent and complementary learned the meanings maintained by a human population, or by identifiable segments of a population, and transmitted from one generation to the next". Rohner's definition is supported by Lenug (2006) and Redding & Witt (2009).

Lively academic discussion has resulted in two major schools of thoughts. The collective centric scholars such as Hofstede tend to generalize their observations into a group or national cultural behaviours. Others lead by Rohner tilt toward the importance of the individual culture definer. Their definition of culture suppresses the idea of creating "cultural boxes". Such an elementary cultural debate might be seen through the literature from leading international business or management studies (Boyacigiller & Adler, 1991; Leung & Bond, 2006; Rohner, 1984; Tung & Verbeke, 2010). This academic discourse leads to the question of which of the streams is more sustainable for management studies, and why?

Concepts: National Culture vs. Corporate Culture

The introduction of the culture concept created extensive enthusiasm among researchers. Such excitement has contributed to the large variety of fields in social science management. Increased academic debated has been noticed in management, marketing, international business or even human-machine interaction.

Cejka (2015) explains (that) Hofstede's model (abbr. HM) is based on the idea of mental programs (Hofstede, 2001), a set of value-driven behaviours shared among individuals within a common culture. Germans, for example, perceive time with punctual preciseness compared to Italians for whom 10-20 minutes do not represent a serious delay (Cateora, et al., 2006) .

The advantage of the HM concept is its robust empirical base (Cejka, 2015); research was carried out in 60 countries with more than 160,600 participants and used quantitative methods (Hofstede, 1984). Hofstede (1984) characterizes culture as "the collective programming of the mind". Originally, HM identified 4 main dimensions in which culture could be assessed: (1) Individualism (ID); (2) Uncertainty avoidance (UA); (3) Power distance (PD); and (4) Masculinity-femininity (MA) (Soares, et al., 2007). Due to the wording limitation of this chapter, the focus will be only on the original 4 dimensions, leaving later additions such as Long-term Orientation undiscussed.

In contrast to Hofstede, some academics suggest that corporate culture or sub-culture offers a more precise insight into the management related disciplines (Chen & Li, 2005; Boyacigiller & Adler, 1991). Orr and Hauser (2008) also suggest that more research reflecting the "21st century" is needed, as the impact of globalization could influence the local cultures.

The introduction of the culture concept created extensive enthusiasm among researchers. Such excitement contributed to the large variety of management fields in social sciences. Increased academic debate can be seen in management, marketing, international business or even human-machine interaction.

As introduced in the previous chapter, there is also evidence of the lively discussion among scholars of management concerning the level one needs to understand culture as a collective construct or not. However, this debate has key implications for cultural management studies (Tung, 2008). Early attempts to scientifically describe culture resulted in "nation-centric" theories such as the one introduced by Hofstede (Hofstede, 1990). The "collective mind program" as it was called gained a lot of attention. Although Hofstede's framework remains the most cited cultural models by Soares, Farhangmehr, & Shoham (2007), it faces a major critique of its methodology and its construct (House, et al., 2004). The latest argument in opposition to Hofstede's work suggests that nation based cultural assessments carry major caveats and may not be the best for addressing management issues (Leung & Bond, 2006). Some authors would argue that his work is obsolete due to its outdated data (Orr & Hauser, 2008). McSweeney (2002) questions its validity and reliability. These critiques have its own importance, since Hofstede's Culture Consequences work is more quoted than any other Social Science book (Orr & Hauser, 2008; Yoo & Bonthu, 2002).

In contrast to Hofstede, some academics suggest that corporate culture or sub-culture offers a more precise insight into management related disciplines (Chen & Li, 2005; Boyacigiller & Adler, 1991). Orr and Hauser (2008) also suggest that more research reflecting the "21st century" is needed, as the impact of the globalization could influence local cultures. Research not based on discrimination or nomological validity is needed (iBit).

Hofstede's defenders praise his work as the most dominant cultural model today (Soares, et al., 2007) even as the number of citations increases. The model was created 30 years ago and it is still considered to be the most influential management thesis assessing culture (Ailon, 2009). Authors (Soares, et al., 2007) supports this claim by demonstrating double digit growth of the phenomena in marketing literature. In rebuttal, Hofstede (2001) pointed out that some of the arguments are only focused on a portion of the research, and entirely ignore critical parts of the original work (Hofstede, 1984; Hofstede, 2002). HM enjoyed support from several qualitative researchers such as Chapman (1996). Hofstede (2002) explains that this is quite strong as it was written by an anthropologist rather than an "accountant". McSweeney's

Table 1. Advantages and disadvantages of National vs. Corporate culture approach (Leung, 2005; Lenartowicz and Roth, 1999)

Currently Used Cultural Assessments							
Cultural Scope	**Research Paradigm**	**Construct**	**Research Method**	**Metrics**	**Strengths**	**Limitations**	**Application in the literature**
National Culture	Centric	Cross-cultural theory	Quantitative, DVI	Nominal	Convenience	Validity, Group Identification	Very much
	Top-down	Indicates effects of the national culture on the individual or organization	Quantitative, DVI	Nominal or Interval	Interval Measures	Sampling	Limited
	Bottom-up	Suggest the influence of individual to the group and the nation	Ethnological Description	N/A	Theory support	Measures not developed, time consuming	Very limited
Organisational Culture	Centric	Culture as such derived from patterns and habits.	Quantitative or Qualitative	Interval or N/A	Interval measures	Sampling or non developed values	Limited
	Community based	Open, non-hierarchical context	Mostly Ethnographical	N/A	Theory support	Measures not developed, time consuming	Very limited

critique is also questionable as it failed to understand a functionalist paradigm suggested by Burrell & Morgan (1979). Williamson (2002) agrees, and further elaborates that McSweeney failed to comprehend the positivist tone which Hofstede employs. On the other hand, the same Williamson (2002) suggests that more research which replicates the original research or tests the robustness of the model is required.

The Table 1 summarizes the advantages and disadvantages of National vs. Corporate culture approaches. This synthesis is based on Leung et al. (2005) and Lenartowicz and Roth.

The summary has identified that organization-centred studies are not so popularly debated in the literature. Therefore, although they are time consuming by nature, they do have a significantly higher research justification compared to nation-focused ones (Gould & Grein, 2005). This conclusion supports (Fletcher & Fang, 2006) who revealed the increasing irrelevancy of nation-based surveys under the rising significance of globalization. That is why Tung and Verkebe (2010) claim intra-national diversity on the sub-cultural level reflects reality better than nation-based studies, as the national cultural score is rather a momentary "snapshot". Tung (Tung, 2008) also introduced the concept of "brain circulation" which makes a nation-based assessment even more inaccurate. This concept, explains Tung, counts on ex-host country nationals returning to their homelands, while nation- based studies fail to do so.

Nevertheless, there is an interdependent relationship between national culture, global culture (or national culture) and perceptions as shown below (Leung, et al, 2005):

Therefore, in order to assess the culture(s) it is important to decide whether the concept of the national culture (NC) is to be considered as an independent variable or a dependent one (Gould & Grein, 2005). One must not fail to consider the complexity of the factors influencing culture. For the purpose

Figure 1. Relationship between national culture, global culture and perceptions (Leung, et al, 2005)

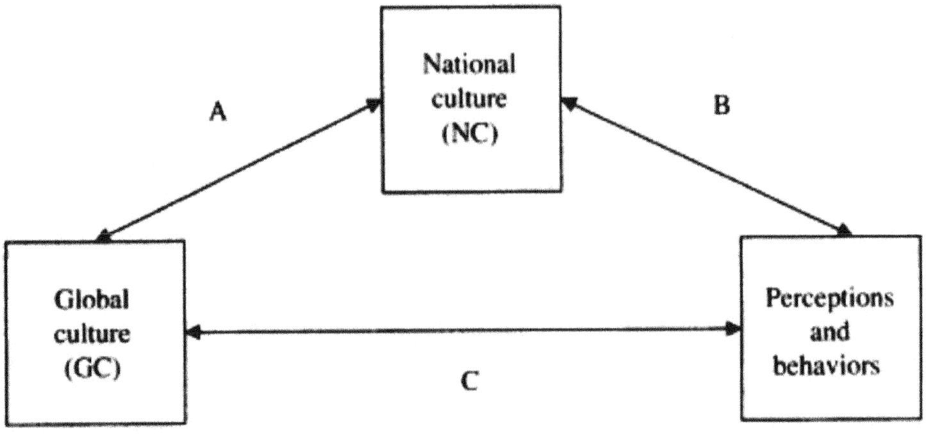

of this study, the fallacies of national culture ought to be avoided by a thorough literature review and by addressing only cultural dimensions related to the carryover of trauma. Multinational organizations operate on a global scale with a lack of resources to explore its market place on the sub-cultural level. This is why understanding national culture plays a vital role, but only an introductory role in one's success.

RESEARCH METHODOLOGY

Pragmatism leaning towards interpretivism was selected as the research tone of this chapter. This is a theoretic, conceptual cross-field literature review intended to explore and synthesize the current concepts from the management, psychology and organisational studies.

The authors selected the following research inquiry approaches, according to King, Keohene & Verba (1994)

1. Research impact by International Social Science Index (Cortez, 2015)
    a. Management journal articles
    b. Journal articles from other scientific fields
    c. Monographies
    d. Scientific literature
2. Chronological order
3. Cross-disciplinary articles
4. Other literature e.g. magazines, newspapers or news agencies

For example: an article from Harvard business review, 2008 is considered superior to the Journal of International Management, 2014.

Such an approach provides this study with sound academic sourcing. However, some updated studies might be overlooked.

Research from the database of the Senate house library of the University of London was used by both researchers: http://encore.ulrls.lon.ac.uk/iii/mobile/home?lang=eng for securing homogeneous outcomes of research inquiries.

To create a conceptual map, a mind mapping approach analogy (Mindomo, 2016; iMindMap, 2016) was modified to create the following

1. Selecting a central concept. This is a starting point of the MAP and represents the researched top
2. Introduce branches representing dependent topics.
3. Find relationships among the concepts.

Scope

Due to the size limitation given by the chapter's length, the scope of this work is to examine leading national culture concepts (Globe, Schwartz, Hofstede and WVS) from conceptual perspective of organisational trauma and its managerial implication. The purpose is to present a conceptual map identifying conceptual relationships and introducing knowledge gaps for further research.

NATIONAL CULTURAL CONCEPTS

Hofstede's model is not the only well-developed and acknowledged model. Schwartz, the World Value Survey, Thompenaars and Globe proposed their own conceptual works explaining nation-based cultural frameworks. The above discussed welcomes conceptual research by drawing a parallel between the national culture model(s) and organizational trauma recovery.

Hofstede's Model

In his research evaluating culture, Cejka (2015) summarizes the 4 elementary Hofstede's dimensions as follows:

1. **Individualism Represents:** "People looking after themselves and their immediate family only, versus people belonging to in-groups that look after them in exchange for loyalty" (Hofstede, 2012) This dimension is bi-polar as it expresses individualism vs. collectivism. The more "collectivist" a country is the less individualism it enjoys. ID introduces social interaction; whether people live in tight families, larger families or they live alone. Chinese culture has difficulty understanding the Western concept of "my or myself" explains Hsu (1971). This is related to the perception of individuality, which in traditional Chinese culture is conceptualized by an emperor who symbolizes the entire Chinese population (Hsu, 1971). Individualism was considered evil by Mao Ze-Tsung, as it reflected the self-perceived greatness of the United States of America (Short, 2001). Etzioni (1975) elaborates more fully, explaining that in a collectivist society, one respects her fiduciary duty towards other members of the community. Countries with the highest ID are those of Anglo-American origins: the USA, Australia and Great Britain as opposed to Latin countries such as Guatemala, Ecuador and Venezuela. The European Marketing Survey of 1997 supported this differentiation.

2. **Uncertainty Avoidance**: "The extent to which people feel threatened by uncertainty and ambiguity and try to avoid these situations" (Hofstede, 2012) Rules, technology and religion help create controls which will reduce uncertain outcomes in the future. For example, Swiss Airlines pilots were supposed to consult the emergency manual in case of an unexpected situation; American Airlines, on the other hand, encourages their crews to cope with the situation first and then check the manual (BBC, 2013). High UA countries would therefore be expected to have a developed bureaucratic system trying to deal with unexpected situations with a strictly defined set of rules. Computer simulations could achieve similar goals, the deployment of scientists or strict control systems, which are so called "rituals". Greece, Belgium and Japan lead the table of UA. Great Britain, Singapore and Sweden scored low on the level of the uncertainty avoidance chart. Similar distinctions were also found in the Values Survey Module (Spector, et al., 2001), 1982 and WVS (2016) supporting the UA chart suggested by Hofstede.
3. **Power Distance:** Is "the extent to which less powerful members of a society accept and expect that power is distributed unequally" (Hofstede, 2012). It could also be understood as a boss-subordinate relationship. This evokes cultural attributes rooted in social inequality such as wealth, power and prestige. Cultures with a high PD will support an elite social class over the welfare of the group. This behaviour is reflected in the corporate culture. It is the elite group of managers who are perceived to have a superior, unquestionable social standard. Those cultures tend to be highly hierarchical with deep respect for elders. Malaysia, Panama and Arab counties topped the PD table opposed to Austria, Nordic countries and New Zealand with the lowest level of PD. World Value Surveys (WVS) researched family values, e.g. "hard work, obedience, independence, free-mind" and find clusters of nations to fit the HM. According to WVS, children in high-PD countries were supposed to strictly follow the values of their parents by being obedient. New Zealanders' children were supported in creativity and innovation. This phenomenon was supported by oth:er studies, e.g. the Spencer-Oatey (1997) comparison of British and Chinese students.
4. **Masculinity:** Represents masculinity/femininity. It describes how individuals behave differently in society based on the gender stereotypes. Feminine culture focuses on relationship, helping others, physical environment. The masculine culture aims at money, success, advancement and career. Mead (2001) characterizes men as "assertive, competitive and tough" and "women as caring and tender". Not only gender differentiation stresses dissimilar values, it also proves different feelings and socializing (Tannen, 1990): "The dominant values in the masculine society are achievement and success; the dominant values in feminine society are caring for others and quality of life".

The Germans, Swiss and Italians scored high on the masculinity side; Nordic countries along with the Netherlands were among the most feminine states (Hofstede & Hofstede, 2005). Women tend to work at the same job position as men in low masculinity countries, earning similar wages (Umans, et al., 2008) (see Figure 2).

GLOBE Model

The GLOBE Leadership and Organisational Behaviour Effectiveness Research (Globe) project followed up on the previous success of Hofstede's study. A team directed by Professor Robert House of Wharton Business School explored the differences and issues surrounding of Hofstede's work. The team investigated 62 countries, where 17,300 front-line managers in 951 organizations were questioned via

Figure 2. Elementary Hofstede's dimensions (Cejka, 2015)

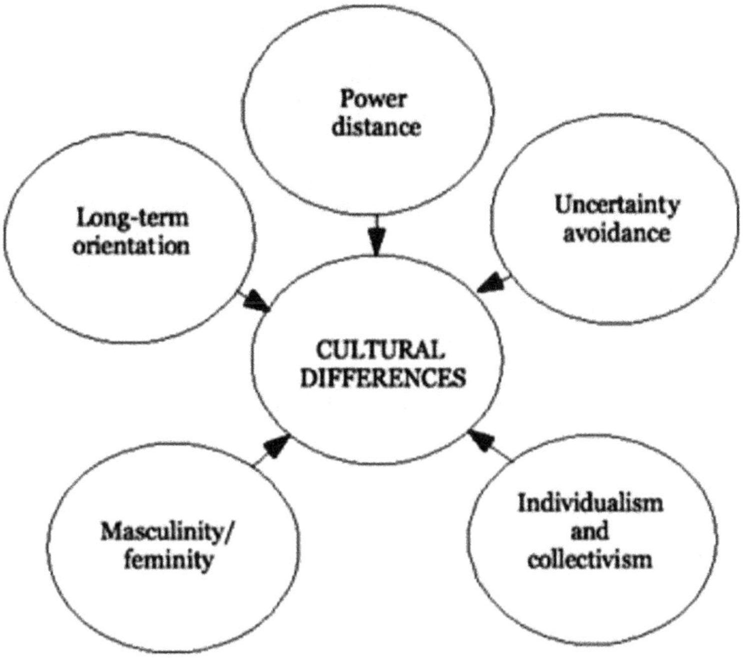

quantitative survey. Nine cultural competencies, grouped into ten cultural clusters were introduced as the result of the research (Javidad & Dastmalchian, 2012).

1. **Performance Orientation**: Refers to the extent to which inhabitants value performance improvement.
2. **Assertiveness Orientation**: Assess the assertiveness in relationships. This is reflected in aggression in negotiations or negotiation styles.
3. **Future Orientation**: Describes how much organizations or cultures plan for the future. Planning or saving might be an example of such behaviours.
4. **Humane Orientation**: Is the degree to which individuals in organizations or societies encourage and reward individuals for being fair, altruistic, friendly, generous, caring, and kind to others.
5. **Collectivism I**: Institutional collectivism - reflects the degree to which organizational and societal, institutional practices encourage and reward collective distribution of resources and collective action.
6. **Collectivism II:** In-group collectivism - reflects the degree to which individuals express pride, loyalty and cohesiveness in their organizations or families.
7. **Gender Egalitarianism**: is the extent to which an organization or a society minimizes gender role differences and gender discrimination.
8. **Power Distance**: is defined as the degree to which members of an organization or society expect and agree that power should be unequally shared.
9. **Uncertainty Avoidance**: is defined as the extent to which members of an organization or society strive to avoid uncertainty by relying on social norms, rituals, and bureaucratic practices to alleviate the unpredictability of future events.

Table 2. Hofstede's and Globe's model comparison

Hofstede's Model	Globe Model
Individualism	Institutional and in-group collectivism, Humane orientation
Uncertainty Avoidance	Uncertainty Avoidance
Power distance	Power distance
Masculine vs. Feminism	Performance orientation, assertiveness, gender egalitarians

Globe and Hofstede's Overlap

Hofstede's and Globe's models overlap to some extent, which is represented in the Table 2.

Shalom Schwartz, an Israeli professor, introduced his cultural model in the 1990s. He introduced the following dimensions:

- **Embeddedness**: Is characterised by the change of avoiding behaviour with focus on traditions. People from such cultures prefer group work and nurturing social relationships which are highly valued as are security and obedience.
- **Harmony**: Cultures focus rather on individual development. External factors are widely accepted and the group is appreciated over individualism. Protection of the environment is highly important.
- **Egalitarian:** Cultures promote social equality with a focus on other members of the community.
- **Autonomy Courtesy**: Is the opposite of embeddness. People in such cultures believe they are responsible for their own choices.
- **Mastery**: Is a culture where one influences the World by their own actions. Independence, courage, ambition, drive and competence are sometimes valued over the benefits of others.

On top of the dimensions introduced, Schwartz grouped them into 3 bi-polar pairs: Embeddness vs. Autonomy, Mastery vs. Harmony and Hierarchy vs. Egalitarianism (Schwartz, 1999) (shown in Figure 3).

World Value Survey

In 1991 a group of social scientists lead by Roland Inglehart started their project covering 100 countries reaching to over 400,000 respondents, covering 90% of the Global population. This research covered not only leading economies, but also regions.

Traditional Values vs. Secular-Rational Values and Survival Values vs. Self-Expression ones were identified.

- **Traditional Values:** Appreciate close family relationships, value religion and respect authority. Divorce, abortion, euthanasia or suicide is rejected in cultures with traditional values. Individuals from these cultures have a high sense of national feeling. Qatar, Jordan or Trinidad represents traditional values cultures.
- **Secular-Rational Values:** Are the opposite of traditional ones. Religion, traditional family norms and authority are taken with more ease, which is typical for Scandinavia.

Figure 3. Schwartz bi-polar pairs of cultural model (Schwartz, 1999)

- **Survival Values:** Are driven by the physical safety and economic security like in Ukraine or Tunisia. A low level of trust and resilience is evident, whilst *self-expression values* tend to focus on the environment, accepting foreigners, and homosexuals and represent gender equality in social interactions. Canada or Australia represents such cultures (Inglehart, et al., 1995). All these values are illustrated in Figure 4.

Thompenaars

Fons Trompenaars and Charles Hampden-Turner published a book in 1997 called Riding the Waves of Culture in which 7 dimensions of culture were introduced. The solid research base of 46,000 managers in 40 countries was questioned over the 10 years of the research.

- **Universalism vs. Particularism:** Is the extent to which rules are applied in all cases or applied according to the individual cases
- **Individualism Versus Communitarianism:** Is similar to Hofstede's Individualism and describes whether an individual is driven by his/her own profit or feels connected to the group which he/she tends to contribute to.
- **Specific vs. Diffuse:** Shows how society considers the consequences. Are they linked or not related?
- **Neutral vs. Emotional:** Determines whether emotions are hidden or shown publicly.

Figure 4. A Cultural map of the world (Inglehart, et al., 1995)

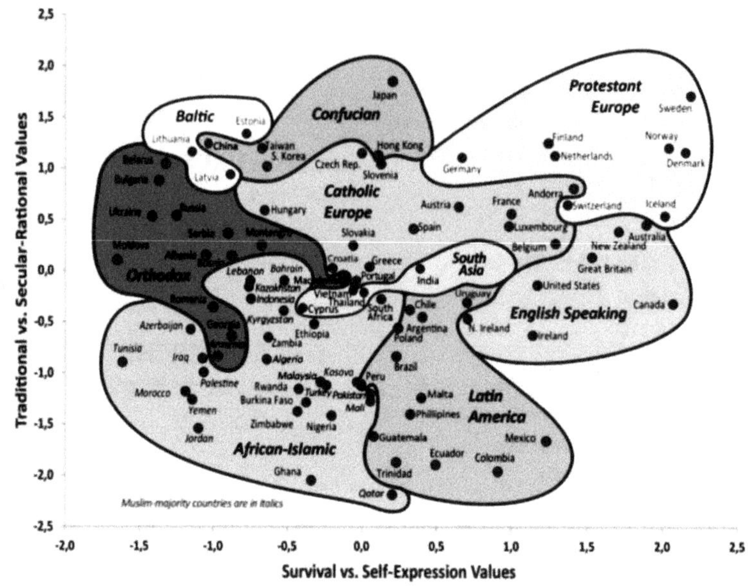

- **Achievement vs. Ascription:** Characterize whether goals are considered to be achieved via individual actions or by affiliations to particular individuals.
- **Sequential vs. Synchronous Time:** Represents understanding time as a sequence of individually managed events or as a flexible fuzzy variable.
- **Internal direction vs. Outer Direction:** Is whether one believes in shaping the external environment or being shaped by other settings (Trompenaars & Hampden-Turner, 1997). The dimensions of culture described are shown in Figure 5.

RESULTS: TRAUMA IMPACT ON ORGANIZATIONS

Emotional conflicts have a strong impact on organizational performance (DeDreu & Weingart, 2002). It has also been pointed out that conflict is more probable in cross-cultural teams due to their misalignment in values and beliefs (von Glinow, et al., 2004). Similar authors suggest that conversation is a sufficient way of getting over a traumatic experience (iBit). However, words alone are sometimes insufficient to get over cultural barriers (Wierzbicka, 1992). For example, Czech does not distinguish between the words "responsible" and "accountable", whereas English speaking individuals feel the contextual difference. Faraj and Xiao (2006) argue that a set of protocols, rules and knowledge sharing are necessary for fast moving organizations, such as hospital emergency units; such rules may ease cultural clashes (von Glinow, et al., 2004). This argument is also supported by authors who see crisis management as a stabilization and transformation of operations (James & Wooten, 2010).

There is a strong agreement in the literature that organizations are defined by the relationships of people – the so-called "nervous system of the organization" (Kahn, et al., 2013). Some authors point out that the relationship system is the key for operations under high uncertainty (Gittel, 2008). However,

Figure 5. Dimensions of culture (Trompenaars & Hampden-Turner, 1997)

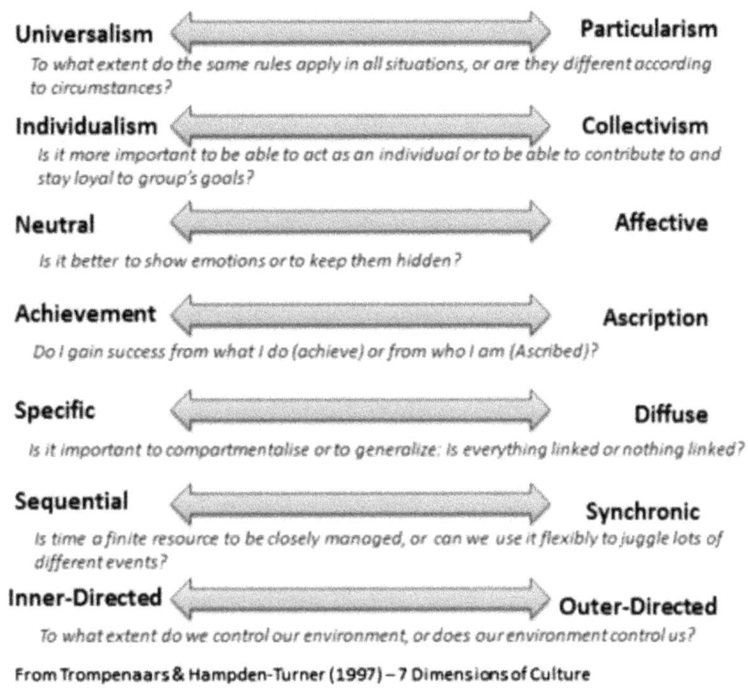

groups of individuals who have experienced trauma tend to demonstrate changed patterns of relating to each other (Kahn, et al., 2013).

Tjosvold (Cheung & Chuah, 1999) suggests that conflict, possibly resulting in trauma is inevitable in an organization, and can have positive or negative consequences depending on how it is managed.

The relational family system describes several dimensions (Olson, 2000): 1] Cohesion, 2] Flexibility and 3] Communication. In terms of cohesion, one may understand how individuals choose to act as an individual or group. Flexibility refers to one's tendencies to change or stability and Communication reflects verbal and non-verbal interactions as well as openness and moral integrity. All three dimensions define culture within a group (Kahn, et al., 2013), which can be severely shifted by the crises (Pearson & Clair, 1998). Kahn, et al., (2013) gave an example of a senior management team experiencing increased anxiety and disruption of their values during the crises. This led to weakened relationships between the team members, lasting even 6 months after the crises ended. Scholars (Walsh & Olson, 1993) also suggest that the level of severity of the aftermath of a crisis is related to the strength of previous bonds. Some authors suggest that a traumatic experience may make the organization stronger in the long term (Clair, et al., 2002). Astrong family-work enrichment provides faster recovery from such distresses or situations (Powell, et al., 2009).

A definition of trauma: "extraordinary events outside the range of usual human experience that overwhelm our coping ability" (Herman, 1997).

Powel, et al. (2009) point out the relationship between family and work cultures. They also stressed that one's culture of origin has an influence on both family and work in the way in which the interpersonal relations are created (Powell, et al., 2009). Other authors (Powell, et al., 2009) also consider individualism/collectivism, humane orientation and specificity/diffusion and gender egalitarianism as

Table 3. Cultural models comparison (Powell, Francesco, & Ling, 2009)

Cultural model	Dimension	Implication
Hofstede Globe	1] Individualism	• Motivation factors • Quality of life focus • Work-family connection • Entrepreneurism • Conflict management • Communication consensus
Globe	2] Humane Orientation	Accountability for someone else's well being
Trompenaars	3] Specificity/ diffusion	• Level of integration vs. atomic existence • Independent linkages in the work
Globe	4]Gender egalitarianism	1. Women tend to smooth out the conflicts

the only family-work relevant cultures. They use examples of Americans coming from highly individualistic cultures which focus rather on individual goals, whereas Chinese individuals would be driven by the shared values of a community. The authors also suggest that higher collectivist countries tend to connect work-family more than individual countries.

Comparison of Models Presented

The researchers also suggest that the involvement of family in solving work problems plays a key role.

1. **Individualism:** Indicates "People looking after themselves and their immediate family only, versus people belonging to in-groups that look after them in exchange for loyalty" (Hofstede, 2012). Some may recognize this dimension as either low and high individuals or collectivism and individualism respectively. The lower "collectivist" a country is, the less individualism it enjoys. People in highly individualist countries tend to care about their own lives, while low individual cultures value interaction within communities or group decision making. Low individual cultures also tend to take care of the elderly and youth as a group, explains Hsu (1971). Etzioni (1975) elaborates more fully, explaining that in low individualistic cultures there is a fiduciary duty towards other members of the community. This is related to the perception of individuality, which in traditional Chinese culture is conceptualized by an emperor who symbolizes the entire Chinese population. Countries with the highest ID are for example the USA, Australia and Great Britain as opposed to Japan, Taiwan, Malaysia or Singapore. The European Marketing Survey of 1997 supported this differentiation.
2. **Humane Orientation:** Might be translated as "the degree to which an organization and society encourages and rewards individuals for being fair, friendly, generous, caring and kind to others" (House, et al., 2004). Some authors suggest that low humane oriented cultures tend to focus on one's own benefits only, tangible benefits are major motivators, the government is responsible for providing support when needed, and there is a low sensitivity towards discrimination. Individuals are interested in the well-being of others in high humane oriented countries, looking for affiliation to the group and are sensitive towards discrimination. When facing an uneasy situation, US workers would try to solve problems individually or in a smaller group, whilst workers in Hong Kong would expect involvement from their top management (Golnaz, 2013).

3. **Specificity/Diffusion:** Refers to the level of a manager's influence over an individual in specific areas of one's life opposed to all areas. This questions whether the employee – manager relationship should extend beyond work related matters and influence his/her personal life as well (van Lieshout & Steurenthaler, 2006). An example is given by Trompenaars & Hampden-Turner (1997) that US managers display friendliness toward their Chinese counterpart not expecting this relationship to develop into deeper levels, whilst Chinese individuals tend to extend the relationship beyond their workplace.

Mitigating Sensitive Trauma in National Culture

Carrying over a trauma is a long lasting and complex process in which a combination of several methods can take place (Lambert & Alhassoon, 2015). Lambert & Alhasoon (2015) pointed out that it is hard to provide a one fit all solution due to the lack of previous research and the large amount of variables such as: types of trauma exposure, the current situation or cultural background. They illustrated this on their research examining trauma-focused therapies on refugees. Mejia (2005) supports Lambert & Alhassoon (2015) as "male and female react differently to traumas" she concludes. She states that "for the male traumas, masculinity plays role in their treatment". However, trauma recovery might take from 2 months to years (Mejia, 2005). It is on the organizational leadership to facilitate organization through the trauma stage by providing stability, processing and grieving, and transcendence (Luxenberg, et al., 2001). Researchers agree that the role of counsellor and communication plays a vital role (Luxenberg, et al., 2001; Mejia, 2005; Lambert & Alhassoon, 2015; Makison & Young, 2012). An example of a special programme is one that was developed in New York City for around 3,700 eligible victims who were workers displaced by 9/11 terrorism. This helped them return back to work, demonstrating the importance of counselling and trauma facilitation for large scale trauma recoveries (Precin, 2010).

Related research on national culture fails to introduce the entire full scale of dimensions from which management applications are suggested (Cejka, 2015); this is usually misleading for the lack of supporting evidence in doing so (Orr & Hauser, 2008; Ailon, 2009; Maseland & van Hoorn, 2009). It has been pointed out in previous sections that following national-culture related dimensions are relevant when addressing organizational trauma phenomena: 1) Hofstede – Individualism, 2) Globe – Human Orientation, 3) Globe – Gender egalitarianism, 4) Trompenaars – Specificity/diffusion. The implications of this on Management will be explained in the next session.

Managerial Implications of National Culture on Trauma in Organizations

When organizations suffer from a trauma, it is important to act quickly to minimize its impact (Kahn, et al., 2013) and prevent subsequent complications from developing (Shen, et al., 2009). This is a hard job for small and medium-sized companies. However, it is even a more challenging endeavour for corporations with cross-cultural teams and multi-national scope (Blake, 1972; Hamilton III & Knouse, 2001). Increased ethical conflicts (Hamilton III & Knouse, 2001), lower operational effectiveness (Huchzemeier & Cohen, 1996) and other risk factors having a high negative impact on the output of multinational enterprises (MNC) lingers in the cross-cultural nature of MNC, summarizes Tong & Reuer (2007).

Hofstede's work introduced Individualism as one of its cultural dimensions. A basic differentiation of cultural division can be two a) low and b) high implication zones. For example, the US individualism score is 91 compared to Taiwan's 17 (Hofstede, 2016). Therefore, one should consider the US as a highly individualistic country, whereas Taiwan should be understood to not value individualism so much (therefore collectivist). Similar logic can be put on the Globe and Trompenaars' findings.

Individualism Implications

Traumatized corporations should advocate for the importance of quality of life as one of its values, while reinforcing work-family connections and creating communication based on the consensus of the community for the low individual countries such as Greater China, Portugal or Malaysia. On the other hand, they should enhance the entrepreneurial spirit of an individual together with providing counselling services. Communication should be carried out by the management addressing the importance of conflict management. An example is given by the reaction of Chinese export-oriented enterprises to the 2009 global economic crisis. Instead of austerity, some (about 30%) of the MNC decided to involve employees in the process to find a solution and kept their compensation intact (Shen & Netto, 2012). This helped organizations to absorb the impact of the external economic shock. During the 2008 Sichuan Earthquake tragedy, the Chinese government relied strongly on the high involvement of volunteers and the Chinese population to help facilitate the swift disaster recovery (Hui, 2009).

Humane Orientation Implications

Cultures of high humane orientation (HO), such as the Philippines, Australia or Canada should support increased peer interaction within the organization during the trauma period. On the other hand, low HO countries, for example Germany, Hungary or Israel ought to let impacted individuals rely on the external support (e.g., governmental or senior leadership help) during the traumas. Israel depended on the help from the US or UN for their economic crisis recovery (Anon., 1977), Arab-Israel Crisis (Ben-Yehuda & Sandler, 1998) or the Middle East Crises (Haney, 1994).

Specificity Implications

Low specificity nations tend to work in larger groups or communicate and involve family members into conflict resolution and trauma carry over. When you get invited for a dinner in China your host shows great hospitality to develop a relationship. Such behaviour has a strong impact on the business (Anon., 2016). Japan, Singapore and China are examples of low specificity countries (Trompenaars & Hampden-Turner, 1997), while high specificity can be expected in Sweden, the UK, Canada or the Czech Republic (Trompenaars & Hampden-Turner, 1997). For the high specific cultures one should invite senior management to provide most of the trauma easing communication. The linkages which were not impacted by the trauma should be supported and strengthened.

For example, when Chinese and Estonians experienced crisis, the management of organizational tactics were investigated and compared. It was determined that Estonia was more efficient as they focused on people, while Chinese companies focused on the economic upturn failed (Alas, et al., 2007) to provide culture sensible communication (Trompenaars & Hampden-Turner, 1997). A similar discovery was made when comparing business crisis communication of US and Japanese airlines. In Japan, extra effort was paid to apologizing to victims and their families, as a culturally sensitive act (Haruta & Hallahan, 2003).

Gender Egalitarianism Implications

Switzerland, Germany and Australia dominate the table as highly egalitarian countries (Trompenaars & Hampden-Turner, 1997). When facing a trauma, an organization should rely on women's natural sensitivity in removing agony. Enterprises located in highly egalitarian societies are advised to create gender diverse engagement teams for mitigating the damage. Yemen, Mali or Liberia share extremely low values in gender equality (United Nations, 2012). Women are often not eligible to be involved in decision making, gatherings or highly valued jobs in these cultures (Hill & King, 1995). Our recommendation is to involve women in trauma, easing groups in low gender egalitarian states, where culturally viable. A study by Lyness & Judiesch (2014) confirmed that gender plays a strong extension of the cross-cultural social role theory. Other authors also promote the importance of mixed gender across the various levels of the organization, explaining they help to absorb external shocks better. There are several examples of how women played a critical role in large traumas such as the Argentinean Economic Crisis (Chejter, 2004), the Sub-Saharan Africa Economic Crisis in 1980s (Howard, 1985; Forje, 1998) or war and economic crises in the UK (Smith, 1987). Organizations can take advantage by continuously planning to increase women's roles during hardships. The findings of the previous chapter are summarized in the below introduced table:

Figure 6. Conceptual Map of Conceptual Relationships between Org. Trauma and Nat. Culture

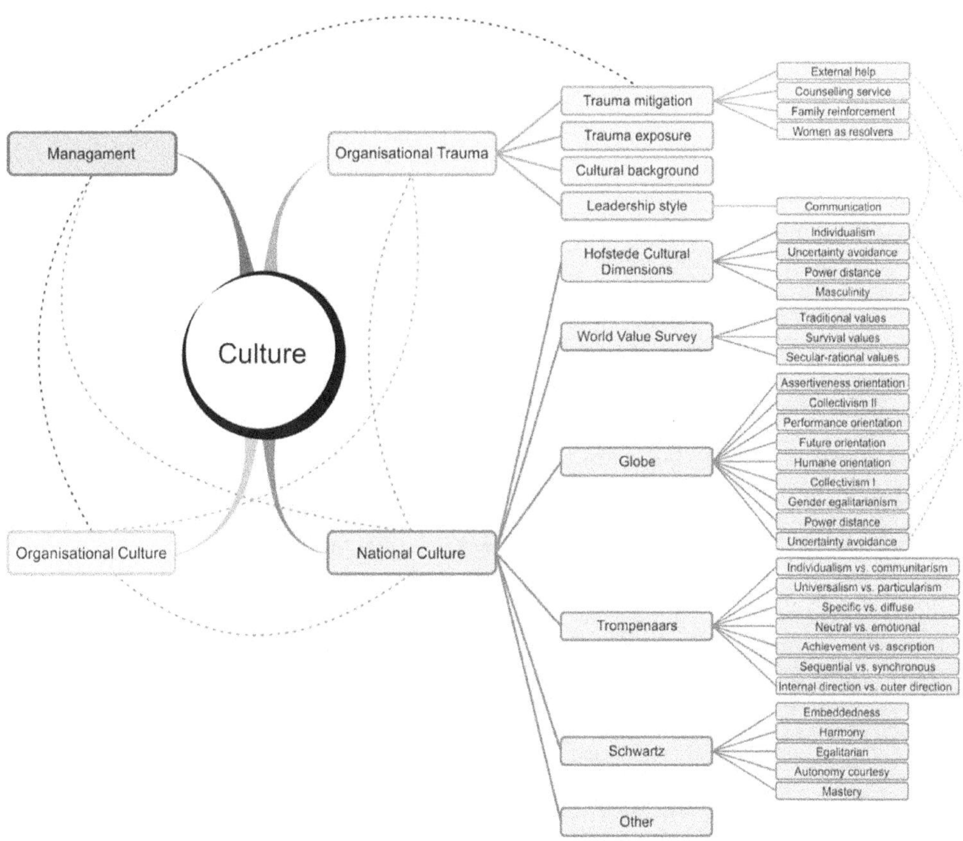

Conceptual Map

The theory discussed in the previous chapters is summarised in the conceptual mind map below (see Figure 6). Each concept is represented by a colour box, where the relationships are marked by the doted lines; blue for commonly acknowledge relationships and red for the direct relationship (e.g. those well described in the literature).

The national culture concept is popular and there are several major studies covering this topic. Each research introduces its own definition of culture and its components, as shown in Figure 7.

It was discovered that some national culture components (across the studies) such as Individualism, Uncertainty Avoidance, Humane Orientation or Gender Egalitarism are closely related to mitigating organisational trauma areas such as the role of women in trauma removal, family importance, implications of counselling services or the importance of external help.

Figure 7. Narrowed Map of the direct conceptual relationships of Org. Trauma Mitigation and National Culture sub-components

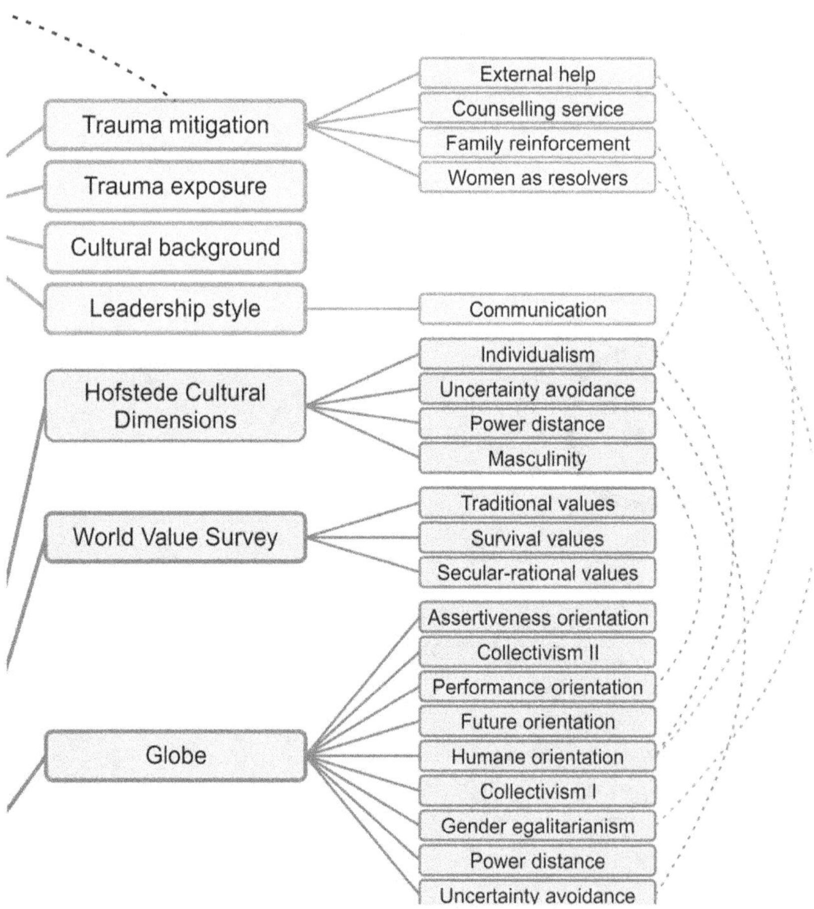

CONCLUSION

External shocks such as the 2009 economic recession, the 2014 Ebola outbreak or the 2015 EU immigration crisis or internal disturbances such as a leadership change, the VW scandal or a company takeover might create external tensions resulting in a crisis or organizational trauma. Trauma has a long-lasting effect on organisational performance. Scholars agree that immediate mitigation actions need to take place, minimizing the further impact on the organization. Several trauma recovery strategies are introduced in the literature. Although the selection process of the best strategy is a complex process, researchers agree that the role of counselling, communication and culture play critical roles. Globalization, multicultural teams and multinational corporations introduce another ramification level to the puzzle of effective trauma recovery.

National culture vs. organizational culture models were critically reviewed in the first section of this chapter. National culture constructs were introduced in the 1980s in the work of Hofstede, Schwartz, Trompenaars or GLOBE. Social science experienced growing citation and expansion of the national culture knowledge in past 20 years. On the other hand, some researchers argue against national culture, pointing out its methodological and structural fallacies. These authors call for research to be carried out on the organizational or sub-cultural level. Although the critique by the authors of this chapter of the "giants" is justified, they also identified sufficient evidence for national culture concepts being relevant constructs for this paper.

The cultural frameworks of GLOBE, Hofstede, Schwartz or Thompenaars were studied in search of the best structure for assessing organizational trauma cultural . It was noticed that none of the frameworks examined can be considered/applied as such, but only Individualism of Hofstede, Specificity of Thompenaars and Globe's Humane Orientation and Gender Egalitarism are cultural dimensions suitable for the further assessment.

The new trauma recovery framework was introduced by suggesting national culture sensitive actions, increasing crisis mitigation efficiency.

- **The Low Individualism:** Culture organization was advised to reinforce the quality of life in their crisis communication, acknowledge and enhance family-work bonds and seek communicational consensus.
- **High Individualism:** Organizations should promote individual entrepreneurism, secure external counselling aid and introduce conflict solution addressing communication.
- **Low Humane Oriented:** Cultures were recommended for providing external professional help (e.g., Psychologists, Psychiatrists) for the trauma sufferers.
- **A High Humane Oriented:** Nation based corporations were directed to facilitate help via peer conversation and engagement.
- **Low Specificity:** Cultures were supposed to work with larger communities/groups and involve families of the impacted individuals.
- **High Specificity:** Cultures, on the other hand, were urged to invite senior management into the active trauma solution and involvement and support individual links within the organization.
- **Low Gender Egalitarian:** Nations were invited to involve women in trauma easing activities.
- **High Gender:** Egalitarian state based organizations were encouraged to strengthen gender differentiation on the trauma engagement teams.

The previously-introduced summary findings are believed to contribute to management science as well to international managerial practice.

The authors believe that this framework is easy to be translated into actionable plans for the severe crisis facing organizations.

RESEARCH LIMITATIONS AND STEPS FORWARD

This work is limited in the scope provided by the chapter's size and nature. The researchers only provided a theoretical analytic-synthetic work based on the review of the leading literature. Although research is applied and expandable, it lacks an empirical test of the theoretical findings. Organisational trauma is a phenomenon combining many fields of social science. Therefore, one deeper review is needed to map out its relationships to culture-related disciplines. Last but not least, this research only operated under the national culture construct lacking the sub-cultural and organizational cultural insight. This research also lacks a deeper examination of organisational trauma, instead exploring its subcomponents that are closer related to the national culture components.

Organisational culture and sub-cultural scholars are invited to build on our findings. We also hope that some researchers will explore this topic in greater depth, such as the research work of the University of Hradec Kralove's researchers (Franěk, et al., 2014).

REFERENCES

Ailon, G. (2009). *Dialog*. Academy of Management Review.

Alas, R., Gao, J., & S, V. (2007). The crisis management in Chinese and Estonian organizations. *Chinese Management Studies,* 18-36.

Anon., (1977). Israel's Economic Crisis. *Journal of Palestine Studies*, 137–145.

Anon. (2016). *International Business Cultures*. Available at: http://www.via-web.de/specific-vs-diffuse-cultures/

BBC. (2013). *News*. Available at: http://www.bbc.com/news/uk-england-somerset-22077051

Ben-Yehuda, H., & Sandler, S. (1998). Crisis Magnitude and Interstate Conflict: Changes in the Arab-Israel Dispute. *Journal of Peace Research, 35*(1), 83–109. doi:10.1177/0022343398035001006

Blake, D. H. (1972). Trade Unions and the Challenge of the Multinational Corporation. *The Annals of the American Academy of Political and Social Science*, *403*(1), 34–45. doi:10.1177/000271627240300104

Boyacigiller, N. A., & Adler, N. J. (1991). The Parochial Dinosaur: Organizational Science in a Global Context. *Academy of Management Review*, 262–290.

Brewis, J., & Ozbilgin, M. (2013). Introducing Recovery and Organization. *Culture and Organization, 19*(5), 371–376. doi:10.1080/14759551.2013.848631

Burrell, G., & Morgan, G. (1979). *Social Paradigms and Organisational Analyses*. Toronto: Ashgate.

Cateora, P. R., Graham, J. L., & Bruning, E. R. (2006). International Marketing (13th ed.). London: McGraw-Hill Ryerson.

Cejka, P. (2015). Pilot validation of Hofstede's original 4 dimensional cultural model and its marketing implications from the perspective of the Czech Republic, Slovakia and Poland. University of Economics.

Champagne, T. (2009). The influence of posttraumatic stress disorder, depression, and sensory processing patterns on occupational engagement: A case study. IOS Press.

Chapman, M. (1996). Social Anthropology, Business Studies and Cultural Issues. *International Studies of Management & Organization*, 3–29. doi:10.1080/00208825.1996.11656692

Chejter, S. (2004). *Argentinian Women Survive Economic Crisis*. Chicago Journals.

Chen, X. P., & Li, S. (2005). Cross-national differences in cooperative decision-making in mixed-motive business contexts: The mediating effect of vertical and horizontal individualism. *Journal of International Business Studies*, *36*(6), 622–636. doi:10.1057/palgrave.jibs.8400169

Cheung, C. C., & Chuah, K. B. (1999). Conflict management styles in Hong Kong industries. *International Journal of Project Management*, *17*(6), 393–399. doi:10.1016/S0263-7863(98)00059-3

Clair, J. A., MacLean, T. L., & Greenberg, D. N. (2002). Teaching Through Traumatic Events: Uncovering the Choices of Management Educators as They Responded to September 11th. *Academy of Management Learning & Education*, *1*(1), 38–54.

Cortez, C. (2015). *Web of Science*. Available at: http://ip-science.thomsonreuters.com/mjl/publist_ssci.pdf

DeDreu, C. K., & Weingart, L. R. (2002). *Task versus relationship conflict, team performance, and team member satisfaction: A meta-analysis*. Denver, CO: Academy of Management.

Dutton, J. E. (2002). Leading in Times of Trauma. *Harvard Business Review*, *80*(1), 54–61. PMID:12964467

Etzioni, A. (1997). *Modern Organizations*. New York: Bearport.

Faraj, S., & Xiao, Y. (2006). *Management Science*. Available at: http://pubsonline.informs.org/doi/ref/10.1287/mnsc.1060.0526

Fletcher, R., & Fang, T. (2006). Assessing the impact of culture on relationship creation and network formation in emerging Asian markets. *European Journal of Marketing*, *40*(3/4), 430–446. doi:10.1108/03090560610648138

Forje, L. C. (1998). Crisis Helps to Demarginalize Women. *Development in Practice*, *8*(2), 211–216. doi:10.1080/09614529853828 PMID:12293703

Franěk, M. (2014). *Organizational and Sociodemographic Determinants of Job Satisfaction in the Czech Republic*. Sage OPEN.

Gittel, J. H. (2008). Relationships and resillience: Care provider responses to pressures from managed care. *The Journal of Applied Behavioral Science*, *XLIV*(1), 25–47. doi:10.1177/0021886307311469

Golnaz, S. (2013). Choosing conflict resolution by culture. *Industrial Management (Des Plaines)*, (September), 11–15.

Gould, S. J., & Grein, A. F. (2005). Think Glocally, Act Glocally: A Culture-Centric Comment on Leung, Bhagat, Buchan, Erez and Gibson (2005). *Journal of International Business Studies*, *40*(2), 237–254.

Hamilton, J. B. III, & Knouse, S. B. (2001). Multinational Enterprise Decision Principles for Dealing With Cross Cultural Ethical Conflicts. *Journal of Business Ethics*, *31*(1), 77–94. doi:10.1023/A:1010793408485

Haney, P. (1994). The Nixon Administration and Middle East Crises: Theory and Evidence of Presidential Management of Foreign Policy Decision Making. *Political Research Quarterly*, *47*(4), 939–959. doi:10.1177/106591299404700410

Haruta, A., & Hallahan, K. (2003). *Cultural issues in airline crisis commnications: A Japan-US comparative study*. Public Relations and Communication.

Herman, J. L. (1997). *Trauma and recovery*. New York: Basic Books.

Herskovitz, E. (1995). Struggling over Subjectivity: Debates about the Self and Alzheimers Disease. *Medical Anthropology Quarterly*, *9*(2), 146–164. doi:10.1525/maq.1995.9.2.02a00030 PMID:7671112

Hill, M. A., & King, E. (1995). Womens Education and Economic Well-Being. *Feminist Economics*, *1*(2), 21–46. doi:10.1080/714042230

Hofstede, G. (1984). Culture's consequences: international differences in work-related values. Beverly Hills, CA: Sage Publications.

Hofstede, G. (1990). Cultural constraints in management theories. *Academz of Management Execitive*, *7*(1).

Hofstede, G. (2001). Culture's consequences: comparing values, behaviors, institutions, and organizations across nations (2nd ed.). Thousand Oaks, CA: Sage Publications.

Hofstede, G. (2002). Dimensions do not exist: A reply to Brandon McSweeney. *Human Relations*, *55*(11), 1355–1361. doi:10.1177/0018726702055011921

Hofstede, G. (2012). *National cultural dimensions*. Available at: http://geert-hofstede.com/national-culture.html

Hofstede, G. (2016). *The Hofstede Centre*. Available at: http://geert-hofstede.com/united-states.html

Hofstede, G., & Hofstede, J. G. (2005). *Cultures and Organizations. Software of the Mind*. New York: McGraw-Hill.

House, R. J. (2004). *Culture, Leadership and Organizations: The GLOBE study of 62 Societes*. Thousand Oaks, CA: Sage.

Howard, R. E. (1985). *Women and the Crisis in Commonwealth Africa*. International Political Science Review.

Hsu, F. L. K. (1971). Filial Piety in Japan and China: Borrowing, Variation and Significance. *Journal of Comparative Family Studies*, 67–74.

Huchzemeier, A., & Cohen, M. A. (1996). Valuing operational flexibility under exchange risk. *Operations Research*, *44*(1), 100–113. doi:10.1287/opre.44.1.100

Hui, L. H. (2009). Politics of Sichuan Earthquake, 2008. *Journal of Contingencies and Crisis Management*, *17*(2), 137–140. doi:10.1111/j.1468-5973.2009.00571.x

iMindMap. (2016). *How to MindMap.* Available at: https://imindmap.com/how-to-mind-map/

Inglehart, R. R., & Abramson, P. (1995). *Value Change in Global Perspective.* University of Michigan Press.

James, E. H., & Wooten, L. P. (2010). *Leading under pressure.* New York: Taylor & Francis.

Javidad, M., & Dastmalchian, A. (2012). Managerial implicaions of the GLOBE project: A study of 62 societies. *Asia Pacific Journal of Human Resources*, 41–58.

Kahn, W. A., Barton, M. A., & Fellows, S. (2013). Organizational Crises and the Disturbance of Relational System. *Academy of Management Review*, *38*(3), 377–396. doi:10.5465/amr.2011.0363

King, G., Keohene, R. O., & Verba, S. (1994). *Designing Social Inquiry.* Princeton, NJ: Princeton University Press.

Lambert, J. E., & Alhassoon, O. M. (2015). Trauma-Focused Therapy for Refugees: Meta-Analytic Findings. *Journal of Counseling Psychology*, *62*(1), 28–37. doi:10.1037/cou0000048 PMID:25485547

Lenartowicz, T., & Roth, K. (1999). A Framework for Culture Assessment. *Journal of International Business Studies*, *30*(4), 781–798. doi:10.1057/palgrave.jibs.8490839

Leung, K., Bhagat, R. S., Buchan, N. R., Erez, M., & Gibson, C. B. (2005). Culture and international business recent advances and their implications for future reserach. *Journal of International Business Studies*, *36*(4), 357–378. doi:10.1057/palgrave.jibs.8400150

Leung, K., & Bond, M. H. (2006). Psycho-logic vs. ecologic: Insights from social axiom dimensions. In *Individuals and Cultures in Multi-level Analysis.* Mahwah, NJ: Lawrence Erlbaum.

LeVine. (1984). *Culture theory: essays on mind, self, and emotion.* Cambridge, UK: Cambridge University Press.

Luxenberg, T. (2001). Complex trauma and disorder of extreme stress (DESNOS) dignosis, part two: Treatment. *Directions in Psychiatry*, 373–392.

Lyness, K. S., & Judiesch, M. K. (2014). Gender Egalitarianism and Work-Life Balance for Managers: Multisource Perspectives in 36 Countries. *Applied Psychology*, *63*(1), 96–129. doi:10.1111/apps.12011

Makison, R. A., & Young, J. S. (2012). Cognitive Behavioral Therapy and the Treatment of Posttraumatic Stress Disorder: Where Counseling and Neuroscience Meet. *Journal of Counseling and Development*, *90*(2), 131–140. doi:10.1111/j.1556-6676.2012.00017.x

Maseland, R., & van Hoorn, A. (2009). Explaining the Negative Correlation between Values and Practices: A Note on the Hofstede–Globe Debate. *Journal of International Business Studies*, *40*(3), 527–532. doi:10.1057/jibs.2008.68

McSweeney, B. (2002). The essentials of scholarship: A reply to Geert Hofstede. *Human Relations*, *55*(11), 1363–1372. doi:10.1177/0018726702555110005

Mead, M. (2001). *Male and Female*. New York: Harper Perennial.

Mejia, X. E. (2005). Gender Matters: Working With Adult Male Survivors of Trauma. *Journal of Counseling and Development*, *83*(1), 29–40. doi:10.1002/j.1556-6678.2005.tb00577.x

Mindomo. (2016). *What is Mind Mapping*. Available at: https://www.mindomo.com/help/mind-mapping.htm

Norburn, D., & Hall, P. D. (1987). The Management Factor in Acquisition Performance. *Leadership and Organization Development Journal*, *8*(3), 23–30. doi:10.1108/eb053618

Olson, D. H. (2000). Circumplex model of marital and family systems. *Journal of Marital and Family Therapy*, *22*(2), 144–167. doi:10.1111/1467-6427.00144

Orr, L. M., & Hauser, W. J. (2008). *A re-inquiry of Hofstede's Cultural Dimensions: A Call for 21st Century Cross-Cultural Research*. Marketing Management Journal.

Orr, L. M., & Hauser, W. J. (2008). *A re-inquiry of Hofstede's cultural dimensions: A call for 21st century cross-cultural research*. Marketing Management Journal.

Orr & Hauser. (2008). *A Re-inquiry of Hofstede's Cultural Dimensions: a Call for 21st Century Cross-cultural research*. The Marketing Management Journal.

Pearson, C. M., & Clair, J. A. (1998). Reframing crisis management. *Academy of Management Review*, *23*, 59–76.

Powell, G. N., Francesco, A. M., & Ling, Y. (2009). Toward culture-sensitive theories of the work-family interface. *Journal of Organizational Behavior*, *30*(5), 597–616. doi:10.1002/job.568

Precin, P. (2010). *Return to work after 9/11* (pp. 3–11). DOI.

Redding, G., & Witt, M. A. (2009). Culture, meaning, and institutions: Rationale in Germany and Japan. *Journal of International Business Studies*, 859–885.

Rohner, R. P. (1984). Toward a conception of culture for crosscultural psychology. *Journal of Cross-Cultural Psychology*, *15*(2), 111–138. doi:10.1177/0022002184015002002

Saint, T. K. (2012). The Long Shadow of Manto's Partition Narratives: "Fictive" Testimony to Historical Trauma. *Social Scientist*, *40*(11/12), 53–62.

Schwartz, S. H. (1999). A Theory of Cultural Values and Some Implications for Work. *Applied Psychology, 48*(1), 23-47.

Shen, J., & Netto, B. D. (2012). Impact of the 2007–09 global economic crisis on human resource. *Asia Pacific Business Review*, *18*(1), 45–64. doi:10.1080/13602381.2011.601163

Shen, Y. C., Hsia, R. Y., & Kuzma, K. (2009). Understanding the Risk Factors of Trauma Center Closures Do Financial Pressure and Community Characteristics Matter? *Medical Care*, *47*(9), 968–978. doi:10.1097/MLR.0b013e31819c9415 PMID:19704354

Short, P. (2001). *Mao: A Life*. London: Holt Paperbacks.

Smith, J. (1987). Transforming Households: Working-Class Women and Economic Crisis. *Social Problems, 34*(5), 416–436. doi:10.2307/800539

Soares, A. M., Farhangmehr, M., & Shoham, A. (2007). Hofstedes dimensions of culture in international marketing studies. *Journal of Business Research, 60*(3), 277–284. doi:10.1016/j.jbusres.2006.10.018

Soares, R. R. (2007). On the Determinants of Mortality Reduction in the Developing World. *Population and Development Review, 1*(July), 247–287. doi:10.1111/j.1728-4457.2007.00169.x

Spector, P. E., Cooper, C., & Sparks, K. (2001). An International Study of the Psychometric Properties of the Hofstede Values Survey Module 1994: A Comparison of Individual and Country/Province Level Results. *Applied Psychology, 50*(2), 269–281. doi:10.1111/1464-0597.00058

Spencer-Oatey, H. (1997). Unequal Relationships in High and Low Power Distance Societies A Comparative Study of Ibtor-Student Role Relations in Britain and China. *Journal of Cross-Cultural Psychology, 28*(3), 284–302. doi:10.1177/0022022197283005

Tannen, D. (1990). *Rethinking Power and Solidarity in Gender and Dominance*. Berkeley, CA: University of Berkeley.

Tong, T. W., & Reuer, J. (2007). Real Options in Multinational Corporations: Organizational Challenges and Risk Implications. *Journal of International Business Studies, 38*(2), 215–230. doi:10.1057/palgrave.jibs.8400260

Trompenaars, F., & Hampden-Turner, C. (1997). *Riding the Waves of Culture: Understanding Cultural Diversity in Business*. London: Nicholas Brealey Publishing.

Tung, L. R. (2008). The cross-cultural research imperative: The need to balance cross-cultural and intra-national diversity. *Journal of International Business Studies, 39*(1), 41–46. doi:10.1057/palgrave.jibs.8400331

Tung, R. L., & Verbeke, A. (2010). Beyond Hofstede and GLOBE: Improving the quality of cross-cultural research. *Journal of International Business Studies, 41*(8), 1299–1274.

Umans, T., Collin, S. O., & Tagesson, T. (2008). Ethnic and gender diversity, process and performance in groups of business students in Sweden. *Intercultural Education, 19*(3).

United Nations. (2012). *Table 4 Gender Inequality Index 2012*. New York: United Nations Development Program.

van Lieshout, S., & Steurenthaler, J. (2006). *Diva-portal.* Available at: http://www.diva-portal.org/smash/get/diva2:119684/FULLTEXT01.pdf

von Glinow, M. A., Shapiro, D. L., & Brett, J. M. (2004). Can we talk, and should we? Managing emotional conflict in multicultural teams. *Academy of Management Review, XIX*(4), 578–592.

Walsh, F., & Olson, D. H. (1993). Utility of the circumplex model with severely dysfunctional family systems. In *Circumplex model: Systematic assessment and treatment of families* (pp. 104–137). New York: Haworth Press.

Wierzbicka, A. (1992). *Semantics, culture, and congnition: Universal human concepts in culture-specific configuations*. New York: Oxford University Press.

Williamson, D. (2002). Forward from a Critique of Hofstedes Model of National Culture. *Human Relations*, *55*(11), 1373–1395. doi:10.1177/0018726702551106

World Value Survey. (2016). Available at: http://www.worldvaluessurvey.org/WVSDocumentationWV1.jsp

Yoo, B., & Bonthu, N. (2002). Book Reviews. *Journal of International Business Studies*, 388–389.

Section 3
Trauma and the Workplace

Chapter 8
Sexual Identities in the Workplace:
Avoiding Organizational Trauma When Disclosure Occurs – Current Perspectives

Robert A. Cleve
The Chicago School of Professional Psychology, USA

İdil Işık
Istanbul Bilgi University, Turkey

Viviane de Castro Pecanha
The Chicago School of Professional Psychology, USA

ABSTRACT

The global progression of human rights advocating for marginalized communities, especially LGBTQ, has seen tremendous change over the past several decades, including the conditions for disclosure of sexual identity in the workplace. The decision-making process of disclosure and the necessity for others to know is key to understanding how best to support and address the potential organizational trauma that may result. Not all disclosure of minority identity is negative and the availability of positive policy development within organizations can assist in smooth transitions toward more equal inclusion and dispel previous heteronormative and heterosexist ideologies. Through increased knowledge about the LGBTQ community and case analysis, a cross cultural lens will be utilized from Brazil, Turkey and the U.S.; prominent sexual identity disclosure perspectives for numerous occupations, as well as recommendations for systemic awareness and change will be offered.

INTRODUCTION

The decision to disclose one's sexual identity can be difficult even under the most optimal of circumstances; in today's politically charged global environments within the broadest context of human rights it can run an entire continuum of challenges. When considered collectively through a cross-cultural lens, the dialogue between universal principles and cultural relativism, as applied to this disclosure decision-

DOI: 10.4018/978-1-5225-2021-4.ch008

making process, should be viewed as interconnected across multiple psychological processes (Berry, Poortinga, Breugelmans, Chasiotis, & Sam, 2013). For the individual, a painstaking cost/benefit analysis utilizing the two disclosure process models (Chaudoir & Fisher, 2010; Cleve, 2012) are critical for any person holding membership in a group identified with a concealable stigmatized identity and includes drug addiction, victims of rape, criminal histories, or sexual minority. Concealable stigmatized identity comprise identities that are not readily visible, but rather require that the person make a decision about whether or not they are shared with another individual in the context of a given situation. These, unfortunately, each contain unique socially negative identifiers.

For those maintaining membership with minority sexual identities, the influence of both internal and relational mediating factors through the decision making process allows one to consider reactions from a relatively broad reference point; individuals, families, colleagues, counselors, supervisors/managers, and specifically, human resource managers can successfully develop a better understanding of inclusive work practices with and within diverse communities. This process can also potentially support institutional and organizational goals for diversity inclusion and may provide a variety of benefits for administrators, managers, staff, and the overall organization (Cunningham & Green, 2007; Saxena, 2014: Stevens, Plaut, & Sanchez-Burks, 2008).

For members of the LGBTQ global community, the cost/benefit analysis includes contemplating a broad spectrum of possible outcomes ranging from acceptance, to tolerance, of being ostracized/ alienated or in the most severe cases, death. The additional requirement of a multilayered analysis (personal, professional, systemic, and organizational) necessitates evaluating the continuum from personal impact to an organizational one, and the layers of this process can become extremely complex. "For sexual minorities, sexual identity disclosure has an impact on workplace commitment and the quality of relationships with coworkers. Gay and bisexual men must weigh the benefits of disclosure with the potential risks for career development" (Mock, Sedlovskaya, & Purdie-Vaughns, 2009, p. 124).

One may question "why is it even necessary to share" such personal information in a work environment. To best understand the 'why' the authors offer definitions and discuss the constructs of heterosexism, homophobia and human rights across several cultural contexts to assist in providing an important discourse on how inherent structures of oppression can create tensions within any system, particularly functional organizations. As the dissonant forces that create these tensions are explored, a plan for navigating or circumventing them can more effectively be established.

The focus of cross-cultural perspectives is essential to the discourse outlined in this chapter and comes from three diverse nations offered from the context of each of the participating authors. One author in the United States, one in Turkey and the third in Brazil, will guide the variety of national perspectives and current ideologies. Each is a university academic with a strong interest in the topics of social justice and advocacy, transformative psychology for stigmatized and marginalized communities; and they have contributed to research work focused on LGBT disclosure decisions for sexual identity.

Research conducted within diverse cultural contexts demonstrates that various types of explicit and non-explicit violence (e.g. homophobia, transphobia, harassment, discrimination, bullying, and stigmatization) towards LGBT individuals in the workplace may potentially generate long lasting traumatic consequences (Ferreira, 2007; Pizer, Sears, Mallory, & Hunter, 2012; Prunas et al., 2016; Siqueira, Saraiva, Carrieri, Lima, & Andrade, 2009; Willis, 2012). Such traumatic consequences include the potential development of psychiatric disorders (e.g. depression, anxiety, and post-traumatic stress), psychological distress, negatively impacting self-esteem, increasing feelings of anger and even suicidal ideation. The additional stress of fundamental religious doctrine that may call for the extinction of family members, who are seen to violate these norms, creates fear through oppression not experienced in all cultures. Known as 'gay honor killings' the phrase was coined in Turkey in 2008 after the murder of Ahmet Yildiz allegedly at the hands of his own father, and has been used on a number of subsequent occasions (Hurtas, 2014).

Despite the extensive range of possible psychological consequences, discrimination in the workplace can additionally impact LGBT employees' wages, job satisfaction, career, promotion opportunities, and overall work productivity (Pizer et al., 2012). Price Waterhouse Cooper, Australia (PwC) in 2016 took the opportunity at the annual 'Midsumma' Festival, a parade and festival supporting the LGBTI community, to interview 500 employees about the perception of workplace. The most important finding from their study indicated, "homophobia is still alive at work" (p. 4); 53% of participants reported witnessing through direct observation or hearing, harassment, discrimination and negative jokes within the past year. Furthermore, violence in the workplace can be exacerbated by a number of factors including race, ethnicity, age, gender, socioeconomic status (SES), and religion. Such factors may affect LGBT individuals on both personal and societal levels. When considering the societal level, it's important to note that in the context of specific countries' laws, cultural and social practices may significantly limit employment opportunities or even preclude workplace benefits (United Nations Human Rights Council, 2015).

In this chapter the authors explore the disclosure process in a cross cultural context, framed within organizations and systems models where LGBT employees may experience a traumatic shift or crisis; when self identification of a member or employee as being gay takes place, recommendations on how to resolve, or hopefully pre-emptively deal with such disclosures in a positive way will be discussed. Organizational culture, sector, and patterns of interpersonal relations create a framework that may turn the disclosure from a negative to an affirming positive experience, ultimately mitigating a traumatic experience both for the individual who is disclosing and for the others who may be impacted by or during that process. Organizational trauma is defined as the emotional impact caused by the internal/external or acute/chronic stressors within the work environment. Formal policies in tandem with informal norms of organizations, structured as social entities, suggest that their systemic functioning can potentially either prevent or enrich possible traumatic experiences for each of their members. This can be evidenced through the examples of the identified professions and organizational settings presented in this chapter.

As businesses and corporations begin to consider the need to develop more inclusive, fair and supportive work environments it is becoming more evident that they are also encouraging anti-discrimination organizational policies and practices through the inclusion of sexual orientation as a protected class (Everly & Schwarz, 2014; Instituto Ethos, 2014; Mahtani & Kernon, 2010; Scobie, 2015; Stein, 2012). The consequence of prominent non-inclusive attitudes can be posited as "organizational trauma" for LGBT people and also for others who witness these organizational interactions. Within business settings these traumatic experiences are viewed as highly possible under conditions of ineffective diversity management and is an important area of concern.

External to the workplace, the recent series of devastating attacks and threats directed toward the global LGBT community; the Orlando killings of 49 LGBT individuals, (Ellis, Fantz, Karimi, & McLaughlin, 2016); threats from ultra-nationalists to successfully disrupt gay pride events in Istanbul, leading to a ban by the government under the guise of safety concerns (The Guardian, 2016), and; religious leaders advocating the "compassionate" killing of gays (The Muslim Issue, 2016) clearly point to considering how current crisis can potentially impact organizations. Such incidents indicate the urgency for accurate information and anti-discrimination policy development to align the rights of all individuals regardless of sexual orientation or gender identity. The claim that the state of the world may be 'improving' for the

LGBT community is likely true only in the sense that governments with separate religious agendas do not immediately revoke rights. However, these issues cannot help but influence workplace organizational and institutional environments and may require protections for a variety of vulnerable populations.

Heterosexism and Homophobia

Defining the constructs of heterosexism and homophobia is a necessary precursor toward developing an understanding of how systemic oppression can lead to organizational trauma that may result from disclosure of sexual identities in the workplace (Badgett, Durso, Kastanis, & Mallory, 2013; Discount, Russell, Gandara, & Sawyer, 2016; King & Cortina, 2010; Pichler, Vama, & Bruce, 2010). In 2003, Louis-Georges Tin, poignantly and quite thoroughly authored and edited the *Dictionary of Homophobia: A Global History of Gay & Lesbian Experience*; the development of this work took place while the author was an esteemed faculty member at the University of Paris. Although originally published in French, it has since been translated into English in 2008 and provides a cross reference of cultural and ideological summaries, indexed alphabetically by topic, geographical region and theological context. It permits the user to explore a variety of critical areas related to homophobia based on the reader's interest and motivation.

In his introduction, Tin (2003) described the need for the development of such a resource through the summation of the etiology and global transmigration of the construct of homophobia as detailed from a variety of scholarly perspectives. Anecdotally, professor Tin lost his appointment at the University of Paris after the publication of this document; it was determined through supporting evidence that it was, in fact, the catalyst for his dismissal. This speaks to the misperception of how evolved the liberties and rights of the LGBT(Q) community in the new millennia actually are and serves notice for the need to remain vigilant in giving voice to realities outside the purview of the macro culture of heteronormativity.

In spite of the twentieth century having witnessed the most progressive advancements for this culture than ever previously documented, dichotomously, this century has also witnessed the greatest atrocities inflicted upon LGBT identified individuals. From North America and Europe's support of gay marriage as being one barometer of the great equalizer of the sexual identities gay and straight, to the aggressive persecution through the McCarthy era, Nazi Germany's internment of gays along with Jews and the litany of murderous acts taking place across the globe, it can easily be questioned what societal tone predominates the discourse of these perceived rights.

To promote an effective discourse on the mechanisms of homophobia one must first operationally define it. Tin (2003) identifies a lack of documented use of this term until 1994 and stated that, "It is, therefore, a recent term with a relatively rich history" (p. 11). The definition of homophobia in its most traditional terms, "the fear of being in a closed space with a homosexual" quickly became inclusive of "an extreme irrational aversion to homosexuality and homosexuals" and ultimately required consideration as a continuum of experiences. The Urban Dictionary's (2016) top definition of homophobia is "the fear that gay men will treat you the way you treat women"; sadly, it suggests how the objectification of women is supported through a heteronormative patriarch of gender binary roles. Even when an attempt is made to position this definition within the context of humor, the societal commentary is obviously negative.

The evolution of homophobia through a socially and culturally constructed lens permits one to look at how the expectation of heteronormative ideologies or heterosexist behavior presumes the role as the only 'normal', effectively extinguishing space for homosexual or gay identities to even exist. Heterosexism is defined as the assumption of superiority without the consideration of alternate sexual identities.

This is especially reflected when an individual is surprised by the observation of discriminatory practice, when, to them, it not only doesn't feel like discrimination, but on a deeper level they have never given thought to the possibility of gay identity to even exist. In totality, this ideology and its lack of even approximating equality for marginalized group's supports the need for diversity acceptance in a variety of spaces including the workplace.

The creation of 'safe spaces' or zones within work environments is often deemed progressive and seen as accepting for LGBTQ populations. There are trainings most often through the human resources department and in some organizations a certification for those who offer a safe space sanctuary in their office (Human Rights Campaign, 2016). Although this is a step in the right direction and promotes tolerance, it is often overlooked that if safe spaces are required, then inherently unsafe spaces exist and this practice serves as evidence to confirm that existence. If there is a systemic awareness of lack of safety for non-heterosexual identities, does it not then become the organizations responsibility to confront the issue of safety for all rather than promoting compartmentalization of this problem?

Tin (2003) correlates this heterocentric view much like the historical reaction to Copernicus discovering that the earth was not the center of the solar system, and eventually discovering that it was but a mere blip on the radar of the universe. Moreover, the religious chaos that ensued as a result of Copernicus' pronouncements did nothing to change that the earth, in fact, revolved around the sun, described as a heretic to challenge man's place in the universe, in much the same way that minority sexualities are demonized.

As gay identity struggles to fit within a heteronormative system as a legitimate sexual identity, the lack of visibility of its existence through the lack of dialogue at a family dinner table (if this even exists in the new millennia), books in schools, and others being free to openly share this identity, provides the catalytic oppression necessary to create potential trauma once it inevitably does emerge. Whether this takes place internally for the individual, or collectively through the societies and consequently organizations, the lack of prior knowledge and positive practical experiences can create an uncomfortable dissonance for all involved.

The organization can be shaken into action when disclosure events occur and whether the structural theory of Minuchin (White, Klein, & Martin 2015) or the work of Bowen's family systems (Titelman, 2014) is used to create an understanding of how homeostasis or the struggle to return to the predictable is actively sought. Everyone within the system becomes activated in both functional and dysfunctional repertoires to steady the course. When this occurs through a coming out or disclosure event, the mobilization of forces can represent a continuum of experiences from the slightly uncomfortable to the polar opposite of full on seismic systemic disruption resulting in organizational traumatization.

The microculture of LGBTQ identities within the macroculture of heteronormative ideologies creates this systemic tension and is further fueled through antagonistic discourse that creates fear of the unknown. It is the irrational fear of gays or the misperception of power that could result by recognizing their existence that allows homophobic myopia and rhetoric to engender concern. Imagine being the gay identity in any particular group when a group member espouses unwarranted fears that lead to sometimes visceral and primal reactions of violence due to a heterosexual person being misperceived as 'gay'. This allows the terminology associated with even the perception of being gay, 'faggot', 'fag', 'homo' being directed toward someone experiencing that fear, and potentially igniting a situation that could be life changing or life ending.

Human Rights

The Universal Declaration of Human Rights (UDHR) was intentionally created to provide a vehicle for all nations to agree on a set of principles that would support basic rights for all humankind. The UDHR was validated on December 10, 1948 through the countries that were signatories for this document. Within the constitutional framework of many countries, a 'Bill of Rights' serves as an addendum to the laws created by governmental systems to protect its citizens; more importantly its role serves as an enforceable means to hold all members of society accountable to advocate and promote Human Rights. At the time of drafting these important documents, the rights for LGBTQ people were not considered due to the high level of invisibility, stigma and hiding any disclosure of sexual orientation. Since the original drafting of these documents, the timeline for and the progression of rights for this population have exponentially increased both in terms of visibility and accountability for discrimination against sexual orientations.

In the work place for the U.S., rights related to sexual orientation are included in policy developed by individual organizations, but are further mandated by laws protecting this group as a vulnerable population in some states. Across nations we see a continuum of support for rights associated with sexual orientation, ranging from non-existent, to countries supporting equality in the highest sense of the word. Although this is most often demonstrated in highly progressive social governments such as Denmark, Sweden and Norway, the modeling of this support for equality of rights serves to make for a more inclusive agenda as more and more Western nations engage this topic for critical consideration (Baird-Remba, 2013). In the workplace this can be identified as support for partner benefits and recognition of 'gay' marriage. There remains dissonance, however, between those who continue to challenge the legitimacy of federal and court ruling on this matter as a means of delaying the enforcement of these laws within their organizations.

In the United States, Hunt (2012) examined the non-discrimination laws and policies in a state by state review and reported for gay identified employees that "17 percent reported being fired because of their sexual orientation, 13 percent reported being denied a promotion as a result of receiving a negative job evaluation, and 20 percent reported being harassed verbally or in writing on the job" (p. 1). The author further reported that although 89% of US-Americans believe that gay and transgender employees are protected under federal law, it remains legal in the majority of states to execute this type of discrimination. The Employment Non-Discrimination Act (ENDA) has yet to be ratified by Congress and would be the protection sought to disallow discrimination based on a person's sexual identity or gender identity whether it is real or perceived.

To date there are a total of 15 states and Washington, D.C. that provide legal protection for sexual and gender identities in the workplace. Some states began with sexual orientation and later added protections for gender, while 10 others passed laws that combined sexual identity and gender as a protected class. It should be noted that these laws apply to both the private and public organizational sectors. In total there are levels of protections against discrimination for gay and transgender identified individuals in 32 states but these workers are only afforded recourse under the law to address discriminatory practices in 21 of those states. The others don't provide any legal recourse and take the form of executive policies that can be rescinded by an organization. Hunt (2012) recommended that in order for gay and transgender individuals to enjoy success in the workplace, Congress should pass ENDA stating, "Policies that create fair workplaces have real, positive impacts on people's lives, and they reflect the best of our country's ideal of granting people equal treatment under the law" (p. 20).

The conditions for human rights in Turkey can be summarized by referring to periodical review reports by a variety of different NGOs. One of them is "The European Region of the International Lesbian, Gay, Bisexual, Trans & Intersex Association" (ILGA Europe) and its "Annual Review of the Human Rights Situation of Lesbian, Gay, Bisexual, Trans and Intersex People in Europe" (2015) covered the period from January to December 2014. The ILGA Europe, collected and presented data on developments at the national level in 49 countries and summarized the adverse conditions in Turkey as follows (p.161):

1. Violence continues to impact the lives of LGBTI individuals, especially those identified as transgender, women have been documented to receive police harassment, indiscriminate citizen attacks, attempted or committed suicide and murdered;
2. The topic of homophobic and transphobic specific crimes has not been included in the government's Democracy Reform Package;
3. The country continues to restrict the freedom to assemble, and;
4. While legal and national establishments continued to ignore sexual and gender identity as a class, it serves to limit employment access, expressive freedoms, and the necessary access to services and goods.

The report also highlighted some positive transitions in Turkey (p.161) as:

1. The courts have for the first time acknowledged equality for gay men that were murdered, providing life sentences for the perpetrators, and addressing hate speech directed toward LGBTI individuals and sexual orientation, and;
2. A number of cities have started LGBTI health services and support of a more inclusive, gay friendly environment.

Göregenli and Serdengeçti (2015) conducted a survey, in a project with the "Kaos Gay and Lesbian Cultural Research and Solidarity Association (Kaos GL)" on the conditions for LGBTI groups in the private sectors of Turkey. They engaged 151 LGBTI individuals and the authors summarized the findings of the research as follows: "On the other hand, participants with open identities in terms of their sexual identities stated they had been exposed to or had witnessed many biased attitudes and discriminatory behaviors. Results of our research unfortunately show that in most of the workplaces in Turkey, there are no procedures or practices that would either protect the LGBTI employees from the negative effects of discrimination or meet their special needs. Furthermore, discrimination based on sexual orientation and gender identity is still not included within the protected grounds in the Constitution and the Labor Law, and this remains the main obstacle, the main legal deficiency against implementation of the "Equal Citizenship" principle for Turkey's LGBTI citizens." (p.7-8)

In Brazil, the country's Bill of Rights from 1998 does not include specific articles that protect the rights of LGBT individuals, with the exception of same sex-marriage, which the Ministry of Justice did amend in 2013. In general, Brazilian citizens' rights, despite their sexual orientations, race, religion affiliation, and social class have the same nationwide status. The Brazilian literature does not address if military personnel can openly discuss their sexual identities, although Brazilian law does not forbid LGBT individuals from entering the Brazilian Armed Forces. Interestingly, a magazine article was identified confirming that the Armed Forces released information that gays are welcomed into Brazilian

Army, even though the information was refuted by several LGBT activists including a Brazilian soldier who went to prison for advocating for LGBT soldiers' rights (O Dia, 2014).

Nonetheless, it is important to mention the achievement of several milestones that were accomplished advocating for the rights of the LGBT population in Brazil. In 2004, the country launched, *Brazil without Homophobia* to fight the violence and discrimination against LGBT persons and to welcome their citizenship. Four years later the first national conference dedicated to promoting a dialogue to discuss the rights of LGBT populations along with the establishment of specific LGBT public policies was held in the country. The results of this conference were the development of an executive national plan to guarantee the rights and citizenship of LGBT Brazilian people. However the effective implementation and enforcement of these initiatives to secure and promote LGBT rights still has much work to be done, otherwise the theory will never be translated into practice (Mello et. al. 2012).

How do human rights translate into policy and procedure development within the more confined context of human resources for organizations? To examine if policy development related to sexual orientation is perceived as protecting gay individuals in the workplace, Tejeda (2006) considered localized protection through corporate discrimination policies. This means that regardless of state or federal laws, at least in the United States, an organization can choose to support vulnerable populations by virtue of their own policy. The author concluded that non-discrimination policy influenced variables relative to perceptions of workplace hostility, promotion opportunity and job satisfaction, and disclosure events influenced career trajectory. It appears that when in an environment that supports diversity and provides written policies that are inclusive of sexual orientation as a protected status, there are better outcomes for the individuals who hold membership within that population. It should be noted that organizations globally could voluntarily make the decision to support non-discrimination policies.

Cross Cultural Framework

Situated within the context of three global economic forces, the United States, Brazil and Turkey have collectively seen the insurgence of fundamentalist religious forces engaging in acts of terrorism previously unknown. Individually each has experienced political upheaval also on an unprecedented historical scale. The presidential election for the 2016-year in the U.S. has attempted to resolve the exponentially dissonant factions of a bi-partisan system struggling to support the model of a traditional democratic process. While the U.S. considers the option of its first female President, Brazil struggles with its past history of military dictatorship along with a long history of political corruption and more recently the impeachment of their first female president. Turkey is attempting to resolve internal strife with their own leaders who appear to support a secular democracy; however, after a failed coup attempt in July of 2016, the rights many have so long struggled to achieve, appear to be fading toward a historically dominant non-secular regime.

Not only are workplace communities affected by the political and economic upheaval for each of these nations but for the LGBT communities, this poses unique challenges when considered from each cultural perspective (King et al., 2010). With a highly conservative platform articulated for the Republican Party in the U.S. - the leaders of that party have articulated that the rights for LGBTQ people will be circumvented if put in a position of power (Drabold, 2016). This ideological platform promotes the essence of heterosexism, as described above, with the assumption that membership within the macro culture of heteronormativity, permits access to rights that may be withheld from others holding inferior or minority sexual orientation. The absence in support of diversity across many demographic markers has stirred behaviors in the political system not witnessed for decades and further appears to support both verbal and physical violence. This potentially could translate into the return of openly discriminatory practices taking place throughout organizations that ascribe to this oppressive rhetoric and could easily be acted out, especially in the workplace.

For the first time in Brazil an official report presenting data on human rights violations against LGBT individuals was released in 2011 and in 2012 a new report was issued comparing the data. In the history of Brazil it can be observed that a paradigmatic movement towards supporting LGBT rights, further discussing heteronormative issues and welcoming diverse perspectives to assist in understanding individuals' sexual identities. Nonetheless, there was a substantial increase in the number of confirmed LGBT crimes and rights' abuses only one year after the first official data report was released. The 2012 report asserted that complaints related to rights' abuses increased 166% from 2011 to 2012 and victims of crimes increased from 1,713 to 4,851 accounting for an outstanding 183% growth. These numbers call for attention and action from the entire Brazilian society, Federal, State and Municipal governments in order to change the current violent scenario against LGBT populations (Secretaria de Direitos Humanos da Presidência da Repúbica, 2012). In a more recent report presented by a Brazilian Group called *Grupo Gay da Bahia* an astonishing statement was presented confirming that Brazil continues to be the leading country of LGBT-hate crimes in the world. LGBT related hate crimes accounted for 326 deaths in the year of 2014 – this means that an LGBT individual is killed every 27 hours (Grupo Gay da Bahia, 2014).

In Turkey, the move toward an increase in non-secular ideologies could potentially encourage 'group markers' to focus on avoiding the support of LGBTQ people as equal citizens and the fragile gains that have been made, like the cancellation of the Pride parade for the past two years has demonstrated, could quickly diminish. The unbridled ascendency of power has demonstrated increased controls placed on journalists, academics, and even military personnel. The public scrutiny of protected and private information could place the LGBTQ community at greater risk making positive outcomes difficult to anticipate.

To explore how freedoms are enjoyed in a cross-cultural context, and understand how each of the countries included in the discussion for this chapter rank on a global scale, Freedom House for the past 75 years has worked to "Defend human rights and promote democratic change, with a focus on political rights, and civil liberties. We act as a catalyst for freedom through a combination of analysis, advocacy, and action". The *Freedom in the World* report (2016) identified through a valid methodological design, each of the countries is scored on both political rights, civil liberties, and an overall aggregate score is included; with 1 being the greatest amount of freedoms and 7 being the least, and the larger the aggregate score the better, the following results were identified for the United States (U.S.), Brazil and Turkey. The U.S. had a political rights score of 1, a civil liberties of 1 and an aggregate score of 90; Brazil received scores for political rights of 2, civil liberties of 2 and an aggregate of 80, and; Turkey was identified with political rights at 3, civil liberties at 4 and an aggregate of 53. Both the U.S. and Turkey are viewed to currently have 'negative trajectories' a decidedly downward trend from the previous year: the U.S. was due to "the cumulative impact of flaws in the electoral system, a disturbing increase in the role of private money in election campaigns and the legislative process, legislative gridlock, the failure of the Obama administration to fulfill promises of enhanced government openness, and fresh evidence of racial discrimination and other dysfunctions in the criminal justice system" (p. 19), and Turkey because of "renewed violence between the government and Kurdish militants, terrorist attacks by the Islamic State group, and intense harassment of opposition members and media outlets by the government and its supporters ahead of November parliamentary elections" (p. 19). Interestingly, Brazil was determined to be relatively stable in spite of a significant political and economic crisis, but at the time of printing that had not yet been resolved, but more importantly, they were not included in the same type of aggressive dissonance or targeted in the same way that other countries experienced.

Disclosure Decisions

The process of deciding to disclose a minority sexual identity in any context can be an emotionally and time-consuming life event (Cleve, 2012). Ragins, Singh, & Cornwell (2007) explored disclosure of sexual orientation specifically in the workplace with a large sample the included 534 self-identified lesbians, gay and bi-sexual employees. The authors approached the study from dual perspectives of those who disclosed in the workplace and compared those with the fears for those who did not. It was discovered that experiences of past discrimination (e.g. bullying, verbal and physical violence) greatly influenced the decision to disclose and for those who chose not to, the factors of job attitude, psychological strain, work environment and career outcomes served as mediators. The majority of employees reported the perception of support, not necessarily evidence of it, within the work environment as a key motivational factor.

A key consideration in discussing the potential impact of sexual orientation disclosure is whether or not it is appropriate or needs to occur at all in a work environment. Part of the cost/benefit analysis must entail the consideration of timing, safety factors, support systems and need. Ward and Winstanley (2005) indicated, "…the decision to come out [at work] is one of the most important career decisions faced by gay employees and one that many others do not have to make" (p. 448). The authors further support the process of 'coming out' as a multi stage rather than singular event and view it as performative by nature of it being a reiterative process; the event being engaged, processed and returned to for further scrutiny and evaluation. The context of the disclosure event is considered an important factor with the workplace being but one in which it takes place.

Cleve (2012) investigated the process of disclosure for gay youth globally, the social and identified cultural mediators that potentially influence life trajectories once disclosure of sexual identity is put into motion. Cleve (2012) utilized a grounded theory design to explore the lived experiences of 24 gay males in Brazil and the U.S. through the collection of in depth narrative responses to a unique interview protocol. The narratives were deconstructed and analyzed utilizing a conceptual framework articulating concealable stigmatized identities, not inclusive of sexual identity. Three primary themes are highlighted in Figure 1 as an end point to the three phase grounded theory analysis process (Charmaz, 2006) and followed the following formatting:

1. Primary coding for each cultural cohort;
2. Combined cohort focused coding, and;
3. Thematic coding.

Congruent with the work of Chaudoir & Fisher (2010), Chaudoir, Fisher, and Simoni (2011), Chaudoir, Earnshaw, and Andel, (2013), and Chaudoir and Quinn, (2016) for disclosure decisions of stigmatized identities, the antecedent and outcomes process are critical for anyone making this very difficult decision. The factors that lead up to the actual event are considered critical, as are the responses that result from that disclosure. When viewed in the context of being positive or negative, they serve to inform the next disclosure event and work in an iterative fashion. Cleve (2012) utilized this framework in identifying three primary themes across two cultural cohorts of gay men that were ultimately identified as internal mediators, relational mediators and post disclosure outcomes.

Figure 1. Disclosure decision model

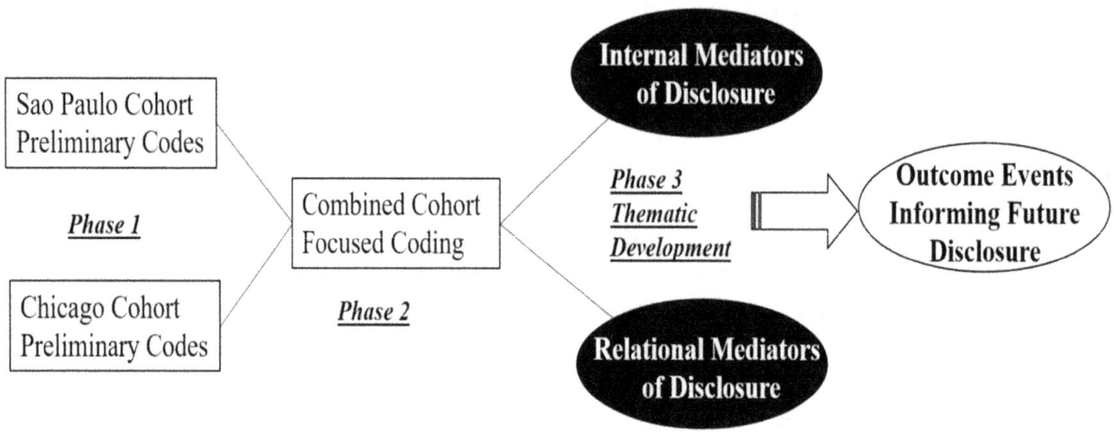

Internal mediators, those which assisted the decision making process through self or internal dialogue and cognitive processing and supported by focused codes included: self acceptance, role of religion, experiences of discrimination, internalizing homophobia, influences of heteronormativity, stages of discovery, access to information and planning for negative outcomes (Figure 2). Each of these mediating factors appeared to play a role in determining both timing for the disclosure and sense of safety tied to attempting the disclosure. The narratives secured that provide evidence supporting the elements of internal mediating process are the following:

1. "Not wanting to live parallel lives was my motivation; I wanted to know what/who I was and decide to live only one life" [self acceptance];
2. "The reality was I was called a faggot every day and nobody cared" [experiences of discrimination];
3. "The religious influence came from him, and it was because of him that I didn't come out. I was afraid of what he would thinking, what he would say, and I never told anyone" [role of religion].

Relation mediators emerged from an analysis that identified: acceptance by others, disclosure events, disclosure factors, disclosure stages, empowering events, identification with others, gender traditions and support systems (Figure 3). Factors that appeared to result post disclosure comprise: taking part in a discourse on rights, cultural identifiers, modeling and educating others, respecting family, formulating self-identities and how participating in events impacts their lives in a positive way. These mediators resulted from the interactions that took place between the person considering disclosure and other significant figures in their lives. Many of the narratives included both powerful and humorous statements from the young men who took part that challenged their trust and sense of empowerment in this process, evidenced in the following:

1. "Some people think that homosexuality is a…just a fling that you have once in your life, you wake up and say, 'Today is summer, I want to be gay; tomorrow is spring, let's be heterosexual" [disclosure factors];

Figure 2. Internal mediators for disclosure decisions

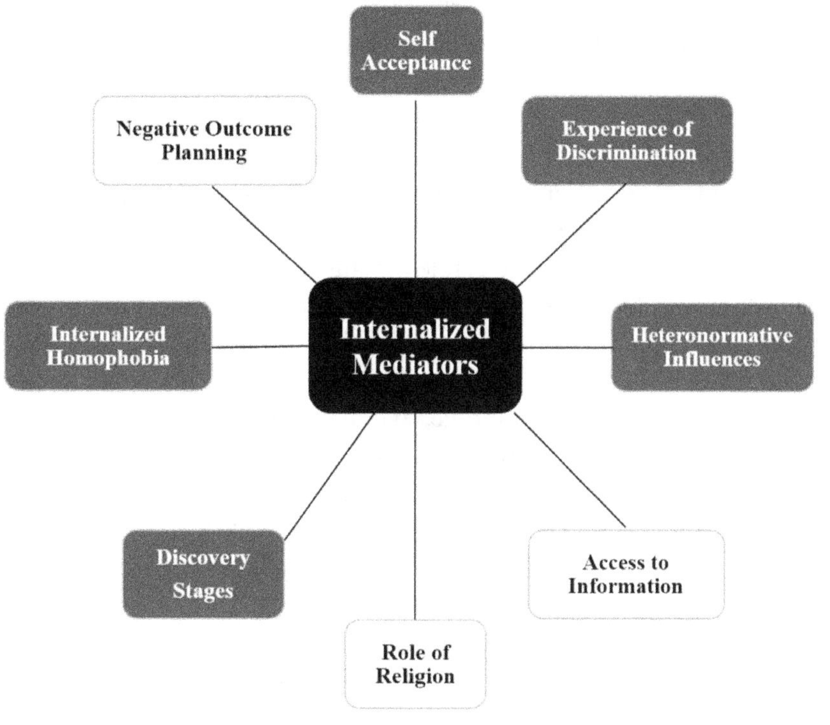

Figure 3. Relational mediators for disclosure decisions

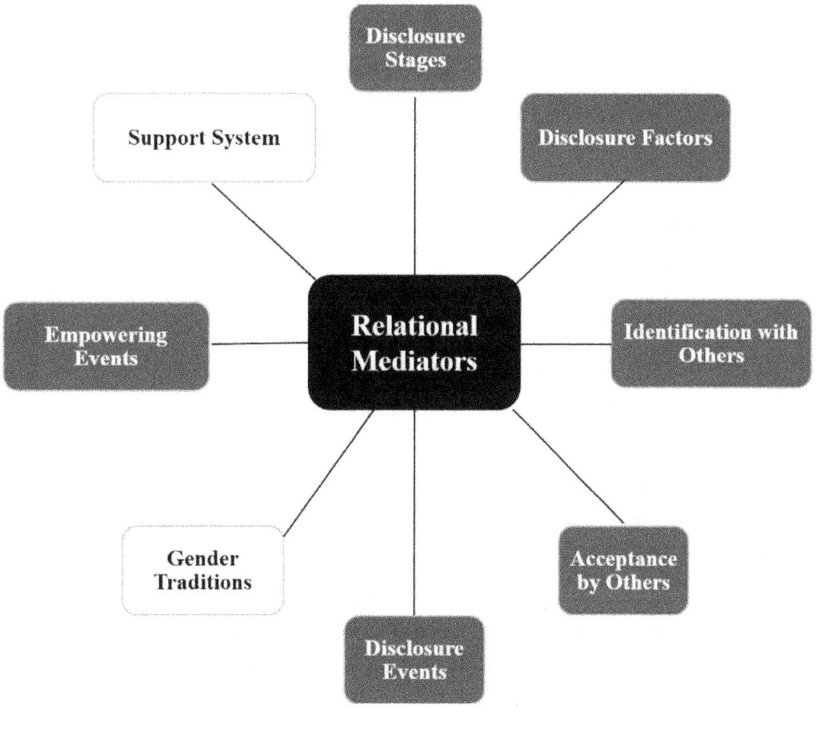

2. "Now it is the real thing, because someone else knows. It was like, I was gay in that moment simply because someone else knew" [disclosure stages], and;
3. "Just give me the summer to [father stated], you know, like to absorb everything; and I did, it was like, that's fair, I understand that is like a shock for you" [acceptance by others].

The authors concluded that although all of the mediators shared characteristics across both cultural cohorts in Brazil and the U.S., to be considered true universalisms would require the addition of a variety of cultures globally. The individual mediating factors did appear weighted for particular categories based on cultural importance and nuance, (e.g. role of religion, access to information, negative outcome planning, gender traditions and support systems), potentially highlighting the role of relativism (Berry et al., 2013). Toward that end of exploring potential universalisms, the primary investigator repeated the study with a purposive sample of Turkish youth (Cleve & Işık, 2013) utilizing the same interview protocol in order to continue working toward the goal of understanding disclosure decisions that may highlight universal characteristics for gay males but also identifying those which may be culture specific or relativistic. There were several additional questions added to include the exploration of career and military experiences for the Turkish cohort and are highlighted below.

LGBTQ Identities

The acronym currently used to identify membership in the gay community, has evolved over the past several decades and even those within the community wonder where this shared stigmatized grouping will lead. Lesbian, Gay, Bisexual, Transgender communities were initially morphed into one group as a means of offering collective support post Stonewall riots in 1969 in New York City, NY. This is quite often used as the marker for the 'gay' civil rights movement. As rights were being negotiated within the borders of the United States, by a variety of advocacy groups, tremendous progress was achieved. Previously most literature cited the acronym as GLBT with no formal logic behind it and more recently LGBT is the preferred order as often it is considered that lesbian women face to broad discriminatory categories of gender and sexual identity.

With the advent of the HIV/AIDS epidemic, first identified in 1981, many gains were lost as the spurious connection between this plague and the gay communities were deemed inseparable. Queer identities emerged in response to the lack of advocacy for this effected community and became a proud moniker for those giving voice to this population who could now be stigmatized on multiple levels; this provided the additional marker moving the acronym to LGBTQ. Homosexuality was sexual behavior that was 'banned' in the U.S. and was only decriminalized as recently as 2003 when the U.S. Supreme Court ruled in Lawrence v. Texas that sodomy laws were unconstitutional.

Krafft-Ebing (1840-1902) initially presented homosexuality as a "severe manifestation of hereditary degeneration" and his treatise *Psychopathia Sexualis*, but later in life he resolved his negative opinion after meeting many homosexual men and argued against sodomy laws in defense of gay identities. Havelock Ellis (1858-1939), another sexologist who argued for a congenital aspect to homosexuality coining the term and naming his book *Sexual Inversion*. Ellis et al. advocated for de-criminalizing homosexuality, arguing that if homosexuality is, in fact, acquired then for logical reasons it would follow that heterosexuality is similarly acquired; acquisition theory then for any particular form of sexuality is incorrect (2016). LGBTQ movement can be viewed as paralleling other movements in society that occurred during the late nineteenth and early twentieth centuries across the U.S. and Europe. Among the most prevalent theories are Social Darwinism, eugenics and moral reform campaigns. Inscribed within such movements were many labels, sexual acts, bodily characteristics and roles relevant to sexual perversions. Sexual proclivities were considered "linked to increasing anxiety about the nature of civilization and evolutionary 'progress'"; the theorists utilizing terms of pathological and degenerate were replete across social movements with homosexuality almost always synonymous with immoral and reprobate (as cited in Dentato, Halkitis, & Orwat, 2013).

Balestrery (*in press*) outlines how the criminalization of homosexuality across the U.S. continued through the twentieth century, and language such as 'sexual psychopathy' in the 1930's served to articulate the concerns of homosexuality as being pathological. Although the American Psychological Association did not remove the term 'homosexuality' as a diagnosable disorder until 1973 it included a significant amount of internal controversy as the discourse about its appropriateness as a sexual classification of perversity and sought to be eliminated. The author further parallels the challenge to remove anti-sodomy laws from the record books with the Supreme Court finally ruling that the unconstitutionality of this privacy violation could and would not be upheld as law in 2003.

Beyond the local and on a global level there is even greater disparity between identifiers of sexual behavior, sexual identity and sexual orientation. The term 'gay' is broadly used to discuss sexual identity, sexual orientation or same sex attraction and replaces the term 'homosexual'; sexual preference is avoided in place of orientation or identity in an attempt to reduce bias and negative stereotypes (APA Publication Manual, 2011, p.74). For the purposes of identification within the workplace, it can again depend greatly on the universality vs. relativism debate.

Case Studies: Corporate, Military and Sports Worlds

Research conducted across diverse cultural contexts demonstrates that the various types of explicit and non-explicit violence (e.g. homophobia, transphobia, harassment, discrimination, bullying, and stigmatization) towards LGBT individuals in the workplace may potentially generate long and lasting traumatic consequences (Ferreira & Siqueira, 2007; Pizer et al., 2012; Prunas et. al., 2016; Siqueira et. al., 2009; Willis, 2012). Such traumatic consequences include the development of psychiatric disorders (e.g. depression, anxiety, and post-traumatic stress), and psychological distress, negatively impacting self-esteem, and potentially increasing feelings of anger and suicidal ideation.

Despite the extensive range of negative psychological consequences, discrimination in the workplace also impacts LGBT employees' wages, job satisfaction, career, promotion opportunities, and overall work productivity (Pizer et al., 2012; Scobie, 2015). Furthermore, violence in the workplace can be exacerbated by a number of factors including race, ethnicity, age, gender, socioeconomic status (SES), and religion affiliations. Such factors may affect LGBT individuals on both personal and societal levels. When considering the societal level, specific countries' laws, cultural and social practices may significantly limit employment opportunities or even deny workplace benefits (United Nations Human Rights Council, 2015).

Corporate

In many parts of world business, corporations have begun to consider the need to develop more inclusive, fair and supportive work environments encouraging anti-discrimination organizational policies and practices (Instituto Ethos, 2014; Everly & Schwarz, 2015; Mahtani & Vernon, 2010; Stein, 2012; Pizer et al., 2012; Scobie, 2015). In spite of this progress, there is still a great deal of prejudice, violence and discrimination in organizational contexts. According to the United Nations 2015 Report on "Violence and Discrimination against LGBT People", harassment and abuse in the workplace remain significantly widespread.

In researching sources of information on the web such as magazines, blogs, and online newspapers, numerous online materials were identified addressing harmful workplace experiences for LGBT individuals working in business corporations across the world. The Williams Institute at University of California Los Angeles (UCLA) School of Law produced a unique report that included the key findings of academic studies researching the impact of discrimination toward LGBT people in both the private and public business sectors (Sears & Mallory, 2011). According to this report, an American national survey using a probability-based sample confirmed that 42% of LGB individuals experienced some form of employment discrimination based on their sexual orientation, at some point in their lives. Additionally, discrimination was increasingly common among LGBT individuals who disclosed their sexual orientation in the workplace when compared to those concealing their sexual identities. Research confirmed that workplace discrimination increases psychological distress, the occurrence of psychiatric disorders such as depression, and health-related problems among those individuals choosing to disclose their sexual orientation. Moreover, discrimination among those coming out is also correlated with reduced job satisfaction, less employment opportunities, decreased income, and increased rates of absenteeism. An expressive 51% of LGBT employees working in the U.S. confirmed that they do not disclose their identity to their co-workers (Sears & Mallory, 2011). In the United Kingdom, 34% of LGBT workers also prefer to conceal their sexual orientations fearing less work promotion opportunities, homophobia and social exclusion (Qvist, 2014). Conversely it should be noted that in the UK 73% chose to disclose. However, the fear of discrimination is a heavy weight in the decision making process for LGBT employees who consider to reveal their sexual identity.

In 1997 Alan Gilmour, took part in an interview with Fortune Magazine. The former Chief Financial Officer (CFO) of Ford Motor Corporation, appointed in 1986, was one of the very first to brave this territory by disclosing his sexual identity after many years with the company. He admitted that being gay was no revelation to him, but he felt that after being passed over for the CEO position twice in subsequent years, it was time to take stock in what was providing meaning in his life. In assessing what disclosure in the workplace would mean, he stated, "they [companies] don't want executive personality being discussed; they want the products to be discussed". He decided to retire from Ford, the first time, in 1995 at the age of 60. "Being gay complicated my life. Gay people don't lie; they dissemble" and distract from the questions about their personal lives. The biggest fear for Gilmour was the possibility of being a diversion away from the business of Ford, the decision making process involved consideration beyond his personal needs and focused on those of the corporation (Fortune, 1997).

The former Chief Executive Officer of British Petroleum (BP) considered one of the most successful British businessmen, Lord Browne of Madinley, discussed homosexuality, homophobia and the challenges LGBT individuals face in the business corporate world in his book *The Glass Closet.* Lord Browne decided to advocate for the benefits of 'coming out' in the business world after having his personal life and sexual orientation exposed by a British tabloid in 2007. Lord Browne privately maintained his sexual orientation during the entire forty-one years he worked for an oil company with a dominant and ingrained 'macho culture', fearing prejudice and discrimination. As a businessman Lord Browne was certain that homophobia was not only harmful to the LGBT employees but also served as an important obstacle that precluded companies in becoming more profitable. Lord Browne stated that the tremendous amount of energy devoted by LGBT workers to conceal their sexual identities could be rerouted and reinvested into the growth of organizations (Aitkenhead, 2014).

There are positive 'coming out' role models in the corporate world in spite of the negative effects and consequences faced by LGBT individuals in the business workplace. The man who played a key role in tripling a well-known international company's revenue is considered one of the most significant 'out' role models in the corporate world. Tim Cook (Apple's CEO) openly disclosed his sexual identity in 2014; this is the first time a *Fortune 500* company's CEO decided to publicly reveal that he was gay (The Economist, 2014). According to Tim Cook, his decision to 'come out' was motivated by the words of Martin Luther King, who once said, "Life's most persistent and urgent question is, 'What are you doing for others?' " In his interview to Bloomberg Technology magazine (2014), he clearly stated, "I'm proud to be gay, and I consider being gay among the greatest gifts God has given me." Tim recognized that being part of a marginalized group contributed to his ability to be more empathetic to the obstacles individuals from minority groups encounter in their daily lives. Regardless of the adversities he faced, Tim described that his sexual orientation built up his confidence to overcome prejudice and discrimination. Although he doesn't call himself a social activist, he recognizes the positive repercussions of his 'coming out' decision – "if hearing that the CEO of Apple is gay can help someone struggling to come to terms with who he or she is, or bring comfort to anyone who feels alone, or inspire people to insist on their equality, then it's worth the trade-off with my own privacy."

The rights of LGBT people in Brazil have not yet been solidified. Federal regulations against homophobia are limited. Advocating for LGBT rights in the Brazilian corporate world still appears to be a voluntary or chosen action. Promoting diversity and equality in Brazilian business environments seems like a tenuous or difficult decision considering that an important portion of Brazilian society still discriminates against LGBT individuals (Instituto Ethos, 2014). Nonetheless, Brazil has begun to witness a positive change in the corporate world as Brazilian executives begin to openly disclose their sexual identities. Ricardo Yuki (Citibank/Brazil risk analyst executive) is one individual contributing to positive change in the Brazilian business scenario when he openly revealed his sexual identity in an interview for an important Brazilian corporate magazine in 2015. Ricardo Yuki said that he had never experienced any type of discrimination in the workplace but believes this is because he had been living a private life, "in a bubble", surrounded by "sophisticated and educated people" (Luders, 2015). Interestingly the information provided in *Exame* magazine described a situation that could be considered a form of prejudice although Ricardo stated exactly the opposite in his interview. Three years ago Ricardo received the most challenging yet attractive job offer of his career – to relocate to Citibank's headquarters in New York and lead a team of 200 employees located across several continents. As an expatriate Ricardo would have the right to receive corporate's support to experience a smooth transition including the necessary benefits to assist his partner's professional relocation (e.g. obtaining a working visa). Ricardo's partner was not able to obtain a visa regardless of the fact that same sex marriage was legal in both Brazil and the State of New York during the time of their anticipated relocation. This was due in part to the fact the housing allowance was regulated by a federal law in the U.S. that precluded supporting his partner as a spouse. In light of this situation, Ricardo decided to stay in Brazil and agreed to travel every fifteen days to the Citibank international branches.

Considering the many stories of LGBT individuals and the experiences revealing their sexual identities in the business corporate world (Aitkenhead, 2014; Bentley, 2015; Hallett, 2016; Reed, 2016; The Economist, 2014) it appears clear that business workplace conditions have enjoyed significant improvements in promoting equality for LGBT employees in specific parts of the world. Although many LGBT individuals still conceal their sexual identities afraid of the discrimination they may experience in the business workplace, the cases reviewed suggest that LGBT employees are feeling more confident in disclosure of their sexual identities; the corporate world appears to be moving toward a more accepting and inclusive environment through embracing diversity in its essence.

Military

Homophobia, heterosexism and discriminatory practices have also been identified in the military field. In the United States the LGBT rights movement began in the beginning of the 20th century (PBS, 2016), in spite of the fact that U.S. military personnel who identify as gay are still facing prejudice and discrimination in the 21st century (Questia, 2016). Until 1993, LGB individuals were banned from serving in the U.S. armed forces in spite of the fact that the majority of North Atlantic Treaty Organization (NATO) countries had already publicly allowed them to do so. In 1993, during the administration of Former President Bill Clinton, the policy *Don't Ask, Don't Tell* (DADT) was officially drafted. This policy basically prohibited U.S. military personnel to engage in homosexual activity or disclose their sexual identities. After 1993, U.S. LGB military personnel were no longer banned from service in the U.S. army forces although they still were actively experiencing prejudice and discrimination. Eighteen years after former President Bill Clinton had signed the DADT, it was revoked during the administration of President Barack Obama, finally permitting LGB U.S. military personnel to openly serve and reveal their sexual identity if they decided to do so, no longer requiring them to be concealed (Questia, 2016).

In spite of the hope that the revocation of the DADT policy in 2011 promised, it appears that LGB U.S. military personnel are still facing prejudice. The DADT policy, as stated above, was officially instituted during the administration of former President Bill Clinton in 1993. During Clinton's election campaign he ran on the platform that all citizens would be granted the opportunity to openly serve in the military despite their sexual orientation, securing huge support from the LGB community. Post-election, DADT was a compromise measure to end the long-standing policy that was instituted during World War II banning LGB people from military service. In reality the prejudice and discrimination experienced by LGB military personnel was very much alive and present in their day-to-day lives falling short of Clinton campaign promises.

Air force soldier Adam says that although the policy was effective, there remained a great deal of work to be done to strengthen and enforce LGBT rights in U.S. Army Forces (Coming Out, 2016). Adam was thrilled when he learned that in 2011, under President Obama, the U.S. Congress revoked the DADT policy; however his excitement did not last long. In his personal 'coming out' story Adam shared that he fully understood that the mindset of the DADT policy was still firmly rooted when he heard a Sergeant, who he once admired, mumble, however loud enough to be heard in the room, you're "fucking faggots". Adam remained silent and even considered that he may feel sad that the policy was rescinded, thus allowing him to avoid retaliation. As Adam described his 'coming out' experience he admits that he decided to disclose his sexual identity to only a few family members and work peers since he ultimately had lost his sense of worth no longer wanted to live in concealment.

To Adam's surprise, his family and peers were extremely supportive and they would even be prepared to defend him during times he actively suffered prejudice (Coming Out, 2016). Unfortunately, his feelings of safety were short lived after he was called for a new work assignment. It did not take him long to realize that he was once again surrounded by intolerance as every five minutes he would hear negative remarks like, "that kid is a faggot", "she's a dyke", and "this is gay, that is gay." The situation become worse when his unit officer made a joke suggesting that Adam was gay without even realizing that he was, in fact, gay identified. This time Adam decided that he would no longer remain silent. Adam had a private conversation with his unit Chief officer and discussed how his comments could be perceived as derogatory especially considering Adam's sexual identity. According to Adam the Chief Officer reassured him that his comments meant no harm and guaranteed that the situation would not happen again (Coming Out, 2016).

All Turkish male citizens between the ages of 20 and 41 are required to execute military service for six to 12 months. Reserve Officers, and the Rank and File groups' serve for a duration of 12 months. The former groups are conscripts holding university degrees of four years or more, and the later with a shorter duration of formal education. Short-term enlisted personnel who have a minimum of 4 years of graduate degrees or more and whose qualifications exceed the reserve officer requirements have the opportunity to complete their military service in 6 months. Following an explorative study about the disclosure process for gay males in the US and Brazil by Cleve (2012), Cleve and Işık collected data (May, 2013) from a disclosure cohort for a male, self-identified gay sample (university students, age range 18-21) in İstanbul, Turkey. Data collected via 11 individual interviews included additional questions about both the career objectives for this target group and their ideas related to mandatory military service in Turkey that may have potential impact on career choices.

The decision to engage in military service for self-identified gay individuals is not an easy task considering the social and physical conditions inherent to serving in the army. One of the participants from Cleve and Işık's interviews (2013) mentioned that "Nothing can force me to be in there with so many men. I won't be able to handle this. I would go mad in there." Gay, bisexual and trans-individuals may receive an exemption from military service if they are open about their identities and agree to accept an exemption report, which is called the "pink report" informally; as the antagonistic name implies it, citizens who are biologically male are not eligible for armed service. This exemption is based on the Turkish Armed Forces' Health Aptitude Regulation which was recently updated but still specifies, "gender identity and behavior disorder" under the category of mental health and disorders (Article # 17/D) with the explanation that includes "cases who have adaptation problems and who are dysfunctional in the context/conditions of army due to their sexual attitudes and behaviors" as Metin Gürcan puts it forward (November, 2015). Another participant briefly and clearly highlight this issue: "I haven't decided yet but I don't want to go and say I have got a sexual dysfunction. That's what the report will say. Yes, they see being homosexual as a psychosexual dysfunction." This specification has twofold effect which is clearly explained in the following extract: "I would do it [military service] if it was my last option. I can't get exemption since my family would know about it. My life would be ruined. Pink report is a kind of labeling because in Turkey being homosexual is not accepted as normal. I won't be able to get a job. I don't think it's necessary to get one. I won't accept it because I'm not doing anything wrong. I have no difference with a heterosexual. Why I have to be stamped? I won't accept it. It would have negative effect on me. It can even change the way I think. I might go into thinking if they are stamping me, there must be something wrong with me. I don't want to do that." Firstly, for non-disclosed or 'closeted' gays, not completing the military service is an obstacle to their gender identity. Getting exemption obliges the individual to disclose which is first of all violation of human rights and also risky for some of the people who are from families and social environment that are homophobic. Secondly, stigma of abnormality is unacceptable.

Beside, getting an exemption report may turn out to be humiliating and traumatic experience. Again a participants from Cleve and Işık's interviews (2013) expressed that "Turkish army is a homophobic place. Until recently they were asking photographic evidence from the homosexuals." Gürcan reported in the Al-Monitor that (November, 2015) "Gays seeking military exemption in Turkey no longer need to provide visual proof of their homosexuality" which is considered as a critical step for respecting human rights." Even with the procedures of exemptions having been recently updated in an affirmative and humanistic direction, the necessity to disclose in order not to enroll in the army does not support a human rights perspective for LGBT individuals. Earlier stories of non-humane regulations and practices related to the exemption process for gay individuals still appear to thrill the people.

The army as an organization is not perceived to be a safe place which is indeed potentially traumatic even if direct exposure to threat doesn't happen. The news in the media appear to cause vicarious trauma as one participant expressed his feelings: "I used to think... Wanted to join the army. I always wanted it. I was going to become a soldier. You know to join [the army]. I wasn't afraid. But you know, I don't want it anymore especially with the conditions of today. However I don't think I would have serious problems when I think about homosexuality. I mean if I have to, I would do it. But again, the idea of [the rape cases] affects me. You know the things that happened recently. You know they could affect [could easily happen to] me. Horrible events… You know I never thought about it. I will try to postpone it as long as I can. If I have to do something like that [join the army]. I don't know what I will do. I don't know what I can do about this."

What we explain about the concurrence of military service as an obligation for male citizens and being self-identified as gay depicts the vicious circle for young people who are at the start of their career. Longer enrollment in the education system allows for the possibility of postponing the mandatory military obligation. One of the participants from Cleve and Işık's study again affirmed this idea by mentioning "I'm not planning to join the military. I will extend my time as a student as long as I can." However, not completing a formal education means that the official employment for particular jobs and organizations which require higher education level wouldn't be possible. Beside, military service is a hurdle for the majority of young men in Turkey since organizations prefer to employ those who had completed this obligation making long-term employment more plausible. As one participant posited that "also there is another option, which is to pay the government instead of doing the military service. I'm totally against this as well, but it's an option." The possibility to buy an exemption from the military service is deployed by the initiatives of the government and Turkish Armed Forces from time to time. It currently costs $8,700 to buy out of military service. Of course this is not a possibility for majority of young adults who are from low social economic status families, who are at the beginning of their own career so that they cannot afford it individually, and because there are minimum age criteria to get this opportunity.

However some of the participants were also thinking that self-identified gay people should have the chance to be in the army if this is what they want to. One participant elaborated the issue from this perspective: "We are a bit out dated in our military service because this is still mandatory. If they say it's mandatory, the gays should be obliged to do it as well. Then there comes the problem of gender identity. The rule says all men should do it. They are denying the patriotic feelings of gay people. I'm not a supporter of that kind of thought but if you want to do that you should be able to do. I think the military should change who they accept and how they treat them."

For those who prefer not to fulfill military obligation, the need to disclose sexual identity without personal consent is challenging in professional settings as well. Göregenli and Serdengeçti's (2015) survey of LGBTI employees which showed that most of the LGBTI private sector employees in Turkey are "obliged to hide their sexual orientation and gender identities in working environments" enlightens this controversial condition. Their study demonstrated the consequences of fulfilling or not fulfilling military service. A self-identified gay male participant from their study mentioned that "I'm exempt from military service because I'm gay. The reason of my exemption was asked during the job interview; I minced words. They smiled saying something like "It's all right, we understand," and afterwards, they didn't call again." (p. 17). The researchers explained, "being exempt from military service causes some participants to be afraid of their sexual identities being disclosed against their will." (p. 20). As another participant mentioned, "I wasn't open. I'm exempt from the military service. I hid that I was exempted; so I told that I served as a soldier." (p.22). As previously explained in the disclosure decision section, concealing sexual identity at social and work settings is in itself a strain, concealing it by using the military service as a cover is an additional burden. Individual's employability and job security is basically dependent how well he hides sexual orientation and how well he pretends being a man who completed military service.

Beside US and Turkey, we meet various cases of LGBT people's in military settings in other countries. In 2007, the case of British soldier presence Lance Bombardier Kerry Fletcher became famous in the UK when she decided to raise a formal complaint against her senior staff sergeant. The openly lesbian identified soldier stated that her senior colleague claimed she was gay because she needed a "real man" in order to change her mind about her sexual identity. Lance was overwhelmed, consumed by panic, and feeling extremely embarrassed, stating, "He was my boss. I thought this was completely out of my control." After the formal complaint was filed, Lance shared that she started to receive disturbing phone calls late at night and her car was damaged twice (The Telegraph, 2008). During the tribunal hearings, Lance described the psychological and physical health problems she experienced as a result of the discrimination and sexual harassment she was forced to tolerate. After 10 years serving the Royal Artillery Lance decided to resign her position fearing further retaliation and persecution. Later in 2008 Lance was informed that the tribunal ruled in her favor and the British Ministry of Defense was mandated to pay her approximately £190,000 (BBC News, 2008). Courageous stories of LGBT military personnel openly sharing their feelings and experiences while serving their countries' armed forces are contributing to empower others those who be suffering in silence.

In 2009, the International Gay and Lesbian Association (IGLA) identified countries that had clear policies permitting LGBT people to serve in the armed forces - Australia, Austria, Bahamas, Belgium, Canada, Czech Republic, Denmark, Estonia, Finland, France, Ireland, Israel, Italy, Lithuania, Netherlands, New Zealand, Norway, Slovenia, South Africa, Sweden, Switzerland and UK (Palm Center, 2009). A more recent list was released in 2011 and included Albania, Argentina, Bermuda, Colombia, Croatia, Germany, Greece, Japan, Luxembourg, Malta, Peru, Philippines, Poland, Romania, Russia, Serbia, Spain, Taiwan, Thailand, Uruguay U.S.; after a comprehensive review examining scholarly articles, books and online material, no additional updates were evident and the current list appears accurate (McPherson, 2011).

In 2010, a study was conducted to examine the experiences of countries of Australia, Canada, Germany, Israel, Italy, the Netherlands, and the UK in relation to permitting LGB individuals to serve in their armed forces (Bensahel, 2010). In these countries the code of conduct for military personnel is equally applied to all service members regardless of their sexual identity. Additionally, no country offered special accommodations related to privacy or separate trainings specific to sexual orientation. Apparently such practices provide a more welcoming environment to LGB personnel considering that few formal complaints addressing sexual orientation harassment were reported. Since the policies in these countries were modified they did not identify a single problem related to recruiting or retaining LGB personnel. In addition, countries' armed forces were not aware of problems related to combat unit performance that were created by LGB personnel serving without restriction. Most important, management and serving personnel confirmed that since the policy was modified unit performance had significantly improved. They attributed performance improvement to the fact that LGB personnel no longer needed to devote energy to hide their sexual identities but rather their energies are reinvested into their work (Bensahel, 2010).

Sports

LGBT workplace discrimination has also been a serious concern in the business of sports (Anderson, 2013; Cavalier, 2011; Cunningham, 2012; Gregory, 2004; Griffin, 1995). In 2014, the online U.S. edition of Reuter's magazine highlighted the story of Michael Sam, a well-known U.S. National Football League (NFL) player, who openly disclosed his gay identity in the media, challenging the boundaries of sport business and sponsoring companies (Richwine & Grover, 2014). Michael Sam was considered the first gay NFL player to openly discuss his sexual orientation in the media. During that time it was questioned if Michael Sam would get contracts with sport companies or if he would suffer any type of discrimination due to his decision to disclose his sexual orientation. After two years, The Guardian published a report confirming the NFL's hostility and bias toward Michael Sam (Moore, 2016).

In Brazil, the story was mirrored with the soccer player Emerson Sheik who shared in his social media a photo kissing one of his male friends on the lips (Alliatti, 2014). The picture had a negative repercussion on the soccer field impacting his ability to continue playing for one of the major soccer clubs in Brazil. Soccer fans decided to respond with violent and discriminatory posts in the social media; fans also brought banners to the soccer games saying that soccer was not a place for queers.

Another controversial case involved the former German soccer player Thomas Hitzlsperger who openly shared in social media his sexual identity (British Broadcasting Corporation Sport - BBC, 2014). Interestingly, Thomas Hitzlsperger's decision was only published after he completed his retirement process. In the soccer business discriminatory practices go above and beyond countries' borders. Sepp Blatter, the former Fédération Internationale de Football Association (FIFA) president, emphatically advised gay soccer fans and players to refrain from having sex while attending the 2022 World Cup in Qatar (BBC Esportes Brasil, 2010). During the 2010 World Cup in South Africa Sepp Blatter, who was at the time still FIFA president, explained (giggling) in a press conference that gay soccer fans should avoid having sex considering that homosexuality is illegal in Qatar. Prompt reactions from world renowned gay athletes promptly flooded social media demanding that Sepp Blatter apologize. Gay athletes agreed that Sepp Blatter's biased speech, in fact, reflects a wider attitude in the soccer industry's discriminating attitudes toward LGBT athletes (BBC Esportes Brasil, 2010).

In Turkey, the most widely known case is of Halil İbrahim Dinçdağ's who used to be a referee in the Turkish Football Federation (TFF) in the city of northeastern Turkey. In 2009 the TFF disseminated the news about Halil İbrahim Dinçdağ that he was gay without his personal consent and he was subsequently dismissed from his organization. He stated, "TFF was thinking that I will show silence when they disclose that I am gay. Instead I initiated court cases. Now I don't have any job, I have been also dismissed from the radio that I used to be programmer. I was intimidated by death because I foul/pollute the identity of Turkish and Black Sea Region people. I am decisive to challenge this and I hope to be the one to stop this injustice in Turkey." (March, 2013). His family showed a very supportive attitude and his brother told him that they would not exclude or discriminate him (May, 2009).

Halil Ibrahim Dinçdağ's case was also cited as an overlap between the discussion of military service, career and trauma as mentioned by one of the participants in Cleve & Işık's (2013) research: "He has got these notes in his military report: Psychosexual disorder and advanced trans-sexuality etc. which are considered against the public morality and an obstacle to serve as a government officer. These mentioned as the conditions that prevent him from performing his military service, which has been based on the decisions of the World Health Organizations in 90s. They have been changed afterwards. But In Turkey, they don't take these changes into account."

Additionally, the General Manager (GM) of the radio that Halil İbrahim Dinçdağ had been working as the programmer since 1994 reported that "I was shocked when I learned the news from TV. He was one of our brother who we loved a lot and who has good human relationships. Beside sports programs, he was sometimes performing religious programs. He was going to Friday prays." GM's incoherency was especially obvious as he states (May, 2009) that; "Our radio has a mission. We can't exclude any person, but it is not possible for our brother to restart working in our radio." In a press conference in 2013, Dinçdağ shared that since the time his sexual identity had been publicly disclosed, he hadn't received responses from any of the150 applications in his job search process. In the same talk he also said, "With the news in 2009, my family and all over Turkey learned of my personal life. I don't want to talk anymore on the pain and trauma that I experienced following this" In a press release dated December 29, 2015, we learn that Halil İbrahim Dinçdağ won his case against the TFF and highlighted, "December 29, 2015 is a day of victory for the challenges of homophobia and the LGBT movement for football in Turkey."

Although the sports field is still marked by discriminatory practices it appears that the world is slowly moving in a healthier and more optimistic direction. This is particularly true in the remarks of the United Nations Secretary-General Ban Ki-moon during the 126th Session of The International Olympic Committee held in Russia (2014). Ban Ki-moon delivered an empowering speech encouraging the Olympic communities to join forces and show that sport has the power to bring people together regardless of their sex, sexual orientation or gender identity (United Nations, 2014).

Another important and positive milestone achieved in the field of sport was the publication of the book *Sexual Orientation and Gender Identity in Sport,* edited by George Cunningham (2012) from the Center for Sport Management and Education in collaboration with Texas A&M University and College Station, Texas. The book encourages a constructive and inclusive view into the relationship of LGBT athletes and the field of sport. Several essays from LGBT activists, coaches, and scholars present their early experiences as athletes as they openly discuss their sexual orientation to compose it. Pat Griffin, an LGBT activist, Professor Emeritus at the University of Massachusetts and one of the authors of the book, proposes an important discussion honoring the success of LGBT equality in sport despite the challenges still faced by LGBT individuals. This initiative serves as a sign of confirmation that it is possible for LGBT athletes to have positive, inclusive and transformational experiences in the sport field including the sport business.

Clearly, LGBT people are still experiencing trauma and discrimination in diverse working settings as illustrated in the stories above. This type of aggression is not limited to geographical boundaries as the stories presented were identified in many parts of the world. The future is likely to see an increase in the number of powerful and inspirational 'coming out' stories positively impacting the lives of those living in concealment. It is expected that such transformational stories and the continuous fight for LGBT rights around the world will consequently result in more inclusive practices advocating for the development of anti-discrimination policies and supportive work environments. The workplace environment is still marked by discriminatory practices; however it appears likely that it is progressively changing and moving in a healthier direction. Workplace conditions have significantly improved encouraging equality for LGBT employees in specific parts of the world. As a result LGBT individuals are able to feel a bit more comfortable and confident that they will not suffer retaliation if they decide to disclose their sexual identities.

SOLUTIONS AND RECOMMENDATIONS

As the discourse on sexual identities continues across a variety of environments, and especially within the workplace, there are several models that can be used to support and address potential organizational trauma from taking place. By understanding and acknowledging the mediating factors that come into play for gay identified individuals considering the disclosure of their sexual identity, it can mitigate potentially awkward or illegal discriminatory practices. The knowledge gained from reviewing historical perspectives and events that have helped the evolution of sexual identity tolerance, equality and acceptance to take place may serve to create more effective and empathic approaches.

It is further critical to not only know what laws are present within a municipality, state, or country, to guide policy development on protection against discriminatory practices but also the current social perspectives that can serve to support marginalized and stigmatized communities within the organization. This can take the form of developing a clearly articulated system of organizational values, the inclusion of diverse populations in formulating those values, and the involvement of both shareholders and stakeholders to provide the broadest assessment and evaluation. The scrutiny of key constructs such as heterosexism and homophobia are critically important for both personal and organizational levels of discrimination and bias to be addressed.

In reviewing the cases of prominent individuals who have voluntarily or involuntarily disclosed their sexual identity, trends and themes can be identified across a continuum of careers including the corporate business world, the business of sports, and the military service. Utilizing a cross-cultural lens to consider how each of these occupations intersect around factors related to sexual identity and disclosure, the authors have provided a brief summary for each of these career paths in the U.S., Brazil and Turkey. This broad context of culture demonstrates how universal and relativistic patterns emerge and are collectively motivated by political, economic, social and moral climates.

In the new millennia, the focus on global human rights for LGBT identified individuals is coming to the forefront of economic, political and social justice discourse. If all people are afforded access to 'human rights', why are marginalized groups classified in ways that limit this right of entry? The ability for social media to quickly, albeit with sometimes-questionable accuracy, share information across the Internet, creates the need for thoughtful and evidence based planning on the part of organizations and businesses. Universal ideologies may define and support collective human rights but access to those rights must be placed in a relativist context as global recognition permitting entree varies along a broad continuum of experiences.

In his seminal work, Murphy (1972) argued that the goal of a global community should ideally include the support of a shared discourse across international boundaries on values and behavioral norms but has instead resulted in failure due to the antagonistic ideologies of sovereign states. Almost a half-century later humankind continues to struggle with this construct of ideological unity. For organizations, access to basic human rights for employees should transpire not only through their human resources department, but also more importantly, at the core of their institutional values. Organizational or collective ideologies can be viewed as 'group markers' (G. Hofstede, G.J. Hofstede, & Minkov, 2010); the way in which groups "penalize deviant symbolic identities and behaviors" differs tremendously across systems but promotes selective membership or inclusion through stated or implicit rules (p. 17). Multinational corporations have concern for their reputations and standing within communities, and with their stakeholders and shareholders. Acknowledging and respecting diverse identities in the workplace and taking preventive measures against the potential trauma that may emerge as a result of disclosure experience in the organizational setting, will convert the organizations into social settings where considerate attitudes inclusively support all forms of diversity.

The benefits for the gay community in having positive role models, male, female and transgender, can be extremely important. Greene, Fisher, Kuper, Andrews, & Mustanski's (2015) qualitative analysis on same-sex relationships and identified the importance of challenging stereotypes against LGBT individuals and their analysis yielded, *"identifying role models and sources of support",* as one of the interventions against homophobic and heteronormative attitudes in addition to "addressing sexual risk and protective behaviors", "improving communication", and "coping with family and relationship violence" (p. 2). The study by Price Waterhouse Cooper, Australia (PwC) in 2016 as mentioned earlier brought forward following factors as critically important:

1. The critical role of leadership;
2. Formal inclusion and diversity strategies being a start but more is needed; and
3. Coming out at work is 'mostly' not considered career limiting.

The authors also incorporated a narrative component, asking employees for ideas to improve the workplace related to decreasing negative heteronormative behaviors and they suggested to: "have leaders who act as role models"; "be more aware that apart from being bi, gay or straight, there are many other orientations" (p. 11), and; minimizing the use of gender specific language toward helping inclusion and even work production. Implementation of these recommendations in the workplace environment may encourage people to voluntarily disclose sexual identities; the use of these approaches by members within the organization may help the emergence of LGBTI role models who are open and successful in organizational life.

These opinions are related certainly to diversity management, which is a critical construct in today's work environment and both local and global organizations are encouraged to invest in their people's time and energy particularly with marginalized and stigmatized groups including LGBT individuals. These efforts should work toward enhancing inclusiveness within the organizational settings in order to:

1. Create non-discriminative policies toward LGBT individuals' selection and placement in available positions;
2. Attain procedural or distributional justice on wages, promotion and other incentives;
3. Give opportunity for career development and the possibility to achieve managerial positions as long as their competencies match the position requirements, and;
4. Engage the LGBT individual in social interactions within or between the network of organizations.

These goals can be attained in an organizational culture with a strong awareness of diversity. Vatansever, Çalışkan and Işık (2015) conducted a grounded theory design on exploring perceptions of global diversity management applications in a multinational company in Turkey. The analysis of the interviews with managers showed that cultural awareness is a critical competency which is defined as a process that starts with "perception of differences" and ends with "not recognizing these differences any more" (p. 49) (i.e., during the interactions, the perception of differences will be eliminated so that the artificial impact of this will diminish and the relations will flow more naturally).

Vatansever et al. (2015) also indicated that culturally aware individuals understand how to derive benefit from differences and act according to the requirements of the social settings in an adaptive manner. The exchanges during this process are not personalized and self-regulation is achieved more effectively. It is proposed that work life will be easier for the LGBT individual if people strive to reach a level of not recognizing differences relative to specific demographic characteristics (age, gender race, and sexual identity). The emerging theory from this research highlights "diversity climate of organizations" coined as a construct which is defined by the following themes (p.42): Firstly, keeping diversity as the "golden rule" so that the initial reaction is always one of inclusion and "so what?" which implies the automatic response toward salient characteristics of people (i.e., unique or distinctive attributes of people is not a big issue). Secondly, trusting that members' will show conscientiousness and will act in a culturally intelligent manner so that external control is not required to ensure inclusiveness within the organization. Thirdly, not "forcing people to fit one size" so that differences are accepted. These themes are very relevant when thinking about the inclusion of LGBT employees, particularly when they are considering disclosure. For instance, a "so what" attitude wouldn't mean that others don't care for or about those who are LGBT, but rather, actively choose to not take issue as a professional in the business setting.

This model further recommends that in organizations where diversity climate is prioritized, diversity management tools inclusive of LGBT identified employees within the corporate processes need to be implemented not only by human resources management but also through the overall organizational vision. All departments and their members have to internalize inclusive approaches as the basic value and the communication channels throughout the company need to incorporate this as a value. Vatansever et al.'s grounded model (2015) also demonstrates the outcomes for this process. The ineffective diversity management would result in interpersonal conflicts, prejudice, deadlocks, and clashes, which may turn into a potentially traumatic experience for all members of the organization.

Further research can be beneficially directed toward continuing to explore how minority sexual identities, specifically LGBT persons can be more effectively appreciated within a global context. With globalization in the work force becoming an increasing reality, the chances of engaging a more diverse clientele and business relationship base is much more likely to occur. This can be achieved across a large participant base inclusive of a variety of career and occupational choices. To view any 'ism' (e.g. sexism, racism, heterosexism, classism, and ageism) as appropriate in the new millennia may create a disservice toward the goal of healthy functioning for any organization.

CONCLUSION

The authors explored how the progression of human rights has served to advocate for stigmatized and marginalized communities, specifically for LGBTQ individuals. The evolution of gay identities and ultimately the ensuing acronym speaks to the levels of discrimination and oppression that has been experienced and was used to inform how sexual identities are considered for disclosure and especially that process as it occurs in the global workplace. Through a cross-cultural lens of case study analysis in the U.S., Brazil and Turkey, for a variety of career options including corporate business contexts, the field of sports and the military, key factors were identified that appear to parallel those processes found in the recent literature. By more explicitly looking at internal and relational mediators, the authors have proposed several recommendations that could serve toward policy development within organizations with the goal of avoiding organizational trauma and disruption among LGBT employees. Exploration of the constructs defined as heterosexism and homophobia can assist managers in increasing self-awareness and self-regulation for managers and employees alike. Sexual identity disclosure can produce both positive and negative outcomes in the workplace and it is recommended that a careful evaluation and assessment of both organizational values and adherence to anti-discrimination laws will best assist in creating an inclusive atmosphere for the LGBT population.

REFERENCES

Aitkenhead, D. (2014, May 24). Lord Browne: 'I though being gay was basically wrong'. *The Guardian*. Retrieved from https://www.theguardian.com/society/2014/may/24/lord-browne-thought-being-gay-wrong-interview-bp-boss-homophobia

Alliatti, A. (2014, February 2). Homossexualidade no esporte: Brasil mantém futebol dentro do armário. *Globo*. Retrieved from http://globoesporte.globo.com/futebol/noticia/2014/02/homossexualidade-no-esporte-brasil-mantem-futebol-dentro-do-armario.html

American Psychological Association. (2010). *Publication manual of the American Psychological Association* (6th ed.). Washington, DC: Author.

Anderson, E. (2013). *Sport, Masculinities and Sexualities*. New York, NY: Routledge Taylor & Francis.

Badgett, M. V. L., Durso, L. E., Kastanis, A., & Mallory, K. (2013). The business impact of LGBT-supportive workplace policies. *The Williams Institute, Executive Summary*, 1-37.

Baird-Remba, R. (2013). 13 countries that are more gay friendly than America. *Business Insider*. Retrieved from http://www.businessinsider.com/worlds-most-gay-friendly-countries-2013-3#denmark-legalized-gay-marriage-in-2012-but-has-recognized-same-sex-domestic-partnerships-since-1989-the-first-country-in-the-world-to-do-so-11

Balestrery, J. (in press). A History of Community: Marching Toward Equality. In M. Dentato (Ed.), *Social Work Practice with the LGBTQ Community: The Intersection of History, Health, Mental Health and Policy Factors*. Oxford University Press.

Bensahel, N. (2010). The Experience of Foreign Militaries. In B. B. Rostker (Ed.), *Sexual orientation and U.S. military personnel policy – an update of RAND's 1993 study* (pp. 275–316). Santa Monica, CA: RAND Corporation.

Bentley, N. (2015, September 2). *Coming out at work: a senior leader's story*. Chartered Management Institute. Retrieved from http://www.managers.org.uk/insights/news/2015/september/coming-out-at-work-a-senior-leaders-story

Berry, J. W., Poortinga, Y. H., Breugelmans, S. M., Chasiotis, A., & Sam, D. L. (Eds.). (2013). *Cross-cultural psychology: Research and applications* (3rd ed.). Cambridge University Press.

Bloomberg Technology Magazine. (2014). *Tim Cook Speaks Up*. Retrieved from http://www.bloomberg.com/news/articles/2014-10-30/tim-cook-speaks-up

British Broadcasting Corporation Sport – BBC. (2014). *Thomas Hitzlsperger: Former Aston Villa player reveals he is gay*. Retrieved from http://www.bbc.com/sport/football/25628806

Cavalier, E. S. (2011). Men at Sport: Gay Mens Experiences in the Sport Workplace. *Journal of Homosexuality, 58*(5), 626–646. PubMeddoi:10.1080/00918369.2011.563662

Charmaz, K. (2006). *Constructing grounded theory: A practical guide through qualitative analysis*. Thousand Oaks, CA: SAGE Publications, Inc.

Chaudoir, S. R., Earnshaw, V. A., & Andel, S. (2013). "Discredited" vs. "discreditable": Understanding how shared and unique stigma mechanisms affect psychological and physical health disparities. *Basic and Applied Social Psychology, 35*, 75–87. doi:10.1080/01973533.2012.746612

Chaudoir, S. R., & Fisher, J. D. (2010). The disclosure processes model: Understanding disclosure decision-making and post-disclosure outcomes among people living with a concealable stigmatized identity. *Psychological Bulletin, 136*(2), 236–256. PubMeddoi:10.1037/a0018193

Chaudoir, S. R., Fisher, J. D., & Simoni, J. (2011). Understanding HIV disclosure: A review and application of the Disclosure Processes Model. *Social Science & Medicine, 72*(10), 1618–1629. PubMeddoi:10.1016/j.socscimed.2011.03.028

Chaudoir, S. R., & Quinn, D. M. (2016). Evidence that anticipated stigma predicts poorer depressive symptom trajectories among emerging adults living with concealable stigmatized identities. *Self and Identity, 15*(2), 139–151. doi:10.1080/15298868.2015.1091378

Cleve, R., & Işık, İ. (2013). *Career Orientations Interview with Gay Males*. Unpublished raw data.

Cleve, R. A. (2012). *Disclosure Decisions of Sexual Identity in Young Adult Males: Emergent Cross-Cultural Themes Utilizing Grounded Theory*. Retrieved from http://search.proquest.com.tcsedsystem.idm.oclc.org/pqdtglobal/docview/1179003386/fulltextPDF/F33E8A259FA429CPQ/1?accountid=34120

Coming Out. (2016). *Before and After 'Don't Ask, Don't Tell'*. Retrieved from http://www.comingout.space/evolving-dont-ask-dont-tell

Cook, T. D. (2014, October 30). Tim Cook speaks up. *Blomberg Technology*. Retrieved from http://www.bloomberg.com/news/articles/2014-10-30/tim-cook-speaks-up

Cunningham, D. D., & Green, D. D. (2007). Diversity as a competitive strategy in the workplace. *Journal of Practical Consulting, 1*(2), 51–55.

Cunningham, G. B. (2012). *Sexual Orientation and Gender Identity in Sport. Texas A&M University*. The Center for Sport Management Research and Education.

Dentato, M. P., Halkitis, P. N., & Orwat, J. (2013). Minority stress theory: An examination of factors surrounding sexual risk behavior in gay and bisexual men who use club drugs. *Journal of Gay & Lesbian Social Services, 24*(4), 509–525. PubMeddoi:10.1080/10538720.2013.829395

Dia, O. (2014). *Exército afirma que aceita gays na tropa - Ativistas da causa homossexual questionam a informação.* Retrieved from http://odia.ig.com.br/noticia/economia/2014-05-11/exercito-afirma-que-aceita-gays-na-tropa.html

Discount, S., Russell, C., Gandara, D., & Sawyer, K. (2016). LGB issues in the workplace 101. *The Industrial-Organizational psychologist, 58*(4), 39–44.

Drabold, W. (2016). Read the Republican platform on same-sex marriage, guns and Wall Street. *Time*. Retrieved from http://time.com/4411842/republican-platform-same-sex-marriage-abortion-guns-wall-street/

Ellis, R., Fantz, A., Karimi, F., & McLaughlin, E. C. (2016). *Orlando shooting: 49 killed, shooter pledged ISIS allegiance.* Retrieved from http://www.cnn.com/2016/06/12/us/orlando-nightclub-shooting/

Eşcinsel hakem: 'Ölüm tehditleri alıyorum' - Akşam. (2013, March 16). Retrieved September 11, 2016, from http://www.aksam.com.tr/yasam/escinsel-hakem-olum-tehditleri-aliyorum-/haber-177758

Eşcinsel olduğunu açıklayan hakem, davayı kazandı. (2015, December 29). Retrieved September 11, 2016, from http://www.ntv.com.tr/turkiye/escinsel-oldugunu-aciklayinca-meslekten-men-edilen-hakem-tffye-actigi-davayi-ka,L1gp9_NgW0ejF02FQyFL_AThe

Esportes Brasil, B. B. C. (2010). *Blatter recomenda que gays evitem 'atividades sexuais' no Catar 22.* Retrieved from http://www.bbc.com/portuguese/noticias/2010/12/101214_blatter_rc.shtml?print=1

European Region of the International Lesbian, Gay, Bisexual, Trans & Intersex Association's report. (2015). *Annual Review of the Human Rights Situation for Lesbian, Gay, Bisexual, Trans and Intersex People in Europe.* Brussels: ILGA Europe.

Everly, B. A., & Schwarz, J. L. (2014). Predictors of the adoption of LGBT-friendly HR policies. *Human Resource Management, 54*(2), 367–384. doi:10.1002/hrm.21622

Ferreira, R. C. (2007). *O Gay no Ambiente de Trabalho: Análise dos Efeitos de ser Gay nas organizações contemporâneas* (Master Thesis). Retrieved from http://repositorio.unb.br/bitstream/10482/3329/1/2007_RenataCostaFerreira.pdf

Ferreira, R. C., & Siqueira, M. V. S. (2007). *O Gay no Ambiente de Trabalho: Análise dos Efeitos de ser Gay nas organizações contemporâneas. XXXI Encontro da ANPAD, Rio de Janeiro.* Retrieved from http://www.anpad.org.br/admin/pdf/EOR-B524.pdf

Florida: Iranian doctor on Islam: Killing gays is an act of 'compassion'. (2016, March). *The Muslim Issue.* Retrieved from https://themuslimissue.wordpress.com/2016/03/30/florida-iranian-doctor-on-islam-killing-gays-is-an-act-of-compassion/

Freedom in the world report. (2016). Retrieved from https://freedomhouse.org/sites/default/files/FH_FITW_Report_2016.pdf

Gay hakemin abisi imam çıktı! (2009, May 18). Retrieved September 11, 2016, from http://www.internethaber.com/gay-hakemin-abisi-imam-cikti-192545h.htm

Gibson, M. (1997). Clitoral corruption: Body metaphors and American doctors' constructions of female homosexuality, 1870-1900. In V. A. Rosario (Ed.), *Science and homosexualities* (pp. 108–132). New York: Academic Press.

Göregenli, M., & Serdengeçti, T. Ş. (2015). *Situation of Lesbian, Gay, Bisexual, Transgender and Intersex Employees in Private Sector in Turkey*. Ankara: Kaos Gey ve Lezbiyen Kültürel Araştırmalar ve Dayanışma Derneği.

Greene, G. J., Fisher, K. A., Kuper, L., Andrews, R., & Mustanski, B. (2015). "Is this normal? is this not normal? there is no set example": Sexual health intervention preferences of LGBT youth in romantic relationships. *Sexuality Research & Social Policy*, *12*(1), 1–14. http://dx.doi.org.tcsedsystem.idm.oclc.org/10.1007/s13178-014-0169-2

Gregory, A. (2004). Rethinking Homophobia in Sports: Legal Protections for Gay and Lesbian Athletes and Coaches. *DePaul Journal of Sports Law & Contemporary Problems*, *2*(2), 264–292.

Gregory, A. (2004). Rethinking Homophobia in Sports: Legal Protections for Gay and Lesbian Athletes and Coaches. *DePaul Journal of Sports Law & Contemporary Problems*, *2*(2), 264–292.

Griffin, P. (1995). Homophobia in Sport. In G. Unks (Ed.), *The Gay Teen: Educational Practice and Theory for Lesbian, Gay and Bisexual Adolescents* (pp. 53–66). New York, NY: Routledge.

Grupo Gay da Bahia. (2014). *Assassinato de Homossexuais (LGBT) No Brasil: Relatório 2014*. Retrieved from https://homofobiamata.files.wordpress.com/2015/01/relatc3b3rio-2014s.pdf

Gürcan, M. (2014, December 10). $8,700 will let young Turks 'buy out' their military service. Retrieved September 07, 2016, from http://www.al-monitor.com/pulse/originals/2014/12/turkey-compulsory-military-service-buy-exemption.html

Gürcan, M. (2015, November 17). *Gays seeking military exemption in Turkey no longer need to provide visual proof of their homosexuality*. Retrieved September 07, 2016, from http://www.al-monitor.com/pulse/originals/2015/11/turkey-military-gay-rights-homosexual-picture.html

Hallett, W. (2016, July 11). *Former Asylum Seeker has now forged a career with UK home office. Gay Star News*. Retrieved from http://www.gaystarnews.com/article/gay-former-asylum-seeker-home-office/#gs.N36Oorg

Hofstede, G., Hofstede, G. J., & Minkov, M. (2010). *Cultures and organizations: Software of the mind*. New York, NY: McGraw-Hill Companies.

Human Rights Campaign. (2016). *Establishing an allies/safe zone program*. Retrieved from http://www.hrc.org/resources/establishing-an-allies-safe-zone-program

Hunt, J. (2012). *A state-by-state examination of non-discrimination laws and policies*. Center for American Progress Action Fund. Retrieved from https://www.americanprogress.org/wp-content/uploads/issues/2012/06/pdf/state_nondiscrimination.pdf

Hurtas, S. (2014). *Honor killings haunt Turkey's gay community*. Retrieved from http://www.al-monitor.com/pulse/originals/2014/05/prejudice-turkey-against-homosexuals.html

Instituto Ethos. (2014). *Business Commitment to LGBT Human Rights*. Retrieved from https://www3.ethos.org.br/wp-content/uploads/2014/12/Manual-LGBT_em-Ingl%C3%AAs_Vers%C3%A3o-Final.pdf

Istanbul authorities ban transgender and gay pride marches. (2016, June). *The Guardian*. Retrieved from https://www.theguardian.com/world/2016/jun/17/istanbul-transgender-gay-pride-marches-ban-alperen-hearths

King, E. B., & Cortina, J. M. (2010). The social and economic imperative of lesbian, gay, bisexual, and transgendered supportive organizational policies. *Industrial and Organizational Psychology: Perspectives on Science and Practice*, *3*(1), 69–78. doi:10.1111/j.1754-9434.2009.01201.x

Luders, G. (2015, April 29). Chefe, sou gay. *Exame*. Retrieved from http://exame.abril.com.br/revista-exame/edicoes/1088/noticias/chefe-sou-gay

Mahtani, S., & Vernon, K. (2010). *Creating Inclusive Workplaces for LGBT Employees - A Resource Guide for Employers in Hong Kong*. Retrieved from http://www.outandequal.org/wp-content/uploads/2015/05/Community-Business-Inclusive-Workplaces-HK-2010.pdf

McPherson, S. (2011, September 22). MAP: Which Countries Enlist Gay Soldiers? *Advocate*. Retrieved from http://www.advocate.com/news/2011/09/22/map-which-countries-enlist-gay-soldiers

Mello, L., Avelar, R. B., & Majora, D. (2012). Por onde andam as políticas públicas para a população LGBT no Brasil. *Sociedade e Estado*, *27*(2), 289–312. doi:10.1590/S0102-69922012000200005

Meyer, I. H., Schwartz, S., & Frost, D. M. (2008). Social patterning of stress and coping: Does disadvantaged social status confer more stress and fewer coping resources? *Social Science & Medicine*, *67*(3), 368–379. PubMeddoi:10.1016/j.socscimed.2008.03.012

Ministry Of National Defense. (2016, March 23). *Military Service Types*. Retrieved September 07, 2016, from http://www.msb.gov.tr/en-US/Askeralma/Content/military-service-types

Mock, S. E., Sedlovskaya, A., & Purdie-Vaughns, V. (2009). Gay and bisexual mens disclosure of sexual orientation in the workplace: Associations with retirement planning. *Journal of Applied Gerontology*, *30*(1), 123–132. doi:10.1177/0733464809358081

Moore, J. (2016, April 26). Cowardly NFL still shows anti-gay bias, two years after Michael Sam's draft. *The Guardian*. Retrieved from https://www.theguardian.com/sport/2016/apr/26/nfl-draft-gay-players-michael-sam

Murphy, C. (1972). Ideological interpretations of human rights. *De Paul Law Review*, *2*, 286–306.

News, B. B. C. (2008). *MoD must pay gay soldier £190,000*. Retrieved from http://news.bbc.co.uk/2/hi/uk_news/england/west_yorkshire/7751036.stm

Palm Center. (2009). *Countries that Allow Military Service by Openly Gay People*. University of California Santa Barbara. Retrieved from http://archive.palmcenter.org/files/active/0/CountriesWithoutBan.pdf

PBS. (2016, August 10). *Timeline: Milestones in the American Gay Rights Movement*. Retrieved from http://www.pbs.org/wgbh/americanexperience/features/timeline/stonewall/

Pichler, S., Vama, A., & Bruce, T. (2010). Heterosexism in employment decisions: The role of job misfit. *The Journal of Applied Psychology, 40*(10), 2527–2555.

Pizer, J. C., Sears, B., Mallory, C., & Hunter, N. D. (2012). Evidence of Persistent and Pervasive Workplace Discrimination Against LGBT People: The Need for Federal Legislation Prohibiting Discrimination and Providing for Equal Employment Benefits. *Loyola of Los Angeles Law Review, 45*, 715–780.

Poteat, V. P., Calzo, J. P., & Yoshikawa, H. (2016). Promoting Youth Agency Through Dimensions of Gay-Straight Alliance Involvement and Conditions that Maximize Associations. *Journal of Youth and Adolescence: a Multidisciplinary Research Publication, 45*(7), 1438–1451. PubMeddoi:10.1007/s10964-016-0421-6

Price Waterhouse Cooper. (2016). *LGBTI perspectives on workplace inclusion.* Retrieved from http://www.pwc.com.au/publications/pdf/workplace-inclusion-survey-jun16.pdf

Prunas, A., Bandini, E., Fisher, A. D., Maggi, M., Pace, V., Quagliarella, L., & Bibi, M. et al. (2016). Experiences of Discrimination, Harassment, and Violence in a Sample of Italian Transsexuals Who Have Undergone Sex-Reassignment Surgery. *Journal of Interpersonal Violence*. doi:10.1177/0886260515624233

Questia. (2016, August 10). *Gays in the military*. Retrieved from https://www.questia.com/library/controversial-topics/gays-in-the-military

Qvist, B. (2014, July 28). Challenges for LGBT people in the workplace and how to overcome them. *The Guardian*. Retrieved from https://www.theguardian.com/sustainable-business/lgbt-employees-discrimination-in-the-workplace-talkpoint

Ragins, B. R., Singh, R., & Cornwell, J. M. (2007). Making the invisible visible: Fear and disclosure of sexual orientation at work. *The Journal of Applied Psychology, 92*(4), 1103–1118. PubMeddoi:10.1037/0021-9010.92.4.1103

Reed, J. (2016, April 11). Entering the workplace drove me back in the closet – until I switched employer. *Gay Star Business*. Retrieved from http://www.gaystarnews.com/article/james-reed-workplace-closet/#gs.PbB63AY

Richwine, L., & Grover, R. (2014, February 10). Analysis: Sponsorship dollars may follow gay NFL hopeful Sam. *Reuters*. Retrieved from http://www.reuters.com/article/us-usa-football-gay-marketing-analysis-idUSBREA1A01J20140211

Saxena, A. (2014). Workforce diversity: A key to improve productivity. *Procedia Economics and Finance, 11*, 76–85. doi:10.1016/S2212-5671(14)00178-6

Scobie, C. (2015). LGBTI in the workplace. *Business Diversity*. Retrieved from https://www.charteredaccountantsanz.com/en/Site-Content/Business-Trends-Insights/Acuity/June-2015/LGBTI-in-the-workplace.aspx#.V-w9HKIrJjc

Sears, B., & Mallory, C. (2011). *Documented evidence of employment discrimination & its effects on LGBT people.* The Williams Institute. Retrieved from http://williamsinstitute.law.ucla.edu/wp-content/uploads/Sears-Mallory-Discrimination-July-20111.pdf

Secretaria de Direitos Humanos da Presidência da Repúbica. (2012). *Relatório sobre Violência Homofobica no Brasil: Ano de 2012*. Retrieved from http://www.sdh.gov.br/assuntos/lgbt/pdf/relatorio-violencia-homofobica-ano-2012

Siqueira, M. V. S., Saraiva, L. A. S., Carrieri, A. P. C., Lima, H. K. B., & Andrade, A. J. A. (2009). Homofobia e Violência Moral no Trabalho no Distrito Federal. *Organizações & Sociedade*, *16*(50), 447–461. doi:10.1590/S1984-92302009000300003

Stein, M. (2012). *Rethinking the Gay and Lesbian movement*. New York, NY: Routledge.

Stevens, F. G., Plaut, V. C., & Sanchez-Burks, J. (2008). Unlocking the benefits of diversity: All-inclusive multiculturalism and positive organizational change. *The Journal of Applied Behavioral Science*, *14*(1), 116–133. doi:10.1177/0021886308314460

Taylor, A., III. (1997). My life as a gay executive. *Fortune Magazine*. Retrieved from: http://archive.fortune.com/magazines/fortune/fortune_archive/1997/09/08/230840/index.htm

Tejeda, M. J. (2006). Nondiscrimination policies and sexual identity disclosure: Do they make a difference in employee outcomes? *Employee Responsibilities and Rights Journal*, *18*(1), 45–59. doi:10.1007/s10672-005-9004-5

The Economist. (2014, November 8). *Gay people in business: out at the top*. Retrieved from http://www.economist.com/news/business/21631046-apples-boss-has-left-closet-being-gay-work-still-struggle-out-top

The Telegraph. (2008). *Lesbian soldier Kerry Fletcher wins case*. Retrieved from http://www.telegraph.co.uk/news/uknews/1575819/Lesbian-soldier-Kerry-Fletcher-wins-case.html

Tin, L. (2003). *The dictionary of homophobia: A global history of gay & lesbian experience*. Vancouver, BC: Arsenal Pulp Press.

Titelman, P. (Ed.). (2014). *Differentiation of self: Bowen family systems theory perspectives*. New York, NY: Taylor & Francis.

Türk Silahlı Kuvvetleri Sağlık Yeteneği Yönetmeliği. (2015, November 12). *Resmi Gazete*. Retrieved September 8, 2016, from http://www.mevzuat.gov.tr/MevzuatMetin/3.5.20158136.pdf

United Nations Human Rights Council. (2015). *Discrimination and violence against individuals based on their sexual orientation and gender identity*. Retrieved from http://www.ohchr.org/EN/Issues/Discrimination/Pages/LGBTUNReports.aspx

Urban Dictionary. (2016). *Definition of homophobia*. Retrieved from http://www.urbandictionary.com/define.php?term=homophobia

Vatansever, Ç., Çalıskan, S., & Isık, I. (2015). Bir Dünya Sirketinin Türkiye'deki Çalısanlarına Göre Çesitliliklerin Yönetimi: Gömülü Kuram Analiziyle Modelleme. *Yönetim Arastırmaları Dergisi*, *12*(1-2), 29–61.

Ward, J., & Winstanley, D. (2005). Coming out at work: Performativity and the recognition and renegotiation of identity. *The Sociological Review*, *53*(3), 447–475. Retrieved from http://www1.udel.edu/soc/tammya/socDev/ward%20winstanley%20coming%20out%20at%20work.pdf. doi:10.1111/j.1467-954X.2005.00561.x

White, J. M., Klein, D. M., & Martin, T. F. (2015). *Family theories: An introduction* (4th ed.). Thousand Oaks, CA: SAGE Publications, Inc.

Willis, P. (2012). Witnesses on the periphery: Young lesbian, gay, bisexual and queer employees witnessing homophobic exchanges in Australian workplaces. *Human Relations*, *65*(12), 1589–1610. doi:10.1177/0018726712457795

KEY TERMS AND DEFINITIONS

Case Analysis: The identification and critical application of relevant case studies.

Disclosure Decisions: The process of analysis for sharing a stigmatized/marginalized concealable identity.

Diversity: The continuum of micro cultures within the macro for workplace organizations and the positioning of LGBT identities within heteronormativity.

Heterosexism: The implicit assumption of inequality and marginalization between gay and heterosexual identity holding heterosexuality as the preferred (only legitimate) for membership.

Human Rights: The rights of humans globally based on the universal declaration of human rights.

LGBTQ: Current minority sexual identity acronym Lesbian, Gay, Bisexual, Transgender and Queer.

Policy Development: The structure of organizational values as applied to employee.

Chapter 9
Impact of Organizational Trauma on Workplace Behavior and Performance:
Workplace Bullying Due to (In)Competency

Ben Tran
Alliant International University, USA

ABSTRACT

Research suggests, according to Branch, Ramsay, and Barker (2013), that a significant number of people are exposed to persistent abusive treatment within the workplace, with the majority of studies within Europe indicating that between 10% and 15% of the workforce are exposed to workplace bullying (Zapf, Escartin, Einarsen, Hoel, & Vartia, 2011), with North American research reporting similar prevalence rates. This is a significant, ongoing dilemma for researchers and practitioners, for which an agreed resolution would be useful because of legal and policy implications. Hence, the purpose of this chapter is on the impact of organizational trauma on workplace behavior and performance based on workplace bullying. The chapter is based on a case study regarding a program that is funded by the Department of Education within a community college in the State of California. The community college is one of four community colleges under the same community college district.

INTRODUCTION

The term *trauma*, is rarely used in conjunction with the term *organization*, as in *organizational trauma*. The term *organizational trauma*, when used, often refers to the health and well-being of an organization being questioned. Hence, *trauma*, when used in an *organizational* setting, is often referred to organizational crisis that can escalate to *organizational trauma* if it reaches and continuously exceeds a level where people involved can no longer cope with the situation. With *organizational trauma* there exists *burnout*. According to Bell, Kulkarni, and Dalton (2003), Maslach (1993) described burnout as having three dimensions:

DOI: 10.4018/978-1-5225-2021-4.ch009

1. Emotional exhaustion,
2. Depersonalization, and
3. Reduced personal accomplishment and commitment to the profession.

Burnout has been conceptualized as a process rather than a condition or state, and some have theorized that it progresses sequentially through each of these dimensions (Maslach, 1993). Maslach and others have examined the interpersonal, and organizational characteristics that contribute to burnout, and confirmed that both individual interpersonal and organizational characteristics can do both at the same time. Of particular interest to this discussion is the finding that organizations can either promote job satisfaction or contribute to burnout (Söderfeldt, Söderfeldt, & Warg, 1995). Individual staff members suffer, and the resulting loss of experienced staff can diminish the quality of client services (Arches, 1991).

Burnout is derived from multiple factors, however, for the purpose of this chapter, focus will be on two interrelated factors: (workplace) bullying and competency [the lack of knowledge, skills, abilities, and other characteristics (KSAOs)]. The first factor in burnout is, workplace bullying, refers to *repeated*, unreasonable actions of individuals (or a group) directed towards an employee (or a group of employees), which are intended to intimate, degrade, humiliate or undermine, or which create a risk to the health or safety of the employees(s). The second factor in burnout is, competency, which consists of knowledge, skills, and abilities and "other" attributes, further referred to as KSAOs (Tran, 2008):

1. Knowledge is usually defined as the degree to which a candidate is required to know certain technical material,
2. Skill indicates adequate performance on tasks requiring the use of tools, equipment, and machinery,
3. Abilities are physical and mental capacities to perform tasks not requiring the use of tools, equipment, or machinery, and
4. Other characteristics include personality, interest, or motivational attributes that indicate a candidate will enjoy certain tasks, rather than whether they can do those tasks (Schneider & Schmitt, 1986: 53).

Workplace bullying often involves an abuse or misuse of power. Bullying behavior creates feelings of defenselessness and injustice in the target and undermines an individual's right to dignity at work. Bullying is different from aggression. Whereas aggression may involve a single act, bullying involves repeated attacks against the target, creating an on-going pattern of behavior. Tough or demanding bosses are not necessarily bullies as long as they are respectful and fair and their primary motivation is to obtain the best performance by setting high yet reasonable expectations. Workplace bullying can be instigated by coworkers, supervisors, contract workers, or labor representatives, and although rare, meek bosses can be also bullied by their direct reports. Some bullying situations involve employees bullying their peers, rather than a supervisor bullying an employee. The term *mobbing* refers to a group of coworkers targeting another worker. Supervisor should intervene immediately to address and stop mobbing behaviors.

In a prevalence study of U.S. workers, 41.4% of respondents reported experiencing psychological aggression at work in the past year, which representing 47 million U.S. workers (Schat, Frone, & Kelloway, 2006). Furthermore, according to other research performed by Pompili, Lester, Innamorati, De Pisa, Iliceto, Puccinno, Fiori, Tatarelli, and Girardi (2008), which focused on the impact of mobbing on the physical health of workers among 102 individuals who were targets of mobbing, 32 subjects (31.4%) had low suicide risk, 17 subjects (16.7%) had a medium suicide risk, and 4 subjects (3.9%) had high suicide risk (Pompili et al., 2008, p. 237). In other words, based on Pompili et al.'s (2008) study, and congruent to Ertureten, Cemalcilar, and Aycan's (2013, p. 206), there appears to be an increase in suicide risk in individuals exposed to mobbing behavior (Ertureten, Cemalcilar, & Aycan, 2013, p. 206). The other important findings deal with issues on how mobbing influences the performance of the individual. Job satisfaction, as well as commitment the employer, decreased in cases of people who were exposed to mobbing. In other words, employees who often consider the work environment as very uncomfortable environment, do not consider it to be a place in which they would like to work (Murphy, 2013; Vveinhardt, 2010) or be committed to.

Hence, the purpose of this chapter is to discuss the impact of organizational trauma on workplace behavior and performance based on workplace bullying, due to the perpetrator's (bully's) knowledge, skills, abilities, and other characteristics (KSAOs) on the staff of the program. The chapter is based on a case study of a program that is funded by the Department of Education within a community college in the State of California. The community college is one of four community colleges under the same community college district. Furthermore, this chapter will also cover bully, specifically bullying in the organizational (workplace) setting, and competency. Specifically, it will examine how lack of competency causes negative dynamics within the program, impacts staff performance, and elicits bullying in prone individuals.

The case study presented here was based on the following research methods:

1. The author communicated with the PROGRAM staff,
2. The author participated in the PROGRAM's staff meetings,
3. The author participated in the PROGRAM's events,
4. The author communicated with staff of the college who are in connection with the PROGRAM, and
5. The author communicated with participants (management level) who were in meetings on programs reviews (regarding learning community programs that are housed in the college).

Due to the fact that since this is only a case study, and also a book chapter, the case itself had to be summarized. In an effort to summarize the case study, only paramount objective information regarding the case, in relations to the topic of *bullying in the workplace* at hand, are included. Hence, the purpose of this chapter is not on identifying and categorizing each individuals' KSAOs in the case study (the PROGRAM) or determining the workplace bullying characteristics (Leymann, 1996; Koonin & Green, 2005). Based on the case study, as a case study, the purpose of this chapter is for readers (students and practitioners) to practice and enhance their skills with being able to identify and categorize workplace bullying behaviors and characteristics (Leymann, 1996; Zapf & Einarsen, 2005) when they are present.

WORKPLACE BULLYING

Mobbing has very negative consequences for the employee, whether from the perspective of health, or from the perspective of work performance. Health problems for victims of mobbing include headaches, stomach disorders, abdominal pains, and often end up in more serious mental disorders (Divincová & Siváková, 2014). For example, according to Sloan et al. (2010), a large study of mobbing behavior in Germany found that almost all (98.7%) of those targeted experienced employment and/or health consequences. Close to half (43.9%) became ill, 68.1% left their employment, and 14.8% were dismissed. The WBI found that 77% of targets changed employment (Namie & Namie, 2009). Dr. Heinz Leymann, who first identified this syndrome, estimated that workplace mobbing was responsible for 15% of suicides in Sweden (Leymann, 1990).

In addition to health problems, victims gradually stop to believe in themselves, and their self-efficacy suffers to the point that they consider themselves as incapable of solving even simple assignments. Not resolving this problem has led to a 20% of cases resulting in suicide (Kozser, 2006). According to Carbo and Hughes (2010, p. 58), a survey carried out by Christine Pearson in 1998, which dealt with the effects of mobbing on the staff, it was found that 37% of respondents reduced their commitment to their employer, 28% left the job in an effort to avoid mobbing, 22% decreased their performance at work, and 12% of respondents left work as a direct result of mobbing (Carbo & Hughes, 2010, p. 58). According to Hoeal, employees who are the target of mobbing in the workplace reduce their performance by an average of 80% compared to normal performance. This research was performed on a sample of employees in Great Britain whose average age was 43 years (Rayner, Hoeal, & Cooper, 2002, p. 135).

BULLYING IN THE WORKPLACE SETTING AT HIGHER EDUCATION INSTITUTION

According to a 2010 survey conducted by the Workplace Bullying Institute, located in the United States, one out of three American workers, 35% equaling to 53.5 million people, have been bullied in the workplace (Farmer, 2011). The United Nations International Labor Organization has also alerted that the issue of workplace bullying is reaching epidemic levels based on survey of 15 European Union countries (International Labor Organization, 2006). With statistics so prominent, the evidence clearly suggests that workplace bullying is rampant throughout most parts of the world. However, despite important advancements in terms of refinement of the construct and understanding of effects of the phenomenon, workplace bullying is still a topic that needs further research (Bowling & Beehr, 2006). This is because research on the antecedents of bullying and on the effect of preventive interventions is still in its infancy—especially for a non-profit workplace, such as higher education institutions.

Research looking into the impact of workplace bullying was first conducted during the 1980's. Dr. Leymann (1990) was the first researcher at the time to explore the effect of mobbing on the victims. According to Einarsen, Hoel, Zapf, and Cooper (2010), both Balducci, Fraccaroli, and Schaufeli (2011) and Leymann (1996) have defined workplace bullying as the prolonged exposure to frequent hostile behaviors at work, such as excessive criticism of one's work, withholding of information which affects performance, spreading rumors, social isolation and the like (Einarsen, Hoel, Zapf, & Cooper, 2010). In the long run, these behaviors may lead to stigmatization and victimization of the exposed individual (Einarsen & Mikkelsen, 2003). Leymann (1990) also defined mobbing as hostile and unethical behavior towards individuals who are unable to defend themselves. Dr. Leymann (1990) compared bullying in the workplace to the act of mobbing, evoking the image of a pack of animals attacking a single even larger animal. According to his research, individuals who had experienced bullying in the workplace were at higher risk of becoming depressed, exhibit signs of anxiety, and displays symptoms of PTSD. Leymann (1990) also introduced a duration criterion into the definition of bullying, stating that in order to be classified as bullying, the behaviors should last more than six months, with at least one interaction per week.

On the other hand, Zapf and Gross (2001), define workplace bullying as consistent exposure to persistent, oppressive, offensive, abusive, intimidating, malicious, or insulting behavior by a manager/supervisor or co-worker. Workplace bullying, can be seen as a continual purposeful behavior that sets bullying behavior apart from in civil treatment (Einarsen, Hoel, Zapf, & Cooper, 2003). As these definitions suggest along with the current literature, there are many different forms and characteristics which define workplace bullying. Mikkelsen and Einarsen (2002) reported that experiences from workplace bullying can be compared to that of losing a loved one due to an unexpected death. The Workplace Bullying Institute, according to Framer (2011), found that males are more consistently in the role of the bully at 62%, while females comprise 58% of those targeted. Workplace bullying can appear in many forms and characteristics, and these forms and characteristics include (Leymann, 1996; Koonin & Green, 2005):

1. Verbal or physical attacks
2. Social isolation and exclusion in the workplace
3. Ridicule and humiliation in front of work colleagues
4. Verbal threats and gestures
5. Assignment of demeaning work tasks
6. Workplace gossip among workers behind a targets back
7. Condescending attitude towards the target
8. "Silent treatment" of the target
9. Belittling the opinion of others
10. Staring, dirty looks, or other forms of negative eye contact

Group "Mobbing" vs. Bullying

Commonly, the terms bullying and mobbing are used more or less synonymously (Namie, 2003), but preferences vary geographically (Sperry, 2009), for based on research, semantically, mobbing has so far been most advanced in Scandinavia, Germany, and Austria. The phenomenon is rather less well recognized in the United States (Davenport, Schwartz, & Elliot, 2005; Kotleras, 2007). Mobbing is a work conflict "in which one person [is] singled out, harassed, and ostracized over a long period of time" (Zapf & Einarsen, 2005, p. 243)", "…not a short episode but a long-lasting wearing-down process, often lasting much longer than one year" (Leymann, 1996, p. 167; Zapf & Einarsen, 2005, p. 248). The systematic and long-term nature of the aggression effectively distinguishes mobbing from normal interpersonal conflict. Leymann and Gustafsson (1996, p. 273) explain how mobbing victims find their trauma "constantly renewed" as "new sources of anxiety occur in a constant stream" while continuing violations of the individual's rights "further undermine his or her self-confidence and psychological health".

With that said, "mobbing…often refers to subtle, less direct forms of aggression as opposed to the physical forms of aggression commonly identified with *bullying*" (Namie & Namie, 2000; Zapf & Einarsen, 2005). Its key elements, in summary, include "Powerlessness, power differences, and loss of control," (Zapf & Einarsen, 2005, pp. 168, 216, 238, 255) which are absent from the other concepts of workplace interpersonal conflict. Leymann (1996), for the purposes of case reporting, defined mobbing as "a social interaction through which one individual is attacked by one or more individuals almost on a daily basis and for periods of many months, bringing the person into an almost helpless position with potentially high risk of expulsion" (p. 168). Westhues (2002) better captures the tenor of mobbing by describing it as "an impassioned, collective campaign by co-workers to exclude, punish, and humiliate targeted workers, ... a desperate urge to crush and eliminate the target [that] travels through the workplace like a virus, infecting one person after another" (pp. 31-32).

Potential Causes of Mobbing

Zapf and Einarsen (2005) synthesize the literature to list four potential causes of mobbing: the organization, the perpetrator, the social work group, and the target. As such, Leymann devised the Leymann Inventory of Psychological Terror (LIPT), an inventory of 45 objective behaviors that were grouped into five categories based on factor analysis (Leyman, 1996, p. 170; Zapf & Einarsen, 2005):

1. **Attacks on Communication Opportunities**: Means being denied opportunities to express oneself. It also includes being told that certain issues either could not be discussed or could be discussed only in a highly artificial, administratively formalized manner preventing expression of one's real concerns;
2. **Attack on Social Relationships**: Goes beyond shunning, and includes overt incitements of subordinates to avoid all contact. A culturally specific variation of this form of psychological assault occurred when one person in authority acted very warm and concerned in one-on-one unofficial situations while deathly cold and impersonally menacing when others were present or in one-on-one official meetings;
3. **Implications on Social Reputation**: Included casting aspersions to one's face regarding one's nationality, making nasty remarks to third parties about one's religion, and spreading false rumors of one's ill health; and
4. **Attacks on the Quality of the Professional and Life Situation**: Includes being assigned to only one minor committee and then designated to chair it only to have its other committee members boycott meetings (Kotleras, 2007, pp. 134-135).
5. **Mobbing and Giftedness**: From the standpoint of the study and treatment of gifted individuals, gifted individuals are often picked as a target of both bullying and mobbing. Since bullying is better recognized than mobbing, it is useful to begin with a brief discussion of the situation of gifted children who may be bullied. The experience of being bullied is a severe matter for every child. Although all children are at risk of being bullied, there is a reason to suppose that not only gifted children are more at risk (Fox & Pope, 2005; Hollingworth, 1930), but also that among gifted children the experience of being the object of bullying is qualitatively different (Peterson & Ray, 2006).
6. **Phases of Mobbing**: According to Shallcross, Sheehan, and Ramsay (2008), there tends of be a pattern in relation to workplace mobbing commencing with a minor conflict that escalates until the target's expulsion from the workplace (Davenport et al., 1999; Leymann, 1996; Resch & Schubinski, 1996). Typically, there are five phases: (1) the initial conflict or critical incident stage, (2) the phase where psychological abuse is increasingly directed at the target, (3) the phase which occurs when management intervenes, often siding with the perpetrators, and increasing the levels of harm, (4) the phase when the target is accused of being *difficult* or *mentally ill* and, (5) a phase marked by the expulsion of the target from their employment (Davenport et al., 1999, p. 38). The mobbing behavior is frequent and enduring, often occurring over a period of months and years (Einarsen et al., 2003, pp. 7-8); Groeglinghoff & Becker, 1996; Leymann, 1996). In some cases, the mobbing continues even after the target's expulsion from the workplace and often causes long-lasting psychological harm. Additionally,

the harm caused can be described as either first, second, or third degree mobbing, analogous to the degree of harm caused by first, second, and third degree *burns* or *scars* (Davenport et al., 1999, p. 39).

Individual Bullying

In contrast to mobbing, bullying is an abusive and harmful behavior directed at a specific target or victim by a single or lone offender (Belak, 2002; Davenport, Schwartz, & Elliott, 2002; Denenberg & Bravernman, 2001; European Foundation for the Improvement of Living and Working Conditions, 2002). The bully may be a peer or supervisor, but other members of the work group are not involved, although others may observe the abuse. Unlike mobbing, there is little or no direct organizational involvement in the abusive behavior. Hence, the consequences of bullying tend to be much less severe than the impact of mobbing. According to the Workplace Bullying and Trauma Institute, workplace bullying is "the repeated mistreatment of one or more employees with a malicious mix of humiliation, intimidation and sabotage of performance". As is the case with childhood bullying, workplace bullies use aggressive or unreasonable behavior to achieve their ends (Daniel, 2006).

Bullying behavior can exist at any level of an organization—bullies can be superiors, subordinates, co-workers and colleagues (Davenport, Schwartz, & Elliott, 1999). Instead of using physical means, however, workplace bullies often operate within the established rules and policies of their organization or their society. For example, according to Daniel (2006), a workplace bully might use the office *rumor mill* to circulate a lie about a co-worker strictly for the purpose of creating a problem for that individual. An employee who dislikes a co-worker for personal reasons may incessantly criticize everything that the individual does or says. While such actions are not necessarily illegal and may not even be against the policy of many organizations, the damage that such actions cause—both to the targeted employee and to workplace morale—is significant. With that said, according to Sperry (2009), mobbing and bullying can be conceptualized along a continuum from healthy social behavior to abusiveness on which bullying is a less severe—that is, milder—form of abusiveness, than mobbing.

1. **Continuum Perspective on Bullying:** Based on Len Sperry's research and consultation experience, Sperry (2009) identified four distinct organization contexts:
    a. **Type I Organizational Contexts**: Represent a workplace setting that is essentially productive and healthy. In such organizations, abusive behavior of any kind is absent. The reason is that the organization's culture, structure, and leadership foster a climate of respect, concern, and caring for employees. Accordingly, such workplace settings are unlikely to support or condone discrimination, sexual harassment, bullying, mobbing, or any other form of abusive behavior or actions;
    b. **Type II Organizational Contexts**: Reflect a workplace setting wherein the abusive behavior of a bully occurs or can occur. The bully may be a peer or supervisor, however, other members of the work group are seldom, if ever, involved, although they may observe the abuse. Typically, there is relatively little or no direct organizational involvement in the abusive behavior. However, the organization's culture, structure, or leaders, can unwittingly foster the negative, abusive behavior by its inaction when it becomes aware of the bully's actions;

c. **Type III Organizational Contexts**: Represent a workplace setting involving moderately abusive behavior or actions. This context is referred to as Mobbing I. It typically involves two or more members of a workplace who engage in the mobbing actions. The work group's supervisor may be directly or indirectly involved in the abusive actions. Indirect involvement means that he or she colludes with the abuse and indirectly supports the mobbing by not making intentional effort to stop it. In contrast to bullying, mobbing requires that the organization supports or, to some degree, is complicit with, the mobbers' actions. The health consequences of Type III are considerably greater than for Type II; and
d. **Type IV Organizational Contexts**: Reflect a workplace involving a very severe abusive action. This context is referred to as *Mobbing II.* The intensity and extent of abusiveness of this type of mobbing is considerably greater than in Type III as is the direct involvement or complicity of the organization. Not surprisingly, the health consequences of this very severe form of mobbing are likely to be more significant than for Type III (Namie & Namie, 2009; Sloan, Matyók, Schmitz, & Short, 2010; Sperry, 2009, pp. 192-193).

According to Len Sperry's professional experience, targets of Mobbing I may recover sufficiently and may even return to their previous positions. On the other hand, victims of Mobbing II are likely to be more impacted and less likely to return to their previous position or, in some instances, to employment anywhere else because of the extent of their disability. Another classification proposed by Einarsen and Raknes (1997), introduces three main sub-categories for bullying, and these are *personal derogation, work related harassment*, and *social exclusion*.

2. **The Bully (The Perpetrator):** Similarly, there is very little research on the psychological profile of those perpetrating workplace bullying and mobbing (Sloan et al., 2010). One of the difficulties in identifying mobbing and bullying is the secretive nature of the behavior (McCord & Richardson, 2001). The offender is difficult to recognize and name because publicly they frequently appear to be helpful and cooperative employees (Lee & Brotheridge, 2006; McCord & Richardson, 2001). Working from their own insecurities and fear of inadequacy, these offenders engage in covert attacks against the *best workers* (McCord & Richardson, 2001). In one study, bullies described themselves as being high on aggressiveness and were found to be low on social competence and high on social anxiety (Einarsen et al., 2003).

In the basis of survey data and clinical observation, Namie (2003) suggested that all bullies are narcissistic and egocentric. Although these individuals may not meet all the criteria for a diagnosis of narcissistic personality disorder in accordance with the *Diagnostic and Statistical Manual of Mental Disorder* (American Psychological Association, 2013), they do exhibit some narcissistic features (Namie, 2003). The perpetrators often face no consequences (Sloan et al., 2010). The European Foundation for the Improvement of Living and Working Conditions (2002) found that only 19.3% were required to change employment, including the 8.2% dismissed. The Workplace Bullying Institute (WBI) found that only 35% of bullies were punished (Namie & Namie, 2009). Targets' isolation and sense of shame, along with the silencing of witnesses, help ensure the permanence of the offender in the organization (Namie & Namie, 2009), because the perpetrators are maintained and the system is left intact, as most cases studies report, the scapegoating and ostracizing continues as administrators and new employees are infected by this workplace virus (Namie & Namie, 2009).

COMPETENCY

Bullying and mobbing silence and marginalize targets as perpetrators seek to prevent targets and witnesses from engaging fully in their work, thereby denying them both supportive relationships and their individual identities. The bully decides to target an individual he or she finds threatening (Sloan et al., 2010). This often involves targeting the "best employees—those who are highly skilled, intelligent, creative, ethical, able to work well with others, and independent" (McCord & Richardson, 2001, p. 2). The targeted individual is ignored, isolated, and excluded from the communication loop (McCord & Richardson, 2001), with their livelihood and health—physical and mental—threatened (Namie & Namie, 2003). If the bullies are in a position of formal power, they may also threaten the target with job loss and exhibit non-compliance with HR rules and company policies (Namie & Namie, 2003). It is sometimes suggested that there are certain personality traits that typify perpetrators and targets. Some of the literature suggests that some targets tend to be trusting, co-operative, conscientious, high achievers, and often loyal to the organizations (Coyne, Seigne, & Randall, 2000; Davenport et al., 1999; Namie & Namie, 2000). This contrasts with the findings from other studies that indicate that there may be personality traits that predispose some people to becoming either a target or a perpetrator (Zapf & Einarsen, 2003). In these studies, perpetrators are sometimes perceived as authoritarian, manipulative, lacking people skills, insensitive, *evil*, sadists, and psychopaths (Davenport et al., 1999, p. 59; McCarthy, 2000, p. 242; Neuman, 2000), while targets are often perceived as *weak* and helpless victims (Neuman & Baron, 2004, p. 185). However, others claim that, sometimes, it is a specific position that is targeted rather than the individual performing the role and that whoever holds that position will be targeted (Einarsen et al., 2003; Leymann & Gustaffson, 1996). In other words, it is not necessarily the person (or the individual in the position/job title) that the perpetrator wants to bully, rather, it is the position (or job title/competencies) that the perpetrator wants and the degree (competencies) that the perpetrator lacks. For example, based on the case study, it is not that Program Specialist 1 (Amanda) was necessarily bullying Counselor 3 (Ethan), but that Program Specialist 1 was bullying the symbolic meaning of the position/title of *counselor* because Program Specialist 1 *lacks education and competencies required.*

Furthermore, a review of the literature by Zapf and Einarsen (2005) suggests that individuals describing themselves "as more achievement-oriented and as more conscientious than their colleagues" (p. 253) are more likely to become bulling and/or mobbing targets. The *perfectionism* that is a virtue of the highly gifted individual is *misunderstood by others*, whereas for the gifted individual this is but an expression of his or her *estheticism* in the same way that a perfect diamond's refraction of light is also beautiful. The target's colleagues know that their work does not stack up by comparison, and they will need no one to tell them so. The gifted individual's perfectionism and estheticism are seen as a threat, even of the gifted individual does not speak about them and does not offer criticism of others. A highly gifted adult cannot obscure his or her presence in such a milieu even through innocuous behavior. Such a presence will become and remain a recognized social fact because gossip, malicious and otherwise, will establish it as such. This malice will enforce the gifted adult's social isolation, probably also intensifying his or her search for the meaning of that social isolation. Highly gifted adults' *difference from others*, exacerbated by *others' misunderstanding* of this difference, offers less capable colleagues the opportunity to establish by rumor and innuendo other socially recognized *facts*, to the detriment of the gifted person, whether those *facts* are actually true or not (Kotleras, 2007; Sloan et al., 2010; Sperry, 2009).

CASE STUDY: THE PROGRAM

The PROGRAM, funded by the U.S. Department of Education, is designed to enhance the capacity of the College to serve its large and diverse student population, specifically Asian [and English as a Second Language (ESL)] students, increase student engagement, and improve educational outcomes for this student cohort (Tran, 2016a). The *predominant* language needed to serve these students is Chinese (Cantonese and Mandarin). The PROGRAM is a special funded program. It is designed to have one full-time director, one part-time program specialist, and three part-time academic counselors. These part-time counselors work different shifts on different days, thus, sometime they may work together on the same shift, whereas other days they do not. The case study presented here, reflects a common organizational injustice within higher education institutions that occurs rather frequently, but is rarely documented and shared due to one's self-preservation (Tran, 2014a).

The Director

The original director of the program who prepared the grant proposal departed soon after the proposal was approved and granted. The PROGRAM searched and selected a new director, *Adam*. Adam has a doctor of philosophy (Ph.D.) degree in psychology and was unemployed for several years prior to becoming the director of the PROGRAM. During the time of unemployment, Adam kept active with sporadic contract opportunities, and has no experience in an educational related industry.

- During several staff meetings after the departure of Program Specialist 1, Adam did not cover anything about the program, but verbally covered all the mistakes and errors that Program Specialist 1 (Amanda) committed during Amanda's tenure, and
- Adam, Amanda, and Bill (Program Specialist 2), respectively inquire and question the status and whereabouts of *Daniel* (Counselor 1) on a regular basis during work hours. Attempts in contacting (calling and texting) Daniel has yet to yield successful results [it is common practice that Daniel arrives to work late and leaves work early without approval (3 hrs.)].

Program Specialist 1 (Amanda)

Amanda originally worked with the original program director. Amanda began as a part-time employee and gradually became a full-time employee due to the budget allowance of the grant. Amanda has two bachelor degrees and eventually obtained a graduate degree in Master of Business Administration (MBA) while serving as a program specialist. Amanda has no prior work experience prior to becoming a Program Specialist for the PROGRAM. Being a Program Specialist was Amanda's *first job* after graduating from college with her undergraduate degrees.

Organizational Injustice: Amanda claimed that the amount of work and expectations placed upon the position exceeds the ability of a part-time program specialist. Amanda requested that the position be upgraded to be a full-time and the request was granted due to the budget allowance of the grant. However, what Amanda did not disclose was the fact that the knowledge, skills, abilities, and other characteristics that are required to perform the position effectively, Amanda did not possess. Amanda later accepted a promotion to become a "*director*" within the college and departed from the PROGRAM.

- During Amanda's tenure with the PROGRAM as a program specialist, a great majority of the work and documentations completed by Amanda were unacceptable by various departments within the college, therefore, repeatedly rejected, and returned to Amanda for continuous revisions, and re-revisions throughout the years,
    - Calculations and maintenance of the program's budget was inaccurate, so much so that not one counselor was paid on time or the correct amount throughout the years, and the accounting department recovered, on behalf of Amanda, a total of $100,000 that Amanda did not even know that the PROGRAM had and was not accounted for due to Amanda's miscalculation and mismanagement with the program's budget [the information (Amanda's miscalculation and mishandling of the PROGRAM's budget) was announced by Adam several times during several staff meetings],
    - The Department of Education reprimanded the PROGRAM as a whole due to Amanda's numerous errors on budget management, record-keeping, record maintenances, and record (data) reporting,
    - During Amanda's tenure with the PROGRAM, Amanda verbally and continuously insulted and demeaned one of the three counselors (Counselor 3: Ethan) in private and in public (in front of Counselor 1: Daniel, Counselor 2: Elaine, and among other individuals who were present), accusing Ethan that Ethan is incompetent, is stupid, is lazy, and is a prevaricator on a weekly basis,
    - During Amanda's tenure with the PROGRAM, Amanda has yet to admit that she is ever wrong or inaccurate, was never fully trained/qualified or did not know how to perform a task, and that she was ever forgetful,
- On more than one occasions, during staff meetings and within other environments, Amanda verbally expressed that she does not understand why she has a "hard time getting along with others" (Amanda mentioned that "I could not identify one person that I do not *hate*" and that Amanda does not understand why Amanda has such difficulty with flexibility and is pervasive across many situations),
- It is common practice that Amanda was rude to students of the PROGRAM, so much so that there are students who call Amanda a *bitch* in the presence of Amanda, whereas other students would call Amanda a *bitch* in the absence of Amanda (including student workers of the PROGRAM),
- It is common practice that Amanda would try to elicit conformations and supports from Bill (Program Specialist 2) by inquiring, "Am I really that rude?", "Am I really that hard to work/get along with?", and "I don't understand why I have such a hard time getting along/working with other people",
    - Amanda ordered Ethan to report directly to Amanda while Daniel and Elaine are to report to the Adam,
    - Amanda informed Daniel, Elaine, and Ethan that the only reason Amanda placed Daniel on the hiring committee for the PROGRAM's Director was because Amanda wanted to team-up with Daniel to assertively advocate for the hiring of the *individual* (Adam) as the Director of the PROGAM (Tran, 2015a),
    - It is common practice that Amanda openly and freely interrupted, spoke over, and cut-off the PROGRAM's former Director and the PROGRAM's current Director, Adam, during all staff meetings, and

- Amanda later received a promotion and became a *Director* for another department and departed from the PROGRAM.
    - After Amanda's departure, several PROGRAM's staff meetings were not about the progress of the PROGRAM, but about the numerous errors made by Amanda that have caused the PROGRAM to be halted, and that these errors have to be resolved, prior to the PROGRAM being able to move forward (Bill was hired to replace Amanda and to remedy Amanda's numerous errors),
    - After the promotion, on behalf of the College's President's request, Amanda was to be mentored by the Adam, one-two times per week (one-two hours per meetings), for one semester (thereafter, the Adam was promoted to become the interim Dean),
    - After being the *Director* for another department for approximately one year, signatures were gathered (among students, staff, and faculties of the college) and hand delivered to the College President, to remove Amanda from one's position due to a vote of no confidence,
    - After Amanda's removal from being the *director*, it was soon discovered that *Amanda* did not pay vendors and workers of the department for services rendered, and for those documents submitted for payments, they are either submitted late and/or completed incorrect (thus rejected),
    - After the removal of Amanda as the *Director* due to a vote of no confidences, an external team of auditors audited the college as a whole, and identified Amanda as the sole individual who single-handedly corrupted the department that she led.
    - After the removal, the Interim Dean (Adam) strongly advocated to the College President for Amanda to return to the PROGRAM to become the PROGRAM's Interim Director,
    - The college granted Adam's request, and Amanda was appointed as Interim Program Director of the PROGRAM. The Interim Program Director (Amanda), upon her return, informed Ethan (one-on-one rather than addressing the entire staff during a staff meeting) behind "closed doors" the following statement: "I do not care what your job description says and I do not care what the union says. If I tell you to do something, you do it, and find a way to do it. Do not ever tell me that you cannot do it or that it is not a part of your job",
    - Upon being the Interim Program Director, Amanda emailed a weekly to-do list to Elaine and Ethan, each list consisted of 10-15 to-do tasks, whereas Amanda's to-do list only consisted of 2-3 tasks. As the week progresses, tasks completed are cross off from the counselors' list, as new tasks are being added on. But Amanda's list remains the same with 2-3 tasks. Eventually, the tasks on Amanda's list became tasks on the counselors' lists (Amanda did not perform any of her own tasks on her list),
    - Throughout Ethan's tenure with the PROGRAM, all ideas, opinions, and suggestions made by Ethan were received by Amanda with silent treatment and/or the answer of "that's stupid" (especially when Amanda became the interim director of the PROGRAM),
    - Upon returning to the PROGRAM as the Interim Program Director, Amanda applied for the PROGRAM's grant renewal from the Department of Education. Due to Amanda's previous numerous errors when Amanda was Program Specialist 1, the grant's budget was several reduced, to the point that the PROGRAM could only afford to have one

part-time counselor (versus having three part-time counselors from previous years), and

- Due to the several reduction of the new budget, Amanda made a *strategic* decision and replaced Elaine and Ethan (Counselor 4 joined and departed from the PROGRAM within one semester) with Counselor 5, Frank (Frank was a new member of the PROGRAM and was in the process of being trained by Elaine and Ethan. Frank only speaks English). Elaine speaks English and Ethan speaks English, Chinese (Cantonese and Mandarin), and limited working Vietnamese.

- After the departure of Elaine and Ethan, it was later revealed to the college as a whole that the PROGRAM's grant renewal (the reduced amount awarded) status from the Department of Education was inaccurate, the PROGRAM's grant renewal request was not reduced, but was *denied* by the Department of Education. The second grant, which focuses on providing services to ESL students, was also *denied* by the Department of Education [not one person listed on the grant proposal was bilingual and no counselor (the sole counselor, Frank, that Amanda *strategically* kept for the purpose of the second grant) listed to the grant proposal to provide services to ESL students was *not* bilingual]. Due to the denial of the two grants from the Department of Education, the PROGRAM was eliminated. Amanda lost her job and departed from the college (Tran, 2016b).

Program Specialist 2 (Bill)

Program Specialist 2, Bill, replaced Amanda after Amanda's departure from PROGRAM. Bill has a Master of Science in Public Policy and Management (MSPPM). Bill was originally the Outreach Specialist for the PROGRAM.

Organizational Injustice: Amanda trained Bill prior to her departure.

- ◦ Technical procedures trained by Amanda were correct, however, forms and documents used, and the completion of these forms and documents were not. As a result, submitted items were unacceptable by various departments within the college, therefore, rejected, and returned to Bill for revision,
- ◦ After the departure of Amanda to become the *director* of another department, Bill verbally expressed that the PROGRAM's staff work for the PROGRAM and not the *Director* (Amanda), therefore, *Amanda* needs to do her own job, because staff are not there to do *Amanda*'s job or carry *Amanda's* responsibilities,
- ◦ Bill, on behalf of Amanda, resolved all of Amanda's mistakes, and reimbursed Ethan [for travels/meetings/conferences and payments that were more than six months late (to date, Amanda has yet to admit fault, or apologize for these late payments that Amanda fell to file according to Bill, Academic Support Services Specialist from the Office of Instructions, and payroll)], and
- ◦ Bill was later terminated (did not receive contract renewal) by the College soon after. Bill was terminated because Bill hired Frank (Frank is friends of Bill) without completing the required procedures and without receiving the approval of the Dean.

Counselors: The first two counselors who started with the original director left the PROGRAM for other opportunities. The PROGRAM recruited and hired new counselors.

Counselor 1 (Daniel)

Daniel is a part-time counselor and has a graduate degree in education (M.S.Ed.) but only introduces himself as having a graduate degree and omitting that it is in education. Daniel only presents himself as having a Master of Science (M.S.) degree [omitting the education (Ed.)] hoping that others will assume that it is a M.S. in counseling and not in education. Daniel originally interviewed for the position with one of the two original counselors but did not receive an offer. Daniel claims that he is bilingual.

- Organizational Injustice: Daniel later received a promotion to become a counselor/coordinator for a special funded position.
    - Daniel claimed to be bilingual only when it is not necessary to be bilingual. When Daniel's bilingual skill is called upon, Daniel has yet to deliver,
    - It is common practice that Daniel is always at least one hour late for work, and leaves work three hours early without approval,
    - Daniel, on several instances, informed Elaine and Ethan that he does not feel comfortable providing academic services to the following three populations: (1) female students, (2) English as a Second Language (ESL) students, and (3) students that Daniel deemed have a disability (but not proven). Daniel contacted Elaine and Ethan on several instances, on their days off, to place students on either of their schedules because students were members of one of the three categories,
    - Daniel was not capable of assisting students with developing a correct comprehensive student educational plan (CSEP), assisting students with financial aid petitions that require developing SEPs or developing a revision of their SEPs, assisting students with petitioning for degrees (either certificate and/or associate degrees), does not feel comfortable interpreting the ESL chart, and does not feel comfortable utilizing and completing counseling documentations,
    - All electronic and hard copies of communication developed and communicated by Daniel are consisted of incomplete sentences and grammatically incorrect sentences (so much so that other counselors within the college had informed Daniel about it without success),
        - Majority of the work completed by Daniel in the PROGRAM had to be revised by either Elaine and/or Ethan based on the Adam's requests and/or Bill's requests,
        - Daniel openly insulted Ethan in public and in the presence of other students, other counselors (including Elaine), and the PROGRAM's staff that Ethan is incompetent, uneducated, and just an overall bad counselor [Daniel openly informed Ethan that Ethan is not as educated, is not as smart, and is not as competent as himself (Daniel), and that Ethan is not his (Daniel's) caliber],
        - Daniel openly insulted Elaine in the presence of the PROGRAM's staff and Ethan, that Elaine is incompetent, as such, Elaine is not able to find another part-time job (because no one wants to hire Elaine),
        - After every student Daniel assisted, Daniel takes a personal fifteen minute break, in addition to Daniel's personal regular smoking breaks,
        - After the arrival of Ethan, based on the quality of the work of Elaine and Ethan, on average, it is common practice that Daniel only assisted approximately one-to-two students per month (students gradually ceased scheduling appointments with Daniel),

- During an off campus retreat among at least five different departments of the college, Daniel arrived an hour late, and during a brainstorming session, to be reported out later by posting them on the wall, every idea/comment/reflection that Daniel wrote were all misspelled and grammatically incorrect. Adam personally requested that Daniel remove all these ideas/comments/reflections prior to having them posted on the wall,
- It is common practice that Daniel removed students' confidential files from the office without approval (it is illegal to remove students' confidential files from the office regardless, especially off of the college campus, and in the possession of Daniel's private resident),
- It is common practice that Daniel received reimbursements for travelling (to meetings, conferences, workshops, trainings, etc.) from Amanda when Daniel did not travel and did not submit receipts for reimbursements. When Bill did not issue reimbursements, Daniel openly (in front of Elaine and Ethan) complained and claimed that reimbursements have always been issued to him even when he did not travel. Bill informed Daniel that it is both unethical and illegal to issue reimbursements for travelling when: 1) no receipts are submitted, thus no record of travelling, or the reason for payment reimbursements, and 2) Daniel did not travel at all. Daniel replied to Bill and said, "Who cares about ethics and the law. Amanda issued reimbursements to me all the time without receipts and even when I did not travel. Amanda did not care about ethics and the law, why should you?",
- Thereafter, Daniel received a promotion to become a Counselor/Coordinator for a special funded position, and after becoming a Counselor/Coordinator, there are evidences that Daniel continued to exhibit the same behavior and demeanor (as when Daniel was a counselor with the PROGRAM),
- Upon departing from the PROGRAM, Daniel took 3 hours lunches [the first hour spent sitting in the PROGRAM's office waiting for Bill to go to lunch (11am-12noon), the second hour was for lunch (12noon-1pm), and the third hour was spent sitting in the PROGRAM's office again (1pm-2pm), with the first and third hour *negatively* and *verbally shouting* and *insulting* Ethan in front of Bill, Ethan, and students of the PROGAM with the following messages: Ethan is a bad counselor, Ethan does not know what one is doing, and if you want to succeed, you do not want to see Ethan. Bill witnessed it all but was too paralyzed to take action since Bill and Daniel are friends],
- For the one month after the departure of Daniel from the PROGRAM, the PROGRAM continued to issue payment to Daniel for the whole month for no work rendered (Daniel collected payments from both positions and the PROGRAM never requested a refund of payment from Daniel), and
- Daniel later departed from the college as a whole after less than one (1) year as the Counselor/Coordinator.
    - After Daniel's departure from the PROGRAM, inappropriate files were found on the computer saved by Daniel,
    - Elaine and Bill assisted the deletion of these inappropriate files, and
    - It appeared that Elaine was offended by the content of these inappropriate files saved by Daniel and did not care for it (these files were not work related and were of an adult nature).

Counselor 2 (Elaine)

Elaine has a graduate degree in counseling (M.S.), specifically in Pupil Personnel Services Credential: School Counseling Designation. Elaine speaks English.

- Organizational Injustice: Elaine is a part-time counselor for the PROGRAM as well as a part-time counselor for another college.
    - Aside from being a counselor for the PROGRAM, it is common for Elaine to perform other duties of the PROGRAM as signed,
    - Elaine revised Daniel's work on a regular basis due to the Adam's and Bill's requests: work related to the PROGRAM and students' CSEP (due to students' requests),
    - Elaine on occasion trained Daniel on completing counseling documentations and on the usage of the Microsoft Office package, and
    - Prior to the arrival of Ethan, Elaine was responsible for cleaning-up and maintaining the counseling room after Daniel.

Counselor 3 (Ethan)

Ethan has a graduate degree in psychology and a Doctor of Psychology (Psy.D.) in Psychology. Ethan is bilingual with a second dialect. Ethan Speaks English, Chinese (Cantonese and Mandarin), and limited working Vietnamese.

- Organizational Injustice: Ethan is a part-time counselor for PROGRAM as well as a counselor part-time counselor for the college's general counseling department.
    - Ethan is generally busy with providing academic services to students of the PROGRAM. Appointments with Ethan are usually made at least one-to-two weeks in advance due to the high demand for Ethan's services and Ethan has an overall rate of above 95% of students who commit to the scheduled appointments,
    - When time permits, Ethan will provide academic services to drop-in students,
    - Based on students' requests and based on Bill's requests, Ethan regularly revised Daniel's CSEP and Daniel's work,
    - Based on students' requests and based on Bill's requests, Ethan assists students with degree petitions, students that previously met with Daniel, but the work was not done (or not done correctly),
    - On occasion, based on the Adam's request, Ethan performs the task of data research and interpretation for the funding of the PROGRAM (contract renewal and the like),
    - On a regular basis, Ethan performed translations (both verbal and written) for the PROGRAM, the ESL Department, and the Disabled Students Programs and Services (DSPS) Department, and
    - Amanda ordered Ethan to clean-up and maintain the counseling office (shared by all three counselors) after Daniel four times a year (each clean-up takes about ½ hour due to the degree of Daniel's uncleanliness—a task previous performed by Elaine). After the departure of Daniel, no clean-up of the counseling room was required, aside from the scheduled janitorial visits.

FUTURE RESEARCH AND RECOMMENDATIONS

However, research is scarce when it comes to correlation between bullying and mobbing, to the following factors: culture, gender, age, sexual orientations, disabilities, and nepotism (Tran, 2014b; Tran, 2016b). Another aspect worth pursuing is education and field of study of the bullies. Does incidence of bullying behavior increase or decrease with education? Are the specific fields where bullying/mobbing is more prevalent? Also, future studies should look into the relationship between nepotism and bullying and/or mobbing behavior.

CONCLUSION

According to Vivian and Hormann (2013), organizational trauma is a collective experience that overwhelms the organization's defensive and protective structures and leaves the entity temporarily vulnerable and helpless or permanently damaged. Traumatic events can be sudden, shocking, and throw the organization into turmoil. Organizational traumatization may also result from repeated damaging actions or the deleterious effects of the nature of an organization's work. Unaddressed organizational trauma, whether sudden or cumulative, causes serious harm and can be catastrophic for organizations. It negatively impacts service delivery, compromises work with clients, and weakens the organization's ability to respond to internal and external challenges. Over time the unhealed effects of trauma and traumatization compromise the organization's fundamental health.

The expertise of Consulting Psychologists (CP), Organizational Psychologists (OP), Organizational Development (OD), and Industrial and Organizational Psychologists (I/O) are often utilized to assess and enhance fundamental health of workplaces. Such psychologists are often housed in Human Resource Development (HRD) and utilize various assessment and intervention strategies when working with individuals and teams in organizational settings to identify and resolve workplace bullying. A comprehensive assessment strategy of a bullying and/or mobbing incident would begin with an assessment of organizational dynamics, along with an assessment of group dynamics and situational factors influencing both perpetrators and victims. It would also include an assessment of individual dynamics of the victims and of the perpetrator. For psychologists, a useful conceptualization of a bullying and/or a mobbing incident accounts for individual, group, and organizational dynamics, because failure to account for any one or two of these three provides a much more limited explanation of the causes and effects of the abusive behavior.

Presumably, guided by this assessment and conceptualization, the psychologist can then plan and implement appropriate and effective interventions. An individual employee's response to abuse in a workplace setting is influenced by individual dynamics, group dynamics, and organizational dynamics. These dynamics can either foster or reduce the likelihood of mobbing and bullying in the workplace. Understanding these sets of dynamic and their possible role in mobbing and bullying can provide a useful framework for assessing, conceptualizing, and planning effective consultation interventions when dealing with workplace abusiveness. The ability to resolving workplace abusiveness plays a part in the ability to recruit and retain human capitals (Tran, 2014c; Tran, 2014d; Tran, 2015b; Tran, 2015c) based on the capital of human's knowledge, skills, abilities, and other characteristics [KSAOs (Tran, 2008; Tran, 2013; Tran, 2014e; Tran, 2015d).

REFERENCES

Arches, J. (1991). Social structure, burnout, and job satisfaction. *Social Work*, *36*(3), 202–206. PMID:2057805

Balducci, C., Fraccaroli, F., & Schaufeli, W. B. (2011). Workplace bullying and its relation with work characteristics, personality, and post-traumatic stress symptoms: An integrated model. *Anxiety, Stress, and Coping*, *24*(5), 499–513. doi:10.1080/10615806.2011.555533 PMID:21347903

Belak, T. (2002). *Emotional abuse in the workplace*. Louisville, KY: Sullivan University.

Bell, H., Kulkarni, S., & Dalton, L. (2003). Organizational prevention of vicarious trauma. *Families in Society*, *84*(4), 463–470. doi:10.1606/1044-3894.131

Bowling, N. A., & Beehr, T. A. (2006). Workplace harassment from the victims perspective: A theoretical model and meta-analysis. *The Journal of Applied Psychology*, *9*(5), 998–1112. doi:10.1037/0021-9010.91.5.998 PMID:16953764

Branch, S., Ramsay, S., & Barker, M. (2013). Workplace bullying, mobbing and general harassment: A review. *International Journal of Management Reviews*, *15*(3), 280–299. doi:10.1111/j.1468-2370.2012.00339.x

Carbo, J., & Hughes, A. (2010). Workplace bullying: Developing a human rights definition from the perspective and experiences of the target. *WorkingUSA: The Journal of Labor and Society*, *13*(9), 387–403. doi:10.1111/j.1743-4580.2010.00297.x

Coyne, I., Seigne, E., & Randall, P. (2000). Predicting workplace victim status from personality. *European Journal of Work and Organizational Psychology*, *9*(3), 335–349. doi:10.1080/135943200417957

Daniel, T. A. (2006). *Bullies in the workplace: A focus on the abusive disrespect of employees*. Society for Human Resource Management. Retrieved on October 29th, 2015, available at http://thepeoplegroupllc.com/wp-content/uploads/2008/04/article-bullies-in-the-workplace.pdf

Davenport, N., Schwartz, R. D., & Elliott, G. P. (1999). *Mobbing: Emotional abuse in the workplace* (1st ed.). Ames, IA: Civil Society Publishing.

Davenport, N., Schwartz, R. D., & Elliott, G. P. (2002). *Mobbing: Emotional abuse in the American workplace* (2nd ed.). Ames, IA: Civil Society Publishing.

Davenport, N., Schwartz, R. D., & Elliott, G. P. (2005). *Mobbing: Emotional abuse in the American workplace* (3rd ed.). Ames, IA: Civil Society Publishing.

Denemberg, R., & Braverman, M. (2001). *The violence prone workplace: A new approach to dealing with hostile, threatening, and uncivil behavior harassment*. Cardiff, UK: Academic Press.

Divincová, A., & Siváková, B. (2014). Mobbing at workplace and its impact on employee performance. *Human Resources Management & Ergonomics*, *8*(2), 20–34.

Einarsen, S., Hoel, H., Xapf, D., & Cooper, C. L. (2003). The concept of bullying at work. In S. Einarsen, H. Hoel, D. Zapf, & C. L. Cooper (Eds.), *Bullying and emotional abuse in the workplace: International perspectives in research and practice* (pp. 3–30). London: Taylor & Francis.

Einarsen, S., Hoel, H., Zapf, D., & Cooper, C. L. (2010). The concept of bullying and harassment at work: The European tradition. In S. Einarsen, H. Hoel, D. Zapf, & C. L. Cooper (Eds.), *Bullying and harassment in the workplace. Developments in Theory, Research, and Practice* (pp. 3–39). Boca Raton, FL: CRC Press. doi:10.1201/EBK1439804896-3

Einarsen, S., & Mikkelsen, E. G. (2003). Individual effects of exposure to bullying at work. In S. Einarsen, H. Hoel, D. Zapf, & C. L. Cooper (Eds.), *Bullying and emotional abuse in the workplace. International Perspectives in Research and Practice* (pp. 127–144). London: Taylor and Francis.

Einarsen, S., & Raknes, B. I. (1997). Harassment at work and the victimization of men. *Violence and Victims, 12*(3), 247–263. PMID:9477540

Ertureten, A., Cemalcilar, Z., & Aycan, Z. (2013). The relationship of downward mobbing with leadership style and organizational attitudes. *Journal of Business Ethics, 116*(1), 205–216. doi:10.1007/s10551-012-1468-2

European Foundation for the Improvement of Living and Working Conditions. (2002). *Study examines 'mobbing' at the workplace*. Retrieved on November 1, 2015, available at http://www.eiro.eurofound.eu.int

Farmer, D. (2011). Workplace bullying: An increasing epidemic creating traumatic experiences for targets of workplace bullying. *The Special Issue on Behavioral and Social Science, 1*(7), 196–203.

Groeblinghoff, D., & Becker, M. (1996). A case study of mobbing and the clinical treatment of mobbing victims. *European Journal of Work and Organizational Psychology, 5*(2), 277–294. doi:10.1080/13594329608414859

Koonin, M., & Green, T. (2005). The emotionally abusive workplace. *Journal of Emotional Abuse, 3*, 71–79.

Kotleras, R. (2007). The workplace mobbing of highly gifted adults: An unremarked barbarism. *Advanced Development Journal, 11*, 130–149.

Lee, R., & Brotheridge, C. (2006). When prey turn predatory: Workplace bullying as a predictor of counter aggression/bullying, coping, and well-being. *European Journal of Work and Organizational Psychology, 15*(3), 352–377. doi:10.1080/13594320600636531

Leymann, H. (1990). Mobbing and psychological terror at workplaces. *Violence and Victims, 5*(2), 119–126. PMID:2278952

Leymann, H. (1996). The content and development of mobbing at work. *European Journal of Work and Organizational Psychology, 5*(2), 165–184. doi:10.1080/13594329608414853

Leymann, H., & Gustaafsson, A. (1996). Mobbing at work and the development of post traumatic stress disorders. *European Journal of Work and Organizational Psychology, 5*(2), 251–275. doi:10.1080/13594329608414858

MaCathy, P. (2000). The bully-victim at work. Transcending boundaries: Integrating people, processes and systems conference, Brisbane, Australia.

Maslach, C. (1993). Burnout: A multidimensional perspective. In W. B. Schaufeli, C. Maslach, & T. Marek (Eds.), *Professional burnout: Recent developments in theory and research* (pp. 19–32). Washington, DC: Taylor & Francis.

McCord, L. B., & Richardson, J. (2001). *Are workplace bullies sabotaging your ability to compete? Learn to identify and extinguish problem behavior.* Retrieved on November 1, 2015, available at http://gbr.pepperdine.edu

Mikkelsen, E. G., & Einarsen, S. (2002). Basic assumptions and symptoms of post-traumatic stress among victims of bullying at work. *European Journal of Work and Organizational Psychology, 11*(1), 87–111. doi:10.1080/13594320143000861

Murphy, S. V. (2013). *Perceptions of bullying in the workplace: A phenomenological study.* Retrieved on November 2, 2015, available at http://media.proquest.com/media/pq/classic/doc/3007474051/fmt/ai/rep/NPDF?_s=5Juw3FglFYcVuIWLovMGiXshEGg%3D

Namie, G. (2003, November/December). Workplace bullying: Escalated incivility. *Ivey Business Journal: Improving the Practice of Management,* 1-6.

Namie, G., & Namie, R. (2000). *The bully at work: What you can do to stop the hurt and reclaim your dignity on the job.* Naperville, IL: Sourcebooks, Inc.

Namie, G., & Namie, R. (2009). *The bully at work: What you can do to stop the hurt and reclaim your dignity on the job.* Naperville, IL: Sourcebooks, Inc.

Neuman, J. (2000). Measuring the costs associated with stress, injustice and workplace bullying. *Proceedings of the Workplace Bullying Conference.*

Neuman, J., & Baron, R. (2004). Aggression in the workplace: A social-psychological perspective. In S. Fox & P. E. Spector (Eds.), *Counterproductive work behaviour: Investigations of actors and targets* (pp. 13–40). Washington, DC: American Psychological Association.

Pompili, M., Lester, D., Innamorati, M., De Pisa, E., Iliceto, P., Puccinno, M., & Girardi, P. et al. (2008). Suicide risk and exposure to mobbing. *Work (Reading, Mass.), 31*(2), 237–243. PMID:18957741

Rayner, C. H., Hoel, H., & Cooper, C. (2002). *Workplace bullying* (1st ed.). London: Cromwell Press. doi:10.4324/9780203302194

Resch, M., & Schubinski, M. (1996). Mobbing-prevention and management in organizations. *European Journal of Work and Organizational Psychology, 5*(2), 295–307. doi:10.1080/13594329608414860

Schat, A. C. H., Frone, M. R., & Kelloway, E. K. (2006). Prevalence of workplace aggression in the U.S. workforce: Findings from a national study. In E. K. Kelloway, J. Barling, & J. Hurrell (Eds.), *Handbook of workplace violence* (pp. 47–89). Thousand Oaks, CA: Sage. doi:10.4135/9781412976947.n4

Schneider, B., & Schmitt, N. (1986). *Staffing organizations* (2nd ed.). HarperCollins Publishers, Inc.

Shallcross, L., Sheehan, M., & Ramsay, S. (2008). Workplace mobbing: Experiences in the public sector. *International Journal of Organizational Behaviour, 13*(2), 56–70.

Sloan, L. M., Matyók, T., Schmitz, C. L., & Short, G. F. L. (2010). A story to tell: Bullying and mobbing in the workplace. *International Journal of Business and Social Science, 1*(3), 87–97.

Söderfeldt, M., Söderfeldt, B., & Warg, L. E. (1995). Burnout in social work. *Social Work, 40*(5), 638–646.

Sperry, L. (2009). Mobbing and bullying: The influence of individual, work group, and organizational dynamics on abusive workplace behavior. *Counseling Psychology Journal: Practice and Research, 61*(3), 190–201.

The American Psychological Association. (2013). *Diagnostic and statistical manual of mental disorders: DSM-5* (5th ed.). American Psychiatric Publishing.

Tran, B. (2008). *Expatriate selection and retention* (Doctoral dissertation). California School of Professional Psychology at Alliant International University, San Francisco, CA.

Tran, B. (2013). Industrial and organizational (I/O) psychology: The roles and purposes of I/O practitioners in global business. In B. Christiansen, E. Turkina, & N. Williams (Eds.), Cultural and technological influences on global business (pp. 175-219). Hershey, PA: IGI Global.

Tran, B. (2014a). Rhetoric of game: Utilizing the game of Tavistock method on organizational politics training. In D. Ruggiero (Ed.), *Cases on societal effects of persuasive games* (pp. 145–174). Hershey, PA: IGI Global. doi:10.4018/978-1-4666-6206-3.ch008

Tran, B. (2014b). Rhetoric of game: Utilizing the game of Tavistock method on organizational politics training. In D. Ruggiero (Eds.), Cases on societal effects of persuasive games (pp. 145-174). Hershey, PA: IGI Global.

Tran, B. (2014c). The foundation of cultural intelligence: Human capital. In B. Christiansen, S. Yildiz, & E. Yildiz (Eds.), Handbook of Research on effective marketing in contemporary globalism (pp. 348-376). Hershey, PA: IGI Global.

Tran, B. (2014d). The human element of the knowledge worker: Identifying, managing, and protecting the intellectual capital within knowledge management. In M. A. Chilton & J. M. Bloodgood (Eds.), Knowledge management and competitive advantage: Issues and potential solutions (pp. 281-303). Hershey, PA: IGI Global.

Tran, B. (2014e). Rhetoric of play: Utilizing the gamer factor in selecting and training employees. In T. M. Connolly, L. Boyle, T. Hainey, G. Baxter, & P. Moreno-Ger (Eds.), Psychology, pedagogy and assessment in serious games (pp. 175-203). Hershey, PA: IGI Global.

Tran, B. (2015a). The next generation of leaders: Women in global leaderships in the hotel management industry. In J. Feng, S. Stocklin, & W. Wang (Eds.), *Educational strategies for the next generation of leaders in hotel management* (pp. 16–42). Hershey, PA: IGI Global. doi:10.4018/978-1-4666-8565-9.ch002

Tran, B. (2015b). Triangulation in organizational research: Validating knowledge in human competence at work. In Research methods: Concepts, methodologies, tools, and applications. Hershey, PA: IGI Global.

Tran, B. (2015c). Triangulation in organizational research: Validating knowledge in human competence at work. In A. Takhar & A. Ghorbani (Eds.), Market research methodologies: Multi-method and qualitative approaches (pp. 93-117). Hershey, PA: IGI Global.

Tran, B. (2015d). Expatriate selection and retention: Identifying and assessing the other characteristics beyond knowledge, skills, and abilities. In A. A. Camillo (Eds.), Handbook of research on global hospitality and tourism management (pp. 468-492). Hershey, PA: IGI Global.

Tran, B. (2016a). Organizational justice: The injustice in the foundation of organizational citizenship behavior within higher education institutions. In N. P. Ololube (Ed.), *Handbook of research on organizational justice and culture in higher education institutions*. Hershey, PA: IGI Global. doi:10.4018/978-1-4666-9850-5.ch001

Tran, B. (2016b). The foundation of (business) ethics' evolution. In I. M. Khosrow-Pour (Ed.), *Encyclopedia of information science and technology* (4th ed.). Hershey, PA: IGI Global.

Vivian, P., & Hormann, S. (2013). *Organizational trauma and healing*. CreateSpace Independent Publishing Platform.

Vveinhardt, J. (2010). The diagnostics of mobbing as discrimination on employee relations aiming to improve the organizational climate in Lithuanian organizations. *Management Theory and Studies for Rural Business and Infrastructure Development*, *21*(2), 173–185.

Westhues, K. (2002). At the mercy of the mob. *Canada's Occupational Health & Safety Magazine*, *18*(8), 30–36.

Zapf, D., & Einarsen, S. (2003). Individual antecedents of bullying: Victims and perpetrators. In S. Einarsen, H. Hoel, D. Zapf, & C. Cooper (Eds.), *Bullying and emotional abuse in the workplace: International perspectives in research and practice* (pp. 165–184). London: Taylor & Francis.

Zapf, D., & Einarsen, S. (2005). Mobbing at work: Escalated conflicts in organizations. In S. Fox & P. E. Spector (Eds.), *Counterproductive work behavior: Investigations of actors and targets* (pp. 237–270). doi:10.1037/10893-010

Zapf, D., Escartin, J., Einarsen, S., Hoel, H., & Vartia, M. (2011). Empirical findings on prevelance and risk groups of bullying in the workplace. In S. Einarsen, H. Hoel, D. Zapf, & C. Cooper (Eds.), *Bullying and harassment in the workplace: Developments in theory, research, and practice* (2nd ed.; pp. 75–106). Boca Raton, FL: CRC Press.

Zapf, D., & Gross, C. (2001). Conflict escalation and coping with workplace bullying: A replication and extension. *European Journal of Work and Organizational Psychology*, *10*(4), 497–522. doi:10.1080/13594320143000834

ADDITIONAL READING

Ashforth, B. E. (1994). Petty tyranny in organizations. *Human Relations*, *47*(7), 755–778. doi:10.1177/001872679404700701

Bakker, A. B., & Demerouti, E. (2007). The job demands-resources model: State of the art. *Journal of Managerial Psychology*, *22*(3), 309–328. doi:10.1108/02683940710733115

Balducci, C., Alfano, V., & Fraccaroli, F. (2009). Relationships between mobbing at work and MMPI-2 personality profile, post-traumatic stress symptoms and suicidal ideation and behaviour. *Violence and Victims*, *24*(1), 52–67. doi:10.1891/0886-6708.24.1.52 PMID:19297885

Bano, S., & Mali, S. (2013). Impact o workplace bullying on organizational outcome. *Pakistan Journal of Commerce and Social Science*, 618-627.

Bobela, J. (2011). *Mobbing*. Retrieved on November 4, 2015, available at http://www.kozsr.sk/page_sk/bozp/sktualnetemy/Mobbing1.pdf

Bowling, N. A., Beehr, T. A., Bennett, M. M., & Watson, C. P. (2010). Target personality and workplace victimization: A prospective analysis. *Work and Stress*, *24*(2), 140–158. doi:10.1080/02678373.2010.489635

Brousse, G., Fontana, L., Ouchchane, L., Boisson, C., Gerbaud, L., Bourguet, D., & Charmoux, A. et al. (2008). Psychopathological features of a patient population of targets of workplace bullying. *Occupational Medicine*, *58*(2), 122–128. doi:10.1093/occmed/kqm148 PMID:18204005

Carden, L. L., & Boyd, R. O. (2013). Workplace bullying, utilizing a risk management framework to address bullying in the workplace. *Southern Journal of Business Ethics*, *5*, 8–17.

Crawshaw, L. (2005). *Coaching abrasive executives: Exploring the use of empathy in constructing less destructive interpersonal management strategies*. Unpublished doctoral dissertation, Fielding Graduate University, Santa Barbara, California, United States of America.

Crawshaw, L. (2007). *Taming the abrasive manager: How to end necessary roughness in the workplace*. San Francisco, CA: Jossey-Bass.

Duffy, M., & Sperry, L. (2012). *Mobbing. Bew York*. Oxford University Press.

Einarsen, S. (1999). The nature and causes of bullying at work. *International Journal of Manpower*, *20*(1), 16–27. doi:10.1108/01437729910268588

Field, E. M. (2011). *Strategies for surviving bullying at work*. Australia: Australia Academic Press.

Hauge, L. J., Skogstad, A., & Einarsen, S. (2007). Relationships between stressful work environments and bullying: Results of a large representative study. *Work and Stress*, *21*(3), 220–242. doi:10.1080/02678370701705810

Hershcovis, M. S. (2011). Incivility, social undermining, bullying…oh my! A call to reconcile constructs within workplace aggression research. *Journal of Organizational Behavior*, *32*(3), 499–519. doi:10.1002/job.689

Hodson, R., Roscigno, V. J., & Lopez, S. H. (2006). Chaos and the abuse of power: Workplace bullying in organizational and interactional context. *Work and Occupations*, *33*(4), 382–416. doi:10.1177/0730888406292885

Hollingworth, L. S. (1930). The child of very supervisor intelligence as a special problem in social adjustment. *The Annals of the American Academy of Political and Social Science*, *149*(3), 151–159. doi:10.1177/000271623014900314

Hoyk, R., & Hershey, P. (2008). *The ethical executive: Becoming aware of the root causes of unethical behavior*. Stanford, CA: Stanford University Press.

Lutgen-Sandvik, P. (2013). *Adult bullying—A nasty piece of work: Translating decade of research on non-sexual harassment, psychological terror, mobbing, and emotional abuse on the job*. CreateSpace Independent Publishing Platform.

Ostling, C. (2014). *Bullying: In the workplace. The secret to overcoming bully bosses and crazy co-workers* (2nd ed.). Amazon Digital Services, Inc.

Peterson, J. S., & Ray, K. E. (2006). Bullying among the gifted: The subjective experience. *Gifted Child Quarterly*, *50*(3), 252–269. doi:10.1177/001698620605000305

Schuster, B. (1996). Rejection, exclusion, and harassment at work and in schools: An integration of results from research on mobbing, bullying, and peer rejection. *European Psychologist*, *1*(4), 293–317. doi:10.1027/1016-9040.1.4.293

Staub, E. (2003). Notes on cultures of violence, cultures of caring and peace, and the fulfillment of basic human needs. *Political Psychology*, *24*(1), 1–21. doi:10.1111/0162-895X.00314

Tehrani, N. (2012). *Workplace bullying: Symptoms and solutions*. Routledge.

Van Heugten, K. (2010). Engaging bystanders as change agents in workplace bullying. Presented at the *7th International Conference on Workplace Bullying and Harassment*, Cardiff, Wales, United Kingdom.

Wrzesniewski, A., Rozin, P., & Bennett, G. (2003). Working, playing and eating: Making the most of most moments. In C. Keyes & J. Haidt (Eds.), *Flourishing: Positive psychology and the life well lived* (pp. 185–204). Washington, D.C.: American Psychological Association. doi:10.1037/10594-008

Zapf, D. (1999). Organizational, work group related and personal causes of mobbing/bullying at work. *International Journal of Manpower*, *20*(1/2), 70–85. doi:10.1108/01437729910268669

KEY TERMS AND DEFINITIONS

Attacks on Communication Opportunities: Means being denied opportunities to express oneself.

Attack on Social Relationships: Means beyond shunning, included overt incitements to subordinates to avoid all contact.

Attacks on the Quality of the Professional and Life Situation: Being assigned to only one minor committee and then designated to chair it only to have its other committee members boycott meetings.

Bully (Perpetrator/Offender): An individual who targets others when he or she finds the other individual as threatening.

Bully(ing): Repeated, unreasonable actions of individuals (or a group) directed towards an employee (or a group of employees), which are intended to intimate, degrade, humiliate or undermine, or which create a risk to the health or safety of the employees(s).

Gifted(ness): An individual who is more competent and skilled compared to the bully (perpetrator/offender).

Implications on Social Reputation: Casting aspersions to one's face regarding one's nationality, making nasty remarks to third parties one's religion, and spreading false rumors of one's ill health.

Incompetence: An individual (the bully/perpetrator/offender) who is working from their own insecurities and fear of inadequacy.

Mobbing: A group of coworkers targeting another worker.

Trauma: Crisis, as in organizational crisis (or crises).

Type I Organizational Contexts: A workplace setting that is essentially productive and healthy.

Types II Organizational Contexts: A workplace setting wherein the abusive behavior of a bully occurs or can occur.

Type III Organizational Contexts: A workplace setting involving moderately abusive behavior or actions.

Type IV Organizational Contexts: A workplace wetting involving a very severe abusive action.

Workplace Bullying: As consistent exposure to persistent, oppressive, offensive, abusive, intimidating, malicious, or insulting behavior by a manager/supervisor or co-worker.

Section 4
Case Studies

Chapter 10
Embracing Organizational Trauma:
Positive Effects of Death Experiences on Organizational Culture – Three Short Case Studies

Mike Szymanski
University of Victoria, Canada

Erik Schindler
University of Victoria, Canada

ABSTRACT

Organizational trauma is traditionally associated with negative effects on organizational behavior and performance. In this chapter the authors seek to answer the question how organizational trauma, and in particular near-death experiences, can positively influence organizational culture in the long term. In doing so, the authors briefly review the recent literature on organizational trauma and near death experiences, and discuss how these negative traumatic experiences can turn into prosocial organizational behaviour. The authors then present three case studies to illustrate how an organization can manage to incorporate near death experiences into its organizational culture in a positive way.

INTRODUCTION

Organizational trauma is an important, yet understudied phenomenon in management research. Recent streams of research in psychology and organizational studies focus on the negative consequences of trauma for organizations and individuals (e.g. Stuart, 1996; Driver, 2007), processes by which organizations may experience trauma (Kahn, 2003), and ways how organizations can help their employees overcome emotional trauma (e.g. deKlerk, 2007; Fischer, 2012). The prevalent assumptions are that organizational trauma negatively affects organizational behaviour, culture, and performance. In this chapter the authors

DOI: 10.4018/978-1-5225-2021-4.ch010

seek to answer the question how organizational trauma can *positively* influence organizational culture in the long term.

In order to do so, the chapter develops as follows: first the authors briefly review the recent literature on organizational trauma in general, and near death experiences in particular. The literature is used to develop a simplified matrix of individual/organizational traumatic experiences. Second, the authors present three case studies to illustrate each cell of the matrix. Each case study focuses on a major organization that at one moment of its existence went through a near death experience and managed to incorporate the event into its organizational culture in a positive way. Next, the authors theorize about potential links between organizational trauma and positive effects on organizational cultures, using the Schein (1996) model of culture. The chapter ends with a concise description of avenues for future research and managerial implications.

BACKGROUND

In the organizational literature, trauma is traditionally associated with significant change in the organization, which bears negative consequences for an employee (Weick, 1988; D'Aveni & MacMillan, 1990). Stein (1991) found that members of an organization perceive sudden unpleasant changes to organizations, such as layoffs, as an equivalent negative emotional load as physical injuries and suggested that in crisis situations the role of a manager is to facilitate the grieving process. Hilton Brown (1997) researched measures organizations might take to deal with challenges to organizational health stemming from organizational trauma. Stuart (1996) elaborated on different types of trauma-causing events in organizations, pointing to organizational change as a significant source of trauma. Amabile and Conti (1999) also suggested that organizations undergoing severe change caused by an unexpected crisis might suffer from trauma. Kahn (2003) compared organizational trauma to individual trauma, suggesting that both constitute a serious threat to the life and integrity of the individual and/or the organization. DeKlerk (2007) proposed that since unresolved emotional trauma might interfere with members' ability to perform, organizational development programs might be instrumental in the healing process within the organization. Driver (2007) suggested that while suffering in organizations has been explored in the literature, its link to existential meaning making is unclear, and proposed that organizational suffering could be a pathway to finding new meaning and fostering positive change. Valikangas, Hoegl, and Gibbert (2009) found that organizations might suffer trauma not only from sudden, unexpected changes, but also from negative results of their intended changes, such as innovation projects. Driver (2009) examined cases of unsuccessful organizational change, suggesting that failed projects lead to negative consequences. Fischer (2012) argued that while turbulence in an organization's environment and its internal dynamics might cause dysfunction and crisis, skilful management of trouble might mobilize resources and lead to productive action. In conclusion, organizational trauma research is gaining significant traction in the organizational behaviour and management literatures. While most scholars focus on negative consequences of unexpected changes in the internal and external environments of organizations, potential positive effects for organizations have also been recognized (e.g. Driver, 2007; Fischer, 2012). In this chapter the authors build on the potential for positive change to organizational culture stemming from near death experiences within the organization.

Death and death awareness is also very much an understudied phenomenon in organizational studies. Social psychologists, however, have studied death and death awareness for decades and two theoretical perspectives have come to dominate the field: terror management theory (TMT) and generativity theory. TMT derives from cultural anthropologist Ernest Becker's (1973) Pulitzer-prize winning The Denial of Death, which argues that human behaviour, and human civilization itself, is ultimately undertaken as a symbolic defence mechanism against our knowledge of the inevitability of our death. Social psychologists, beginning with Greenberg, Pyszczynski, and Solomon (1986) have expanded this into a theory based on the anxiety surrounding death. In TMT, this anxiety results from the contrast and conflict between two opposing states – the awareness of our inevitable death (presumed, in TMT, to be a uniquely human capacity), and the instinctual need for survival, which we share with all animals (Burke, Martens, & Faucher, 2010). Thus, TMT focuses on self-protective motivations – the desire to defend one's identity and image – as our buffer against this death anxiety. Generativity theory is based on Erik Erikson's (1998) eight-stage theory of psychosocial development. In each stage, the individual faces a psychosocial challenge or crisis; a healthy individual will successfully complete this challenge. Each stage builds upon the challenges faced in previous stages, and should an individual not resolve the psychosocial crisis of a particular stage, he or she can expect this crisis or challenge to recur throughout life. In the penultimate stage (Care), which occurs at midlife, the individual experiences a crisis of generativity vs. stagnation. This is an ego crisis, to either make a positive contribution to society and future generations, thus finding meaning in life, or to succumb and experience despair and a fear of death. In contrast to TMT, generativity theory states that death awareness results in the individual focusing on the betterment of society itself.

Grant and Wade-Benzoni (2009), writing from a managerial perspective, reconciled TMT and generativity theory by discussing two discrete psychological pathways that the individual experiences when navigating an awareness of or exposure to death: a 'hot' death anxiety pathway and a 'cool' death reflection pathway. Death anxiety is an emotional state of death awareness processed by a 'hot' or experiential psychological system, where the individual engages in self-protective behaviours as predicted by TMT; death reflection is a 'cool' cognitive state, where individuals ruminate and contemplate their mortality and purpose, leading to the generative, positive contributions to society as predicted by generativity theory. The psychological pathway engaged by the individual upon his or her awareness of death depends on how he or she gains this awareness – the antecedent Grant and Wade-Benzoni (2009) term the mortality cue. Grant and Wade-Benzoni (2009) develop a typology of mortality cues along three dimensions – self-relevance, source, and exposure. Self-relevance cues are divided into personal cues, where the employee's own life is directly threatened, and vicarious cues, where the employee's life is not directly threatened but he or she is exposed to those whose lives are. Source cues are divided into internal mortality cues, which occur at the workplace and external cues that occur outside the workplace. Finally, exposure cues are divided into chronic cues – lasting, recurring events - and acute cues – short-lived intermittent events.

Although Grant and Wade-Benzoni's (2009) mortality cue typology shows us that the individual at work can become aware of death in a variety of ways, here we focus on a specific situation where the individual gains death awareness – near-death experience – and particularly near-death experiences of a sudden, traumatic nature. Near-death experience, defined most succinctly as a close brush with death (Appleby, 1989) has been virtually unstudied by organizational scholars, yet is far more common that one might expect, with over half of all Americans being exposed to life-threatening trauma at least once, and fully one quarter more than once (Kessler, Sonnega, Bromet, Hughes, & Nelson, 1995; Greyson, 2001). However, in the medical literature the construct is well developed; much of this literature focuses on the physiological or pharmacological states associated with dying, or the psychological processes related to the perceived threat of death (Owens, Cook, & Stevenson, 1990). Many of those who have a near-death experience report symptoms congruent with posttraumatic stress disorder (Greyson, 2001; Kessler et al., 1995). Reconciling this evidence with Grant and Wade-Benzoni's (2009) psychological pathways and mortality cue typology, we expect that a near-death experience, at onset, would be experienced by the 'hot' death anxiety pathway, as the individual has nearly died him- or herself or has been directly exposed to someone who has died or nearly so. This is a clearly a traumatic event, and the individual, logically, will not be in a 'cool' reflective state. Self-relevance mortality cues will be either personal (if the individual has a near-death experience) or vicarious (if he/she does not), source mortality cues will be either internal or external, depending on where the near-death experience occurs, and the authors expect a near-death experience to be an acute mortality cue. Following TMT, the authors expect the individual to engage in self-protective behaviours at the workplace.

The authors believe that organizations can also experience near-death experiences of a sudden nature, which we demonstrate through case examples in this chapter. Although research on sudden near-death experiences for organizations is nearly nonexistent, Hamilton (2006) examined the role of loss of legitimacy in sudden organizational death. She defined sudden organizational death as "an organization's rapid and substantial loss of customers, clients, and market value that is unanticipated based on previous organizational trends." (Hamilton, 2006: 330). The organization is left in a permanently debilitated state, causing it to lose its ability to self-govern, relinquish its organizational identity, and cease operations in its existing form.

The authors propose to extend this definition to discuss sudden organizational near-death experience through a simple amendment: instead of an ultimate ceasing of operations, an organization experiencing a sudden organizational near-death experience does recover. Thus, we define sudden organizational near-death experience as an organization's rapid and substantial loss of customers, clients, and market value that is unanticipated based on previous organizational trends, but from which it does recover. This recovery could take a multitude of forms, ranging from anywhere between back to business as usual with few and/or superficial changes, to a substantially altered organizational state and culture. It can be expected that individual organizational members will experience this as a highly emotive event, triggering the 'hot' death anxiety pathway and self-protective behaviours.

In this chapter, the authors are interested in how these self-protective behaviours that individuals and organizations engage in after a near death experience change over time towards prosocial behaviours, where individuals and organizations effect positive change for themselves and their organizations. Brief and Motowildo (1986) have given us a three part definition of prosocial organizational behaviors: these are behaviors that are performed by a member of an organization, directed toward an individual, group, or organization with whom he or she interacts while carrying out his or her organizational role, and are performed with the intention of promoting the welfare of the individual, group, or organization toward which they are directed (p. 711). We predict that the amount, or degree, of prosocial organizational behavior will depend on the amount of exposure the individuals in the organization have to the near-death experience – the greater the exposure, the greater the amount of prosocial behavior. The literature around positive change deriving from negative events as having greater impact than changes deriving from positive events supports this concept: Baumeister, Bratslavsky, Finkenauer, and Vohs (2001), in a thorough review of this general hypothesis, found that negative events have greater power than positive events, whether they be everyday events or major life events such as trauma. Cameron (2008) notes the paradox behind negative events and positive organizational change: negative events, as proposed by evolutionary theory (Darwin, 2003), lead individuals and living systems to a quick, strong response when their existence is threatened. As these life-threatening events can signal evolutionary maladaptation, they act as a corrective influence or motivation to adapt to changed circumstances (Taylor, 1991) – in short, they lead to the recognition for the need for positive change, which we believe will lead to prosocial organizational behavior. To explain how this process occurs, the authors turn back to the discussion on the 'hot' death awareness pathway and the 'cool' death reflection pathway.

As mentioned before, individuals who have a near-death experience or are directly exposed to death in their organizational context will likely experience this with the 'hot' death awareness pathway; this is a highly anxiety-provoking situation. However, no individual can remain in a permanent state of high anxiety; as the immediacy of the near-death experience recedes and the individual and his or her organization begin to recover and regain some form of stability, the hot death anxiety pathway will begin to subside, and the individual will re-enter a more 'normal' state. It is at this time that we predict the individual will switch death awareness pathways and he or she will begin to follow the 'cool' reflective pathway, where he or she will be able to reflect on his or her experience and begin the process of adding prosocial change to the organization. We see support for this theorizing from the medical literature surrounding near-death experience. In an early work investigating individual reactions to community disasters, Tyhurst (1951) discussed what he termed the 'natural history' of reaction to acute disaster. This natural history consists of three overlapping phases: a period of impact, a period of recoil, and a posttraumatic period. Interestingly, during Tyhurst's (1954) first two periods the individual tends to focus on the self and self-preservation to the point that social interactions are primarily driven by self-serving motivations, while during the posttraumatic period the individual begins to focus on the future, on others, and on civil society again. This process mirrors the transition from the 'hot' death anxiety state to the 'cool death reflection state that we are proposing. More recently, scholars have found the aftermath of such near death experiences to be transforming at personal, religious, spiritual, and societal levels (e.g. Khanna & Greyson, 2014), while a recent review of the literature surrounding the changes experienced by individuals after a near-death experience noted several characteristic changes of particular interest to organizational scholars: a new sense of purpose or mission, increased compassion and love for others, lower concern for material gain, recognition, or status; higher self-esteem; a greater desire to serve others; a search for knowledge; and a heightened focus on the present (Noyes, Fenwick, Holden, & Christian, 2009).

Furthermore, the 'hot' and 'cool' pathways outlined by Grant and Wade-Benzoni (2009) might be extendable to the organizational level. Although organizations, in and of themselves, are not living, feeling entities, organizational members most certainly are; these organizational states would be the aggregate effect of individual organizational members' states. In other words, organizational 'hot' and 'cool' states depend on the pathways that the organizational members are following at a particular point in time. Under normal circumstances, where organizational members have not been exposed to a near-death experience, the organization will be in a 'cool' state – if either of these pathways are being followed at all. In a similar vein, should exposure to a near-death experience be limited to the individual level, where certain organizational members are exposed to a near-death experience but the greater majority of organizational members are not, the organization will likely continue or remain in a 'cool' reflective state. This does not, of course, preclude the possibility that those organizational members directly exposed to a near-death experience will enact prosocial organizational behaviours upon returning to the 'cool' death reflective pathway after the immediate crises has resolved. At the organizational level, however, these prosocial behaviours might be expected to be somewhat limited in their scope and scale – simply put, not enough organizational members have experienced the 'hot' death awareness pathway to effect organization-wide prosocial change upon returning to the 'cool' death reflection pathway. As the near-death experience, however, expands in scope and scale to be at the organizational level or at the individual level and organizational level simultaneously, this process is expected to change. Here, the vast majority of organizational members – leadership, management, and employees – experience the 'hot' death awareness pathway in reaction to the near-death experience. As organizational members transition to the 'cool' death reflection pathway post-trauma, they are both searching for and receptive to the potential for prosocial organizational behavior, and this organization-wide receptivity to positive change leads to prosocial organizational behavior enacted at the organizational level. This follows a fundamental assumption of organizational culture – that events with a high degree of emotional potential or load have the potential to be deeply rooted in both organizations and individuals. These emotive events lead to change.

ORGANIZATIONS EMBRACING ORGANIZATIONAL TRAUMA

In this chapter the authors use three sport organizations to examine the potential positive effect of organizational trauma, and specifically near-death experience, on organizational culture. Although the world of sports may seem unique, it can be also seen as a microcosm of society at large (Madigan & Delaney, 2009). Sport provides researchers with a rich context within which to study various organizational phenomena (Wolfe et al., 2005). An abundance of information resulting from media scrutiny and transparency of sport organizations (Goff & Tollison, 1990) offer a unique opportunity to study the effect of organizational trauma on organizational culture. In fact, sport organizations have already been used to study very subtle, emotionally loaded phenomena such as escalating commitment (Staw & Hoang, 1995) or determinants of perception of rivalry (Kilduff, Elfenbein, & Staw, 2010).

In terms of case selection, the authors follow Pettigrew (1990) and Eisenhardt (1989) to choose extreme (and polar) cases where the phenomenon of interest is "transparently observable." The following three are by no means the only organizations that have suffered organizational trauma, nor the only ones that used traumatic events to shape organizational culture. What they have in common are near-death experiences that influenced their organizational cultures. Table 1 indicates the level where near-death experiences occurred in the described organizations.

Table 1. A simplified matrix of individual/organizational traumatic experiences

<table>
<tr><th>Level</th><th colspan="3">Individual</th></tr>
<tr><td rowspan="3">Organization</td><td>Near-death Experience</td><td>No</td><td>Yes</td></tr>
<tr><td>No</td><td>-</td><td>Organization I</td></tr>
<tr><td>Yes</td><td>Organization II</td><td>Organization III</td></tr>
</table>

Organization I: Near Death Experience at the Individual Level Only

Sport Lisboa e Benfica is a sports club based in Lisbon, Portugal. Founded in 1904, Benfica is one of the most successful teams in Portuguese association football with over 70 domestic and international titles. In January 2004 the team was struck by the sudden death of Miklos Feher. The Hungarian footballer died suddenly on January 25th at the stadium in Guimaraes, during a local league game between Benfica and Vitoria. Feher came on as a substitute in the 60th minute of the match. In stoppage time, Benfica's Fernando Aguilar scored the match-winning goal. Feher ran to him and celebrated with his teammates. A minute later Feher was cautioned by the referee for a foul, but calmly accepted the yellow card and smiled at the referee. The "ultima sorrisa do Fehcr" ("the last smile of Feher") is a picture that hit the front pages of Portuguese newspapers the next day as after just walking a few steps Feher stopped, leaned over, and then fell limply on the pitch. Feher was immediately taken to a nearby hospital, but a 90-minute attempt at resuscitation was unsuccessful. The 24-year-old died without regaining consciousness. Feher had died of a heart attack, which, considering his good health and exercise regime, was entirely unexpected. His sudden death came as a shock to his teammates, Benfica supporters, and the entire football community. Benfica Lisbon has done a lot to commemorate Feher. The Board of the Portuguese club decided to retire Feher's number; no Benfica player will ever wear number 29 again. Feher's photograph was placed in the club's locker room, so that he will always be close to his teammates as they prepare for a match. After winning the 2004-2005 Portuguese league season, the entire team travelled to Hungary to present Feher's parents with a championship medal. Later on, one of the stands at Benfica's home ground, the Estadio da Luz in Lisbon, was named after the player, and the club established a museum commemorating Miklos Feher in the city of Gyor, Hungary – which the club continues to maintain.

Organization II: Near Death Experience at the Organizational Level Only

Borussia Dortmund, also known as BVB 09, is a German sports club based in Dortmund. Founded in 1909, Borussia has been one of the most successful professional football clubs in Germany, winning eight championships and three national cups. After a golden age in the 1990s, the club ran into serious financial trouble as a result of poor management and unsatisfactory performance on the field. In 2004 Borussia was on the verge of collapse. After signing numerous expensive star players, the team failed to live up to its potential and incurred heavy financial losses, which, according to some unofficial sources, amounted to EUR 120 million. In 2005 the club was on the brink of bankruptcy. At that time, Reinhald Rauball became the new president of the organization and Hans-Joachim Watzke was hired as a new managing director. Due to Borrusia's heavy debt load the organization was forced to the sell their stadium and to introduce drastic austerity measures. Finally, a loan from their major rivals, Bayern Munchen, helped the team regain financial stability. Borussia hired a new head coach, Jurgen Klopp, who created a new, competitive team out of low profile signings and graduates of the club's academy. Between 2008 and 2015 the team won two German Championships (along with placing second twice in the Bundesliga), one German Cup, two German Supercups and also came second in the UEFA Champions League. Most importantly, the new management engrained passion and a winning mentality back into the organization.

Organization III: Near Death Experience at the Individual and Organizational Level

Torino Football Club is a professional Italian association football club based in Turin. Founded in 1906, the club is among the most successful teams in Italy. In the 1940s the *Grande Torino,* one of the strongest teams of that era, won five consecutive league titles. This successful era in the club's history ended abruptly on May 4th, 1949, when a plane carrying the whole team crashed near Turin, killing everyone on board, including players, coaching staff and two executives. The 1949 plane crash not only decimated one of the strongest teams of that time in Europe, but also has left a seemingly unhealed stigma on the entire organization and its supporters. The crash changed a powerful winning machine into a much weaker team that has spent the past six decades hovering between the elite and the second tier of Italian football.

DISCUSSION

Organizational culture is a crucial element of every organization; hence it comes as no surprise that it has received much scholarly attention. While it is impossible to summarize all research on organizational culture in a single piece, a number of fundamental studies must be noted. Ouchi (1980; 1982) compared organizations to clans having a strong culture to help them with goal incongruence and performance ambiguity. Barney (1986) proposed that organizational culture might be a source of sustained competitive advantage.

Schein (1992 ; 2004) identifies three levels of culture: (1) artifacts; (2) espoused values; and (3) basic underlying assumptions. Artifacts include any tangible and easily identifiable elements characteristic for a given organization, such as dress codes, architecture, and signs and memorabilia. An outsider may easily recognize these artifacts. Espoused values are an organization's stated values and rules of behaviour, both among its members and towards individuals outside of the organization. Ideally, these values reflect shared basic assumptions, i.e. the deeply embedded values and ways of thinking of the world. These assumptions are not only difficult to understand by individuals outside of the organization, but also the organizational members may not be aware of their existence.

Organizational responses to organizational trauma, particularly traumatic near death experiences, might have an effect on various levels of organizational culture, depending on the context of the near death experience and its level – individual, organizational, or both. The case of Benfica, where the death of Feher and the near-death experience of organizational members happened at the individual level, illustrates how symbols, such as the retired number and player's memorial bust in the main hallway of Benfica's stadium, are used to symbolically engrave the individual and the experience in the collective memory of the organization (Schwartz, 1982). While a change of artifacts is crucial for successful organizational change, they must be tied to deeper levels of organizational culture to have a significant effect on the organization (Higgins & Mcallaster, 2004). In this case the visible artifacts are important acts, but they do not change neither the espoused values of the organization, nor the basic underlying assumptions. Presenting Feher's family with a medal and retiring his number were admirable and emotional gestures, thus having a significant impact on organizational culture (Rafaeli & Vilnai-Yavetz, 2004); however, these were one time acts that did not turn into rituals, hence could not change the organizational culture in terms of values or practices, and organizational strategy and culture remained the same (Deal & Kennedy, 1982; Islam & Zyphur, 2009). Similarly, the Vancouver Canucks, a National Hockey League organization in Vancouver, Canada, experienced the same type of traumatic event as Benfica in 2011, when one of their players, Rick Rypien, committed suicide after a struggle with clinical depression. Following his death, the team honoured Rypien with a ceremony prior to one of their home games, the family was presented with a jersey, and the organization made a donation to a local foundation helping youth and young adults cope with mental health issues. While all these gestures were important symbols, they have not changed the deeper levels of organizational culture. Using an example from other industries beside sport, Steve Jobs' death in 2011 might be seen as a similar case. Apple had lost its leader and an important asset, but its very existence was not under direct threat; hence, there have been no fundamental changes to Apple's organizational culture. Death of a founder or a leader might be seen to have a more profound effect, but since it does not endanger the very existence of a large organization, the effect on organizational culture is very limited as near death experience at the individual level appears to trigger the "hot" pathway (Grant & Wade-Benzoni, 2009) in individuals only, while the organization is still in a "cool" cognitive state. The result is a superficial change in organizational culture (at the artifacts level only) that helps organizational members deal with the "hot" death anxiety state, but the deeper levels of organizational culture remain unchanged.

Proposition 1: Near death experience at the individual level only results in a change of symbolic artefacts, but not espoused values or basic underlying assumptions.

The second case, the near bankruptcy at Borussia Dortmund, illustrates how an organizational near death experience might lead to deeper changes, including radical changes in strategy and espoused values. Before its 2005 ordeals, Borussia was a wealthy organisation, spending millions on transfer fees (a net of EUR 25 million in 2000; 27 million in 2001; 9 million in 2002; and 13 million in 2003). Previous successes and good financial standing created a culture fostering irresponsible investment, which even when not successful was initially covered by other sources of revenue. However, as losses mounted and were mirrored by a lack of success on the football pitch, this strategy and culture of profligate spending led to a near bankruptcy in 2005. The change in the club's strategy was substantial. After 2005 Borussia stopped paying high transfer fees and began making profits on the transfer market – a net of EUR 3 million in 2005, 5 million in 2006, 8 million in 2012, and 23 million in 2015, along with balanced transfer revenue/spending in all other seasons. Borrusia's significant spending in 2014 was balanced by its enormous profits in 2012 and 2013, and yet it was ill received by the club's supporters, for whom large transfer fees were a reminder of the events of the last decade. In 2015, the organization returned to its more conservative financial strategy. Interestingly, Borrusia's conservative financial strategy has had not only positive effects on the club's financial status, but also has had some unexpected negative consequences. Despite recent successes in the Bundesliga and in European competitions, the club has refused to discuss improved contracts with its top players, consequently losing two of them to their fierce rival (and one time rescuer), Bayern Munchen. In this case, the new organizational culture and new financial strategy has led to unexpected consequences, raising questions about whether the financial strategy was just a strategy, or whether there was a deeper understanding of the underlying assumptions of sensible management. A proper alignment of strategy with deeper levels of organizational culture is key for achieving sustainable competitive advantage (e.g. Schneider, 2000; Hatch & Schultz, 2001; Zheng, Yang, & McLean, 2010). General Motors' bankruptcy in 2008 and the subsequent government bailout might serve as another example of a sudden near death experience at the organization level. Since 2008, the company has paid back its rescue package and is now in good financial standing. The most significant change occurred at the corporate strategy and structure level, with the simplification of decision-making processes and the introduction of financial austerity, but the changes to GM's corporate culture's deeper levels – the basic underlying assumptions – are still ongoing.

Proposition 2: Near death experience at the organizational level results in a change of artifacts and of espoused values, but not of basic underlying assumptions.

The 1949 tragedy has significantly changed both the strategy and culture of Torino. Before the plane crash, Torino were a major, high profile, team, attracting worldwide attention. The tragedy triggered an emotional response not only among Torino supporters, but also throughout Italy. Although the club has never achieved the same status in sport, the organization has managed to embrace this experience and has created a strong organizational culture. The 1949 plane crash has become a founding myth of Torino's new organizational culture (Meek, 1988; McWhinney & Batista, 1988) and ever since the club has consciously built a romantic aura around the team. All new incoming players have to visit the crash site on their first day at the club as a part of their introduction, which can be seen as a ritual ingraining organizational culture into the new organizational member (Deal & Kennedy, 2000) and a form of communicating organizational values (Pacanowsky & O'Donnell-Trujillo, 1983). Pettigrew (1979) recognized the role of examining rituals, which are a form of symbolism, in studying organizational culture. Rites and ceremonial behaviours are important elements shaping and strengthening organizational culture (Young, 1965; Trice & Beyer, 1984). An annual memorial ceremony at the 1949 crash site serves the same purpose of bringing all members of the organization and its stakeholders together to refresh its founding myth and reinforce organizational assumptions and values. At the strategy level, the size of Torino's museum exceeds by far the sport stature of the club, showing how important history is to the organization. The club has also recognized the roles of their key stakeholders, their supporters, in maintaining organizational culture (Jones, Felps, & Bigley, 2007); hence Torino had the first official organized supporters' group in Italy. In sum, the death of organizational members and the threat of death to the organization triggered a strong emotive reaction, which has affected all three levels of organizational culture. Artifacts, such as the welcome ritual and annual memorial ceremony, are closely tied to the espoused values of a close-knit group of organizational members and stakeholders, with the tragedy as a founding myth leading to the constant struggle for survival as the underlying assumption.

Cantor Fitzgerald, a financial services company, might be seen as a similar business case. Cantor Fitzgerald's corporate headquarters was located in the World Trade Center and were destroyed on September 11th, 2001. The company lost 658 out of its 960 New York head office employees. Immediately after the attack, corporate management promised to keep the company alive and vowed to financially support the families of its killed employees. Moreover, The Cantor Fitzgerald Relief Fund has continued to support victims of natural disasters, such as Hurricane Sandy and the Moore, Oklahoma tornado. A company that before 2001 exhibited an organizational culture typical of financial services firms has embraced philanthropy as an integral part of its organizational culture only after a near death experience at both the individual and organizational levels. The immediate threat to the members of the organization triggered the "hot" death awareness pathway (Grant & Wade-Benzoni, 2009). The threat to organizational existence triggered a "cool" death reflection response from the organization, but because of organizational trauma following the 9/11 events, a search for new existential meaning began (Driver, 2007). As a result, all levels of Cantor Fitzgerald's organizational culture have been deeply changed.

Proposition 3: Near death experience at both the organizational and individual level results in a change of artifacts, espoused values, and basic underlying assumptions.

The sport context provided a common denominator for the three aforementioned case studies, but the phenomenon of traumatic events changing organizational culture is not limited to sport organizations. To better understand differences in levels of cultural changed caused by near death experience, one may look at recent events at Western companies' subcontractor facilities in Asia. In 2010-2011 a wave of suicides occurred at Foxconn, a Chinese manufacturing subcontractor to Apple, Dell, Hewlett-Packard and many more. In this 2-year period alone, 22 employees attempted suicide, because of numerous labour abuses. Unwanted media attention forced the company to attempt a corporate culture change. However, the change was limited to installing suicide prevention netting, introducing prayer sessions, and encouraging employees to sign no-suicide pledges. Because the near death experience did not threaten the actual existence of the entire organization, the effect of these traumatic events was limited to the very superficial level of organizational culture, with the basic underlying assumptions and organizational values remaining virtually unchanged. Only two years later, another traumatic event occurred in Savar Upazila, Bangladesh, where a commercial building named Rana Plaza collapsed, causing the deaths of over 1,100 people. Rana Plaza housed a number of garment-manufacturing subcontractors of several well-known Western clothing brands, such as Benetton, El Corte Ingles, Mango, and Walmart. While the event did not directly threaten the Western companies, it did raise questions about their existing business model based on exploitive supply-chain arrangements. A week after the collapse an accord aiming for improvement of labour conditions in Bangladeshi garment factories was signed by leading Western fashion retailers. As a result, over 1,500 locations have been inspected for potential hazards, potentially preventing many more incidents. The magnitude of the near death experience and potential risk to the existence of the business model forced cost-oriented organizations to forego some of their profit for a positive change in organizational culture, at least at the artefacts and espoused values levels.

Finally, it is noteworthy that it is not merely the sheer number of affected individuals that constitutes the difference between the first and the last case study. Undoubtedly, the magnitude of trauma as measured by the number of organizational members suffering plays a role in the amount of emotional loading generated in individuals, but it is the direct threat to the very existence of the organization that triggers the change mechanisms in its culture at deeper levels.

SOLUTIONS AND RECOMMENDATIONS FOR PRACTITIONERS

As Friedrich Nietzsche (1888), a German philosopher, wrote "What does not kill me, makes me stronger". Even the worst ordeals can eventually bring positive contributions. Organizations experience both prosperity and times of trouble, the latter sometimes being in the form of traumatic events. Outstanding managers can turn these events and experiences into both positive reinforcements of organizational culture and an impetus for change. However, traumatic events turn into positive experience only when consciously reflected upon. Near-death experiences within an organization require careful analysis, a closer look from all sides, in a variety of contexts and at multiple levels, to be fully understood and to internalize lessons learned and changes made. Merely experiencing a traumatic event does not in and of itself create a positive effect on organizational culture, but a lesson consciously learned from it might have a long-term positive impact on the organization.

Organizations learn and evolve through experience (Cyert & March, 1963) and effective managers must know how to take advantage of various kinds of experiences and changes. Schein argues that nowadays it is not enough to manage "change," but managers face the challenge of managing a "surprise" (Schein, 1993: 85). Sudden traumatic events constitute a great challenge to an organization's members and to the organization itself, but they also have a significant emotional loading that can be used to "unfreeze" (Lewin, 1951) the current status quo and introduce critical changes to organizational culture. Schein (1993) proposes that organizations learn faster when members experience three stages: (1) disconfirmation, i.e. an ascertainment that the current state is imperfect; (2) creation of guilt or anxiety, i.e. a state of strong emotional shock; (3) and creation of psychological safety. With the high emotional loading of sudden traumatic events, the first two stages occur naturally, therefore the role of the manager should be the swift introduction of important changes and then providing psychological safety to reinforce the effect of positive change, and freeze the new positive state (Lewin, 1951).

FUTURE RESEARCH DIRECTIONS

In this chapter the authors only briefly outline potential positive implications of traumatic events and near death experiences on organizational culture; however, they do suggest to scholars some new avenues for future research. One of these avenues is the role of leadership in turning organizational trauma into positive culture reinforcement or transformation. Hilton Brown (1997) recognized the role of leaders in combating organizational trauma and improving organizational health. Positive Organizational Scholarship (POS) also offers some insight into the role of leaders in creating a nurturing work environment. Cameron and Caza (2002) described the role of leadership virtues in organizational life, stressing that leaders play an especially important role under conditions of organizational injury and trauma, such as downsizing. Dutton, Frost, Worline, Lilius, and Kanov (2002) studied personal tragedies caused by natural disasters and found that during times of pain and confusion, leaders can trigger a compassionate response throughout the organization, hence increasing bonds among organizational members and attachment to the organization (Dutton et al., 2002: 54). Schein (2006) also stressed the role of leaders in changing organizational culture. It would be worthwhile to study differences in leadership behaviours (and their outcomes) in organizations after suffering near-death experiences at the individual and organizational levels to better understand the potential for positive cultural change.

Another interesting research avenue is the role of competitors in surviving organizational trauma and learning from near-death experiences. Both Borussia Dortmund and Torino received immediate help from their direct competitors (financial and sporting, respectively) to overcome and ease the organizational trauma. Similarly, Apple, now the most valuable brand worldwide, received an emergency loan from Microsoft in 1997. These actions, so contrary to fundamental institutional logics of the world of sport and business, must have made an impact on the organizational cultures of all affected parties. Surprisingly, the organizational literature offers little insight into this phenomenon. A stream of research on co-opetition (e.g. Bengtsson & Kock, 2000; Walley, 2007; Brandenburger & Nalebuff, 2011) focuses mostly on an ongoing or project-based cooperation of competitors, but there are virtually no studies on organizations directly saving their competitors. However, the trust literature sheds some light on this issue and might be a useful starting point for future analysis (Banarjee, Bowie, & Pavone, 2006).

Lastly, empirical research on near-death experiences in and of organizations is sorely needed. As most research on death awareness and near-death experience comes from social psychology, scholars know very little about how this plays out in an organizational setting. Similarly, little is known about factors accompanying near death experiences and other traumatic events within and around organizations. Perhaps qualitative research describing organizational members' experiences in near-death situations would be beneficial in expanding on the ideas proposed in this chapter, and would bring about a host of new research questions that would broaden and deepen academic and practitioner knowledge on this undeniably tragic yet all too frequent topic – hopefully leading to more positive, prosocial outcomes both for organizational members and organizations themselves.

CONCLUSION

There is little doubt that organizational trauma is an important, yet understudied phenomenon. It can affect not only individual members (Weick, 1988; Stein, 1991), but also an entire organization (Amabile & Conti, 1999; Kahn, 2003). Research has shown that organizational trauma might negatively affect individual and organizational performance (Fischer, 2012; Valikangas et al., 2009; deKlerk, 2007). However, organizational trauma and its underlying causes, such as near death experiences, might also trigger positive organizational changes (Driver, 2007). The three above described organizations survived near death experiences and managed to incorporate them into their organizational culture at different levels. However, the underlying mechanisms and processes leading from near death experiences to positive organizational culture change require more conceptual and empirical research.

REFERENCES

Amabile, T. M., & Conti, R. (1999). Changes in the work environment for creativity during downsizing. *Academy of Management Journal*, *42*(6), 630–640. doi:10.2307/256984

Appleby, L. (1989). Near death experience. *BMJ: British Medical Journal*, *298*(6679), 976–977. doi:10.1136/bmj.298.6679.976 PMID:2499387

Banerjee, S., Bowie, N. E., & Pavone, C. (2006). An ethical analysis of the trust relationship. In R. Bachmann & A. Zaheer (Eds.), *Handbook of trust research* (pp. 303–343). Cheltenham, UK: Edward Elgar. doi:10.4337/9781847202819.00026

Baumeister, R. F., Bratslavsky, E., Finkenauer, C., & Vohs, K. D. (2001). Bad is stronger than good. *Review of General Psychology*, *5*(4), 323–370. doi:10.1037/1089-2680.5.4.323

Becker, E. (1997). *The denial of death* (2nd ed.). New York, NY: Free Press.

Bengtsson, M., & Kock, S. (2000). Coopetition" in business Networks—to cooperate and compete simultaneously. *Industrial Marketing Management*, *29*(5), 411–426. doi:10.1016/S0019-8501(99)00067-X

Brandenburger, A. M., & Nalebuff, B. J. (2011). *Co-opetition*. New York, NY: Doubleday.

Brief, A. P., & Motowidlo, S. J. (1986). Prosocial organizational behaviors. *Academy of Management Review*, *11*(4), 710–725.

Cameron, K., & Caza, A. (2002). Organizational and leadership virtues and the role of forgiveness. *Journal of Leadership & Organizational Studies*, *9*(1), 33–48. doi:10.1177/107179190200900103

Cameron, K. S. (2008). Paradox in positive organizational change. *The Journal of Applied Behavioral Science*, *44*(1), 7–24. doi:10.1177/0021886308314703

Cyert, R. M., & March, J. G. (1963). *A behavioral theory of the firm*. Englewood Cliffs, NJ: Prentice-Hall.

Darwin, C. (2003). *The origin of species*. New York: Signet Classics.

DAveni, R. A., & MacMillan, I. C. (1990). Crisis and the content of managerial communications: A study of the focus of attention of top managers in surviving and failing firms. *Administrative Science Quarterly*, *35*(4), 634–657. doi:10.2307/2393512

Deal, T. E., & Kennedy, A. A. (1982). *Organization cultures: The rites and rituals of organization life*. Reading, UK: Addison-Wesley.

Deal, T. E., & Kennedy, A. A. (2000). *Corporate cultures: The rites and rituals of corporate life*. New York, NY: Basic Books.

deKlerk, M. (2007). Healing Emotional Trauma in Organizations: An OD Framework and Case Study. *Organization Development Journal*, *25*(2), 49–55.

Delaney, T., & Madigan, T. (2009). *Sports: why people love them!* Lanham, MD: University Press of America.

Driver, M. (2007). Meaning and suffering in organizations. *Journal of Organizational Change Management*, *20*(5), 611–632. doi:10.1108/09534810710779063

Driver, M. (2009). From loss to lack: Stories of organizational change as encounters with failed fantasies of self, work and organization. *Organization*, *16*(3), 353–369. doi:10.1177/1350508409102300

Dutton, J. E., Frost, P. J., Worline, M. C., Lilius, J. M., & Kanov, J. M. (2002). Leading in times of trauma. *Harvard Business Review*, *80*(1), 54–61. PMID:12964467

Eisenhardt, K. M. (1989). Building theories from case study research. *Academy of Management Review*, *14*(4), 532–550.

Erikson, E. H., & Erikson, J. M. (1998). *The life cycle completed (extended version)*. New York, NY: WW Norton & Company.

Fischer, M. D. (2012). Organizational turbulence, trouble and trauma: Theorizing the collapse of a mental health setting. *Organization Studies*, *33*(9), 1153–1173. doi:10.1177/0170840612448155

Goff, B. L., & Tollison, R. D. (Eds.). (1990). *Sportometrics (No. 11)*. College Station, TX: Texas A&M University Press.

Grant, A. M., & Wade-Benzoni, K. A. (2009). The hot and cool of death awareness at work: Mortality cues, aging, and self-protective and prosocial motivations. *Academy of Management Review*, *34*(4), 600–622. doi:10.5465/AMR.2009.44882929

Greenberg, J., Pyszczynski, T., & Solomon, S. (1986). The causes and consequences of a need for self- esteem: A terror management theory. In R. F. Baumeister (Ed.), *Public self and private self* (pp. 189–212). New York: Springer. doi:10.1007/978-1-4613-9564-5_10

Greyson, B. (2001). Posttraumatic stress symptoms following near-death experiences. *The American Journal of Orthopsychiatry*, *71*(3), 368–373. doi:10.1037/0002-9432.71.3.368 PMID:11495339

Hamilton, E. A. (2006). An exploration of the relationship between loss of legitimacy and the sudden death of organizations. *Group & Organization Management*, *31*(3), 327–358. doi:10.1177/1059601106286885

Hatch, M. J., & Schultz, M. (2001). Are the strategic stars aligned for your corporate brand? *Harvard Business Review*, *79*(2), 128–134. PMID:11213687

Higgins, J. M., & Mcallaster, C. (2004). If you want strategic change, dont forget to change your cultural artifacts. *Journal of Change Management*, *4*(1), 63–73. doi:10.1080/1469701032000154926

Hilton Brown, E. (1997). Improving organizational health by addressing organizational trauma. *Journal of Organizational Change Management*, *10*(2), 175–178. doi:10.1108/09534819710160835

Hopper, E. (2012). *Trauma and organizations*. London, UK: Karnac Books.

Islam, G., & Zyphur, M. J. (2009). Rituals in organizations: A review and expansion of current theory. *Group & Organization Management*, *34*(1), 114–139. doi:10.1177/1059601108329717

Jones, T. M., Felps, W., & Bigley, G. A. (2007). Ethical theory and stakeholder-related decisions: The role of stakeholder culture. *Academy of Management Review*, *32*(1), 137–155. doi:10.5465/AMR.2007.23463924

Kahn, W. A. (2003). The revelation of organizational trauma. *The Journal of Applied Behavioral Science*, *39*(4), 364–380. doi:10.1177/0021886303261954

Keidel, R. W., Bell, S. M., & Lewis, K. J. (1994). Rethinking organizational design. *The Academy of Management Executive*, *8*(4), 12-30.

Kessler, R. C., Sonnega, A., Bromet, E., Hughes, M., & Nelson, C. B. (1995). Posttraumatic stress disorder in the National Comorbidity Survey. *Archives of General Psychiatry*, *52*(12), 1048–1060. doi:10.1001/archpsyc.1995.03950240066012 PMID:7492257

Khanna, S., & Greyson, B. (2014). Near-death experiences and spiritual well-being. *Journal of Religion and Health*, *53*(6), 1605–1615. doi:10.1007/s10943-013-9723-0 PMID:23625172

Kilduff, G. J., Elfenbein, H. A., & Staw, B. M. (2010). The psychology of rivalry: A relationally dependent analysis of competition. *Academy of Management Journal*, *53*(5), 943–969. doi:10.5465/AMJ.2010.54533171

Lewin, K. (1951). *Field Theory in Social Science*. Harper & Row.

McWhinney, W., & Batista, J. (1988). How remythologizing can revitalize organizations. *Organizational Dynamics*, *17*(2), 46–58. doi:10.1016/0090-2616(88)90018-6

Meek, V. L. (1988). Organizational culture: Origins and weaknesses. *Organization Studies*, *9*(4), 453–473. doi:10.1177/017084068800900401

Noyes, R., Fenwick, P., Holden, J. M., & Christian, S. R. (2009). Aftereffects of pleasurable Western adult near-death experiences. In J. M. Holden, B. Greyson, & D. James (Eds.), *The handbook of near-death experiences: Thirty years of investigation* (pp. 41–62). Santa Barbara, CA: Praeger/ABC-CLIO.

Ouchi, W. G. (1980). Markets, bureaucracies, and clans. *Administrative Science Quarterly*, *25*(1), 129–141. doi:10.2307/2392231

Ouchi, W. G. (1982). *Theory z*. Avon.

Owens, J., Cook, E. W., & Stevenson, I. (1990). Features of near-death experience in relation to whether or not patients were near death. *Lancet*, *336*(8724), 1175–1177. doi:10.1016/0140-6736(90)92780-L PMID:1978037

Pacanowsky, M. E., & ODonnell-Trujillo, N. (1983). Organizational communication as cultural performance. *Communication Monographs*, *50*(2), 126–147. doi:10.1080/03637758309390158

Pettigrew, A. M. (1990). Longitudinal field research on change: Theory and practice. *Organization Science*, *1*(3), 267–292. doi:10.1287/orsc.1.3.267

Rafaeli, A., & Vilnai-Yavetz, I. (2004). Emotion as a connection of physical artifacts and organizations. *Organization Science*, *15*(6), 671–686. doi:10.1287/orsc.1040.0083

Schein, E. H. (1992). *Organizational culture and leadership* (2nd ed.). San Francisco, CA: John Wiley & Sons.

Schein, E. H. (1993). SMR forum: How can organizations learn faster? The challenge of entering the green room. *Sloan Management Review*, *34*(2), 85–92.

Schein, E. H. (1996). Culture: The missing concept in organization studies. *Administrative Science Quarterly*, *41*(2), 229–240. doi:10.2307/2393715

Schein, E. H. (2006). *Organizational culture and leadership* (Vol. 356). John Wiley & Sons.

Schneider, W. E. (2000). Why good management ideas fail: The neglected power of organizational culture. *Strategy and Leadership*, *28*(1), 24–29. doi:10.1108/10878570010336001

Schwartz, B. (1982). The social context of commemoration: A study in collective memory. *Social Forces*, *61*(2), 374–402. doi:10.1093/sf/61.2.374

Staw, B. M., & Hoang, H. (1995). Sunk costs in the NBA: Why draft order affects playing time and survival in professional basketball. *Administrative Science Quarterly*, *40*(3), 474–494. doi:10.2307/2393794

Stein, H. F. (1991). Metaphors of organizational trauma and organizational development: A case example. *Organization Development Journal*, *9*(4), 22–30.

Stuart, R. (1996). The trauma of organizational change. *Journal of European Industrial Training*, *20*(2), 11–16. doi:10.1108/03090599610110420

Taylor, S. E. (1991). Asymmetrical effects of positive and negative events: The mobilization- minimization hypothesis. *Psychological Bulletin*, *110*(1), 67–85. doi:10.1037/0033-2909.110.1.67 PMID:1891519

Tyhurst, J. S. (1951). Individual reactions to community disaster: The natural history of psychiatric phenomena. *The American Journal of Psychiatry*, *107*(10), 764–769. doi:10.1176/ajp.107.10.764 PMID:14819372

Välikangas, L., Hoegl, M., & Gibbert, M. (2009). Why learning from failure isnt easy (and what to do about it): Innovation trauma at Sun Microsystems. *European Management Journal*, *27*(4), 225–233. doi:10.1016/j.emj.2008.12.001

Walley, K. (2007). Coopetition: An introduction to the subject and an agenda for research. *International Studies of Management & Organization*, *37*(2), 11–31. doi:10.2753/IMO0020-8825370201

Weick, K. E. (1988). Enacted sensemaking in crisis situations. *Journal of Management Studies*, *25*(4), 305–317. doi:10.1111/j.1467-6486.1988.tb00039.x

Wolfe, R. A., Weick, K. E., Usher, J. M., Terborg, J. R., Poppo, L., Murrell, A. J., & Jourdan, J. S. et al. (2005). Sport and organizational studies exploring synergy. *Journal of Management Inquiry*, *14*(2), 182–210. doi:10.1177/1056492605275245

Zheng, W., Yang, B., & McLean, G. N. (2010). Linking organizational culture, structure, strategy, and organizational effectiveness: Mediating role of knowledge management. *Journal of Business Research*, *63*(7), 763–771. doi:10.1016/j.jbusres.2009.06.005

KEY TERMS AND DEFINITIONS

Artifacts: Tangible and easily identifiable elements characteristic for a given culture.

Basic Underlying Assumptions: Deeply embedded values and ways of thinking of the world shared by members of a given culture.

Espoused Values: Stated values and rules of behaviour, both among members of a culture and towards individuals outside of the culture.

Generativity Theory: Predictive theory of creative behaviour of individuals, proposed by Robert Epstein in the 1980s.

Near Death Experience: A state when an organization and its members witnessed and/or suffered from a sudden, traumatic event at either organizational or individual level.

Organizational Culture: Collective values, beliefs, informal rules, and principles shared by organizational members.

Organizational Death: An organization's rapid and substantial loss of customers, clients, and market value that is unanticipated based on previous organizational trends, but from which it does recover.

Positive Organizational Scholarship: A stream of research focusing on organizations providing their members with a supportive and safe environment, in which they can flourish.

Chapter 11
An Organizational Trauma Intervention: A Case From Turkey

Bülent Kılıç
Koç University, Turkey

ABSTRACT

The aim of this chapter is to describe a trauma experienced among blue collar employees at the XYZ car factory in Turkey. Demonstrations led to a halt of production after the representative union signed higher salary at another factory. After the consensus among the parties the production was restarted. However, the trauma and its symptoms emerged. Conflicts and polarization rose among the workers and the employer decided to conduct an intervention program. This study focuses on the pre-intervention, pilot intervention and main intervention programs. Descriptive quotations related to the trauma and the implications of the intervention program are discussed in the light of a theoretical framework. In the present paper, a brief background of the automotive industry and labor unions will be presented. The theoretical perspective is put forward, the implemented program is described, and the descriptive findings are presented then the findings and implications are discussed.

INTRODUCTION

The Automotive Industry and Labor Unions in Turkey

The automotive industry in Turkey is quite developed. Both cars and their components are manufactured in Turkey. Most of the factories producing cars and their components are located in Bursa, one of the northwestern cities of Turkey. In this text, the factories and unions involved have been given fictitious names, both because of confidentiality and to allow the author to explain the situation with more details and accuracy. The narration is thus made more convenient for the reader.

In a majority of the factories in the automotive sector as well as in other manufacturing industries, labor unions sign collective labor agreements for a three-year period with the employers. When the last

DOI: 10.4018/978-1-5225-2021-4.ch011

contracts were signed in December 2014 by the Representative Union, there were two different labor unions at ABC factory. It was uncertain which of the competing labor unions was going to represent the workers there and therefore a collective labor agreement could not be signed. A court decided in May 2015 that the Representative Union should represent the workers and this union signed the agreement after the court decision. Hence the agreement at ABC factory was signed six months later than the collective agreements signed at other factories.

According to the collective labor agreement signed in December 2014 workers were paid 6 Turkish Lira (TL) (2.25USD) per hour while workers at ABC factory were paid 8 TL (3.00USD) per hour because of their late contract. This inequality created a lot of tension in the labor market and among the workers in Bursa. Demonstrations against the union Representative Union started at one of the factories. The protests then spread to other big factories in Bursa. The production at XYZ factory was suspended for a period of time in 2015. The protests ended after a consensus between representatives of the workers, the union and the employers. They agreed upon a one-time payment of 1000 TL (275USD) to those workers who were receiving the lower hourly salary.

The Organizational Trauma from the Perspective of the Workers

The protests at XYZ factory had started in the cafeteria with workers banging their cutlery on the tables. They later grew bigger and even led to a halt of production in some ateliers. While some workers were very upset over the inequality in pay others joined the protests out of solidarity for their friends. A majority of the senior workers (more than 15 years of employment) preferred not to join the demonstrations as well as some of the younger workers.

Demonstrations were held peacefully and there was no vandalism, no sabotage and no damage done to the factory facilities. After the stop of production for nine days, the workers took up their work again. Conflicts and polarizations emerged among the workers after the production was restarted. The workers were now divided into several groups and subgroups. These groups can be categorized as follows:

1. Broadly we can categorize all workers as the ones who had joined the protests and the ones who did not.
2. Representative Union members,
3. Members of Alternative Union,
4. Those without a union membership,
5. Superiors of blue collar workers, namely Main Production Team Leaders (MTL) and Lean Team Leaders (LTL),
6. Workers joining the protests at first and then returning to their jobs out of fear of losing their employment,
7. Workers taking part of the protests until the end regardless of union membership status.

Workers who had taken part of the demonstration until the end accused their colleagues who had not participated at all or had participated for a while of being traitors. They claimed that they had received the compensation payment thanks to their effort but that the others did not really deserve this payment.

The psychological atmosphere in the factory had again became unproductive and the morale among the workers was low. Upon this the HR department decided that an intervention was needed to restore a positive working climate. A team of social scientists and practitioners were invited to develop and implement an intervention program to heal the trauma experienced. The author was the team leader of the project, conducted focus group meetings, designed and implemented the intervention program with a group of psychologists. Moreover, the author also attended meetings with the Human Resources department, Production department and the CEO.

THEORETICAL BACKGROUND

Perceived Equity, Organizational Commitment and Organizational Trauma

Equity is based on an employee's job inputs and outputs (Adams, 1965). Inputs can be defined as effort, training, experience and seniority which are contributed to the job by the worker. Outcomes are distribution of pay, career advancement opportunities, promotions and fringe benefits which refer to the perceived fairness of treatment of the employee as compared to others. In the present study, *pay* -cash income-, is considered to be the primary determinant of the organizational trauma. The basic premise of this approach is that there is a general balance in the labor market because the majority of the blue collar workers in that industrial region are represented by the same labor union. Perceived unfairness led to the demonstrations and organizational trauma. The connection of blue collar workers to their employers is through their salary. This pay is determined by the capital value of their skills and productivity (Jovanovic, 1979). Research shows that the amount of income is negatively correlated to turnover intentions and turnover while being positively related to the intent to stay (Zenger, 1992). Despite these findings although the pay at the XYZ factory is not high the turnover rate is relatively low. The factory is a highly reputable workplace to work at for a regular blue collar worker. Therefore, the loyalty to the company among the employees is quite high. This could also be seen during the protests, the workers paid high attention to protect the factory facilities and they acted as if they were the owners of the workplace.

The average retention rate is relatively high 9-10 years at XYZ factory which also demonstrates that people's commitment and loyalty are high. Higher levels of organizational commitment might have mediated the effects of job stressors and trauma (Bakker, Demerouti, De Boer, & Schaufeli, 2003a; Bakker, Demerouti, & Schaufeli, 2003b; Glazer & Kruse, 2008). It has also been put forward that affective organizational commitment is a coping source in times of organizational stress and trauma (Schmidt & Diestel, 2012). Due to the high commitment and loyalty of the workers at the XYZ factory the workers did not resign even though they had experienced trauma. The high levels of commitment were also a positive factor for the workers coping with the trauma.

Job Insecurity, Emotional Exhaustion and Organizational Trauma

Job insecurity can be defined as anxieties about the continuity of one's future employment or the perceived threat of losing one's current job (Sverke, Hellgren, & Näswall, 2002). Dekker and Schaufeli (1995) found that job insecurity may cause emotional exhaustion and reduced well-being. Emotional exhaustion is a state of depletion and fatigue which is a component of burnout (Maslach & Jackson, 1981).

Literature shows a negative correlation between job insecurity and psychological health (Cheng & Chan, 2008; Sverke et al., 2002). As mentioned above some workers joined the protests and then went back their jobs before the demonstrations ended. They were highly anxious about losing their jobs. The trauma of this group of employees had two aspects. They perceived threat of losing the job and being discriminated by their friends because they did not continue to participate in the protests until the end. As a result, this group of workers experienced a more severe trauma than the other workers.

In crisis and trauma situations there are different approaches on how to intervene. In this project the intervention program was partially based on the Critical Incident Stress Debriefing (CISD) method. In the following section this approach will be briefly described.

Critical Incident Stress Debriefing (CISD)

The Critical Incident Stress Debriefing (CISD) model was developed by Mitchell and Everly (1995). It was developed especially for small, homogeneous groups who have encountered a significant traumatic event. It focuses on the reduction of distress and a restoration of morale, friendship and group cohesion. The CISD is a structured group story-telling model which aims to normalize participants' reactions to a critical incident and facilitate their recovery. It is recommended to be used in the aftermath of an important traumatic event that has generated strong reactions among a group of employees. In the group meetings, participants first introduce themselves then the moderator facilitates more emotionally intense exchanges regarding the trauma, and concludes with a psychoeducational component intended to increase the dialogue in the group. In the present project, the first five phases of the model were conducted and then the rest of the intervention program was designed based on the needs of the employees. As recommended in this model in each group two psychologists facilitated the program.

CISD is a seven phase small group trauma intervention process (Mitchell and Everly, 1996, pp.101-114). The used first five phases are explained as follows:

1. **Introduction:** In this phase the facilitators introduce themselves and describe the process. They give the instructions and rules for the conduct of CISD and encourage the participants to engage actively in the process. One of the essential rules is that every single participant has the right to express his/her feelings, thoughts and experiences without being judged and interrupted. The facilitators intervene in any case of inconvenient interruption and disrespectful behavior.
2. **Fact:** In this phase the participants begin to talk. It is important for the participants to know each other before sharing how the events impacted them because it is easier to speak of what happened to people you know. The important thing at this stage for the facilitator is to give the participants an opportunity to express themselves. Each participant is given a chance to speak and share their thoughts and experiences. The facilitator supports in lowering the anxiety and lets the group know that they have control of the discussion. The usual question used to start the fact phase is "Can you give a brief overview of what happened in the situation from your point of view? We are going to give everybody an opportunity to speak if they wish. If you do not wish to say anything you can remain silent and we will continue with the next person."
3. **Thoughts:** This is the transition stage from the cognitive to the affective domain. It is always easier to speak about one's thoughts than to focus on the emotional and more painful aspects of the event. The typical question addressed in this phase is "What was your first thought or your most prominent thought during the event? Everybody is given an opportunity to speak if they wish. Participants who do not want to say something, may remain silent.
4. **Reactions:** The reaction phase is the core of the Critical Incident Stress Debriefing. It focuses on the impact of the trauma on the participants. Anger, frustration, fear, disappointment, uncertainty, sadness, loss, confusion, and other emotions may emerge. The essential question in this phase is

"What was the most critical moment of this event for you personally?" The facilitators listen carefully and encourage participants to add something if they wish. When the group runs out of issues or concerns that they wish to Express, the team moves on to the discussion in the next phase, the symptoms phase, which will lead the group from the affective domain toward the cognitive domain.

5. **Symptoms:** In this phase the facilitators ask, "How has this tragic experience affected your life?" or "What cognitive, physical, emotional, or behavioral symptoms have you been dealing with since this event?" The team members listen carefully for common symptoms associated with exposure to traumatic events. The CISD facilitators use the signs and symptoms of trauma presented by the participants as a kicking off point for the teaching and reentry phases of the model.

METHOD

The Intervention Program

Participants

A total of 300 participants took part in the project. Main Production Team Leaders (MTL), Lean Team Leaders (LTL), Representative Union member workers, Alternative Union member workers and workers without membership to a union.

Pre-Intervention Stage

The focus group method was conducted at this stage of the project. A total of 90 workers participated in the focus groups and each group were made up of 15-20 workers. Depending on the categories of the workers, uniform groups were composed such as only Representative Union members, Alternative Union members, workers without union membership and superiors of workers. The meetings were held for two hours and two psychologists took notes and one psychologist facilitated the meetings. The main questions in these meetings were as follows:

What did they experience during the demonstrations and post-demonstration period?
What were the reasons behind the trauma?
What were their needs and expectations after the conflicts?

The Pilot Intervention

A one-day intervention program was developed based on the data collected from the focus group studies. The program was conducted in four groups of 10 workers each. The participants were selected by HR representatives and workers' immediate supervisors. Individuals who were showing symptoms of post-traumatic stress behavior were advised to participate in the program.

The program consisted of two parts. In the first part the workers were asked in groups of two to debrief what they had experienced and to what extent they had been affected by the events. After debrief each partner made a summary of the other partner's story to the whole group. The aim of the second part of the program was to enhance dialogue and cooperation between the workers. Core values like solidarity, friendship, loyalty to the workplace and its culture were emphasized.

Figure 1. Reasons of the organizational trauma

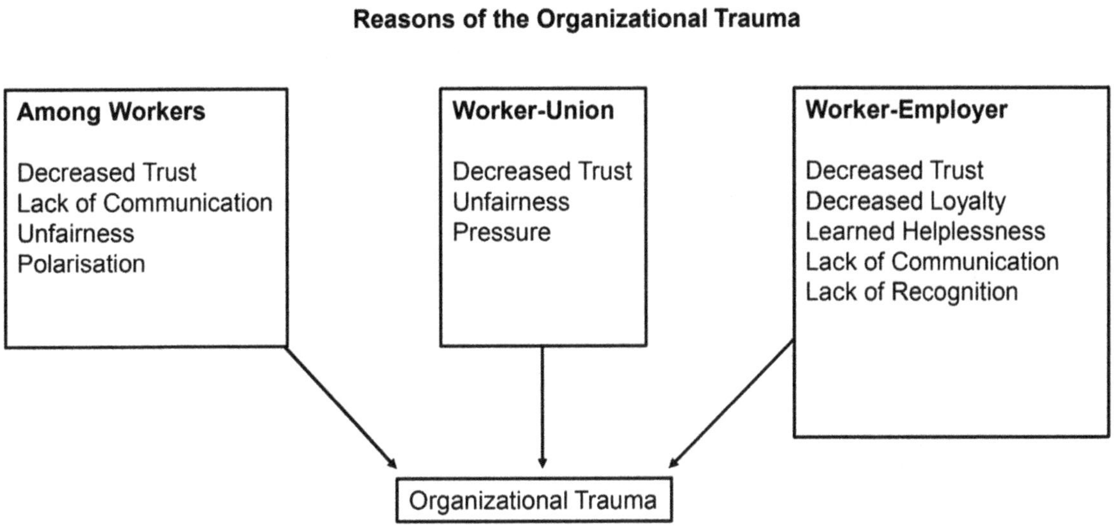

The Main Intervention

After the completion of the pre-intervention program and pilot implementation, the results were presented to the production managers, HR managers and the CEO. It was decided to continue and implement the program with slight modifications to a group of 200 workers. Based on the Conservation of Resources Theory (COR) the experts decided to ask the workers what made them motivated to stay in this workplace, despite all the negative experiences and grievances. In this main intervention, the groups were not uniform but mixed. Team leaders, workers with membership of different unions were put together with others with no union membership. This was done on purpose to reduce the polarization among the different groups of workers and to enhance communication. Bringing the different groups together allowed a better communication and exchange of ideas, a better understanding of each other's point of view.

Figure 1 shows and briefly summarizes the reasons of the trauma. The origin of the trauma was the union. (1) At the beginning workers reacted against the union in a democratic way, (2) then they reacted against the employer and (3) finally the restlessness emerged among workers.

DESCRIPTIVE FINDINGS

The following section presents the findings of the intervention program including positive and negative quotations and descriptions from workers.

Decrease in Trust

Research shows that co-worker trust has a positive impact on common support, conflict management and group unity (Erdem, 2003; Wang & Lu, 2012). In this case, the trust among co-workers seems to rely more on personal traits than other types of organizational relationships (Erdem & Ozen-Aytemur,

2014). The trust dynamic of co-worker relationships was damaged by the protests. People who discontinued the protest and went back to their jobs were discriminated by those who continued until the end of the demonstrations. When the production restarted workers were polarized although they work in the assembly line next to each other.

Below are some quotations from the participants related to trust.

We were working in the atelier. Some colleagues brought soft drinks. They drank the drinks and then one of them said throw away the rest instead of offering us some. They are angry with us because we stopped protesting and went back to work. They no longer trust us. (A worker who quit the protests)

I no longer trust the union because the representatives did not keep their promises. They signed a contract which did not include conditions that had been promised. (A worker without a union membership)

This movement was a workers' movement. It was not a movement of the unions. We did our best to keep it a workers' movement but some people who saw this as an opportunity to turn it into a union movement and they polarized people. (A worker without a union membership)

Commitment and Solidarity (to the Workplace and Among the Workers)

One group of workers stated in unison that they were ready to compensate the loss incurred during the protests by working day and night and that they were not expecting any extra payment.

I am sorry to say that I no longer feel as loyal as before and that my commitment is not as high as it used to be. However, if I get my fair pay I will still do my best. (The Alternative Union worker)

We are no longer a XYZ family. We are just a family of workers. (A worker without a union membership)

We who participated in the protests experienced real fraternity. People we did not know before shared their food with us, we remembered our shared values and felt that we were a family. (The Alternative Union worker)

Being in the Middle

The management pressured us (the team leaders) to persuade our subordinates to end the protests and go back to work. Some of our most trusted colleagues were angry with us and cursed us. Now we have to work together with them. Our relationship was ruined. (A senior MTL)

I was stuck between my family and co-workers. My family did not want me to participate in the protests while out of solidarity to my co-workers I felt obliged to participate. (An LTL)

The Need for Nurture and Compensation

[XYZ received a World Class Manufacturing Award in the previous years. It was marked by a yellow flag]. The yellow flag was received thanks to our efforts. The management says that we achieved this all

together so why don't we share the success all together? We love our job and workplace; we are proud of working here but the financial conditions challenge us. The factory is making a profit but this doesn't reflect on us. They say we are a family. If we are a family, they should nurture us. (The Representative Union worker)

The Need for Change and Learned Helplessness

All these things happen because the relationship between the workers and the employer has been weakened by the protests. When we voice our expectations the communication ends. Nobody listens to us. Nothing changes. I have lost my belief in change. (The Alternative Union worker)

A worker who has been working for three years at ABC receives a payment of 2200TL (760USD) a month while I who have been working here for nine years only get 1600TL (550USD) per month. If this situation is not solved I don't believe anything is going to change. (The Alternative Union worker)

Lessons Learned

Turkey and XYZ has to change. We are hopeful for the next contract period 2017. The greatest gain of the protests was to learn our legal rights. (A worker participated in the Main Intervention)

Expectation of Reciprocity and Empathy

We were expected to come up with a solution while we never felt that they (the union and the management) were making the same effort. (The Alternative Union worker)

How can they expect our motivation to increase without fair payment? It is impossible. If I were in the employer's position I would probably not wish to increase the payment. But I expect the employer show empathy to us as well. (The Alternative Union worker)

Polarization

Right now polarization is being provoked between those who participated in the protests and those who did not. This is not right. We are all humans and we all work for the same company. (A Worker without a union membership)

Injustice / Unfairness

They told us we did not deserve the compensation payment because we had not joined the protests. I could not touch the money for a whole month because I felt bad. I even wanted to give it back as it was not my rightful money. (A worker without a union membership)

If a question like did you join the protest or not is asked at career advancement interviews, then how can we talk about equality and justice? (The Representative Union worker)

Emotional vs. Rational Approaches

During the project one of the salient behaviors of workers was their negative affectivity. Constant complaining adversely affects resilience and motivation of people. It was observed that both the complaining party and people around lose their enthusiasm and show no energy.

However, there were also examples of rational and mature approaches.

We are all interdependent. I should perform at my best so that the person after me in the assembly line also can perform at his best and the job is completed with high quality.(The Representative Union worker)

During the intervention program I had the chance to speak with a man from the representative union who previously during the protests had publicized my name as one of the leaders of the protests. I think the other parties involved should be rational and focus on finding a solution. (Alternative Union Member Worker)

Reactions on the Representative Union

We are here to prevent similar traumas from occurring next year 2017. This is wrong. I am paying my union membership but what does the union do for me? The working conditions are not improved. The union representatives have to improve the conditions for everybody but they only work for themselves. (A worker with Alternative Union Membership)

I believe in rights and justice. Although I am a member of the Representative Union I don't see that they are taking any positive action on behalf of us. I think the union is pro employer. Still, I don't complain I am here to earn money there is no place for emotions.

I should not need to be friends with the union representatives to get my legal rights and services. It should be enough to pay the membership fee. (A Representative Union worker)

DISCUSSION

The intervention program regarding the organizational trauma will be discussed based on the theory of Conservation of Resources. COR is a theory of *stress* and *motivation*. It emphasizes occupational stress and strain. Hobfoll (1989) defined resources as "those objects, personal characteristics, conditions, or energies that are valued by the individual" (p. 516). According to the COR theory "individuals are seen as motivated to obtain, retain, foster and protect those things they value" (Westman, Hobfoll, Chen, Davidson and Laski, 2005, p. 168).

The theory has two principles:

1. **The Primacy of Resource Loss:** This principle states that given equal amounts of loss and gain, loss will have a greater impact.
2. **Resource Investment:** The second principle indicates that human beings have to invest resources in order to protect against resource loss, recover from loss, and gain resources.

These principles have three implications. The first two will be covered and discussed below as they are more relevant to this case.

Implication

Those with alternative resources are more resilient to resource loss and are more able to acquire resources. Those with limited resources are more vulnerable to resource loss less capable of resource gain. To exemplify, during the protests younger workers were more active than senior workers. Young workers are more vulnerable to resource loss based on the fact that they have relatively limited resources and they have a long time ahead of them to their retirement. Due to these reasons young workers are more reactive and sensitive and display significant signs of trauma.

Implication

Those with limited resources are not only more vulnerable to resource loss but initial resource loss can also be the basis of future losses. In this case, the starting point of the protests was the 2 TL difference per hour that the other factory workers were being paid. The younger workers might have believed that their future losses will be higher than just the 2 TL.

Psychological Resources of the Workers

At the end of the intervention program the workers were asked what motivated them to keep working at the factory in spite of all trauma experienced. In other words, what were the resources that encouraged them to stay?

Some of the named resources are listed below:

1. "We like our workplace."
2. "We have responsibilities towards our families."
3. "I like my profession."
4. "I still have hope for the next collective contract period 2017."
5. "I have faith in God. God will not make me suffer."
6. "If I quit here I have to start from scratch again."
7. "This is a professional company. I have compensation rights, social benefits, and long term gains. If I stay here I can leave after 15 years and buy my family a house with the money.

The intervention program made the workers aware of their resources. These resources play an important role in the retention of the workers. Although many were traumatized and felt burned out they remembered the positive aspects of working at the factory and this made them more engaged and willing to keep on working there.

Emotional Exhaustion and the Cultural Perspective

Wilson et al (2015) found that there is a significant relationship between conservation of resources and emotional exhaustion among blue collar workers. The intervention program started in July 2015 and was completed in November 2015. During this period one of the salient behavior of workers was grievance. They were complaining about their working conditions and their pay. On top of this, the trauma changed the working climate adversely. The workers were in a state of constant complaint which lowered motivation and concentration. Emotional exhaustion and low psychological well-being might lead to a decrease in motivation and concentration problems. When this occurs, according to the COR theory, employees might seek to protect resources through putting less effort into their work which is lower motivation (Wright & Cropanzano, 1998).

Beside the COR theory the impact of the trauma can be discussed through a cultural perspective. Societies are categorized as hierarchical versus egalitarian. One of the cultural dimensions of Hofstede is Power Distance. Power Distance is defined as the extent to which the less powerful members of organizations and institutions (like the family) accept and expect that power is distributed unequally (Hofstede 2011, p 9). High power distance countries such as Turkey are hierarchical. In hierarchical societies, individuals believe that resources, rights, and roles should be distributed based on differences in status, i.e. giving a larger office to a manager. These individuals strictly adhere to stratified role differentiation and devote their efforts to maintaining it because it supports their own perceived values and interests. Thus conformity is expected even in cases of inequity. This might explain the starting point of the conflicts. The Representative Union signed off a higher wage to the ABC factory workers in the assumption that this would be accepted by the other factory workers. The Union thought that the workers at the other factories would conform and not protest the inequity, as inequities are a widespread phenomenon in the Turkish work life. The reaction of the workers was in other words unexpected.

Masculinity versus *Femininity*, is another cultural dimension defined by Hofstede (1980). It is a societal, not an individual characteristic and refers to the distribution of values between the genders. According to Hofstede, societies can be grouped as assertive-competitive (masculine) and modest-caring (feminine) in the masculinity-femininity continuum (Hofstede, 2011). It was found that Turkey is described as high in femininity and low in masculinity (Hofstede, 1980). This means that men and women should be modest and caring. There is strong sympathy and support for the weak. In other words, the reactions of people in Turkey are generally more emotional and caring. The workers expected a supporting attitude both from the union and the employer. The inclination to act based on emotions might have made the workers more sensitive to the impact of the trauma as at XYZ the workplace friendship and solidarity among workers was negatively affected (Trompenaars, Hampden-Turner, 2012).

CONCLUSION AND PRACTICAL IMPLICATIONS

This chapter describes the events that took place between May and November 2015 at XYZ factory in Bursa, Turkey. The signing of a labor union agreement including a higher hourly wage at ABC factory led to a series of unexpected events. The collective labor agreement at XYZ and another factory had been signed off 2 TL lower just six months before the agreement was signed with ABC. This discrepancy in pay led to an uproar among the workers. Protests and demonstrations took place. Although production was continued after a halt of nine days the protests and demonstrations had created a trauma which affected the workers' morale.

The intervention program gave the workers the possibility to voice their traumatic experiences and demands and also face colleagues whom they no longer trusted. An effort was made to heal the collective trauma. Communication channels were reestablished, a positive psychological work climate was instilled and values like solidarity and friendship were emphasized. The upper management at XYZ initiated a psychological counselling program for the affected workers. Every worker who wishes to get individual psychological support has the right to six sessions of paid therapy. Some workers who have finished their first six sessions are continuing by their own means.

The Human Resources department has reported some positive feedback about the implications of the intervention program. Workers have enhanced the dialogue and slightly reduced the polarization. Although working conditions are still the same the morale and friendship are revived.

At the end of the project the HR department was advised to take the actions listed below.

- Giving the workers training and support on living and learning with stress and burnout
- Facilitate awareness of the symptoms of post-traumatic stress disorder
- Support and invest in social activities
- Continue in developing coaching and mentoring skills of MTL and LTLs' regarding trauma and its impacts.
- Leadership models that emphasize Turkish cultural norms and values such as paternalistic leadership (Aycan, 2006) and Nurturant-Task Leadership (Sinha, 1980; 1995) were recommended to be implemented during the training and development of MTL's and LTL's.
- The MTL and LTL's should act as role models in managing stress and burn-out. They should on one hand be paternalistic and nurturant and on the other hand be professional and disciplined.

In conclusion, people's deference and conformity is a common attitude in Turkey. However, equity is an essential phenomenon in work-life. Each party in this event (the employees, employer and the union) had new insights. Especially the new generation of workers are aware of their rights regarding International Labor Organization contracts. They are sensitive and alert to any inequities and expect fair pay. They cannot be expected to conform with unfair conditions like the elder generations did. The Unions have to be more careful when signing contracts in the future. They have to preserve the rights of all workers in an equal way. Unfair contracts can disrupt the balance of the whole industry. It may lead to both financial loss and trauma for all stakeholders and damage the trust in unions. The employer has to realize that blue collar workers are one of the most important assets. These groups have to be trained and their psychological well-being has to be maintained. Further investments should be done to prevent events like this from happening in the future.

REFERENCES

Adams, J. S. (1965). Inequity in social exchange. *Advances in Experimental Social Psychology*, *2*, 267–299. doi:10.1016/S0065-2601(08)60108-2

Aycan, Z. (2006). Paternalism: Towards Conceptual refinement and operationalization. In K. S. Yang, K. K. Hwang, & U. Kim (Eds.), *Scientific Advances in Indigenous Psychologies: Empirical, Philosophical, and Cultural Contributions* (pp. 445–466). London: Cambridge University Press. doi:10.1007/0-387-28662-4_20

Bakker, A., Demerouti, E., & Schaufeli, W. (2003b). Dual processes at work in a call center: An application of the job demands–resources model. *European Journal of Work and Organizational Psychology*, *12*(4), 393–417. doi:10.1080/13594320344000165

Bakker, A. B., Demerouti, E., De Boer, E., & Schaufeli, W. B. (2003a). Job demands and job resources as predictors of absence duration and frequency. *Journal of Vocational Behavior*, *62*(2), 341–356. doi:10.1016/S0001-8791(02)00030-1

Cheng, G. H. L., & Chan, D. K. S. (2008). Who suffers more from job insecurity? A meta-analytic review. *Applied Psychology*, *57*(2), 272–303. doi:10.1111/j.1464-0597.2007.00312.x

Dekker, S., & Schaufeli, W. (1995). The effects of job insecurity on psychological health and withdrawal: A longitudinal study. *Australian Psychologist*, *30*(1), 57–63. doi:10.1080/00050069508259607

Erdem, F. (2003). Optimal trust and teamwork: From groupthink to team think. *Work Study*, *52*(5), 229–233. doi:10.1108/00438020310485958

Erdem, F., & Özen-Aytemur, J. (2014). Context-specific dimensions of trust in manager, subordinate and co-worker in organizations. *Journal of Arts and Humanities*, *3*(10), 28–40.

Glazer, S., & Kruse, B. (2008). The role of organizational commitment in occupational Stress models. *International Journal of Stress Management*, *15*(4), 329–344. doi:10.1037/a0013135

Grandey, A. A. (2003). When the show must go on: Surface acting and deep acting as determinants of emotional exhaustion and peer-rated service delivery. *Academy of Management Journal*, *46*(1), 86–96. doi:10.2307/30040678

Hobfoll, S. E. (1989). Conservation of resources: A new attempt at conceptualizing stress. *The American Psychologist*, *44*(3), 513–524. doi:10.1037/0003-066X.44.3.513 PMID:2648906

Hofstede, G. (1980). *Culture's consequences: International differences in work-related values*. Beverly Hills, CA: Sage Publications.

Hofstede, G. (2011). Dimensionalizing Cultures: The Hofstede Model in Context. *Online Readings in Psychology and Culture*, *2*(1), 1–26. doi:10.9707/2307-0919.1014

Jovanovic, B. (1979). Job matching and the theory of turnover. *Journal of Political Economy*, *87*(5), 972–990. doi:10.1086/260808

Maslach, C., & Jackson, S. E. (1981). The measurement of experienced burnout. *Journal of Organizational Behavior*, *2*(2), 99–113. doi:10.1002/job.4030020205

Mitchell, J. T., & Everly, G. S. Jr. (1995). Critical incident stress debriefing (CISD) and the prevention of work-related traumatic stress among high risk occupational groups. In G. S. Everly Jr & J. M. Lating (Eds.), *Psychotraumatology* (pp. 267–280). New York: Plenum Press. doi:10.1007/978-1-4899-1034-9_16

Mitchell, J. T., & Everly, G. S. (1996). *Critical incident stress debriefing: An operations Manual* (2nd ed.). Ellicott City, MD: Chevron.

Schmidt, K. H., & Diestel, S. (2012). The relation of self-control demands to job strain: The moderating role of organizational commitment. *Applied Psychology, 61*(3), 479–497. doi:10.1111/j.1464-0597.2011.00479.x

Sinha, J. B. P. (1980). *The nurturant task leader*. New Delhi: Concept.

Sinha, J. B. P. (1995). *The cultural context of leadership and power*. New Delhi: Sage Publications.

Sverke, M., Hellgren, J., & Näswall, K. (2002). No security: A meta-analysis and review of job insecurity and its consequences. *Journal of Occupational Health Psychology, 7*(3), 242–264. doi:10.1037/1076-8998.7.3.242 PMID:12148956

Trompenaars, F., & Hampden-Turner, C. (2012). *Riding the waves of culture*. New York: McGraw-Hill.

Wang, H., & Lu, Y. (2012). Trust governance based on active interpersonal strategy. *Nankai Business Review International, 3*(2), 128–144. doi:10.1108/20408741211244361

Wilson, R. A., Perry, S. J., Witt, L. A., & Griffeth, R. W. (2015). The exhausted short-timer: Leveraging autonomy to engage in production deviance. *Human Relations, 68*(11), 1693–1711. doi:10.1177/0018726714565703

Wright, T. A., & Cropanzano, R. (1998). Emotional exhaustion as a predictor of job performance and voluntary turnover. *The Journal of Applied Psychology, 83*(3), 486–493. doi:10.1037/0021-9010.83.3.486 PMID:9648526

Zenger, T. R. (1992). Why do employers only reward extreme performance? Examining the relationships among performance, pay, and turnover. *Administrative Science Quarterly, 37*(2), 198–219. doi:10.2307/2393221

KEY TERMS AND DEFINITIONS

Collective Labor Agreement: The collective labor agreements represent a central regulatory instrument in the relationship between employer and employee, and unions represent the employees. Such agreements should rest to a large extent on the norms that form the basis of the countries' labor laws.

Co-Worker Trust: A positive attitude on common support and conflict management. Showing solidarity and trustworthiness to co-workers.

Emotional Exhaustion: A psychological state of depletion and fatigue.

Equity: A worker perceives that the proportion of his inputs to outcomes and the proportion of other's inputs to outcomes are equal.

Job Insecurity: Anxieties about the continuity of one's future employment.

Organizational Loyalty: Identification with the organization, protecting the organization's reputation, image and even facilities as a whole.

Organizational Trauma: A major crisis that occurs at the workplace and affects the psychological health of employees adversely.

Polarization: The sharp division of a work group into opposing parts.

Psychological Resources: Being optimistic and having the ability to find meaning in one's life.

Section 5

Healing

Chapter 12
Foundations and Future of Well-Being:
How Personality Influences Happiness and Well-Being

Vidya S. Athota
University of Notre Dame, Australia

ABSTRACT

This chapter begins by exploring subjective well-being and its origins dating back to ancient thinkers such as Aristotle. It discusses two main forms of subjective well-being; eudaimonic and hedonic well-being. The chapter then delves into the roles of personality, emotional intelligence, positive emotions, economics and religion in influencing subjective well-being. Measures of well-being are discussed as well as the notion of the Hedonic Treadmill and how it operates with the Set-point Theory of happiness. In addition, this chapter also presents the latest research from neuroscience and discusses how neuroscience potentially challenges personality and set-point theories. A few practical steps for subjective well-being are also discussed. Overall, this chapter covers the historical and contemporary theories of subjective well-being and explores a new positive direction on the association of personality, health and subjective well-being.

INTRODUCTION

The pursuit of happiness and wellbeing has recently gained attention among academics despite being a subject of inquiry since ancient times. Aristotle, in his book *Nicomachean Ethics*, spent a great deal discussing *eudaimonia*, which translates as 'happiness' or 'well-being'. The Aristotelian concept of eudaimonia has provided a mechanism for recent theories on wellbeing and positive psychology. The association between personality, health, and well-being has relationship with moral philosophy and positive psychology. Traditionally psychology has focused on the negative side of human behavior patterns. Whereas, recent theories on well-being argue for new ground, based on human strengths. Furthermore, the study of personality traits has provided further clarity to the mechanisms of wellbeing. In addition

DOI: 10.4018/978-1-5225-2021-4.ch012

to personality, this chapter also takes into account concepts from moral philosophy, neuroscience, and positive psychology in addressing wellbeing. Overall, the goal of this paper is to describe various approaches to wellbeing.

BACKGROUND

Subjective Well-Being

The concept of subjective well-being refers to an individual's evaluation of overall life satisfaction and feelings (Kesebir & Diener, 2008; Marks & Shah, 2005; Seiligman & Csikszentmihalyi, 2000). It includes positive and negative evaluation of cognitive, emotional, economic and social aspects of one's life. Interventions such as positive thinking, exercise, eating well and spirituality help to promote subjective well-being (Ryff, 2014). Life satisfaction (including pleasure and enjoyment), personal development (engagement in life, social cohesion, curiosity and resilience), and general social wellbeing (positive attitudes and belongingness in social activities) are important dimensions of subjective well-being (Marks & Shah, 2005). Well-being and happiness is also associated with success in various domains of life (Lyubomirsky, King, & Diener, 2005).

Origins of Research on Well-Being

The underpinnings of well-being are ancient and have existed since Aristotle's times. For Aristotle, the essential philosophical roots of *eudaimonia* (happiness) were not about feeling good or satisfying hedonistic appetites, but rather practicing and acting according with virtue, (i.e "activity of the soul in accord with virtue" (p.11) and exercising unique human potential (Ryff, 1989; 2014). Aristotle banded virtues such as courage, temperance, patience, friendliness, and honor that can lead to *eudaimonia*. Similarly, philosophers Socrates and Plato, were in tune with the good life as the result of practicing virtuous living. Aristotle was the disciple of Plato and Plato was the disciple of Socrates. Similar to Aristotle, Plato suggested that desire and doing good things leads to happiness (Plato, 1999). In addition to Aristotle's *eudaimonia*, ataraxia which is aimed at finding happiness within, existed among Greeks (Leahey, 2000). Similar to Aristotle, other Stoic philosophers endorsed happiness as the result of leading a virtuous life. The current notion of subjective well-being in positive psychology is slightly contrasted with Aristotle's *eudaimonia* despite its underpinnings of ancient views on happiness.

The research on subjective well-being in positive psychology has focused on the hedonic view of well-being. Yet the Aristotelian concept of *eudemonia* has been used by recent scholars on wellbeing (e.g. Seligman, 2002). The positive psychology notions of 'flourishing', 'wellbeing' and 'happiness' are also used in the Aristotelian view of *eudemonia*. Seligman has contributed to positive psychology through utilizing ideas from moral philosophy. Living well in terms of intellectually, and morally is associated with happiness (Spieker, 1999). A healthy life is acting virtually and employing excellence in physical and mental activities leading to sustainable happiness. Based on this tradition, practicing excellence in virtues leads to a state of well-being.

Peterson and Seligman (2005) proposed 24 signature strengths which are further grouped in 6 virtue clusters (Seligman, Steen, Perk & Peterson, 2005); they are, Wisdom and knowledge (creativity, curiosity, open-mindedness, love of learning, perspective and wisdom); Courage (Authenticity, Bravery,

Persistence, Vitality/Zest); Humanity (Kindness, love, social intelligence); Justice (Fairness, Leadership, Teamwork); Temperance (Forgiveness, Modesty, Prudence, Self-regulation); and Transcendence (Appreciation of beauty and excellence, Gratitude, Hope, Humor, Religiousness). Some of these signature strengths (e.g. Justice, Courage) are inspired by Aristotle's book Nicomachean Ethics and theological roots (e.g. Temperance and Transcendence). Overall, Aristotle's view of *eudemonia* is a subjective view and current theories are more accommodative of a prescriptive view of wellbeing and happiness (Kesebir & Diener, 2008). Both the subjective and prescriptive views are important based on their positive influence on human wellbeing.

The Influence of Moral Philosophy on Well-Being

It is evident that the current theories on well-being have integrated ancient Aristotle's *eudaimonia.* As Aristotle suggested that "living well and doing well "are important aspects of *eudaimonia* (happiness or wellbeing) (p. 3), Seligman (2011) similarly states, "if we want to flourish and if we want to have well-being, we must indeed minimize our misery; but in addition, we must have positive emotion, meaning, accomplishment, and positive relationships" (p.57).

Table 1 Classification of 6 virtues and 24 character strengths

Virtue and Strength	Definition
1. Wisdom and knowledge Creativity Curiosity Open-mindedness Love of learning Perspective 2. Courage Authenticity Bravery Persistence Zest 3. Humanity Kindness Love Social intelligence 4. Justice Fairness Leadership Teamwork 5. Temperance Forgiveness Modesty Prudence Self-regulation 6. Transcendence Appreciation of beauty and excellence Gratitude Hope Humor Religiousness	Cognitive strengths that entail the acquisition and use of knowledge Thinking of novel and productive ways to do things Taking an interest in all of ongoing experience Thinking things through and examining them from all sides Mastering new skills, topics, and bodies of knowledge Being able to provide wise counsel to others Emotional strengths that involve the exercise of will to accomplish goals in the face of opposition, external or internal Speaking the truth and presenting oneself in a genuine way *Not* shrinking from threat, challenge, difficulty, or pain Finishing what one starts Approaching life with excitement and energy Interpersonal strengths that involve "tending and befriending" others Doing favors and good deeds for others Valuing close relations with others Being aware of the motives and feelings of self and others Civic strengths that underlie healthy community life Treating all people, the same according to notions of fairness and justice Organizing group activities and seeing that they happen Working well as member of a group or team Strengths that protect against excess Forgiving those who have done wrong Letting one's accomplishments speak for themselves Being careful about one's choices; *not* saying or doing things that might later be regretted Regulating what one feels and does Strengths that forge connections to the larger universe and provide meaning Noticing and appreciating beauty, excellence, and/or skilled performance in all domains of life Being aware of and thankful for the good things that happen Expecting the best and working to achieve it Liking to laugh and tease; bringing smiles to other people Having coherent beliefs about the higher purpose and meaning of life

Source: Seligman, M. E. P., Steen, T. A., Park, N., & Peterson, C. (2005), Positive psychology progress: Empirical validation of interventions. *American Psychologist*, 60, 410-421. (p. 412)

Forms of Well-Being

As discussed above, there are two main forms of well-being; eudaimonic and hedonic well-being. Eudaimonism is based on Aristotle's view of virtues and Hedonic well-being refers to pleasure orientation. There is conceptual overlap between Aristotle's *eudaimonia* and current theories of psychological well-being. Philosophical theories of happiness provide underpinnings to recent positive psychology theories.

Ryff (2014) utilized philosophical, developmental and clinical psychology to put forth her concept of well-being that contains six key components; autonomy, environmental mastery, personal growth, positive relations with others, purpose in life, and self-acceptance. These components have their foundations Rogers, Maslow and Jung theories (See Figure 1). Ryff has tried to address the question "What constitutes essential features of well-being?" (p.11). Ryff has substituted Aristotle's virtues with dimensions of psychological well-being; purpose in life, autonomy, personal growth, environmental mastery, positive relationships, and self-acceptance. Life satisfaction was strongly associated with Environmental mastery and self-acceptance (Ryff, 1989). Ryff also integrated concepts from Aristotle' *eudaimonia*, mental health and life span development to propose positive psychological functioning.

Table 2 outlines definitions of Ryff 's (2014) model of psychological well-being that includes six key components; autonomy, environmental mastery, personal growth, positive relations with others, purpose in life, and self-acceptance.

Figure 1. Ryff's (2014) core dimensions of psychological well-being
Source: Ryff, C.D. (2014). Psychological Well-Being Revisited: Advances in the Science and Practice of Eudaimonia, Psychther Psychosom, 83, 10-28. (Page 11)

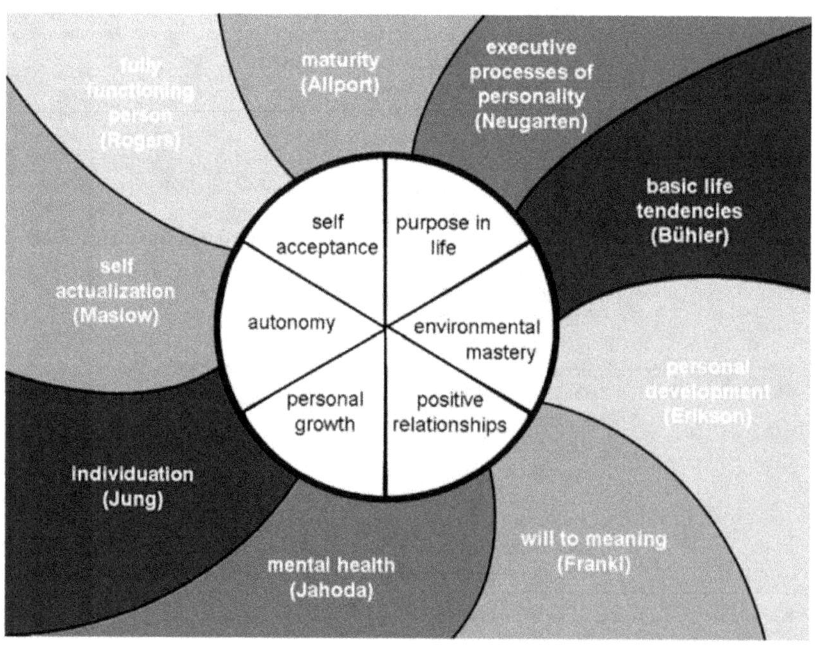

Table 2. Definitions of theory-guided dimensions of well-being

Autonomy High scorer: Is self-determining and independent; able to resist social pressures to think and act in certain ways; regulates behavior from within; evaluates self by personal standards.
Low scorer: Is concerned about the expectations and evaluations of others; relies on judgments of others to make important decisions; conforms to social pressures to think and act in certain ways.
Environmental mastery
High scorer: Has a sense of mastery and competence in managing the environment; controls complex array of external activities; makes effective use of surrounding opportunities; able to choose or create contexts suitable to personal needs and values.
Low scorer: Has difficulty managing everyday affairs; feels unable to change or improve surrounding context; is unaware of surrounding opportunities; lacks sense of control over external world.
Personal growth
High scorer: Has a feeling of continued development; sees self as growing and expanding; is open to new experiences; has sense of realizing his or her potential; sees improvement in self and behavior over time; is changing in ways that reflect more self-knowledge and effectiveness.
Low scorer: Has a sense of personal stagnation; lacks sense of improvement or expansion over time; feels bored and uninterested with life; feels unable to develop new attitudes or behaviors.
Positive relations with others
High scorer: Has warm, satisfying, trusting relationships with others; is concerned about the welfare of others; capable of strong empathy, affection and intimacy; understands give and take of human relationships.
Low scorer: Has few close, trusting relationships with others; finds it difficult to be warm, open, concerned about others; is isolated and frustrated in interpersonal relationships; not willing to make compromises to sustain important ties with others.
Self-acceptance
High scorer: Possesses a positive attitude toward the self; acknowledges and accepts multiple aspects of self, including good and bad qualities; feels positive about past life.
Low scorer: Feels dissatisfied with self; is disappointed with what has occurred in past life; is troubled about certain personal qualities; wishes to be different than what he or she is.

Source: Ryff, C.D. (2014). Psychological Well-Being Revisited: Advances in the Science and Practice of Eudaimonia, *Psychther Psychosom,* 83, 10-28. (Page 3)

Causes of Well-Being

Individual Differences

The study of psychological well-being has been an important aspect of personality and health psychology. Even though well-being was and has been the main area of interest for Aristotle and the study of positive psychology, empirical and longitudinal studies point out that personality provides effective scientific foundation to subjective well-being (Steel, Schmidt, & Shultz, 2008; Diener & Lucas, 1999). Diener and Lucas (1999) suggested that subjective well-being is the result of personality traits. There is a relationship between subjective well-being and personality traits (Steel, Schmidt, & Shultz, 2008). Personality plays a significant role in predicting subjective wellbeing (DeNeve & Cooper, 1998).

The Big Five personality traits known as Extraversion, Neuroticism, Agreeableness, Conscientiousness and Openness (see Table 3) have been linked to much research on well-being. Research suggests that individuals who score high on conscientiousness and low on neuroticism maintain health-promoting behaviors (Bogg & Roberts, 2004). Similarly, the same personality traits (high conscientiousness and

Table 3. The big five personality factors

Big Five Dimensions	Facet
Extraversion	Sociable, Assertiveness, Energetic, Outgoing, Activity, Excitement-seeking, Enthusiastic, Warmth
Agreeableness	Warm, Trusting, Altruism, Compliance Modesty, Tender-mindedness
Conscientiousness	Competence, Keep things in Order, Dutifulness, Achievement striving, Maintain Self-discipline, Deliberation
Neuroticism	Anxious, Irritable, Self-consciousness, Impulsiveness Vulnerability, Less-confident
Openness	Curious, Imaginative, Aesthetics, Wide interests, Unconventional

Source: John, O. P., & Srivastava, S. (1999). The Big-Five trait taxonomy: History, measurement, and theoretical perspectives. In L. A. Pervin & O. P. John (Eds.), *Handbook of personality: Theory and research* (Vol. 2, pp. 102–138). New York: Guilford Press.

low in neuroticism) predict healthy sleep patterns (Duggan, Friedman, McDevitt, & Mednick, 2004). Research also points to positive correlation between agreeableness and conscientiousness (DeNeve & Seligman, 2002; Lucas, 2008). Therefore, agreeableness and conscientiousness influence health behaviors.

Conscientious individuals by trait exhibit self-control, diligence, goal-oriented behavior, life satisfaction and positive health behaviors (Friedman, 2000; Israel & Moffitt, 2014). Therefore, individuals who score high on Conscientiousness are likely to live longer. Research also suggests that Extraversion is positively associated with subjective well-being and Neuroticism is negatively associated with subjective well-being (Lucas, 2008) and greater happiness (Cost & McCrae, 1980). All these associations point to personality playing a "substantial role" in predicting subjective wellbeing (Diener and Lucas, 1999). Individuals who score high on Extraversion positively respond to social interactions and Neurotic individuals intensely respond to negative experiences. Neuroticism has been associated with poor mental health such as depression (Enns aa& Cox, 1997) and increased mortality (Shipley, et.al. 2007). Generally, individuals with high Extraversion and Conscientiousness, low Neuroticism are associated with wellbeing (Ryff, Keyes & Shmotkin, 2002). Individuals with high conscientious report positive mental well-being due to their sense of confidence (Löckenhoff, Sutin et al., 2008). Life experience plays a pivotal role in providing stimuli for personality traits and influencing well-being (Larsen and Ketelaar, 1991). Based on the empirical evidence personality is a better predictor of long-term subjective well-being (Steel, Schmidt, & Shultz, 2008).

Type A and Type B Personality Factors

Individuals with Type A personality are defined as competitive, ambitious, impatience, aggressive, hostile and show physical tenseness; whereas individuals with Type B personality are defined as easy going, less hostile and relatively leading calm lives (Caracciolo & Molinari, 1986). Individuals with Type B personality maintain effective social support and lead reasonably relaxed lives. Therefore, Type B individuals have more well-being orientation compared to Type A personality individuals. Their "upright" and "laid back" nature has a direct influence on subjective wellbeing:

- **Emotional intelligence:** Emotional Intelligence can further shed light on the association of personality, health and well-being. Both from the trait and emotional perspective, emotional intelligence sheds further understanding of subjective well-being. The ability to understand, manage own emotions is an integral part of emotional intelligence (Mayer & Salovey, 1997; Salovey,

Mayer, & Caruso, 2002). Moral emotions have significant influence on wellbeing. They are the result of concern for conscious response to right and wrong (Kroll, Egan, Erickson, Carey, & Johnson 2004). Recently Athota and O'Connor (2014) established a moral component of emotional intelligence. According to Salovey and Mayer (1990), emotional competence is an ability to understand and control emotions, both in the self and in others. Responding to empathetic emotions avoids psychological conflict and positively influences experience of wellbeing. Goleman (1995) suggested that emotional control (expressing emotions at the right time to the right degree) is the bedrock of character, which has similarities to Aristotle's *eudaimonia* concept. Research also suggests that positive emotions play an important role and act as a buffer to deal with tough situations in life and promote subjective wellbeing (Kahneman & Krueger, 2006; Seligman, 2002). Responding to empathetic feelings also influences psychological wellbeing (Pizarro & Salovey, 2002). New paradigms for emotional intelligence are still evolving (MacCan & Roberts, 2008). Further empirical work is needed in specifically targeting subjective well-being;

- **Positive emotions:** The importance of flourishing through positive emotions and activities is encouraged (Fredrickson, 1998; Ryff, 2014; Seligman, 2011). Positive emotions have been associated with longevity (Danner, Snowdon, & Friesen, 2001). Positive emotions are directly associated with overall success and health (Lyubomirsky, King, & Diener, 2005). Health benefits include fewer colds (Cohen, Alper, Doyle, Treanor, & Turner, 2006), reduced risk of cardiovascular disease (Boehm & Kubzansky, 2012) and mortality (Chida & Steptoe, 2008). Positive emotions influence overall cognitive abilities, that help individuals to utilize their ideas effectively (Fredrickson, 1998) and increase personal resources like mindfulness, social support and decrease illness symptoms (Fredrickson, Cohn, Coffey, Pek, & Finkel, 2008). Positive emotions have the ability to influence the cognitive aspect and biochemistry of individuals. Therefore, induced positive memories can also have a potential positive effect on health;
- **Religiosity:** According to Divine Command Theory, happiness is achieved through divine laws and morals given in sacred texts. The philosophical foundations of this theory have conceptual overlap with Aristotle's concept of *eudaimonia.* Professor Andrew Clark and Dr. Orsolya Lelkes in their longitudinal study in 2005 found that religious people maintain higher wellbeing. Specific activities such as church going and prayer provide a buffer against stressful events of life and leave a positive impact on life quality. Individuals with intrinsically motivated religious beliefs like Mother Theresa, operate with empathy. Research suggests that empathy helps to understand the needs of others and promotes positive social interaction (Eisenberg, Shea, Carlo, & Knight, 1991; Haidt, 2006; Pizzaro, 2000). Furthermore, the Sermon on the Mount by Jesus of Nazareth makes an association between virtues of humility, compassion and happiness (Matthew 5, New International Version). Research also points to moral emotions resolves emotional conflict and facilitates altruistic behavior (Kroll, Egan, Erickson, Carey, & Johnson 2004). Belief in positive religious teaching helps in dealing with existential crisis as well as terror management. Overall, subjective well-being is enhanced through participation of religious practices and prayers (Diener et al. 1999).

Measures of Well-Being

Despite the popularity of the concept of subjective well-being, evidence points to measures of subjective well-being in its early stage. One of the main reasons is that well-being is a multidimensional concept and there are potential challenges in measuring well-being. The existing research has relied on self-report scales. Well-being is generally associated with life satisfaction, using the Life Satisfaction Index. (Neugarten, Havigburst, & Tobin,1961); Fordyce Emotions Questionnaire (Fordyce, 1988); and Subjective Happiness Scale (Lyubomirsky & Lepper, 1999). The Ryff Scales of Psychological wellbeing (Ryff & Keyes, 1995) utilized theory-guided dimensions of well-being to measure self-acceptance, positive relations with others, autonomy, environmental mastery, personal life and personal growth. Despite a few available scales, the qualities of self-reports also need to be improved (Kahneman and Krueger 2006; Schwarz and Strack 1999). A battery of advanced longitudinal and experimental measures are needed to measure experiences, biological traits, and cognitive abilities. Caution must be exercised in measuring wellbeing as Daniel Kohonmen indicates that there are different ways of achieving well-being. Some caution must be exercised in measuring well-being.

Hedonic Treadmill: Heritability and Well-Being

Research suggests that genetics plays an important role in wellbeing. Over all our hedonic methods make individuals happy to an extent. Genetics factors have been found to play role in subjective wellbeing. Research conducted among fraternal twins at University of Minnesota found that genetics play an important role in the experience of happiness. Lykken and Tellegen (1996), in their 10-year longitudinal twin study found that genetic factors generally influence 44 -52% of subjective well-being. Approximately 10% of well-being is due to life circumstances and 40% of well-being is due to general attitude influence subjective well-being. Recent research also points out that 80% of wellbeing is the result of genes (Nes, Roysamb, Tambs, Harris, and Reichborn-Kjennerud, 2006). Therefore, long-term well-being is the result of internal characteristics (Steel, Schmidt, & Shultz, 2008).

The notion of the Hedonic Treadmill operates with the Set-point Theory of happiness. According to this theory, individuals have fixed or average range happiness and well-being in response to their experiences. Brickman and Campbell (1971) suggested that an individual's state of happiness depends on inbuilt psychological mechanisms. Despite positive and negative experiences and circumstances, adaptation occurs quickly, and people can get back to their original state of nature within two months (Suh, Diener, & Fujita, 1996). Brickman and Campbell described this a *hedonic treadmill*. Research also suggests that lottery winners and accident victims are not going to be forever happy or sad (Brickman, Coates, & Jahoff-Bulman, 1978). The definition by David Myers (1992) provides further clarification, "The point can- not be overstated: *Every* desirable experience—passionate love, a spiritual high, the pleasure of a new possession, the exhilaration of success—is transitory" (p. 53). Earlier personality theories also supported this notion of a set point (Costa and McCrea, 1980).

Challenge to Traditional Set-Point Theory of Happiness

The Set-point theory was challenged by Easterlin (2005). Easterlin (2005) suggested that some tough experiences are life changing and leave permanent scars. Recent development in the theories of personality also suggests that personality can change, this points to some kind of hope for misery (Davidson & Lutz, 2008; Lutz, Slagter, Dunne, & Davidson, 2008). Hope can play a pivotal role in promoting psychological well-being (Valle, Huebner, & Suldo, 2006). The Hedonic Treadmill concept still complements personality theory despite of recent research development. Recent development in neuroscience has the potential to pause a challenge to the influence of traditional personality and set-point theory on subjective well-being.

Brain science explains that human experiences significantly influence neural activity in the brain (Ramachandran & Oberman, 2006). There are 100 billion neurons in the human brain. Each neuron makes 1000 to 10,000 contacts with other neurons in the brain. Vence, Roberson, McGuinnies, and Fazel, (2010) suggest, "the process by which the brain and nervous system produce morphological and structural changes in the brain in response to environmental stimuli" p. 29). Positive feelings are the result of brain activity in the left side of the pre-frontal cortex and negative feelings are due to the brain activity in the right side of the brain. Compassionate meditative experiences significantly influence changes in brain activity due to increased activity in left pre-frontal cortex (Lutz, Slagter, Dunne, & Davidson, 2008). Therefore our positive and negative experiences, emotions and actions immensely influence neurons in our brain (Davidson & Lutz, 2008). Professor Richard Davidson from the University of Wisconsin-Madison, a leading neuroscientist, suggests that changes in the brain are possible through training the mind. These recent neuroscience findings may challenge traditional set-point theory and provide further hope for increased wellbeing or happiness.

Well-Being through Meaning

Victor Frankl, in his book, *Man's search for meaning*, suggested that a will to meaning is the key to leading a satisfied life. Frankl invented *Logotherapy,* which means "therapy through meaning'. Frankl's personal experience in a concentration camp gives him an authentic position to comment on human misery. Helping suffering people was the primary source of Frankl's motivation to find meaning in life. Meaning does not come easily but a deeper understanding of the human condition and creating hope through helping creates meaning. Instead of focusing on psychological afflictions, meaning can be found by focusing on the positive side of human strengths. One's ultimate meaning of life is unique to one's own life and situation. Therefore, meaning cannot be invented but must be discovered according one's own values.

Economics and Well-Being

The concept of subjective wellbeing has also become a subject of interest for economists, sociologists and policy makers in order to improve quality of life. Subjective wellbeing of individuals is valuable at an individual level as well as societal level (Diener & Seligman, 2004). Research has established the association between happiness and income (Diener and Suh, 1997; Kahneman and Krueger, 2006; Rojas, 2007; Zhou, 2012). The influence of income on people's feelings and behavior is complex. The extent of individual's happiness to income is limited, both positive and negative experiences of wealth eventually fade with time (Diener, Lucas, & Scollon, 2006). Kahneman and Deaton (2010) examined whether money influences happiness and wellbeing among 1,000 US residents. An annual income of up to $75,000 influenced health, emotional well-being and subjective well-being. It was concluded that wealth is associated with satisfaction but happiness is not guaranteed. Low income negatively influenced emotional well-being and subjective well-being (Kahneman and Deaton, 2010).

Figure 2. High income improves evaluation of life but not emotional well-being (Kahneman and Deaton, 2010)

Note: Positive affect, blue affect, stress, and life evaluation in relation to household income (Kahneman & Deaton, 2010)

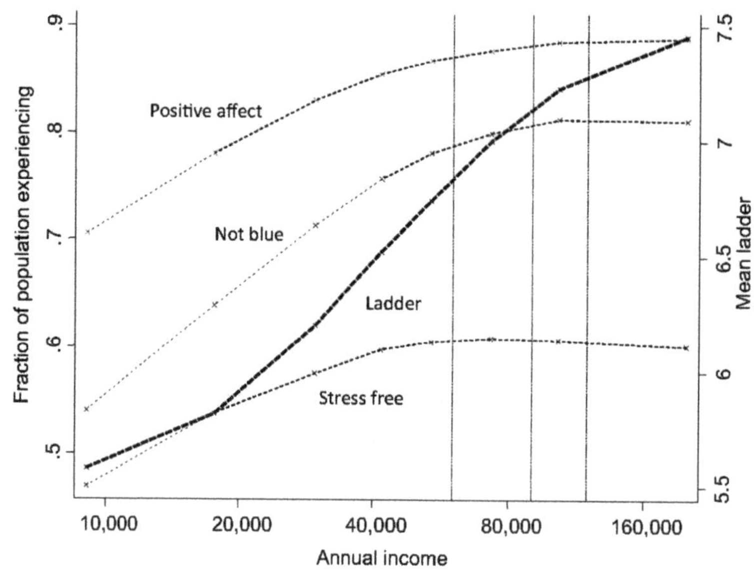

Practical Tools for Health and Well-Being

According to World Health Organization (1946), Health and well-being is holistic, where complete achievement is of physical, mental and social well-being. Despite personality and genetic explanations for well-being, some practical tools can be employed to enhance well-being. Research suggests that positive health habits can be very beneficial in influencing subjective well-being.

Positive habits such as healthy nutrition, physical exercise, social relationships and resting well are important to enhancing well-being. Healthy nutrition involves a diet that consists of 45% to 65% carbohydrates, 20% to 35% healthy fats, 10% to 35% protein. Physical exercise that involves walking, aerobic exercise and swimming can also be very useful. Strong social relationships also play an important role in enhancing well-being. Furthermore, it is also important to have enough rest and holidays to rejuvenate health and wellbeing.

Using Technology to Your Advantage

In the age of technology, where facebook, emails, apps…etc. constantly demand our attention, it is important to use them positively and set up healthy boundaries in order to protect our health and well-being. Research suggests that individuals who score high on Extraversion and Neuroticism are likely to practice excessive internet usage (Widyanto & McMurran 2004; Wolfradt & Doll 2001).

Recent devices such as a wrist step count like Fitbit can help to track physical activity and sleep habits. There may be some health benefits in using technology like this.

In her book, *The How of Happiness: A New Approach to Getting the Life You Want,* Sonja Lyubomirsky (2007) suggested 12 activities to enhance happiness "express gratitude, cultivate optimism,

Figure 3. Utilizing Fitbit to track physical activity
Source: http://help.fitbit.com

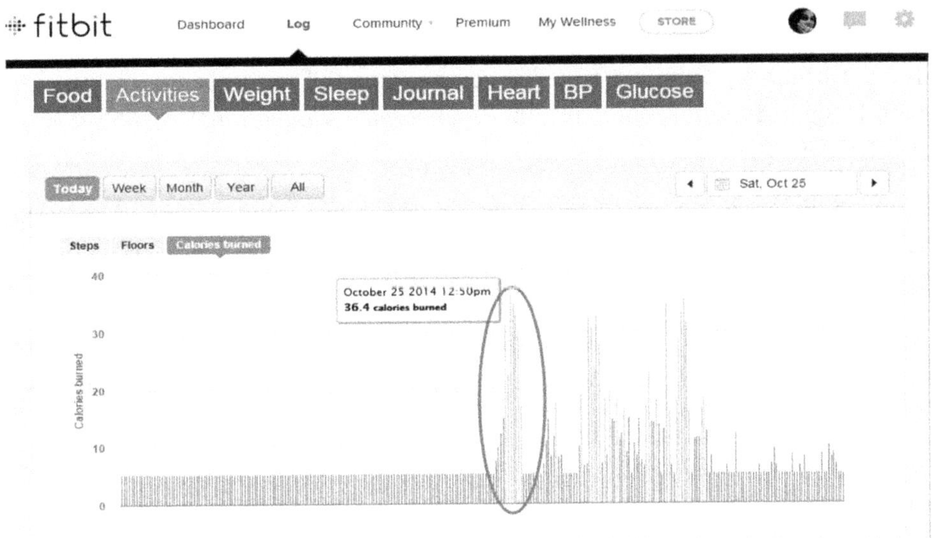

avoid overthinking and social comparison, practicing acts of kindness, nurturing social relationships, developing strategies for coping, learning to forgive, increasing flow experiences, savoring life's joys, committing to your goals, practicing religion and spirituality, and taking care of your body." (p. 2-3). These can help as a proactive measure to protect health and well-being. Purposeful engagement of various activities that promote growth and self-realization assist in living healthy lives (Ryff, 2014). Further advances in well-being research ought to be done on how personality can be changed, and in the influence of change on health and well-being. Each of us is different with our unique values and manual for health and wellbeing. Further empirical research is required on the role of values in health and wellbeing.

CONCLUSION

In this chapter we have reviewed the association between personality, health, and well-being as well as the foundational conceptual links with ancient philosophy and positive psychology. The ancient concept of happiness from Aristotle's *eudaimonia* and current theories of positive psychology provide mechanisms for wellbeing. Ancient and modern views of happiness and subjective well-being contrast yet conceptually overlap in their applications. It was found that certain personality traits are effective predictors of subjective well-being. Personality theories have further provided a set-point theory of happiness and well-being. The new developments in neuroscience is challenging the set-point nature of well-being.

REFERENCES

Aristotle, . (1925). *The Nicomachean ethics* (D. Ross, Trans.). New York: Oxford University Press.

Aristotle, . (1984). *The Complete Works of Aristotle*. Princeton, NJ: Princeton University Press.

Athota, V. S., & OConnor, P. J. (2014). How approach and avoidance constructs of personality and trait emotional intelligence predict core human values. *Learning and Individual Differences*, *31*, 51–58. doi:10.1016/j.lindif.2013.12.009

Boehm, J. K., & Kubzansky, L. D. (2012). The hearts content: The association between positive psychological well-being and cardiovascular health. *Psychological Bulletin*, *138*(4), 655–691. doi:10.1037/a0027448 PMID:22506752

Bogg, T., & Roberts, B. W. (2004). Conscientiousness and health-related behaviors: A meta-analysis of the leading behavioral contributors to mortality. *Psychological Bulletin*, *130*(6), 887–919. doi:10.1037/0033-2909.130.6.887 PMID:15535742

Brickman, P., & Campbell, D. T. (1971). Hedonic relativism and planning the good society. In M. H. Appley (Ed.), *Adaptation level theory: A symposium* (pp. 287–302). New York: Academic Press.

Brickman, P., Coates, D., & Jahoff-Bulman, R. (1978). Lottery winners and victims: Is happiness relative? *Journal of Personality and Social Psychology*, *36*(8), 917–927. doi:10.1037/0022-3514.36.8.917 PMID:690806

Caracciolo, S., & Molinari, S. (1986). Convergent validity of Self- Reported Type A Behavior Pattern of Patients with Coronary Artery Disease. *Psychological Reports*.

Chida, Y., & Steptoe, A. (2008). Positive psychological well- being and mortality: A quantitative review of prospective observational studies. *Psychosomatic Medicine*, *70*(7), 741–756. doi:10.1097/PSY.0b013e31818105ba PMID:18725425

Clark, A., & Lelkes, O. (2005). *Deliver us from Evil: Religion as Insurance*. Paris: PSE.

Cohen, S., Alper, C. M., Doyle, W. J., Treanor, J. J., & Turner, R. B. (2006). Positive emotional style predicts resistance to illness after experimental exposure to rhinovirus or Influenza A virus. *Psychosomatic Medicine*, *68*(6), 809–815. doi:10.1097/01.psy.0000245867.92364.3c PMID:17101814

Costa, P. T. Jr, & McCrae, R. R. (1980). Influence of extra- version and neuroticism on subjective well-being: Happy and unhappy people. *Journal of Personality and Social Psychology*, *38*(4), 668–678. doi:10.1037/0022-3514.38.4.668 PMID:7381680

Danner, D. D., Snowdon, D. A., & Friesen, W. V. (2001). Positive emotions in early life and longevity: Findings from the nun study. *Journal of Personality and Social Psychology*, *80*(5), 804–813. doi:10.1037/0022-3514.80.5.804 PMID:11374751

Davidson, R. J., & Lutz, A. (2008). Buddhas brain: Neuroplasticity and meditation. *Signal Processing Magazine*, *25*(1), 176–174. doi:10.1109/MSP.2008.4431873 PMID:20871742

DeNeve, K. M., & Cooper, H. (1998). The happy personality: A metaanalysis of 137 personality traits and subjective well-being. *Psychological Bulletin*, *124*(2), 197–229. doi:10.1037/0033-2909.124.2.197 PMID:9747186

Diener, E., Lucas, R. E., & Scollon, C. N. (2006). Beyond the hedonic treadmill: Revising the adaptation theory of well-being. *The American Psychologist*, *61*(4), 305–314. doi:10.1037/0003-066X.61.4.305 PMID:16719675

Diener, E., & Lucas, R. R. (1999). Personality and subjective well-being. In E. Kahneman, E. Diener, & N. Schwarz (Eds.), *Well-being: The foundations of hedonic psychology* (pp. 213–229). New York: Russell Sage Foundation.

Diener, E., & Seligman, M. E. P. (2002). Very happy people. *Psychological Science, 13*(1), 81–84. doi:10.1111/1467-9280.00415 PMID:11894851

Diener, E., & Seligman, M. E. P. (2004). Beyond money: Toward an economy of well-being. *Psychological Science in the Public Interest, 5*(1), 1–31. doi:10.1111/j.0963-7214.2004.00501001.x PMID:26158992

Diener, E., & Suh, E. (1997). Measuring quality of life: Economic, social and subjective indicators. *Social Indicators Research, 40*(1/2), 189–216. doi:10.1023/A:1006859511756

Diener, E., Suh, E. M., Lucas, R. E., & Smith, H. L. (1999). Subjective well-being: Three decades of progress. *Psychological Bulletin, 125*(2), 276–302. doi:10.1037/0033-2909.125.2.276

Duggan, A. K., Friedman, S. H., McDevitt, D. E., & Mednick, C. S. (2004). Personality and Healthy Sleep: The Importance of Conscientiousness and Neuroticism. *PLoS ONE, 9*, 1–11. PMID:24651274

Enns, M. W., & Cox, B. J. (1997). Personality dimensions and depression: Review and commentary. *Canadian Journal of Psychiatry, 42*(3), 274–284. PMID:9114943

Fordyce, M. W. (1988). A review of research on the Happiness Measures: A sixty second index of happiness and mental health. *Social Indicators Research, 20*(4), 355–381. doi:10.1007/BF00302333

Fredrickson, B. L. (1998). What good are positive emotions? *Review of General Psychology, 2*(3), 300–319. doi:10.1037/1089-2680.2.3.300 PMID:21850154

Fredrickson, B. L., Cohn, A. M., Coffey, A. K., Pek, J., & Finkel, M. S. (2008). Open Hearts Build Lives: Positive Emotions, Induced Through Loving-Kindness Meditation, Build Consequential Personal Resources. *Journal of Personality and Social Psychology, 5*(5), 1045–1062. doi:10.1037/a0013262 PMID:18954193

Friedman, H. S. (2000). Long-term relations of personality and health: Dynamisms, mechanisms, tropisms. *Journal of Personality, 68*(6), 1089–1107. doi:10.1111/1467-6494.00127 PMID:11130733

Israel, S., & Moffitt, E. T. (2014). Assessing Conscientious Personality in Primary Care: An Opportunity for Prevention and Health Promotion. *Developmental Psychology, 50*(5), 1475–1477. doi:10.1037/a0036113 PMID:24773110

John, O. P., & Srivastava, S. (1999). The Big-Five trait taxonomy: History, measurement, and theoretical perspectives. In L. A. Pervin & O. P. John (Eds.), *Handbook of personality: Theory and research* (Vol. 2, pp. 102–138). New York: Guilford Press.

Kahneman, D., & Deaton, A. (2010). High income improves evaluation of life but not emotional well-being. *Proceedings of the National Academy of Sciences of the United States of America, 107*(38), 16489–16493. doi:10.1073/pnas.1011492107 PMID:20823223

Kahneman, D., & Krueger, A. (2006). Developments in the measurement of subjective well-being. *The Journal of Economic Perspectives, 20*(1), 3–24. doi:10.1257/089533006776526030

Kesebir, P., & Diener, E. (2008). In pursuit of happiness: Empirical answers to philosophical questions. *Perspectives on Psychological Science*, *3*(2), 117–125. doi:10.1111/j.1745-6916.2008.00069.x PMID:26158878

Larsen, J. R., & Ketelaar, T. (1991). Personality and Susceptibility to Positive Negative Emotional State. *Journal of Personality and Social Psychology*, *61*(1), 132–140. doi:10.1037/0022-3514.61.1.132 PMID:1890584

Leahey, T. H. (2000). *A history of psychology*. Upper Saddle River, NJ: Prentice Hall.

Löckenhoff, C. E., Sutin, A. R., Ferrucci, L., & Costa, P. T. Jr. (2008). Personality traits and subjective health in the later years: The association between NEO-PI-R and SF-36 in advanced age is influenced by health status. *Journal of Research in Personality*, *42*(5), 1334–1346. doi:10.1016/j.jrp.2008.05.006

Lutz, A., Slagter, H. A., Dunne, J. D., & Davidson, R. J. (2008). Attention regulation and monitoring in meditation. *Trends in Cognitive Sciences*, *12*(4), 163–169. doi:10.1016/j.tics.2008.01.005 PMID:18329323

Lykken, D., & Tellegen, A. (1996). Happiness is a stochastic phenomenon. *Psychological Science*, *7*(3), 186–189. doi:10.1111/j.1467-9280.1996.tb00355.x

Lyubomirsky, S., King, L., & Diener, E. (2005). The benefit of frequent positive affect: Does hap- piness lead to success? *Psychological Bulletin*, *131*(6), 803–855. doi:10.1037/0033-2909.131.6.803 PMID:16351326

Lyubomirsky, S., & Lepper, H. S. (1999). A measure of subjective happiness: Preliminary reliability and construct validation. *Social Indicators Research*, *46*(2), 137–155. doi:10.1023/A:1006824100041

MacCann, C., & Roberts, R. D. (2008). New Paradigms for Assessing Emotional Intelligence: Theory and Data. *Emotion (Washington, D.C.)*, *8*(4), 540–551. doi:10.1037/a0012746 PMID:18729584

Marks, N., & Shah, H. (2005). A well-being manifesto for a flourishing society. *Journal of Mental Health Promotion*, *3*(4), 9-15. Retrieved from www.neweconomics.org

Mayer, J. D., & Salovey, P. (1997). What is emotional intelligence? In P. Salovey & D. Sluyter (Eds.), *Emotional development and emotional intelligence: Implications for educators* (pp. 3–31). New York: Basic Books.

Myers, D. (1992). *The pursuit of happiness*. New York: Morrow.

Nes, R. B., Roysamb, E., Tambs, K., Harris, J. R., & Reichborn-Kjennerud, T. (2006). Subjective well-being: Genetic and environmental contributions to stability and change. *Psychological Medicine*, *36*(07), 1033–1042. doi:10.1017/S0033291706007409 PMID:16749947

Neugarten, B. L., Havighurst, R., & Tobin, S. (1961). The measurement of life satisfaction. *Journal of Gerontology*, *16*(2), 134–143. doi:10.1093/geronj/16.2.134 PMID:13728508

Peterson, C., & Seligman, M. E. P. (2004). *Character strengths and virtues: A handbook and classification*. Oxford, UK: Oxford University Press.

Pizarro, D. A., & Salovey, P. (2002). On being and becoming a good person: The role of emotional intelligence in moral development and behavior. In J. Aronson (Ed.), *Improving academic achievement: Impact of psychological factors on education* (pp. 247–266). San Diego, CA: Academic Press. doi:10.1016/B978-012064455-1/50015-4

Platow. (1999). *Platow: The symposium* (C. Gill, Trans.). New York: Penguin Classics.

Ramachandran, V. S., & Oberman, L. M. (2006). Broken Mirrors: A Theory of Autism. *Scientific American, 295*(5), 62–69. doi:10.1038/scientificamerican1106-62 PMID:17076085

Rojas, M. (2007). Heterogeneity in the relationship between income and happiness: A conceptual-referent-theory explanation. *Journal of Economic Psychology, 28*(1), 1–14. doi:10.1016/j.joep.2005.10.002

Ryff, C., & Keyes, C. (1995). The structure of psychological well-being revisited. *Journal of Personality and Social Psychology, 69*(4), 719–727. doi:10.1037/0022-3514.69.4.719 PMID:7473027

Ryff, C. D. (1989). Happiness is everything, or is it? Ex- plorations on the meaning of psychological well-being. *Journal of Personality and Social Psychology, 57*(6), 1069–1081. doi:10.1037/0022-3514.57.6.1069

Ryff, C. D. (2013). Eudaimonic well-being and health: Mapping consequences of self-realization. In A. S. Waterman (Ed.), *The best within us. Positive psychology perspectives on eudaimonia* (pp. 77–98). Washington, DC: American Psychological Association. doi:10.1037/14092-005

Ryff, C. D. (2014). Psychological Well-Being Revisited: Advances in the Science and Practice of Eudaimonia. *Psychotherapy and Psychosomatics, 83*(1), 10–28. doi:10.1159/000353263 PMID:24281296

Ryff, C. D., Keyes, C. L. M., & Shmotkin, D. (2002). Optimizing well-being: The empirical encounter of two traditions. *Journal of Personality and Social Psychology, 82*(6), 1007–1022. doi:10.1037/0022-3514.82.6.1007 PMID:12051575

Salovey, P., Mayer, J. D., & Caruso, D. (2002). The positive psychology of emotional intelli- gence. In C. R. Snyder & S. J. Lopez (Eds.), *Handbook of positive psychology* (pp. 159–171). New York: Oxford University Press.

Schwarz, N., & Strack, F. (1999). Reports of subjective well-being: Judgment processes and their methodological implications. In D. Kahneman, E. Diener, & N. Schwarz (Eds.), *Well being: The founda- tions of hedonic psychology*. New York: Russell Sage.

Seligman, M., & Csikszentmihalyi, M. (2000). Positive Psychology: An introduction. *The American Psychologist, 55*(1), 5–14. doi:10.1037/0003-066X.55.1.5 PMID:11392865

Seligman, M. E. P. (2002). *Authentic happiness: Using the new positive psychology to realize your potential for lasting fulfilment*. New York: Free Press.

Seligman, M. E. P. (2011). *Flourish: A visionary new understanding of happiness and well-being*. New York: Simon & Schuster.

Seligman, M. E. P., Steen, T. A., Park, N., & Peterson, C. (2005). Positive psychology progress: Empirical validation of interventions. *The American Psychologist, 60*(5), 410–421. doi:10.1037/0003-066X.60.5.410 PMID:16045394

Shipley, B. A., Weiss, A., Der, G., Taylor, M., & Deary, I. J. (2007). Neuroticism, extraversion, and mortality in the UK Health and Lifestyle Survey: A 21-year prospective cohort study. *Psychosomatic Medicine*, *69*(9), 923–931. doi:10.1097/PSY.0b013e31815abf83 PMID:17991814

Steel, P., Schmidt, J., & Shultz, J. (2008). Refining the Relationship between Personality and Subjective Well-being. *Psychological Bulletin*, *134*(1), 138–161. doi:10.1037/0033-2909.134.1.138 PMID:18193998

Suh, E., Diener, E., & Fujita, F. (1996). Events and subjective well-being: Only recent events matter. *Journal of Personality and Social Psychology*, *70*(5), 1091–1102. doi:10.1037/0022-3514.70.5.1091 PMID:8656337

Valle, M. F., Huebner, E. S., & Suldo, S. M. (2006). An analy- sis of hope as a psychological strength. *Journal of School Psychology*, *44*(5), 393–406. doi:10.1016/j.jsp.2006.03.005

Vence, E. D., Roberson, J. A., McGuinnies, M. T., & Fazel, L. P. (2010). How neuroplasticity and cognitive reserve protect cognitive functioning. *Journal of Psychological Nursing*, *48*(4), 23–30. PMID:20349891

Widyanto, L., & McMurran, M. (2004). The psychometric properties of the Internet Addiction Test. *Cyberpsychology & Behavior*, *7*(4), 443–450. doi:10.1089/cpb.2004.7.443 PMID:15331031

Wolfradt, U., & Doll, J. (2001). Motives of adolescents to use the Internet as a function of personality traits, personal and social factors. *Journal of Educational Computing Research*, *24*(1), 13–27. doi:10.2190/ANPM-LN97-AUT2-D2EJ

World Health Organization. (1946). Preamble to the Constitution of the World Health Organization as adopted by the International Health Conference, New York, 19–22 June 1946; signed on 22 July 1946 by the representatives of 61 States (Official Records of the World Health Organization, no. 2, p. 100) and entered into force on 7 April 1948.

Zhou, H. (2012). A New Framework of Happiness Survey and Evaluation of National Wellbeing. *Social Indicators Research*, *108*(3), 491–507. doi:10.1007/s11205-011-9888-4

Chapter 13
The Potential of Spirituality for the Treatment of Organizational Trauma

Dušan Kučera
University of Economics, Czech Republic

ABSTRACT

The spiritual approach in dealing with organizational trauma is still relatively uncommon in business management literature. This chapter attempts to show the complexity of the problem through getting over the traditional framework of managerial psychology as defined by modern Western thought. Inspired by the holistic concept of man, the author transcends the usual managerial horizon and introduces a new perspective, which touches on the problem of the meaning of work within the context of the purpose of human life. The description of traumatic experiences in an organization is connected with feelings of guilt, the crisis of the concept of justice, the problem of forgiveness, and finding the inner energy to overcome the trauma and huge disappointment. Organizational trauma may develop into a personal and organizational crisis. This chapter tackles the potential of spirituality (human faith and hope) that gives a new meaning to life and work. Spirituality is connected with some religious systems. It can be instrumental in finding an appropriate treatment.

INTRODUCTION

The phenomenon of organizational trauma is a frequently discussed topic in the academy, and it is also demanded for practical help among managers and entrepreneurs. This chapter describes the ongoing discussion about possible psychological and practical personal assistance, with an emphasis on the potential of spirituality for understanding and treatment of organizational trauma. The following pages explain the spiritual perspective of a human being and also offer suggestions for practical application of spiritual help in the form of pastoral psychology. Since the spiritual context of trauma is a very complex issue, the following paragraphs draw attention to basic anthropological thinking and different demonstrations of a traumatic experience within an organization.

DOI: 10.4018/978-1-5225-2021-4.ch013

Professional literature refers to the phenomenon of trauma primarily as a psychological and psychiatric problem, which has a certain bearing on functioning of the affected organization through the affected staff. However, managerial literature almost never relates the topic of trauma to spirituality. The nature of organizational trauma can become such a huge managerial problem that the organization has to discontinue its activities. Anngwyn St. Just (2006) warns organizations about negative consequences of broken relationships and threatened organizational system. Therefore managers and employees should exhaust all possibilities of its treatment, including the spiritual dimension. Managers need to be able to understand the problem and help each other or at least refer the employees affected with trauma to professional and complex help. Most managers and entrepreneurs may not be sufficiently and adequately trained to do so. Yet, employees affected by organizational trauma still expect to be helped.

Generally, a traumatized person believes that it is a task of an *expert* to help them. But it is important to realize that a human trauma is not a merely general HR or health issue, to be dealt with in a purely psychological or medical way. An organizational trauma involves a whole range of symptoms, which make up an integral whole. The problem of organizational trauma is primarily an anthropological one, with physical, psychological, social and spiritual impact, and in an organization also with organizational and managerial impact.

The following pages examine a wide range of traumatic impact in terms of our understanding of anthropology within a holistic perspective, which includes the spiritual aspect of a human being. Logically, spirituality is also related to a specific understanding of religious concepts, which is understood in this study as the next level of spiritual potential. The spiritual and religious perspectives may cause specific problems based on the common understanding of economy and management. Therefore, this chapter explains the limitations of the Western scientific thinking, while also offering a new perspective by considering organizational trauma and its treatment in terms of spirituality. an Because human spirituality not only entails a great positive energy but also some dangerous strains, one of the paragraphs is dedicated to this important concern. Finally, this chapter discusses the necessary post-traumatic growth.

The author uses his own pastoral and managerial experience acquired during the last twenty-five years in HR departments of international companies. The study of pastoral psychology and management theories provides a rich inspiration to consider spirituality as a way to help traumatized people in an organi zation.

A BASIS FOR DEALING WITH ORGANIZATIONAL TRAUMA

Organizational trauma poses a challenge for managers and their team members, who have to cope with the complexity of its symptoms. This chapter focuses on organizational trauma and will not touch on the other specific types of trauma, e.g. trauma in a clinic environment, HIV trauma, family crises, post war symptoms (Vietnam, Persian Gulf) or the situation in New York after 9/11, which have been very well documented and systematically researched even from the perspective of spirituality and pastoral psychology (Swain, 2011).

Definitions

There are many definitions of the word *trauma*. The etymological meaning of the original Greek word is *wound, damage* (Wiktionary). In order to define organizational trauma generally, so that it applies to a very negative experience in an organization, let us describe it first according to Hughes, Kinder & Cooper (2012):

The organizational trauma is a result of critical events happening in an organization. Organizational trauma expresses itself in a response of the members of an organization to the set of negative circumstances demonstrated by different traumatic effects depending on diagnostics.

Organizational trauma is usually affected by many factors we cannot influence. But what we actually can influence by spiritual means is individual trauma. In order to understand an individual trauma in an organization, a formal concept of trauma, formulated by the Substance Abuse and Mental Health Services Administration (SAMHSA), will be of interest:

An individual trauma results from an event, a series of events, or a set of circumstances that is experienced by an individual as physically or emotionally harmful or threatening and that has lasting adverse effects on the individual's functioning and physical, social, emotional, or spiritual well-being. (SAMHSA, 2014a)

SAMHSA (2014b) also uses a broader definition of trauma as:

a sudden and forceful event that overwhelms a person's ability to respond to it, recognizing that a trauma need not involve actual physical harm to oneself; an event can be traumatic if it contradicts one's worldview and overpowers one's ability to cope.

In summarizing the first three definitions of trauma mentioned, we can say that a trauma is a very serious and long-lasting wound for individuals as members of groups and whole organizations. It is so serious that reasonableness and rationality as such do not suffice to solve it because traumatized people facing the critical reality are not capable of communicating pragmatically. This is caused mainly by the tendency of some people to suppress the tragic event (into their inner world) and deny it (before the outer world). Naturally, traumatized people do not believe that their colleagues would be able to understand them and that the organization would not lose its reputation. The result of a traumatic experience is regression, isolation, attempts to rationalize, but after these attempts fail, personal isolation, feeling of powerlessness and a shock of self- and world-understanding ensue. Organizational trauma is actually a rift in interactions between individuals as team members and their social environment.

The following definitions show the direct effect of the individual trauma on an organization in which the traumatized person works. A trauma is described as:

...a stressful event or situation of shorter or longer duration with an exceptional threat of a catastrophic scale, which would cause deep despair to almost everybody." (Dilling & Freyberger, as cited in Paterno, 2012, p. 3)

The American sociologist Kai Erikson makes a distinction between *individual trauma* and *collective trauma*. Every individual trauma of any of the employees can have very negative effects on the organization, considering the *wounded* person who cannot be effective or responsible in his/her working position any more:

By individual trauma I mean a blow to the psyche that breaks through one's defenses so suddenly and with such brutal force that one cannot react to it effectively... They suffered deep shock as a result of their exposure to death and devastation, and, as so often happens in catastrophes of this magnitude, they withdrew, feeling numbed, afraid, vulnerable, and very lonely.

By collective trauma, on the other hand, I mean a blow to the basic tissues of social life that damages the bonds attaching people together and impairs the prevailing sense of communality. The collective trauma works its way slowly and even insidiously into the awareness of those who suffer from it, so it does not have the quality of suddenness normally associated with trauma. But it is a form of shock all the same, a gradual realization that the community no longer exists as an effective source of support and that an important part of the self has disappeared.

The last quotation of Erikson combines the individual trauma with the collective trauma as follows:

'I' continues to exist, though damaged and maybe even permanently changed. 'You' continues to exist, though distant and hard to relate to. But 'we' no longer exists as a connected pair or as linked cells in a larger communal body. (Erikson, 1976: Everything in its Path. Destruction of Community in Buffalo Creek Flood, pp.153–154, as cited in Saul, 2009, p. 3)

Reasons and Consequences of a Trauma

The previous definitions were concentrated on individual trauma; the last four selected definitions will help us understand the essence of organizational trauma. To sum up, there are many reasons why organizations face trauma:

- Personal failure, failure of human morals (corruption);
- Organizational failure (wrong decision of management, bankruptcy);
- Technological disaster (e.g. BP Company in the Gulf of Mexico 2010, Fukushima 2011).

The concrete effects on the organization can be as follows:

- Loss of human resources for effective and stable organizational process (personal crises, disease, accident, death);
- Necessity to recruit new employees;
- Necessary restructuring of some departments or the whole organization;
- Tragic consequences when a traumatized employee commits suicide (cases from recent years in the Chinese company Foxconn, French Telecom and others);
- Disruption of the organization due to disruption of relationships with customers and suppliers;
- Destruction of the company or its technology and equipment by disasters (natural, industrial, financial, terrorist).

Complex Challenge for Organizations

Reasons as well as consequences of trauma show the complexity of the trauma phenomenon. In anthropological terms, trauma relates to psychosis and emotional wounds of individuals, teams, managers, and naturally even their families (Kleber, Figley & Gersons, 2013).

The responsibility for a trauma lies on the side of the organization management, employees and the social environment. An individual employee can be held responsible because of his/her failure, which influences the organization. The organization can be held responsible because of its failures, which influence the employees and their immediate families and friends or the whole region. A trauma represents a very intense crisis and sadness for both parties. They lose the ability to communicate, the sense of trust and social safety. The worst scenario of organizational trauma is connected with catastrophic events, near-death experiences of some individuals, hazards to life, injury and fear. We have to agree with many scholars (Dutton, Frost, Worline, Lilius & Kanov, 2002) who confirm that the phenomenon of organizational trauma is very complex and therefore it poses a big challenge to the survival of an organization.

Complex Challenge for the Leadership

Key leadership qualities are based on the ability to have a vision, to analyze the current situation, to search for solutions and treatment, to choose the right procedures, to innovate, to be flexible, to communicate in crisis, to recognize priorities and show new ways out of critical situations, etc. (Covey, 2000). In this chapter, we also include the ability to understand and assist in solving one of the most difficult problems – organizational trauma (Argenti, 2002). Argenti describes some critical situations and gives advice to leaders on how to uplift the morals and strengthen communication channels in the organization, bear in mind the safety of employees, while not neglecting the main business operations. The whole decision-making processes during any crisis are based on specific *non-technical* skills.

Our short overview of related perspectives shows that the subject has an interdisciplinary character (Blüm, 1983; Figley, 2012). The complexity of trauma in an organization therefore cannot be grasped only by several selected traditional disciplines. Managers are typically well trained in solving different financial, economical, material, technical and informational issues. Business schools prepare future managers for business strategy, effective production, and project management. But the process of trauma treatment depends on a different set of skills. In critical organizational situations, the management needs to have good analytical skills, communicative competence, social and emotional intelligence (as described in classical textbooks on leadership). Another very important skill is spiritual intelligence (Zohar&Marshall, 2000). Zohar and Marshall aptly define spiritual intelligence as:

- An ability to believe in special values which are the strongest motivation;
- An ability to be spontaneous at important moments in life;
- An ability to have a complex vision with the capacity to transcend the visible situation and accept the vocation to serve;
- A tendency to ask about reasons and a specific kind of independence based on one's own worth.

It is not necessary to think immediately about religion but certainly about virtues of humility, compassion and positivism. The perspective of managers is typically physical and empirical. The owners of companies and top managers expect that every problem will be solved in some way, preferably quickly (e.g. with some pills, short holiday for the individual and some steps of crisis management for the organization). However, organizational trauma originates in a deeply negative human experience and disappointment experienced in an organization. The manifestation of organizational trauma is described as a physical, psychological, social and spiritual disease of the whole human being, which has a tendency to resign oneself to anything in a critical situation within an organization (Briere & Scott, 2006). This individual form of trauma has a tremendous impact on the whole organization and its function.

The author agrees with Frommberger (2014), who defines trauma as a specific disease which pertains to a completely different category than medicine and psychology can handle. This approach is supported by Saul (2009), who explains also the relationships between team members and groups, their style of communication, and the organization's credibility among other partners. It may happen that a management which is otherwise technologically well-equipped and financially skilled encounters the human beings affected by an organizational trauma almost unarmed. Every manager will try to solve the crisis using some steps of problem solving. All this needs a certain level of staff rationality and discipline. But in the case of an organizational trauma, people can be so profoundly shocked that according to Cottis (2008) they are even emotionally unable to cooperate with the management and finally prevent any intended therapy, which would have to be based on the ability of intellectual communication.

A very strong example of practical leadership was provided by Mayor Rudi Giuliani in New York City after the 9/11 terrorist attacks on the World Trade Center. He earned the reputation of a good leader thanks to his decisive position. He acted immediately in favor of the sufferers, he was empathetic, followed his natural instincts, provided maximum support and hope to the people, and addressed the long-term consequences for the whole district. In such situations, even death and its meaning for future generations is an important topic (Miller, 2011). Interestingly, the spiritual and religious perspective did play a big role for Giuliani in treatment of the American trauma after the terrorist attack (Saul, 2011).

THE SIGNIFICANCE OF HUMAN SPIRITUALITY FOR THE TREATMENT OF TRAUMA

The word *spirituality* comes from the Latin term *spiritus*, which is understood as an inner energy directed inside, a thought-oriented personal power. Milan Balabán explains spirituality as an intention of human activity (Balabán, 2012). In Hebrew thinking, *spirit* (*ruah*) is conceived as *breath* or *wind*, i.e. dynamic force in motion – even if everything else became paralyzed. In Hebrew the word *ruah* is feminine, which suggests something fertile, maternal and life oriented. Similarly, the ancient *wisdom* (*sapientia*) was worshiped as a goddess because of her spiritual orientation. It is a pity that in contrast with the very dynamic original meaning of human spirit, the Western understanding of spirituality is often reduced to a static psychological description of human psyche.

Human Spirituality in an Organization

Spirituality views the world, including life and work in an organization from the perspective oriented to the complex meaning and long term goals of human work in a complex (universal) way.

Max Weber (2003) suggests that not only organizations and companies but also capitalism itself has its *spirit*. He understands the *spirit of capitalism* as based on protestant roots. Entrepreneurs and workers are *called* to support and develop their professions and organization in society. Weber's explanations confirm that entrepreneurs are focused on as effective a creation of values as possible. The *spirit of capitalism* also arises as an important factor in times when the organization is in a crisis.

Spirituality considers the implications of the historical development of an organization which suddenly breaks down during a critical disaster. It assesses the values that transcend material values and rational speculations and looks for possible lessons that can be learned by overcoming organizational trauma. Spirituality follows an outlook for the future and is thus focused on the principle of hope, trust in values and vision of future development, which does not directly depend on a present success. Spirituality offers a way of relating to everything, including disasters and ensuing traumas. The spiritual perspective transcends the horizontal level (social relations) of human existence and leads to the vertical level (relation to the purpose and meaning of life and work in universal and eternal context). S It transcends ordinary personal empirical experience, pure rationality and current feelings or opinions and comments of others. This does not mean that the spiritual person ignores them. The spiritual person is familiar with these perspectives, but at the same time stays critical of them. The spiritual perspective does not accept any cheap answers and rejects superficial solutions.

Hans Joas (2008) points out that spirituality is a universal human phenomenon, which has been unjustly dismissed by modern society and which is now being laboriously rediscovered, but is still subject to many suspicions. Following Carl Gustav Jung, Joas re-describes his concept with a new language and shows that spirituality is a universal phenomenon which needs to be taken into account when dealing with organizational trauma. It is a phenomenon which forms human organizations, whether managers and entrepreneurs realize it or not. If the spiritual perspective is neglected, the organization misses an essential chance to understand and deal with a human individual in a traumatic situation. Our main suggestion is to incorporate human anthropology and spiritual perspective of economy and leadership in managerial education (Kučera, 2015).

The fact that we seek a solution indicates that there is a belief that this seeking makes sense. Even organizational trauma itself does not have to be seen as a no-win situation. The traumatized human beings are undermined, but with this belief they probably will not break down completely. They rebel against the misfortune and quite naturally do not want to become reconciled to it. The trauma causes some difficulties and they are perceived as a threat. But that is one of the results of human transcendence which is value-oriented and is not indifferent to any dimension of trauma. In this perspective, it is important to look for a spiritual context for solving an organizational trauma based on mutual trust.

Limitations of the Psychological Approach

The importance of a spiritual perspective in trauma treatment becomes more obvious when it is compared with the position of classical psychology. The nature of trauma deeply touches on the spiritual dimension, which should be psychologically identified, reflected, and interpreted. But there are some essential differences between spirituality and psychology. Reimund Blühm describes general limits of psychology which can serve us as a starting point for spirituality and pastoral psychology (1983, pp. 35-37):

- Psychology gathers its knowledge mainly through observation, surveys and experimentation. On the other hand, spiritual perspective is concerned with value orientation;
- Psychology strives to understand and describe human personality in categories (an important perspective for psychotherapy, psycho-diagnostics and clinical psychology), whereas spiritual

perspective strives to understand human personality in terms of a higher, deeper and long-term spiritual orientation;

- Psychology is a descriptive science about human behavior. Spiritual perspective also summarizes the normative value orientation of human thinking and acting;
- Psychology is concerned with the possibilities of human development; however, it does not define its own solid value system concerning spiritual orientation. Therefore it needs spirituality;
- Blühm says (p. 36) that *psychology* in a narrow sense actually *does not exist*. It is not a unified, closed science which would be able to determine itself. It explores a whole range of other influences on the human's psychological state like motivation, life and work conditions, and relational processes. But only philosophical and spiritual perspectives endow motivation with spiritual power, its vertical and universal anchor;
- Psychology examines processes of human consciousness, feelings and emotions through experiments. Spirituality endows human conscience with a transcendent personal relationship which empowers people to overcome the negative impact of their environment;
- Psychology touches on an analysis and searching of the sense of human potential, whereas spiritual perspective fills it up with a future oriented vision, value and meaning.

A classic example of understanding the limitations of traditional psychology and the potential of spirituality for trauma treatment is the depth psychology of Sigmund Freud. It is primarily his interpretation of the subconscious mind and dreams full of sexual frustrations (2007). In the situation of organizational trauma, this kind of analysis would not be of much help. But Freud's disciples Alfred Adler and Carl Gustav Jung opened Freud's perspective to new horizons. Alfred Adler shifted the attention of classical psychology to a deeper definition of feelings generally, particularly feelings of inferiority. Adler very successfully identifies the role of life and work purpose and the meaning of human community (Adler, 1998). Another very important and critical disciple of Freud was Carl Gustav Jung with his collective unconscious, archetypes and a whole system of psychological symbolism, imagination, intuition, and focus on the goal. This approach is known as teleology (study of purpose or design), which is expressed by human beings in all cultures as well as religions (Jung, 1967).

Adler and Jung were the first to diverge from Freud's dogmatism of concentrating on human libido and sexuality as the reason of psychological failures. Unlike Freudian psychoanalysis, which perceives human subconscious as a disturbing trash dump of frustrations, they see the subconscious as a path to deeper realms of a human being, which can then be reflected in successful life, work and sense of belonging. In fact, Adler and Jung as the first psychologists showed that the *spiritual* perspective of a human being and the *archetypes* play an important role in a person's life and work. Therefore spirituality is very important when dealing with organizational trauma. For the treatment of a trauma, it is also very important to realize that spiritual thinking transcends even Jung's *descriptive* and *relative* methodology and has a courage to open a higher perspective which does not fully depend on human instincts.

The same boundaries apply not only to classical psychology but also to the limits of personal coaching. There are circumstances where even personal coaching based on personal psychology does not help. Clients with traumatic experiences have to be referred to a psychiatrist and also to skilled pastoral psychologists. Many scholars (Heinonen, Lindors, Laaksonen, & Knekt, 2012) describe the circumstances in which clients need more than just psychological advice or personal coaching. These circumstances occur when:

- Cooperation with a psychologist or a coach is not efficient;
- The client keeps going in circles around seemingly *resolved* issues;
- The client keeps returning to a topic (e.g. organizational trauma, misfortune, disaster) that cannot be resolved solely by individual coaching methods;
- The client remains obsessed by his/her gloomy past and the coach is not able to orient him/her to the future with new hope and decision;
- The client does not have the capacity for self-reflection and shows limitations of his/her cognitive functions.

These are the reasons why this chapter emphasizes the potential of spirituality for solving organizational trauma after psychological methods have been exhausted.

POTENTIAL OF THE SPIRITUAL PERSPECTIVE

Pastoral Psychology

In every organization, there should be individuals or members of management able to recognize if their employees need spiritual help, which can come in the form of pastoral psychology.

Blüm (1983) describes pastoral psychology as professional and very personal, as spiritual care exercised by spiritually trained psychologists, advisers and pastors. Pastoral care is characterized by encouragement and support of a traumatized person in his/her stressful and traumatic test of faith in life and sense of work. Pastoral care is in general offered in a community of spiritual people or believers (church communities). In the Christian context, we speak about pastoral care based on the belief in God and the human example and teachings of Jesus.

Pastoral psychology follows the principles of hope and accompanies the traumatized people in overcoming their personal crises and tragedies. Pastoral psychology promises a special empathetic working environment associated with high expectations and demands on the personal, moral, but also professional standards of pastoral psychologists or pastors. Pastoral psychology and spiritual help is based on the professional ability to help concrete people in their particular situations.

Spiritual Ways of Interpreting Trauma

Right at the beginning it must be admitted that in a critical situation even pastoral workers cannot help immediately. Even a specialist in pastoral care knows that first it is necessary to secure vital functions, soothe the patient, let him/her rest, sleep and recover his/her physical and mental energy. Therapy begins with these fundamental functions and then it unfolds in spiritual development of the traumatized person step by step. The particularity of spiritual care resides in a professional approach of the caring professionals which allows them to see the whole range of traumatic manifestations (Wilking, Biberacher & Volker, 2012). Let us formulate the most important characteristics of traumatized people who need pastoral care:

- Traumatized people seem to be helpless and hopeless. Their physical and mental energy is exhausted and blocked;

- Their confrontation with reality, which is so surprising, shocking and startling for the organization, completely disarms and paralyzes the involved persons;
- The ultimate critical spiritual situation of a traumatic experience we have to be prepared for is that the injured persons find themselves on the border of life and death;
- We have to be aware about the limitations of humanistic psychology, particularly when the traumatized person experiences recurring critical memories and threatening dreams (Rambo, 2010);
- Traumatized people often have the tendency to undermine one's own life and work purpose saying e.g.: *"I did my best, but what was the point in all that? It all went wrong!"*
- Very dangerous is the tendency to lose the vision for the future (nothing matters, a collapse of values) and emphasize personal limits of physical existence and health;
- In the social environment there are limits to cultural acceptance when the person hears certain judgments e.g.: *"You are considered bankrupt, you failed to conform, and you found yourself on the edge of society."*
- Questioning of values – what is the point of any effort?
- A big challenge for spiritual care is loss of motivation and inner energy to search for ways out, for a fresh start or desire for something else;
- A very difficult situation we have to face when the person is sinking into fatefulness with an inclination to say: *"I am out of luck and I cannot influence my tragic destiny."*
- In organizational trauma, we frequently face the phenomenon of burnout;
- A serious challenge for pastors is human indifference, strong sadness, apathy and hate or reluctance to talk about traumatic experiences;
- Finally the traumatized person tries to withdraw, is deeply disappointed, skeptic about everything, and loses all the desire to live and work for the same or perhaps for any organization.

With respect to these points, the intervention of a spiritual therapist is not only needed after the event, but is also desirable before the trauma. A person may be struggling with extreme doubts, be they personal or professional, before an occupational trauma occurs. Spiritual orientation can be built up over the course of time on the principle of hope and mutual trust in practical acts. It is the spiritual education that can help everybody *prepare* for all situations related to trauma.

Spiritual Characteristics of Organizational Trauma and its Treatment

The spiritual role of a pastoral psychologist is to spend time with the affected persons, listen to them, try to understand them, and hold *them by their hand* before giving any explanations or advice. Pastoral psychology opens some concrete horizons for clients:

- New relationship to hope, renewed trust in the meaning of their life, job and future;
- Strengthening of human values by progressive conversations and involvement by being there for the other person;
- Spiritual conversations can help the affected person to understand that some things also happen without direct personal fault. Pastoral conversation can create awareness that we all live in an environment where there is not only the capacity for good, but also for evil;
- Spiritual accents can facilitate necessary forgiveness for all those involved in an organizational crisis and trauma;

- Encouragement to leave the person's own isolation and meet other people (colleagues, friends, family, church community). Positive fellowship can help to overcome loneliness, natural concentration on feelings of guilt and incomprehension of others.

People respond to trauma in various ways, but the main prerequisites for spiritual trauma treatment are:

- The need to have someone who will be ready to understand all the depths and consequences of the trauma, accept them, have enough patience and, despite all its heaviness, open a new horizon leading to treatment;
- Offering possibilities regarding the meaning of life, transcending common rationality and feelings;
- Offering possibilities regarding the meaning of work, exceeding material and financial values;
- Dealing empathetically with feelings of guilt (*"Could I have prevented this? Did I neglect to do something?"*);
- Showing understanding of the evil involved in the organizational accident;
- Searching for a new relationship to the world, to the organization, to the people in the organization (co-workers, management, etc.) and to God;
- Sympathy for feelings of perceived injustice (*"Why a certain accident happened, why to me, to us, why here and now?"*);
- Inspiring willingness to forgive actors in the tragedy for their possible failures;
- Searching together for a renewed hope and a new perspective for the future;
- Searching for personal faith (in the meaning of life, efforts before any accident, future vision, and the value of human endeavor itself);
- Offering personal attendance and responding to the need of the traumatized person to have someone who will be there, will listen to his/her laments, complaints and questions, and carefully start a new conversation;
- Offering spiritual energy for a fresh start;
- Offering a wise combination of humanistic psychology and pastoral psychology which will help the person to understand the phenomenon of trauma in all its breadth and depth.

In order to heal a trauma, almost all the above mentioned requirements and characteristics have to be met. Even this listing shows the limitation of approaches based on non-spiritual foundations (pure rational speculation, natural psychology, classical medicine, statistical and sociological analyses, the factor of time itself without any specific intention of conversation or therapeutic aiming). This listing also shows that there is a potential and room for a spiritual perspective to understand the scope and depth of the trauma and search for therapeutic possibilities.

The typical spiritual accent of pastoral psychology is based on religion. The common fundamentals of spiritual empathy are love of neighbors, readiness for self-sacrifice, charity and service as nourished almost by all religious teachings, in Western society traditionally by Judaism and Christianity.

SPIRITUALITY AND RELIGION

One of the deepest secrets of spirituality is the insight that life and justice are frequently contradictory or in a mutual tension. For example, people can learn something new even through evil and sometimes trough an accident. Even illness can be deliberately used as a lesson of a higher level of understanding of negative experiences. The example of a general lesson learned from disasters is only the beginning of what some theologians have in mind. It is well described in Martin Luther's *theology of the cross* (Trueman, 2005). Also many mystics asked about the meaning of pain. Some of them even tried to vicariously bear the burden of the evil in this world through their own suffering and its acceptance in their own life. The Christian cross is a familiar symbol which represents an intersection where horizontal tragedy of our lives is crossed by a new vertical hope (see Figure 1).

This general spiritual perspective found many cultural and religious forms throughout human history and is extensively described in literature. From the point of view of a historian of capitalism and economy, the role of Judaism and Christianity in basic spiritual sets of world religions is obvious. Naturally, in a large part of the world, the Muslim or other concepts of values in society also play an important role.

Immanuel Kant understood religion as recognition of moral law (categorical imperative or divine command). Friedrich Hegel spoke about the Absolute Spirit (absolute knowledge) with an emphasis on the whole. Friedrich Schleiermacher understood religion as an awareness of infinity, as contemplating eternity. All these and other meanings carry a great potential for innovative thinking, which is most needed in situations of disappointment, crisis and trauma.

The Potential of Christian Spirituality for Trauma Treatment

Spirituality is based on assumptions which are known from world religious systems. They consist of a whole range of important points which are included in many religions and which are communicated to people who have suffered from a trauma. Western society is influenced mostly by Christianity.

Figure 1. Symbol of cross (Source: http://www.flaticon.com/free-icon/cross_140151#term=cross&page=2&position=67)

There are basically two ways in which spiritual practices can help with organizational trauma: personal conversations with traumatized people and private workshops. Pastors and pastoral psychologists can foster the following:

- Awareness of the fact that the world was created by a personal God who freely decided to do so (the position of Judaism, Christianity and also Islam);
- Awareness of the fact that the world was created for us, for human work and life as a safe place with its natural structures and laws;
- Awareness that even human life and human society as a whole, including human organizations, can grow and develop if it abides by a certain relationship and regulations and divine advice;
- Awareness that if there has been any kind of a mistake, error or disaster (sin), there is always a way out. Basically, no situation is hopeless;
- Awareness that the *Creator* has affections for His creation and cares about it. Christianity derives this belief from the old prophetic message and the story of Jesus Christ, who (although he did not have to) entered the human world affected by evil, understood it, suffered at the hands of it, but taught and showed people a way out;
- Awareness that the accident and the ensuing trauma have happened and that the victims cannot change anything about it, except for their attitude toward it. Everything is in the *hands of God*;
- The traumatized person should know that the others respect him/her as a human being, regardless of what happened and why;
- Pastoral care can also offer a prayer for the person and his/her future. This typical pastoral service can help to encourage him/her to trust and believe in a new future (with God);
- Spiritual care can explain the vertical religious relationship between man and God or recover it and deepen it especially if the people in question are already spiritually oriented in any way.

Christian pastoral psychology leaves enough space for the affected person who can freely communicate with God, even expressing his/her disagreement, discontent, trauma and anger. Of essential importance is the already mentioned spirituality of cross and human sufferings.

The Potential of Religion for Treatment of Organizational Trauma

A typical characteristic of the Judeo-Christian perspective is a personal relationship between man and God which can be deepened and developed, given the perspective described in biblical books and other literature. What are the other religious traditions?

- It is important for Western readers to realize that Eastern spiritual sources also offer a valuable perspective on how to deal with trauma. Hindu meditation (in the form of yoga, which strives for a harmonic relationship between the body and the spirit) offers spiritual openness to a new inspiration from the *infinity of the universe*. Hinduism seeks a realistic way of treatment paradoxically beyond human rational speculation. Another concept of Hinduism is divinity in the soul of every human being. In a specific but nonetheless professional way, even Hinduism can treat human trauma by internally harmonizing the traumatized person (see Figure 2);
- Figure 3, known as the *Dharmachakra wheel*, is the symbol of 8 or 24 main Hindu qualities (Love, Courage, Patience, Peace, Goodness, Faith, Self-Control, Self- Sacrifice, Truthfulness,

Righteousness, Justice, Mercy, Gracefulness, Humility, Loyal, Sympathy, Spiritual Knowledge, Forgiveness, Honesty, Hope etc.). All the qualities are in this symbol connected in human heart;

- Buddhism (which is a philosophy rather than a religion) offers *mystical concentration of internal enlightenment*. It manifests itself as a contemplation of spiritual focus on meditation which frees the spirit of man from its longing for the world (present organizational crises) and of any connection to secular interests (Weber, 2013). This approach demands a completely different life philosophy and a very strong personality, as it requires deep concentration on the given objective;
- In Confucianism, there is an emphasis on the practical and moral values of life, social ethics, harmony with the universe and the ubiquitous accent on *wisdom*. The Eastern concept of wisdom is completely different from the Western concept of *cleverness* and pure information about the situation. In Confucian wisdom, it is important that human relationships, justice, sincerity, and spiritual understanding of the whole world find their meaning and personal position in the world order (Küng, 2006). It means that traumatized people can find in Confucianism specific moral power for overcoming personal or organizational trauma;
- In Taoism, the focus is on a holistic conception of man and of the world. Although this ancient Chinese philosophy reflects all the antitheses in the world, at the same time it aims for holistic harmony. Figure 4 illustrates this philosophy.

Modern entrepreneurs and managers make use of some features of Taoism. Even in European countries, some workplaces and consulting institutions of Chinese medicine now operate. What does Taoism offer for management? There are the following aspects:

- The concept of life and work is considered as the *right path*;
- The use of a combination of work with a value-oriented *spirit*. Taoism offers the use of holistic, dialectic and dynamic duality of good and evil, happiness and misfortune instead of the static and bipolar world. Some lecturers use the principles of Taoism for personal problem solving (Fang-Faubereb, 2011);
- The traditional symbol of Taoism operates with the phenomenon of universality and helps us understand life and work with two opposing energies of the universe and society/ organization. This model can be very useful in problem solving methods by involvement and processing of Tao elements, e.g.:
    - **Yin:** The female part of the world (moon, night, weakness, softness in work);
    - **Yang:** The male part of the world (sun, day, strength, clarity, hardness in work);
    - The black dot in the white field and the white dot in the black field symbolize the parts of opposing powers in the respective fields;
    - The curve inside the circle indicates that the opposites are not always clear-cut and absolute, but that sometimes they overlap with one another;
    - The whole principle of the paradox in this world and our organizations is illustrated by the duality, unity in diversity and the dynamic process of change within a single unit.

All these points can broaden the spiritual perspective of managers in organizations through deeper perception of trauma treatment:

Figure 2. Hindu position of yoga (Source: http://www.flaticon.com/free-icon/relax_141906#term=yoga&page=1&position=27)

Figure 3. Dharmachakra wheel (Source: http://www.flaticon.com/free-icon/dharma_144515#term=dharma&page=1&position=2)

- In Shintoism, there is the *path of the gods* called Shinto. In this ancient and yet still thriving Japanese religion, there is a great deal of respect for something that exceeds humanity and can become part of an individual via a harmonization ritual. Many rituals of devotion to oneself, family, group, company and country are known. What originates in the old Shintoist tradition is the well-known accent on continuous improvement and excellence as seen in the *Kaizen* philosophy. This concept has played an important role in building post-war automotive industry (e.g. Toyota).

Figure 4. Yin Yang (Source: http://www.flaticon.com/free-icon/yin-yang-symbol-variant_33900#term=yin%20yang&page=1&position=12)

Shintoism as well as the whole Japanese tradition celebrates life symbolized as the position on a mountain and the path towards the sun (Fujisawa, 1959).

Finally, Hans Küng (2008) described the religious meaning of life and work in modern society step by step, although in this field it is always necessary to differentiate between a healthy spirituality (religion) and a superstition. However, from a brief overview it is clear that the spiritual perspective plays an important role in post-modern society. From it, the traumatized organization can derive a renewed awareness of order, sense of high targets and desire to carry on.

Dangers of Spiritual Approaches

This part discusses the necessary precautions against a possible misuse of spirituality and frequent faults in spiritual help. For the practical purpose let us mention but a few examples:

- It requires extreme patience and sensitivity on the part of both the pastor and the client, because the trauma and its effects can last very long, and its treatment is individual. Some traumatic symptoms can stay until the end of a person's life;
- There may be an unwillingness or a lack of readiness of the pastor to empathize, or understand the client's situation;
- Pastoral psychologists need to be able to convince the patient to change and take on new attitudes. Many patients want the change and improvement to happen quickly;
- A very dangerous approach is to reproach traumatized people or talk to their conscience, e.g. *"Aren't you yourselves guilty after all? You should admit it and ask for forgiveness. After that you will find inner peace..."*;

- Some well-meaning spiritual consoling comments can be perceived as patronizing, and can actually deepen the feeling of guilt (e.g. *"Take it easy..."; "things happen..."; "there is no sin big enough that it cannot be forgiven..."; "do you feel as if you were in a deep hole from which there is no way out?"* and the like);
- Especially pastors must avoid inappropriate choice of quotations or insensitively used biblical texts which some clerics like to quote;
- Some pastoral psychologists may appear to be minimizing the trauma with statements such as *"This will pass," "Everything will eventually work out," "Keep smiling", "Don't worry," and "Keep your head up."*

On the one hand, religion and spirituality can be really helpful for traumatized people in an organization. On the other hand religious fundamentalism, unprofessional approach and intolerance can cause more harm than any secular psychologist.

Spirituality in the Traditional Scientific Environment

Herbert Pietschmann (2001) tried to analyze typical differences between Western scientific thinking and the holistic approach typical of the spiritual perspective. The emphasis on the complexity of the spiritual perspective is in a certain contrast or tension to the modern scientific concept.

It is known from the history of philosophy and science that science has been fragmented and specialized since Rene Descartes (Anzenbacher, 2002). Western thinking typically focuses on the logic that every effect has a clear cause, which, when solved, solves everything. In the case of a trauma, this logic is not sufficient. Even the typical scientific approach based on an experiment and its repeatability will not help resolve trauma.

According to Pietschmann, the boundaries and limitations of modern science are connected with modern empiricism. It is the typical scientific emphasis on human experience (*emperia*), which tends to neglect the whole context of human existence. It is really very difficult to include a larger sphere of being-in-the-world or the experience of other people and previous generations who are not part of a specific scientific study in a scientific analysis and description. In a traumatic situation, there are actually not many really natural and logical solutions.

We thus speak about a scientific consideration which questions some rational principles at the moment of an organizational trauma. For example: medication can soothe the trauma, enable the affected person to sleep and suppress his/her emotions. A sociologist can definitely describe the destructive social impact on a working team, family and friends. Psychological approaches are very interesting and can offer in-depth analysis and explanation of all causes, and various psychological ways to find a solution and overcome the issue. However, the question is whether purely natural, rational tools suffice for treatment of an organizational trauma. The question is a pressing one because a traumatized person finds him/herself in a value-related crisis, crisis of purpose, a crisis of his/her future and further engagement. Strong organizational trauma even *breaks down* the whole person and calls for a holistic treatment.

The only thing the traumatized person can hope for is the principle of hope itself. The spiritual perspective teaches us that the person should not break down after all, that he/she will hear a word of hope and think of a way out into a new future. But this path towards the future frequently requires a very long journey full of inner obstacles which are difficult to name, but which require the person to wait, persist, trust that something will change, and be prepared to carefully take the first step out of the trauma and its burden toward a new life.

It is the critical situation and trauma that leads a traumatized person very markedly towards self-transcendence. In an ordinary situation when everything goes well it does not seem that anybody needs this effort and care. A trauma, however, is a moment of a sudden and unexpected change, which leads the affected person to a completely different way of thinking and perception of the world. This gives rise to the opportunity to find a solution and overcome the trauma in general and organizational trauma in particular.

FURTHER RESEARCH AND READING RECOMMENDATIONS

The phenomenon of organizational trauma is a part of a very broad context. Its interdisciplinary character opens many other perspectives. Besides references used in this chapter, readers may find the following recommendations useful:

- On the place of spirituality in human thinking, spiritual accents of anthropology and existential meaning of life and work:
  - Frankl, V. (1997), *Man's Search for Ultimate Meaning*. New York;
  - Joas, H. (2014). *Faith as an Option: Possible Futures for Christianity.* Stanford;
  - Kenyon, G.M. (2000). *Philosophical foundations of existential meaning.* London;
  - WACH, J. (1972): *Types of Religious Experience. Christian and Non-Christian.* University of Chicago Press;
- On general therapy of organizational trauma:
  - Antioch University. (2007). *Organizational Trauma: A Phenomenological Study of Leaders in Traumatized Organizations.* Los Angeles;
  - Dutton, J.E., Frost, P.J., Worline, M.C., Lilius, J.M. & Kanov, J.M. (2002) *Leading in Times of Trauma.* Harward Business Review, 1/2002;
  - Levine, P. A. (2007). *Waking the Tiger. The Innate Capacity to Transform Overwhelming Experiences.* Altamira-Becht Haarlem;
  - Vivian, P. & Hormann, S. (2013). *Organizational Trauma and Healing.* Publishing house is acquired to Amazon.com;
- On the role of spirituality and spiritual therapy which is also applicable to organizational trauma:
  - Říčan, P. (2004): *Spirituality – the story of a concept in the psychology of religion.* Archiv für Religionspsychologie, 26, 135-156;
  - Hormann, S., & Vivian, P. (2005). *Toward an understanding of traumatized organizations and how to intervene in them.* Traumatology: An International Journal, 11(3), 159-169;
  - Handbook of posttraumatic growth: *Research and practice.* (Especially 291-310). New Jersey;
  - Shaw, A., Joseph, S. & Linely, P.A. (2005). *Religion, spirituality, and posttraumatic growth: a systematic review.* Mental Health, Religion & Culture. 8, 1-11;

- Linely, P.A. (2003). *Positive adaptation to trauma: Wisdom as both process and outcome.* Journal of Traumatic Stress.16, 601-610;
- Derrick, H. (2004). *Dealing with trauma of unemployment Job Seekers organization aims at handling problems of downsizing in corporate America.* The Atlanta Journal the Atlanta Constitution;
- Ishita, A. & Peeyush, K. (2015). *Spirituality and quality of life: A study among members of a spiritual organization in Delhi, India.* Indian Journal of Health and Wellbeing6, 963-967;
- Wimberly, E. P. (2011). *Story Telling and Managing Trauma: Health and Spirituality at Work.* Journal of Health Care for the Poor and Underserved, Emergency Preparedness: Ethical Faith-Health Leadership. 8, 48-57;
- Afful, I. & Williams, A. (2015). *Crisis management: the spiritual aspects of victim recovery in serious crime.* International Journal of Emergency Services4 (1), 50-64.

CONCLUSION

The spiritual perspective carries a considerable potential for treatment of an organizational trauma. Modern society, organizations and companies are built and managed by people. This implies that the natural human desire for harmony between *heaven and earth*, between the ideal and the reality of an organization must not be ignored. When people are unsuccessful in an organization, they will try to seek inner harmony. They know that life and active involvement in an organization means a specific form of tension and struggle. Therefore they need the inner energy in order to be able to face all the negative influences. Organizational trauma is one of the strongest situations for opening up latent spiritual and religious potential. This conclusion is supported by many scholars and practitioners.

Viktor Schermer (2007) writes that even the most confirmed atheists or existentialists struggle with life purpose. Psychological studies by Rudolf Říčan (2007) show that while the concept of "religion" is getting narrower, the concept of *spirituality* is getting larger. Whereas *religion* is perceived as old, obsolete, rigid, conservative, connected with the church institution, then especially in developed Western and industrial countries, "spirituality" is starting to be perceived as open, more free and with a positive potential. The spiritual perspective can even bring about an improved personal stability in technocratic society and counterbalance the one-sided Western way of thinking by the more spiritual Eastern approach.

The spiritual attitude to a trauma also corresponds with a natural human interest for a better and deeper understanding of a tragic situation. Dealing with an organizational trauma can become a spiritual experience described as a *unique experience*, perhaps as a seemingly irrational moment (Otto, 1998). Rudolf Otto, who is considered a breakthrough thinker by experts in religious studies, did not find a better term for the deepest spiritual level than *numinousness* and *mysteriousness* (an awe-arousing and fascinating secret). Such perspective has even substantially influenced our everyday thinking and behavior and can help both managers and employees who are struggling with organizational trauma.

On the other hand, the German philosopher Friedrich Schleiermacher (1768-1844) warned against a too great optimism connected to spirituality. Actually the spiritual approach is not an easy one and might not be suitable for those who are not prepared for it (Schleiermacher 2012). Schleiermacher describes spirituality as *looking out for infinity*, for one's *place in the universe.* Spirituality can develop human self-understanding in ways which cannot be achieved in the situation of success and happiness, but which open up in the situation of trauma and crisis.

Naturally, such a perspective is possible only from the spiritual point of view. Spiritual energies are also at work when the traumatized person becomes healed and returns back to him/herself and turns a new leaf. The achievement of these spiritual goals is based on the long and systemic work of entrepreneurs, managers and employees as members of a team.

REFERENCES

Adler, A. (1998). *Social Interest: Adler's Key to the Meaning of Life* (1st ed.). London, UK: Oneworld Publications.

Anzenbacher, A. (2002). *Einführung in die Philosophie* (1st ed.). Freiburg, Germany: Herder.

Argenti, A. P. (2002, October). Crisis Communication: Lessons from 9/11. Brighton, MA: Harvard Business Publishing.

Balabán, M. (2012). Kořeny a květy biblických pojmů [Roots and flowers of biblical terminology]. Benešov, Czech Republic: Eman.

Blühm, R. (1983). *Handbuch der Seelsorge* (1st ed.). Berlin, Germany: Evangelische Verlagsanstalt.

Briere, J., & Scott, C. (2006). *Principles of Trauma Therapy: A Guide to Symptoms, Evaluation, and Treatment* (1st ed.). London, UK: Sage Publications.

Cottis, T. (2008). *Intellectual Disability, Trauma and Psychotherapy* (1st ed.). Oxon, UK: Routledge.

Covey, S. R. (2000). *The 7 Habits of Highly Effective People* (2nd ed.). Philadelphia: Running Press.

Dutton, E. J., Frost, J. P., Worline, C. M., Lilius, M. J. & Kanov, M. J. (2002, January). *Leading in Times of Trauma*. Brighton, MA: Harvard Business Publishing.

Fang, T., & Faureb, G. O. (2011, May). Chinese communication characteristics: A Yin Yang perspective. *International Journal of Intercultural Relations, Amsterdam, Netherlands, 35*(3), 320–333. doi:10.1016/j.ijintrel.2010.06.005

Figley, R. Ch. (Ed.). (2012). *Encyclopedia of Trauma: An Interdisciplinary Guide* (1st ed.). London, UK: Sage Publications. doi:10.4135/9781452218595

Freud, S. (2007). *The Psychology of Love* (1st ed.). London, UK: Penguin Publishing Group.

Frommberger, U. (2014). Post-traumatic stress disorder – a diagnostic and therapeutic challenge. *Deutsches Ärzteblatt International, Cologne, Germany, 111*(5), 59–65. PMID:24612528

Fujisawa, C. (1959). *Zen and Shinto: A History of Japanese Philosophy*. New York: Philosophical Library.

Heinonen, E., Lindors, O., Laaksonen, M., & Knekt, P. (2012, May). Therapistsprofessional and personal characteristics as predictors of outcome in short- and long-term psychotherapy. *Journal of Affective Disorders, London, UK, 138*(3), 301–312. doi:10.1016/j.jad.2012.01.023 PMID:22335889

Hughes, R., Kinder, A., & Cooper, L. C. (Eds.). (2012). *International Handbook of Workplace Trauma Support* (1st ed.). Malden, MA: Wiley-Blackwell. doi:10.1002/9781119943242

Joas, H. (2008). *Do We Need Religion? On the Experience of Self-Transcendence* (1st ed.). Oxon, UK: Routledge.

Jung, C. G. (1967). Symbols of transformation (2nd ed.). Princeton University Press.

Kleber, J. R., Figley, R. Ch., & Gerson, P. R. B. (Eds.). (2013). *Beyond Trauma: Cultural and Societal Dynamics* (1st ed.). Berlin, Germany: Springer Science & Business Media.

Kučera, D. (2015). Weberova teze „ducha kapitalismu" jako podnět pro hledání spirituálních potenciálů v podnikatelském a manažerském prostředí.(Weber's "spirit of capitalism" thesis as a starting point for finding spiritual potentials in business and management environment.) Acta Oeconomica Pragensia, University of Economics, Prague, Czech Republic, 5, 24–44. doi: 10.18267/j.aop.484

Küng, H. (2008). *Spurensuche: Die Weltreligionen auf dem Weg* (2nd ed.). München, Germany: Piper Verlag.

Miller, E. (2011). Finding meaning at Ground Zero for future generations: Some reflections a decade after 9/11. *International Social Science Review, 86*(3-4), 113-133. Retrieved from http://search.proquest.com.zdroje.vse.cz/ docview/921995269?pq-origsite=summon

Otto, R. (1958). *The Idea of the Holy* (1st ed.). Oxford, UK: Oxford University Press.

Paterno, D. (2012). *Posttraumatisches Wachstum und Sinnerleben – Sinnressourcen für die Traumatherapie* (Master's Thesis). University Innsbruck, Faculty of Psychology and Sport Science. Retrieved July 9, 2016 from http://www.sinnforschung.org/wp-content/uploads/ 2012/04/ Diplomarbeit_Home pageversion.pdf

Pietschmann, H. (2001). *Merits and Limits of Applying the Scientific Method to Human Society*. Luton, UK: The Pantaneto Forum. Retrieved from http:// www.pantaneto.co.uk/issue2/pietschmann.htm

Rambo, S. (2010). *Spirit and Trauma: A Theology of Remaining* (1st ed.). Louisville, KY: Westminster John Knox Press.

Říčan, P. (2007). *Psychologie náboženství a spirituality* (1st ed.). Psychology of religion and spiritualityPraha, Czech Republic: Portál.

Rogers, D. C. F. (2002). *Pastoral Care for Post-Traumatic Stress Disorder: Healing the Shattered Soul* (3rd ed.). Philadelphia: Haworth Press.

SAMHSA. (2014a). *Concept of Trauma and Guidance for a Trauma-Informed Approach*. U.S. Department of Health and Human Services. Substance Abuse and Mental Health Services Administration Office of Policy, Planning and Innovation. Retrieved from http://store.samhsa.gov/shin/content//SMA14-4884/SMA14-4884.pdf

SAMHSA. (2014b). *Trauma-Informed Care in Behavioural Health Services*. Treatment Improvement Protocol (TIP) Series, No. 57. Centre for Substance Abuse Treatment (US).Rockville (MD): Substance Abuse and Mental Health Services Administration (US). Retrieved from http://www.ncbi.nlm.nih.gov/books/NBK207192/

Saul, J. (2009). Collective Trauma, Collective Healing: Promoting Community Resilience in the Aftermath of Disaster. New York: Routledge.

Saul, M. H. (2011, September 2). City News: Invite Clergy to 9/11 Event, Giuliani Says. *Wall Street Journal*, p. A17. Retrieved from http://search.proquest.com.zdroje.vse.cz/docview/886974828?pq-origsite=summon

Schermer, V. L. (2007). Duch a duše [Spirit and Soul]. Praha, Czech Republic: Triton.

Schleiermacher, F. (2012). On Religion: Speeches to its Cultured Despisers (2nd ed.). Cambridge University Press.

St. Just, A. (2006). *Relative balance in an unstable world. A search for new models for Trauma Education and Recovery* (1st ed.). Heidelberg, Germany: Carl-Auer Verlag.

Swain, S. (2011). *Trauma and Transformation at Ground Zero: A Pastoral Theology* (1st ed.). Minneapolis, MN: Fortress Press.

Trueman, C. E. (2005). *Luther's Theology of the Cross*. Retrieved from http://www.opc.org/new_horizons/NH05/10b.html

Weber, M. (2003). The Protestant Ethic and the Spirit of Capitalism. New York: Dover Publications. (first published 1958)

Wiktionary. (n.d.). *Trauma*. Retrieved from https://en.wiktionary.org/wiki/ trauma#Etymology

Zohar, D., & Marshall, I. (2000). *Spiritual Intelligence. The Ultimate Intelligence* (1st ed.). London, UK: Bloomsbury Publishing Plc.

KEY TERMS AND DEFINITIONS

Faith: A perspective of thinking based on chosen authorities formulating something which is considered true and important for personal life.

Hope: A perspective of thinking oriented to the future. Hope is based on the trust in the meaning of life and special values.

Meaning (of Work): An accepted value orientation based on belief in the meaning and importance of one's own work. In practice it is manifested by certain attitudes and effort.

Pastoral Psychology: A professional and spiritual or religious oriented care exercised by specifically educated psychologists, advisers or pastors.

Religiosity: A general human frame of thinking and behavior based on belief in supernatural beings and phenomena. It does not necessarily have to be connected with any religious institution.

Religion: A formally organized or institutionalized group of people based on special declaration of beliefs.

Spirituality: An internal human ability to perceive what transcends physical reality. It implicates personal openness to an experience of mystery and becomes the most important orientation.

Trauma (Organizational): A serious psychological wound based on a very negative and critical experience in professional life. Organizational trauma is composed of individual traumas of particular members.

Treatment (of Trauma): Professional effort aiming to help a traumatized person to overcome the experienced crisis and find a new perspective and internal energy for life and work.

Chapter 14
The Role of Leaders in Facilitating Healing After Organizational Trauma

Lynda Byrd-Poller
The George Washington University, USA

Jennifer L. Farmer
Renewed Mindset LLC, USA

Valerie Ford
ISP Global Communications LLC, USA

ABSTRACT

Effective 21st century organizations build cultures that adapt to an unpredictable and changing environment. However, organizational change can be traumatic. This chapter endeavors to make a contribution to knowledge about organizational trauma and leader behaviors - specifically what leaders can do when there are signs of trauma in the organization due to organizational change. Trauma is a psychosocial response to a perceived or actual event beyond one's control that results in personal feelings of overwhelming helplessness. Moreover, this chapter will examine how leader behaviors influence employee engagement and professional identity. The chapter provides background information about employee engagement in general and its positioning inside a broader framework called work-related well-being. The authors also link professional identity to the trauma of organizational change.

INTRODUCTION

Leaders are constantly responding to the external pressures of change and the internal choreography that aims to improve organizational performance. External factors such as changing demographics, government mandates, industry regulations, technological advancements, socio-cultural shifts, and global competition, all present unique challenges that leave organizations in a constant state of change. This

DOI: 10.4018/978-1-5225-2021-4.ch014

change leaves individuals within organizations grasping for a sense of stability, meaning, and direction; but even when that wish is granted, there may also be a set of traumatic responses that follow.

Research on organizational change often focuses on employee resistance (Piderit, 2000). However, trauma resulting from organizational change is rarely explored. As a result, this chapter discusses the nature of trauma in an organization in search of stability, well-being and improved performance. This chapter will serve as the introduction to the authors' intended research in the field of organizational trauma. When change invokes trauma, the authors posit that there is a negative impact on professional identity and employee engagement. Consequently, leaders must enact certain key behaviors to restore a healthy working environment. Lastly, this chapter will provide insights about the role of the leader in restoring and cultivating a healthy organizational culture.

BACKGROUND

In management literature, studies have demonstrated time and again that the organization's climate influences the psychological well-being of its employees and, therefore, the health of the organization (Vivian & Hormann, 2015). This knowledge has gone beyond concerns about the failure to provide for individual needs and has identified conditions in which the psychological health of employees can decline even when given challenging and interesting tasks. One such condition that threatens individual and organizational health is trauma. The trauma concept was first introduced in the clinical discipline and describes an emotional response to a terrible event, such as an accident or natural disaster (De Klerk, 2007). Organizational trauma typically focuses on the collective and is part of the organizational development domain. In organizations, trauma may result from a single devastating event, the effects of several harmful events, or cumulative trauma (Vivian & Hormann, 2015).

A review of the literature demonstrates that one of the most glaring issues concerning the construct of organizational trauma is that there is not a single, unifying definition for the concept. Much of the current research concerning organizational trauma emphasizes the responses to catastrophic events and has been studied at different levels of analysis and in varying contexts. For example, prior studies have focused on cumulative trauma disorders that define and describe trauma in terms of physical ailments such as carpal tunnel syndrome and other health issues (Brenner, Fairris & Ruser, 2004). Other studies define organizational trauma as a collective experience that leaves the organization temporarily vulnerable or permanently damaged (Vivian & Hormann, 2005).

Still, other scholars describe organizational trauma as a process in which organizations experience trauma in the form of dysfunctional patterns that can be seen in individuals, groups and behaviors in the organization (Kahn, 2003). Finally, De Klerk (2007) conceptualizes trauma by focusing on unresolved emotional trauma and how it blocks the capacity of individuals to be effective within the organization. All of these definitions of organizational trauma are broad, overarching concepts that provide little direction for practitioners who want to improve organizational performance. As a result, leaders who are concerned about trauma in their organizations must first determine which definition to use and then tailor that to their specific organization.

Conceptual Framework

Figure 1 presents a model of the hypothesized relationship between the behaviors of leaders and employees in the context of an organizational trauma caused by organizational change. This conceptual framework illustrates the authors' belief that trauma caused by organizational change can influence employee behaviors and may be expressed as a decline in professional identity and decreased engagement. The authors also believe that there are specific leader behaviors that can provide needed support for employees when traumatic symptoms are present. Through the exploration of these relationships, the authors intend to gain insights into leader behaviors that positively influence engagement and professional identity. Organizations experience continuous cycles of change and within its culture, there are many things that may contribute to trauma and work-related well-being. For example, leader behaviors influence organizational culture and employee behavior is influenced by the stability and instability of organizational culture.

There are some assumptions to be noted regarding the authors' conceptual framework. The authors believe that individuals and organizations experience trauma. For the purposes of this chapter, trauma is defined as a psychosocial response to a perceived or actual event beyond one's control that results in personal feelings of overwhelming helplessness (Herman, 1992; Stuart, 1996; Smollan & Sayers, 2009). Leaders must constantly respond to the external pressures of reform and the internal management of those pressures in an attempt to improve organizational performance. The authors believe constant states of change lead to traumatic responses and if leaders do not address the trauma, the trauma can proliferate; therefore, coping with constant change is critical to organizational success (Cawsey & Deszca, 2007).

Figure 1. Conceptual framework

Another assumption of the authors is the belief that leadership is a process of influencing others to understand and agree on establishing goals. Leaders affect and are affected by their followers. Thus, defining leadership as a process makes it available to everyone and not just a chosen few (Yukl, 2006). The authors also propose that leaders and employees are more context-bound and have more sophisticated behavioral ranges than might be overtly conveyed by the limitations of the authors' writing. Finally, the subtle nuances of the leader-follower relationship and the resilience of employees are also assumptions the authors hold about how behavior operates in an organizational context.

The remainder of this chapter explores the concepts in the conceptual framework and outlines the areas for further exploration and research. This chapter endeavors to make a contribution to literature, and later research, about organizational trauma and leader behaviors; specifically what leaders can do when there are signs of trauma in the organization due to organizational change. Taken as a whole, this chapter seeks to understand the leader behaviors that best support professional identity and engagement when there is evidence of trauma due to organizational change. Moreover, this chapter will examine the relationships between leader behaviors enacted to restore engagement and rebuild professional identity.

Challenges of Organizational Change

Managing change is one of the major challenges that organizations face and coping with constant change is critical to organizational success (Cawsey & Deszca, 2007 and DeVose, 2014). This challenge can result in structural and strategic changes which lead to downsizing, outsourcing and even mergers throughout the organization. Accordingly, members of the organization often find themselves in periods of what Kahn (2003) calls "stuckness" or caught in patterns that frustrate them and their capacities to do what they would like to do. Change management also involves processes used to help employees and the organization transition and adapt to change (DeVose, 2014). When organizational change is well planned and implemented successfully, it helps assure an organization's continued survival, which may result in many tangible benefits, including operational efficiencies and employee satisfaction. On the contrary, a poorly planned and unsuccessful organizational change process can be very frustrating and stressful for all involved and often results in lack of productivity (Kotter, 1999).

Trauma in Organizations

Failed attempts to properly implement organizational change can often result in trauma. Trauma can overwhelm an individual's capacity to modulate their feelings and to organize their thinking (van der Kolk, 1996). If left unresolved, trauma can present a significant barrier to employee performance within many organizations (De Klerk, 2007). Symonds (1975) posits that both the original experience of trauma and its ongoing impact on affect and cognition can lead to feelings of ineffectiveness which may cause withdrawal from other people who might be helpful, such as managers and coworkers. In other cases, change from unhealthy organizational cultures to healthier, more engaging cultures may still invoke trauma, especially when the change is from oppressive, autocratic leadership, rather than leadership that is democratic, tolerant and transformational. With the increase of organizational trauma resulting from numerous change events, leaders must be equipped to help facilitate the healing process.

Leading the Healing Process

Many human motivations, cognitions, and behavioral consequences are rooted in suffering, despair and pain. We must embrace people's powerful sense of loss and learn how to help them adapt to the trauma of even the most devastating loss. Learning to lead the healing of organizational trauma, facilitating people to contentment with their pasts and to find meaning in loss is an essential competency for organizational development (OD) professionals. (De Klerk, 2007, p. 40)

The authors of this chapter theorize that not only must OD professionals learn to facilitate the healing process, so must leaders at every level of the organization. In cases where organizational trauma exists, leaders must exhibit certain behaviors that help to restore organizational health and well-being. These leader behaviors will be explored later in this chapter.

Recognizing Symptoms of Trauma

To facilitate the healing process, leaders must be able to recognize symptoms of trauma in order to implement an appropriate response. According to De Klerk (2007, 2013), organizations can respond to trauma by acknowledging it, providing safety, symbolizing it, and allowing and dealing with emotions. Scholars in recent years have shed more light on the trauma symptoms that may result from major organizational change. Table 1 highlights common symptoms and descriptions of trauma in organizations.

Leaders must pay close attention to symptoms that members of the organizational demonstrate. This is extremely important since De Klerk (2007) suggests that organizational trauma not only affects those who are directly involved in the traumatic event, but also those who are indirectly involved. Survivor and witness accounts of traumatic events were documented by Allen, Freeman, Russell, Reizenstein, & Rentz (2001) and Baruch & Hind (2000). Although organizational trauma originates at the individual level, an individual may have a tendency to project his or her trauma into the larger organizational system, especially if the trauma experience is of high intensity (De Klerk, 2007). Consequently, the individual trauma leads to group trauma and ultimately widespread organizational trauma. If leaders do not address trauma swiftly and appropriately, it could mean organizational death.

While many view organizational downsizing and restructuring as the major causes of trauma, there are many other triggers of organizational trauma. For example, emotional trauma can also be incited by any event with sufficient emotional power to overwhelm employees and overcome their usual coping abilities (De Klerk, 2007). De Klerk (2007) lists betrayal of trust, invasion of personal space, various forms of harassment, and abuse of power, as key triggers for trauma. Surprisingly, success in the workplace can also lead one to experience emotional trauma which can be the result of increased responsibilities, loneliness, loss of peer acceptance, envy and confusion of gender roles (De Klerk, 2007). With the increase of women in the workplace, viewpoints on traditional gender roles may be challenged.

Table 1. Trauma symptoms following major organizational change. (Adapted from "Healing Emotional Trauma in Organizations: An O.D. Framework and Case Study," by Mias deKlerk, 2007, Organization Development Journal, Volume 25, No.2, p. 36. Adapted with permission.)

Symptom	Description
Aggression	Intention to cause harm to, or within, the organization.
Anxiety	Anticipation that uncertain danger is about to happen, which causes unhealthy nervousness.
Apprehension	A dreaded and fearful anticipation that something bad will happen to oneself in the organization.
Cynicism	Having distrust of the actions and intentions of others, accompanied by skepticism, suspicion and sarcastic or sneering responses.
Decreased commitment	Reduced willingness to take up time or energy to fulfill obligations.
Diminished loyalty	Reduced feelings of allegiance to the organization or its members.
Disorientation	Being confused about what is happening and how to proceed.
Distrust	Losing faith or confidence about the organization's trustworthiness and honesty.
Emotional numbness	Apathy, demonstrated by absence of emotional sensations and reactions such as feeling good, bad, happy or sad.
Fear	Being scared, usually accompanied desires to fight or flee.
Helplessness	Feeling unable to cope with one's circumstances.
Higher absenteeism and turnover	Being more inclined to take sick leave or resign.
Lack of focus	Inability to concentrate clearly on one's work.
Lack of involvement	Employees' reluctance to immerse themselves in their work or the organization.
Perceptions of betrayal	Feeling that the organization was disloyal, unfaithful and deceitful in "delivering" oneself to a worse situation.
Rejection	The experience of not being accepted, but rather being pushed aside by the organization.
Sadness	Intense feelings of unhappiness, grief and sorrow.
Uncertainty	Being undecided and not knowing what to do or where to go with one's actions.
Withdrawal	Removing oneself emotionally from organizational obligations and relations.

Figure 2. Steps to facilitate the trauma healing (De Klerk, 2007)

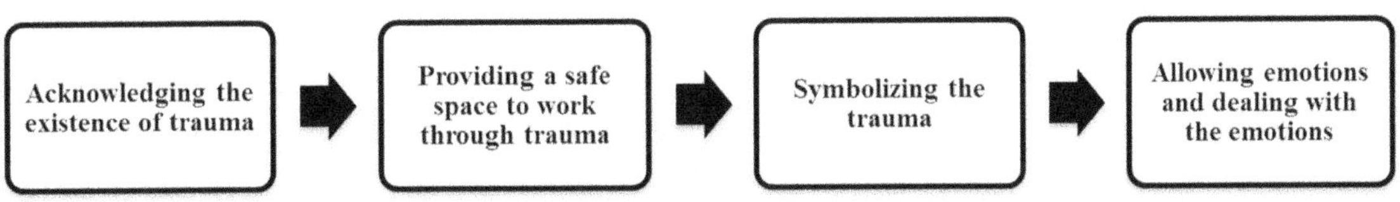

Facilitating the Healing Process

Once leaders are able to identify the symptoms of organizational trauma highlighted in Table 1, they must move forward swiftly to facilitate the healing process. De Klerk (2007) proposes a therapeutic model for healing emotional trauma. Figure 2 highlights the four integrated steps of this model:

1. Acknowledging the existence of trauma;
2. Providing a safe space to work through the trauma;
3. Symbolizing the trauma; and
4. Allowing emotions and dealing with the emotions.

Step 1: Acknowledging the Existence of Trauma

In the first and most important step of the De Klerk (2007) therapeutic model for healing, organizations must take the time to acknowledge the existence of organizational trauma and be willing to address it. This step allows trauma to be dealt with openly – allowing "victims, survivors, witnesses, and even the perpetrators, to reach contentment with their respective pasts" (De Klerk, 2007, p.38).

Trauma is described as a wound, which helps to symbolize emotional injuries and any associated hurt and pain. Similarly, the metaphor helps organizations understand how the wound must heal – like a physical wound, an emotional wound needs to be opened and cleaned in order to heal. Trauma should be symbolized and experiences brought into awareness, accepted and acknowledged. Before employees can move on to acceptance and healing, the wounds of emotional trauma are opened, the problem is named, and emotions are symbolized.

It is important to note that the leader cannot be excluded in the trauma healing process – they are participants that must deal with their own symptoms of trauma. If facilitated properly, this step of the model allows leadership to contribute to an effective healing process, supported by leader behaviors that include sensitivity to the traumatic effects of change, compassion, empathetic listening skills, awareness of their own emotions, and vulnerability to show their own pain and sorrow (De Klerk, 2006).

Step 2: Providing a Safe Space to Work through the Trauma

The second step of the De Klerk (2007) model is important due to the way many people experience trauma – one person may come through an event with no traumatic symptoms, while another might struggle for years as a result of a traumatic event. It is important to note that most trauma sufferers are not familiar with the affects, so many of them may think they are to blame for their trauma, or feel there is something wrong with them because others do not seem to have the same problems (De Klerk, 2007). Since the symptoms of trauma can often be associated with weakness, many individuals may have a tendency to hide these feelings in fear of being stigmatized. In order to alleviate trauma, it is critical for leaders to provide a safe space where people feel free to express their hurt, anger and helplessness without embarrassment, judgment, or moralization.

Step 3: Symbolizing the Trauma

The third step of the De Klerk (2007) model uses narratives as a way for healing trauma wounds. Experiences are brought into awareness, through the development and telling of stories. Developing and telling stories help employees bring order to the insensibility and chaos of certain recollections and emotions. Niederhoffer and Pennebaker (2005) posit that putting upsetting experiences into words allows people to stop inhibiting their thoughts and feelings, organize their thoughts and find meaning in their traumas. Much power is seen in speaking the unspeakable – creative energy can be released when the barriers of denial and suppression are removed. The narrative approach has been effective in dealing with the trauma of downsizing, mergers, restructuring, workplace abuse, betrayal and harassment (De Klerk, 2007).

Step 4: Allowing Emotions and Dealing with the Emotions

The last step in the De Klerk (2007) healing model highlights the connection between trauma, loss and grief. Since trauma is associated with loss and loss is associated with grief, grieving is a critical component of the healing process. Grieving is a process of emotional healing that requires time and patience so that conflicts may be worked through appropriately. The attempt to resolve trauma prematurely may leave employees stuck in anger, pain and resentment. Mourning is critical to resolving trauma.

Humor is an important factor that adds to the success of all these steps. Lefcourt (2005) highlights humor as an excellent way to deal with trauma and to recover from illness. While emotionally intense, these therapeutic interventions ultimately render some humor and laughter. Similar to humor, laughter helps the person distance themselves from grief, allowing them to recover and enjoy life more fully.

Healing Trauma through Forgiveness

In cases of organizational trauma, leaders have an especially important role to play in demonstrating virtuous behaviors (Cameron & Caza, 2002). In addition to the model outlined above, forgiveness is seen as a critical virtuous behavior. "Organizational forgiveness, then, is the capacity to foster collective abandonment of justified resentment, bitterness, and blame, and instead it is the adoption of positive, forward looking approaches in response to harm or damage" (Cameron & Caza, 2002, p. 39). Additionally, behaviors attributed to transformational leadership may provide a path toward healing organizational trauma. Transformational leaders expand and elevate the interests of their employees and attempt to increase awareness and acceptance of the organization's mission (Bass, 1985; Kelloway & McKee, 2007). Transformational leadership and how it can impact organizational trauma also will be explored in this chapter.

Cameron (2002) suggests that leaders can play two virtuous roles in fostering forgiveness and, consequently, the healing which allows the organization to move forward, focusing on a common goal:

Role 1: Leaders provide meaning and vision: In one role, leaders acknowledge the trauma, harm and injustice that the organizational members may have experienced, but define the occurrence of events as an opportunity to move forward. The important aspect of the role is to associate outcomes (i.e. products and services) with a higher purpose that provides personal meaning for organizational members. It is important to note that forgiveness is not an excuse for mediocrity. It should assist in facilitating excellence.

Role 2: Leaders provide legitimacy and support: This role allows leaders to communicate that human development and human welfare are just as important as the organization's financial bottom-line. It is believed that this support allows organizational members to move past injury or trauma.

Moving beyond trauma requires organizational compassion. Organizational compassion is the process in which organizational members collectively notice, feel and respond to pain in their organizations (Kanov, Maitlis, Worline, Dutton, Frost & Lilius, 2004). Organizational culture is one of the key determinants of the healing process after trauma. It can be expressed in both visible and embedded ways in terms of policies and procedures, as well as expectations and norms. While trauma is inevitable, the type of culture an organization has will determine how it will respond in difficult times and how employees engage with the organization.

Engagement and Well-Being

Work-related well-being is a result of the interaction between an individual and their work environment (Muchiri, Pintelon, Gelders, & Martin, 2011; Samad, et al., 2015). A greater part of the literature on well-being at work asserts that it is an affective state in which positive feelings occur more frequently than negative ones (Diener, 1999; Taris & Schaufeli, 2015). Further, well-being at work is partially a function of helping employees do what is right for them by allowing them to implement behaviors that positively influence engagement and other emotions at work (Harter, et al., 2002). Broader definitions of well-being have been proposed that include behavioral and motivational aspects (Harter, Schmidt, & Keyes, 2014; Taris & Schaufeli, 2015). Additionally, the research postulates that well-being can be measured as a context-free (i.e., general life roles) or as a domain-specific construct (e.g., work, school, etc.) and can be studied at the individual, team/group and organizational level (Rothmann, 2008; Taris & Schaufeli, 2015).

The study of well-being suggests that organizations are interested in the construct because of its impact on organizational outcomes, such as job satisfaction, organizational commitment, turnover intentions and engagement. Engagement is an aspect of work-related well-being that comprises how employees feel at work (Schaufeli & Salanova, 2014). Research also has linked employee engagement to higher rates of profitability, growth, increased staff performance, decreased staff turnover, and improved employee well-being, and is considered to be an important business driver for organizational success (Kumar & Pansari, 2015; Swarnalatha & Prasanna, 2013; Taris & Kompier, 2003; Wright & Cropanzano, 2000). Of interest to this chapter are two components of well-being: employee engagement and professional identity and what leadership behaviors can positively impact them after a trauma. Engagement is a complex concept that is influenced by many elements in the organization, including culture, communication, trust, respect and leadership (Swarnalatha & Prasanna, 2013).

The origin of the theories and models of engagement stem from two primary areas of research: job burnout and employee well-being (Maslach & Leiter, 1997) and Kahn's (1990) ethnographic study on personal engagement and disengagement. Although engagement has been studied for more than two decades, it is important to note that the definition and meaning of the construct has been problematic from the beginning (Harter, Schmidt, & Hayes, 2002; Kumar & Pansari, 2015; Schaufeli & Bakker, 2004; Swarnalatha & Prasanna, 2013). There continues to be confusion, disagreement, and a lack of consensus regarding the meaning and uniqueness of employee engagement among scholars and practitioners due partly to the conceptual overlap of engagement with other, more established constructs such as job satisfaction and organizational commitment (Bakker, Albrecht, & Leiter, 2011; Cole, Walter, Bedeian, & O'Boyle, 2012).

The first definition of engagement in the scholarly literature was presented by Kahn (1990) more than 25 years ago. Kahn defined engagement as "the harnessing of organization members' selves to their work roles." In engagement, people employ and express themselves physically, cognitively, and emotionally when performing in their work roles" (p. 694). The physical component of this definition refers to the energy a person exerts in performing their job. The emotional factor is all about personal commitment and connection to their work, and finally, the cognitive component refers to the job itself and how an individual becomes so absorbed in their work that they can forget about everything else (Kahn, 1990; May, Gilson & Harter, 2004).

In his seminal study, Kahn explored the psychological conditions of personal engagement and disengagement at work and determined that a person's degree of engagement was a function of the experience of three psychological conditions: psychological meaningfulness, psychological safety, and psychological availability (Kahn, 1990). More than a decade later, the first empirical study to investigate Kahn's theory was conducted by May, Gilson, and Harter (2004) who confirmed that meaningfulness, safety, and availability were in fact, significantly related to engagement. In a recent study, Kahn's theory was tested again and it was determined that when individuals are engaged they invest their hands (focus physical effort on the pursuit of role-related goals), head (are cognitively vigilant), and heart (are emotionally connected and present) in their performance (Ashforth & Humphrey, 1995; Rich, Lepine, & Crawford, 2010).

A second influential definition of engagement has its origins in the literature on job burnout (Kumar & Pansari, 2015; Maslach & Leiter, 1997; Maslach, Schaufeli, & Leiter, 2001). In this line of research, engagement is characterized by energy, involvement, and efficacy—the direct opposites of the burnout dimensions of exhaustion, cynicism, and inefficacy. Other researchers extended engagement research beyond burnout with a focus on employees' basic needs, asserting that engaged employees perceive their work to be meaningful, their workplace to be safe and the resources to do their job sufficient (Kumar & Pansari, 2015).

Engagement and Transformational Leadership

Scholars have made great strides in the past fifteen years in identifying workplace variables related to engagement (Harter, Schmidt, & Hayes, 2002; Schaufeli & Bakker, 2004). Recently, there has been emerging evidence which suggests that organizations are beginning to recognize the impact that leadership has on its employees and organizational outcomes (Muchiri, et al., 2011; Samad, et al., 2015). For example, one study determined that leaders are critical elements of the work environment and can influence how employees view their work (Christian, Garza, & Slaughter, 2011).

Three decades of research and a number of meta-analyses on transformational leadership establish that it is positively associated with leadership effectiveness and a number of organizational outcomes across many types of organizations, situations, levels of analyses and cultures (Avolio, et al., 2009). Likewise, over the last 100 years, many theories have been proposed that describe the leadership styles that make effective leadership possible (Avolio, Walumbwa, & Weber, 2009). Leadership style is a set of behaviors that leaders use to influence the actions of followers (Bass & Riggio, 2006).

Other research suggests that transformational leaders are able to inspire passion and identification with work amongst their employees (Bass & Avolio, 2007; Macey & Schneider, 2008). Research has established that transformational leadership has characteristics that are predicted to improve employee well-being through increased engagement and identity (Shuck & Herd, 2012). For example, Kelloway et al. (2012) assert that components of transformational leadership as proposed by Bass and Avolio (1994) are relevant to employee psychological well-being. Promotion of followers' processes of learning and self-improvement, strong relationships with each of their subordinates as well as direct communication are further characteristics of transformational leadership that improve employee health, well-being and work performance (Arnold, et al., 2007).

Initially, the primary focus in leadership research was on the individual leader, but now, the field has evolved to include followers, peers, work setting or context and culture (Avolio, et al., 2009). Furthermore, leadership is no longer described as individual characteristics or differences, but is depicted in models, such as dyadic, shared, relational, strategic, global, and as a complex social dynamic (Avolio, 2007; Yukl, 2006). Probably, the most important thing the authors have learned from the leadership literature is that leadership does not exist in a vacuum; instead it is grounded in relationships (Bennis, 2007).

Transformational leadership theory characterizes leadership as something that happens when leaders expand and elevate the interests of their employees, increase awareness and acceptance of the mission of the group and motivate employees to look beyond their own self-interest for the greater good (Arnold, Turner, Barling, Kelloway, & McKee, 2007; Bass, 1985; Kelloway, Turner, Barling, & Loughlin, 2012). Transformational leadership is about leaders who inspire commitment to a clear vision as well as guide and transform the organization to a central mission (Avolio, et al., 2009; Bass, 1985; Bass & Avolio, 1994; Burns, 1978; Zhu, Avolio, & Walumbwa, 2009).

Existing research supports the notion of a relationship between transformational leadership and levels of engagement (Brief & Weiss, 2002). In fact, in a previous study, followers were found to consider their work as more important and more aligned with their values when they had a transformational leader (Bono & Judge, 2003). Also, the transformational perspective on leadership is theoretically connected to Kahn's views on employee engagement in which leaders create the environment where engagement flourishes or fades (Kahn, 1990, 2010). Kahn's psychological conditions—meaningfulness, safety and availability are posited to be the predecessors to engagement (Kahn, 1990). Scholars and practitioners have also contended that employees will have higher levels of engagement when their basic and especially their higher order needs have been taken care of by the leaders in the organization (Harter, et al., 2002).

How then does transformational leadership impact employee engagement in an effort to restore well-being? In the conceptual framework, Kahn's (1990) theory of employee engagement was selected for its holistic approach. In this sense, work engagement is more than just the investment of a single aspect of the self; it represents the investment of multiple dimensions (physical, emotional, and cognitive) so that the experience is simultaneous and holistic (Kahn, 1992; Rich, et al., 2010). Also, transformational leadership was selected to be part of the conceptual framework because of its holistic leadership approach. In the conceptual framework, work-related well-being can potentially be restored through leadership behaviors that are attributed to the four "I's" of transformational leadership—idealized influence, intellectual stimulation, inspirational motivation, and individual consideration (Bass & Bass, 2008).

A fundamental behavior in transformational leadership is idealized influence and refers to leaders who act as a role model. Leaders who display these behaviors build loyalty and commitment with little regard for their own self-interests (Bass & Bass, 2008). When leaders set the example for followers, the followers' sense of values and contributions will increase, and as a result, they will engage their whole self in work. In fact, Kahn (1990) claimed that when employees have trust in their leaders, they will be more willing to invest themselves in their work because they feel psychologically safe (Christian, et al., 2011).

Another core behavior of transformational leadership that has been linked to employee engagement is individualized consideration. When leaders display individualized consideration behaviors, they pay attention to individual followers' needs and act as a coach and mentor (Bass & Avolio, 2007). This behavior can include discussing and empathizing with the needs of individual employees, making personal connections and showing genuine compassion and encouraging personal growth (Bass & Avolio, 2007).

Bass (1985) established that transformational leaders stimulate followers to go beyond their own basic needs to support the needs of the organization's mission and purpose when they exhibit inspirational motivation behaviors. As a result of these motivating behaviors, followers are likely to find more meaning in their work, be more innovative and make significant contributions to the organization (Shin & Zhou, 2003). By helping improve followers' sense of self-determination, psychological meaningfulness and safety, engagement might also improve as well, since psychological meaningfulness and safety are antecedents to engagement (Zhu, Avolio, & Walumbwa, 2009).

Through intellectual stimulation behaviors, leaders encourage their followers to be more creative problem solvers by questioning their assumptions and solving problems with fresh perspectives (Bass & Bass, 2008). Also, intellectually stimulating leaders create a supportive organizational culture which can play a role in the development of employees' feelings of engagement (Avolio & Bass, 2002).

Several studies support a positive relationship between transformational leadership and well-being and engagement (Arnold, Turner, Barling, Kelloway, & McKee, 2007; Nielsen, Yarker, Randall, & Munir, 2009). The research has demonstrated that leaders that display positive affect and charisma through transformational leadership tend to produce similar levels of activation and positive affect in their followers (George, 2000). Therefore, the authors expect that employee engagement will be positively related to transformational leadership and contribute to restoring overall health and well-being to an organization.

Organizational Change and Professional Identity

As discussed previously, there are many sources of trauma in the workplace. The most likely, but least obvious source of trauma is change (Nadler & Tushman, 1989). Trauma exists even when the change shifts the culture from ongoing conflict to a culture of collaboration (Bloom & Sreedhar, 2008; Bloom, 2012). Nadler and Tushman (1989) examined large-scale, re-creation organizational change and found that this type of organizational change entails shifts in values, processes, culture and leader behavior – they call this frame-breaking change. They further confirm the idea that strategic wholesale changes within the organization come with levels of intensity. "Intensity relates to the severity of the change and, in particular, the degree of shock, trauma, or discontinuity created throughout the organization" (Nadler & Tushman, 1989, p. 196).

Organizations undergo shifts as they grow, learn and develop. Large shifts in organizational culture can be traumatic if members in the organization are not given the opportunity to prepare and deal with the change (Nadler & Tushman, 1989). Changes in the organization, whether strategic or incremental, alter the culture and affect the people within the organization. As an organization works to change its image and identity, it too undergoes traumatic processes that not only affect organizational identification, but the self-concept of its employees (Van Dick, Wagner, & Lemmer, 2004).

An individual's identity is a social process that weaves together the idiosyncratic truths of an individual and their environment (Berger & Luckmann, 1967; Hogg, Terry & White, 1995; Owens, Robinson, & Smith-Lovin, 2010). Identity theory is a useful lens in examining the social nature of self, allowing the study of separate, multiple identities that reside within the self-system and their relationship in organizational culture. According to Burke and Tully (1977) an individual's identity depends on the meaning that the self prescribes to certain social roles or situations. Identity is formed through a reciprocal social dance of feedback between the self and its social environment. The type of feedback provided from the social environment influences the perception of one's self identity.

An identity is formed by the process of identification; in which, the individual evaluates and accepts others' evaluation of self within various social structures (Stets & Burke, 2000). Identities are related to the positions that individuals hold as well as what it means to display that identity. Professional identity is defined by Fagermoen (1997) as the values and beliefs held by employees that guide thinking, actions, and interactions with others. Professional identity is socially constructed and relies on the interactions and exchange between and among other social partners. Organizational studies support the principles of social identity theories because this theory helps to explain how individuals come to identify with the organization and this becomes socialized into its culture (Van Dick, Wagner, & Lemmer, 2004). Ibarra (1999) offers a definition for professional identity as "the constellation of attributes, beliefs, values, motives, and experiences in terms of which people define themselves in a professional role (p. 764-5).

Professional Identity and Trauma

The identity of employees is associated with their work achievements and personal accomplishments. Their identities are related to how they view themselves in the role and, in turn this view of self is connected to their feelings of adequacy and satisfaction (Berger & Luckmann, 1967; Burke, 2004). Professional identities are also demonstrated through the various roles enacted. "Roles serve to confirm or disconfirm the self-concepts of those who occupy them, as well as provide ways for individuals to broaden their self-concepts" (Cohen, Fink, Gadon, & Willits, 1984, p. 198). Burke and Reitzes' (1981) study clarified the relationship between identity performances and behaviors – the choices or decisions that are made by an individual whether to engage in a particular role identity. They determined that an individual's identity is used to help the individual maneuver through social interactions and meanings. When an individual experiences traumatic encounters, the effects on the self tend to be similar to those one would experience with grief (Bloom, 2012). Life after any traumatic episode begins with the process of readjusting one's self to a changed set of life circumstances and emphasizes identity work that arrives at a new sense of self (Lutgen-Sandvik, 2008).

Sudden organizational changes can come with large wakes of stress and residual sprays of post-traumatic stress symptoms, making it difficult to perform effectively (Braverman, 1992). "Organizational identification has been shown to be positively associated with employees' work-related attitudes in times of change" (Van Dick, Wagner, & Lemmer, 2004, p. 135). Cohen, Fink, Gadon, and Willits (1984) posit change can also cause defensive practices meant to protect the individual. They also asserted, when one's identity is traumatized, the challenge for leaders is two-fold: recognizing the signs of defensiveness and masking, and determining the best way to respond to increase opportunities for learning.

While traumatic stressors may be more evident in catastrophic natural events, these same stressors become less obvious when change is less pronounced and on-going. The way that individuals rebound once the work environment shifts depends on the how they see themselves. Bandura (1989) describes an individual's belief that he or she possesses the ability to successfully enact a role or behavior in a given situation as self-efficacy. He posits that an individual's belief about themselves serves as the motivation and basis for engaging action. Stuart (1996) suggests that individuals can either see themselves as victims or survivors. The difference is a matter of empowerment that allows the individual to be resolute and engaging. Being a survivor suggests a restorative quality that trauma is not all-consuming, but instead has a finite end, an escape, and a recuperative hope for something better.

Restoring a Healthy Organizational Culture after Trauma

Organizations are made up of communities, formal and informal units or sub-systems that exchange experiences, knowledge, and common understandings (Wenger, 1998). Since organizations function as communities, the identity of individuals is shaped by the group. Landau's (2007) research suggests that organizations are able to work, through the collective efforts of community members, to achieve resilience thus allowing the community the ability to confront and overcome the symptoms of trauma. "The role relationships people establish with others become important sources of stability in their lives; they count on them to help maintain personal identity, a basic sense of adequacy, and a sense of worth" (Cohen, Fink, Gadon, & Willits, 1984, p. 254). Braverman (1992) encourages group support in the aftermath of trauma, suggesting that an open and communicative organizational culture helps to mitigate traumatic symptoms.

Brown (1997) asserts that in order to get to a healthier state of organizational culture, it is vital to solicit the natural resilience within the self and use the energy surrounding traumatic episodes to power the healing process. Nurturing the health and well-being of the organization and its members is very much an organic, non-linear and delicate process in which special attention must be given to observing the signs of trauma and honoring the dignity of everyone. Leadership has a critical role in addressing trauma in organizations and helping individuals maintain a sense of dignity and remain engaged in the work of the organization.

Leading a change initiative is demanding and seemingly contradictory to work-related well-being because often it is the leader who is the initiator of change within the organization (Stuart, 1996). The choices that leaders make can cause changes in the organization that shift or strain individuals' sense of self and challenge identities. Cohen, Fink, Gadon, and Willits (1984), suggest that it is vital to the success of the change initiative for leaders to understand how individuals are processing the change and how they see their identities and roles. The self-concept of the employee will influence the ability of the organization to meet its goals and objectives.

Unhealthy work environments lend themselves to the emergence of "Toxic Leaders" (Lipman-Blumen, 2004). Toxic leaders are subtly or overtly abusive, violating the basic standards of human respect, courtesy and the rights of the people who report to them. Toxic leaders tend to be power hungry; using and often abusing the power they have (Bloom, 2012). Unhealthy environments erode self-identities that cause defensive behaviors that protect the individual from feeling uncomfortable or having to change established self-views (Cohen, Fink, Gadon, & Willits, 1984). Unhealthy or toxic environments make it difficult to trust, learn and grow. The trauma of working in an unhealthy, unsafe environment promotes feelings of vulnerability and disorder (Stuart, 1996).

Creating or restoring an organization to a healthy state of well-being is no small or easy task. Bloom (2012) suggests in order to create and sustain a healthy environment, the desired culture must be explicit, visualized, articulated and planned to promote a supportive, conscious and deliberate environment. "One of the most demanding aspects of leadership is to create a positive culture that engages employees at a personal level" (Bryant 2011, p. 202). Bryant also suggests that leaders can make more of an effort to make organizations self-governing by fostering a culture that encourages employees to make decisions for themselves and work and learn collaboratively. Finally, it is suggested that leaders trying to rebuild healthy work cultures after years of workplace violence, aggression and disentanglement must establish and adhere to policies that protect and ensure the dignity of its members (Brown, 1997; Vickers, 2001).

Leadership Behaviors that Facilitate Healing after Trauma

Brown (1997) maintains that trauma and transition are fundamental organizational health issues and while there is no protection against trauma, it can potentially feed creativity and growth if a healthy transition is initiated. So, what kind of leadership or leader behaviors are needed after an organizational trauma has occurred? When an organizational trauma occurs, the result leaves employees feeling anxious, withdrawn, fearful, hopeless and filled with distrust (De Klerk, 2007). Transformational leaders can help address these issues by raising followers' aspirations and activating higher order values, such that followers identify with the leader and his or her mission and vision, feel better about their work and try to perform beyond simple transactions and basic expectations (Bass, 1985).

Research on organizational trauma focuses on how leaders can help their organizations heal (Brown, 1997; Nielsen, Yarker, Randall, & Munir, 2009; Samad, Reaburn, Davis, & Ahmed, 2015). Leadership is always more challenging in difficult times and tough problems require innovative ways to address them. Organizations continuously face uncertainty and challenges that run the gamut from failures to terrorism. However, in times of difficulty and change, leader behaviors such as support, empowerment and a high-quality relationship between leaders and their followers might prevent stress, and improve employees' affective well-being (Schaufeli & Enzmann, 1998).

When an individual experiences trauma, there is an overwhelming reaction to events that have been forcefully and intimately experienced for which a person feels powerless to cope (Stuart, 1996). During times of trauma, leaders have a critical responsibility to address the trauma head on and stabilize the organization while offering hope and remaining calm and compassionate (Brown, 1997; Hormann & Vivian, 2005). Additionally, leadership must focus on ways to help people bounce back from negative events and restore their well-being through the search for meaning, connection and self-awareness (Hormann & Vivian, 2005). Scholars and practitioners alike agree that the quality of leadership is one of the single biggest factors contributing to work engagement, character development, task performance, and creativity (Ghadi, Fernando, & Caputi, 2013; Judge & Piccolo, 2006; Nielsen, et al., 2009; Piccolo & Colquitt, 2004; Shin & Zhou, 2003). Thus, the kinds of leadership needed to guide organizations through difficult times must emphasize perspectives, visions and models that help meet the challenges of a changing workplace (Shuck & Herd, 2012).

The behaviors attributed to transformational leadership might make it a suitable approach for organizations that have experienced a trauma because transformational leaders that embody these behaviors affect employees at both the instrumental and symbolic levels (Bass & Riggio, 2006; Judge & Piccolo, 2006). Additionally, transformational leadership behaviors also could positively impact organizational trauma through the psychological conditions of meaningfulness, safety and availability. The Four I's of transformational leadership foster attentiveness, connection, and focus in followers (Ashforth & Humphrey, 1995; Kahn, 1990; Kelloway, et al., 2012).

Table 2 depicts the Four I's of transformational leadership and the corresponding organizational trauma symptoms as defined by Allen, Freeman, Russell, Reizenstein & Rentz, (2001) and cited by De Klerk (2007) for which they possibly help to improve and restore well-being.

Table 2. Transformational leadership styles and trauma symptoms

Transformational Leadership Style	Organizational Trauma Symptoms
Idealized Influence – Build relationships based on trust, sets the example and serve as a positive role model for followers	Distrust, diminished loyalty, cynicism, perceptions of betrayal
Intellectual Stimulation – take people places they have never been before by stimulating them to challenge assumptions, reframe problems and devise new solutions	Disorientation, decreased commitment
Inspirational Motivation– Get people excited about going to new places by inspiring meaning and challenge	Lack of focus, emotional numbness, lack of involvement
Individual Consideration – act as coach and mentor and enabling others to act on their own by paying special attention to followers and their needs	Having distrust of the actions and intentions of others, accompanied by skepticism, suspicion and sarcastic or sneering responses

Transformational Leadership and its Impact on Well-Being

If leadership can change the way in which employees engage with their organizations, then it may have great consequences for employee self-concept and professional identity. Accordingly, tying sense of self to the collective is an important piece of leadership effectiveness (De Cremer & Van Knippenberg, 2002). Aligned with this idea of identity and the collective, transformational leaders encourage followers to achieve more by focusing on their values and helping to align these values with those of the organization (Bass, 1985; Burns, 1978).

A conceptual relationship has been drawn between transformational leadership behavior, employee engagement and professional identity in the context of organizational trauma. The authors also believe that there are specific leadership behaviors that can provide needed support for employee behavior when traumatic symptoms are present. This relationship has implications for organizations looking to increase engagement levels and foster professional identity after a trauma in order to restore well-being and a healthy organizational culture.

FUTURE RESEARCH DIRECTIONS

This chapter discusses the conceptual relationship between organizational trauma, organizational change, transformational leadership behaviors and their influence on engagement and professional identity. An examination of the relationships between the constructs in this chapter is a logical next step for research. Future research will seek to validate this conceptual framework and further the understanding of organizational trauma. Additional study is needed to further understanding of organizational trauma - especially those experiences that are not the result of catastrophic events but instead manifest themselves in the subtleties and nuances of organizational life. Research on organizational trauma as an unintended consequence of seemingly positive organizational change is another interesting research direction. The authors' future research aims to explore organizational trauma and how transformational leadership can facilitate healing, and restore engagement and professional identity. Our intention is to contribute to the literature and to inform practice regarding the signs and symptoms of organizational trauma with a focus on which leader behaviors are most effective when it is present. Exploring the experiences of practitioners regarding organizational trauma and seeking to understand the impact that trauma can have on the organization may help to close this research gap.

CONCLUSION

This chapter endeavors to stimulate research in the field of organizational trauma. As the exploration of the construct evolves, a unifying definition and a unified community of scholars and practitioners may potentially emerge. Prior research has shown that organizational trauma is real and is most easily identified when there are catastrophic events. However, more focus is needed on incidents that do not make the headlines, but have just as great an impact on individuals in the organization that experience them. We live and work in a complex world in which change is inevitable and expected. Therefore continued research on organizational trauma will be an important step forward for leaders and organizations that are interested in managing change and maintaining the well-being of its employees.

For all the progress that has been made regarding the study of organizational trauma, there is still plenty of work to be done. The authors focused on one aspect of the phenomenon and its relationship to other constructs. It has been posited that organizational trauma is a concept that is under-investigated, yet it has significant implications for organizations when it is not addressed. Organizations that seek to establish and maintain healthy work cultures should know how to identify trauma so that they can put strategies in place to deal with it. The objectives of this chapter have been to contribute to the conversation on organizational trauma, providing scholars and practitioners with insights on potential behaviors that leaders can use to restore well-being and accelerate healing through engagement and professional identity when organizational trauma occurs.

REFERENCES

Allen, T. D., Freeman, D. M., Russell, J. E., Reizenstein, R. C., & Rentz, J. O. (2001). Survivor reactions to organizational downsizing: Does time ease the pain? *Journal of Occupational and Organizational Psychology*, *74*(2), 145–164. doi:10.1348/096317901167299

Arnold, K. A., Turner, N., Barling, J., Kelloway, E. K., & McKee, M. C. (2007). Transformational leadership and psychological well-being: The mediating role of meaningful work. *Journal of Occupational Health Psychology*, *12*(3), 193–203. doi:10.1037/1076-8998.12.3.193 PMID:17638487

Ashforth, R. E., & Humphrey, R. H. (1995). Emotion in the workplace: A reappraisal. *Human Relations*, *48*(2), 97–125. doi:10.1177/001872679504800201

Avolio, B. (2007). Promoting more integrative strategies for leadership theory-building. *The American Psychologist*, *62*(1), 25–33. doi:10.1037/0003-066X.62.1.25 PMID:17209677

Avolio, B. J., & Bass, B. M. (2002). *Manual for the multifactor leadership questionnaire (Form 5X)*. Redwood City, CA: Mindgarden.

Avolio, B. J., Walumbwa, F. O., & Weber, T. J. (2009). Leadership: Current theories, research, and future directions. *Annual Review of Psychology*, *60*(1), 421–449. doi:10.1146/annurev.psych.60.110707.163621 PMID:18651820

Bakker, A. B., Albrecht, S. L., & Leiter, M. P. (2011). Key questions regarding work engagement. *European Journal of Work and Organizational Psychology*, *20*(1), 4–28. doi:10.1080/1359432X.2010.485352

Bandura, A. (1989). Social cognitive theory. In R. Vasta (Ed.), Annals of child development: Six theories of child mental health development (vol. 6, pp. 1-60). Greenwich, CT: JAI Press.

Bass, B. M. (1985). *Leadership and Performance Beyond Expectations*. New York: Free Press.

Bass, B. M., & Avolio, B. J. (1994). *Improving organizational effectiveness through transformational leadership*. Thousand Oaks, CA: Sage Publications.

Bass, B. M., & Avolio, B. J. (2007). Developing transformational leadership: 1992 and beyond. *Journal of European Industrial Training*, *14*(5), 25–33.

Bass, B. M., & Bass, R. (2008). *The Bass handbook of leadership: Theory, research, and managerial applications*. New York: Free Press.

Bass, B. M., & Riggio, R. E. (2006). *Transformational Leadership* (2nd ed.). Mahwah, NJ: Lawrence Erlbaum Associates.

Bennis, W. (2007). The challenges of leadership in the modern world: Introduction to the special issue. *The American Psychologist*, *62*(1), 2–5. doi:10.1037/0003-066X.62.1.2 PMID:17209674

Berger, L., & Luckmann, T. (1967). The foundations of knowledge in everyday life. In *The social construction of reality*. New York: Anchor Books, Doubleday.

Bloom, S. L. (2012). *Building resilient workers and organisations: The Sanctuary Model of organisational change. In Workplace bullying: Symptoms and solutions* (pp. 260–277). Hove, UK: Routledge.

Bloom, S. L., & Sreedhar, S. Y. (2008). The sanctuary model of trauma-informed organizational change. *Reclaiming Children and Youth*, *17*(3), 48–53.

Bono, J. E., & Judge, T. A. (2003). Core self-evaluations: A review of the trait and its role in job satisfaction and job performance. *European Journal of Personality*, *17*(S1), S5–S18. doi:10.1002/per.481

Braverman, M. (1992). Post-trauma crisis intervention in the workplace. In *Stress and well-being at work: Assessments and interventions for occupational mental health*, (pp. 299-316). Academic Press.

Brief, A., & Weiss, H. (2002). Organizational behavior: Affect in the workplace. *Annual Review of Psychology*, *53*(1), 279–307. doi:10.1146/annurev.psych.53.100901.135156 PMID:11752487

Brown, E. H. (1997). Improving organizational health by addressing organizational trauma. *Journal of Organizational Change Management*, *10*(2), 175–178. doi:10.1108/09534819710160835

Bryant, A. (2011). *The corner office: Indispensable and unexpected lessons from CEOs on how to lead and succeed*. New York: Times Books.

Burke, P. (2004). Identities and social structure: The 2003 Cooley-Mead award address. *Social Psychology Quarterly*, *67*(1), 5–15. doi:10.1177/019027250406700103

Burke, P., & Reitzes, D. (1981). The Link between identity and role performance. *Social Psychology Quarterly*, *44*(2), 83–92. doi:10.2307/3033704

Burns, J. M. (1978). *Leadership*. New York: Harper and Row.

Cameron, K., & Caza, A. (2002). Organizational and leadership virtues and the role of forgiveness. *Journal of Leadership & Organizational Studies*, *9*(1), 33–48. doi:10.1177/107179190200900103

Cawsey, T. F., & Deszca, G. (2007). Toolkit for organizational change. *Sage (Atlanta, Ga.)*.

Christian, M. S., Garza, A. S., & Slaughter, J. E. (2011). Work engagement: A quantitative review and test of its relations with task and contextual performance. *Personnel Psychology*, *64*(1), 89–136. doi:10.1111/j.1744-6570.2010.01203.x

Cohen, A., Fink, S., Gadon, H., & Willits, R. (1984). *Effective Behavior in Organizations* (3rd ed.). Homewood, IL: Richard D. Irwin, Inc.

Cole, M. S., Walter, F., Bedeian, A. G., & OBoyle, E. H. (2012). Job burnout and employee engagement a meta-analytic examination of construct proliferation. *Journal of Management*, *38*(5), 1550–1581. doi:10.1177/0149206311415252

De Cremer, D., & Van Knippenberg, D. (2002). How do leaders promote cooperation? The effects of charisma and procedural fairness. *The Journal of Applied Psychology*, *87*(5), 858–866. doi:10.1037/0021-9010.87.5.858 PMID:12395810

De Klerk, J. J. (2006 October). *Learning to lead organizational trauma: A positive advancement in leadership development*. Paper presented at the Gallup Leadership Institute Summit, Washington, DC.

De Klerk, M. (2007). Healing emotional trauma in organizations: An OD framework and case study. *Organization Development Journal*, *25*(2).

De Vose, C. (2014). *Successfully leading needed organization change: Strategies for leading change and managing resistance*. Retrieved from ProQuest Dissertations & Theses Global. (Accession Order No. AAT 3703633)

Diener, E., Suh, E., Lucas, R., & Smith, H. (1999). Subjective well-being: Three decades of progress. *Psychological Bulletin*, *125*(2), 276–302. doi:10.1037/0033-2909.125.2.276

Fagermoen, M. S. (1997). Professional identity: Values embedded in meaningful nursing practice. *Journal of Advanced Nursing*, *25*(3), 434–441. doi:10.1046/j.1365-2648.1997.1997025434.x PMID:9080267

George, J. M. (2000). Emotions and leadership: The role of emotional intelligence. *Human Relations*, *53*(8), 1027–1055. doi:10.1177/0018726700538001

Ghadi, M. Y., Fernando, M., & Caputi, P. (2013). Transformational leadership and work engagement: The mediating effect of meaning in work. *Leadership and Organization Development Journal*, *34*(6), 532–550. doi:10.1108/LODJ-10-2011-0110

Harter, J. K., Schmidt, F. L., & Hayes, T. L. (2002). Business-unit-level relationship between employee satisfaction, employee engagement, and business outcomes: A meta-analysis. *The Journal of Applied Psychology*, *87*(2), 268–279. doi:10.1037/0021-9010.87.2.268 PMID:12002955

Harter, J. K., Schmidt, F. L., & Keyes, C. L. M. (2014). Well-being in the workplace and its relationship to business outcomes: A review of the Gallup studies. *Flourishing: Positive Psychology and the Life Well-Lived, 2,* 205-224.

Herman, J. L. (1992). Complex PTSD: A syndrome in survivors of prolonged and repeated trauma. *Journal of Traumatic Stress*, *5*(3), 377–391. doi:10.1002/jts.2490050305

Hogg, M. A., Terry, D. J., & White, K. M. (1995). A tale of two theories: A critical comparison of identity theory with social identity theory. *Social Psychology Quarterly*, *58*(4), 255–269. doi:10.2307/2787127

Hormann, S., & Vivian, P. (2005). Toward an understanding of traumatized organizations and how to intervene in them. *Traumatology*, *11*(3), 159–169. doi:10.1177/153476560501100302

Ibarra, H. (1999). Provisional selves: Experimenting with image and identity in professional adaptation. *Administrative Science Quarterly*, *44*(4), 764–791. doi:10.2307/2667055

Judge, T. A., & Piccolo, R. F. (2006). Transformational and transactional leadership: A meta-analytic test of their relative validity. *The Journal of Applied Psychology*, *89*(5). PMID:15506858

Kahn, W. A. (1990). Psychological conditions of personal engagement and disengagement at work. *Academy of Management Journal*, *33*(4), 692–724. doi:10.2307/256287

Kahn, W. A. (2003). The revelation of organizational trauma. *The Journal of Applied Behavioral Science*, *39*(4), 364–380. doi:10.1177/0021886303261954

Kahn, W. A. (2010). The essence of engagement: Lessons from the field. In S. L. Albrecht (Ed.), *Handbook of Employee Engagement: Perspectives, Issues, Research and Practice* (pp. 20–30). Cheltenham, UK: Edward Elgar. doi:10.4337/9781849806374.00008

Kanov, J. M., Maitlis, S., Worline, M. C., Dutton, J. E., Frost, P. J., & Lilius, J. M. (2004). Compassion in organizational life. *The American Behavioral Scientist*, *47*(6), 808–827. doi:10.1177/0002764203260211

Kelloway, K. E., Turner, N., Barling, J., & Loughlin, C. (2012). Transformational leadership and employee psychological well-being: The mediating role of employee trust in leadership. *Work & Stress: An International Journal of Work. Health & Organisations*, *26*(1), 39–55.

Kotter, J. P. (1999). *John P. Kotter on what leaders really do*. Harvard Business Press.

Kumar, V., & Pansari, A. (2015). Measuring the Benefits of Employee Engagement. *MIT Sloan Management Review*, *56*(4), 67.

Lefcourt, H. M. (2005). Humor. In C. R. Snyder & S. J, Lopez (Eds.), Handbook of positive psychology (pp. 619-629). Oxford, UK: Oxford University Press.

Lipman-Blumen, J. (2006). *The allure of toxic leaders: Why we follow destructive bosses and corrupt politicians-and how we can survive them.* Oxford University Press.

Lutgen-Sandvik, P. (2008). Intensive remedial identity work: Responses to workplace bullying trauma and stigmatization. *Organization, 15*(1), 97–119. doi:10.1177/1350508407084487

Macey, W. H., & Schneider, B. (2008). The meaning of employee engagement. *Industrial and Organizational Psychology: Perspectives on Science and Practice, 1*(1), 3–30. doi:10.1111/j.1754-9434.2007.0002.x

Maslach, C., & Leiter, M. P. (1997). *The truth about burnout.* San Francisco, CA: Jossey-Bass.

Maslach, C., Schaufeli, W. B., & Leiter, M. P. (2001). Job burnout. *Annual Review of Psychology, 52*(1), 397–422. doi:10.1146/annurev.psych.52.1.397 PMID:11148311

May, D. R., Gilson, R. L., & Harter, L. M. (2004). The psychological conditions of meaningfulness, safety and availability and the engagement of the human spirit at work. *Journal of Occupational and Organizational Psychology, 77*(1), 11–37. doi:10.1348/096317904322915892

Muchiri, P., Pintelon, L., Gelders, L., & Martin, H. (2011). Development of maintenance function performance measurement framework and indicators. *International Journal of Production Economics, 131*(1), 295–302. doi:10.1016/j.ijpe.2010.04.039

Nadler, D. A., & Tushman, M. L. (1989). Organizational frame bending: Principles for managing reorientation. *The Academy of Management Executive, 3*(3), 194–204. doi:10.5465/AME.1989.4274738

Niederhoffer, K. G., & Pennebaker, J.W. (2009). *Sharing one's story: On the benefits of writing or talking about emotional experience.* Academic Press.

Nielsen, K., Yarker, J., Randall, R., & Munir, F. (2009). The mediating effects of team and self-efficacy on the relationship between transformational leadership and job satisfaction and psychological well-being in healthcare professionals. *International Journal of Nursing Studies, 46*(9), 1236–1244. doi:10.1016/j.ijnurstu.2009.03.001 PMID:19345946

Northouse, P. G. (2007). *Leadership: Theories and practices.* Academic Press.

Owens, T., Robinson, D., & Smith-Lovin, L. (2010). Three faces of identity. *Annual Review of Sociology, 36*(23), 1–23.

Piccolo, R. F., & Colquitt, J. A. (2004). Transformational leadership and job behaviors: The mediating role of core job characteristics. *Academy of Management Journal, 49*(2), 327–340. doi:10.5465/AMJ.2006.20786079

Piderit, S. K. (2000). Rethinking resistance and recognizing ambivalence: A multidimensional view of attitudes toward an organizational change. *Academy of Management Review, 25*(4), 783–794.

Rich, B. L., Lepine, J. A., & Crawford, E. R. (2010). Job engagement: Antecedents and effects on job performance. *Academy of Management Journal, 53*(3), 617–635. doi:10.5465/AMJ.2010.51468988

Rothmann, S. (2008). Job satisfaction, occupational stress, burnout and work engagement as components of work-related well-being. *SA Journal of Industrial Psychology, 34*(3), 11–16. doi:10.4102/sajip.v34i3.424

Samad, A., Reaburn, P., Davis, H., & Ahmed, E. (2015). *An Empirical Study on the Effect of Leadership Styles on Employee well-being and Organizational Outcomes within an Australian Regional University.* Paper presented at the Australasian Conference on Business and Social Sciences, Sydney, Australia.

Schaufeli, W. B., & Bakker, A. B. (2004). Job demands, job resources, and their relationship with burnout and engagement: A multi-sample study. *Journal of Organizational Behavior*, *25*(3), 293–315. doi:10.1002/job.248

Schaufeli, W. B., & Enzmann, D. (1998). *The Burnout Companion to Study and Practice*. Philadelphia, PA: Taylor & Francis, Inc.

Schaufeli, W. B., & Salanova, M. (2014). Burnout, Boredom and Engagement in the Workplace. In M. C. W. Peeters, J. d. Jonge, & T. W. Taris (Eds.), *An Introduction to Contemporary Work Psychology* (pp. 293–320). John Wiley & Sons, Ltd.

Shin, S. J., & Zhou, J. (2003). Transformational leadership, conservation, and creativity: Evidence from Korea. *Academy of Management Journal*, *46*(3), 703–714.

Shuck, B., & Herd, A. M. (2012). Employee engagement and leadership: Exploring the convergence of two frameworks and implications for Leadership in HRD. *Human Resource Development Review*, *11*(2), 156–181. doi:10.1177/1534484312438211

Smollan, R. K., & Sayers, J. G. (2009). Organizational culture, change and emotions: A qualitative study. *Journal of Change Management*, *9*(4), 435–457. doi:10.1080/14697010903360632

Stets, J., & Burke, P. (2000). Identity theory and social identity theory. *Social Psychology Quarterly*, *63*(3), 224–237. doi:10.2307/2695870

Stuart, R. (1996). The trauma of organizational change. *Journal of European Industrial Training*, *20*(2), 11–16. doi:10.1108/03090599610110420

Swarnalatha, C., & Prasanna, T. S. (2013). Employee engagement: The concept. *International Journal of Management Research and Review*, *3*(12), 3872–3880.

Symonds, M. (1975). Victims of violence: Psychological effects and after effects. *American Journal of Psychoanalysis*, *35*(1), 19–26. doi:10.1007/BF01248422 PMID:1155652

Taris, T. W., & Schaufeli, W. B. (2015). Individual Well-being and Performance at Work: A conceptual and theoretical overview. In M. V. V. R. Peccei (Ed.), *Well-being and performance at work: The role of context* (pp. 15–34). London: Taylor & Francis.

Van der Kolk, B.A. (1996). *The complexity of adaptation to trauma: Self-regulation, stimulus discrimination, and characterological development.* Academic Press.

Van Dick, R., Wagner, U., & Lemmer, G. (2004). Research note: The winds of change—Multiple identifications in the case of organizational mergers. *European Journal of Work and Organizational Psychology*, *13*(2), 121–138. doi:10.1080/13594320444000038

Vickers, M. H. (2001). Bullying as unacknowledged organizational evil: A researchers story. *Employee Responsibilities and Rights Journal*, *13*(4), 205–217. doi:10.1023/A:1014975203542

Vivian, P., & Hormann, S. (2015). Persistent Traumatization in Nonprofit Organizations. *OD Practitioner, 47*(1), 25–30.

Wenger, E. (1998). Communities of practice: Learning as a social system. *Systems Thinker, 9*(5), 2-3.

Yukl, G. (2006). *Leadership in organizations* (6th ed.). Saddle River, NJ: Prentice Hall.

Zhu, W., Avolio, B. J., & Walumbwa, F. O. (2009). Moderating role of follower characteristics with transformational leadership and follower work engagement. *Group & Organization Management, 34*(5), 590–619. doi:10.1177/1059601108331242

KEY TERMS AND DEFINITIONS

Employee Engagement: The full participation and expression of self--physically, cognitively, and emotionally--through work roles.

Identity Theory: A philosophy that considers multiple perceptions and meanings of self as a result of the interchange between the self and self-in-role.

Identity: The psychosocial marker of the self that is projected in and shaped by social systems.

Organizational Change: The way an organization recognizes and responds to shifts in the environment and organizational culture through modifications in its thinking, practices, structures, and services.

Transformational Leadership: A style of leadership where leaders and followers/employees work together to identify the needed change, create a vision to guide the change and execute the change together.

Trauma: A psychosocial response to a perceived or actual event beyond one's control that result in personal feelings of overwhelming helplessness.

Work-Related Well-Being: A broad and encompassing construct that takes into account the physical and emotional health of employees.

Compilation of References

Abrahamson, E. (2004). *Change without pain: How managers can overcome initiative overload, organizational chaos, and employee burnout.* Boston, MA: Harvard Business School Press.

Abulnour, A. H. (2014). The post-disaster temporary dwelling: Fundamentals of provision, design and construction. *Housing and Building National Research Center Journal, 10*, 10–24.

Ace, W., & Parker, S. (2010). Overcoming change fatigue through focused employee engagement. *OD Practitioner, 42*(1), 21–25.

Ackoff, R. L. (2006). Why few organizations adopt systems thinking. *Systems Research and Behavioral Science, 23*(5), 705–708. doi:10.1002/sres.791

Ackoff, R. L., & Strümpfer, J. P. (2003). Terrorism: A systemic review. *Systems Research and Behavioral Science, 20*(3), 287–294. doi:10.1002/sres.544

Adams, J. S. (1965). Inequity in social exchange. *Advances in Experimental Social Psychology, 2*, 267–299. doi:10.1016/S0065-2601(08)60108-2

Adams, R. E., Boscarino, J. A., & Figley, C. R. (2006). Compassion fatigue and psychological distress among social workers: A validation study. *The American Journal of Orthopsychiatry, 76*(1), 103–108. doi:10.1037/0002-9432.76.1.103 PMID:16569133

Adizes, I. (1979). Organizational passagesdiagnosing and treating lifecycle problems of organizations. *Organizational Dynamics, 8*(1), 3–25. doi:10.1016/0090-2616(79)90001-9

Adler, A. (1998). *Social Interest: Adler's Key to the Meaning of Life* (1st ed.). London, UK: Oneworld Publications.

Ailon, G. (2009). *Dialog*. Academy of Management Review.

Aini, M. S., & Fakhrul-Raz, A. (2013). Latent errors of socio-technical disasters: A Malaysian case study. *Safety Science, 51*(1), 284–292. doi:10.1016/j.ssci.2012.07.004

Aitkenhead, D. (2014, May 24). Lord Browne: 'I though being gay was basically wrong'. *The Guardian*. Retrieved from https://www.theguardian.com/society/2014/may/24/lord-browne-thought-being-gay-wrong-interview-bp-boss-homophobia

Alarcon, G., Eschleman, K. J., & Bowling, N. A. (2009). Relationships between personality variables and burnout: A meta-analysis. *Work & Stress: An International Journal of Work, Health, & Organisations, 23*(3), 244–263.

Alas, R., Gao, J., & S, V. (2007). The crisis management in Chinese and Estonian organizations. *Chinese Management Studies,* 18-36.

Allen, T. D., Freeman, D. M., Russell, J. E., Reizenstein, R. C., & Rentz, J. O. (2001). Survivor reactions to organizational downsizing: Does time ease the pain? *Journal of Occupational and Organizational Psychology*, *74*(2), 145–164. doi:10.1348/096317901167299

Alliatti, A. (2014, February 2). Homossexualidade no esporte: Brasil mantém futebol dentro do armário. *Globo*. Retrieved from http://globoesporte.globo.com/futebol/noticia/2014/02/homossexualidade-no-esporte-brasil-mantem-futebol-dentro-do-armario.html

Amabile, T. M., & Conti, R. (1999). Changes in the work environment for creativity during downsizing. *Academy of Management Journal*, *42*(6), 630–640. doi:10.2307/256984

American Psychiatric Association. (1980). *Diagnostic and statistical manual of mental disorders* (3rd ed.). Washington, DC: Author.

American Psychiatric Association. (2000). Diagnostic and statistical manual of mental disorders (4th ed.). Rev. Washington DC: Author.

American Psychiatric Association. (2013). *Diagnostic and statistical manual of mental health* (5th ed.). Washington, DC: Author.

American Psychological Association. (2010). *Publication manual of the American Psychological Association* (6th ed.). Washington, DC: Author.

American Psychological Association. (2013). DSM 5. American Psychiatric Association.

American Psychological Association. (2015). *Stress in America. Paying With Our Health.* Retrieved December 3, 2015, from https://www.apa.org/news/press/releases/stress/2014/stress-report.pdf

Anderson, E. (2013). *Sport, Masculinities and Sexualities*. New York, NY: Routledge Taylor & Francis.

Andersson, L. M., & Pearson, C. M. (1999). Tit for tat? The spiraling effect of incivility in the workplace. *Academy of Management Review*, *24*(3), 452–471. doi:10.5465/AMR.1999.2202131

Andreassen, C. S. (2014). Workaholism: An overview and current status of the research. *Journal of Behavioral Addictions*, *3*(1), 1–11. doi:10.1556/JBA.2.2013.017 PMID:25215209

Andreoli, A., & Damsa, C. (2005). Stress, dissociation ou trauma psychique? Incidence des travaux francophones dans le débat international. *Revue Francophone du Stress et du Trauma*, *5*(2), 61–65.

Annarelli, A., & Nanino, F. (2015). *Strategic and operational management of organizational resilience: Current state of research and future directions*. Retrieved from: http://www.sciencedirect.com/science/article/pii/S0305048315001590

Anon., (1977). Israel's Economic Crisis. *Journal of Palestine Studies*, 137–145.

Anon. (2016). *International Business Cultures.* Available at: http://www.via-web.de/specific-vs-diffuse-cultures/

Antonacopoulou, E., & Sheaffer, Z. (2014). Learning in crisis: rethinking the relationship between organizational learning and crisis management. *Journal of Management Inquiry, 23*(1), 5-21.

Anzenbacher, A. (2002). *Einführung in die Philosophie* (1st ed.). Freiburg, Germany: Herder.

Anzieu, D. B., Chabert, J., Chouvier, B., Ciccone, A., Clancier, A., … Vidal, J. P. (1986). *L'Oeuvre Ouverte.* Paper presented at the Journées d'Etudes de Psychologie Sociale Clinique Organisées par le C.O.R sur le thème L'œuvre Ouverte: Autour Du Concept De Moi-Peau Et Des Travaux De Didier Anzieu.

Anzieu, D., & Séchaud, E. (1995). *Le moi-peau.* Dunod.

Appelbaum, S. H., Patton, E., & Shapiro, B. (2003). The early retirement incentive program: A downsizing strategy. *Journal of European Industrial Training*, *27*(1), 22–35. doi:10.1108/03090590310456500

Appleby, L. (1989). Near death experience. *BMJ: British Medical Journal*, *298*(6679), 976–977. doi:10.1136/bmj.298.6679.976 PMID:2499387

Appleton, A. A., Buka, S. L., Loucks, E. B., Gilman, S. E., & Kubzansky, L. D. (2013). Divergent associations of adaptive and maladaptive emotion regulation strategies with inflammation. *Health Psychology*, *32*(7), 748–756. doi:10.1037/a0030068 PMID:23815767

Arches, J. (1991). Social structure, burnout, and job satisfaction. *Social Work*, *36*(3), 202–206. PMID:2057805

Argenti, A. P. (2002, October). Crisis Communication: Lessons from 9/11. Brighton, MA: Harvard Business Publishing.

Aristotle, . (1925). *The Nicomachean ethics* (D. Ross, Trans.). New York: Oxford University Press.

Aristotle, . (1984). *The Complete Works of Aristotle*. Princeton, NJ: Princeton University Press.

Armstrong-Stassen, M. (2005). Coping With Downsizing: A Comparison of Executive-Level and Middle Managers. *International Journal of Stress Management*, *12*(2), 117–141. doi:10.1037/1072-5245.12.2.117

Arnetz, B. B. (2005). Subjective indicators as a gauge for improving organizational well being. An attempt to apply the cognitive activation theory to organizations. *Psychoneuroendocrinology*, *30*(10), 1022–1026. doi:10.1016/j.psyneuen.2005.03.016 PMID:15955637

Arnold, K. A., Turner, N., Barling, J., Kelloway, E. K., & McKee, M. C. (2007). Transformational leadership and psychological well-being: The mediating role of meaningful work. *Journal of Occupational Health Psychology*, *12*(3), 193–203. doi:10.1037/1076-8998.12.3.193 PMID:17638487

Ashforth, R. E., & Humphrey, R. H. (1995). Emotion in the workplace: A reappraisal. *Human Relations*, *48*(2), 97–125. doi:10.1177/001872679504800201

Association for Talent Development. (2013). *$164.2 Billion Spent on Training and Development by U.S. Companies*. Retrieved February 10, 2016, from https://www.td.org/Publications/Blogs/ATD-Blog/2013/12/ASTD-Releases-2013-State-of-the-Industry-Report

Athota, V. S., & OConnor, P. J. (2014). How approach and avoidance constructs of personality and trait emotional intelligence predict core human values. *Learning and Individual Differences*, *31*, 51–58. doi:10.1016/j.lindif.2013.12.009

Atluri, V., Jubas, J., Patel, D., & Schneider, J. (2012). *Mobile industry at a crossroads*. Retrieved from https://tmt.mckinsey.com/

Aubourg, L. (2015, November 25). This is what happened at the Bataclan Concert Hall during the Paris attacks. *Vice News*. Retrieved August 16, 2016, from https://news.vice.com/article/this-is-what-happened-at-the-bataclan-concert-hall-during-the-paris-attacks

Audergon, A. (2004). Collective trauma: The nightmare of History. *Psychotherapy and Politics International*, *2004*(1), 16–31. doi:10.1002/ppi.67

Avolio, B. (2007). Promoting more integrative strategies for leadership theory-building. *The American Psychologist*, *62*(1), 25–33. doi:10.1037/0003-066X.62.1.25 PMID:17209677

Avolio, B. J., & Bass, B. M. (2002). *Manual for the multifactor leadership questionnaire (Form 5X)*. Redwood City, CA: Mindgarden.

Avolio, B. J., Walumbwa, F. O., & Weber, T. J. (2009). Leadership: Current theories, research, and future directions. *Annual Review of Psychology*, *60*(1), 421–449. doi:10.1146/annurev.psych.60.110707.163621 PMID:18651820

Aycan, Z. (2006). Paternalism: Towards Conceptual refinement and operationalization. In K. S. Yang, K. K. Hwang, & U. Kim (Eds.), *Scientific Advances in Indigenous Psychologies: Empirical, Philosophical, and Cultural Contributions* (pp. 445–466). London: Cambridge University Press. doi:10.1007/0-387-28662-4_20

Badgett, M. V. L., Durso, L. E., Kastanis, A., & Mallory, K. (2013). The business impact of LGBT-supportive workplace policies. *The Williams Institute, Executive Summary*, 1-37.

Baird-Remba, R. (2013). 13 countries that are more gay friendly than America. *Business Insider.* Retrieved from http://www.businessinsider.com/worlds-most-gay-friendly-countries-2013-3#denmark-legalized-gay-marriage-in-2012-but-has-recognized-same-sex-domestic-partnerships-since-1989-the-first-country-in-the-world-to-do-so-11

Baker, D. (2006). *Fairness in downsizing: Judgement and complexity.* Adelaide: University of South Australia.

Bakker, A. B., Albrecht, S. L., & Leiter, M. P. (2011). Key questions regarding work engagement. *European Journal of Work and Organizational Psychology*, *20*(1), 4–28. doi:10.1080/1359432X.2010.485352

Bakker, A. B., Demerouti, E., & Burke, R. (2009). Workaholism and relationship quality: A spillover-crossover perspective. *Journal of Occupational Health Psychology*, *14*(1), 23–33. doi:10.1037/a0013290 PMID:19210044

Bakker, A. B., Demerouti, E., De Boer, E., & Schaufeli, W. B. (2003a). Job demands and job resources as predictors of absence duration and frequency. *Journal of Vocational Behavior*, *62*(2), 341–356. doi:10.1016/S0001-8791(02)00030-1

Bakker, A. B., Demerouti, E., & Euwema, M. C. (2005). Job Resources Buffer the Impact of Job Demands on Burnout. *Journal of Occupational Health Psychology*, *10*(2), 170–180. doi:10.1037/1076-8998.10.2.170 PMID:15826226

Bakker, A. B., & Heuven, E. (2006). Emotional dissonance, burnout, and in-role performance among nurses and police officers. *International Journal of Stress Management*, *13*(4), 423–440. doi:10.1037/1072-5245.13.4.423

Bakker, A., Demerouti, E., & Schaufeli, W. (2003b). Dual processes at work in a call center: An application of the job demands–resources model. *European Journal of Work and Organizational Psychology*, *12*(4), 393–417. doi:10.1080/13594320344000165

Balabán, M. (2012). Kořeny a květy biblických pojmů [Roots and flowers of biblical terminology]. Benešov, Czech Republic: Eman.

Balducci, C., Fraccaroli, F., & Schaufeli, W. B. (2011). Workplace bullying and its relation with work characteristics, personality, and post-traumatic stress symptoms: An integrated model. *Anxiety, Stress, and Coping*, *24*(5), 499–513. do i:10.1080/10615806.2011.555533 PMID:21347903

Balestrery, J. (in press). A History of Community: Marching Toward Equality. In M. Dentato (Ed.), *Social Work Practice with the LGBTQ Community: The Intersection of History, Health, Mental Health and Policy Factors.* Oxford University Press.

Bandura, A. (1989). Social cognitive theory. In R. Vasta (Ed.), Annals of child development: Six theories of child mental health development (vol. 6, pp. 1-60). Greenwich, CT: JAI Press.

Banerjee, S., Bowie, N. E., & Pavone, C. (2006). An ethical analysis of the trust relationship. In R. Bachmann & A. Zaheer (Eds.), *Handbook of trust research* (pp. 303–343). Cheltenham, UK: Edward Elgar. doi:10.4337/9781847202819.00026

Barger, N., & Kirby, L. (1995). *The challenge of change in organizations: Helping employees thrive in the New Frontier.* Mountain View, CA: Davies-Black Publishing.

Baron, R. A., Franklin, R. J., & Hmieleski, K. M. (2016). Why entrepreneurs often experience low, not high, levels of stress: The joint effects of selection and psychological capital. *Journal of Management*, *42*(3), 742–768. doi:10.1177/0149206313495411

Barrick, M. R., & Mount, M. K. (1991). The Big Five Personality Dimensions and Job Performance: A meta-analysis. *Personnel Psychology*, *44*(1), 1–26. doi:10.1111/j.1744-6570.1991.tb00688.x

Barrois, C. (1998). *Les névroses traumatiques*. Paris: Editions Dunod.

Bar-Sela, G., Lulav-Grinwald, D., & Mitnik, I. (2012). Balint group meetings for oncology residents as a tool to improve therapeutic communication skills and reduce burnout level. *Journal of Cancer Education*, *27*(4), 786–789. doi:10.1007/s13187-012-0407-3 PMID:22923383

Baruch, Y., & Hind, P. (2000). Survivor syndrome - a management myth? *Journal of Managerial Psychology*, *15*(1), 29–45. doi:10.1108/02683940010305289

Bass, B. M. (1985). *Leadership and Performance Beyond Expectations*. New York: Free Press.

Bass, B. M., & Avolio, B. J. (1994). *Improving organizational effectiveness through transformational leadership*. Thousand Oaks, CA: Sage Publications.

Bass, B. M., & Avolio, B. J. (2007). Developing transformational leadership: 1992 and beyond. *Journal of European Industrial Training*, *14*(5), 25–33.

Bass, B. M., & Bass, R. (2008). *The Bass handbook of leadership: Theory, research, and managerial applications*. New York: Free Press.

Bass, B. M., & Riggio, R. E. (2006). *Transformational Leadership* (2nd ed.). Mahwah, NJ: Lawrence Erlbaum Associates.

Bassuk, E. L., Unick, G. J., Paquette, K., & Richard, M. K. (2016). Developing an Instrument to measure organizational trauma-informed care in human services: The TICOMETER. *Psychology of Violence*. 10.1037/vio0000030

Bathia, M. S. (Ed.). (2009). *Dictionary Of Psychology And Allied Sciences*. New Age International Pvt Ltd Publisher.

Baumeister, R. F., Bratslavsky, E., Finkenauer, C., & Vohs, K. D. (2001). Bad is stronger than good. *Review of General Psychology*, *5*(4), 323–370. doi:10.1037/1089-2680.5.4.323

BBC News. (2015, December 9). Paris attacks: What happened on the night? *BBC News*. Retrieved August 16, 2016, from http://www.bbc.com/news/world-europe-34818994

BBC. (2013). *News*. Available at: http://www.bbc.com/news/uk-england-somerset-22077051

Becker, E. (1997). *The denial of death* (2nd ed.). New York, NY: Free Press.

Beehr, T. A., Jex, S. M., Stacy, B. A., & Murray, M. A. (2000). Work stressors and coworker support as predictors of individual strain and job performance. *Journal of Organizational Behavior*, *21*(4), 391–405. doi:10.1002/(SICI)1099-1379(200006)21:4<391::AID-JOB15>3.0.CO;2-9

Beehr, T. A., & Newman, J. E. (1978). Job stress, employee health, and organizational effectiveness: A facet analysis, model, and literature review. *Personnel Psychology*, *31*(4), 665–699. doi:10.1111/j.1744-6570.1978.tb02118.x

Beer, M., & Nohria, N. (2000). Cracking the code of change. *Harvard Business Review*, *78*(3), 133–141. PMID:11183975

Belak, T. (2002). *Emotional abuse in the workplace*. Louisville, KY: Sullivan University.

Belenky, G. (1987). *Contemporary studies in combat psychiatry*. Westport, CT: Greenwood Press.

Bell, H., Kulkarni, S., & Dalton, L. (2003). Organizational prevention of vicarious trauma. *Families in Society*, *84*(4), 463–470. doi:10.1606/1044-3894.131

Bengtsson, M., & Kock, S. (2000). Coopetition" in business Networks—to cooperate and compete simultaneously. *Industrial Marketing Management*, *29*(5), 411–426. doi:10.1016/S0019-8501(99)00067-X

Bennis, W. (2007). The challenges of leadership in the modern world: Introduction to the special issue. *The American Psychologist*, *62*(1), 2–5. doi:10.1037/0003-066X.62.1.2 PMID:17209674

Bensahel, N. (2010). The Experience of Foreign Militaries. In B. B. Rostker (Ed.), *Sexual orientation and U.S. military personnel policy – an update of RAND's 1993 study* (pp. 275–316). Santa Monica, CA: RAND Corporation.

Bentley, N. (2015, September 2). *Coming out at work: a senior leader's story*. Chartered Management Institute. Retrieved from http://www.managers.org.uk/insights/news/2015/september/coming-out-at-work-a-senior-leaders-story

Ben-Yehuda, H., & Sandler, S. (1998). Crisis Magnitude and Interstate Conflict: Changes in the Arab-Israel Dispute. *Journal of Peace Research*, *35*(1), 83–109. doi:10.1177/0022343398035001006

Berger, L., & Luckmann, T. (1967). The foundations of knowledge in everyday life. In *The social construction of reality*. New York: Anchor Books, Doubleday.

Berry, J. W., Poortinga, Y. H., Breugelmans, S. M., Chasiotis, A., & Sam, D. L. (Eds.). (2013). *Cross-cultural psychology: Research and applications* (3rd ed.). Cambridge University Press.

Beylerian, M., & Kleiner, B. H. (2003). The downsized workplace. *Management Research News, 26*(2/3/4), 97–108.

Bianchi, R., Schonfeld, I. S., & Laurent, E. (2014). Is burnout a depressive disorder? A reexamination with special focus on atypical depression. *International Journal of Stress Management*, *21*(4), 307–324. doi:10.1037/a0037906

Blackie, L. E. R., Jayawickreme, E., Forgeard, M. J. C., & Jayawickreme, N. (2015). The protective function of personal growth initiative among a genocide-affected population in Rwanda. *Psychological Trauma: Theory, Research, Practice, and Policy*, *7*(4), 333–339. doi:10.1037/tra0000010 PMID:26147518

Blake, D. H. (1972). Trade Unions and the Challenge of the Multinational Corporation. *The Annals of the American Academy of Political and Social Science*, *403*(1), 34–45. doi:10.1177/000271627240300104

Blankstein, K. R., & Dunkley, D. M. (2002). Evaluative Concerns, Self-critical, and Personal Standards Perfectionism: A Structural Equation Modeling Strategy. In G. L. Flett & P. L. Hewitt (Eds.), *Perfectionism: Theory, Research, and Treatment* (pp. 285–315). Washington, DC: American Psychological Association. doi:10.1037/10458-012

Blau, G., & Andersson, L. (2005). Testing a measure of instigated workplace incivility. *Journal of Occupational and Organizational Psychology*, *78*(4), 595–614. doi:10.1348/096317905X26822

Bloomberg Technology Magazine. (2014). *Tim Cook Speaks Up*. Retrieved from http://www.bloomberg.com/news/articles/2014-10-30/tim-cook-speaks-up

Bloom, S. (2006). *Organizational stress as a barrier to trauma-sensitive change and system transformation*. Alexandria, VA: National Technical Assistance Center for State Mental Health Planning Pulications and Reports.

Bloom, S. L. (2012). *Building resilient workers and organisations: The Sanctuary Model of organisational change. In Workplace bullying: Symptoms and solutions* (pp. 260–277). Hove, UK: Routledge.

Bloom, S. L., & Farragher, B. (2011). *Destroying sanctuary: The crisis in human service delivery systems*. New York, NY: Oxford University Press.

Bloom, S. L., & Sreedhar, S. Y. (2008). The sanctuary model of trauma-informed organizational change. *Reclaiming Children and Youth*, *17*(3), 48–53.

Bluen, S. D., Barling, J., & Burns, W. (1990). Predicting sales performance, job satisfaction, and depression using the Achievement Strivings and Impatience/Irritability dimensions of Type A behavior. *The Journal of Applied Psychology*, *75*(2), 212–216. doi:10.1037/0021-9010.75.2.212

Blühm, R. (1983). *Handbuch der Seelsorge* (1st ed.). Berlin, Germany: Evangelische Verlagsanstalt.

Blyth, A. (2003). The art of survival. *People Management*, *9*(9), 38–40.

Boehm, J. K., & Kubzansky, L. D. (2012). The hearts content: The association between positive psychological well-being and cardiovascular health. *Psychological Bulletin*, *138*(4), 655 691. doi:10.1037/a0027448 PMID:22506752

Bogg, T., & Roberts, B. W. (2004). Conscientiousness and health-related behaviors: A meta-analysis of the leading behavioral contributors to mortality. *Psychological Bulletin*, *130*(6), 887–919. doi:10.1037/0033-2909.130.6.887 PMID:15535742

Bokenberger, K., Pedersen, N. L., Gatz, M., & Dahl, A. K. (2014). The Type A behavior pattern and cardiovascular disease as predictors of dementia. *Health Psychology*, *33*(12), 1593–1601. doi:10.1037/hea0000028 PMID:24364377

Bonanno, G., Brewin, C., Kaniasty, K., & La Greca, A. (2010). Weighing the costs of disaster: Consequences, risks, and resilience in individuals, families and communities. *Psychological Science in the Public Interest*, *11*(1), 1–49. doi:10.1177/1529100610387086 PMID:26168411

Bonebright, C. A., Clay, D. L., & Ankenmann, R. D. (2000). The relationship of workaholism with work–life conflict, life satisfaction, and purpose in life. *Journal of Counseling Psychology*, *47*(4), 469–477. doi:10.1037/0022-0167.47.4.469

Bono, J. E., & Judge, T. A. (2003). Core self-evaluations: A review of the trait and its role in job satisfaction and job performance. *European Journal of Personality*, *17*(S1), S5–S18. doi:10.1002/per.481

Booth, J., Connelly, L., Lawrence, M., Chalmers, C., Joice, S., Becker, C., & Dougall, N. (2015). Evidence of perceived psychosocial stress as a risk factor for stroke in adults: A meta-analysis. *BMC Neurology*, *15*(233). doi:10.1186/s12883-015-0456-4 PMID:26563170

Boronson, W., & Burgess, L. (1992). Survivors' syndrome. *Across the Board*, *29*(11), 41–45.

Boudrias, J. S., Desrumaux, P., Gaudreau, P., Nelson, K., Brunet, L., & Savoie, A. (2011). Modeling the experience of psychological health at work: The role of personal resources, social-organizational resources, and job demands. *International Journal of Stress Management*, *18*(4), 372–395. doi:10.1037/a0025353

Bovey, W. H., & Hede, A. (2001). Resistance to organizational change: The role of cognitive and affective processes. *Leadership and Organization Development Journal*, *22*(8), 372–382. doi:10.1108/01437730110410099

Bovornusvakool, W., Vodanovich, S. J., Ariyabuddhiphongs, K., & Ngamake, S. T. (2012). Examining the antecedents and consequences of workaholism. *The Psychologist Manager Journal*, *15*(1), 56–70. doi:10.1080/10887156.2012.649994

Bowling, N. A., & Beehr, T. A. (2006). Workplace harassment from the victims perspective: A theoretical model and meta-analysis. *The Journal of Applied Psychology*, *9*(5), 998–1112. doi:10.1037/0021-9010.91.5.998 PMID:16953764

Bowling, N. A., & Eschleman, K. J. (2010). Employee personality as a moderator of relationships between work stressors and counterproductive work behavior. *Journal of Occupational Health Psychology*, *15*(1), 91–103. doi:10.1037/a0017326 PMID:20063961

Bowman, B., Bhamjee, F., Eagle, G., & Crafford, A. (2009). A qualitative study of the multiple impacts of external workplace violence in two Western Cape communities. *South African Journal of Psychology. Suid-Afrikaanse Tydskrif vir Sielkunde*, *39*(3), 300–313. doi:10.1177/008124630903900305

Boyacigiller, N. A., & Adler, N. J. (1991). The Parochial Dinosaur: Organizational Science in a Global Context. *Academy of Management Review*, 262–290.

Boyd, W. (1998). *Armadillo*. London: Hamish Hamilton.

Bozeman, B. (2011a). The 2010 BP Gulf of Mexico oil spill: Implications for theory of organizational disaster. *Technology in Society*, *33*(3-4), 244–252. doi:10.1016/j.techsoc.2011.09.006

Bozeman, B. (2011b). Toward a theory of organizational implosion. *American Review of Public Administration*, *41*(2), 119–140. doi:10.1177/0275074010381781

Brady, B. R., Vodanovich, S. J., & Rotunda, R. (2008). The impact of workaholism on work-family conflict, job satisfaction, and perception of leisure activities. *The Psychologist Manager Journal*, *11*(2), 241–263. doi:10.1080/10887150802371781

Brady, J. L., Guy, J. D., Poelstra, P. L., & Brokaw, B. F. (1999). Vicarious traumatization, spirituality, and the treatment of sexual abuse survivors: A national survey of women psychotherapists. *Professional Psychology, Research and Practice*, *30*(4), 386–393. doi:10.1037/0735-7028.30.4.386

Bragg, K. (1997). Being a gay or lesbian professional in a psychiatric hospital for adolescents. *Journal of Gay & Lesbian Social Services*, *6*(4), 25–38. doi:10.1300/J041v06n04_03

Bramsen, I. (1995). *The longterm psychological adjustment of World War II survivors in the Netherlands*. Delft: Eburon Press.

Branch, S., Ramsay, S., & Barker, M. (2013). Workplace bullying, mobbing and general harassment: A review. *International Journal of Management Reviews*, *15*(3), 280–299. doi:10.1111/j.1468-2370.2012.00339.x

Brandenburger, A. M., & Nalebuff, B. J. (2011). *Co-opetition*. New York, NY: Doubleday.

Brand, J. E. (2015). The Far-Reaching Impact of Job Loss and Unemployment. *Annual Review of Sociology*, *41*(1), 359–375. doi:10.1146/annurev-soc-071913-043237 PMID:26336327

Brandt, C. P., Zvolensky, M. J., Vujanovic, A. A., Gover, K. W., Hogan, J., Bakhshaie, J., & Gonzalez, A. (2015). The mediating role of anxiety sensitivity in the relation between avoidant coping and posttraumatic stress among trauma-exposed HIV+ individuals. *Psychological Trauma: Theory, Research, Practice, and Policy*, *7*(2), 146–153. doi:10.1037/a0037236 PMID:25793690

Braverman, M. (1992). Post-trauma crisis intervention in the workplace. In *Stress and well-being at work: Assessments and interventions for occupational mental health*, (pp. 299-316). Academic Press.

Brenner, M. D., Fairris, D., & Ruser, J. (2004). Flexible work practices and occupational safety and Health: Exploring the Relationship between cumulative trauma disorders and workplace transformation. *Industrial Relations*, *43*(1), 242–266. doi:10.1111/j.0019-8676.2004.00325.x

Breslau, N., & Davis, G. C. (1992). Posttraumatic stress disorder in an urban population of young adults: Risk factors for chronicity. *Journal of Psychiatry*, *149*, 671–675. PMID:1575259

Breuer, J., & Freud, S. (1973). *Studies on Hysteria: Physical Mechanisms of Hysteria*. New York: Penguin.

Brewin, C. R., Andrews, B., & Valentine, J. D. (2000). Meta-Analysis of Risk Factors for Posttraumatic Stress Disorder in Trauma-Exposed Adults. *Journal of Consulting and Clinical Psychology*, *68*(5), 748–766. doi:10.1037/0022-006X.68.5.748 PMID:11068961

Brewis, J., & Őzbilgin, M. (2013). Introducing recovery and organization. *Culture and Organization*, *19*(5), 371–376. doi:10.1080/14759551.2013.848631

Brickman, P., & Campbell, D. T. (1971). Hedonic relativism and planning the good society. In M. H. Appley (Ed.), *Adaptation level theory: A symposium* (pp. 287–302). New York: Academic Press.

Brickman, P., Coates, D., & Jahoff-Bulman, R. (1978). Lottery winners and victims: Is happiness relative? *Journal of Personality and Social Psychology*, *36*(8), 917–927. doi:10.1037/0022-3514.36.8.917 PMID:690806

Brief, A. P., & Motowidlo, S. J. (1986). Prosocial organizational behaviors. *Academy of Management Review*, *11*(4), 710–725.

Brief, A., & Weiss, H. (2002). Organizational behavior: Affect in the workplace. *Annual Review of Psychology*, *53*(1), 279–307. doi:10.1146/annurev.psych.53.100901.135156 PMID:11752487

Briere, J., & Scott, C. (2006). *Principles of Trauma Therapy: A Guide to Symptoms, Evaluation, and Treatment* (1st ed.). London, UK: Sage Publications.

Bringselius, L. (2014). Employee objections to organizational change: A framework for addressing management responses. *Organization Development Journal*, *32*(1), 41–54.

British Broadcasting Corporation Sport – BBC. (2014). *Thomas Hitzlsperger: Former Aston Villa player reveals he is gay*. Retrieved from http://www.bbc.com/sport/football/25628806

Britt, T. W., Adler, A. B., & Bartone, P. T. (2001). Deriving benefits from stressful events: The role of engagement in meaningful work and hardiness. *Journal of Occupational Health Psychology*, *6*(1), 53–63. doi:10.1037/1076-8998.6.1.53 PMID:11199257

Brockner, J. (1988). The effects of work layoffs on survivors: Research, theory, and practice. In B. M. Staw & L. L. Cummings (Eds.), Research in organizational behavior (pp. 213–255). Greenwich, CT: JAI Press.

Brough, P., Dollard, M. F., & Tuckey, M. R. (2014). Theory and methods to prevent and manage occupational stress: Innovations from around the globe. *International Journal of Stress Management*, *21*(1), 1–6. doi:10.1037/a0035903

Brown, E. H. (1997). Improving organizational health by addressing organizational trauma. *Journal of Organizational Change Management*, *10*(2), 175–178. doi:10.1108/09534819710160835

Brown, J., Mulhern, G., & Joseph, S. (2005). Incident-related stressors, locus of control, and psychological distress among firefighters in Northern Ireland. *Journal of Traumatic Stress*, *15*(2), 191–168. PMID:12013068

Brown, K. W., & Ryan, R. M. (2003). The benefits of being present: Mindfulness and its role in psychological well-being. *Journal of Personality and Social Psychology*, *84*(4), 822–848. doi:10.1037/0022-3514.84.4.822 PMID:12703651

Brunborg, G. S. (2008). Core self-evaluations: A predictor variable for job stress. *European Psychologist*, *13*(2), 96–102. doi:10.1027/1016-9040.13.2.96

Bryant, A. (2011). *The corner office: Indispensable and unexpected lessons from CEOs on how to lead and succeed*. New York: Times Books.

Bughin, J., Chui, M., & Manyika, J. (2013). *Ten IT-enabled business trends for the decade ahead*. Retrieved from http://www.mckinsey.com/insights/high_tech_telecoms_internet/ten_it-enabled_business_trends_for_the_decade_ahead

Bughin, J., Ferruz-Aguilar, P., Gil-Gómez, J., & Spittaels, S. (2013). *Evolve or perish: Digital Darwinism for telecom companies*. Retrieved from http://www.mckinsey.com/~/media/mckinsey/dotcom/client_service/Telecoms/PDFs/Evolve_or_Perish.ashx

Burke, R. J. (2012). International Handbook of Workplace Trauma Support. In R. Hughes, A. Kinder, & C. L. Cooper (Eds.), Workplace Trauma Support. Wiley-Blackwell.

Burke, R. J. (2012). Organizations: Causes, Consequences, and Remedies. International Handbook of Workplace Trauma Support, 71.

Burke, R. J. (2012). The trauma impact on organizations: causes, consequences, and remedies. In R. Hughes, A. Kinder, & C.L. Cooper (Ed.), International handbook of workplace trauma support (pp. 71-86). Noida, India: John Wiley & Sons. doi:10.1002/9781119943242.ch5

Burke, P. (2004). Identities and social structure: The 2003 Cooley-Mead award address. *Social Psychology Quarterly*, *67*(1), 5–15. doi:10.1177/019027250406700103

Burke, P., & Reitzes, D. (1981). The Link between identity and role performance. *Social Psychology Quarterly*, *44*(2), 83–92. doi:10.2307/3033704

Burke, R. J. (2005). Hospital restructuring stressors, support, and nursing staff perceptions of unit functioning. *The Health Care Manager*, *24*(1), 21–28. doi:10.1097/00126450-200501000-00004 PMID:15825816

Burke, W. W. (2011). *Organization change: Theory and Practice* (3rd ed.). Thousand Oaks, CA: Sage Publications.

Burke, W. W., & Jackson, P. (1991). Making the SmithKline Beecham merger work. *Human Resource Management*, *30*(1), 69–87. doi:10.1002/hrm.3930300105

Burke, W. W., & Litwin, G. H. (1992). A causal model of organizational performance and change. *Journal of Management*, *18*(3), 523–545. doi:10.1177/014920639201800306

Burnes, B. (2009). *Managing Change* (5th ed.). London, UK: FT/Prentice Hall.

Burnes, B., & Jackson, P. (2011). Success and failure in organizational change: An exploration of the role of values. *Journal of Change Management*, *11*(2), 133–162. doi:10.1080/14697017.2010.524655

Burns, J. M. (1978). *Leadership*. New York: Harper and Row.

Burrell, G., & Morgan, G. (1979). *Social Paradigms and Organisational Analyses*. Toronto: Ashgate.

Busby, J. S., & Iszatt-White, M. (2016). Rationalizing violation: Ordered accounts of intentionality in the breaking of safety rules. *Organization Studies*, *37*(1), 35–53. doi:10.1177/0170840615593590

Business & Human Rights Resource Centre. (2015, August 27). *Hagens Berman: Class action filed against Nestlé for slave labor, human trafficking used to produce top-selling pet food*. Business & Human Rights Resource Centre. Retrieved August 16, 2016, from http://www.businesswire.com/news/home/20150827006036/en/Hagens-Berman-Class-Action-Filed-Nestl%C3%A9-Slave#.VeCqmZerog4

Business & Human Rights Resource Centre. (2015, September 1). *Nestlé's response*. Business & Human Rights Resource Centre. Retrieved August 16, 2016, from http://business-humanrights.org/sites/default/files/documents/BHRRC%20Response_Thailand%20Slave%20Labour_English%2002%2009%2015.docx

Byrne, A., Dionisi, A. M., Barling, J., Akers, A., Robertson, J., Lys, R., & Dupré, K. et al. (2014). The depleted leader: The influence of leaders diminished psychological resources on leadership behaviors. *The Leadership Quarterly*, *25*(2), 344–357. doi:10.1016/j.leaqua.2013.09.003

Byron, K., & Peterson, S. (2002). The impact of a large-scale traumatic event on individual and organizational outcomes: Exploring employee and company reactions to September 11, 2001. *Journal of Organizational Behavior, 23*(8), 895–910. doi:10.1002/job.176

Cameron, K., Quinn, R., DeGraff, J., & Thakor, A. (2006). Competing values leadership: Creating value in organizations. MPG Books Group. doi:10.4337/9781847201560

Cameron, K. S. (1994). Strategies for Successful Organizational Downsizing. *Human Resource Management, 33*(2), 189–211. doi:10.1002/hrm.3930330204

Cameron, K. S. (2008). Paradox in positive organizational change. *The Journal of Applied Behavioral Science, 44*(1), 7–24. doi:10.1177/0021886308314703

Cameron, K., & Caza, A. (2002). Organizational and leadership virtues and the role of forgiveness. *Journal of Leadership & Organizational Studies, 9*(1), 33–48. doi:10.1177/107179190200900103

Cameron, K., & Quinn, R. (2011). *Diagnosing and changing organizational culture: Based on the competing values framework*. San Francisco, CA: Jossey-Bass.

Capielo, C., Delgado-Romero, E. A., & Stewart, A. E. (2015). A focus on an emerging Latina/o population: The role of psychological acculturation, acculturative stress, and coping on depression symptoms among central Florida Puerto Ricans. *Journal of Latina/o Psychology (Savannah, Ga.), 3*(4), 209–223.

Caracciolo, S., & Molinari, S. (1986). Convergent validity of Self- Reported Type A Behavior Pattern of Patients with Coronary Artery Disease. *Psychological Reports.*

Carbo, J., & Hughes, A. (2010). Workplace bullying: Developing a human rights definition from the perspective and experiences of the target. *WorkingUSA: The Journal of Labor and Society, 13*(9), 387–403. doi:10.1111/j.1743-4580.2010.00297.x

Carlson, E. B., Furby, L., Armstrong, L., & Shlaes, J. (1997). A conceptual framework for the long-term psychological effects of traumatic childhood abuse. *Child Maltreatment, 2*(3), 272–295.

Carper, W. B., & Snizek, W. E. (1980). The nature and types of organizational taxonomies: An overview. *Academy of Management Review, 5*, 55–75.

Cascio, W. F. (2002). *Managing Human resources* (9th ed.). San Francisco: Berrett-Koehler Publishers.

Cateora, P. R., Graham, J. L., & Bruning, E. R. (2006). International Marketing (13th ed.). London: McGraw-Hill Ryerson.

Cavaiola, A., & Lavender, N. (2000). *Toxic coworkers: How to deal with dysfunctional people on the job. Working with narcissists, borderlines, sociopaths, schizoids, and others*. Oakland, CA: New Harbinger Publications Inc.

Cavalier, E. S. (2011). Men at Sport: Gay Mens Experiences in the Sport Workplace. *Journal of Homosexuality, 58*(5), 626–646. PubMeddoi:10.1080/00918369.2011.563662

Cawsey, T. F., & Deszca, G. (2007). Toolkit for organizational change. *Sage (Atlanta, Ga.).*

Caza, B., & Cortina, L. M. (2007). From insult to injury: Explaining the impact of incivility. *Basic and Applied Social Psychology, 29*(4), 335–350. doi:10.1080/01973530701665108

Cejka, P. (2015). Pilot validation of Hofstede's original 4 dimensional cultural model and its marketing implications from the perspective of the Czech Republic, Slovakia and Poland. University of Economics.

Champagne, T. (2009). The influence of posttraumatic stress disorder, depression, and sensory processing patterns on occupational engagement: A case study. IOS Press.

Chapman, M. (1996). Social Anthropology, Business Studies and Cultural Issues. *International Studies of Management & Organization*, 3–29. doi:10.1080/00208825.1996.11656692

Charcot, J.-M. (1887). *Leçons sur les maladies du système nerveux faites à la Salpêtrière*. Paris: Progrèm Médical Delahaye & Lecrosnie.

Charmaz, K. (2006). *Constructing grounded theory: A practical guide through qualitative analysis*. Thousand Oaks, CA: SAGE Publications, Inc.

Charpentier, R. (1917). Allocution de M. René Charpentier. *Annales Médico-Psychologiques*, *74*(8), 273–329.

Chaudoir, S. R., & Fisher, J. D. (2010). The disclosure processes model: Understanding disclosure decision-making and post-disclosure outcomes among people living with a concealable stigmatized identity. *Psychological Bulletin, 136*(2), 236–256. PubMeddoi:10.1037/a0018193

Chaudoir, S. R., Fisher, J. D., & Simoni, J. (2011). Understanding HIV disclosure: A review and application of the Disclosure Processes Model. *Social Science & Medicine, 72*(10), 1618–1629. PubMeddoi:10.1016/j.socscimed.2011.03.028

Chaudoir, S. R., Earnshaw, V. A., & Andel, S. (2013). "Discredited" vs. "discreditable": Understanding how shared and unique stigma mechanisms affect psychological and physical health disparities. *Basic and Applied Social Psychology, 35*, 75–87. doi:10.1080/01973533.2012.746612

Chaudoir, S. R., & Quinn, D. M. (2016). Evidence that anticipated stigma predicts poorer depressive symptom trajectories among emerging adults living with concealable stigmatized identities. *Self and Identity*, *15*(2), 139–151. doi:10.1080/15298868.2015.1091378

Chauvin, C., Lardjane, S., Morel, G., Clostermann, J. P., & Langard, B. (2013). Human and organizational factors in maritime accidents: Analysis of collisions at sea using the HFACS. *Accident; Analysis and Prevention*, *59*, 26–37. doi:10.1016/j.aap.2013.05.006 PMID:23764875

Chejter, S. (2004). *Argentinian Women Survive Economic Crisis*. Chicago Journals.

Cheng, G. H. L., & Chan, D. K. S. (2008). Who suffers more from job insecurity? A meta-analytic review. *Applied Psychology*, *57*(2), 272–303. doi:10.1111/j.1464-0597.2007.00312.x

Cheng, Y., Chen, C. W., Chen, C. J., & Chiang, T. L. (2005). Job insecurity and its association with health among employees in the Taiwanese general population. *Social Science & Medicine*, *61*(1), 41–52. doi:10.1016/j.socscimed.2004.11.039 PMID:15847960

Chen, M. C., Chen, K. M., & Chu, T. P. (2015). Caregiver burden, health status, and learned resourcefulness of older caregivers. *Western Journal of Nursing Research*, *37*(6), 767–780. doi:10.1177/0193945914525280 PMID:24608748

Chen, X. P., & Li, S. (2005). Cross-national differences in cooperative decision-making in mixed-motive business contexts: The mediating effect of vertical and horizontal individualism. *Journal of International Business Studies*, *36*(6), 622–636. doi:10.1057/palgrave.jibs.8400169

Cheung, C. C., & Chuah, K. B. (1999). Conflict management styles in Hong Kong industries. *International Journal of Project Management*, *17*(6), 393–399. doi:10.1016/S0263-7863(98)00059-3

Chida, Y., & Steptoe, A. (2008). Positive psychological well- being and mortality: A quantitative review of prospective observational studies. *Psychosomatic Medicine*, *70*(7), 741–756. doi:10.1097/PSY.0b013e31818105ba PMID:18725425

Chipunza, C., & Berry, D. M. (2010). The relationship among survivor qualities – attitude, commitment and motivation – after downsizing. *African Journal of Business Management*, *4*(5), 604–613.

Christian, M. S., Garza, A. S., & Slaughter, J. E. (2011). Work engagement: A quantitative review and test of its relations with task and contextual performance. *Personnel Psychology*, *64*(1), 89–136. doi:10.1111/j.1744-6570.2010.01203.x

Clair, J. A., MacLean, T. L., & Greenberg, D. N. (2002). Teaching Through Traumatic Events: Uncovering the Choices of Management Educators as They Responded to September 11th. *Academy of Management Learning & Education*, *1*(1), 38–54.

Clanton, L. D., Rude, S. S., & Taylor, C. (1992). Learned resourcefulness as a moderator of burnout in a sample of rehabilitation providers. *Rehabilitation Psychology*, *37*(2), 131–140. doi:10.1037/h0079105

Clark, A., & Lelkes, O. (2005). *Deliver us from Evil: Religion as Insurance*. Paris: PSE.

Clavelle, P. R. (2009). Consulting to the intelligence community: An employee assistance program model. *Consulting Psychology Journal: Practice and Research*, *61*(1), 14–24. doi:10.1037/a0015101

Cleve, R. A. (2012). *Disclosure Decisions of Sexual Identity in Young Adult Males: Emergent Cross-Cultural Themes Utilizing Grounded Theory*. Retrieved from http://search.proquest.com.tcsedsystem.idm.oclc.org/pqdtglobal/docview/1179003386/fulltextPDF/F33E8A259FA429CPQ/1?accountid=34120

Cleve, R., & Işık, İ. (2013). *Career Orientations Interview with Gay Males*. Unpublished raw data.

Cleve, R., & Dentato, M. P. (in press). Emergent cross-cultural themes of sexual identity disclosure. *Journal of Homosexuality*.

Cohen, A., Fink, S., Gadon, H., & Willits, R. (1984). *Effective Behavior in Organizations* (3rd ed.). Homewood, IL: Richard D. Irwin, Inc.

Cohen, S., Alper, C. M., Doyle, W. J., Treanor, J. J., & Turner, R. B. (2006). Positive emotional style predicts resistance to illness after experimental exposure to rhinovirus or Influenza A virus. *Psychosomatic Medicine*, *68*(6), 809–815. doi:10.1097/01.psy.0000245867.92364.3c PMID:17101814

Cole, M. S., Walter, F., Bedeian, A. G., & OBoyle, E. H. (2012). Job burnout and employee engagement a meta-analytic examination of construct proliferation. *Journal of Management*, *38*(5), 1550–1581. doi:10.1177/0149206311415252

Columbia Accident Investigation Board. (2003). *Columbia Accident Report* (vol. 1). Burlington, Ontario: Apoge. Retrieved May, 6, 2016 from http://www.nasa.gov/columbia/home/CAIB_Vol1.html

Coming Out. (2016). *Before and After 'Don't Ask, Don't Tell'*. Retrieved from http://www.comingout.space/evolving-dont-ask-dont-tell

Constantinides, P. (2013). The failure of foresight in crisis management: A secondary analysis of the Mari disaster. *Technological Forecasting and Social Change*, *80*(9), 1657–1683. doi:10.1016/j.techfore.2012.10.017

Conway, S. (1993). Advice from a corporate casualty. *Industry Week*, *242*, 22–24.

Cook, T. D. (2014, October 30). Tim Cook speaks up. *Blomberg Technology*. Retrieved from http://www.bloomberg.com/news/articles/2014-10-30/tim-cook-speaks-up

Cooper, C. L., & Lu, L. (2016). Presenteeism as a global phenomenon. *Cross Cultural & Strategic Management*, *23*(2), 216–231. doi:10.1108/CCSM-09-2015-0106

Cornand, C., & Gimet, C. (2012). The 2007–2008 financial crisis: Is there evidence of disaster myopia? *Emerging Markets Review*, *13*(3), 301–315. doi:10.1016/j.ememar.2012.02.001

Cortez, C. (2015). *Web of Science.* Available at: http://ip-science.thomsonreuters.com/mjl/publist_ssci.pdf

Cortina, L. M., Magley, V. J., Williams, J., & Langhout, R. (2001). Incivility in the workplace: Incidence and impact. *Journal of Occupational Health Psychology*, *6*(1), 64–80. doi:10.1037/1076-8998.6.1.64 PMID:11199258

Costa, P. T. Jr, & McCrae, R. R. (1980). Influence of extra- version and neuroticism on subjective well-being: Happy and unhappy people. *Journal of Personality and Social Psychology*, *38*(4), 668–678. doi:10.1037/0022-3514.38.4.668 PMID:7381680

Cottis, T. (2008). *Intellectual Disability, Trauma and Psychotherapy* (1st ed.). Oxon, UK: Routledge.

Courtois, C. A. (2008). Complex trauma, complex reactions: Assessment and treatment. *Psychological Trauma: Theory, Research, Practice, and Policy, S*(1), 86-100.

Covey, S. R. (2000). *The 7 Habits of Highly Effective People* (2nd ed.). Philadelphia: Running Press.

Cox, B. J., MacPherson, P. S. R., Enns, M. W., & McWilliams, L. A. (2004). Neuroticism and self-criticism associated with posttraumatic stress disorder in a nationally representative sample. *Behavior Therapy*, *42*(1), 105–114. doi:10.1016/S0005-7967(03)00105-0 PMID:14744527

Cox, C. B., Johnson, J., & Coyle, T. (2015). Coping styles moderate the relationship between exposure to community violence and work-related outcomes. *Journal of Occupational Health Psychology*, *20*(3), 348–358. doi:10.1037/a0038556 PMID:25528686

Coyle-Shapiro, J. A. (2002). A psychological contract perspective on organizational citizenship behavior. *Journal of Organizational Behavior*, *23*(8), 927–946. doi:10.1002/job.173

Coyne, I., Seigne, E., & Randall, P. (2000). Predicting workplace victim status from personality. *European Journal of Work and Organizational Psychology*, *9*(3), 335–349. doi:10.1080/135943200417957

Coze, J. C. L. (2013). What have we learned about learning from accidents? Post-disasters reflections. *Safety Science*, *51*(1), 441–453. doi:10.1016/j.ssci.2012.07.007

Craigie, M., Osseiran-Moisson, R., Hemsworth, D., Aoun, S., Francis, K., Brown, J., & Rees, C. et al. (2016). The influence of trait-negative affect and compassion satisfaction on compassion fatigue in Australian nurses. *Psychological Trauma: Theory, Research, Practice, and Policy*, *8*(1), 88–97. doi:10.1037/tra0000050 PMID:25961866

Crocq, L. (2007). Traumatismes psychiques: prise en charge psychologique des victimes. Paris: Masson.

Crocq, L. (1992). Le syndrome de répétition dans la névrose traumatique. Ses variations cliniques, sa signification. *Perspectives Psy*, *32*(2), 59–65.

Crocq, L. (1999). *Les traumatismes psychiques de guerre*. Paris: Odile Jacob.

Crocq, L. (2001). Le traumatisme psychique dans la pensée psychiatrique francophone: Introduction. In M. De Clercq & F. Lebigot (Eds.), *Les traumatismes psychiques*. Paris: Masson.

Crocq, L. (2002). Persée, la Méduse et l'effroi. *Revue Francophone du Stress et du Trauma*, *2*(3), 133–138.

Crocq, L., & De Verbizier, J. (1989). Le traumatisme psychologique dans l'oeuvre de Pierre Janet. *Annales Médico-Psychologiques*, *147*, 983–987.

Crompton, S. (2014). *What's stressing the stressed? Main sources of stress among workers.* Retrieved December 2, 2015, from http://www.statcan.gc.ca/pub/11-008-x/2011002/article/11562-eng.htm

Cruz, J. (2014). Memories of trauma and organizing: Market womens susu groups in post-conflict Liberia. *Organization, 21*(4), 447–462. doi:10.1177/1350508414527254

Cunningham, D. D., & Green, D. D. (2007). Diversity as a competitive strategy in the workplace. *Journal of Practical Consulting, 1*(2), 51–55.

Cunningham, G. B. (2012). *Sexual Orientation and Gender Identity in Sport. Texas A&M University.* The Center for Sport Management Research and Education.

Cyert, R. M., & March, J. G. (1963). *A behavioral theory of the firm.* Englewood Cliffs, NJ: Prentice-Hall.

Cygielstrejch, A. (1916). La psychologie de la panique pendant la guerre. *Annales Médico-Psychologiques, 7*, 172–192.

Dagan, K., Itzhaky, H., & Ben-Porat, A. (2015). Therapists working with trauma victims: The contribution of personal, environmental, and professional-organizational resources to secondary traumatization. *Journal of Trauma & Dissociation, 16*(5), 592–606. doi:10.1080/15299732.2015.1037038 PMID:26158393

Dahles, H., & Susilowati, T. P. (2015). Business resilience in times of growth and crisis. *Annals of Tourism Research, 51*, 34–50. doi:10.1016/j.annals.2015.01.002

Daniel, T. A. (2006). *Bullies in the workplace: A focus on the abusive disrespect of employees.* Society for Human Resource Management. Retrieved on October 29th, 2015, available at http://thepeoplegroupllc.com/wp-content/uploads/2008/04/article-bullies-in-the-workplace.pdf

Daniels, A. C. (2000). *Bringing out the best in people: How to apply the astonishing power of position reinforcement.* New York, NY: McGraw-Hill.

Danna, K., & Griffin, R. W. (1999). Health and wellbeing in the workplace: A review and synthesis of the literature. *Journal of Management, 25*(3), 357–384. doi:10.1177/014920639902500305

Danner, D. D., Snowdon, D. A., & Friesen, W. V. (2001). Positive emotions in early life and longevity: Findings from the nun study. *Journal of Personality and Social Psychology, 80*(5), 804–813. doi:10.1037/0022-3514.80.5.804 PMID:11374751

Darwin, C. (2003). *The origin of species.* New York: Signet Classics.

DAveni, R. A., & MacMillan, I. C. (1990). Crisis and the content of managerial communications: A study of the focus of attention of top managers in surviving and failing firms. *Administrative Science Quarterly, 35*(4), 634–657. doi:10.2307/2393512

Davenport, N., Schwartz, R. D., & Elliott, G. P. (1999). *Mobbing: Emotional abuse in the workplace* (1st ed.). Ames, IA: Civil Society Publishing.

Davenport, N., Schwartz, R. D., & Elliott, G. P. (2002). *Mobbing: Emotional abuse in the American workplace* (2nd ed.). Ames, IA: Civil Society Publishing.

Davidson, R. J., & Lutz, A. (2008). Buddhas brain: Neuroplasticity and meditation. *Signal Processing Magazine, 25*(1), 176–174. doi:10.1109/MSP.2008.4431873 PMID:20871742

Davis, C., Keilis-Borok, V., Kossobokov, V., & Soloviev, A. (2012). Advance prediction of the March 11, 2011 Great East Japan Earthquake: A missed opportunity for disaster preparedness. *International Journal of Disaster Risk Reduction, 1*, 17–32. doi:10.1016/j.ijdrr.2012.03.001

Day, A. L., & Jreige, S. (2002). Examining Type A behavior pattern to explain the relationship between job stressors and psychosocial outcomes. *Journal of Occupational Health Psychology*, *7*(1), 109–120. doi:10.1037/1076-8998.7.2.109 PMID:12003364

De Clercq, M. (1999). Les répercussions psychiatriques et psycho-sociales des catastrophes et trauma graves. *Médecine de Catastrophe - urgences collectives, 2*(3–4), 73-78. doi:10.1016/S1279-8479(00)80006-3

De Clercq, M., & Lebigot, F. (2001). *Les traumatismes psychiques*. Paris: Masson.

De Cock, C., Vachhani, S., & Murray, S. (2013). Putting into question the imaginary of recovery: A dialectical reading of the global financial crisis and its aftermath. *Culture and Organization*, *19*(5), 396–412. doi:10.1080/14759551.2013.815618

De Cremer, D., & Van Knippenberg, D. (2002). How do leaders promote cooperation? The effects of charisma and procedural fairness. *The Journal of Applied Psychology*, *87*(5), 858–866. doi:10.1037/0021-9010.87.5.858 PMID:12395810

De Cuyper, N., Raeder, S., Van der Heijden, B. I. J. M., & Wittekind, A. (2012). Psychodynamics of normal and neurotic perfectionism. *Journal of Occupational Health Psychology*, *17*(2), 162–174. doi:10.1037/a0027348 PMID:22352292

De Hoogh, A. H. B., & Den Hartog, D. H. (2009). Neuroticism and locus of control as moderators of the relationships of charismatic and autocratic leadership with burnout. *The Journal of Applied Psychology*, *94*(4), 1058–1067. doi:10.1037/a0016253 PMID:19594244

De Klerk, J. J. (2006 October). *Learning to lead organizational trauma: A positive advancement in leadership development.* Paper presented at the Gallup Leadership Institute Summit, Washington, DC.

De Klerk, M. (2007). Healing emotional trauma in organizations: An OD framework and case study. *Organization Development Journal*, *25*(2).

De Klerk, M. (2007, Summer). Healing Emotional Trauma in Organisations: An O.D. Framework and Case Study. *Organization Development Journal*, *25*(2), 49–55.

De Klerk, M. (2007, Summer). Healing Emotional Trauma in Organizations: An O.D. Framework and Case Study. *Organization Development Journal*, *25*(2), 49–55.

de Klerk, S. (2007). Healing emotional trauma in organizations: An O.D. framework and case study. *Organization Development Journal*, *25*, 49–55.

De Soir, E. (2009). Le modèle CRASH. *Revue internationale de psychosociologie et de gestion des comportements organisationnels, 36*, 157-198. doi: 10.3917/rips.036.0157

De Soir, E., Daubechies, F., & Van den Steene, P. (2012). *Stress et trauma dans les services de police et de secours.* Antwerpen, Apeldoorn: Maklu Uitgevers.

De Vitte, H., Vandoorne, J., Verlinder, R., & De Cuyper, N. (2005). Outplacement and Re-Employment Measures during Organizational Restructuring in Belgium: Overview of the Literature and Results of Qualitative Research. *Journal of European Industrial Training*, *29*(2), 148–164. doi:10.1108/03090590510585109

De Vose, C. (2014). *Successfully leading needed organization change: Strategies for leading change and managing resistance.* Retrieved from ProQuest Dissertations & Theses Global. (Accession Order No. AAT 3703633)

Deal, T. E., & Kennedy, A. A. (1982). *Organization cultures: The rites and rituals of organization life*. Reading, UK: Addison-Wesley.

Deal, T. E., & Kennedy, A. A. (2000). *Corporate cultures: The rites and rituals of corporate life*. New York, NY: Basic Books.

DeDreu, C. K., & Weingart, L. R. (2002). *Task versus relationship conflict, team performance, and team member satisfaction: A meta-analysis*. Denver, CO: Academy of Management.

Defraia, G. S. (2013). Organizational outcomes following traumatic workplace incidents: A practice-based exploration of impact of incident severity level. *Social Work in Mental Health*, *11*(5), 404–433. doi:10.1080/15332985.2013.784224

Dekker, S., & Schaufeli, W. (1995). The effects of job insecurity on psychological health and withdrawal: A longitudinal study. *Australian Psychologist*, *30*(1), 57–63. doi:10.1080/00050069508259607

DeKlerk, M. (2007). Healing emotional trauma in organizations: An O.D. Framework and Case study. *Organization Development Journal*, *25*(2), 49–56.

deKlerk, M. (2007). Healing Emotional Trauma in Organizations: An OD Framework and Case Study. *Organization Development Journal*, *25*(2), 49–55.

Delaney, T., & Madigan, T. (2009). *Sports: why people love them!* Lanham, MD: University Press of America.

Demerouti, E., Bakker, A. B., & Leiter, M. (2014). Burnout and job performance: The moderating role of selection, optimization, and compensation strategies. *Journal of Occupational Health Psychology*, *19*(1), 96–107. doi:10.1037/a0035062 PMID:24447224

Denemberg, R., & Braverman, M. (2001). *The violence prone workplace: A new approach to dealing with hostile, threatening, and uncivil behavior harassment*. Cardiff, UK: Academic Press.

DeNeve, K. M., & Cooper, H. (1998). The happy personality: A metaanalysis of 137 personality traits and subjective well-being. *Psychological Bulletin*, *124*(2), 197–229. doi:10.1037/0033-2909.124.2.197 PMID:9747186

Denollet, J. (2000). Type D personality a potential risk factor refined. *Journal of Psychosomatic Research*, *49*(4), 255–266. doi:10.1016/S0022-3999(00)00177-X PMID:11119782

Denollet, J. (2005). DS14: Standard assessment of negative affectivity, social inhibition, and Type D personality. *Psychosomatic Medicine*, *67*(1), 89–97. doi:10.1097/01.psy.0000149256.81953.49 PMID:15673629

Denollet, J. (2012). Type D or not Type D: That's the question. *The European Health Psychologist Bulletin of the European Health Psychology Society*, *14*(3), 58–63.

Denollet, J., Martens, E. J., Nyklíček, I., Conraads, V. M., & de Gelder, B. (2008). Clinical events in coronary patients who report low distress: Adverse effect of repressive coping. *Health Psychology*, *27*(3), 302–307. doi:10.1037/0278-6133.27.3.302 PMID:18624593

Dentato, M. P., Halkitis, P. N., & Orwat, J. (2013). Minority stress theory: An examination of factors surrounding sexual risk behavior in gay and bisexual men who use club drugs. *Journal of Gay & Lesbian Social Services, 24*(4), 509–525. PubMeddoi:10.1080/10538720.2013.829395

Devine, K., Reay, T., Stainton, L., & Collins-Nakai, R. (2003). Downsizing outcomes: Better a victim than a survivor? *Human Resource Management*, *42*(2), 109–124. doi:10.1002/hrm.10071

Dewitt, R. L., Trevino, L. K., & Mollica, K. A. (2003). Stuck in the middle: A control based model of managers' reactions to subordinates' layoffs. *Journal of Managerial Issues*, *15*, 32–49.

Dia, O. (2014). *Exército afirma que aceita gays na tropa - Ativistas da causa homossexual questionam a informação.* Retrieved from http://odia.ig.com.br/noticia/economia/2014-05-11/exercito-afirma-que-aceita-gays-na-tropa.html

Diener, E., Lucas, R. E., & Scollon, C. N. (2006). Beyond the hedonic treadmill: Revising the adaptation theory of well-being. *The American Psychologist*, *61*(4), 305–314. doi:10.1037/0003-066X.61.4.305 PMID:16719675

Diener, E., & Lucas, R. R. (1999). Personality and subjective well-being. In E. Kahneman, E. Diener, & N. Schwarz (Eds.), *Well-being: The foundations of hedonic psychology* (pp. 213–229). New York: Russell Sage Foundation.

Diener, E., & Seligman, M. E. P. (2002). Very happy people. *Psychological Science*, *13*(1), 81–84. doi:10.1111/1467-9280.00415 PMID:11894851

Diener, E., & Seligman, M. E. P. (2004). Beyond money: Toward an economy of well-being. *Psychological Science in the Public Interest*, *5*(1), 1–31. doi:10.1111/j.0963-7214.2004.00501001.x PMID:26158992

Diener, E., & Suh, E. (1997). Measuring quality of life: Economic, social and subjective indicators. *Social Indicators Research*, *40*(1/2), 189–216. doi:10.1023/A:1006859511756

Diener, E., Suh, E. M., Lucas, R. E., & Smith, H. L. (1999). Subjective well-being: Three decades of progress. *Psychological Bulletin*, *125*(2), 276–302. doi:10.1037/0033-2909.125.2.276

DiPofi, J. A. (2002). Organizational diagnostics: Integrating qualitative and quantitative methodology. *Journal of Change Management*, *15*(2), 156–168. doi:10.1108/09534810210423053

Discount, S., Russell, C., Gandara, D., & Sawyer, K. (2016). LGB issues in the workplace 101. *The Industrial-Organizational psychologist*, *58*(4), 39–44.

Divincová, A., & Siváková, B. (2014). Mobbing at workplace and its impact on employee performance. *Human Resources Management & Ergonomics*, *8*(2), 20–34.

Doherty, N., & Horsted, J. (1995). Helping survivors stay on board. *People Management*, *1*(1), 26–31.

Dolan, C. A., Adler, A. B., Thomas, J. L., & Castro, C. A. (2005). Operations Tempo and Soldier Health: The Moderating Effect of Wellness Behavior. *Military Psychology*, *17*(3), 157–174. doi:10.1207/s15327876mp1703_3

Dombo, E. A., & Gray, C. (2013). Engaging spirituality in addressing vicarious trauma in clinical social workers: A self-care model. *Social Work & Christianity*, *40*(1), 89–104.

Doulatabad, S. N., Mohamadhosaini, S., Shirazi, H. R. G., & Mohebbi, Z. (2015). Nursing students in Iran identify the clinical environment stressors. *International Journal of Nursing Practice*, *21*(3), 297–302. doi:10.1111/ijn.12276 PMID:24840020

Dowbiggin, I. (1985). Degeneration and Hereditarianism in French Mental Medicine, 1840-1890: Psychiatric Theory as Ideological Adaptation. In W. F. Bynum, R. Porter, & M. Shepherd (Eds.), *The Anatomy of Madness: Essays in the History of Psychiatry* (Vol. 1, pp. 188–232). London: Tavistock.

Downs, A. (1995). *Corporate executions: The ugly truth about layoffs: How corporate greed is shattering lives, companies, and communities.* New York: American Management Association.

Drabold, W. (2016). Read the Republican platform on same-sex marriage, guns and Wall Street. *Time*. Retrieved from http://time.com/4411842/republican-platform-same-sex-marriage-abortion-guns-wall-street/

Dragano, N., Verde, P. E., & Siegrist, J. (2005). Organisational downsizing and work stress: Testing synergistic health effects in employed men and women. *Journal of Epidemiology and Community Health*, *59*(8), 694–699. doi:10.1136/jech.2005.035089 PMID:16020648

Driver, M. (2003). Nothing clinical, just business? Reflections on psychoanalytically grounded organizational diagnosis and intervention. *Human Relations*, *56*(1), 39–59. doi:10.1177/0018726703056001449

Driver, M. (2007). Meaning and suffering in organizations. *Journal of Organizational Change Management*, *20*(5), 611–632. doi:10.1108/09534810710779063

Driver, M. (2009). From loss to lack: Stories of organizational change as encounters with failed fantasies of self, work and organization. *Organization*, *16*(3), 353–369. doi:10.1177/1350508409102300

Dueweke, A. R., Hurtado, G., & Hovey, J. D. (2015). Protective psychosocial resources in the lives of Latina migrant farmworkers. *Journal of Rural Mental Health*, *39*(3-4), 162–177. doi:10.1037/rmh0000038

Duggan, A. K., Friedman, S. H., McDevitt, D. E., & Mednick, C. S. (2004). Personality and Healthy Sleep: The Importance of Conscientiousness and Neuroticism. *PLoS ONE*, *9*, 1–11. PMID:24651274

Dutton, E. J., Frost, J. P., Worline, C. M., Lilius, M. J. & Kanov, M. J. (2002, January). *Leading in Times of Trauma*. Brighton, MA: Harvard Business Publishing.

Dutton, J.E., Frost, P. J., Worline, M.C., Lilius, J.M., & Kanov, J. M. (2002, January). Leading in Time of Trauma. *Harvard Business Review*, 55-61.

Dutton, J. E. (2002). Leading in Times of Trauma. *Harvard Business Review*, *80*(1), 54–61. PMID:12964467

Dutton, J. E., Frost, P. J., Worline, M. C., Lilius, J. M., & Kanov, J. M. (2002). Leading in times of trauma. *Harvard Business Review*, *80*(1), 54–61. PMID:12964467

Dwyer, D. J., & Arbelo, M. (2012). The role of social cognition in downsizing decisions. *Journal of Managerial Psychology*, *27*(4), 383–405. doi:10.1108/02683941211220199

Edwards, A. S. (1928). Intelligence as the capacity for variability or versatility of response. *Psychological Review*, *35*(3), 198–210. doi:10.1037/h0073234

Eijckelhof, B. H., Huysmans, M. A., Bruno, G. J. L., Blatter, B. M., van Dieën, J. H., Dennerlein, J. T., & van der Beek, A. J. (2013). The effects of workplace stressors on muscle activity in the neck-shoulder and forearm muscles during computer work: A systematic review and meta-analysis. *European Journal of Applied Physiology*, *113*(12), 2897–2912. doi:10.1007/s00421-013-2602-2 PMID:23584278

Einarsen, S., Hoel, H., Xapf, D., & Cooper, C. L. (2003). The concept of bullying at work. In S. Einarsen, H. Hoel, D. Zapf, & C. L. Cooper (Eds.), *Bullying and emotional abuse in the workplace: International perspectives in research and practice* (pp. 3–30). London: Taylor & Francis.

Einarsen, S., Hoel, H., Zapf, D., & Cooper, C. L. (2010). The concept of bullying and harassment at work: The European tradition. In S. Einarsen, H. Hoel, D. Zapf, & C. L. Cooper (Eds.), *Bullying and harassment in the workplace. Developments in Theory, Research, and Practice* (pp. 3–39). Boca Raton, FL: CRC Press. doi:10.1201/EBK1439804896-3

Einarsen, S., & Mikkelsen, E. G. (2003). Individual effects of exposure to bullying at work. In S. Einarsen, H. Hoel, D. Zapf, & C. L. Cooper (Eds.), *Bullying and emotional abuse in the workplace. International Perspectives in Research and Practice* (pp. 127–144). London: Taylor and Francis.

Einarsen, S., & Raknes, B. I. (1997). Harassment at work and the victimization of men. *Violence and Victims*, *12*(3), 247–263. PMID:9477540

Eisenhardt, K. M. (1989). Building theories from case study research. *Academy of Management Review*, *14*(4), 532–550.

Elhai, J. D., Grubaugh, A. L., Kashdan, T. B., & Frueh, B. C. (2008). Empirical examination of a proposed refinement to posttraumatic stress disorders symptom criteria using the National Comorbidity Survey Replication data. *The Journal of Clinical Psychiatry*, *69*(4), 597–602. doi:10.4088/JCP.v69n0411 PMID:18294026

Elliott, T. R., & Gramling, S. E. (1990). Personal assertiveness and the effects of social support among college students. *Journal of Counseling Psychology*, *37*(4), 427–436. doi:10.1037/0022-0167.37.4.427

Elliott, T. R., Shewchuk, R., Hagglund, K., Rybarczyk, B., & Harkins, S. (1996). Occupational Burnout, Tolerance for Stress, and Coping Among Nurses in Rehabilitation Units. *Rehabilitation Psychology*, *41*(4), 267–284. doi:10.1037/0090-5550.41.4.267

Ellis, R., Fantz, A., Karimi, F., & McLaughlin, E. C. (2016). *Orlando shooting: 49 killed, shooter pledged ISIS allegiance*. Retrieved from http://www.cnn.com/2016/06/12/us/orlando-nightclub-shooting/

Emold, C., Schneider, N., Meller, I., & Yagil, Y. (2011). Communication Skills, working environment and burnout among oncology nurses. *European Journal of Oncology Nursing*, *15*(4), 358–363. doi:10.1016/j.ejon.2010.08.001 PMID:20863757

Employee Assistance Trade Association. (2009). *Selecting and Strengthening Employee Assistance Programs: A Purchaser's Guide.* Retrieved December 3, 2015 from https://www.easna.org/wp-content/uploads/2010/08/EASNA-PURCHSERS-GUIDE-TO-EAPs-FINAL-102209.pdf

Employee Assistance Trade Association. (2013). *Code of Ethics.* Retrieved February 11, 2016 from http://www.easna.org/research-and-best-practices/what-is-eap/code-of-ethics/

Enns, M. W., & Cox, B. J. (1997). Personality dimensions and depression: Review and commentary. *Canadian Journal of Psychiatry*, *42*(3), 274–284. PMID:9114943

Erdem, F. (2003). Optimal trust and teamwork: From groupthink to team think. *Work Study*, *52*(5), 229–233. doi:10.1108/00438020310485958

Erdem, F., & Özen-Aytemur, J. (2014). Context-specific dimensions of trust in manager, subordinate and co-worker in organizations. *Journal of Arts and Humanities*, *3*(10), 28–40.

Eriebach, A. C., Amundson, N. E., Borgen, W., & Jordan, S. A. (2004). Survivors of downsizing: Helpful and hindering experiences. *Career Development Quarterly*. Retrieved on January 5, 2016 from http://www.allbusiness.com/human-resources/workforce-management-hiring/770709-1.html

Erikson, K. (1995). Notes on trauma and community. In C. Caruth (Ed.), Trauma: explorations in memory (pp. 183–199). Academic Press.

Erikson, E. H., & Erikson, J. M. (1998). *The life cycle completed (extended version)*. New York, NY: WW Norton & Company.

Eriksson, C. B., Lopes, C. B., Foy, D. W., Sabin, M., Ager, A., Snider, L., & Simon, W. et al. (2013). Predeployment mental health and trauma exposure of expatriate humanitarian aid workers: Risk and resilience factors. *Traumatology*, *19*(1), 41–48. doi:10.1177/1534765612441978

Ertureten, A., Cemalcilar, Z., & Aycan, Z. (2013). The relationship of downward mobbing with leadership style and organizational attitudes. *Journal of Business Ethics*, *116*(1), 205–216. doi:10.1007/s10551-012-1468-2

Ervasti, J., Kivimäki, M., Dray-Spira, R., Head, J., Goldberg, M., Pentti, J., & Virtanen, M. et al. (2016). Psychosocial factors associated with work disability in men and women with diabetes: A pooled analysis of three occupational cohort studies. *Diabetic Medicine*, *33*(2), 208–207. doi:10.1111/dme.12821 PMID:26036141

Eşcinsel hakem: 'Ölüm tehditleri alıyorum' - Akşam. (2013, March 16). Retrieved September 11, 2016, from http://www.aksam.com.tr/yasam/escinsel-hakem-olum-tehditleri-aliyorum-/haber-177758

Eşcinsel olduğunu açıklayan hakem, davayı kazandı. (2015, December 29). Retrieved September 11, 2016, from http://www.ntv.com.tr/turkiye/escinsel-oldugunu-aciklayinca-meslekten-men-edilen-hakem-tffye-actigi-davayi-ka,L1gp9_NgW0ejF02FQyFL_AThe

Eskildson, L. (1997). Surviving and thriving in a hypercompetitive economy. *National Productivity Review*, *16*(2), 9–24. doi:10.1002/npr.4040160203

Esportes Brasil, B. B. C. (2010). *Blatter recomenda que gays evitem 'atividades sexuais' no Catar 22*. Retrieved from http://www.bbc.com/portuguese/noticias/2010/12/101214_blatter_rc.shtml?print=1

Etzioni, A. (1997). *Modern Organizations*. New York: Bearport.

European Agency for Safety and Health at Work. (2014). *Calculating the costs of work-related stress and psychosocial risks – A literature review.* Retrieved December 3, 2015 from https://osha.europa.eu/en/tools-and-publications/publications/literature_reviews/calculating-the-cost-of-work-related-stress-and-psychosocial-risks

European Foundation for the Improvement of Living and Working Conditions. (2002). *Study examines 'mobbing' at the workplace*. Retrieved on November 1, 2015, available at http://www.eiro.eurofound.eu.int

European Region of the International Lesbian, Gay, Bisexual, Trans & Intersex Association's report. (2015). *Annual Review of the Human Rights Situation for Lesbian, Gay, Bisexual, Trans and Intersex People in Europe*. Brussels: ILGA Europe.

Everly, B. A., & Schwarz, J. L. (2014). Predictors of the adoption of LGBT-friendly HR policies. *Human Resource Management*, *54*(2), 367–384. doi:10.1002/hrm.21622

Evers, Prochaska, Castle, Johnson, Prochaska, Harrison, … Pope. (2012). Development of an individual well-being scores assessment. *Psychology of Well-Being: Theory, Research and Practice.*

Factor, R., Mahalel, D., & Yair, G. (2007). The social accident: A theoretical model and a research agenda for studying the influence of social and cultural characteristics on motor vehicle accidents. *Accident; Analysis and Prevention*, *39*(5), 914–921. doi:10.1016/j.aap.2006.12.015 PMID:17291438

Fagermoen, M. S. (1997). Professional identity: Values embedded in meaningful nursing practice. *Journal of Advanced Nursing*, *25*(3), 434–441. doi:10.1046/j.1365-2648.1997.1997025434.x PMID:9080267

Faheem, Q. J., & Khan, A. M. (2013). Association of downsizing with survivor's organizational commitment, work motivation and psychological wellbeing in secondary and tertiary sectors of economy of Pakistan. *Journal of Behavioural Science*, *23*(1), 68–79.

Fang, T., & Faureb, G. O. (2011, May). Chinese communication characteristics: A Yin Yang perspective. *International Journal of Intercultural Relations, Amsterdam, Netherlands*, *35*(3), 320–333. doi:10.1016/j.ijintrel.2010.06.005

Faraj, S., & Xiao, Y. (2006). *Management Science.* Available at: http://pubsonline.informs.org/doi/ref/10.1287/mnsc.1060.0526

Farh, C. I. C., & Chen, Z. (2014). Beyond the individual victim: Multilevel consequences of abusive supervision in teams. *The Journal of Applied Psychology*, *99*(6), 1074–1095. doi:10.1037/a0037636 PMID:25111251

Farmer, D. (2011). Workplace bullying: An increasing epidemic creating traumatic experiences for targets of workplace bullying. *The Special Issue on Behavioral and Social Science*, *1*(7), 196–203.

Farragher, B., & Yanosy, S. (2005). Creating a trauma-sensitive culture in residential treatment. *Therapeutic Communities*, *26*(1), 93–109.

Fein, A. H., & Isaacson, N. S. (2009). Echoes of Columbine the emotion work of leaders in school shooting sites. *The American Behavioral Scientist*, *52*(9), 1327–1346. doi:10.1177/0002764209332549

Felix, E., Afifi, T., Kia-Keating, M., Brown, L., Afifi, W., & Reyes, G. (2015). Family functioning and posttraumatic growth among parents and youth following wildfire disasters. *The American Journal of Orthopsychiatry*, *85*(2), 191–200. doi:10.1037/ort0000054 PMID:25822609

Fenichel, O. (1945). *The psychoanalytic theory of neurosis*. New York: Norton & Company Inc.

Ferenczi, S., Abraham, K., Simmel, E., & Jones, E. (1921). Psychoanalysis and the war neuroses. *The International Psycho-Analytical Library*, *2*, 1–59.

Ferreira, R. C. (2007). *O Gay no Ambiente de Trabalho: Análise dos Efeitos de ser Gay nas organizações contemporâneas* (Master Thesis). Retrieved from http://repositorio.unb.br/bitstream/10482/3329/1/2007_RenataCostaFerreira.pdf

Ferreira, R. C., & Siqueira, M. V. S. (2007). *O Gay no Ambiente de Trabalho: Análise dos Efeitos de ser Gay nas organizações contemporâneas. XXXI Encontro da ANPAD, Rio de Janeiro*. Retrieved from http://www.anpad.org.br/admin/pdf/EOR-B524.pdf

Ferris, P. A., Sinclair, C., & Kline, T. J. (2005). It Takes Two to Tango: Personal and Organizational Resilience as Predictors of Strain and Cardiovascular Disease Risk in a Work Sample. *Journal of Occupational Health Psychology*, *10*(3), 225–238. doi:10.1037/1076-8998.10.3.225 PMID:16060726

Feuerhahn, N., Kühnel, J., & Kudielka, B. M. (2012). Interaction effects of effort-reward imbalance and overcommitment on emotional exhaustion and job performance. *International Journal of Stress Management*, *19*(2), 105–131. doi:10.1037/a0028338

Fida, R., Paciello, M., Tramontano, C., Barbaranelli, C., & Farnese, M. L. (2015). Yes I can: The protective role of personal self-efficacy in hindering counterproductive work behavior under stressful conditions. *Anxiety, Stress, and Coping*, *28*(5), 479–499. doi:10.1080/10615806.2014.969718 PMID:25265506

Figley, C. R. (1982). *Traumatization and comfort: Close relationships may be hazardous to your health*. Conference on Families and Close Relationships: Individuals in social interaction, Lubbock, TX.

Figley, C. R. (1995). Systemic traumatization: Secondary traumatic stress disorder in family therapists. In R. H. Mikesell, D.-D. Lusterman, & S. H. McDaniel (Eds.), *Integrating family therapy: Handbook of family psychology and systems theory* (pp. 571–581). Washington, DC: American Psychological Association. doi:10.1037/10172-033

Figley, C. R. (Ed.). (1995). *Compassion Fatigue: Coping with secondary traumatic stress disorder in those who treat the traumatized*. Florence, KY: Brunner/Mazel.

Figley, R. Ch. (Ed.). (2012). *Encyclopedia of Trauma: An Interdisciplinary Guide* (1st ed.). London, UK: Sage Publications. doi:10.4135/9781452218595

Fiorey, R. M. (2010). *Mitigating PTSD: Emotionally intelligent leaders* (Doctoral dissertation). Retrieved from PsycEXTRA. (Accession Order No. ADA526234)

Fischer, M. D. (2012). Organizational turbulence, trouble and trauma: Theorizing the collapse of a mental health setting. *Organization Studies*, *33*(9), 1153–1173. doi:10.1177/0170840612448155

Fisher, S. R., & White, M. A. (2000). Downsizing in a learning organization: Are there hidden costs? *Academy of Management Review*, *25*(1), 244–251. doi:10.5465/AMR.2000.2791613

Fleishman, E. A., & Quaintance, M. K. (1984). *Taxonomies of human performance*. New York, NY: Academic Press.

Fletcher, R., & Fang, T. (2006). Assessing the impact of culture on relationship creation and network formation in emerging Asian markets. *European Journal of Marketing*, *40*(3/4), 430–446. doi:10.1108/03090560610648138

Florida: Iranian doctor on Islam: Killing gays is an act of 'compassion'. (2016, March). *The Muslim Issue*. Retrieved from https://themuslimissue.wordpress.com/2016/03/30/florida-iranian-doctor-on-islam-killing-gays-is-an-act-of-compassion/

Foa, E. B., Riggs, D. S., & Gershuny, B. S. (1995). Arousal, numbing, and intrusion: Symptom structure of PTSD following assault. *The American Journal of Psychiatry*, *152*(1), 116–120. doi:10.1176/ajp.152.1.116 PMID:7802101

Foa, E. B., & Rothbaum, B. O. (1998). *Treating the trauma of rape*. New York: Guilford Press.

Folkman, S., & Lazarus, R. S. (1985). If it changes it must be a process: Study of emotion and coping during three stages of a college examination. *Journal of Personality and Social Psychology*, *48*(1), 150–170. doi:10.1037/0022-3514.48.1.150 PMID:2980281

Ford, B. Q., Mauss, I. B., Troy, A. S., Smolen, A., & Hankin, B. (2014). Emotion regulation moderates the risk associated with the 5-HTT gene and stress in children. *Emotion (Washington, D.C.)*, *14*(5), 930–939. doi:10.1037/a0036835 PMID:24866526

Fordyce, M. W. (1988). A review of research on the Happiness Measures: A sixty second index of happiness and mental health. *Social Indicators Research*, *20*(4), 355–381. doi:10.1007/BF00302333

Forje, L. C. (1998). Crisis Helps to Demarginalize Women. *Development in Practice*, *8*(2), 211–216. doi:10.1080/09614529853828 PMID:12293703

Fox, S., Amichai-Hamburger, Y., & Evans, E. A. (2001). The Power of Emotional Appeals in Promoting Organizational Change Programs [and Executive Commentary]. *The Academy of Management Executive (1993-2005)*, *15*(4), 84-95. doi: 10.2307/4165788

Fox, J. A., & Savage, J. (2009). Mass murder goes to college: An examination of changes on college campuses following Virginia Tech. *The American Behavioral Scientist*, *52*(10), 1227–1245. doi:10.1177/0002764209332558

Franěk, M. (2014). *Organizational and Sociodemographic Determinants of Job Satisfaction in the Czech Republic*. Sage OPEN.

Fredrickson, B. L. (1998). What good arc positivc cmotions? *Review of General Psychology*, *2*(3), 300 319. doi:10.1037/1089-2680.2.3.300 PMID:21850154

Fredrickson, B. L., Cohn, A. M., Coffey, A. K., Pek, J., & Finkel, M. S. (2008). Open Hearts Build Lives: Positive Emotions, Induced Through Loving-Kindness Meditation, Build Consequential Personal Resources. *Journal of Personality and Social Psychology*, *5*(5), 1045–1062. doi:10.1037/a0013262 PMID:18954193

Freedom in the world report. (2016). Retrieved from https://freedomhouse.org/sites/default/files/FH_FITW_Report_2016.pdf

Freud, S., & Breuer, J. (1893). Preliminary Communication. Studies on Hysteria, 2(17).

Freud, S., & Breuer, J. (1956). Etudes sur l'hystérie (7th ed.). Paris: PUF.

Freud, S. (1918). *Reflections on war and death*. New York: Moffat, Yard & Co.

Freud, S. (2001). Some points for a comparative study of organic and hysterical paralyses. In J. Strachey & A. Strachey (Eds.), *Standard edition of the complete Psychological Works of Sigmund Freud, 1*. London: Hogarth. (Original work published 1893)

Freud, S. (2007). *The Psychology of Love* (1st ed.). London, UK: Penguin Publishing Group.

Friedman, H. S. (2000). Long-term relations of personality and health: Dynamisms, mechanisms, tropisms. *Journal of Personality, 68*(6), 1089–1107. doi:10.1111/1467-6494.00127 PMID:11130733

Friedman, M. (1977). Type A behavior pattern: Some of its pathophysiological components. *Bulletin of the New York Academy of Medicine, 53*(7), 593–604. PMID:196708

Friedman, M., & Rosenman, R. H. (1959). Association of Specific Overt Behavior Pattern with Blood and Cardiovascular Findings: Blood cholesterol level, blood clotting time, incidence of arcus senilis, and clinical coronary artery disease. *Journal of the American Medical Association, 169*(12), 1286–1296. doi:10.1001/jama.1959.03000290012005 PMID:13630753

Frommberger, U. (2014). Post-traumatic stress disorder – a diagnostic and therapeutic challenge. *Deutsches Ärzteblatt International, Cologne, Germany, 111*(5), 59–65. PMID:24612528

Frost, P. J. (2004). Handling toxic emotions: New challenges for leaders and their organization. *Organizational Dynamics, 33*(2), 111–127. doi:10.1016/j.orgdyn.2004.01.001

Frost, R. O., Heimberg, R. G., Holt, C. S., Mattia, J. I., & Neubauer, A. L. (1993). A comparison of two measures of perfectionism. *Personality and Individual Differences, 14*(1), 119–126. doi:10.1016/0191-8869(93)90181-2

Frost, R. O., Marten, P., Lahart, C., & Rosenblate, R. (1990). The Dimensions of Perfectionism. *Cognitive Therapy and Research, 14*(5), 449–468. doi:10.1007/BF01172967

Frueh, B. C., Elhai, J. D., & Kaloupek, D. G. (2004). Unresolved issues in the assessment of trauma exposure and posttraumatic reactions. In G. M. Rosen (Ed.), *Posttraumatic stress disorder: issues and controversies* (pp. 63–84). New York, NY: Wiley. doi:10.1002/9780470713570.ch4

Fujisawa, C. (1959). *Zen and Shinto: A History of Japanese Philosophy*. New York: Philosophical Library.

Gabriel, Y. (2012). Organizations in a state of darkness: Towards a theory of organizational Miasma. *Organization Studies, 33*(9), 1137–1152. doi:10.1177/0170840612448154

Gabriel, Y., Gray, D. E., & Goregaokar, H. (2013). Job loss and its aftermath among managers and professionals: Wounded, fragmented and flexible. *Work, Employment and Society, 27*(1), 56–72. doi:10.1177/0950017012460326

Gaher, R. M., Simons, J. S., Hahn, A. M., Hofman, N. L., Hansen, J., & Buchkoski, J. (2014). An experience sampling study of PTSD and alcohol-related problems. *Psychology of Addictive Behaviors, 28*(4), 1013–1025. doi:10.1037/a0037257 PMID:25134021

Gallavan, D. B., & Newman, J. L. (2013). Predictors of burnout among correctional mental health professionals. *Psychological Services, 10*(1), 115–122. doi:10.1037/a0031341 PMID:23421364

Gallego-Toledo, J. M. (2015). *The Relationship between perceived frequency of change and the wellbeing of telecom professionals*. Ann Arbor, MI: UMI Dissertation Services.

Gallos, J. V. (2008). Learning from the toxic trenches. *Journal of Management Inquiry, 17*(4), 354–367. doi:10.1177/1056492608320580

Gallup Consulting. (2011). *State of the global workplace 2011*. Retrieved from http://www.gallup.com/strategicconsulting/145535/State-Global-Workplace-2011.aspx

Gallus, J. A., Walsh, B. M., van Driel, M., Gouge, M. C., & Antolic, E. (2013). Intolerable cruelty: A multilevel examination of the impact of toxic leadership on U.S. military units and service members. *Military Psychology*, *25*(6), 588–601. doi:10.1037/mil0000022

Gandolfi, F. (2008). Reflecting on downsizing: What have mangers learned? *S.A.M. Advanced Management Journal*, *73*(2), 46–55.

Gantt, S. P., & Hopper, E. (2012). *Two perspectives on a trauma in a training group: The systems-centred approach and the theory of incohesion. In Trauma and organizations* (pp. 233–254). London: Karnac Books.

Gay hakemin abisi imam çıktı! (2009, May 18). Retrieved September 11, 2016, from http://www.internethaber.com/gay-hakemin-abisi-imam-cikti-192545h.htm

George, J. M. (2000). Emotions and leadership: The role of emotional intelligence. *Human Relations*, *53*(8), 1027–1055. doi:10.1177/0018726700538001

Gersons, B. P. R., & Carlier, I. V. E. (1992). Post-Traumatic Stress Disorder: The History of a Recent Concept. *The British Journal of Psychiatry*, *161*(6), 742–748. doi:10.1192/bjp.161.6.742 PMID:1483159

Ghadi, M. Y., Fernando, M., & Caputi, P. (2013). Transformational leadership and work engagement: The mediating effect of meaning in work. *Leadership and Organization Development Journal*, *34*(6), 532–550. doi:10.1108/LODJ-10-2011-0110

Gibson, M. (1997). Clitoral corruption: Body metaphors and American doctors' constructions of female homosexuality, 1870-1900. In V. A. Rosario (Ed.), *Science and homosexualities* (pp. 108–132). New York: Academic Press.

Gilmore, G. (1994). Coping with the realities of rightsizing. *Risk Management*, *41*, 42–46.

Gittel, J. H. (2008). Relationships and resillience: Care provider responses to pressures from managed care. *The Journal of Applied Behavioral Science*, *XLIV*(1), 25–47. doi:10.1177/0021886307311469

Giustiniano, L., Cunha, M. P., & Clegg, S. (2016). Organizational zemblanity. *European Management Journal*, *34*(1), 7–21. doi:10.1016/j.emj.2015.12.001

Glazer, S., & Kruse, B. (2008). The role of organizational commitment in occupational Stress models. *International Journal of Stress Management*, *15*(4), 329–344. doi:10.1037/a0013135

Goff, B. L., & Tollison, R. D. (Eds.). (1990). *Sportometrics (No. 11)*. College Station, TX: Texas A&M University Press.

Goldman, K. D., & Schmalz, K. J. (2004). The Matrix Method of literature reviews. *Health Promotion Practice*, *5*(1), 5–7. doi:10.1177/1524839903258885 PMID:14965430

Goldratt, E. (2010, July 17). *Overcoming resistance to change: Isn't it obvious?* [YouTube]. The World with Theory of Constraints. Retrieved from https://youtu.be/hcz1aZ60k7w

Goldsmith, J., Ferrell, B., Wittenberg-Lyles, E., & Ragan, S. L. (2013). Palliative care communication in oncology nurses. *Clinical Journal of Oncology Nursing*, *17*(2), 163–167. doi:10.1188/13.CJON.163-167 PMID:23538251

Goleman, D. (1995). *Emotional intelligence: Why it can matter more than IQ*. New York: Bantam.

Goleman, D. (1998). *Working with Emotional Intelligence*. New York: Bantam.

Golnaz, S. (2013). Choosing conflict resolution by culture. *Industrial Management (Des Plaines)*, (September), 11–15.

Gombault, A. (2002). Clinique d'une crise d'identité organisationnelle. L'adolescence du Grand Louvre. Paper presented at the Actes de la 11 è Conférence de l'Association Internationale de Management Stratégique (AIMS).

Goodman, J. (2016, February 11). Paris attacks: Le Bataclan to reopen before end of 2016. *Entertainment Weekly*. Retrieved August 16, 2016, from http://www.ew.com/article/2016/02/11/le-bataclan-reopen-2016-paris-attacks

Goodman, P. S., Ramanujam, R., Carroll, J. S., Edmondson, A. C., Hofmann, D. A., & Sutcliffe, K. M. (2011). Organizational errors: Directions for future research. *Research in Organizational Behavior*, *31*, 151–176. doi:10.1016/j.riob.2011.09.003

Goodstein, L. D., & Burke, W. W. (1991). Creating successful organization change. *Organizational Dynamics*, *19*(4), 4–17. doi:10.1016/0090-2616(91)90050-J

Göregenli, M., & Serdengeçti, T. Ş. (2015). *Situation of Lesbian, Gay, Bisexual, Transgender and Intersex Employees in Private Sector in Turkey*. Ankara: Kaos Gey ve Lezbiyen Kültürel Araştırmalar ve Dayanışma Derneği.

Gould, S. J., & Grein, A. F. (2005). Think Glocally, Act Glocally: A Culture-Centric Comment on Leung, Bhagat, Buchan, Erez and Gibson (2005). *Journal of International Business Studies*, *40*(2), 237–254.

Gowan, M. A. (2012). Employability, well-being and job satisfaction following a job loss. *Journal of Managerial Psychology*, *27*(8), 780–798. doi:10.1108/02683941211280157

Grandey, A. A. (2003). When the show must go on: Surface acting and deep acting as determinants of emotional exhaustion and peer-rated service delivery. *Academy of Management Journal*, *46*(1), 86–96. doi:10.2307/30040678

Grant, A. M., & Wade-Benzoni, K. A. (2009). The hot and cool of death awareness at work: Mortality cues, aging, and self-protective and prosocial motivations. *Academy of Management Review*, *34*(4), 600–622. doi:10.5465/AMR.2009.44882929

Grant, S., & Langan-Fox, J. (2006). Occupational stress, coping and strain: The combined/interactive effect of the Big Five traits. *Personality and Individual Differences*, *41*(4), 719–732. doi:10.1016/j.paid.2006.03.008

Grawitch, M. J., Gottschalk, M., & Munz, D. C. (2006). The path to a healthy workplace: A critical review linking healthy workplace practices, employee wellbeing, and organizational improvements. *Consulting Psychology Journal: Practice and Research*, *58*(3), 129–147. doi:10.1037/1065-9293.58.3.129

Greenberg, J., Pyszczynski, T., & Solomon, S. (1986). The causes and consequences of a need for self- esteem: A terror management theory. In R. F. Baumeister (Ed.), *Public self and private self* (pp. 189–212). New York: Springer. doi:10.1007/978-1-4613-9564-5_10

Greene, G. J., Fisher, K. A., Kuper, L., Andrews, R., & Mustanski, B. (2015). "Is this normal? is this not normal? there is no set example": Sexual health intervention preferences of LGBT youth in romantic relationships. *Sexuality Research & Social Policy*, *12*(1), 1–14. http://dx.doi.org.tcsedsystem.idm.oclc.org/10.1007/s13178-014-0169-2

Greenglass, E. R., Burke, R. J., & Moore, K. A. (2003). Reactions to increased workload: Effects on professional efficacy on nurses. *Applied Psychology*, *52*(4), 580–597. doi:10.1111/1464-0597.00152

Gregory, A. (2004). Rethinking Homophobia in Sports: Legal Protections for Gay and Lesbian Athletes and Coaches. *DePaul Journal of Sports Law & Contemporary Problems*, *2*(2), 264–292.

Gregory, B. T., Harris, S. G., Armenakis, A. A., & Shook, C. L. (2009). Organizational culture and effectiveness: A study of values, attitudes, & organizational outcome. *Journal of Business Research*, *62*(7), 673–679. doi:10.1016/j.jbusres.2008.05.021

Greiner, B. A., Krause, N., Ragland, D. R., & Fisher, J. M. (1998). Objective stress factors, accidents, and absenteeism in transit operators: A theoretical framework and empirical evidence. *Journal of Occupational Health Psychology*, *3*(2), 130–146. doi:10.1037/1076-8998.3.2.130 PMID:9585913

Greyson, B. (2001). Posttraumatic stress symptoms following near-death experiences. *The American Journal of Orthopsychiatry*, *71*(3), 368–373. doi:10.1037/0002-9432.71.3.368 PMID:11495339

Griffin, P. (1995). Homophobia in Sport. In G. Unks (Ed.), *The Gay Teen: Educational Practice and Theory for Lesbian, Gay and Bisexual Adolescents* (pp. 53–66). New York, NY: Routledge.

Griffin, R. W., & Lopez, Y. P. (2005). Bad behavior in organizations: A review and typology for future research. *Journal of Management*, *31*(6), 988–1005. doi:10.1177/0149206305279942

Griffin, R. W., & O'Leary-Kelly, A. M. (2004). *The dark side of organizational behavior*. San Francisco, CA: Jossey-Bass – A Wiley Imprint.

Griffin, R. W., & O'Leary-Kelly, A. M. (2004). *The dark side of organizational behaviour*. San Francisco: Jossey-Bass.

Groeblinghoff, D., & Becker, M. (1996). A case study of mobbing and the clinical treatment of mobbing victims. *European Journal of Work and Organizational Psychology*, *5*(2), 277–294. doi:10.1080/13594329608414859

Grupo Gay da Bahia. (2014). *Assassinato de Homossexuais (LGBT) No Brasil: Relatório 2014*. Retrieved from https://homofobiamata.files.wordpress.com/2015/01/relatc3b3rio-2014s.pdf

Guiho-Bailly, M. P., & Guillet, D. (2005). Psychopathologie et psychodynamique du travail. *EMC - Toxicologie-Pathologie*, *2*(3), 98-110. doi:10.1016/j.emctp.2005.04.001

Gürcan, M. (2014, December 10). $8,700 will let young Turks 'buy out' their military service. Retrieved September 07, 2016, from http://www.al-monitor.com/pulse/originals/2014/12/turkey-compulsory-military-service-buy-exemption.html

Gürcan, M. (2015, November 17). *Gays seeking military exemption in Turkey no longer need to provide visual proof of their homosexuality*. Retrieved September 07, 2016, from http://www.al-monitor.com/pulse/originals/2015/11/turkey-military-gay-rights-homosexual-picture.html

Haas, J. E., Hall, R. H., & Johnson, N. J. (1966). Toward an empirically derived taxonomy of organizations. In R. V. Bowers (Ed.), Studies on Behavior in Organizations (pp. 157-180). Athens, GA: University of Georgia.

Hallett, W. (2016, July 11). *Former Asylum Seeker has now forged a career with UK home office. Gay Star News*. Retrieved from http://www.gaystarnews.com/article/gay-former-asylum-seeker-home-office/#gs.N36Oorg

Hamachek, D. E. (1978). Psychodynamics of normal and neurotic perfectionism. *Psychology: A Journal of Human Behavior*, *15*(1), 27-33.

Hamilton, E. A. (2006). An exploration of the relationship between loss of legitimacy and the sudden death of organizations. *Group & Organization Management*, *31*(3), 327–358. doi:10.1177/1059601106286885

Hamilton, J. B. III, & Knouse, S. B. (2001). Multinational Enterprise Decision Principles for Dealing With Cross Cultural Ethical Conflicts. *Journal of Business Ethics*, *31*(1), 77–94. doi:10.1023/A:1010793408485

Haney, P. (1994). The Nixon Administration and Middle East Crises: Theory and Evidence of Presidential Management of Foreign Policy Decision Making. *Political Research Quarterly*, *47*(4), 939–959. doi:10.1177/106591299404700410

Hansbrough, T. K., & Jones, G. E. (2014). Inside the minds of narcissists: How narcissistic leaders cognitive processes contribute to abusive supervision. *Zeitschrift fur Psychologie mit Zeitschrift fur Angewandte Psychologie*, *222*(4), 214–220. doi:10.1027/2151-2604/a000188

Hardiman, P., & Simmonds, J. G. (2013). Spiritual well-being, burnout and trauma in counselors and psychotherapists. *Mental Health, Religion & Culture*, *16*(10), 1044–1055. doi:10.1080/13674676.2012.732560

Harrison, R. L., & Westwood, M. J. (2009). Preventing vicarious traumatization of mental health therapists: Identifying protective practices. *Psychotherapy (Chicago, Ill.)*, *46*(2), 203–219. doi:10.1037/a0016081 PMID:22122619

Harter, J. K., Schmidt, F. L., & Keyes, C. L. M. (2014). Well-being in the workplace and its relationship to business outcomes: A review of the Gallup studies. *Flourishing: Positive Psychology and the Life Well-Lived, 2,* 205-224.

Harter, Schmidt, & Hayes. (2002). Business-Unit-Level Relationship Between Employee Satisfaction, Employee Engagement, and Business Outcomes: Meta-Analysis, . *The Journal of Applied Psychology*, *87*(2), 268–279.

Harter, J. K., Schmidt, F. L., & Hayes, T. L. (2002). Business-unit-level relationship between employee satisfaction, employee engagement, and business outcomes: A meta-analysis. *The Journal of Applied Psychology*, *87*(2), 268–279. doi:10.1037/0021-9010.87.2.268 PMID:12002955

Hart, P. (1991). Irving L. Janis Victims of Groupthink. *Political Psychology*, *12*(2), 247–278. doi:10.2307/3791464

Hartung, C. M., Canu, W. H., Cleveland, C. S., Lefler, E. K., Mignogna, M. J., Fedele, D. A., & Clapp, J. D. et al. (2013). Stimulant Medication Use in College Students: Comparison of Appropriate Users, Misusers, and Nonusers. *Psychology of Addictive Behaviors*, *27*(3), 832–840. doi:10.1037/a0033822 PMID:24059834

Haruta, A., & Hallahan, K. (2003). *Cultural issues in airline crisis commnications: A Japan-US comparative study*. Public Relations and Communication.

Hatch, M. J., & Schultz, M. (2001). Are the strategic stars aligned for your corporate brand? *Harvard Business Review*, *79*(2), 128–134. PMID:11213687

Havranek, M. M., Bolliger, B., Ross, S., Pryce, C. R., Quednow, B. B., & Seifritz, E. (2016). Uncontrollable and unpredictable stress interacts with subclinical depression and anxiety scores in determining anxiety response. *Stress: The International Journal of the Biology of Stress*, *19*(1), 53–62. doi:10.3109/10253890.2015.1117449 PMID:26669536

Hay Group. (2004, March 4). *A culture for learning: An investigation into the values and beliefs associated with effective schools*. Retrieved from http://www.haygroup.com/Downloads/uk/misc/Culture_for_Learning.pdf

Health and Safety Executive. (2015). *Work related Stress, Anxiety and Depression Statistics in Great Britain 2015*. Retrieved December 2, 2015, from http://www.hse.gov.uk/statistics/causdis/stress/

Hebl, M. R., Madera, J. M., & Martinez, L. R. (2014). Personnel selection. In F. T. L. Leong, L. Comas-Díaz, G. C. Nagayama Hall, V. C. McLoyd, & J. E. Trimble (Eds.), APA handbook of multicultural psychology, Vol. 2: Applications and training. APA handbooks in psychology (pp. 253-264). Washington, DC: American Psychological Association. doi:10.1037/14187-015

Heinonen, E., Lindors, O., Laaksonen, M., & Knekt, P. (2012, May). Therapistsprofessional and personal characteristics as predictors of outcome in short- and long-term psychotherapy. *Journal of Affective Disorders, London, UK, 138*(3), 301–312. doi:10.1016/j.jad.2012.01.023 PMID:22335889

Helgeson, V. S., Reynolds, K. A., & Tomich, P. L. (2006). A meta-analytic review of benefit finding and growth. *Journal of Consluting and Clinical Psychology, 74*(5), 797-816.

Hensel, J. M., Ruiz, C., Finney, C., & Dewa, C. S. (2015). Meta-analysis of risk factors for secondary traumatic stress in therapeutic work with trauma victims. *Journal of Traumatic Stress*, *28*(2), 83–91. doi:10.1002/jts.21998 PMID:25864503

Herman, J. (1992). *Trauma and Recovery: The Aftermath of Violence – from Domestic Abuse to Political Terror*. New York, NY: Basic Books.

Herman, J. L. (1992). Complex PTSD: A syndrome in survivors of prolonged and repeated trauma. *Journal of Traumatic Stress*, *5*(3), 377–391. doi:10.1002/jts.2490050305

Herman, J. L. (1997). *Trauma and recovery*. New York: Basic Books.

Herskovitz, E. (1995). Struggling over Subjectivity: Debates about the Self and Alzheimers Disease. *Medical Anthropology Quarterly*, *9*(2), 146–164. doi:10.1525/maq.1995.9.2.02a00030 PMID:7671112

Herzberg, F. (2003). One more time: How do you motivate employees? *Harvard Business Review*, *81*(1), 87–96. PMID:12545925

Higgins, J. M., & Mcallaster, C. (2004). If you want strategic change, dont forget to change your cultural artifacts. *Journal of Change Management*, *4*(1), 63–73. doi:10.1080/1469701032000154926

Hill, M. A., & King, E. (1995). Womens Education and Economic Well-Being. *Feminist Economics*, *1*(2), 21–46. doi:10.1080/714042230

Hobfoll, S. E. (1989). Conservation of resources: A new attempt at conceptualizing stress. *The American Psychologist*, *44*(3), 513–524. doi:10.1037/0003-066X.44.3.513 PMID:2648906

Hofstede, G. (1984). Culture's consequences: international differences in work-related values. Beverly Hills, CA: Sage Publications.

Hofstede, G. (1990). Cultural constraints in management theories. *Academz of Management Execitive,7*(1).

Hofstede, G. (2001). Culture's consequences: comparing values, behaviors, institutions, and organizations across nations (2nd ed.). Thousand Oaks, CA: Sage Publications.

Hofstede, G. (2012). *National cultural dimensions.* Available at: http://geert-hofstede.com/national-culture.html

Hofstede, G. (2016). *The Hofstede Centre.* Available at: http://geert-hofstede.com/united-states.html

Hofstede, G. (1980). *Culture's consequences: International differences in work-related values*. Beverly Hills, CA: Sage Publications.

Hofstede, G. (2002). Dimensions do not exist: A reply to Brandon McSweeney. *Human Relations*, *55*(11), 1355–1361. doi:10.1177/0018726702055011921

Hofstede, G. (2011). Dimensionalizing Cultures: The Hofstede Model in Context. *Online Readings in Psychology and Culture*, *2*(1), 1–26. doi:10.9707/2307-0919.1014

Hofstede, G. H., Hofstede, G. J., & Minkov, M. (2010). *Cultures and organizations: Software of the mind: Intercultural cooperation and its importance for survival* (3rd ed.). McGrawHill.

Hofstede, G., Hofstede, G. J., & Minkov, M. (2010). *Cultures and organizations: Software of the mind.* New York, NY: McGraw-Hill Companies.

Hofstede, G., & Hofstede, J. G. (2005). *Cultures and Organizations. Software of the Mind.* New York: McGraw-Hill.

Hogan, R., Hogan, J., & Roberts, B. W. (1996). Personality measurement and employment decisions: Questions and answers. *The American Psychologist*, *51*(5), 469–477. doi:10.1037/0003-066X.51.5.469

Hogg, M. A., Terry, D. J., & White, K. M. (1995). A tale of two theories: A critical comparison of identity theory with social identity theory. *Social Psychology Quarterly*, *58*(4), 255–269. doi:10.2307/2787127

Holloway, E., & Kusy, M. (2010). Detox your workplace. *Marketing Health Services*, *30*(3), 24–27. PMID:20804081

Holmes, T. H., & Rahe, R. H. (1967). The Social Readjustment Rating Scale. *Journal of Psychosomatic Research*, *11*(2), 213–218. doi:10.1016/0022-3999(67)90010-4 PMID:6059863

Hong, G., Cho, Y., Jintae-Froese, F., & Shin, M. (2016). The effect of leadership styles, rank, and seniority on affective organizational commitment. *Cross Cultural & Strategic Management*, *23*(2), 340–362. doi:10.1108/CCSM-03-2014-0034

Hong, O., Chin, D. L., Phelps, S., Feld, J., & Vogel, S. (2012). Occupational injuries, duty status, and factors associated with injuries among firefighters. *Workplace Health and Safety*, *60*(10), 517–523. doi:10.3928/21650799-20121116-08 PMID:23163314

Hoobler, J. M., & Brass, D. J. (2006). Abusive supervision and family undermining as displaced aggression. *The Journal of Applied Psychology*, *91*(5), 1125–1133. doi:10.1037/0021-9010.91.5.1125 PMID:16953773

Hopper, E. (2012). *A theory of Incohesion: Aggregation/massification as the fourth basic assumption in the unconscious life of groups and group-like social systems. In Trauma and organizations* (pp. xxxi–li). London: Karnac Books.

Hopper, E. (2012). *Trauma and organizations*. London, UK: Karnac Books Ltd.

Hormann, S. (2007). *Organizational trauma: A phenomenological study of leaders in traumatized organizations* (Doctoral dissertation). Antioch University, Ohio.

Hormann, S. D. L. (2007). *Organizational trauma: A phenomenological study of leaders in traumatized organizations* (AAI3276967). PsycINFO database.

Hormann, S., & Vivian, P. (2005). Toward An Understanding of Traumatized Organizations and How to Intervene in Them. *Traumatology*, *11*(3), 159–169. doi:10.1177/153476560501100302

Horowitz, M. (1986). Stress-response syndromes: A review of posttraumatic and adjustment disorder. *Hospital & Community Psychiatry*, *37*, 241–249. PMID:3957267

House, R. J. (2004). *Culture, Leadership and Organizations: The GLOBE study of 62 Societes*. Thousand Oaks, CA: Sage.

Howard, R. E. (1985). *Women and the Crisis in Commonwealth Africa*. International Political Science Review.

Hsu, F. L. K. (1971). Filial Piety in Japan and China: Borrowing, Variation and Significance. *Journal of Comparative Family Studies*, 67–74.

Huchzemeier, A., & Cohen, M. A. (1996). Valuing operational flexibility under exchange risk. *Operations Research*, *44*(1), 100–113. doi:10.1287/opre.44.1.100

Hughes, R., Kinder, A., & Cooper, C. L. (2012). *International handbook of workplace trauma support*. Noida, India: John Wiley & Sons. doi:10.1002/9781119943242

Hui, L. H. (2009). Politics of Sichuan Earthquake, 2008. *Journal of Contingencies and Crisis Management*, *17*(2), 137–140. doi:10.1111/j.1468-5973.2009.00571.x

Human Rights Campaign. (2016). *Establishing an allies/safe zone program*. Retrieved from http://www.hrc.org/resources/establishing-an-allies-safe-zone-program

Hunt, J. (2012). *A state-by-state examination of non-discrimination laws and policies*. Center for American Progress Action Fund. Retrieved from https://www.americanprogress.org/wp-content/uploads/issues/2012/06/pdf/state_nondiscrimination.pdf

Hurtas, S. (2014). *Honor killings haunt Turkey's gay community*. Retrieved from http://www.al-monitor.com/pulse/originals/2014/05/prejudice-turkey-against-homosexuals.html

Hwang, G., & Lee, J. (2000). The process innovation in a competitive telecommunications market: A case study. *Total Quality Management,11*(4/5/6), S728-S733.10.1080/09544120050008138

Hystad, S. W., Eid, J., & Brevik, J. I. (2011). Effects of psychological hardiness, job demands, and job control on sickness absence: A prospective study. *Journal of Occupational Health Psychology*, *16*(3), 265–278. doi:10.1037/a0022904 PMID:21728435

Hyungju, K., Stein, H., & Bouwer, U. I. (2016). Assessment of accident theories for major accidents focusing on the MV SEWOL disaster: Similarities, differences, and discussion for a combined approach. *Safety Science*, *82*, 410–420. doi:10.1016/j.ssci.2015.10.009

Hyun, J. K., Kang, H. S., & Swanger, N. (2009). Burnout and engagement: A comparative analysis using the Big Five personality dimensions. *International Journal of Hospitality Management*, *28*(1), 96–104. doi:10.1016/j.ijhm.2008.06.001

Ibarra, H. (1999). Provisional selves: Experimenting with image and identity in professional adaptation. *Administrative Science Quarterly*, *44*(4), 764–791. doi:10.2307/2667055

Igic, I., Ryser, S., & Elfering, A. (2013). Does work stress make you shorter? An ambulatory field study of daily work stressors, job control, and spinal shrinkage. *Journal of Occupational Health Psychology*, *18*(4), 469–480. doi:10.1037/a0034256 PMID:24099165

Igo, T., & Skitmore, M. (2006). Diagnosing the organizational culture of an Australian engineering consultancy using the competing values framework. *Construction Innovation*, *6*(2), 121–139. doi:10.1108/14714170610710659

iMindMap. (2016). *How to MindMap*. Available at: https://imindmap.com/how-to-mind-map/

Inglehart, R. R., & Abramson, P. (1995). *Value Change in Global Perspective*. University of Michigan Press.

Institute of Work, Health and Organizations. (2004). *Protecting Workers' Health (Series 3)*. Retrieved from http://www.who.int/occupational_health/publications/stress/en/

Institute of Work, Health and Organizations. (2008). *Towards the Development of a European Framework for Psychosocial Risk Management at the Workplace*. Retrieved from http://www.prima-ef.org/preliminary-report.html

Instituto Ethos. (2014). *Business Commitment to LGBT Human Rights*. Retrieved from https://www3.ethos.org.br/wp-content/uploads/2014/12/Manual-LGBT_em-Ingl%C3%AAs_Vers%C3%A3o-Final.pdf

Islam, G., & Zyphur, M. J. (2009). Rituals in organizations: A review and expansion of current theory. *Group & Organization Management*, *34*(1), 114–139. doi:10.1177/1059601108329717

Israel, S., & Moffitt, E. T. (2014). Assessing Conscientious Personality in Primary Care: An Opportunity for Prevention and Health Promotion. *Developmental Psychology*, *50*(5), 1475–1477. doi:10.1037/a0036113 PMID:24773110

Istanbul authorities ban transgender and gay pride marches. (2016, June). *The Guardian*. Retrieved from https://www.theguardian.com/world/2016/jun/17/istanbul-transgender-gay-pride-marches-ban-alperen-hearths

Jackson, S. E., Schuler, S. W., & Werner, S. (2009). *Managing Human Resources*. Mason, OH: Cengage Learning.

Jamal, F. Q., & Khan, A. M. (2013). Association of downsizing with survivor's organizational commitment, work motivation and psychological well-being in secondary and tertiary sectors of economy of Pakistan. *Journal of Behavioural Science*, *23*(1), 1–25.

Jamal, M., & Baba, V. V. (2003). Type A behavior, components, and outcomes: A study of Canadian employees. *International Journal of Stress Management*, *10*(1), 39–50. doi:10.1037/1072-5245.10.1.39

James, E. H., & Wooten, L. P. (2010). *Leading under pressure*. New York: Taylor & Francis.

Janet, P. (1889). *L'automatisme psychologique*. Paris: Alcan.

Janet, P. (1904). L'amnésie et la dissociation des souvenirs par l'émotion. *Journal für Psychologie*, *1*, 417–453.

Janoff-Bulman, R. (1985). The aftermath of victimization: Rebuilding shattered assumptions. In C. R. Figley (Ed.), *Trauma and its wake: The study and Treatment of Post-Traumatic Stress Disorder*. Brunner-Mazel.

Javidad, M., & Dastmalchian, A. (2012). Managerial implicaions of the GLOBE project: A study of 62 societies. *Asia Pacific Journal of Human Resources*, 41–58.

Jerabek, I., & Muoio, D. (2011). *Type A Personality and Striving for Success*. Unpublished raw data.

Jerabek, I., & Muoio, D. (2012a). *Why emotional intelligence matters more than traditional intelligence*. Unpublished raw data.

Jerabek, I., & Muoio, D. (2013a). *The Hardy Personality*. Unpublished raw data.

Jerabek, I., & Muoio, D. (2013b). *The Power of a Positive Mindset*. Unpublished raw data.

Jerabek, I., & Muoio, D. (2013c). *The Pitfalls of Perfectionism*. Unpublished raw data.

Jerabek, I., & Muoio, D. (2013d). *Protective Factor of High Self-esteem*. Unpublished raw data.

Jerabek, I., & Muoio, D. (2014a). *Self-made martyr: Locus of control and victim mentality*. Unpublished raw data.

Jerabek, I., & Muoio, D. (2014b). *Goal Achievement and Coaching*. Unpublished raw data.

Jerabek, I., & Muoio, D. (2014c). *Emotional Intelligence and Life Satisfaction*. Unpublished raw data.

Jerabek, I., & Muoio, D. (2015a). *The Splendors and Miseries of Workaholics*. Unpublished raw data.

Jerabek, I., & Muoio, D. (2015b). *The Role of Management in Turnover*. Unpublished raw data.

Jin, Y., Liu, B. F., Anagondahalli, D., & Austin, L. (2014). Scale development for measuring publics emotions in organizational crises. *Public Relations Review*, *40*(3), 509–518. doi:10.1016/j.pubrev.2014.04.007

Joas, H. (2008). *Do We Need Religion? On the Experience of Self-Transcendence* (1st ed.). Oxon, UK: Routledge.

John, O. P., & Srivastava, S. (1999). The Big-Five trait taxonomy: History, measurement, and theoretical perspectives. In L. A. Pervin & O. P. John (Eds.), *Handbook of personality: Theory and research* (Vol. 2, pp. 102–138). New York: Guilford Press.

John, P., Arnon, E., & James, T. (2000). Cynicism about organizational change. *Group & Organization Management*, *25*(2), 132–153. doi:10.1177/1059601100252003

Jonason, P. K., Slomski, S., & Partyka, J. (2012). The Dark Triad at work: How toxic employees get their way. *Personality and Individual Differences*, *52*(3), 449–453. doi:10.1016/j.paid.2011.11.008

Jones, C. A. (2002). Victim perspective of bank robbery trauma and recovery. *Traumatology*, *8*(4), 191–204. doi:10.1177/153476560200800402

Jones, D. W. (1982). The Vietnams of Michael Herr and Tim OBrien: Tales of Disintegration and Integration. *Canadian Review of American Studies*, *13*(3), 309–200. doi:10.3138/CRAS-013-03-03

Jones, T. M., Felps, W., & Bigley, G. A. (2007). Ethical theory and stakeholder-related decisions: The role of stakeholder culture. *Academy of Management Review*, *32*(1), 137–155. doi:10.5465/AMR.2007.23463924

Jovanovic, B. (1979). Job matching and the theory of turnover. *Journal of Political Economy*, *87*(5), 972–990. doi:10.1086/260808

Judge, T. A., & Piccolo, R. F. (2006). Transformational and transactional leadership: A meta-analytic test of their relative validity. *The Journal of Applied Psychology*, *89*(5). PMID:15506858

Jung, C. G. (1967). Symbols of transformation (2nd ed.). Princeton University Press.

Kahneman, D., & Deaton, A. (2010). High income improves evaluation of life but not emotional well-being. *Proceedings of the National Academy of Sciences of the United States of America*, *107*(38), 16489–16493. doi:10.1073/pnas.1011492107 PMID:20823223

Kahneman, D., & Krueger, A. (2006). Developments in the measurement of subjective well-being. *The Journal of Economic Perspectives*, *20*(1), 3–24. doi:10.1257/089533006776526030

Kahn, W. A. (1990). Psychological conditions of personal engagement and disengagement at work. *Academy of Management Journal*, *33*(4), 692–724. doi:10.2307/256287

Kahn, W. A. (2003). The revelation of organizational trauma. *The Journal of Applied Behavioral Science*, *39*(4), 364–380. doi:10.1177/0021886303261954

Kahn, W. A. (2010). The essence of engagement: Lessons from the field. In S. L. Albrecht (Ed.), *Handbook of Employee Engagement: Perspectives, Issues, Research and Practice* (pp. 20–30). Cheltenham, UK: Edward Elgar. doi:10.4337/9781849806374.00008

Kahn, W. A. (2011). Treating organizational wounds. *Organizational Dynamics*, *40*(2), 75–84. doi:10.1016/j.orgdyn.2011.01.001

Kahn, W. A., Barton, M. A., & Fellows, S. (2013). Organizational Crises and the Disturbance of Relational System. *Academy of Management Review*, *38*(3), 377–396. doi:10.5465/amr.2011.0363

Kalimo, R., Taris, T. W., & Schaufeli, W. B. (2003). The effects of Past and Anticipated Future Downsizing on Survivor Well-Being: An Equity Perspective. *Journal of Occupational Health Psychology*, *8*(2), 91–109. doi:10.1037/1076-8998.8.2.91 PMID:12703876

Kammeyer-Mueller, J. D., Judge, T. A., & Scott, B. A. (2009). The role of core self-evaluations in the coping process. *The Journal of Applied Psychology*, *94*(1), 177–195. doi:10.1037/a0013214 PMID:19186903

Kanov, J. M., Maitlis, S., Worline, M. C., Dutton, J. E., Frost, P. J., & Lilius, J. M. (2004). Compassion in organizational life. *The American Behavioral Scientist*, *47*(6), 808–827. doi:10.1177/0002764203260211

Kantur, D., & İşeri-Say, A. (2012). Organizational resilience: Conceptual integrative framework. *Journal of Management & Organization*, *18*(06), 762–773. doi:10.1017/S1833367200000420

Kaplan, R. S. (2005). How the balanced scorecard complements the McKinsey 7-S model. *Strategy and Leadership*, *33*(3), 41–46. doi:10.1108/10878570510594442

Kardiner, A., & Spiegel, H. (1947). *War stress and neurotic illness*. New York: Paul B. Hoeber Inc.

Kates, N., Greiff, B. S., & Hagen, D. Q. (1990). *The Psychosocial Impact of Job Loss*. Washington, DC: American Psychiatric Association.

Kauffman, J. (2005). Lost in space: A critique of NASAs crisis communications in the Columbia disaster. *Public Relations Review*, *31*(2), 263–275. doi:10.1016/j.pubrev.2005.02.013

Keidel, R. W., Bell, S. M., & Lewis, K. J. (1994). Rethinking organizational design. *The Academy of Management Executive*, *8*(4), 12-30.

Kelloway, K. E., Turner, N., Barling, J., & Loughlin, C. (2012). Transformational leadership and employee psychological well-being: The mediating role of employee trust in leadership. *Work & Stress: An International Journal of Work. Health & Organisations*, *26*(1), 39–55.

Kendra, J. M., & Wachtendorf, T. (2003). Elements of resilience after the world trade center disaster: Reconstituting New York Citys emergency operations center. *Disasters*, *27*(1), 37–53. doi:10.1111/1467-7717.00218 PMID:12703151

Kesebir, P., & Diener, E. (2008). In pursuit of happiness: Empirical answers to philosophical questions. *Perspectives on Psychological Science*, *3*(2), 117–125. doi:10.1111/j.1745-6916.2008.00069.x PMID:26158878

Kessler, R. C., Sonnega, A., Bromet, E., Hughes, M., & Nelson, C. B. (1995). Posttraumatic stress disorder in the National Comorbidity Survey. *Archives of General Psychiatry*, *52*(12), 1048–1060. doi:10.1001/archpsyc.1995.03950240066012 PMID:7492257

Khanna, S., & Greyson, B. (2014). Near-death experiences and spiritual well-being. *Journal of Religion and Health*, *53*(6), 1605–1615. doi:10.1007/s10943-013-9723-0 PMID:23625172

Kibel, H. D. (2012). *A study in institutional change: The experience of trauma and the role of rumour in a case of paranoiagenesis. In Trauma and organizations* (pp. 3–22). London: Karnac Books.

Kiefer, T. (2005). The real reason people won't change. *Harvard Business Review*, *79*(10), 85–92.

Kilduff, G. J., Elfenbein, H. A., & Staw, B. M. (2010). The psychology of rivalry: A relationally dependent analysis of competition. *Academy of Management Journal*, *53*(5), 943–969. doi:10.5465/AMJ.2010.54533171

Killian, K. D. (2008). Helping till it hurts? A multimethod study of compassion fatigue, burnout, and self-care in clinicians working with trauma survivors. *Traumatology*, *14*(2), 32–44. doi:10.1177/1534765608319083

King, E. B., & Cortina, J. M. (2010). The social and economic imperative of lesbian, gay, bisexual, and transgendered supportive organizational policies. *Industrial and Organizational Psychology: Perspectives on Science and Practice*, *3*(1), 69–78. doi:10.1111/j.1754-9434.2009.01201.x

King, G., Keohene, R. O., & Verba, S. (1994). *Designing Social Inquiry*. Princeton, NJ: Princeton University Press.

Kinzie, J. D., & Goetz, R. R. (1996). A Century of Controversy Surrounding Posttraumatic Stress-Spectrum Syndromes: The Impact on DSM-III and DSM-IV. *Journal of Traumatic Stress*, *9*(2), 159–179. doi:10.1002/jts.2490090202 PMID:8731540

Kirby, R., Shakespeare-Finch, J., & Palk, G. (2011). Adaptive and maladaptive coping strategies predict posttrauma outcomes in ambulance personnel. *Traumatology*, *17*(4), 25–34. doi:10.1177/1534765610395623

Klarner, P., By, R. T., & Diefenbach, T. (2011). Employee emotions during organizational change—Towards a new research agenda. *Scandinavian Journal of Management*, *27*(3), 332–340. doi:10.1016/j.scaman.2011.06.002

Kleber, J. R., Figley, R. Ch., & Gerson, P. R. B. (Eds.). (2013). *Beyond Trauma: Cultural and Societal Dynamics* (1st ed.). Berlin, Germany: Springer Science & Business Media.

Kleber, R. J., & Brom, D. (1992). *Coping with trauma*. Amsterdam: Swets & Zeitlinger.

Klein, S., & Alexander, D. (2011). The impact of trauma within organisations. In Managing trauma in the workplace: Supporting workers and organisations (pp. 117-138). Routledge/Taylor et Francis Group.

Kleinberg, J. (2012). Building individual resilience and organizational hardiness: addressing post-trauma worker's block. In E. Hopper (Ed.), Trauma and organizations (pp. 255-276). London, UK: Karnac Books Ltd.

Kleinberg, J. (2014). Corruptogenic organizations. *International Journal of Group Psychotherapy*, *64*(4), 420–443. doi:10.1521/ijgp.2014.64.4.420 PMID:25188561

Kleinberg, J. (2016). How organizational hunger may have contributed to the American Psychological Association's scandal over the ethics of torture. *International Journal of Group Psychotherapy*. doi:10.1080/00207284.2016.1176482

Klein, K. J., & Kozlowski, S. W. J. (2013). *Multilevel Theory, Research, and Methods in Organizations: Foundations, Extensions, and New Directions*. Wiley.

Kobasa, S. C. (1979). Stressful life events, personality, and health: An inquiry into hardiness. *Journal of Personality and Social Psychology*, *37*(1), 1–11. doi:10.1037/0022-3514.37.1.1 PMID:458548

Koninckx, G., & Teneau, G. (2010). *Résilience organisationnelle: Rebondir face aux turbulences*. Brussels/Paris: De Boeck Supérieur

Koonin, M., & Green, T. (2005). The emotionally abusive workplace. *Journal of Emotional Abuse*, *3*, 71–79.

Kotleras, R. (2007). The workplace mobbing of highly gifted adults: An unremarked barbarism. *Advanced Development Journal*, *11*, 130–149.

Kotsou, I., Nelis, D., Grégoire, J., & Mikolajczak, M. (2011). Emotional plasticity: Conditions and effects of improving emotional competence in adulthood. *The Journal of Applied Psychology*, *96*(4), 827–839. doi:10.1037/a0023047 PMID:21443316

Kotter, J. (2011, March 23). *John Kotter- Dealing with resistance to change* [YouTube]. Retrieved from https://youtu.be/Wdroj6F3VlQ

Kotter, J. (1995). Leading change: Why transformation efforts fail. *Harvard Business Review*, *73*(2), 59–67. doi:10.1002/npr.10055

Kotter, J. P. (1999). *John P. Kotter on what leaders really do*. Harvard Business Press.

Kotter, J. P., & Schlesinger, L. A. (2008). Choosing strategies for change. *Harvard Business Review*, *86*(7/8), 130–139. PMID:10240501

Koubaridis, A. (2015, June 5). *Every six weeks an emergency services worker in Australia commits suicide*. Retrieved August 16, 2016, from http://www.news.com.au/finance/work/every-six-weeks-an-emergency-services-worker-in-australia-commits-suicide/news-story/728bedaac0840e4a6214c0e525324d44

Kozlowski, S. W. J., Chao, G. T., Smith, E. M., & Hedlund, J. (1993). Organisational downsizing: Strategies, interventions, and research implications. *International Review of Industrial and Organizational Psychology*, *8*, 263–332.

Kraepelin, E. (1899). *Ein Lehrbuch für Studierende und Aertze (vols. 1-2)*. Leipzig: Johann Ambrosius Barth.

Krystal, H. (1988). *Integration and Self Healing: Affect – Trauma – Alexithymia*. New York: Routledge.

Kübler-Ross, E. (2005). *On Grief and Grieving: Finding the Meaning of Grief Through the Five Stages of Loss*. New York: Simon & Schuster Ltd.

Kučera, D. (2015). Weberova teze „ducha kapitalismu" jako podnět pro hledání spirituálních potenciálů v podnikatelském a manažerském prostředí.(Weber's "spirit of capitalism" thesis as a starting point for finding spiritual potentials in business and management environment.) Acta Oeconomica Pragensia, University of Economics, Prague, Czech Republic, 5, 24–44. doi: 10.18267/j.aop.484

Kumar, P., Gupta, S., Agarwal, M., & Singh, U. (2016). Categorization and standardization of accidental risk-criticality levels of human error to develop risk and safety management policy. *Safety Science*, *85*, 88–98. doi:10.1016/j.ssci.2016.01.007

Kumar, V., & Pansari, A. (2015). Measuring the Benefits of Employee Engagement. *MIT Sloan Management Review*, *56*(4), 67.

Küng, H. (2008). *Spurensuche: Die Weltreligionen auf dem Weg* (2nd ed.). München, Germany: Piper Verlag.

Kurian, A. G., Currier, J. M., Rojas-Flores, L., Herrera, S., & Foster, J. D. (2016). Meaning, Perceived Growth, and Posttraumatic Stress Among Teachers in El Salvador: Assessing the Impact of Daily Spiritual Experiences. *Psychology of Religion and Spirituality*, *8*(4), 289–297; Advance online publication. doi:10.1037/rel0000070

Kusy, M., & Holloway, E. (2009). *Toxic workplace! Managing toxic personalities and their systems of power*. San Francisco, CA: John Wiley & Sons, Inc.

Kusy, M., & Holloway, E. (2010). Cultivating a culture of respectful engagement. *Leader to Leader*, *2010*(58), 50–56. doi:10.1002/ltl.442

Lacan, J. (1973). *Les quatre concepts fondamentaux de la psychanalyse*. Paris: Seuil.

Lagerveld, S. E., Blonk, R. W. B., Brenninkmeijer, V., Wijngaards-de Meij, L., & Schaufeli, W. B. (2012). Work-focused treatment of common mental disorders and return to work: A comparative outcome study. *Journal of Occupational Health Psychology*, *17*(2), 220–234. doi:10.1037/a0027049 PMID:22308965

Lambert, J. E., & Alhassoon, O. M. (2015). Trauma-Focused Therapy for Refugees: Meta-Analytic Findings. *Journal of Counseling Psychology*, *62*(1), 28–37. doi:10.1037/cou0000048 PMID:25485547

Lambert, J. E., Benight, C. C., Harrison, E., & Cieslak, R. (2012). The Firefighter Coping Self-Efficacy Scale: Measure development and validation. *Anxiety, Stress, and Coping*, *25*(1), 79–91. doi:10.1080/10615806.2011.567328 PMID:21476153

Larsen, J. L., Clauss-Ehlers, C. S., & Cosden, M. A. (2015). An exploration of army wives responses to spousal deployment: Stressors and protective factors. *Couple and Family Psychology: Research and Practice*, *4*(4), 212–228. doi:10.1037/cfp0000049

Larsen, J. R., & Ketelaar, T. (1991). Personality and Susceptibility to Positive Negative Emotional State. *Journal of Personality and Social Psychology*, *61*(1), 132–140. doi:10.1037/0022-3514.61.1.132 PMID:1890584

Lasebikan, V. O., & Oyetunde, M. O. (2012). Burnout among Nurses in a Nigerian General Hospital: Prevalance and Associated Factors. *ISRN Nursing*, *2012*(1), 1-6.

Lazarus, R. S. (1993). Coping Theory and Research: Past, Present, and Future. *Psychosomatic Medicine*, *55*(3), 234–247. doi:10.1097/00006842-199305000-00002 PMID:8346332

Leahey, T. H. (2000). *A history of psychology*. Upper Saddle River, NJ: Prentice Hall.

Leana, C. R., & Feldman, D. C. (1988). Individual responses to job loss: Perceptions, reactions, and coping behaviors. *Journal of Management*, *14*(3), 375–389. doi:10.1177/014920638801400302

Lebigot, F. (2001). Prises en charge psychothérapeutiques psychodynamiques. In Les traumatismes psychiques. Paris: Masson.

Lebigot, F. (2002). L'effroi du traumatisme psychique. Le regarder en face ou s'en protéger. *Revue Francophone du Stress et du Trauma, 2*(3), 139–146.

Lebigot, F. (2004). Le traumatisme psychique. *Revue Francophone du Stress et du Trauma, 4*(1), 5–11.

Lebigot, F. (2005). *Traiter les traumatismes psychiques. Cliniques et prise en charge.* Paris: Editions Dunod.

Lee, G., & Teo, A. (2005). Organizational restructuring: Impact on trust and work satisfaction. *Asia Pacific Journal of Management, 22*(1), 23–39. doi:10.1007/s10490-005-6416-6

Lee, R., & Brotheridge, C. (2006). When prey turn predatory: Workplace bullying as a predictor of counter aggression/bullying, coping, and well-being. *European Journal of Work and Organizational Psychology, 15*(3), 352–377. doi:10.1080/13594320600636531

Lefcourt, H. M. (2005). Humor. In C. R. Snyder & S. J, Lopez (Eds.), Handbook of positive psychology (pp. 619-629). Oxford, UK: Oxford University Press.

Lefebvre, P., & Barbes, S. (184). L'Hystérie de guerre: Étude comparative de ses manifestations au cours de deux derniers conflits mondiaux. *Annales Médico-Psychologiques, 142*(February), 262–266.

Leidner, D. E., Pan, G., & Pan, S. L. (2009). The role of IT in crisis response: Lessons from the SARS and Asian tsunami disasters. *The Journal of Strategic Information Systems, 18*(2), 80–99. doi:10.1016/j.jsis.2009.05.001

Leiter, M. P., Gascón, S., & Martínez-Jarreta, B. (2010). Making sense of work life: A structural model of burnout. *Journal of Applied Social Psychology, 40*(1), 57–75. doi:10.1111/j.1559-1816.2009.00563.x

Leiter, M. P., Laschinger, H., Day, A., & Oore, D. (2011). The impact of civility interventions on employees social behavior, distress, and attitudes. *The Journal of Applied Psychology, 96*(6), 1258–1274. doi:10.1037/a0024442 PMID:21744942

Lemogne, C., Schuster, J. P., Levenstein, S., Melchior, M., Nabi, H., Ducimetière, P., & Consoli, S. M. et al. (2015). Hostility and the risk of peptic ulcer in the GAZEL cohort. *Health Psychology, 34*(2), 181–185. doi:10.1037/hea0000129 PMID:25110845

Lenartowicz, T., & Roth, K. (1999). A Framework for Culture Assessment. *Journal of International Business Studies, 30*(4), 781–798. doi:10.1057/palgrave.jibs.8490839

Lengnick-Hall, C. A., Beck, T. E., & Lengnick-Hall, M. L. (2011). Developing a capacity for organizational resilience through strategic human resource management. *Human Resource Management Review, 21*(3), 243–255. doi:10.1016/j.hrmr.2010.07.001

Lennerfors, T. T. (2013). Organizational diaspora: The aftermath of the Saléninvest bankruptcy. *Culture and Organization, 19*(5), 430–450. doi:10.1080/14759551.2013.824447

Leon, S. C., Visscher, L., Sugimura, N., & Lakin, B. L. (2008). Person-job match among frontline staff working in residential treatment centers: The impact of personality and child psychopathology on burnout experiences. *The American Journal of Orthopsychiatry, 78*(2), 240–248. doi:10.1037/a0013946 PMID:18954187

Leppaniemi, A. K. (2009). Update on global trends in trauma. *Trauma, 11*(1), 37–47. doi:10.1177/1460408608100461

Leroy, H., Palanski, M., & Simons, T. (2012). Authentic leadership and behavioral integrity as drivers of follower commitment and performance. *Journal of Business Ethics, 107*(3), 255–264. doi:10.1007/s10551-011-1036-1

Lester, D. L., Parnell, J. A., & Carraher, S. (2003). Organizational life cycle: A five-stage empirical scale. *The International Journal of Organizational Analysis, 11*(4), 339–354. doi:10.1108/eb028979

Leung, K., Bhagat, R. S., Buchan, N. R., Erez, M., & Gibson, C. B. (2005). Culture and international business recent advances and their implications for future reserach. *Journal of International Business Studies*, *36*(4), 357–378. doi:10.1057/palgrave.jibs.8400150

Leung, K., & Bond, M. H. (2006). Psycho-logic vs. ecologic: Insights from social axiom dimensions. In *Individuals and Cultures in Multi-level Analysis*. Mahwah, NJ: Lawrence Erlbaum.

Levi, L., Sauter, S. L., & Shimomitsu, T. (1999). Work-related stress - its time to act. *Journal of Occupational Health Psychology*, *4*(4), 394–396. doi:10.1037/1076-8998.4.4.394 PMID:10526843

LeVine. (1984). *Culture theory: essays on mind, self, and emotion*. Cambridge, UK: Cambridge University Press.

Lewin, K. (1951). *Field Theory in Social Science*. Harper & Row.

Leymann, H. (1990). Mobbing and psychological terror at workplaces. *Violence and Victims*, *5*(2), 119–126. PMID:2278952

Leymann, H. (1996). The content and development of mobbing at work. *European Journal of Work and Organizational Psychology*, *5*(2), 165–184. doi:10.1080/13594329608414853

Leymann, H., & Gustaafsson, A. (1996). Mobbing at work and the development of post traumatic stress disorders. *European Journal of Work and Organizational Psychology*, *5*(2), 251–275. doi:10.1080/13594329608414858

Li, J., Zhang, M., Loerbroks, A., Angerer, P., & Siegrist, J. (2014). Work stress and the risk of recurrent coronary heart disease events: A systematic review and meta-analysis. *International Journal of Occupational Medicine and Environmental Health*, *28*(1), 8–19. PMID:26159942

Lilly, M. M., & Pierce, H. (2013). PTSD and depressive symptoms in 911 telecommunicators: The role of peritraumatic distress and world assumptions in predicting risk. *Psychological Trauma: Theory, Research, Practice, and Policy*, *5*(2), 135–141. doi:10.1037/a0026850

Lindwall, M., Gerber, M., Jonsdottir, I. H., Börjesson, M., & Ahlborg, G. Jr. (2014). The relationships of change in physical activity with change in depression, anxiety, and burnout: A longitudinal study of Swedish healthcare workers. *Health Psychology*, *33*(11), 1309–1318. doi:10.1037/a0034402 PMID:24245832

Lindy, J., Green, B., & Grace, M. (1987). The stressor criterion and posttraumatic stress disorder. *The Journal of Nervous and Mental Disease*, *175*, 269–272. doi:10.1097/00005053-198705000-00004 PMID:3572377

Linstead, S., Maréchal, G., & Griffin, R. W. (2014). Theorizing and researching the dark side of organization. *Organization Studies*, *35*(2), 165–188. doi:10.1177/0170840613515402

Linton, D. K., & Power, J. L. (2013). The personality traits of workplace bullies are often shared by their victims: Is there a dark side to victims? *Personality and Individual Differences*, *54*(6), 738–743. doi:10.1016/j.paid.2012.11.026

Lipman-Blumen, J. (2006). *The allure of toxic leaders: Why we follow destructive bosses and corrupt politicians-and how we can survive them*. Oxford University Press.

Liu, C., Li, C., Fan, J., & Nauta, M. M. (2015). Workplace conflict and absence/lateness: The moderating effects of core self-evaluation in China and the United States. *International Journal of Stress Management*, *22*(3), 243–269. doi:10.1037/a0039163

Li, Y., Wang, Z., Yang, L. Q., & Liu, S. (2016). The crossover of psychological distress from leaders to subordinates in teams: The role of abusive supervision, psychological capital, and team performance. *Journal of Occupational Health Psychology*, *21*(2), 142–153. doi:10.1037/a0039960 PMID:26652269

Lo Bue, S., Taverniers, J., Mylle, J., & Euwema, M. (2013). Hardiness promotes work engagement, prevents burnout, and moderates their relationship. *Military Psychology*, *25*(2), 105–115. doi:10.1037/h0094952

Locke, E. A., & Latham, G. P. (2009). What should we do about motivation theory? *Academy of Management Review*, *29*, 388–403.

Löckenhoff, C. E., Sutin, A. R., Ferrucci, L., & Costa, P. T. Jr. (2008). Personality traits and subjective health in the later years: The association between NEO-PI-R and SF-36 in advanced age is influenced by health status. *Journal of Research in Personality*, *42*(5), 1334–1346. doi:10.1016/j.jrp.2008.05.006

López-Fuentes, I., & Calvete, E. (2015). Building resilience: A quantitative study of Spanish women who have suffered intimate partner violence. *The American Journal of Orthopsychiatry*, *85*(4), 339–351. doi:10.1037/ort0000070 PMID:26011382

Lubit, R. H. (2008). *Coping with toxic managers, subordinates.... and other difficult people: Using emotional intelligence to survive and prosper*. Upper Saddle River, NJ: FT Press.

Luders, G. (2015, April 29). Chefe, sou gay. *Exame*. Retrieved from http://exame.abril.com.br/revista-exame/edicoes/1088/noticias/chefe-sou-gay

Luszczynska, A., Benight, C. C., & Cieslak, R. (2009). Self-efficacy and health-related outcomes of collective trauma: A systematic review. *European Psychologist*, *14*(1), 51–62. doi:10.1027/1016-9040.14.1.51

Lutgen-Sandvik, P. (2008). Intensive remedial identity work: Responses to workplace bullying trauma and stigmatization. *Organization*, *15*(1), 97–119. doi:10.1177/1350508407084487

Lutz, A., Slagter, H. A., Dunne, J. D., & Davidson, R. J. (2008). Attention regulation and monitoring in meditation. *Trends in Cognitive Sciences*, *12*(4), 163–169. doi:10.1016/j.tics.2008.01.005 PMID:18329323

Luxenberg, T. (2001). Complex trauma and disorder of extreme stress (DESNOS) dignosis, part two: Treatment. *Directions in Psychiatry*, 373–392.

Lykken, D., & Tellegen, A. (1996). Happiness is a stochastic phenomenon. *Psychological Science*, *7*(3), 186–189. doi:10.1111/j.1467-9280.1996.tb00355.x

Lyness, K. S., & Judiesch, M. K. (2014). Gender Egalitarianism and Work-Life Balance for Managers: Multisource Perspectives in 36 Countries. *Applied Psychology*, *63*(1), 96–129. doi:10.1111/apps.12011

Lyubomirsky, S., King, L., & Diener, E. (2005). The benefit of frequent positive affect: Does hap- piness lead to success? *Psychological Bulletin*, *131*(6), 803–855. doi:10.1037/0033-2909.131.6.803 PMID:16351326

Lyubomirsky, S., & Lepper, H. S. (1999). A measure of subjective happiness: Preliminary reliability and construct validation. *Social Indicators Research*, *46*(2), 137–155. doi:10.1023/A:1006824100041

MaCathy, P. (2000). The bully-victim at work. Transcending boundaries: Integrating people, processes and systems conference, Brisbane, Australia.

MacCann, C., & Roberts, R. D. (2008). New Paradigms for Assessing Emotional Intelligence: Theory and Data. *Emotion (Washington, D.C.)*, *8*(4), 540–551. doi:10.1037/a0012746 PMID:18729584

Macey, W. H., & Schneider, B. (2008). The meaning of employee engagement. *Industrial and Organizational Psychology: Perspectives on Science and Practice*, *1*(1), 3–30. doi:10.1111/j.1754-9434.2007.0002.x

Maddi, S. R. (2013). Personal hardiness as the basis for resilience. In S. R. Maddi (Ed.), *Hardiness: Turning stressful circumstances into resilient growth* (pp. 7–17). New York: Springer. doi:10.1007/978-94-007-5222-1_2

Mahtani, S., & Vernon, K. (2010). *Creating Inclusive Workplaces for LGBT Employees - A Resource Guide for Employers in Hong Kong*. Retrieved from http://www.outandequal.org/wp-content/uploads/2015/05/Community-Business-Inclusive-Workplaces-HK-2010.pdf

Makawatsakul, N., & Kleiner, B.H. (2003). The effect of downsizing on morale and attrition. *Management Research News, 26*(2/3/4), 52-62.

Maki, N. E. (2005). The Responses of Male and Female Managers to Workplace Stress and Downsizing. *North American Journal of Psychology*, *7*(2), 295–312.

Makison, R. A., & Young, J. S. (2012). Cognitive Behavioral Therapy and the Treatment of Posttraumatic Stress Disorder: Where Counseling and Neuroscience Meet. *Journal of Counseling and Development*, *90*(2), 131–140. doi:10.1111/j.1556-6676.2012.00017.x

Malarewicz, J. A. (2012). *Systémique et entreprise: Mettre en oeuvre une stratégie de changement*. Pearson Education France.

Malik, M. I., & Ahmad, D. M. (2011). Lucky or unlucky people: Layoff Survivors. *Far East Journal of Psychology and Business*, *2*(3), 23–35.

Mandel, T., Dunkley, D. M., & Moroz, M. (2015). Self-critical perfectionism and depressive and anxious symptoms over 4 years: The mediating role of daily stress reactivity. *Journal of Counseling Psychology*, *62*(4), 703–717. doi:10.1037/cou0000101 PMID:26191980

Mandemakers, J. J., & Monden, C. S. (2013). Does the effect of job loss on psychological distress differ by educational level? *Work, Employment and Society*, *27*(1), 73–93. doi:10.1177/0950017012460312

Mansell, W. (2015, November 18). *Eagles of death metal share first message since Paris attack*. Retrieved August 16, 2016, from http://www.idigitaltimes.com/eagles-death-metal-share-first-message-paris-attack-491231

Mantler, J., Matejicek, A., Matheson, K., & Anisman, H. (2005). Coping With Employment Uncertainty: A Comparison of Employed and Unemployed Workers. *Journal of Occupational Health Psychology*, *10*(3), 200–209. doi:10.1037/1076-8998.10.3.200 PMID:16060724

Marais, A., & Stuart, A. D. (2005). The role of temperament in the development of post-traumatic stress disorder amongst journalists. *South African Journal of Psychology. Suid-Afrikaanse Tydskrif vir Sielkunde*, *35*(1), 89–105. doi:10.1177/008124630503500106

Marks, N., & Shah, H. (2005). A well-being manifesto for a flourishing society. *Journal of Mental Health Promotion*, *3*(4), 9-15. Retrieved from www.neweconomics.org

Marmar, C. R., Weiss, D. S., & Metzler, T. J. (1996). Characteristics of emergency services personnel related to peritraumatic dissociation during critical incident exposure. *The American Journal of Psychiatry*, *153*(7), 94–102. doi:10.1176/ajp.153.7.94 PMID:8659646

Martinez, M. E., Morales, O., Rodríguez, O., Rosa, W., & Sánchez, S. (2009). Civilidad, incivilidad y el bienestar asociado al trabajo en un grupo de personas empleadas en Puerto Rico[Civility, incivility and the wellbeing associated with the workplace on a group of Puerto Rican employees]. *Revista Interamericana de Psicología Ocupacional*, *28*(1), 45–55.

Martin, G., Farndale, E., Paauwe, J., & Stiles, P. G. (2016). Corporate governance and strategic human resource management: Four archetypes and proposals for a new approach to corporate sustainability. *European Management Journal*, *34*(1), 22–35. doi:10.1016/j.emj.2016.01.002

Maseland, R., & van Hoorn, A. (2009). Explaining the Negative Correlation between Values and Practices: A Note on the Hofstede–Globe Debate. *Journal of International Business Studies*, *40*(3), 527–532. doi:10.1057/jibs.2008.68

Maslach, C. (1993). Burnout: A multidimensional perspective. In W. B. Schaufeli, C. Maslach, & T. Marek (Eds.), *Professional burnout: Recent developments in theory and research* (pp. 19–32). Washington, DC: Taylor & Francis.

Maslach, C. (2003). *Burnout: The cost of caring*. Cambridge, MA: Marlor Books.

Maslach, C., & Jackson, S. E. (1981). The measurement of experienced burnout. *Journal of Organizational Behavior*, *2*(2), 99–113. doi:10.1002/job.4030020205

Maslach, C., Jackson, S. E., & Leiter, M. P. (1996). *The Maslach Burnout Inventory* (3rd ed.). Palo Alto, CA: Consulting Psychologists Press.

Maslach, C., & Leiter, M. P. (1997). *The truth about burnout*. San Francisco, CA: Jossey-Bass.

Maslach, C., & Leiter, M. P. (2008). Early predictors of job burnout and engagement. *The Journal of Applied Psychology*, *93*(3), 498–512. doi:10.1037/0021-9010.93.3.498 PMID:18457483

Maslach, C., Schaufeli, W. B., & Leiter, M. P. (2001). Job burnout. *Annual Review of Psychology*, *52*(1), 397–422. doi:10.1146/annurev.psych.52.1.397 PMID:11148311

Matthiessen, S. B., & Einarsen, S. (2004). Psychiatric distress and symptoms of PTSD among victims of bullying at work. *British Journal of Guidance & Counselling*, *32*(3), 335–356. doi:10.1080/03069880410001723558

Mawritz, M. B., Dust, S. B., & Resick, C. J. (2014). Hostile climate, abusive supervision, and employee coping: Does conscientiousness matter? *The Journal of Applied Psychology*, *99*(4), 737–747. doi:10.1037/a0035863 PMID:24512026

May, D. R., Gilson, R. L., & Harter, L. M. (2004). The psychological conditions of meaningfulness, safety and availability and the engagement of the human spirit at work. *Journal of Occupational and Organizational Psychology*, *77*(1), 11–37. doi:10.1348/096317904322915892

May, D., Wesche, J. S., Heinitz, K., & Kerschreiter, R. (2014). Coping with destructive leadership: Putting forward an integrated theoretical framework for the interaction process between leaders and followers. *Zeitschrift fur Psychologie mit Zeitschrift fur Angewandte Psychologie*, *222*(4), 203–213. doi:10.1027/2151-2604/a000187

Mayer, J. D., Caruso, D. R., & Salovey, P. (2000). Emotional intelligence meets traditional standards for an intelligence. *Intelligence*, *27*(4), 267–298. doi:10.1016/S0160-2896(99)00016-1

Mayer, J. D., & Salovey, P. (1997). What is emotional intelligence? In P. Salovey & D. Sluyter (Eds.), *Emotional development and emotional intelligence: Implications for educators* (pp. 3–31). New York: Basic Books.

Mazzetti, G., Schaufeli, W. B., & Guglielmi, D. (2014). Are workaholics born or made? Relations of workaholism with person characteristics and overwork climate. *Journal of Counseling Psychology*, *62*(4), 703–717.

McBride, N. (2015). *The application of an extended hierarchy theory in understanding complex organizational situations: The case of FIReControl*. Retrieved from http://onlinelibrary.wiley.com/doi/10.1002/sres.2350/epdf

McCord, L. B., & Richardson, J. (2001). *Are workplace bullies sabotaging your ability to compete? Learn to identify and extinguish problem behavior*. Retrieved on November 1, 2015, available at http://gbr.pepperdine.edu

McGonagle, A. K., Beatty, J. E., & Joffe, R. (2014). Coaching for workers with chronic illness: Evaluating an intervention. *Journal of Occupational Health Psychology*, *19*(3), 385–398. doi:10.1037/a0036601 PMID:24796227

McKelvey, B. (1975). Guidelines for the empirical classification of organizations. *Administrative Science Quarterly, 20*(4), 509–525. doi:10.2307/2392019

McNally, R. J. (2003). Progress and controversy in the study of posttraumatic stress disorder. *Annual Review of Psychology, 54*(1), 229–252. doi:10.1146/annurev.psych.54.101601.145112 PMID:12172002

McPherson, S. (2011, September 22). MAP: Which Countries Enlist Gay Soldiers? *Advocate*. Retrieved from http://www.advocate.com/news/2011/09/22/map-which-countries-enlist-gay-soldiers

McSweeney, B. (2002). The essentials of scholarship: A reply to Geert Hofstede. *Human Relations, 55*(11), 1363–1372. doi:10.1177/0018726702551100 5

McWhinney, W., & Batista, J. (1988). How remythologizing can revitalize organizations. *Organizational Dynamics, 17*(2), 46–58. doi:10.1016/0090-2616(88)90018-6

Mead, M. (2001). *Male and Female*. New York: Harper Perennial.

Meek, V. L. (1988). Organizational culture: Origins and weaknesses. *Organization Studies, 9*(4), 453–473. doi:10.1177/017084068800900401

Meier, L. L., Semmer, N. K., Elfering, A., & Jacobshagen, N. (2008). The double meaning of control: Three-way interactions between internal resources, job control, and stressors at work. *Journal of Occupational Health Psychology, 13*(3), 244–258. doi:10.1037/1076-8998.13.3.244 PMID:18572995

Meier, L., & Spector, P. (2013). Reciprocal effects of work stressors and counterproductive work behavior: A five-wave longitudinal study. *The Journal of Applied Psychology, 98*(3), 529–539. doi:10.1037/a0031732 PMID:23379915

Mejia, X. E. (2005). Gender Matters: Working With Adult Male Survivors of Trauma. *Journal of Counseling and Development, 83*(1), 29–40. doi:10.1002/j.1556-6678.2005.tb00577.x

Mello, L., Avelar, R. B., & Majora, D. (2012). Por onde andam as políticas públicas para a população LGBT no Brasil. *Sociedade e Estado, 27*(2), 289–312. doi:10.1590/S0102-69922012000200005

Mendonça, D., & Wallace, W. A. (2015). Factors underlying organizational resilience: The case of electric power restoration in New York City after 11 September 2001. *Reliability Engineering & System Safety, 141*, 83–91. doi:10.1016/j.ress.2015.03.017

Messenger, A. (2003). *Breakthrough research by DBM finds Investment in outplacement services positively impacts the bottom line*. Thomson DBM. Retrieved January 5, 2016, from http://www.amgr.com/pdf/02-06-03OPCReturnOnInvestment.pdf

Meyer, I. H., Schwartz, S., & Frost, D. M. (2008). Social patterning of stress and coping: Does disadvantaged social status confer more stress and fewer coping resources? *Social Science & Medicine, 67*(3), 368–379. PubMeddoi:10.1016/j.socscimed.2008.03.012

Micale, M. S., & Lerner, P. (Eds.). (2001). Traumatic Pasts. History, Psychiatry, and Trauma in the Modern Age, 1870-1930. New York: Cambridge University Press.

Micale, M. S. (1985). The Salpêtrière in the Age of Charcot: An Institutional Perspective on Medical History in the Late Nineteenth Century. *Journal of Contemporary History, 20*(October), 703–731. doi:10.1177/002200948502000411 PMID:11617298

Micale, M. S. (1996). Paradigm and Ideology in Psychiatric History Writing: The Case of Psychoanalysis. *The Journal of Nervous and Mental Disease, 184*(3), 146–152. doi:10.1097/00005053-199603000-00002 PMID:8600217

Mikkelsen, E. G., & Einarsen, S. (2002). Basic assumptions and symptoms of post-traumatic stress among of bullying at work. *European Journal of Work and Organizational Psychology*, *11*(1), 87–111. doi:10.1080/13594320143000861

Miller, E. (2011). Finding meaning at Ground Zero for future generations: Some reflections a decade after 9/11. *International Social Science Review, 86*(3-4), 113-133. Retrieved from http://search.proquest.com.zdroje.vse.cz/docview/921995269?pq-origsite=summon

Miller, D. (1996). Equality management-towards a materialist approach. *Gender, Work and Organization*, *3*(4), 202–214. doi:10.1111/j.1468-0432.1996.tb00060.x

Miller, D., & Freisen, P. H. (1980). Momentum and revolution in organizational adaptation. *Academy of Management Journal*, *23*(4), 591–614. doi:10.2307/255551

Mindomo. (2016). *What is Mind Mapping.* Available at: https://www.mindomo.com/help/mind-mapping.htm

Ministry Of National Defense. (2016, March 23). *Military Service Types.* Retrieved September 07, 2016, from http://www.msb.gov.tr/en-US/Askeralma/Content/military-service-types

Mitchell, J. T., & Everly, G. S. (1996). *Critical incident stress debriefing: An operations Manual* (2nd ed.). Ellicott City, MD: Chevron.

Mitchell, J. T., & Everly, G. S. Jr. (1995). Critical incident stress debriefing (CISD) and the prevention of work-related traumatic stress among high risk occupational groups. In G. S. Everly Jr & J. M. Lating (Eds.), *Psychotraumatology* (pp. 267–280). New York: Plenum Press. doi:10.1007/978-1-4899-1034-9_16

Mitchell, M. S., & Ambrose, M. L. (2007). Abusive supervision and workplace deviance and the moderating effects of negative reciprocity beliefs. *The Journal of Applied Psychology*, *92*(4), 1159–1168. doi:10.1037/0021-9010.92.4.1159 PMID:17638473

Moate, R. M., Gnilka, P. B., West, E. M., & Bruns, K. L. (2016). Stress and burnout among counselor educators: Differences between adaptive perfectionists, maladaptive perfectionists, and nonperfectionists. *Journal of Counseling and Development*, *94*(2), 161–171. doi:10.1002/jcad.12073

Mock, S. E., Sedlovskaya, A., & Purdie-Vaughns, V. (2009). Gay and bisexual mens disclosure of sexual orientation in the workplace: Associations with retirement planning. *Journal of Applied Gerontology*, *30*(1), 123–132. doi:10.1177/0733464809358081

Moody, C., Fuks, N., Peláez, S., & Smith, N. G. (2015). Without this, I would for sure be already dead: A qualitative inquiry regarding suicide protective factors among trans adults. *Psychology of Sexual Orientation and Gender Diversity*, *2*(3), 266–280. doi:10.1037/sgd0000130

Moore, J. (2016, April 26). Cowardly NFL still shows anti-gay bias, two years after Michael Sam's draft. *The Guardian.* Retrieved from https://www.theguardian.com/sport/2016/apr/26/nfl-draft-gay-players-michael-sam

Moore, S., Grunberg, L., & Greenberg, E. (2004). Repeated Downsizing Contact: The Effects of Similar and Dissimilar Layoff Experiences on Work and Well-Being Outcomes. *Journal of Occupational Health Psychology*, *9*(3), 247–257. doi:10.1037/1076-8998.9.3.247 PMID:15279519

Moreno-Jiménez, B., Bustos, R., Matallana, A., & Miralles, T. (1997). La Evaluación del burnout: Problemas y Alternativas. El CBB como evaluación de los elementos del proceso[A burnout evaluation: Problems and alternatives. The CBB as an evaluation tool of process elements]. *Revista de Psicología del Trabajo y de las Organizaciones*, *13*(2), 185–207.

Morgan, G. (2011). Reflections on Images of Organization and its implications for organization and environment. *Organization & Environment*, *24*(4), 459–478. doi:10.1177/1086026611434274

Moules, N. J., Simonson, K., Prins, M., Angus, P., & Bell, J. M. (2004). Making room for grief: Walking backwards and living forward. *Nursing Inquiry, 11*(2), 99–107. doi:10.1111/j.1440-1800.2004.00204.x PMID:15154889

Muchiri, P., Pintelon, L., Gelders, L., & Martin, H. (2011). Development of maintenance function performance measurement framework and indicators. *International Journal of Production Economics, 131*(1), 295–302. doi:10.1016/j.ijpe.2010.04.039

Müeller, A., Heiden, B., Herbig, B., Poppe, F., & Angerer, P. (2016). Improving Well-being at Work: A Randomized Controlled Intervention Based on Selection, Optimization, and Compensation. *Journal of Occupational Health Psychology, 21*(2), 169–181. doi:10.1037/a0039676 PMID:26322438

Murphy, S. V. (2013). *Perceptions of bullying in the workplace: A phenomenological study*. Retrieved on November 2, 2015, available at http://media.proquest.com/media/pq/classic/doc/3007474051/fmt/ai/rep/NPDF?_s=5Juw3FglFYcVuIWLovMGiXshEGg%3D

Murphy, C. (1972). Ideological interpretations of human rights. *De Paul Law Review, 2*, 286–306.

Muscalu, E., & Muntean, S. (2013). Motivation - A stimulating factor for increasing human resource management performance. *Review of International Comparative Management, 14*(2), 303-309.

Mutch, C. (2015). Leadership in times of crisis: Dispositional, relational and contextual factors influencing school principals actions. *International Journal of Disaster Risk Reduction, 14*, 186–194. doi:10.1016/j.ijdrr.2015.06.005

Myer, R. A., & Moore, H. B. (2006). Crisis in context theory: An ecological model. *Journal of Counseling and Development, 84*(2), 139–147. doi:10.1002/j.1556-6678.2006.tb00389.x

Myers, D. (1992). *The pursuit of happiness*. New York: Morrow.

Nadler, D. A., & Tushman, M. L. (1989). Organizational frame bending: Principles for managing reorientation. *Academy of Management Executive, 3*(3), 194-204. doi:10.5465/AME.1989.4274738

Nadler, D. A., & Tushman, M. L. (1980). A model for diagnosing organizational behavior. *Organizational Dynamics, 9*(2), 35–51. doi:10.1016/0090-2616(80)90039-X

Namie, G. (2003, November/December). Workplace bullying: Escalated incivility. *Ivey Business Journal: Improving the Practice of Management,* 1-6.

Namie, G., & Namie, R. (2000). *The bully at work: What you can do to stop the hurt and reclaim your dignity on the job*. Naperville, IL: Sourcebooks, Inc.

Nandkeolyar, A. K., Shaffer, J. A., Li, A., Ekkirala, S., & Bagger, J. (2014). Surviving an abusive supervisor: The joint roles of conscientiousness and coping strategies. *The Journal of Applied Psychology, 99*(1), 138–150. doi:10.1037/a0034262 PMID:23978107

National Institute for Occupational Safety and Health (NIOSH) – Center for Disease Control and Prevention. (1999). *Stress At Work* (Publication No. 99-101). Retrieved from http://www.cdc.gov/niosh/topics/stress/

Nes, R. B., Roysamb, E., Tambs, K., Harris, J. R., & Reichborn-Kjennerud, T. (2006). Subjective well-being: Genetic and environmental contributions to stability and change. *Psychological Medicine, 36*(07), 1033–1042. doi:10.1017/S0033291706007409 PMID:16749947

Neugarten, B. L., Havighurst, R., & Tobin, S. (1961). The measurement of life satisfaction. *Journal of Gerontology, 16*(2), 134–143. doi:10.1093/geronj/16.2.134 PMID:13728508

Neuman, J. (2000). Measuring the costs associated with stress, injustice and workplace bullying. *Proceedings of the Workplace Bullying Conference.*

Neuman, J., & Baron, R. (2004). Aggression in the workplace: A social-psychological perspective. In S. Fox & P. E. Spector (Eds.), *Counterproductive work behaviour: Investigations of actors and targets* (pp. 13–40). Washington, DC: American Psychological Association.

Neves, P. (2014). Taking it out on survivors: Submissive employees, downsizing, and abusive supervision. *Journal of Occupational and Organizational Psychology, 87*(3), 507–534. doi:10.1111/joop.12061

News, B. B. C. (2008). *MoD must pay gay soldier £190,000.* Retrieved from http://news.bbc.co.uk/2/hi/uk_news/england/west_yorkshire/7751036.stm

Niederhoffer, K. G., & Pennebaker, J.W. (2009). *Sharing one's story: On the benefits of writing or talking about emotional experience.* Academic Press.

Nielsen, K., Yarker, J., Randall, R., & Munir, F. (2009). The mediating effects of team and self-efficacy on the relationship between transformational leadership and job satisfaction and psychological well-being in healthcare professionals. *International Journal of Nursing Studies, 46*(9), 1236–1244. doi:10.1016/j.ijnurstu.2009.03.001 PMID:19345946

Nixon, A. E., Mazzola, J. J., Bauer, J., Krueger, J. R., & Spector, P. E. (2011). Can work make you sick? A meta-analysis of the relationships between job stressors and physical symptoms. *Work & Stress: An International Journal of Work. Health & Organisations, 25*(1), 1–22.

Nizielski, S., Hallum, S., Schütz, A., & Lopes, P. N. (2013). A note on emotion appraisal and burnout: The mediating role of antecedent-focused coping strategies. *Journal of Occupational Health Psychology, 18*(3), 363–369. doi:10.1037/a0033043 PMID:23834450

Noer, D. (1993). Four new realities. *Executive Excellence, 10*(11), 16–17.

Noer, D. M. (1993). *Healing the wounds.* San Francisco, CA: Jossey-Bass Inc.

Noer, D. M. (2010a). *Healing the wounds: overcoming the trauma of layoffs and revitalizing downsized organizations, revised & updated.* San Francisco: Jossey-Bass.

Noer, D. M. (2010b). Six crucial leadership competencies for an era of downsizing. *Leader to Leader, 2010*(56), 8–11. doi:10.1002/ltl.407

Norburn, D., & Hall, P. D. (1987). The Management Factor in Acquisition Performance. *Leadership and Organization Development Journal, 8*(3), 23–30. doi:10.1108/eb053618

Noronha, E., & DCruz, P. (2005). Achieving downsizing. Managerial perspectives. *Global Business Review, 6*(1), 77–94. doi:10.1177/097215090500600106

Norris, F. H., Friedman, M. J., Watson, P., Byrne, C. M., Diaz, E., & Kaniasty, K. (2002). 60,000 disaster victims speak: Part I. An empirical review of the empirical literature, 1981–2001. *Psychiatry: Interpers. Biol. Process., 65*(3), 207–239. doi:10.1521/psyc.65.3.207.20173 PMID:12405079

Northouse, P. G. (2007). *Leadership: Theories and practices.* Academic Press.

Novak, R. J., & Davidson, S. (2013). Journalists reporting on hazardous events: Constructing protective factors within the professional role. *Traumatology, 19*(4), 313–322. doi:10.1177/1534765613481854

Noyes, R., Fenwick, P., Holden, J. M., & Christian, S. R. (2009). Aftereffects of pleasurable Western adult near-death experiences. In J. M. Holden, B. Greyson, & D. James (Eds.), *The handbook of near-death experiences: Thirty years of investigation* (pp. 41–62). Santa Barbara, CA: Praeger/ABC-CLIO.

Nuttman-Shwartz, O. (2015). Shared resilience in a traumatic reality: A new concept for trauma workers exposed personally and professionally to collective disaster. *Trauma, Violence & Abuse*, *16*(4), 466–475. doi:10.1177/1524838014557287 PMID:25427830

OBoyle, E. H. Jr, Forsyth, D. R., Banks, G. C., & McDaniel, M. A. (2012). A meta-analysis of the Dark Triad and work behavior: A social exchange perspective. *The Journal of Applied Psychology*, *97*(3), 557–579. doi:10.1037/a0025679 PMID:22023075

OConnor, R. C., & OConnor, D. B. (2003). Predicting Hopeless and Psychological Distress: The Role of Perfectionism and Coping. *Journal of Counseling Psychology*, *50*(3), 362–372. doi:10.1037/0022-0167.50.3.362

Olde, E., van der Hart, O., Kleber, R., & van Son, M. (2006). Posttraumatic stress following childbirth: A review. *Clinical Psychology Review*, *26*(1), 1–16. doi:10.1016/j.cpr.2005.07.002 PMID:16176853

O'Leary-Kelly, A. M., Griffin, R. W., & Glew, D. J. (1996). Organization-motivated aggression: A research framework. *Academy of Management Review*, *21*(1), 225–253. doi:10.5465/AMR.1996.9602161571

Olson, D. H. (2000). Circumplex model of marital and family systems. *Journal of Marital and Family Therapy*, *22*(2), 144–167. doi:10.1111/1467-6427.00144

Orr & Hauser. (2008). *A Re-inquiry of Hofstede's Cultural Dimensions: a Call for 21st Century Cross-cultural research.* The Marketing Management Journal.

Orr, L. M., & Hauser, W. J. (2008). *A re-inquiry of Hofstede's cultural dimensions: A call for 21st century cross-cultural research.* Marketing Management Journal.

Orr, L. M., & Hauser, W. J. (2008). *A re-inquiry of Hofstede's Cultural Dimensions: A Call for 21st Century Cross-Cultural Research.* Marketing Management Journal.

Orth, U., & Wieland, E. (2006). Anger, hostility, and posttraumatic stress disorder in trauma-exposed adults: A meta-analysis. *Journal of Consulting and Clinical Psychology*, *74*(4), 698–706. doi:10.1037/0022-006X.74.4.698 PMID:16881777

Otto, R. (1958). *The Idea of the Holy* (1st ed.). Oxford, UK: Oxford University Press.

Ouchi, W. G. (1980). Markets, bureaucracies, and clans. *Administrative Science Quarterly*, *25*(1), 129–141. doi:10.2307/2392231

Ouchi, W. G. (1982). *Theory z.* Avon.

Owens, J., Cook, E. W., & Stevenson, I. (1990). Features of near-death experience in relation to whether or not patients were near death. *Lancet*, *336*(8724), 1175–1177. doi:10.1016/0140-6736(90)92780-L PMID:1978037

Owens, T., Robinson, D., & Smith-Lovin, L. (2010). Three faces of identity. *Annual Review of Sociology*, *36*(23), 1–23.

Pacanowsky, M. E., & ODonnell-Trujillo, N. (1983). Organizational communication as cultural performance. *Communication Monographs*, *50*(2), 126–147. doi:10.1080/03637758309390158

Pack, M. (2014). Vicarious resilience: A multilayered model of stress and trauma. *Affilia: Journal of Women & Social Work*, *29*(1), 18–29. doi:10.1177/0886109913510088

Paddison, L. (2015, December 30). From VW to Brazil's mining disaster: 5 corporate scandals that defined 2015. *The Guardian*. Retrieved August 16, 2016, from http://www.theguardian.com/sustainable-business/2015/dec/30/vw-exxon-lobbying-brazil-mining-tragedy-toshiba-corporate-scandals-greenwashing-climate-change

Palm Center. (2009). *Countries that Allow Military Service by Openly Gay People*. University of California Santa Barbara. Retrieved from http://archive.palmcenter.org/files/active/0/CountriesWithoutBan.pdf

Palmieri, P. A., & Fitzgerals, L. F. (2005). Confirmatory factor analysis of posttraumatic stress symptoms in sexually harassed women. *Journal of Traumatic Stress*, *18*(6), 657–666. doi:10.1002/jts.20074 PMID:16382424

Papazoglou, K. (2013). Conceptualizing police complex spiral trauma and its applications in the police field. *Traumatology*, *19*(3), 196–209. doi:10.1177/1534765612466151

Park, H. (2011). Man-made disasters: A cross-national analysis. *International Business Review*, *20*(4), 466–476. doi:10.1016/j.ibusrev.2010.08.004

Park, H. I., Beehr, T. A., Han, K., & Grebner, S. I. (2012). Demands-abilities fit and psychological strain: Moderating effects of personality. *International Journal of Stress Management*, *19*(1), 1–33. doi:10.1037/a0026852

Paterno, D. (2012). *Posttraumatisches Wachstum und Sinnerleben – Sinnressourcen für die Traumatherapie* (Master's Thesis). University Innsbruck, Faculty of Psychology and Sport Science. Retrieved July 9, 2016 from http://www.sinnforschung.org/wp-content/uploads/ 2012/04/ Diplomarbeit_Home pageversion.pdf

Paterson, J. M., & Cary, J. (2002). Organizational justice, change anxiety, and acceptance of downsizing: Preliminary tests of an AET-based model. *Motivation and Emotion*, *26*(1), 83–103. doi:10.1023/A:1015146225215

Patnaik, J. B. (2011). Role of work culture in improving organizational health. *Amity Journal of Applied Psychology*, *2*(1), 40–48.

Paton, D. (2005). Posttraumatic growth in protective services professionals: Individual, cognitive and organizational influences. *Traumatology*, *11*(4), 335–346. doi:10.1177/153476560501100411

Paul, R., & Thompson, C. (2006). Employee assistance program responses to large scale traumatic events. *Journal of Workplace Behavioral Health*, *21*(3-4), 1–19. doi:10.1300/J490v21n03_01

PBS. (2016, August 10). *Timeline: Milestones in the American Gay Rights Movement*. Retrieved from http://www.pbs.org/wgbh/americanexperience/features/timeline/stonewall/

Pearlman, L. A. (1999). Self-care for trauma therapists: Ameliorating vicarious traumatization. In B. H. Stamm (Eds.), Secondary traumatic stress: Self-care issues for clinicians, researchers, and Educators (pp. 51-64). Baltimore, MD: Sidran Press.

Pearlman, L. A., & Mac Ian, P. S. (1995). Vicarious traumatization: An empirical study of the effects of trauma work on trauma therapists. *Professional Psychology, Research and Practice*, *26*(6), 558–565. doi:10.1037/0735-7028.26.6.558

Pearlman, L. A., & Saakvitne, K. W. (1995). *Trauma and the therapist: Countertransference and vicarious traumatization in psychotherapy with incest survivors*. New York, NY: W.W. Norton and Company.

Pearson, C. M., Andersson, L. A., & Porath, C. L. (2005). Workplace Incivility. In S. Fox & P. E. Spector (Eds.), *Counterproductive workplace behavior: Investigations of actors and targets* (pp. 256–309). Washington, DC: American Psychological Association. doi:10.1037/10893-008

Pearson, C. M., Andersson, L. M., & Porath, C. L. (2000). Assessing and attacking workplace incivility. *Organizational Dynamics*, *29*(2), 123–137. doi:10.1016/S0090-2616(00)00019-X

Pearson, C. M., Andersson, L. M., & Wegner, J. W. (2001). When workers flout convention: A study of workplace incivility. *Human Relations*, *54*(11), 1387–1419. doi:10.1177/00187267015411001

Pearson, C. M., & Clair, J. A. (1998). Reframing crisis management. *Academy of Management Review*, *23*, 59–76.

Pekkarinen, L., Elovainio, M., Sinervo, T., Heponiemi, T., Aalto, A. M., Noro, A., & Finne-Soveri, H. (2013). Job demands and musculoskeletal symptoms among female geriatric nurses: The moderating role of psychosocial resources. *Journal of Occupational Health Psychology*, *18*(2), 211–219. doi:10.1037/a0031801 PMID:23458058

Pereira, A. (2015, December 4). Chennai floods: Decoding the city's worst rains in 100 years. *The Indian Express*. Retrieved August 16, 2016, from http://indianexpress.com/article/india/india-news-india/chennai-floods-rains-jayalalithaa-imd-reasons-rescue-news-updates/

Pereira-Lima, K., & Loureiro, S. R. (2015). Burnout, anxiety, depression, and social skills in medical residents. *Psychology Health and Medicine*, *20*(3), 353–362. doi:10.1080/13548506.2014.936889 PMID:25030412

Peterson, C., & Seligman, M. E. P. (2004). *Character strengths and virtues: A handbook and classification*. Oxford, UK: Oxford University Press.

Peterson, C., & Seligman, M. E. P. (2004). *Character strengths and virtues: A handbook and classification*. American Psychological Association.

Pettersson, E., & Burnson, R. (2015, August 28). Nestle accused of putting fish from slave labor in cat food. *Bloomberg*. Retrieved August 16, 2016, from http://www.bloomberg.com/news/articles/2015-08-27/nestle-accused-of-putting-fish-from-slave-labor-in-cat-food

Pettigrew, A. M. (1990). Longitudinal field research on change: Theory and practice. *Organization Science*, *1*(3), 267–292. doi:10.1287/orsc.1.3.267

Piccolo, R. F., & Colquitt, J. A. (2004). Transformational leadership and job behaviors: The mediating role of core job characteristics. *Academy of Management Journal*, *49*(2), 327–340. doi:10.5465/AMJ.2006.20786079

Pichler, S., Vama, A., & Bruce, T. (2010). Heterosexism in employment decisions: The role of job misfit. *The Journal of Applied Psychology*, *40*(10), 2527–2555.

Piderit, S. K. (2000). Rethinking resistance and recognizing ambivalence: A multidimensional view of attitudes toward an organizational change. *Academy of Management Review*, *25*(4), 783–794.

Pietschmann, H. (2001). *Merits and Limits of Applying the Scientific Method to Human Society*. Luton, UK: The Pantaneto Forum. Retrieved from http:// www.pantaneto.co.uk/issue2/pietschmann.htm

Pinder, C. C., & Moore, L. F. (1979). The resurrection of taxonomy to aid the development of middle range theories of organizational behavior. *Administrative Science Quarterly*, *24*(1), 99–118. doi:10.2307/2989878

Pinel, P. (1798). *Nosographie philosophique, ou la method de l'analyse appliquée à la Médecine*. Paris: Richard, Caille, & Ravier.

Pizarro, D. A., & Salovey, P. (2002). On being and becoming a good person: The role of emotional intelligence in moral development and behavior. In J. Aronson (Ed.), *Improving academic achievement: Impact of psychological factors on education* (pp. 247–266). San Diego, CA: Academic Press. doi:10.1016/B978-012064455-1/50015-4

Pizer, J. C., Sears, B., Mallory, C., & Hunter, N. D. (2012). Evidence of Persistent and Pervasive Workplace Discrimination Against LGBT People: The Need for Federal Legislation Prohibiting Discrimination and Providing for Equal Employment Benefits. *Loyola of Los Angeles Law Review*, *45*, 715–780.

Plant, K. L., & Stanton, N. A. (2012). Why did the pilots shut down the wrong engine? Explaining errors in context using Schema Theory and the Perceptual Cycle Model. *Safety Science*, *50*(2), 300–315. doi:10.1016/j.ssci.2011.09.005

Plater, Z. (2010). Learning from disasters: Twenty-one years after the Exxon Valdez oil spill, will reactions to the Deepwater Horizon blowout finally address the systematic flaws revealed in Alaska? *Environmental Law Reporter*, *40*, 391–408.

Platow. (1999). *Platow: The symposium* (C. Gill, Trans.). New York: Penguin Classics.

Pompili, M., Lester, D., Innamorati, M., De Pisa, E., Iliceto, P., Puccinno, M., & Girardi, P. et al. (2008). Suicide risk and exposure to mobbing. *Work (Reading, Mass.)*, *31*(2), 237–243. PMID:18957741

Poteat, V. P., Calzo, J. P., & Yoshikawa, H. (2016). Promoting Youth Agency Through Dimensions of Gay-Straight Alliance Involvement and Conditions that Maximize Associations. *Journal of Youth and Adolescence: a Multidisciplinary Research Publication*, *45*(7), 1438–1451. PubMeddoi:10.1007/s10964-016-0421-6

Powell, G. N., Francesco, A. M., & Ling, Y. (2009). Toward culture-sensitive theories of the work-family interface. *Journal of Organizational Behavior*, *30*(5), 597–616. doi:10.1002/job.568

Powell, M., Cassematis, P., Benson, M., Smallbone, S., & Wortley, R. (2014). Police officers strategies for coping with the stress of investigating Internet child exploitation. *Traumatology: An International Journal*, *20*(1), 32–42. doi:10.1037/h0099378

Powley, E. H., & Piderit, S. K. (2008). Tending wounds elements of the organizational healing process. *The Journal of Applied Behavioral Science*, *44*(1), 134–149. doi:10.1177/0021886308314842

Precin, P. (2010). *Return to work after 9/11* (pp. 3–11). DOI.

Price Waterhouse Cooper. (2016). *LGBTI perspectives on workplace inclusion.* Retrieved from http://www.pwc.com.au/publications/pdf/workplace-inclusion-survey-jun16.pdf

Pross, C., & Schweitzer, S. (2010). The culture of organizations dealing with trauma: Sources of work-related stress and conflict. *Traumatology*, *16*(4), 97–108. doi:10.1177/1534765610388301

Prunas, A., Bandini, E., Fisher, A. D., Maggi, M., Pace, V., Quagliarella, L., & Bibi, M. et al. (2016). Experiences of Discrimination, Harassment, and Violence in a Sample of Italian Transsexuals Who Have Undergone Sex-Reassignment Surgery. *Journal of Interpersonal Violence*. doi:10.1177/0886260515624233

Pugh, D. S., Hickson, D. J., & Hinings, C. R. (1969). An empirical taxonomy of work organizations. *Administrative Science Ouarterly*, *14*(1), 115–126. doi:10.2307/2391367

Questia. (2016, August 10). *Gays in the military*. Retrieved from https://www.questia.com/library/controversial-topics/gays-in-the-military

Qvist, B. (2014, July 28). Challenges for LGBT people in the workplace and how to overcome them. *The Guardian*. Retrieved from https://www.theguardian.com/sustainable-business/lgbt-employees-discrimination-in-the-workplace-talkpoint

Rafaeli, A., & Vilnai-Yavetz, I. (2004). Emotion as a connection of physical artifacts and organizations. *Organization Science*, *15*(6), 671–686. doi:10.1287/orsc.1040.0083

Rafferty, A. E., & Griffin, M. A. (2006). Perceptions of organizational change: A stress and coping perspective. *The Journal of Applied Psychology*, *91*(5), 1154–1162. doi:10.1037/0021-9010.91.5.1154 PMID:16953776

Ragins, B. R., Singh, R., & Cornwell, J. M. (2007). Making the invisible visible: Fear and disclosure of sexual orientation at work. *The Journal of Applied Psychology*, *92*(4), 1103–1118. PubMeddoi:10.1037/0021-9010.92.4.1103

Raju, E., & Becker, P. (2013). Multi-organisational coordination for disaster recovery: The story of post-tsunami Tamil Nadu, India. *International Journal of Disaster Risk Reduction*, *4*, 82–91. doi:10.1016/j.ijdrr.2013.02.004

Ramachandran, V. S., & Oberman, L. M. (2006). Broken Mirrors: A Theory of Autism. *Scientific American*, *295*(5), 62–69. doi:10.1038/scientificamerican1106-62 PMID:17076085

Rambo, S. (2010). *Spirit and Trauma: A Theology of Remaining* (1st ed.). Louisville, KY: Westminster John Knox Press.

Ramírez-Velázquez, J. (2006). *El Estudio de las Emociones en el Ámbito Laboral* [A study of emotions in the workplace]. Presentation at V Congreso National AMET: Trabajo y Reestructuración: Los Retos del Nuevo Siglo.

Ramsey, R. D. (2004). Humanizing a downsized workplace. *Super Vision*, *65*(7), 3–5.

Rayner, C. H., Hoel, H., & Cooper, C. (2002). *Workplace bullying* (1st ed.). London: Cromwell Press. doi:10.4324/9780203302194

Reason, J. (2000). Human error: Models and management. *British Medical Journal*, *320*(7237), 768–771. doi:10.1136/bmj.320.7237.768 PMID:10720363

Reason, J. (2002). *Managing the risks of organizational accidents*. Burlington: Ashgate.

Redding, G., & Witt, M. A. (2009). Culture, meaning, and institutions: Rationale in Germany and Japan. *Journal of International Business Studies*, 859–885.

Reed, J. (2016, April 11). Entering the workplace drove me back in the closet – until I switched employer. *Gay Star Business*. Retrieved from http://www.gaystarnews.com/article/james-reed-workplace-closet/#gs.PbB63AY

Regehr, C., Hill, J., & Glancy, G. D. (2000). Individual predictors of traumatic reactions in firefighters. *The Journal of Nervous and Mental Disease*, *188*(6), 333–339. doi:10.1097/00005053-200006000-00003 PMID:10890341

Regehr, C., Hill, J., Goldberg, G., & Hughes, J. (2003). Postmortem inquiries and trauma responses in paramedics and firefighters. *Journal of Interpersonal Violence*, *18*(6), 607–622. doi:10.1177/0886260503251131

Reichers, A. E., Wanous, J. P., & Austin, J. T. (1997). Understanding and managing cynicism about organizational change. *The Academy of Management Executive*, *11*(1), 48–59. doi:10.5465/AME.1997.9707100659

Resch, M., & Schubinski, M. (1996). Mobbing-prevention and management in organizations. *European Journal of Work and Organizational Psychology*, *5*(2), 295–307. doi:10.1080/13594329608414860

Restubog, S. L. D., Scott, K. L., & Zagenczyk, T. J. (2011). When distress hits home: The role of contextual factors and psychological distress in predicting employees responses to abusive supervision. *The Journal of Applied Psychology*, *96*(4), 713–729. doi:10.1037/a0021593 PMID:21280933

Ribeiro, V. F., Filho, C. F., Valenti, V. E., Ferreira, M., de Abreu, L. C., de Carvalho, T. D., & Ferreira, C. et al. (2014). Prevalence of burnout syndrome in clinical nurses at a hospital of excellence. *International Archives of Medicine*, *7*(22), 1–14. PMID:24860618

Říčan, P. (2007). *Psychologie náboženství a spirituality* (1st ed.). Psychology of religion and spiritualityPraha, Czech Republic: Portál.

Rice, D., & Dreilinger, C. (1991). After the downsizing. *Training & Development*, *45*(5), 41–44.

Rice, K. G., & Van Arsdale, A. C. (2010). Perfectionism, perceived stress, drinking to cope, and alcohol-related problems among college students. *Journal of Counseling Psychology*, *57*(4), 439–450. doi:10.1037/a0020221

Rich, B. L., Lepine, J. A., & Crawford, E. R. (2010). Job engagement: Antecedents and effects on job performance. *Academy of Management Journal*, *53*(3), 617–635. doi:10.5465/AMJ.2010.51468988

Richwine, L., & Grover, R. (2014, February 10). Analysis: Sponsorship dollars may follow gay NFL hopeful Sam. *Reuters*. Retrieved from http://www.reuters.com/article/us-usa-football-gay-marketing-analysis-idUSBREA1A01J20140211

Rimé, B. (2005). *Le partage social des émotions*. Paris: Presses universitaires de France.

Riolli, L., & Savicki, V. (2003). Optimism and Coping as Moderators of the Relation Between Work Resources and Burnout in Information Service Workers. *International Journal of Stress Management*, *10*(3), 235–252. doi:10.1037/1072-5245.10.3.235

Riolli, L., & Savicki, V. (2010). Coping effectiveness and coping diversity under traumatic stress. *International Journal of Stress Management*, *17*(2), 97–113. doi:10.1037/a0018041

Riordan, C. M., & Griffeth, R. W. (1995). The opportunity for friendship in the workplace: An underexplored construct. *Journal of Business and Psychology*, *10*(2), 141–154. doi:10.1007/BF02249575

Robinson, M. D., Moeller, S. K., Buchholz, M. M., Boyd, R. L., & Troop-Gordon, W. (2012). The regulatory benefits of high levels of affect perception accuracy: A process analysis of reactions to stressors in daily life. *Emotion (Washington, D.C.)*, *12*(4), 785–795. doi:10.1037/a0029044 PMID:22775136

Rodwell, J. J., & Fernando, J. W. (2015). Improving employee outcomes among an often-neglected occupational group in healthcare: Stimulating work and job control keep hospital administrators happy. *International Journal of Stress Management*, *22*(4), 395–419. doi:10.1037/a0039358

Rogers, D. C. F. (2002). *Pastoral Care for Post-Traumatic Stress Disorder: Healing the Shattered Soul* (3rd ed.). Philadelphia: Haworth Press.

Rohner, R. P. (1984). Toward a conception of culture for crosscultural psychology. *Journal of Cross-Cultural Psychology*, *15*(2), 111–138. doi:10.1177/0022002184015002002

Rojas, M. (2007). Heterogeneity in the relationship between income and happiness: A conceptual-referent-theory explanation. *Journal of Economic Psychology*, *28*(1), 1–14. doi:10.1016/j.joep.2005.10.002

Rose, A., & Krausmann, E. (2013). An economic framework for the development of a resilience index for business recovery. *International Journal of Disaster Risk Reduction*, *5*, 73–83. doi:10.1016/j.ijdrr.2013.08.003

Rose, M. (2003). Good Deal, Bad Deal? Job Satisfaction in Occupations. *Work, Employment and Society*, *17*(3), 503–530. doi:10.1177/09500170030173006

Rothmann, S. (2008). Job satisfaction, occupational stress, burnout and work engagement as components of work-related well-being. *SA Journal of Industrial Psychology*, *34*(3), 11–16. doi:10.4102/sajip.v34i3.424

Roussy, G., & Lhermitte, J. (1919). *Les psychonévroses de guerre*. Paris: Masson.

Ryff, C. D. (1989). Happiness is everything, or is it? Ex- plorations on the meaning of psychological well-being. *Journal of Personality and Social Psychology*, *57*(6), 1069–1081. doi:10.1037/0022-3514.57.6.1069

Ryff, C. D. (2013). Eudaimonic well-being and health: Mapping consequences of self-realization. In A. S. Waterman (Ed.), *The best within us. Positive psychology perspectives on eudaimonia* (pp. 77–98). Washington, DC: American Psychological Association. doi:10.1037/14092-005

Ryff, C. D. (2014). Psychological Well-Being Revisited: Advances in the Science and Practice of Eudaimonia. *Psychotherapy and Psychosomatics*, *83*(1), 10–28. doi:10.1159/000353263 PMID:24281296

Ryff, C. D., Keyes, C. L. M., & Shmotkin, D. (2002). Optimizing well-being: The empirical encounter of two traditions. *Journal of Personality and Social Psychology*, *82*(6), 1007–1022. doi:10.1037/0022-3514.82.6.1007 PMID:12051575

Ryff, C., & Keyes, C. (1995). The structure of psychological well-being revisited. *Journal of Personality and Social Psychology*, *69*(4), 719–727. doi:10.1037/0022-3514.69.4.719 PMID:7473027

Rzeszutek, M., Partyka, M., & Gołąb, A. (2015). Temperament traits, social support, and secondary traumatic stress disorder symptoms in a sample of trauma therapists. *Professional Psychology, Research and Practice*, *46*(4), 213–220. doi:10.1037/pro0000024

Saakvitne, K. W., Tennen, H., & Ameck, G. (1998). Exploring thriving in the context of clinical trauma theory: Constructivist self-development theory. *The Journal of Social Issues*, *54*(2), 279–299. doi:10.1111/j.1540-4560.1998.tb01219.x

Sahdev, K. (2004). Revisiting the survivor syndrome: The Role of Leadership in Implementing downsizing. *European Journal of Work and Organizational Psychology*, *13*(2), 165–196. doi:10.1080/13594320444000056

Saint, T. K. (2012). The Long Shadow of Manto's Partition Narratives: "Fictive" Testimony to Historical Trauma. *Social Scientist*, *40*(11/12), 53–62.

Saldaña, J. (2013). *The Coding Manual for Qualitative Researchers*. London: Sage Publications Ltd.

Salmona, M. (2013). *Le livre noir des violences sexuelles*. Dunod.

Salovey, P., Mayer, J. D., & Caruso, D. (2002). The positive psychology of emotional intelli- gence. In C. R. Snyder & S. J. Lopez (Eds.), *Handbook of positive psychology* (pp. 159–171). New York: Oxford University Press.

Samad, A., Reaburn, P., Davis, H., & Ahmed, E. (2015). *An Empirical Study on the Effect of Leadership Styles on Employee well-being and Organizational Outcomes within an Australian Regional University*. Paper presented at the Australasian Conference on Business and Social Sciences, Sydney, Australia.

SAMHSA. (2014a). *Concept of Trauma and Guidance for a Trauma-Informed Approach*. U.S. Department of Health and Human Services. Substance Abuse and Mental Health Services Administration Office of Policy, Planning and Innovation. Retrieved from http://store.samhsa.gov/shin/content//SMA14-4884/SMA14-4884.pdf

SAMHSA. (2014b). *Trauma-Informed Care in Behavioural Health Services*. Treatment Improvement Protocol (TIP) Series, No. 57. Centre for Substance Abuse Treatment (US).Rockville (MD): Substance Abuse and Mental Health Services Administration (US). Retrieved from http://www.ncbi.nlm.nih.gov/books/NBK207192/

Saul, J. (2009). Collective Trauma, Collective Healing: Promoting Community Resilience in the Aftermath of Disaster. New York: Routledge.

Saul, M. H. (2011, September 2). City News: Invite Clergy to 9/11 Event, Giuliani Says. *Wall Street Journal*, p. A17. Retrieved from http://search.proquest.com.zdroje.vse.cz/docview/886974828?pq-origsite=summon

Sauter, S. L., Murphy, L. R., & Hurrell, J. J. (1990). Prevention of work-related psychological disorders: A national strategy proposed by the National Institute for Occupational Safety and Health (NIOSH). *The American Psychologist*, *45*(10), 1146–1158. doi:10.1037/0003-066X.45.10.1146 PMID:2252233

Saxena, A. (2014). Workforce diversity: A key to improve productivity. *Procedia Economics and Finance*, *11*, 76–85. doi:10.1016/S2212-5671(14)00178-6

Schaluf, I. M., Ahmadun, F., & Scariff, A. R. (2003). Technological disaster factors. *Journal of Loss Prevention in the Process Industries*, *16*(6), 513–521. doi:10.1016/j.jlp.2003.08.002

Schat, A. C. H., Frone, M. R., & Kelloway, E. K. (2006). Prevalence of workplace aggression in the U.S. workforce: Findings from a national study. In E. K. Kelloway, J. Barling, & J. Hurrell (Eds.), *Handbook of workplace violence* (pp. 47–89). Thousand Oaks, CA: Sage. doi:10.4135/9781412976947.n4

Schaufeli, W. B., & Bakker, A. B. (2004). Job demands, job resources, and their relationship with burnout and engagement: A multi-sample study. *Journal of Organizational Behavior*, *25*(3), 293–315. doi:10.1002/job.248

Schaufeli, W. B., Bakker, A. B., van der Heijden, F. M. M. A., & Prins, J. T. (2009). Workaholism among medical residents: It is the combination of working excessively and compulsively that counts. *International Journal of Stress Management*, *16*(4), 249–272. doi:10.1037/a0017537

Schaufeli, W. B., & Enzmann, D. (1998). *The Burnout Companion to Study and Practice*. Philadelphia, PA: Taylor & Francis, Inc.

Schaufeli, W. B., & Salanova, M. (2014). Burnout, Boredom and Engagement in the Workplace. In M. C. W. Peeters, J. d. Jonge, & T. W. Taris (Eds.), *An Introduction to Contemporary Work Psychology* (pp. 293–320). John Wiley & Sons, Ltd.

Schein, E. H. (1992). *Organizational culture and leadership* (2nd ed.). San Francisco, CA: John Wiley & Sons.

Schein, E. H. (1993). SMR forum: How can organizations learn faster? The challenge of entering the green room. *Sloan Management Review*, *34*(2), 85–92.

Schein, E. H. (1996). Culture: The missing concept in organization studies. *Administrative Science Quarterly*, *41*(2), 229–240. doi:10.2307/2393715

Schermer, V. L. (2007). Duch a duše [Spirit and Soul]. Praha, Czech Republic: Triton.

Schiro, J.B., & Baker, R.L. (2009). Downsizing and organizational change survivors and victims: mental health issues. *The International Journal of Applied Management and Technology,7*(1), 91-121.

Schleiermacher, F. (2012). On Religion: Speeches to its Cultured Despisers (2nd ed.). Cambridge University Press.

Schmidt, K. H., & Diestel, S. (2012). The relation of self-control demands to job strain: The moderating role of organizational commitment. *Applied Psychology*, *61*(3), 479–497. doi:10.1111/j.1464-0597.2011.00479.x

Schmitt, A., Den Hartog, D. N., & Belschak, F. D. (2015). Is outcome responsibility at work emotionally exhausting? Investigating employee proactivity as a moderator. *Journal of Occupational Health Psychology*, *20*(4), 491–500. doi:10.1037/a0039011 PMID:25798719

Schmitt, A., & Klarner, P. (2015). From snapshot to continuity: A dynamic model of organizational adaptation to environmental changes. *Scandinavian Journal of Management*, *31*(1), 3–13. doi:10.1016/j.scaman.2014.06.003

Schneider, B., & Schmitt, N. (1986). *Staffing organizations* (2nd ed.). HarperCollins Publishers, Inc.

Schneider, W. E. (2000). Why good management ideas fail: The neglected power of organizational culture. *Strategy and Leadership*, *28*(1), 24–29. doi:10.1108/10878570010336001

Schuler, R. S. (1980). Definition and conceptualization of stress in organizations. *Organizational Behavior and Human Performance*, *25*(2), 189–202. doi:10.1016/0030-5073(80)90063-X

Schwartz, S. H. (1999). A Theory of Cultural Values and Some Implications for Work. *Applied Psychology, 48*(1), 23-47.

Schwartz, B. (1982). The social context of commemoration: A study in collective memory. *Social Forces*, *61*(2), 374–402. doi:10.1093/sf/61.2.374

Schwarz, N., & Strack, F. (1999). Reports of subjective well-being: Judgment processes and their meth- odological implications. In D. Kahneman, E. Diener, & N. Schwarz (Eds.), *Well being: The founda- tions of hedonic psychology*. New York: Russell Sage.

Scire, P. (2007). *Applying Grief Stages to Organizational Change. An attributional analysis of Kubler-Ross Model of dying*. Cambridge, MA: Harvard University.

Scobie, C. (2015). LGBTI in the workplace. *Business Diversity*. Retrieved from https://www.charteredaccountantsanz.com/en/Site-Content/Business-Trends-Insights/Acuity/June-2015/LGBTI-in-the-workplace.aspx#.V-w9HKIrJjc

Scott, K. S., Moore, K. S., & Miceli, P. (1997). An exploration of the meaning and consequences of workaholism. *Human Relations*, *50*(3), 287–314. doi:10.1177/001872679705000304

Sears, B., & Mallory, C. (2011). *Documented evidence of employment discrimination & its effects on LGBT people*. The Williams Institute. Retrieved from http://williamsinstitute.law.ucla.edu/wp-content/uploads/Sears-Mallory-Discrimination-July-20111.pdf

Secretaria de Direitos Humanos da Presidência da Repúbica. (2012). *Relatório sobre Violência Homofobica no Brasil: Ano de 2012*. Retrieved from http://www.sdh.gov.br/assuntos/lgbt/pdf/relatorio-violencia-homofobica-ano-2012

Seligman, M. E. P. (2002). *Authentic happiness: Using the new positive psychology to realize your potential for lasting fulfilment*. New York: Free Press.

Seligman, M. E. P. (2011). *Flourish: A visionary new understanding of happiness and well-being*. New York: Simon & Schuster.

Seligman, M. E. P., & Csikszentmihalyi, M. (2000). Positive psychology: An introduction. *The American Psychologist*, *55*(1), 5–14. doi:10.1037/0003-066X.55.1.5 PMID:11392865

Seligman, M. E. P., Steen, T. A., Park, N., & Peterson, C. (2005). Positive psychology progress: Empirical validation of interventions. *The American Psychologist*, *60*(5), 410–421. doi:10.1037/0003-066X.60.5.410 PMID:16045394

Sellers, R. D., Fogerty, T. J., & Parker, L. M. (2014). Mobility and structural change through traumatic organizational events. *Journal of Accounting & Organizational Change*, *10*(3), 382–408. doi:10.1108/JAOC-02-2011-0007

Setti, I., & Argentero, P. (2014). The role of mindfulness in protecting firefighters from psychosomatic malaise. *Traumatology: An International Journal*, *20*(2), 134–141. doi:10.1037/h0099398

Seymour, K. (2009). Women, gendered work and gendered violence: So much more than a job. *Gender, Work and Organization*, *16*(2), 238–265. doi:10.1111/j.1468-0432.2009.00437.x

Shallcross, L., Sheehan, M., & Ramsay, S. (2008). Workplace mobbing: Experiences in the public sector. *International Journal of Organizational Behaviour*, *13*(2), 56–70.

Shapiro, J., Astin, J., Shapiro, S. L., Robitshek, D., & Shapiro, D. H. (2011). Coping with loss of control in the practice of medicine. *Families, Systems & Health*, *29*(1), 15–28. doi:10.1037/a0022921 PMID:21417521

Sheffi, Y. (2005). *The resilient enterprise*. Cambridge, MA: Ballinger.

Shen, J., & Netto, B. D. (2012). Impact of the 2007–09 global economic crisis on human resource. *Asia Pacific Business Review*, *18*(1), 45–64. doi:10.1080/13602381.2011.601163

Shen, Y. C., Hsia, R. Y., & Kuzma, K. (2009). Understanding the Risk Factors of Trauma Center Closures Do Financial Pressure and Community Characteristics Matter? *Medical Care*, *47*(9), 968–978. doi:10.1097/MLR.0b013e31819c9415 PMID:19704354

Shepard, B. C. (2013). Between harm reduction, loss and wellness: On the occupational hazards of work. *Harm Reduction Journal, 10*(5). doi:10.1186/1477-7517-10-5 PMID:23548032

Sherman, M. D., & Thelen, M. H. (1998). Distress and professional impairment among psychologists in clinical practice. *Professional Psychology, Research and Practice, 29*(1), 79–85. doi:10.1037/0735-7028.29.1.79

Shin, S. J., & Zhou, J. (2003). Transformational leadership, conservation, and creativity: Evidence from Korea. *Academy of Management Journal, 46*(3), 703–714.

Shipley, B. A., Weiss, A., Der, G., Taylor, M., & Deary, I. J. (2007). Neuroticism, extraversion, and mortality in the UK Health and Lifestyle Survey: A 21-year prospective cohort study. *Psychosomatic Medicine, 69*(9), 923–931. doi:10.1097/PSY.0b013e31815abf83 PMID:17991814

Short, P. (2001). *Mao: A Life*. London: Holt Paperbacks.

Shuck, B., & Herd, A. M. (2012). Employee engagement and leadership: Exploring the convergence of two frameworks and implications for Leadership in HRD. *Human Resource Development Review, 11*(2), 156–181. doi:10.1177/1534484312438211

Shull, A. C., Church, A. H., & Burke, W. W. (2014). Something old, something new. *OD Practitioner, 46*(4), 23–30.

Simuth, J., & Sarmany-Schuller, I. (2010). Online learning barriers. In *Technological Developments in Education and Automation* (pp. 113–118). New York: Springer. doi:10.1007/978-90-481-3656-8_21

Sinha, J. B. P. (1980). *The nurturant task leader*. New Delhi: Concept.

Sinha, J. B. P. (1995). *The cultural context of leadership and power*. New Delhi: Sage Publications.

Siomkos, G. J. (2000). Managing airline disasters: The role of consumer safety perceptions and sense-making. *Journal of Air Transport Management, 6*(2), 101–108. doi:10.1016/S0969-6997(99)00030-7

Siqueira, M. V. S., Saraiva, L. A. S., Carrieri, A. P. C., Lima, H. K. B., & Andrade, A. J. A. (2009). Homofobia e Violência Moral no Trabalho no Distrito Federal. *Organizações & Sociedade, 16*(50), 447–461. doi:10.1590/S1984-92302009000300003

Siu, O. L., Cooper, C. L., & Phillips, D. R. (2014). Intervention studies on enhancing work well-being, reducing burnout, and improving recovery experiences among Hong Kong health care workers and teachers. *International Journal of Stress Management, 21*(1), 69–84. doi:10.1037/a0033291

Sklet, S. (2006). Safety barriers: Definition, classification, and performance. *Journal of Loss Prevention in the Process Industries, 19*(5), 494–506. doi:10.1016/j.jlp.2005.12.004

Skogstad, A., Aasland, M. S., Nielsen, M. B., Hetland, J., Matthiesen, S. B., & Einarsen, S. (2014). The relative effects of constructive, laissez-faire, and tyrannical leadership on subordinate job satisfaction: Results from two prospective and representative studies. *Zeitschrift fur Psychologie mit Zeitschrift fur Angewandte Psychologie, 222*(4), 221–232. doi:10.1027/2151-2604/a000189

Sliter, M. T., Pui, S. Y., Sliter, K. A., & Jex, S. M. (2011). The differential effects of interpersonal conflict from customer and coworkers: Trait anger as a moderator. *Journal of Occupational Health Psychology, 16*(4), 424–440. doi:10.1037/a0023874 PMID:21688916

Sliter, M., & Yuan, Z. (2015). Workout at work: Laboratory test of psychological and performance outcomes of active workstations. *Journal of Occupational Health Psychology, 20*(2), 259–271. doi:10.1037/a0038175 PMID:25347682

Sloan, L. M., Matyók, T., Schmitz, C. L., & Short, G. F. L. (2010). A story to tell: Bullying and mobbing in the workplace. *International Journal of Business and Social Science, 1*(3), 87–97.

Smith, G. (2015, July 21). Toshiba just lost its CEO to a huge accounting scandal. *Fortune*. Retrieved August 16, 2016, from http://fortune.com/2015/07/21/toshiba-just-lost-its-ceo-to-a-huge-accounting-scandal/

Smith, J. (1987). Transforming Households: Working-Class Women and Economic Crisis. *Social Problems, 34*(5), 416–436. doi:10.2307/800539

Smith, M. Y., Redda, W. H., Peyserb, C., & Vool, D. (1999). Posttraumatic stress disorder in cancer.: A review. *Psycho-Oncology, 8*(6), 521–537. doi:10.1002/(SICI)1099-1611(199911/12)8:6<521::AID-PON423>3.0.CO;2-X PMID:10607985

Smollan, R. K., & Sayers, J. G. (2009). Organizational culture, change and emotions: A qualitative study. *Journal of Change Management, 9*(4), 435–457. doi:10.1080/14697010903360632

Soares, A. M., Farhangmehr, M., & Shoham, A. (2007). Hofstedes dimensions of culture in international marketing studies. *Journal of Business Research, 60*(3), 277–284. doi:10.1016/j.jbusres.2006.10.018

Soares, R. R. (2007). On the Determinants of Mortality Reduction in the Developing World. *Population and Development Review, 1*(July), 247–287. doi:10.1111/j.1728-4457.2007.00169.x

Söderfeldt, M., Söderfeldt, B., & Warg, L. E. (1995). Burnout in social work. *Social Work, 40*(5), 638–646.

Sousa, C. A., Haj-Yahia, M. M., Feldman, G., & Lee, J. (2013). Individual and collective dimensions of resilience within political violence. *Trauma, Violence & Abuse, 14*(3), 235–254. doi:10.1177/1524838013493520 PMID:23793902

Spector, P. E., Cooper, C., & Sparks, K. (2001). An International Study of the Psychometric Properties of the Hofstede Values Survey Module 1994: A Comparison of Individual and Country/Province Level Results. *Applied Psychology, 50*(2), 269–281. doi:10.1111/1464-0597.00058

Spencer-Oatey, H. (1997). Unequal Relationships in High and Low Power Distance Societies A Comparative Study of Ibtor-Student Role Relations in Britain and China. *Journal of Cross-Cultural Psychology, 28*(3), 284–302. doi:10.1177/0022022197283005

Sperry, L. (2009). Mobbing and bullying: The influence of individual, work group, and organizational dynamics on abusive workplace behavior. *Counseling Psychology Journal: Practice and Research, 61*(3), 190–201.

Spetch, A., Howland, A., & Lowman, R. L. (2011). EAP utilization patterns and employee absenteeism: Results of an empirical, 3-year longitudinal study in a national Canadian retail corporation. *Consulting Psychology Journal: Practice and Research, 63*(2), 110–128. doi:10.1037/a0024690

Sprung, J. M., & Jex, S. M. (2012). Work locus of control as a moderator of the relationship between work stressors and counterproductive work behavior. *International Journal of Stress Management, 19*(4), 272–291. doi:10.1037/a0030320

St. Just, A. (2006). *Relative balance in an unstable world. A search for new models for Trauma Education and Recovery* (1st ed.). Heidelberg, Germany: Carl-Auer Verlag.

Stamm, B. H. (Ed.). (1999). *Secondary traumatic stress: Self-care issues for clinicians, researchers, and educators.* Baltimore, MD: Sidran Press.

Stanley, D. J., Meyer, J. P., & Topolnytsky, L. (2005). Employee cynicism and resistance to organizational change. *Journal of Business and Psychology, 19*(4), 429–459. doi:10.1007/s10869-005-4518-2

Statistic Brain Research Institute. (2015). *Stress Statistics.* Retrieved November 30, 2015, from http://www.statisticbrain.com/stress-statistics/

Staw, B. M., & Hoang, H. (1995). Sunk costs in the NBA: Why draft order affects playing time and survival in professional basketball. *Administrative Science Quarterly, 40*(3), 474–494. doi:10.2307/2393794

Steel, P., Schmidt, J., & Shultz, J. (2008). Refining the Relationship between Personality and Subjective Well-being. *Psychological Bulletin*, *134*(1), 138–161. doi:10.1037/0033-2909.134.1.138 PMID:18193998

Stein, H. F. (1991). Metaphors of organizational trauma and organizational development: A case example. *Organization Development Journal*, *9*(4), 22–30.

Steinkamp, M. (2014). *Behind the masks of silence: How leaders can overcome organizational trauma* (Unpublished master's thesis). INSEAD, Fontainebleau.

Stein, M. (2007). Toxicity and the unconscious experience of the body at the employee–customer interface. *Organization Studies*, *28*(8), 1223–1242. doi:10.1177/0170840607079527

Stein, M. (2012). *Rethinking the Gay and Lesbian movement*. New York, NY: Routledge.

Stenson, J. (2006). Disaster management as a tool for sustainable development: A case study of cyanide leaching in the gold mining industry. *Journal of Cleaner Production*, *14*(3-4), 230–233. doi:10.1016/j.jclepro.2005.03.003

Stets, J., & Burke, P. (2000). Identity theory and social identity theory. *Social Psychology Quarterly*, *63*(3), 224–237. doi:10.2307/2695870

Stevens, F. G., Plaut, V. C., & Sanchez-Burks, J. (2008). Unlocking the benefits of diversity: All-inclusive multiculturalism and positive organizational change. *The Journal of Applied Behavioral Science*, *14*(1), 116–133. doi:10.1177/0021886308314460

Stone, K. B. (2010). *Relationships between organizational performance and change factors and manufacturing firms´ leanness*. Retrieved from http://dspace.library.colostate.edu/webclient/DeliveryManager/digitool_items/csu01_storage/2011/04/22/file_1/96022

Stone, K. B. (2015). Burke-Litwin Organizational Assessment Survey: Reliability and Validity. *Organization Development Journal*, *33*(2), 33–50.

Stoneman, Z., & Jinnah, H. A. (2015). Stress on the farm: Father stress and its association with unsafe farm behaviors of youth. *Journal of Rural Mental Health*, *39*(2), 73–80. doi:10.1037/rmh0000026

Strauss, A. L., & Corbin, J. (1998). *Basics of qualitative research: Grounded theory procedures and techniques* (2nd ed.). Thousand Oaks, CA: Sage.

Stuart, R. (1996). The trauma of organizational change. *Journal of European Industrial Training*, *20*(2), 11–16. doi:10.1108/03090599610110420

Sue, D. et al.. (1990). *Understanding abnormal behavior* (3rd ed.). Boston: Houghton Mifflin company.

Suh, E., Diener, E., & Fujita, F. (1996). Events and subjective well-being: Only recent events matter. *Journal of Personality and Social Psychology*, *70*(5), 1091–1102. doi:10.1037/0022-3514.70.5.1091 PMID:8656337

Sverke, M., Hellgren, J., & Näswall, K. (2002). No security: A meta-analysis and review of job insecurity and its consequences. *Journal of Occupational Health Psychology*, *7*(3), 242–264. doi:10.1037/1076-8998.7.3.242 PMID:12148956

Swain, S. (2011). *Trauma and Transformation at Ground Zero: A Pastoral Theology* (1st ed.). Minneapolis, MN: Fortress Press.

Swarnalatha, C., & Prasanna, T. S. (2013). Employee engagement: The concept. *International Journal of Management Research and Review*, *3*(12), 3872–3880.

Swider, B. W., & Zimmerman, R. D. (2010). Born to burnout: A meta-analytic path model of personality, job burnout, and work outcomes. *Journal of Vocational Behavior*, *76*(3), 487–506. doi:10.1016/j.jvb.2010.01.003

Symonds, M. (1975). Victims of violence: Psychological effects and after effects. *American Journal of Psychoanalysis*, *35*(1), 19–26. doi:10.1007/BF01248422 PMID:1155652

Szeto, A. C. H., & Dobson, K. S. (2013). Mental disorders and their association with perceived work stress: An investigation of the 2010 Canadian Community Health Survey. *Journal of Occupational Health Psychology*, *18*(2), 191–197. doi:10.1037/a0031806 PMID:23458060

Tahnee, N., & Griffin, B. (2015). Here today but not gone tomorrow: Incivility affects after-work and next-day recovery. *Journal of Occupational Health Psychology*, *20*(2), 218–225. doi:10.1037/a0038376 PMID:25402225

Taj, M., & Aquino, M. (2016, February 23). *Peru pipeline leaks in Amazon; two rivers polluted, agency says* (A. Hay, Ed.). Retrieved August 16, 2016, from http://uk.reuters.com/article/us-peru-oil-spill-idUKKCN0VW064

Tannen, D. (1990). *Rethinking Power and Solidarity in Gender and Dominance*. Berkeley, CA: University of Berkeley.

Tansel, B. (1995). Natural and manmade disasters: Accepting and managing risks. *Safety Science*, *20*(1), 91–99. doi:10.1016/0925-7535(94)00070-J

Taris, T. W., & Schaufeli, W. B. (2015). Individual Well-being and Performance at Work: A conceptual and theoretical overview. In M. V. V. R. Peccei (Ed.), *Well-being and performance at work: The role of context* (pp. 15–34). London: Taylor & Francis.

Tavakoli, S., Lumley, M. A., Hijazi, A. M., Slavin-Spenny, O. M., & Parris, G. P. (2009). Effects of assertiveness training and expressive writing on acculturative stress in international students. *Journal of Counseling Psychology*, *56*(4), 590–596. doi:10.1037/a0016634 PMID:20357910

Tavousi, M. N. (2014). Job stress and affective well being: The mediating effects of core self-evaluations. *Journal of Iranian Psychologists*, *10*(38), 103–122.

Taylor, A., III. (1997). My life as a gay executive. *Fortune Magazine*. Retrieved from: http://archive.fortune.com/magazines/fortune/fortune_archive/1997/09/08/230840/index.htm

Taylor, S. E. (1991). Asymmetrical effects of positive and negative events: The mobilization- minimization hypothesis. *Psychological Bulletin*, *110*(1), 67–85. doi:10.1037/0033-2909.110.1.67 PMID:1891519

Tehrani, N. (2011). *Managing trauma in the workplace: Supporting workers and organisations*. New York, NY: Routledge/Taylor & Francis Group.

Tejeda, M. J. (2006). Nondiscrimination policies and sexual identity disclosure: Do they make a difference in employee outcomes? *Employee Responsibilities and Rights Journal*, *18*(1), 45–59. doi:10.1007/s10672-005-9004-5

Terr, L. C. (1994). Childhood traumas. *Psychotraumatology: Key papers and core concepts in post-traumatic stress*, 301.

The American Psychological Association. (2013). *Diagnostic and statistical manual of mental disorders: DSM-5* (5th ed.). American Psychiatric Publishing.

The Conference Board. (2008). *Executive Coaching Fee Survey*. Retrieved February 10, 2016, from https://www.conference-board.org/pdf_free/councils/TCBCP006.pdf

The Economist. (2014, November 8). *Gay people in business: out at the top*. Retrieved from http://www.economist.com/news/business/21631046-apples-boss-has-left-closet-being-gay-work-still-struggle-out-top

The Telegraph. (2008). *Lesbian soldier Kerry Fletcher wins case*. Retrieved from http://www.telegraph.co.uk/news/uknews/1575819/Lesbian-soldier-Kerry-Fletcher-wins-case.html

Theorell, T., Hammarström, A., Aronsson, G., Träskman Bendz, L., Grape, T., Hogstedt, C., & Hall, C. et al. (2015). A systematic review including meta-analysis of work environment and depressive symptoms. *BMC Public Health, 15*(1), 1–14. doi:10.1186/s12889-015-1954-4 PMID:26232123

Tin, L. (2003). *The dictionary of homophobia: A global history of gay & lesbian experience*. Vancouver, BC: Arsenal Pulp Press.

Titelman, P. (Ed.). (2014). *Differentiation of self: Bowen family systems theory perspectives*. New York, NY: Taylor & Francis.

Toker, S., Shirom, A., Melamed, S., & Armon, G. (2012). Work characteristics as predictors of diabetes incidence among apparently healthy employees. *Journal of Occupational Health Psychology, 17*(3), 259–267. doi:10.1037/a0028401 PMID:22746366

Tomaka, J., Palacios, R., Schneider, K. T., Colotla, M., Concha, J. B., & Herrald, M. M. (1999). Assertiveness predicts threat and challenge reactions to potential stress among women. *Journal of Personality and Social Psychology, 76*(6), 1008–1021. doi:10.1037/0022-3514.76.6.1008 PMID:10402683

Tong, T. W., & Reuer, J. (2007). Real Options in Multinational Corporations: Organizational Challenges and Risk Implications. *Journal of International Business Studies, 38*(2), 215–230. doi:10.1057/palgrave.jibs.8400260

Torkelson, E., & Muhonen, T. (2003). Coping strategies and health symptoms among women and men in a downsizing organization. *Psychological Reports, 92*(3), 899–907. doi:10.2466/pr0.2003.92.3.899 PMID:12841464

Törnroos, M., Hintsanen, M., Hintsa, T., Jokela, M., Pulkki-Råback, L., Hutri-Kähönen, N., & Keltikangas-Järvinen, L. (2013). Associations between Five-Factor Model traits and perceived job strain: A population-based study. *Journal of Occupational Health Psychology, 18*(4), 492–500. doi:10.1037/a0033987 PMID:24099167

Tran, B. (2008). *Expatriate selection and retention* (Doctoral dissertation). California School of Professional Psychology at Alliant International University, San Francisco, CA.

Tran, B. (2013). Industrial and organizational (I/O) psychology: The roles and purposes of I/O practitioners in global business. In B. Christiansen, E. Turkina, & N. Williams (Eds.), Cultural and technological influences on global business (pp. 175-219). Hershey, PA: IGI Global.

Tran, B. (2014b). Rhetoric of game: Utilizing the game of Tavistock method on organizational politics training. In D. Ruggiero (Eds.), Cases on societal effects of persuasive games (pp. 145-174). Hershey, PA: IGI Global.

Tran, B. (2014c). The foundation of cultural intelligence: Human capital. In B. Christiansen, S. Yildiz, & E. Yildiz (Eds.), Handbook of Research on effective marketing in contemporary globalism (pp. 348-376). Hershey, PA: IGI Global.

Tran, B. (2014d). The human element of the knowledge worker: Identifying, managing, and protecting the intellectual capital within knowledge management. In M. A. Chilton & J. M. Bloodgood (Eds.), Knowledge management and competitive advantage: Issues and potential solutions (pp. 281-303). Hershey, PA: IGI Global.

Tran, B. (2014e). Rhetoric of play: Utilizing the gamer factor in selecting and training employees. In T. M. Connolly, L. Boyle, T. Hainey, G. Baxter, & P. Moreno-Ger (Eds.), Psychology, pedagogy and assessment in serious games (pp. 175-203). Hershey, PA: IGI Global.

Tran, B. (2015b). Triangulation in organizational research: Validating knowledge in human competence at work. In Research methods: Concepts, methodologies, tools, and applications. Hershey, PA: IGI Global.

Tran, B. (2015c). Triangulation in organizational research: Validating knowledge in human competence at work. In A. Takhar & A. Ghorbani (Eds.), Market research methodologies: Multi-method and qualitative approaches (pp. 93-117). Hershey, PA: IGI Global.

Tran, B. (2015d). Expatriate selection and retention: Identifying and assessing the other characteristics beyond knowledge, skills, and abilities. In A. A. Camillo (Eds.), Handbook of research on global hospitality and tourism management (pp. 468-492). Hershey, PA: IGI Global.

Tran, B. (2014a). Rhetoric of game: Utilizing the game of Tavistock method on organizational politics training. In D. Ruggiero (Ed.), *Cases on societal effects of persuasive games* (pp. 145–174). Hershey, PA: IGI Global. doi:10.4018/978-1-4666-6206-3.ch008

Tran, B. (2015a). The next generation of leaders: Women in global leaderships in the hotel management industry. In J. Feng, S. Stocklin, & W. Wang (Eds.), *Educational strategies for the next generation of leaders in hotel management* (pp. 16–42). Hershey, PA: IGI Global. doi:10.4018/978-1-4666-8565-9.ch002

Tran, B. (2016a). Organizational justice: The injustice in the foundation of organizational citizenship behavior within higher education institutions. In N. P. Ololube (Ed.), *Handbook of research on organizational justice and culture in higher education institutions*. Hershey, PA: IGI Global. doi:10.4018/978-1-4666-9850-5.ch001

Tran, B. (2016b). The foundation of (business) ethics' evolution. In I. M. Khosrow-Pour (Ed.), *Encyclopedia of information science and technology* (4th ed.). Hershey, PA: IGI Global.

Travagione, A., & Cross, B. (2006). Diminishing the social network in organizations: Does there need to be such a phenomenon as „survivor syndrome" after downsizing? *Strategic Change*, *15*(1), 1–13. doi:10.1002/jsc.743

Trompenaars, F., & Hampden-Turner, C. (1997). *Riding the Waves of Culture: Understanding Cultural Diversity in Business*. London: Nicholas Brealey Publishing.

Trompenaars, F., & Hampden-Turner, C. (2012). *Riding the waves of culture*. New York: McGraw-Hill.

Trueman, C. E. (2005). *Luther's Theology of the Cross*. Retrieved from http://www.opc.org/new_horizons/NH05/10b.html

Tung, L. R. (2008). The cross-cultural research imperative: The need to balance cross-cultural and intra-national diversity. *Journal of International Business Studies*, *39*(1), 41–46. doi:10.1057/palgrave.jibs.8400331

Tung, R. L., & Verbeke, A. (2010). Beyond Hofstede and GLOBE: Improving the quality of cross-cultural research. *Journal of International Business Studies*, *41*(8), 1299–1274.

Türk Silahlı Kuvvetleri Sağlık Yeteneği Yönetmeliği. (2015, November 12). *Resmi Gazete*. Retrieved September 8, 2016, from http://www.mevzuat.gov.tr/MevzuatMetin/3.5.20158136.pdf

Turner, M. E., & Pratkanis, A. R. (1998). A social identity maintenance model of groupthink. *Organizational Behavior and Human Decision Processes*, *73*(2), 210–235. doi:10.1006/obhd.1998.2757 PMID:9705803

Tuxford, L. M., & Bradley, G. L. (2015). Emotional job demands and emotional exhaustion in teachers. *Educational Psychology*, *35*(8), 1006–1024. doi:10.1080/01443410.2014.912260

Tyhurst, J. S. (1951). Individual reactions to community disaster: The natural history of psychiatric phenomena. *The American Journal of Psychiatry*, *107*(10), 764–769. doi:10.1176/ajp.107.10.764 PMID:14819372

Umans, T., Collin, S. O., & Tagesson, T. (2008). Ethnic and gender diversity, process and performance in groups of business students in Sweden. *Intercultural Education*, *19*(3).

United Nations Human Rights Council. (2015). *Discrimination and violence against individuals based on their sexual orientation and gender identity*. Retrieved from http://www.ohchr.org/EN/Issues/Discrimination/Pages/LGBTUNReports.aspx

United Nations. (2012). *Table 4 Gender Inequality Index 2012*. New York: United Nations Development Program.

Urban Dictionary. (2016). *Definition of homophobia*. Retrieved from http://www.urbandictionary.com/define.php?term=homophobia

US Chemical Safety & Hazard Investigation Board. (2007). *Refinery Explosion and Fire, BP Texas City 23 March 2005*. Washington, DC: Author.

Vahtera, J., Kivimaki, M., & Pentti, J. (1997). Effect of organizational downsizing on health of employees. *Lancet*, *350*(9085), 1124–1128. doi:10.1016/S0140-6736(97)03216-9 PMID:9343499

Välikangas, L., Hoegl, M., & Gibbert, M. (2009). Why learning from failure isnt easy (and what to do about it): Innovation trauma at Sun Microsystems. *European Management Journal*, *27*(4), 225–233. doi:10.1016/j.emj.2008.12.001

Valle, M. F., Huebner, E. S., & Suldo, S. M. (2006). An analy- sis of hope as a psychological strength. *Journal of School Psychology*, *44*(5), 393–406. doi:10.1016/j.jsp.2006.03.005

Van Beek, I., Taris, T. W., & Schaufeli, W. B. (2011). Workaholic and work engaged employees: Dead ringers or worlds apart? *Journal of Occupational Health Psychology*, *16*(4), 468–482. doi:10.1037/a0024392 PMID:21787085

Van De Voorde, K., Paauwe, J., & Van Veldhoven, M. (2012, December). Employee Well-being and the HRM-Organizational Performance Relationship: A Review of Quantitative Studies. *International Journal of Management Reviews*, *14*(4), 391–407. doi:10.1111/j.1468-2370.2011.00322.x

Van der Hart, O., Brown, P., & Van der Kolk, B. A. (1989). Pierre Janets Treatment of Post-Traumatic Stress. *Journal of Traumatic Stress*, *2*(4), 379–395. doi:10.1002/jts.2490020404

Van der Hart, O., & Friedman, B. (1989). A Reader's Guide to Pierre Janet on Dissociation: A Neglected Intellectual Heritage. *Dissociation*, *2*, 3–16.

Van der Hart, O., Nijenhuis, E., & Steele, K. (2006). *The haunted Self: Structural dissociation and the treatment of chronic traumatization*. New York: Norton.

Van der Hoeven, R., & Sziraczki, G. (1998). *Lessons from privatization: Labour issues in developing and transitional countries*. Geneva, Switzerland: ILO Publications.

Van der Kolk, B.A. (1996). *The complexity of adaptation to trauma: Self-regulation, stimulus discrimination, and characterological development*. Academic Press.

Van der Tooren, M., & Rutte, C. (2016). Explaining Emotional Exhaustion and Work Engagement: The role of job demands-resources and Type D Personality. *International Journal of Stress Management*; Advanced online publication. doi:10.1037/a0039754

van der Velden, P. G., Bosmans, M. W. G., Bogaerts, S., & Veldhoven, M. J. P. M. (2014). Social organizational stressors and post-disaster mental health disturbances: A longitudinal study. *Psychiatry Research*, *219*(1), 177–182. doi:10.1016/j.psychres.2014.05.032 PMID:24915898

Van Dick, R., Wagner, U., & Lemmer, G. (2004). Research note: The winds of change—Multiple identifications in the case of organizational mergers. *European Journal of Work and Organizational Psychology*, *13*(2), 121–138. doi:10.1080/13594320444000038

Van Doorn, R. A., & Hülsheger, U. R. (2015). What makes employees resilient to job demands? The role of core self-evaluations in the relationship between job demands and strain reactions. *European Journal of Work and Organizational Psychology*, *24*(1), 76–87. doi:10.1080/1359432X.2013.858700

van Lieshout, S., & Steurenthaler, J. (2006). *Diva-portal.* Available at: http://www.diva-portal.org/smash/get/diva2:119684/FULLTEXT01.pdf

Van Mol, M. M. C., Kompanje, E. J. O., Benoit, D. D., Bakker, J., & Nijkmap, M. D. (2015). The prevalence of compassion fatigue and burnout among healthcare professionals in intensive care units: A systematic review. *PLoS ONE*, *10*(8), e0136955. doi:10.1371/journal.pone.0136955 PMID:26322644

Vanhala, S., & Tuomi, K. (2006). HRM, Company Performance and Employee Well-being. Management Revue, 17(3), 241-255.

Vanhala, S., & Tuomi, K. (2006). HRM, Company Performance and Employee Well-being. *Management Review*.

Vatansever, Ç., Çalıskan, S., & Isık, I. (2015). Bir Dünya Sirketinin Türkiye'deki Çalısanlarına Göre Çesitliliklerin Yönetimi: Gömülü Kuram Analiziyle Modelleme. *Yönetim Arastırmaları Dergisi*, *12*(1-2), 29–61.

Vence, E. D., Roberson, J. A., McGuinnies, M. T., & Fazel, L. P. (2010). How neuroplasticity and cognitive reserve protect cognitive functioning. *Journal of Psychological Nursing*, *48*(4), 23–30. PMID:20349891

Venkataramani, V., Labianca, G., & Grossier, T. (2013). Positive and negative workplace relationships, social satisfaction, and organizational attachment. *The Journal of Applied Psychology*, *98*(6), 1028–1039. doi:10.1037/a0034090 PMID:23915428

Veronese, G., Pepe, A. (2015). Sense of coherence as a determinant of psychological well-being across professional groups of aid workers exposed to war trauma. *Journal of Interpersonal Violence*.

Vickers, M. H. (2001). Bullying as unacknowledged organizational evil: A researchers story. *Employee Responsibilities and Rights Journal*, *13*(4), 205–217. doi:10.1023/A:1014975203542

Vickers, M. H., & Kouzmin, A. (2001). Resilience in organizational actors and rearticulating voice: Towards a humanistic critique of New Public Management. *Public Management Review*, *3*(1), 95–119. doi:10.1080/14616670010009478

Victor, B., & Cullen, J. (1988). The organizational bases of ethical work climates. *Administrative Science Quarterly*, *33*(1), 101–125. doi:10.2307/2392857

Vinkers, C. H., Joëls, M., Milaneschi, Y., Kahn, R. S., Penninx, B. W. J. H., & Boks, M. P. M. (2014). Stress exposure across the life span cumulatively increases depression risk and is moderated by neuroticism. *Depression and Anxiety*, *31*(9), 737–745. doi:10.1002/da.22262 PMID:24753162

Vinokur, A., & Selzer, M. L. (1975). Desirable versus undesirable life events: Their relationship to stress and mental distress. *Journal of Personality and Social Psychology*, *32*(2), 329–337. doi:10.1037/0022-3514.32.2.329 PMID:1239500

Vitinius, F., Sonntag, B., Barthel, Y., Brennfleck, B., Kuhnt, S., Werner, A., & Keller, M. et al. (2013). KoMPASS – Design, implementation, and experiences concerning a structured communication skills training for physicians dealing with oncology. *PPmP: Psychotherapie Psychosomatik Medizinische Psychologie*, *63*(12), 482–488. PMID:23677627

Vivian, P., & Hormann, S. (2002). Trauma and Healing in Organizations. *O.D. The Practitioner*, *34*(4), 52–57.

Vivian, P., & Hormann, S. (2013). *Organizational trauma and healing*. CreateSpace Independent Publishing Platform.

Vivian, P., & Hormann, S. (2013). *Organizational Trauma and Healing*. CreateSpace Independent Publishing Platform.

Vivian, P., & Hormann, S. (2015). Persistent Traumatization in Nonprofit Organizations. *OD Practitioner*, *47*(1), 25–30.

von Glinow, M. A., Shapiro, D. L., & Brett, J. M. (2004). Can we talk, and should we? Managing emotional conflict in multicultural teams. *Academy of Management Review*, *XIX*(4), 578–592.

Voss, E., & Maack, P. (2007). *Overview of restructuring in Europe*. Hamburg, Germany: European Trade Union Confederation. ETUC.

Voss, T. (2007). *Overview of restructuring in Europe. European Trade Union Confederation*. European Commission.

Vveinhardt, J. (2010). The diagnostics of mobbing as discrimination on employee relations aiming to improve the organizational climate in Lithuanian organizations. *Management Theory and Studies for Rural Business and Infrastructure Development*, *21*(2), 173–185.

Waclawski, J. (2002). Large-scale organizational change and performance: An empirical examination. *Human Resource Development Quarterly*, *13*(3), 289–305. doi:10.1002/hrdq.1032

Waisfisz, R. (2015). *Constructing the best culture to perform*. Helsinki, Finland: Itim Publications.

Walley, K. (2007). Coopetition: An introduction to the subject and an agenda for research. *International Studies of Management & Organization*, *37*(2), 11–31. doi:10.2753/IMO0020-8825370201

Walsh, F., & Olson, D. H. (1993). Utility of the circumplex model with severely dysfunctional family systems. In *Circumplex model: Systematic assessment and treatment of families* (pp. 104–137). New York: Haworth Press.

Wang, H., & Lu, Y. (2012). Trust governance based on active interpersonal strategy. *Nankai Business Review International*, *3*(2), 128–144. doi:10.1108/20408741211244361

Wang, S. M., Lai, C. Y., Chang, Y. Y., Huang, C. Y., Zauszniewski, J. A., & Yu, C. Y. (2015). The relationships among work stress, resourcefulness, and depression level in psychiatric nurses. *Archives of Psychiatric Nursing*, *29*(1), 64–70. doi:10.1016/j.apnu.2014.10.002 PMID:25634877

Ward, J., & Winstanley, D. (2005). Coming out at work: Performativity and the recognition and renegotiation of identity. *The Sociological Review*, *53*(3), 447–475. Retrieved from http://www1.udel.edu/soc/tammya/socDev/ward%20winstanley%20coming%20out%20at%20work.pdf. doi:10.1111/j.1467-954X.2005.00561.x

Waring, A. (2015). Managerial and non-technical factors in the development of human-created disasters: A review and research agenda. *Safety Science*, *79*, 254–267. doi:10.1016/j.ssci.2015.06.015

Weber, M. (2003). The Protestant Ethic and the Spirit of Capitalism. New York: Dover Publications. (first published 1958)

Weick, K. E. (1988). Enacted sensemaking in crisis situations. *Journal of Management Studies*, *25*(4), 305–317. doi:10.1111/j.1467-6486.1988.tb00039.x

Weisbord, M. R. (1971). Eight most important issues managers should look into. *Industrial Management (Des Plaines)*, *13*(6), 11.

Weisbord, M. R. (1976). Organizational Diagnosis: Six places to look for trouble with or without a theory. *Group & Organization Studies*, *1*(4), 430–447. doi:10.1177/105960117600100405

Wenger, E. (1998). Communities of practice: Learning as a social system. *Systems Thinker, 9*(5), 2-3.

Werther, W. B. Jr. (2003). Strategic change and leader-follower alignment. *Organizational Dynamics*, *32*(1), 32–45. doi:10.1016/S0090-2616(02)00136-5

Westhues, K. (2002). At the mercy of the mob. *Canada's Occupational Health & Safety Magazine*, *18*(8), 30–36.

White, J. M., Klein, D. M., & Martin, T. F. (2015). *Family theories: An introduction* (4th ed.). Thousand Oaks, CA: SAGE Publications, Inc.

White, P. N., & Rollins, J. C. (1981). Rape: A family crisis. *Family Relations*, *30*(1), 103–109. doi:10.2307/584243

Widyanto, L., & McMurran, M. (2004). The psychometric properties of the Internet Addiction Test. *Cyberpsychology & Behavior*, *7*(4), 443–450. doi:10.1089/cpb.2004.7.443 PMID:15331031

Wierzbicka, A. (1992). *Semantics, culture, and congnition: Universal human concepts in culture-specific configuations*. New York: Oxford University Press.

Wiktionary. (n.d.). *Trauma*. Retrieved from https://en.wiktionary.org/wiki/ trauma#Etymology

Williamson, D. (2002). Forward from a Critique of Hofstedes Model of National Culture. *Human Relations*, *55*(11), 1373–1395. doi:10.1177/001872670255511006

Willis, P. (2012). Witnesses on the periphery: Young lesbian, gay, bisexual and queer employees witnessing homophobic exchanges in Australian workplaces. *Human Relations*, *65*(12), 1589–1610. doi:10.1177/0018726712457795

Willsher, K. (2014, March 19). Orange France investigates second wave of suicides among staff. *The Guardian*. Retrieved from https://www.theguardian.com

Wilson, J. P. (1989). A person-environment approach to traumatic stress reactions. In J. Wilson (Ed.), Trauma, transformation and healing: An integrative approach to theory, research, and post-traumatic therapy, (pp. 75-110). New York: Brunner/Mazel.

Wilson, J. P., Harel, Z., & Kahana, B. (Eds.). (1988). Human Adaptation to Extreme Stress From the Holocaust to Vietnam. New York: Springer Science.

Wilson, J. P. (1994). The Historical Evolution of PTSD Diagnostic Criteria: From Freud to DSM-IV. *Journal of Traumatic Stress*, *7*(4), 1994. doi:10.1002/jts.2490070413 PMID:7820357

Wilson, R. A., Perry, S. J., Witt, L. A., & Griffeth, R. W. (2015). The exhausted short-timer: Leveraging autonomy to engage in production deviance. *Human Relations*, *68*(11), 1693–1711. doi:10.1177/0018726714565703

Wolfe, R. A., Weick, K. E., Usher, J. M., Terborg, J. R., Poppo, L., Murrell, A. J., & Jourdan, J. S. et al. (2005). Sport and organizational studies exploring synergy. *Journal of Management Inquiry*, *14*(2), 182–210. doi:10.1177/1056492605275245

Wolfradt, U., & Doll, J. (2001). Motives of adolescents to use the Internet as a function of personality traits, personal and social factors. *Journal of Educational Computing Research*, *24*(1), 13–27. doi:10.2190/ANPM-LN97-AUT2-D2EJ

World Health Organization. (1946). Preamble to the Constitution of the World Health Organization as adopted by the International Health Conference, New York, 19–22 June 1946; signed on 22 July 1946 by the representatives of 61 States (Official Records of the World Health Organization, no. 2, p. 100) and entered into force on 7 April 1948.

World Value Survey. (2016). Available at: http://www.worldvaluessurvey.org/WVSDocumentationWV1.jsp

Wright, T. A., & Cropanzano, R. (1998). Emotional exhaustion as a predictor of job performance and voluntary turnover. *The Journal of Applied Psychology*, *83*(3), 486–493. doi:10.1037/0021-9010.83.3.486 PMID:9648526

Yablon, Y. B. (2015). Positive school climate as a resilience factor in armed conflict zones. *Psychology of Violence*, *5*(4), 393–401. doi:10.1037/a0039600

Yoo, B., & Bonthu, N. (2002). Book Reviews. *Journal of International Business Studies*, 388–389.

Young, C. (2012). Losing a Job: The Nonpecuniary Cost of Unemployment in the United States. *Social Forces, 91*(2), 609–634. doi:10.1093/sf/sos071

Yukl, G. (2006). *Leadership in organizations* (6th ed.). Saddle River, NJ: Prentice Hall.

Zacher, H., Jimmieson, N. L., & Bordia, P. (2014). Time pressure and coworker support mediate the curvilinear relationship between age and occupational well-being. *Journal of Occupational Health Psychology, 19*(4), 462–475. doi:10.1037/a0036995 PMID:24885685

Zaloznay, M. (2015). Does authoritarianism breed corruption? Reconsidering the relationship between authoritarian governance and corrupt exchanges in bureaucracies. *Law & Social Inquiry, 40*(2), 345–376. doi:10.1111/lsi.12076

Zandberg, L. J., Rosenfield, D., McLean, C. P., Powers, M. B., Asnaani, A., & Foa, E. B. (2016). Concurrent treatment of posttraumatic stress disorder and alcohol dependence: Predictors and moderators of outcome. *Journal of Consulting and Clinical Psychology, 84*(1), 43–56. doi:10.1037/ccp0000052 PMID:26460570

Zapf, D., & Einarsen, S. (2003). Individual antecedents of bullying: Victims and perpetrators. In S. Einarsen, H. Hoel, D. Zapf, & C. Cooper (Eds.), *Bullying and emotional abuse in the workplace: International perspectives in research and practice* (pp. 165–184). London: Taylor & Francis.

Zapf, D., & Einarsen, S. (2005). Mobbing at work: Escalated conflicts in organizations. In S. Fox & P. E. Spector (Eds.), *Counterproductive work behavior: Investigations of actors and targets* (pp. 237–270). doi:10.1037/10893-010

Zapf, D., Escartin, J., Einarsen, S., Hoel, H., & Vartia, M. (2011). Empirical findings on prevelance and risk groups of bullying in the workplace. In S. Einarsen, H. Hoel, D. Zapf, & C. Cooper (Eds.), *Bullying and harassment in the workplace: Developments in theory, research, and practice* (2nd ed.; pp. 75–106). Boca Raton, FL: CRC Press.

Zapf, D., & Gross, C. (2001). Conflict escalation and coping with workplace bullying: A replication and extension. *European Journal of Work and Organizational Psychology, 10*(4), 497–522. doi:10.1080/13594320143000834

Zellars, K. L., Tepper, B. J., & Duffy, M. K. (2002). Abusive supervision and subordinates organizational citizenship behavior. *The Journal of Applied Psychology, 87*(6), 1068–1076. doi:10.1037/0021-9010.87.6.1068 PMID:12558214

Zenger, T. R. (1992). Why do employers only reward extreme performance? Examining the relationships among performance, pay, and turnover. *Administrative Science Quarterly, 37*(2), 198–219. doi:10.2307/2393221

Zheng, W., Yang, B., & McLean, G. N. (2010). Linking organizational culture, structure, strategy, and organizational effectiveness: Mediating role of knowledge management. *Journal of Business Research, 63*(7), 763–771. doi:10.1016/j.jbusres.2009.06.005

Zhou, H. (2012). A New Framework of Happiness Survey and Evaluation of National Wellbeing. *Social Indicators Research, 108*(3), 491–507. doi:10.1007/s11205-011-9888-4

Zhou, Z. E., Yan, Y., Che, X. X., & Meier, L. L. (2015). Effect of workplace incivility on end-of-work negative affect: Examining individual and organizational moderators in a daily diary study. *Journal of Occupational Health Psychology, 20*(1), 117–130. doi:10.1037/a0038167 PMID:25347686

Zhu, W., Avolio, B. J., & Walumbwa, F. O. (2009). Moderating role of follower characteristics with transformational leadership and follower work engagement. *Group & Organization Management, 34*(5), 590–619. doi:10.1177/1059601108331242

Zohar, D., & Marshall, I. (2000). *Spiritual Intelligence. The Ultimate Intelligence* (1st ed.). London, UK: Bloomsbury Publishing Plc.

About the Contributors

Richard Brunet-Thornton, FRSA, MIM, MBA, Ph.D. Dr. Brunet-Thornton holds two full-time positions in both Montréal (Canada) and Prague (Czech Republic). As an assistant professor at VŠE, his expertise encompasses Cross-Cultural Management and Communications, Knowledge Management, Project Management, and Academic Writing. His area of speciality is the Czech Republic. In addition, he is a native speaker of both French and English. He has published numerous articles in various scholarly journals and textbooks as well as holding various editorial positions in numerous journals. On the application side, he is responsible for an international business practice with the fifth largest global IS/IT consultancy. In this field, his expertise is in telephony. During his many years of business tenure, Dr. Brunet-Thornton has worked on every continent within the telecommunications domain.

* * *

Pablo Alonso Pena is a research fellow with the Royal Military Academy. As a PhD student in a co-directed thesis at Université Catholique de Louvain and Université libre de Bruxelles, his research involves the study of Organizational Trauma.

Vidya Sagar Athota teaches HR and Business Psychology in the School of Business at the University of Notre Dame Australia. Dr Athota holds a PhD from the University of New South Wales. He has published papers in high-impact international journals and has presented papers at a number of domestic and international conferences. His current research involves the study of human personality, cognition, non-cognitive skills and ethics in the context of workplace success. Dr Athota's expertise also includes management diagnostics and multi-perspective assessments in the areas of personality, and social, cognitive and entrepreneurial skills. He has provided services to various business organisations, including Fortune 500, and is a visiting research fellow at the Centre for Innovative Assessments, New York.

Lynda Byrd-Poller earned her doctorate in Human and Organizational Learning from The George Washington University. She currently serves as the Director of Human Resources, Strategic Planning & Professional Learning for Charles City County Public Schools and serves as an adjunct professor in GWU Organizational Leadership & Learning graduate studies. She has experience in education, leadership, organization sciences, and human resources development. Her research interests include organizational and adult learning, leadership, diversity and cultural studies as well as other areas of social science.

Pavel Cejka received his Ph.D. from University of Economics in Prague. He also holds master degrees from University of St Andrews, National Sun Yat-sen University and University of Hradec

Kralove. Pavel has spent past 10 years in business working living in Taiwan, the Czech Republic and UK, working for Asus, 3M and Tableau. His research focuses on cross-cultural aspects of international marketing and management. Pavel is an active lecturer at University of Economics, Prague and National Sun Yat-sen University.

Robert A. Cleve is an associate professor at The Chicago School of Professional Psychology in the International Psychology PhD program since 2013. He has been a counseling clinician (MA, LCPC) for the past 22 years, receiving his MA degree in School and Community psychology from Wayne State University and has worked in a variety of therapeutic settings including, mental health with children and adolescents, addictions counseling, private practice, inpatient psychiatric hospital settings and served director of a residential treatment facility for the adult chronically mentally ill population. His cross-cultural research interests include exploring disclosure decisions for LGBTQ youth globally. He supports qualitative methodology believing in its utility to add depth and breadth to the scientific psychological literature. He serves as an executive and board member for a number of LGBT non-profit organizations involved in providing mental health and social services, youth residential services and youth job training and development.

Erik de Soir (1965), in 1988, obtained a Master in Social & Military Sciences at the Royal Military Academy in Brussels. In 1992, after a short operational career as an Infantry Officer, he became a Lecturer in Psychology at the Department of Behavioral Sciences of the Royal Military Academy. In 2009, he was assigned as Commander of the Psychosocial Support Section to the Well-being Department of the Belgian Defence. He is currently attached to Department of Scientific and Technological Research of Defence at the Royal Higher Institute of Defence. Erik De Soir has a PhD in Psychology (Utrecht University, 2015), a PhD in Social & Military Sciences (Royal Military Academy, 2015), a Postgraduate Psychotherapy Training in Systemic Marital, Family & Sex Therapy (Catholic University of Leuven, 1998), a Master's Degree in Clinical Psychology (Catholic University of Leuven, 1995) and a Postgraduate Degree in Disaster Management & Disaster Medicine (Catholic University of Leuven, 1991).

Jennifer L. Farmer earned her doctorate in Human and Organizational Learning from The George Washington University. She also has an MBA from Florida Agricultural and Mechanical University (FAMU). Jennifer is the Founder and Chief Executive Officer of Renewed Mindset, LLC, which focuses on assisting organizations in achieving their diversity and inclusion, team and organizational goals through consultation, analysis, training, and collaboration. Jennifer's career and scholarly research interests include workplace diversity and inclusion, organizational culture, global leadership, organizational development, organizational learning, and human capital management.

Valerie Ford earned her doctorate in Human and Organizational Learning from The George Washington University in Washington, DC. Her research interests comprise a broad range of topics, including how data and information technology change behaviors and processes in organizations, understanding the changing nature of organizations and teams in the 21st century, and fostering organizational creativity and innovation to generate new processes and products. Her experience in MIS has given her a keen awareness of the technology issues in corporate environments and she feels fortunate to experience and investigate behavior in organizations as both a scholar and a practitioner.

Juan M. Gallego has 20 years of experience in international business. He has held executive positions in the USA, Latin America, Europe and China. He worked for Nokia for 17 years, opening up the Latin American market and also led the Global account team of Telefonica (Latin America, Europe and Morocco), prior to leading the strategy and sales development Nokia account team for China Mobile, the largest operator in the world. In his consulting, focused on organizational development, culture awareness, organizational culture analysis and corporate executive trainings he led and facilitated projects in sales, organizational development, coaching leadership and merger & acquisitions in the USA, Latin America, Europe and Hong Kong. Dr. Gallego lectures at the University of Colorado (Colorado Springs) and Regis University. His education includes a Doctorate of Psychology (Psy.D.), with a specialization in Organizational Consulting and a Master of International Management from Thunderbird School of Global Management.

Idil Işık, PhD, is Assistant Professor and the program director in Organizational Psychology Master's Program at Istanbul Bilgi University, Turkey. Her academic focus is more on quantitative, qualitative, and mixed research methodologies. She applies her focus to the behavioral dynamics at work including social identity, diversity, human rights, disadvantaged groups and mistreatments in workplaces, and occupational safety and health. She earned her psychology undergraduate degree from Boğaziçi University, Turkey; Masters and PhD degree on Organizational Behavior from Marmara University, Turkey. She is currently teaching advanced quantitative and qualitative research methods courses in her institution to develop the students' skills for SPSS and MAXQDA consequently. She is actively and intensively using diverse analytic tools both in her academic research, in the process of advising to undergraduate and graduate students in their thesis, and also in teaching of qualitative and quantitative research courses. She can be reached at idil.isik@bilgi.edu.tr.

Ilona Jerabek, Ph.D., is the president of PsychTests AIM Inc. PsychTests offers an extensive collection of psychological assessments used in a wide variety of professional and personal settings, from pre-employment screening to therapy, academic research to life coaching. Dr. Jerabek obtained a doctoral degree in clinical sciences from the Medical School of Sherbrooke University and trained in psychiatric genetics as part of her post-doctoral fellowship at McGill University. Dr. Jerabek has been involved in numerous projects, and continues to work in the capacity of a test developer, project manager, scientific advisor, subject matter expert, compatibility expert and business and HR consultant. She has been actively involved in a variety of projects with companies such as Reebok, Major League Baseball, FX Networks, Move.com, Land Rover, Psychology Today, Discovery Channel, Proctor & Gamble, Hickory Farms, True.com, France Telecom, Cosmopolitan, CosmoGirl, Glamour and Glam.com and many others.

Rolf J. Kleber, Ph.D., is Emeritus Professor of Psychotraumatology, Utrecht University as well as Past Director Research of Arq Psychotrauma Foundation. He was a lecturer at the University of California, Irvine (U.S.A.) and held academic positions at several Dutch universities. Prof. Kleber has conducted and supervised research projects on posttraumatic stress disorder treatment outcome, work related trauma and intervention programs, late sequelae of war stress, psychosocial consequences of disasters, health issues of refugees, and cross-cultural aspects of mental health. He is also a consultant in mental health care after major life events and emergencies in The Netherlands and abroad. Prof. Kleber has published various articles and books on stress, coping with trauma and cross-cultural psychology.

Dušan Kučera graduated from the Evangelical Theological Faculty of Charles University in Prague in 1986, and later completed a course in pastoral psychology at the Theological Seminary in Friedensau, Germany and Andrews University, MI, USA. He worked as a pastor, editor and teacher for 7 years. In 1994 he changed to a secular position and worked as an HR manager for several international companies, most importantly (10 years) for the automotive company ŠKODA AUTO/VOLKSWAGEN. In 2002 he finished an international study of his MBA and PhD program at the University of Economics, Prague, where he now works as the Assistant Professor for Managerial Responsibility and Business Ethics in master courses and International MBA programs, and as a lecturer in company courses.

Jan Leysen is professor at the Royal Military Academy in Brussels where he is the head of the Department of Economics, Management and Leadership, and Dean of the Faculty of Social and Military Sciences. He is internal consultant to the Belgian Ministry of Defence in the domain of strategic and performance management. He equally consulted several Belgian public administrations in these domains. Professor Leysen is author and co-author of articles and communications, mainly on performance management in defence and in the public sector and on decision making. He directs the Research Group on Risk-, Crisis- and Disastermanagement at the Royal Military Academy.

Hana Mohelská, Ph.D. is the Head of the Department of Management at the Faculty of Informatics and Management of the University Hradec Králové. She has worked in the private sector as a managing director before joining the University of Hradec Králové. Her research focus involves areas such as Knowledge Management, Management, Business Economics, Human Resource Management, virtual teams, motivation and incentive systems. As a lecturer, she teaches managerial methods, modern managerial methods and HRM.

Deborah Muoio is a researcher, test developer, and blogger for PsychTests AIM Inc. Her love for writing, psychology, and self-discovery have come together in the creation of over 300 mental health, IQ, career, and personality tests and articles. She received her Bachelor's degree in Psychology from Concordia University in Montreal, Canada, and has collaborated on projects for Major League Baseball, Psychology Today, Reebok, Cosmo, and many others.

Viviane de Castro Pecanha, Ph.D., is a clinical and research psychologist in São Paulo, Brazil. Since 1998, Dr. Pecanha has worked to advance research and education on addictive and impulse control disorders. Dr. Pecanha co-founded an NGO providing pro bono professional training and clinical services in the diagnosis and treatment of addictive and impulse control disorders. In 2005, Dr. Pecanha attended the University of California - Los Angeles to research addictive disorders; she was invited to join The Chicago School of Professional Psychology's Los Angeles Campus to develop the Clinical Psychology Ph.D. Program. In 2009, she returned to Brazil, teaching online for the International Psychology Ph.D. Program at The Chicago School, furthering its global mission by directing TCS Education System initiatives in Brazil. Dr. Pecanha is Associate Department Chair of the International Psychology Ph.D. Program and Director of the MA Program in International Psychology for The Chicago School's Online Campus.

Erik Schindler is a PhD Candidate in International Management and Organization at the Sardul S. Gill Graduate School, part of the Peter B. Gustavson School of Business at the University of Victoria,

Canada. His research interests lie in organizational trauma and near-death experiences, and in the transfer of knowledge and best practices both cross-culturally and cross-sectorally.

Jozef Simuth received his PhD degree in psychology at Comenius University, Slovakia. He works as a management consultant specializing in employee development focusing on psychological factors influencing effectiveness of soft skills training, e-learning and holistic approach to personal development. He worked as a coordinator of outplacement projects for major corporations in Slovakia. He has 19 years of experience in University education at international universities in various roles in academic management as well as teaching, teacher training, research and student counseling. Jozef is a member of Slovak Association of Psychologists and Education, Learning, Styles and Individual Differences Network.

Michel Sylin is an Organisational psychologist (Université libre de Bruxelles, Brussels – 1990) with a specialization in Work Sciences (1992) and got his PhD in Psychology at the ULB (1996). Is the head of the "Centre de Recherche en Psychologie des Organisations et des Istitutions" at the ULB. He is Professor at the Faculty of Psychology and Educational Sciences and at the faculty of Philosophy and Social Sciences of the ULB.

Mike Szymanski is a Ph.D. candidate at the Gustavson School of Business. He holds a master's degree in strategic management from the Warsaw School of Economics and a master's degree in American culture from the University of Warsaw. Mike's research focuses on the potential effect of bicultural individuals on organizational performance in international settings. Before starting his Ph.D. training, Mike spent time working in strategic management consulting.

Ben Tran received his Doctor of Psychology (Psy.D.) and his Master of Arts (M.A.) from the California School of Professional Psychology (CSPP) at Alliant International University (AIU), in San Francisco, California. Dr. Tran is a Senior Vocational Rehabilitation Counselor, Qualified Rehabilitation Professional (SVRC-QRP), with the State of California, Department of Rehabilitation, in San Francisco, California. Dr. Tran's research interests are: domestic and expatriate recruitment, selection, training, evaluation, and retention; organizational and international organizational behavior and ethics; minorities in organizations; gender and sexuality; gendered communication; and persons with disabilities and accommodations.

Stephan Van den Broucke (1959) is Professor of Public Health Psychology at the Université Catholique de Louvain, Belgium. He has supervised a large number of national and international research projects in the areas of health promotion planning and evaluation, health inequalities, capacity building, and health literacy, and authored more than 70 peer-reviewed international publications and several books. Prof. Van den Broucke is associate editor of Health Promotion International, Executive Board Member of the International Union for Health Promotion and Education and Advisory Board Member of the Asian Health Literacy Association, and has been an expert adviser for the European Commission and a technical adviser for the WHO and for the Open Science Foundation. He has been an invited professor at various universities across Europe, Latin America and Asia.

Index

A

B

C

D

E

F

G

H

I

J

L

M

N

O

Stay Current on the Latest Emerging Research Developments

Become an IGI Global Reviewer for Authored Book Projects

The overall success of an authored book project is dependent on quality and timely reviews.

In this competitive age of scholarly publishing, constructive and timely feedback significantly decreases the turnaround time of manuscripts from submission to acceptance, allowing the publication and discovery of progressive research at a much more expeditious rate. Several IGI Global authored book projects are currently seeking highly qualified experts in the field to fill vacancies on their respective editorial review boards:

Applications may be sent to:
development@igi-global.com

Applicants must have a doctorate (or an equivalent degree) as well as publishing and reviewing experience. Reviewers are asked to write reviews in a timely, collegial, and constructive manner. All reviewers will begin their role on an ad-hoc basis for a period of one year, and upon successful completion of this term can be considered for full editorial review board status, with the potential for a subsequent promotion to Associate Editor.

If you have a colleague that may be interested in this opportunity,
we encourage you to share this information with them.

www.ingramcontent.com/pod-product-compliance
Lightning Source LLC
LaVergne TN
LVHW060359300926
849162LV00006B/1302
* 9 7 8 1 5 2 2 5 2 0 2 1 4 *